Microeconomic Analysis

Microeconomic Analysis

(SECOND REVISED EDITION)

R.R. Barthwal
Former Professor of Economics
Department of Humanities and Social Sciences
Indian Institute of Technology
Kanpur (U.P.)

Publishing Globally

NEW AGE INTERNATIONAL (P) LIMITED, PUBLISHERS
New Delhi • Bangalore • Chennai • Cochin • Guwahati
Hyderabad • Kolkata • Lucknow • Mumbai
Visit us at **www.newagepublishers.com**

Published by New Age International (P) Ltd., Publishers
First Edition : 1992
Second Revised Edition: 2012

BRANCHES

- **Bangalore** 37/10, 8th Cross (Near Hanuman Temple), Azad Nagar, Chamarajpet, Bangalore-560 018
  Tel.: (080) 26756823, Telefax: 26756820, **E-mail: bangalore@newagepublishers.com**
- **Chennai** 26, Damodaran Street, T. Nagar, Chennai-600 017
  Tel.: (044) 24353401, Telefax: 24351463, **E-mail: chennai@newagepublishers.com**
- **Cochin** CC-39/1016, Carrier Station Road, Ernakulam South, Cochin-682 016
  Tel.: (0484) 2377004, Telefax: 4051303, **E-mail: cochin@newagepublishers.com**
- **Guwahati** Hemsen Complex, Mohd. Shah Road, Paltan Bazar, Near Starline Hotel, Guwahati-781 008
  Tel.: (0361) 2513881, Telefax: 2543669, **E-mail: guwahati@newagepublishers.com**
- **Hyderabad** 105, 1st Floor, Madhiray Kaveri Tower, 3-2-19, Azam Jahi Road, Nimboliadda, Hyderabad-500 027
  Tel.: (040) 24652456, Telefax: 24652457, **E-mail: hyderabad@newagepublishers.com**
- **Kolkata** RDB Chambers (Formerly Lotus Cinema) 106A, 1st Floor, S.N. Banerjee Road, Kolkata-700 014
  Tel.: (033) 22273773, Telefax: 22275247, **E-mail: kolkata@newagepublishers.com**
- **Lucknow** 16-A, Jopling Road, Lucknow-226 001
  Tel.: (0522) 2209578, 4045297, Telefax: 2204098, **E-mail: lucknow@newagepublishers.com**
- **Mumbai** 142C, Victor House, Ground Floor, N.M. Joshi Marg, Lower Parel, Mumbai-400 013
  Tel.: (022) 24927869, Telefax: 24915415, **E-mail: mumbai@newagepublishers.com**
- **New Delhi** 22, Golden House, Daryaganj, New Delhi-110 002
  Tel.: (011) 23262368, 23262370, Telefax: 43551305, **E-mail: sales@newagepublishers.com**

ISBN: 978-81-224-3220-6

₹ 295.00

C-12-03-6210

Printed in India at Lalit Printers and Binders, Delhi.

Typeset at River Edge and In-house, New Delhi.

PUBLISHING FOR ONE WORLD

NEW AGE INTERNATIONAL (P) LIMITED, PUBLISHERS
4835/24, Ansari Road, Daryaganj, New Delhi-110002
Visit us at **www.newagepublishers.com**

Preface to the Second Edition

Microeconomics is a basic and fairly matured branch of economics. It has not changed much during the last twenty years except intensification of mathematical exposition of the subject particularly the game theoretic models. Such developments of microeconomics are useful for advance level students. At undergraduate level for which this book is written, the present syllabus of the subject is adequate. In view of this, I have not revised the book too much except filling some gaps and giving some examples. I also introduced some new lines of microeconomic theory which are providing serious challenges to the present neo-classical theory. The last chapter of this book contains, such theories under titles the 'transaction cost theory', the 'property right theory' and the 'agency theory.' With these changes, the book becomes more comprehensive in coverage and up-to-date for students of Indian universities and technical institutes.

R.R. Barthwal

Preface to the First Edition

Microeconomics, comprising a set of principles that govern production, exchange and consumption of goods and services, is the foundation of the entire economic theory. The study of economics begins with microeconomic analysis because it deals with those fundamental laws which help in optimum allocation of economic resources and, hence, price determination for goods and services including factors of production. This is the core or basic theme of the economic theory as a whole. Keeping in mind, the important role of microeconomics, I decided to write this textbook. The need for this was felt by me after gaining the experience of teaching introductory microeconomics to engineering students of Indian Institute of Technology, Kanpur for a number of years. I consider engineers as 'practical economists' whose task is to plan, design, execute, and run industrial projects and other ventures. Apart from technical and managerial skills, they need a sound knowledge of the basic principles of microeconomics with in-built emphasis on their practical applications. I strongly feel that professionals, engineers and others associated with the running of business enterprises and other economic activities should be taught complete and consistent microeconomics in a systematic way. Existing textbooks in the subject designed for them give only an abridged version of it. This book has been written with this purpose in mind. However, it is not only to serve to specific needs of engineering students but other categories of readers also, In fact, this book is useful to all students interested in economic theory whatever may be their areas of study. Primarily, it is meant for undergraduate students of engineering and economics but the honours and post-graduate students of economics are also likely to benefit by the material presented in the book.

The book covers a wide range of topics in its various chapters. The first-two chapters deal with introductory aspects of the subject such as its scope, methods of study, major branches, basic economic problems of modern societies and the role of microeconomics in solving them. Chapter 3 provides the basic concepts related to demand, supply, price-determination and elasticities. All this is intermediate economics which helps in understanding the contents of the later chapters. The theory of consumer behaviour is given in Chapter 4. The next two chapters deal with the theories of production and cost; and the analysis of pricing and output decisions under different market situations is spread-over in Chapters 7 to 10. Chapter 11 contains the theories for factor price determination. The general equilibrium analysis and welfare economics are now integral parts of modern microeconomics. These are covered in Chapters 12 and 13 respectively. Finally, Chapter 14 contains an epilogue to the microeconomic analysis presented in this book. It deals with the new directions in development of microeconomics and their compatibility with the neo-classical theory of the firm. The entire analysis presented in the book is a synthesis of the classical, neo-classical and modern approaches to the subject. It is a reading of the economic theory which is of course abstract in nature being based on a number of simplifying assumptions. However, an attempt is made in the book to keep the degree of abstraction at the minimal level, and much emphasis is laid on examining the concepts and laws of the economic theory in the light of their practical applicability. On the whole this book provides analytically rigorous but readable treatment of microeconomics. I hope this will meet the requirements and expectations of the students of Indian universities and institutes of high learning for whom it is written.

A number of colleagues in my department encouraged me to write this book. I am thankful to all of them. My thanks are also due to Mr. V.N. Katiyar and Mr. S.K. Khullar who typed the bulky manuscript of the book with patience and skill.

Financial assistance for preparation of the manuscript of the book came from the Continuing Education Cell of the Quality Improvement Programme (Q.I.P.) of the Indian Institute of Technology, Kanpur. I express my deep appreciation to the authorities of the programme for this generous help.

December, 1991

R.R. Barthwal

Contents

CHAPTER 1

Scope and Methods of Economics

1.1 WHAT IS ECONOMICS?

It is customary to begin the study of a subject with its definition. We are also following this practice in this book. In a definition we make a precise statement of the essential nature of a thing. This provides the bounds or limits in which to confine ourselves while studying the subject. This is applicable to the study of economics also.

Economics is quite an old discipline. Its development in the contemporary form was a continuous process. Perhaps the beginning was made by the Greek philosopher, Aristotle, who, in his two books, *Economica* confined the study of economics to household management and acquiring, guarding and making proper use of wealth. In fact, the word 'economics' has been derived from the Greek words *oikos* meaning a house and '*nemein*' meaning to manage. So, economics means managing a household with limited funds. The concept of frugal use of one's limited resources in managing a household has been extended to macro level which gave birth to the term 'economy' implying the manner in which a particular society organises its resources for maximum production of desired goods.

There is no consensus among economists about a precise definition of economics. Several approaches have been followed in the past in this regard. The current position is that there are perhaps, as many specific definitions as there are economics instructors. Broadly speaking, the various definitions of economics can be put together under four categories depending upon the emphasis of particular aspects. These are (*i*) 'Wealth', (*ii*) 'Welfare', (*iii*) 'Scarcity', and (*iv*) 'Growth'.

The earlier economists defined economics as the 'science of wealth'. Economics was regarded as the science which studied production and consumption of wealth. Adam Smith (1776), who is regarded as 'Father of Economics', in fact, gave the title of his famous book as *An Enquiry into the Nature and Causes of the Wealth of Nations*.[1] This is nothing but a definition of economics adopted by the earlier classical economists. It clearly indicates the wealth approach used in defining the scope of economics. Similarly, J.S. Mill, another leading classical economist, defined economics as "the practical science of the production and distribution of wealth."[2]

1. Adam Smith, '*An Enquiry Into the Nature and Causes of the Wealth of Nations*' (1776), Ed. Edwin Cannan; Modern Library, N.Y. 1937 Edition.
2. J.S. Mill, *Principles of Political Economy*, Edited by W.J. Ashley, New Impression, London/N.Y., Longmans, Green and Co., 1920, Ch. 1.

The other leading economists of the past, such as J.B. Say, Nassau Senior, and W.S. Jevons also defined economics or political economy as it used to be called then, using wealth approach. They all contended that the subject matter of economics was not happiness but wealth. The term 'wealth' in these definitions was taken as "riches or abundance of money or scarce goods having exchange value." This is a quite narrow approach used to define wealth by the classical economists. In fact, 'wealth', as we define today, means scarce goods and services capable to satisfy human wants. If this concept of wealth was taken into account by the classical economists, there would not have been any problem in accepting their definition of economics. But the classical economists by narrowing down the concept of wealth to material and money only invited criticism of economics from several authors even during their own times. Carlyle, for example, characterised economics as the Gospel of Mammon, a 'dismal science' that teaches selfishness and love of money. Ruskin dubbed it as "a basterd science, the science of getting rich." He emphasized that living, and not getting rich, should be the end of human endeavour. In view of this and other limitations these definitions of economics were found unsatisfactory.

Towards the end of 19th century, Alfred Marshall suggested a new definition of economics. According to him, wealth was not the end itself but a means to the end of achieving human welfare. Keeping in mind the link between wealth and human welfare, he defined economics as follows:

> "Political Economy or Economics, is a study of mankind in the ordinary business of lifes: it examines that part of individual and social action which is most closely connected with the attainment and with the use of the material requisites of well-being."[3]

This definition treats economics as a social science. The primary emphasis placed by Marshall while defining economics is on the study of mankind and the material requisites of well-being. Wealth, which is in the form of material requisites is a means to welfare, *i.e.*, as a source of the betterment of human lot. To make economics an exact, precise and universal science, Marshall excluded all those activities of human life which cannot be quantified and which are of non-material nature. By doing so, Marshall has opened his definition of economics to criticism as there might be several non-material things such as services of doctors, lawyers and teachers which are equally relevant for human welfare as the material requisites, yet they have been excluded by him. Pigou, a disciple of Marshall, tried to remove this ambiguity regarding the scope of economics. He simply defined economics as "that part of welfare which can be brought directly or indirectly within the measuring rod of money."[4] This definition extends the scope of economic analysis to all goods, material and non-material, which command a price in the economic system. Pigou, in his approach to define economics, laid major emphasis on the study of human actions in relation to material or economic welfare itself.

The 'welfare' definition of economics, as developed by Marshall, has been well accepted by a number of economists. However, it is not free from criticism. Serious objections have been raised by Lionel Robbins.[5] The first one was regarding the treatment of economics as a social science rather than as a human science. A social science studies individuals as members of a society. An isolated individual like a Sadhu or a 'Robinson Crusoe' will be outside the scope of economic analysis if we accept Marshall's definition. In practice, human beings, whether they are isolated or members of an organised community, do face economic problems arising out of the scarcity of resources. A study

3. Alfred Marshall, Principles of Economics (8th Edition), London, MacMillan, 1956, p. 1.
4. A. C. Pigou, Economics of welfare, MacMillan (4th Ed.) 1948, p. 1.
5. Lionel Robbins, An Essay on the Nature and Significance of Economic Science; London, MacMillan, 1935. Chapter 1, pp. 1-21.

of their behaviour is as relevant for economic analysis as the study of social behaviour. The appropriate approach for the study of economics is therefore to treat it as a 'human science' rather than a social science. Although Marshall argued for the study of "individual and social actions" in economics still by relating their activities to the measuring rod of money he and his follower Pigou restricted the scope of economics to the study of persons living in organised communities using some kind of currency for exchange. This implies a social science approach rather than human science approach used in the study of economic science by Marshall. It is difficult to say that this was a wrong approach. Economists like Robbins may not agree with this but there is a large number of economists even today who strongly support or follow Marshall in defining economics.

A second limitation of Marshallian approach to define economics is related to its classificatory nature. In Marshall's definition, economics is concerned with certain groups of commodities (*i.e.*, material requisites of well-being) rather than certain aspects of human or social activities. According to Robbins, the division of human activities into 'material' and 'non-material' is unscientific and illogical. All individual and social activities, such as production, distribution and consumption of goods and services (*i.e.*, material and non-material) under the influence of scarcity come under the scope of economic science.

Another drawback with Marshall's approach is that it focussed on "the study of mankind in the ordinary business of life." What is the meaning of this? It implies that individual and social actions in the extraordinary business of life such as famines, wars, and other similar situations, fall outside the scope of economics. But economics is relevant under all situations, whether ordinary or extraordinary.

In conclusion, we can say that, although there are some limitations or drawbacks with Marshall's welfare definition of economics, yet it is well accepted by economists.

Lionel Robbins who was dissatisfied with the Marshallian definition of economics gave his own definition using the scarcity notion. According to him:

"Economics is the science which studies human behaviour as a relationship between ends and scarce means which have alternative uses."[6]

In this definition, the term 'ends' indicates human wants *i.e.*, man has several ends or wants to serve. Resources or means, such as income or quantities of goods and services or time or any other thing with the use of which the wants can be satisfied are limited in supply. When means are scarce or limited in supply, all ends or wants cannot be met. In this situation, a choice of the ends to be met with the limited resources, is to be made. The means are capable of satisfying any subset of wants, *i.e.*, they can be put on alternative uses. If we choose one subset of ends or wants for satisfaction the other will remain unsatisfied. When we have several ends and limited means, a judicious choice or decision is to be made regarding selection of the wants for satisfaction. This is a very important aspect of human behaviour which we study in economics. The end and means relationship can be examined from the view point of a consumer or a producer or any other economic actor like a trader, financer or public authority. Robbins' definition provides us with an analytical framework for the study of economics. It is superior than the 'wealth' and 'welfare' definitions. The concept of welfare is implicit in this definition and 'wealth' is taken as means, which is always scarce.

There are some limitations with Robbins' definition. It treats economics as a positive science. The normative or ethical aspects of economics have not been taken into account. Further, economic problems do not always arise from scarcity. A problem can arise from abundance as well, as we see in over-production of agricultural goods sometime. In many situations, production may be low

6. *Ibid.*, p. 16.

because of inefficient management. Robbins did not examine these aspects. The definition proposed by him is static in nature. It fails to incorporate dynamic adjustments, particularly the growth aspect of the economy into consideration. These are some of the problems associated with the scarcity definition of economics. By and large, it is widely accepted and explains the meaning of economics in an unambiguous way.

To incorporate dynamic aspects of economic analysis Paul A. Samuelson suggested a better definition of economics. His definition is branded as the 'growth definition'. According to this:

> Economics is the study of how men and society choose, with or without money, to employ scarce productive resources which could have alternative uses, to produce various commodities over time, and distribute them for consumption now and in future among various people and groups of society.[7]

This definition is wider in scope than the other definitions. It has taken into account whatever Robbins wanted to say. Apart from that, it has been extended to problems of making economic choices under dynamic setting, *i.e.*, for present as well as for future. Another feature of this definition is that it takes into account both money economy and barter economy since the problem of choice or economising exists in both the types of economies.

From the above discussion we find that the definition of economics has been a controversial issue right from the beginning of the discipline itself. As Edwin Seligman observed: "Economics has suffered more than any other discipline from the malaise of polemics about definition and methods."[8] Today, we are in a bit of confusion as to which definition is to be accepted finally. Looking at the contents of the various definitions and comparing them, we may agree that Samuelson's growth definition is the most appropriate. It presents the choice or economising problem in its dynamic setting by taking care of past, present and future. It is wider in scope. It has taken into account production, distribution, consumption, etc., in relation to monetary as well as barter economies. Further, positive as well as normative aspects of the subject have also been taken care of by this definition.

Considering the difficulties of or controversies in defining economics, some economists argue that there is no need of defining the subject at all as it provides us with virtually nothing. Maurice Dobb, for example, says: "The search for logically concise definition of one's subject-matter, which is so popular today, must generally be barren, and when pushed to an extreme, must result in emptying ideas of real content and attaining little but an arid and scholastic dogmatism."[9] Similarly, Gunnar Myrdal expressed his views saying that "such definitions are both unnecessary and undesirable. They are unnecessary for the one concept which an economist need not define precisely is 'Economics'. No argument can possibly be affected by such a definition, just as no chemist can draw any scientific conclusions from a definition of the chemistry."[10] One may or may not agree with this kind of views. It is a debatable question. But a definition of the subject seems to be necessary in order to delimit it and make it precise and exact and scientific in nature. It is true that economics "as a human science or social science will have linkages with subjects like Politics, Psychology, Sociology, etc., but it does not mean that all of these subjects should be integrated together. There will be no bounds for such a study. There is, no doubt, diversity in economic thinking but that is because of its normative aspects. The basic core, based on the scarcity concept, is however, similar everywhere in every situation and the science of economics from this account is universal in nature.

---

7. Paul A. Samuelson, *Economics*; McGraw-Hill, (6th Ed.), 1964, p. 5.
8. Edwin R.A. Seligman (1937), *Encyclopaedia of Social Sciences*, vol. v. p. 344.
9. Maurice Dobb, *Political Economy and Capitalism*; London: G. Routledge 1953, p. 173.
10. Gunnar Myrdal, *The Political Elements in the Development of Economic Theory*; Harvard University Press (1954), p. 155.

1.2 IS ECONOMICS A SCIENCE?

Science is defined as a systematic knowledge derived from observation, study, and experimentation carried on in order to determine the nature or principle of what is being studied. The essence of a scientific method that is applied to all sciences can be summarised in terms of the following steps:

(*a*) Define or identify the problem or phenomenon to be investigated in an explicit manner.
(*b*) Hypothesize the possible relationships between the most important factors relating to the phenomenon.
(*c*) From the hypothesis establish predictions or conclusions about the phenomenon using deductive reasoning.
(*d*) Test the prediction or conclusions using actual observations. If conclusions are not true then go back to step (*b*) in order to improve them by adopting alternative hypothesis.

The discipline of science discipline will adopt such methodology of study. A few examples of sciences can be cited such as Physics, Chemistry, Zoology, Geology, etc. Can we include economics in this category? The answer is not simple. Some economists argue that economics is a science but others do not agree with this view. In order to understand the exact nature of economics, let us compare it with a physical science like Physics. In Physics or in other physical sciences we study the behaviour of 'matter'. A 'matter' is inanimate. Such an object shows stable responses when we study it using the scientific method as mentioned above. That is, we conduct experiments or observe the nature of the matter, analyse facts and draw conclusions and finally develop the general theory about it. Such a theory or relationship will be stable because of homogeneity of the object being studied. Most of the sciences show this kind of stable relationship.

Now, take a subject like economics. As we have mentioned earlier, in this discipline we study human behaviour, *i.e.*, the responses of a man (or men) which is an animate, *i.e.*, a living body. The study of such a body resembles with the study of physical sciences. We conduct experiments or make observations regarding the nature of the body, analyse them, draw conclusions, test them and generalise in the form of a theory. Responses reflected by such an enquiry may not be quite stable like that of physical sciences. This is because of heterogeneity of behaviour of the animate body, *i.e.*, a man. While in the case of a science we can predict the behaviour of a matter to some external stimulus with certainty, it would not be easy in the case of an animate object. The predictions in this case will be subjected to some uncertainty. However, the approach to the study, *i.e.*, the method of analysis and generalisation is exactly similar in both the cases and so from this, we can say that economics, like physics or chemistry, is a science. There are, of course, some differences between the two, *i.e.*, physics or any other science subject and economics, such as: (*a*) Theories of physics (or any other science) are universally valid but the theories of economics are not so because they are affected by the heterogeneity of human behaviour across the globe. (*b*) Prediction in economics are not so accurate as in pure sciences. (*c*) Controlled experiments in economics are not possible as in the case of pure sciences. This is because economic theories are subjected to multiplicity of causation, that is, there are several factors which affect human behaviour related to economic aspects. All such factors cannot be controlled just as we control some variables in a laboratory experiment of a science for the study of certain phenomenon.

The conclusion we draw from this is that economics is a science but the degree of perfection of this science is less when it is compared with the pure sciences.

Some economists argue that economics is an art. Like a science, an art is also a systematic body of knowledge. It is a system of rules or procedure for the attainment of a given end. It lays emphasis on the formulation of percepts immediately applicable to policy. A science teaches us to know a phenomenon but an art tells us how to do a thing. Economics has a dimension in it which takes it very near to an art. This aspect we find in normative economics in which a society, based on the basis of its value judgements, fixes the norms to solve its economic problems. In business management, we study several rules and procedures to achieve the goal of profit or sales maximisation. We may call this an art of running the business. These are important aspects of economics particularly when it is to be used for some practical purposes, *i.e.*, in policy. So, we can say that economics, apart from its scientific nature, is also an art. To develop a body of knowledge like economics we need both scientific approach as well as that of the art. The two are complementary attributes of the subject. They should not be treated as competing attributes. After all, economics is a social science so we cannot altogether eliminate the aspects of the art from its study.

1.3 METHODS OF ECONOMIC ANALYSIS

There are two general methods used in the scientific study of a subject. One is the 'deductive' method and the other is 'inductive' method. A deductive method deduces conclusions about the phenomenon under study from certain fundamental assumptions or truths or axioms through a process of logical arguments. The axioms are established on a-priori basis through some other methods. They are theoretical abstractions derived from the real world. Such axioms or theoretical abstractions or hypotheses are analysed further using logical arguments which leads to logical conclusions about the object of study. The conclusions are used in theoretical interpretation of the real world again. In this way, we develop a theory using the deductive method.

The inductive method is based on historical data or facts generated through experiments. They are collected, analysed and then conclusions are derived about the behaviour of the object of study. This method is also called 'historical' or 'empirical' method. In sciences, we do find considerable application of this method.

At present, there is a dispute among economists regarding methodological choice for economic analysis. One group of present and past economists, known as "Extreme A-priorism School", argues that economic theories are not amenable for verification on empirical basis. The leading economists in this group are: Mill, Mises, Robbins and Knight. The second group of economists, called as "Ultra-Empiricism School", argues that all economic theories can be verified or deduced from the facts. Hutchinson and Machlup are leaders of the school. There is a third group of economists led by Samuelson which follows the middle approach. It is called as 'Logical Positivism'. According to this, the basic assumptions of economics cannot be verified empirically but the conclusions derived from them can be verified using the facts or data. This approach is being followed mostly in contemporary economic analysis.[11]

As the name 'logical positivism' connotes, it is the methodology for positive economic analysis. The emphasis in this type of economic analysis is given to the predictive powers of a model. A model which gives better predictions will be closer to reality and hence the assumptions behind the model will be valid in a greater degree as compared to the assumptions of the model which produces inferior

11. For full discussion on the methods see the readings listed at the end of this chapter.

or less accurate predictions. Predictive power of a model or theory as a basis for its acceptance or rejection is the essence of the method of logical positivism. The method is popular in economic analysis on this account.

1.4 LINKS OF ECONOMICS WITH OTHER DISCIPLINES

There are several divisions of knowledge and in each division we find a number of disciplines. For example, Humanities is a division of knowledge in which subjects like language, literature, fine arts, philosophy and music, etc., are covered. This branch of knowledge is concerned with human thoughts and relations therein as distinguished from the sciences. Economics does not interact much with such disciplines.

Consider natural sciences, such as Physics, Chemistry, to some extent Maths, Zoology, Botany, Geology, etc. In these disciplines, we derive systematic knowledge from observations, study and experiment carried on, in order to determine the nature or principles of what is being studied. Economics is not having links with these disciplines. However, several laws of economics resemble the laws of pure or biological sciences. Growth of a firm, for example, resembles the growth of bio-organism.

Now consider applied sciences, such as Engineering. There is a considerable link between such sciences and economics as both are destined to solve human problems of resource scarcity and welfare impeding constraints for mankind.

There is a very important branch of knowledge called Social Science. In this, we study man and his institutions. All such disciplines are interlinked together to some extent as they are parts of the entire social system. Economics interacts with them in a big way. Consider the link between Sociology and Economics. Sociology covers the study of social aspects of human life. It deals with groups of people or society as a whole, its norms, values, sanctions, and host of social institutions such as marriage and family, caste and kins, etc. The economic aspects of such things cannot be isolated completely. There will be several social constraints on economic activities. For example, charging of interest on loans is prohibited under Islam. If there is no interest on loans it may create disincentives for saving and investment. But an economist has to take such constraints into account. Cows are worshiped by Hindus so they cannot be killed for food in India but in Muslim or Christian countries they are important sources of meat for human consumption. Several such examples can be given to cite links of Economics with Sociology. Similarly, Political Science and Economics are linked together. The social preference system, which provides the ultimate aims of economic development, comes under the scope of political science. Economics cannot be ignored while taking decisions on social aims or objectives. Whether there should be price control or not is decided by the politicians, so we can very easily see the vital links between Politics and Economics. Examples showing links between Economics and other social sciences can be given in the similar ways.

Economics is much linked with Statistics and Mathematics. Statistics provides the methodology of data collection, tabulation, analysis and hypothesis testing or what we call as decision-making. This is what we need in economic analysis. Mathematics deals with quantities and their relationships or attributes, etc., by using numbers and symbols. We do have such problems in Economics. It is, therefore, closely linked with Mathematics. Mathematics provides preciseness and economy of words in theorising economic principles. It is difficult to study Economics without the help of Mathematics and Statistics. Non-mathematical approach to study economics is not capable of resolving the rapidly growing complexities of the discipline, as we find today.

1.5 SOME BASIC BRANCHES OF ECONOMICS

Economic theory can be classified into some basic divisions on the basis of the subject matter or approach adopted for the study of the object. Some of these divisions are as follows:

(i) Microeconomics and Macroeconomics

Microeconomics is a study of small parts of an economy. This is what we mean by the term 'micro' attached to it. It is a branch of economics which deals with the study of economic behaviour of the individual unit such as a consumer, a family, a firm, an industry and a factor of production. It refers to the study of price determination. Both the products as well as factor price determination come under the scope of microeconomics. From this, it is also called as Price Theory. The prices of individual commodities or factors of production are determined through the study of markets for them. The approach to the study in microeconomics is partial equilibrium analysis which means equilibrium of the individual commodity or factor markets. Topics like welfare economics, optimising over time, etc., are also covered in microeconomics.

Macroeconomics is a study of economic system as a whole. It deals with aggregate national income, total consumption of goods and services, total savings and investment, unemployment, inflation, etc., in the economy. It concentrates on the equilibrium of the entire economy. Alternatively, it is called Income Theory, as the focus in macroeconomics will be on income determination rather than prices. By 'income' we mean the aggregate national income of a country and its components. Along with the income we do find general price level and other aggregates such as real output, total employment, etc., in an economy when we study its macroeconomics.

Both, micro and macroeconomics are quite useful from practical point of view, that is to solve a host of problems which an individual and a society face in real life. At the individual or household level, we are faced with several economic problems. What jobs are there to do? How much do they pay? How should we allocate our limited income on various goods and services? How to maintain our family expenditure in the situation of rising prices? Why wages are changing? All such questions can be answered with the help of microeconomic analysis. A businessman is concerned with getting adequate return from his investment. How to get it; why his profits are not adequate; how should he conduct his business; what price he should charge for his product; how much he should spend on advertisement; how much labour he should engage in production; etc.? There are the problems which can be tackled through the study of microeconomics. From the point of view of a society, we have problems of inflation, unemployment. under-production or over-production of goods and services, depressions in economic activities, regional disparities in economic development, slow growth of economy as a whole, trade deficits, inadequate money for financing development projects, etc. A study of macroeconomics helps considerably to solve such problems through proper formulation of national economic policies. Apart from consumers, producers, and governments there will be other agencies or persons associated with economic decision-making, such as traders, bankers, international financial bodies, and planning commissions. All of them require a knowledge of economics for efficient decision-making related to their activities. Best use of economic resources from the point of view of everybody as well as of the society as a whole is imperative which is to be achieved somehow. Economics provides the way for this.

As defined above, microeconomics is a study of the individual units while macroeconomic of the aggregates in the economy of a country. Several microeconomic studies throw light on macro economic problems. A study of individual family budgets, for example, is quite useful to understand the pattern of aggregate consumption of goods and services in the community. Microeconomics provides strong base for welfare economics which leads us directly in the realm of macroeconomics. We can cite several other examples for microfoundations of macroeconomics.[12] There are, however, situations when simple microeconomic aggregation leads us to different conclusion than what is revealed by the macroeconomics. This is not a paradox but a kind of confusion or fallacy called by logicians the "fallacy of composition." It is defined as a "fallacy in which what is true of a part is, on that account alone, alleged to be true of the whole."[13] A few examples for this may be cited as:

(*a*) If one farmer works hard his income increases, but if all farmers work hard and nature cooperates total farm income may fall.

(*b*) Higher price in one industry may benefit its firms but if the prices of everything bought and sold increase in the same proportion, no one would be better off.

(*c*) Attempts of individuals to save more in depression may lessen total savings of the community.

(ii) Positive and Normative Economics

These two are very important types of economic theory. Positive Economics deals with analysis of facts. It tries to answer the questions: What is; What was; or What will be? Normative or Ethical Economics, on the other hand deals with the questions like 'what ought to be'. It is based on value judgements as one thing which is preferred by one person may not be liked by another. So the answer to the question, 'what ought to be', depends on individual judgements or values. Society or community as a whole synchronises such value choices of its individuals and set the norms for their fulfilment.

In positive economics we study the economic principles. It aims at derivation, testing and implementation of prediction or making hypotheses about economic behaviour. The theory of positive economics provides a "good enough" explanation of economic phenomena, *i.e.*, the theory is verifiable empirically. The predictions made on the basis of such hypotheses may be used in public policy formulation. For example, an analysis of consumer behaviour provides us empirically testable demand functions for goods and services on the basis of which we can forecast total market demand for them or find the effects of the demand factors like income, prices, etc., on the quantity demanded of goods and services. Similarly, production theory in economics helps us in proper utilisation of inputs, determination of the effects of public policies like taxation, price control on business activities, etc.

In normative economics we go through economic policies. When economics is used for some practical purpose, *i.e.*, achievement of some goal or objective we design a policy for this. A policy is nothing but a course of action adopted by the government or a representative body of people to achieve a goal. The normative economics is concerned with this. Basically, the purpose of normative economic theory is to compare the properties and implications of alternative social decision rules. Positive economics plays very important role in normative economics. All social decision rules must be derived by taking into account the behaviour of relevant economic actors like consumers or producers and the constraints imposed by the resource scarcity. The microeconomic theory, which is a major branch of positive economics, plays an important role in this regard.

To know the difference between positive and normative aspects let us consider the following statements:

12. E. Roy, Weintraub, *Microfoundations: The Compatibility of Microeconomics and Macroeconomics;* Cambridge University Press, 1979.
13. Paul A. Samuelson; *Economics* 6th Ed. McGraw-Hill 1964, p. 11.

'It is difficult to break the atom'
'Scientists should not break the atom'.

The first statement is a positive one but the second one is a normative. If there are disagreements over positive statements, they can approximately be settled by reference to facts, that is, accept that statement which is supported by the facts. The disagreements over normative statements, however, cannot be settled merely by examining the facts. They will depend on the values or choices of decision-making party or parties.

(iii) Static Economics and Dynamic Economics

This is another way of classifying economic theory. Static Economics or Economic Statics refers to that type of economic analysis in which time element does not enter as a variable. All variables in this type of economic analysis relate to the same point or period of time. The theory of price determination for commodities and factors of production is a good example for static analysis.

Dynamic Economics or Economic Dynamics, on the other hand, deals with the type of economic analysis in which time element enters explicitly in some form or the other. Some variables of the relationships of this type of economic analysis will belong to different time period either with a 'lag' or with a 'lead' time. For example, current supply of a commodity in the market may be related to its price in the previous year (or period) and when we use such supply relationship together with the demand for the commodity, to determine its current price, it will be a dynamic economic analysis. Time element comes into picture in this example, in the form of price-lag to determine current supply or demand and hence current price of the commodity. Similarly, investment in the current period for production of a commodity may be analysed on the basis of change in sales of that commodity over the past year. The analysis of economic development or growth over time, technological change overtime, trade cycles in an economy, theory of investment, etc., are other examples of dynamic economics.

The study of economic dynamics is much more meaningful than that of static economics. In static economic analysis we make several assumptions, such as constant tastes, preferences, fashions, technology over-time, perfect mobility of factors of production, instantaneous adjustments in commodity and factor markets, and so on. Some of the assumptions may not be realistic. The study of economic dynamics helps us to remove unrealistic assumptions from the analysis and thus helps in developing a more realistic theory for study or better policy for implementation.

Although dynamic economic analysis is informative, comprehensive and realistic in nature, it is very much complex and difficult to conduct with precision. It is beyond the average capacity of human-being to take into account all complexities of real life for study. Present day economists, therefore, use dynamic framework for the analysis of economic problems in limited cases such as market adjustments, growth theories, investment planning, etc. Bulk of economics, at present, is economic statics. The situations of changes in this type of economics are taken care of by the method of comparative static. The results of one equilibrium state under static situation are compared with the results of another equilibrium state at another point of time. By such comparison we take into account the effect of time on the economic phenomenon. Such an effect is coming via changes in some variables overtime which, in turn, affect the equilibrium position.

1.6 ECONOMIC LAWS OR PRINCIPLES AND ECONOMIC THEORY

Economic theory is the core of economic science. It is the foundation for the study of the allocation of scarce resources and several other problems that are derived from this central core of economics. In a simple way, we can define economic theory as 'deriving the implications of purposive behaviour of consumers, producers, and other economic agents from the interaction of the tastes and constraints facing them.'[14] This definition recognises three basic elements of the economic theory. First, economic units are assumed to seek and achieve some goal that depends on taste and preferences of the units. Second, the goal or objective is achieved in a consistent manner. Third, they are not free to make any choice, rather this depends on the constraints which arise because of scarcity of resources. For example, consumers are assumed to maximise the utility derived from the goods and services of their choices purchased from the market place. The choice of goods and services available to the consumers is limited by the availability of money income. How to achieve the goal of maximising utility in this situation is the task of the economic theory to tell us.

Economic theories or models and the economic laws or principles derived from them are generalisations or abstractions of complex real life situations related to economic behaviour. Most of the economic phenomena are too complex to be described fully. What economists do is to take the most fundamental factors into account while developing a theory leaving the minor ones as constant or unchanged. Further, all the data required for the study of economic behaviour may not be available. So, some kind of simplification or abstraction is necessary to develop a theory in economics. The role of assumptions is very much crucial in this aspect. The theories or laws or principles of economics are valid in terms of averages/or statistical probabilities are associated with their validity in practice.

1.7 THE TASK AHEAD

The objective of this book is to provide a basic course of economic analysis to its readers mostly undergraduate students. The basic course in economic analysis starts with Microeconomics or what we call alternatively as Price Theory. This lays down the foundations for courses like macroeconomics, industrial economics, welfare economics, managerial economics and a number of other applied branches of the discipline. The emphasis will be given in the book on positive economic analysis relevant for economic decision making. Immediately in the next chapter we will go through the alternative economic systems and the basic economic problems of all societies. This will be followed by the other topics like demand and supply concepts, consumer behaviour, production theory, commodity pricing, factor pricing, etc., in the subsequent chapters.

SUGGESTED READINGS

Friedman, M., *The Methodology of Positive Economics in Essays in Positive Economics,* University of Cambridge Press, 1953.

Hutchinson, T.W., *The Significance and Postulates of Economic Theory,* A. Kolly 1938.

Keynes, J.N., *The Scope and Methods of Political Economy;* Macmillan, 1891.

14. Robert Russel and Wilkinson, M., *Microeconomics: A Synthesis of Modern & Neo Classical Theory,* John Wiley & Sons, N. Y., 1979, p. 2.

Liebhafsky, H. H., *The Nature of Price Theory;* The Dorrey Press, Homewood Illinois, 1968.
McKenzie, R.B., *The Limits of Economic Science;* Kluber Nijhoff Pub. Co. 1983.
Nagel, E., Assumptions in Economic Theory, *American Economic Review,* Vol. 53, 1963. pp. 211-219.
Robbins, L., *An Essay on the Nature and Significance of Economic Science,* Macmillan, 1935.
Samuelson, P.A., *Foundations of Economic Analysis,* Harvard University Press, 1947.

REVIEW QUESTIONS

1. What are the various approaches adopted by economists to define economics? Why economists could not reach a consensus regarding the precise definition of this discipline? Explain in brief.
2. Robbin's approach to define economics is regarded as the best one at present. Do you agree or not with this contention? Give justification for your answer.
3. What are the differences between the definitions of economics as given by Marshall, Robbins and Samuelson?
4. Some people consider economics as a science while others as an art. Why it is so? Discuss this completely.
5. What type of method of study, inductive or deductive or anything like that, you would like to suggest for the study of economics? Give reasons for your answer.
6. Some economists interpret economics as an inter-disciplinary subject in view of its strong linkages with several other subjects. What is your opinion about this? How do you justify the linkages of economics with other disciplines of social sciences, pure sciences and applied sciences?
7. How microeconomics is different from macroeconomics? What are the specific advantages of studying microeconomics from the point of view of society as a whole and individual decision makers like a producer, an engineer and like that?
8. Discuss the nature of the following branches of economics:
   (*a*) Positive and Normative Economics.
   (*b*) Static and Dynamic Economics.
9. How do you define the term 'theory'? Do you consider that the economic theories are necessary to understand the economic behaviour of human beings? Examine with full arguments.

CHAPTER 2

Alternative Economic Systems and Basic Economic Problems of Every Society

The economic systems prevailing in the world, at present, are quite complex and varied in nature. In spite of differences in the economic systems, however, we find certain basic economic problems existing in every society. The study of economics will be concerned, by and large, to find the solutions to such problems. In this chapter, we will go through a brief description of the problems and their implications for the economic theory as well as for the economic policy of different societies. Before we present this material it will be useful for us to have an idea of the competing economic systems since solution of problems depends, to a great extent, on the type of economy.

2.1 ALTERNATIVE ECONOMIC SYSTEMS

By the term 'economic system' we mean a complex organised body or structure of interconnected economic activities related to production, distribution and consumption of goods and services concerned with social administration. The major economic systems, seen at present, are Free Market Economy or Capitalism, Socialism, Communism, Mixed Economy and Fascism. The main features of these systems are as follows:

(i) Free Market Economy or Capitalism

An economy is said to be free-market economy or capitalistic if the following conditions are satisfied:

(*a*) There is perfect competition in the economy. Everybody tries to maximise his own gains or self-interest. The social gain or interest is automatically taken to be maximised in this situation. A simple addictive principle is being applied here, *i.e.*, social gain is the sum of gains of individuals. In terms of Adam Smith, this is called the principle of 'invisible hands.'[1] Persuasion of self interest by individual members of society is taken as a force or 'invisible hands' to achieve the best good for all.

1. Adam Smith, *The Wealth of Nations* (1776), Republished by Modern Library, N.Y. 1937, Book IV, Chapter 2.

(*b*) There is a right of private property in the economy. Business units and properties, including the money invested therein, are owned by private individuals. It implies that the means of production are owned by them and there is nothing like public sector in the economy.

(*c*) There is no government interference of any kind in the economic activities of individuals. Government simply takes taxes from individuals and business units to maintain law and order in the system. This is 'laissez faire' system. Individuals are free in this system to choose any economic activity for themselves. Government has nothing to do with this.

This type of economy is regulated by the market itself. Prices of different commodities and services are determined by their respective markets in which demand and supply forces interact. The investment pattern or what we call as resource allocation is also done by the markets.

There is no economy in the world where the above conditions are found in full. U.S.A. and some other Western economies are known as 'capitalistic economy' but they are not hundred per cent so.

The major drawback of this type of economy is that there is no control over individuals performing different economic activities. When there is full freedom in the system and control mechanism is absent the very foundation of the perfect competition is eroded leading thereby to imperfections in the economy and non-operation of the principle of 'invisible hands'. The free market economy is just like a bus without a driver in which every passenger is fighting to take control of its wheels. You can imagine what will happen in such a situation. The system of capitalism eventually leads to exploitation and self-degeneration. 'Survival of the fittest' is the basic principle that really applies to the competitive system of free-market economy.

(ii) Socialistic Economy or Socialism

This is another popular form of the economic system. The main features of this system are as follows:

(*a*) *Government (or public) ownership of Productive Resources:* All productive resources, *i.e.*, the means of production, except labour, are owned by the state under socialism. The state, in fact, owns the resources on behalf of the society as a whole. Alternatively, we call it as public ownership or collective ownership of the resources. The private sector in which enterprises are owned by individuals does not exist in this type of economy.

(*b*) *Centralised Planning Mechanism:* Both, resource allocation and pricing decisions are undertaken by a centralised body. Market mechanism will not be in operation in this type of economy. Production of goods and services is undertaken for uses keeping in mind the needs of consumption, rather than profit.

(*c*) *Redistribution of Income:* This is a very important goal of socialistic economy. Imbalances in income distribution in the society are corrected through proper adaptation of economic policies and their implementation. Some of the examples of economic measures through which the goal of income redistribution can be achieved are: government taxes on swollen incomes, restriction on inheritance of wealth, provision of social security benefits, equal job opportunities, granting of minimum need base income to poors, and so on. It does not mean that there would not be differences in incomes of people under socialism, but such difference will result from differences in skills and efficiency of individuals in the society.

(*d*) *Peaceful and Democratic Revolution:* There is no scope of violent movements for socio-economic changes under socialism. It advocates peaceful and gradual extension of government ownership of enterprises and other resources. The changes in the pattern of economic activities are brought through democratic ways involving masses.

Socialism is an ideal economic system in principle, but some people believe that this is inefficient as individuals lack motivation under this type of economy. Their rights, including incomes, are protected by the state; so, they do not bother to work hard to improve their lots. In spite of this potential limitation of socialism, it is becoming popular day by day and a large number of countries are coming under the cover of some type of socialism. It may be Christian Socialism, state or Marxian Socialism, guild or fabian socialism or of any other type.

(iii) Communism

This system was conceived of by Karl Marx. He called it by the name of "Scientific Socialism". Under this system, the means of production are owned by workers (and not by the state) and there is a militant workers movement to protect their interests. These two features make it significantly different from socialism. The other characteristics of socialism, *e.g.*, centralised planning and income redistribution in the society are also applicable to communism. There is no scope for exploitation of workers even by the state under this system of economy.

There is no country where the above mentioned conditions, are satisfied. Even the Russian economy, which was claimed to be communistic, was not fully so.

(iv) Mixed Economy

This is a mixture of both free market economy and socialism. Free market sector contains a large number of private enterprises owned by individuals or groups of individuals. Socialistic sector contains similarly several critical industries of the economy owned exclusively by the state. Thus, a mixed economy will have private as well as public sectors within its scope. The private sector of such an economy will be governed by the norm of self-interest but it has to keep in mind the economic interest of the community at large. It plays vital role in the economic reconstruction and development of a country. Industries, which are left free for private sector, are decided by the government. It reserves vital economic sectors like power generation and distribution, oil and natural gas, iron and steel, atomic energy, transport and communication, etc., for public or state ownership in the larger interest of the community. Profiteering is strictly checked in these industries. The emphasis is given on low price and availability of larger output of such industries for greater benefit of masses.

The system of mixed economy makes the best of the free market economy and socialistic economy. Freedom for economic choices, efficiency, and growth with social justice are some cannons of mixed economy. Most of the world economies are mixed at present. The degree of the 'mixture' of the two systems differs across the countries. Indian economy, for example, is judged on the basis of investment allocation and is 60 per cent free market oriented and 40 per cent socialistic. American economy, on the other hand, may be around 90 per cent 'free' and 10 per cent state owned.

Prices of goods and services are allowed to be determined under this system freely by the markets, but if they cross a limit then state regulates them. The task of resource allocation in the public or state sector is assigned to a centralised body, such as planning commission. This body, on behalf of the government, decides the norms for resource allocation in the private sector. The government will have considerable powers to regulate the economy.

(v) Fascism or Dictatorship

This is more a political system than an economic one. It is usually characterised by a one-man dictatorship. Hitler's Germany, Mussolini's Italy, Franco's Spain, Salazar's Portugal are a few examples of Fascism. What type of economy exists under Fascism is difficult to say. Each one may have its own norms. Some may prefer socialistic grab while others capitalistic. But it is clear that the central government of the country will have considerable economic powers under Fascism. Trade union activities and personal freedom will be curtailed significantly under this system and economic interests of the ruling dictator or 'Junta' will be taken care of fully. Since the economic system under fascism cannot be defined, it is difficult to visualize how pricing and resource allocation decisions will be made in this type of political system.

A brief summary of the major 'isms' or economic systems has been presented above. Our objective is not to go through the economic policies relevant for these different types of economics. Our objective in this study is simply to go through the basic theories or laws or principles of micro-economics. What type of economic system is most suitable to this or whether the basic laws of economics are independent of the types of isms prevailing in the world will be understood in a meaningful way only when we go through the theories we intend to study and the assumptions or abstractions behind them.

2.2 BASIC ECONOMIC PROBLEMS OF EVERY SOCIETY

Economists have identified six basic economic problems that are faced by all societies whether capitalistic or socialistic or mixed economy or any other type. The societies do differ on the basis of the types of economies or economic systems as we have seen in the previous section, but the core economic problems they face are identical. Economists try to find out how decisions on such core problems are arrived at in various societies and how governments and other organisations play meaningful roles in this direction. The problems are (*i*) What to produce; (*ii*) How to produce, (*iii*) For whom to produce, (*iv*) Full utilisation of resources, (*v*) Attainment of maximum economic efficiency and (*vi*) Growth of the economy. A brief description of these problems would give us a clear picture of their nature and implications for economic analysis.

(i) What to Produce?

This is perhaps the most fundamental economic problem of all societies. It is concerned with identification of those goods and services which are to be produced by a country. That is, a country has to decide in some way or other what collection of goods and services will mostly satisfy the needs of its citizen and in what quantities the goods and services are to be produced. Bombs or houses; cloth, medicines, cosmetics, etc., or machines; roads or railways or any combination of these or other goods are a few examples which throw enough light on the nature of the problem of 'What to produce'? How this problem is solved? It depends on the type of economic system. In a free market *i.e.*, capitalistic or even in mixed economy an analysis of consumer's expenditure patterns will help to answer the question 'What to produce'? The goods and services on which consumers are willing to spend their money should be produced. In a centralised economy where consumers are not having much freedom to choose way the commodities they need to satisfy their wants the government decides on the selection of goods and services for production. It may be based on some well defined norms, such as provision of essential goods for consumption, discouraging of consumption and production of luxury goods; emphasis on production of machines rather than consumer goods and so on. In economics we have the theory of demand or the theory of consumer behaviour that is concerned with the study of consumers' expenditure patterns and this helps identification of combination of goods and services for production in the economy.

(ii) How to Produce?

Goods and services wanted by the society are to be produced. How to produce them? This is a technological and organisational problem of production. Factors of production like men and machines cooperate together in transforming or fabricating of raw materials in the form of end products for consumers. Several problems are associated with this kind of economic activity such as:

(*a*) What resources should be used in production of goods and services, more machines or more men? This is the problem of choice of production techniques.

(*b*) What goods should be produced by large plants and what by small scale units or cottage industries? This is the problem of size and organisation of production units.

(*c*) What should be produced in public sector *i.e.*, in government factories and what in private factories? This is the problem of ownership of productive resources.

(*d*) Where should the goods and services be produced? This is the problem of location of industries.

There may be several other such problems. A society has to take decisions on solution of all problems related to production of goods and services. A study of the theory of production and cost helps us in answering or finding solutions to the questions raised above.

(iii) For whom to Produce?

One can say that goods and services are produced for consumers since they buy them and satisfy their wants. This is correct, but consumers can buy goods and services they need only when they have the money for this. Consumers supply various factors of production to the society in the form of labour, savings, *e.g.*, capital, property on rental basis for use in production and entrepreneurship. For all this, they get a share in production which is their income and from such income they buy goods and services. For whom to produce is the problem related to the distribution of net product (*i.e.*, total revenue minus value of material consumed) among the factors of production. How to do this? What should be the share of workers, rentiers, moneylenders, and residual income *e.g.*, profit from the production of goods and services? What should be the basis of such income distribution at enterprise level as well as at the national level? A study of the theory of distribution provides us with answers to such questions.

(iv) The Problem of Resource Utilisation

Production of goods and services is always constrained by the scarcity of relevant resources. When resources are scarce, one would expect that they are utilised fully but there are examples in different societies of under-utilisation of resources in spite of demand for goods and services in whose production the resources can be used. In India, for example, 30 per cent of arable land has been unutilised till 1970. Overall capacity utilisation (weighted average) in Indian industries for the period 1970–82 varied between 72.9 and 85.2 per cent. In specific industries, capacity utilisation figures for the year 1981 were: Textiles 84 per cent, Chemicals 73 per cent, Electricity generation 43 per cent, Ferrous Metals 60 per cent. Similarly, we can cite examples of unemployment of skilled manpower like engineers, doctors, trained teachers and so on. What are the reasons for such unemployment or under-utilisation of productive resources is a big question that economists try to answer. This is an important aspect to be studied in economics.

(v) The Problem of Efficiency

Productive resources at the disposal of a society may be utilised fully. But this itself is not a guarantee that they are being utilised in the most desirable way. The phrase "desirable way" has normative connotation. A society has to spell it out. However, for the sake of simplicity, we may take the stand that 'full utilisation of resources in the most desirable way' means optimisation of production and consumption in the economy. Without going into details at this stage, production is said to be inefficient if it would be possible to reallocate resources and to produce more of at least one product without simultaneously producing less of any other product.

The goods (including services) that are produced, are said to be inefficiently distributed if it would be possible to redistribute them among individuals in the society and make at least one person better off without simultaneously making anyone worse off.

Inefficiencies in both, production and consumption are to be reduced. That is the same thing as saying that production and consumption in the society has to be efficient. What are the conditions or laws for attainment of efficiency in production and consumption is studied under welfare economics. The economic system has to give maximum welfare to the people for whom it works.

(vi) The Problem of Growth of Economy

The problem of growth of economy is quite serious in most of the countries, particularly under-developed and developing ones. By 'growth' we mean increase in productive capacity and actual production of goods and services from year to year. More goods and services are required by a country overtime because of necessity to meet the demands of growing population. Apart from this, the standard of living of people improves overtime due to the impact of education and development of science and technology. Thus, they need varieties of goods and services which meet their requirements. An economy has to make necessary arrangements for production of greater amount as well as greater varieties of goods and services. Economies have to make all efforts for this. It implies growth of the economy. It is, however, not very easy to achieve the objective of growth of the economy. There will be several constraints to this which are to be removed. What is to be the rate of growth, what is the appropriate way to achieve growth and development of the economy? These are vital questions for which a society must find answers. These problems are studied under the theories of economic development and growth.

The six problems, as discussed above, are fundamental and common to all economies. The first three problems, *i.e.*, 'What to Produce', 'How to Produce' and 'For Whom to Produce' together forming a 'triology' of economic problems are normally considered more fundamental than the other three but we emphasize that all of them are of equal importance in the context of contemporary economic complexities. The different economic systems try to solve these problems in different ways. In a free market economy these problems are solved by a system of prices. In mixed economy they are solved partly by prices and partly by government. While in a centralised economy the price system may not be in operation to solve them but a set of public norms or directions by the government do the job of solving them. In brief, we can say that the basic economic problems of different societies are solved in different ways – by customs, instinct, fiat and decree, and largely by a price system.

2.3 THE PRODUCTION POSSIBILITY CURVE AND BASIC ECONOMIC PROBLEMS

A production possibility curve depicts the frontier showing different combinations of various goods that can be produced from a given amount of resources. In other words, the curve shows full production possibilities at full employment or full use of resources. In practice, a society will be producing several goods from the fixed quantities of different resources. To draw a production possibility curve in such a situation is impossible. So, we have to abstract or simplify the reality. Let us assume that a society produces two goods – one is 'bread' representing consumer goods and another 'guns' representing machines and war goods. Only one composite type of resource is used to produce these two products. The society intends to use its resource fully in production of goods. From the given or fixed quantity of the resource it can produce only 'bread' or only 'guns' or any of its combination. It is further assumed that the quality of the resource is at maximum level, otherwise there may be a possibility of producing more of both the goods if quality of the resource goes up. The production possibility curve for this simplified case, *i.e.*, two goods and one resource, can be shown graphically as follows:

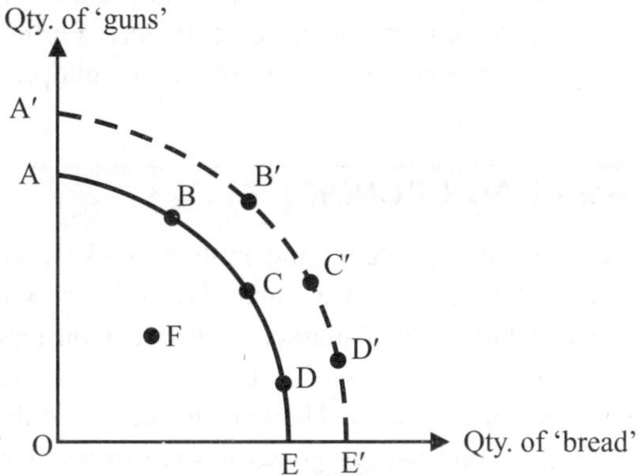

Fig. 2.1 Production Possibility Curve (PPC)

ABCDE shows the production possibility curve in this diagram. From the given quantity of the resource (say R°) the society can produce either OA units of 'guns' or OE units of 'bread' or any combination of these two goods, such as shown by points B or C or D on the PPC. If the society wants to produce more 'bread' it has to reduce production of 'guns' and vice versa. When resources are fully utilised it will not be able to produce more of both the goods. Substitution of one good for the other is inevitable. The frontier A to E shows full utilisation of resources, so the fourth basic economic problem mentioned in the previous section is solved if we operate along the boundary A to E. The first economic problem, *i.e.*, 'What to Produce' is also 'solved' when the society picks up the combination of two goods from a large number of combinations shown by the PPC. Actually, how it is done depends on the goal of the society, such as revenue maximisation or profit maximisation. This type of analysis will be presented later on in this book under the theory of production.

How to produce two goods selected cannot be explicitly explained through the production possibility curve. We can simply make a statement that the society makes efficient choice of methods with proper allocation of inputs including factors of production to the various industries. Production has to be efficient, (refer problem 5; in the previous section) for this the techniques should be chosen in such a way that society gets the outputs shown by the PPC. Any point inside the production possibility curve, such as shown by F, will depict inefficient production and under-utilisation of resources.

For 'Whom to Produce', *i.e.*, the distribution problem of output cannot be deduced from the PPC diagram. The growth problem, *i.e.*, increase in productive capacity of economy can be very well explained with the help of the PPC. We know that for an increase in productive capacity of an economy we need more resources. An increase in resources means production of at least more of a good without simultaneously decreasing production of the other goods. This implies a shift of the production possibility curve to outward, the one shown by the new p.p.c. A′ B′ C′ D′ E′ in Fig. 2.1. The curve will shift parallel to the right if more resources are available, other things, such as society's preference for goods and state of technology remaining unchanged. This type of a shift in p.p.c. indicates a balanced growth of sectors. Change in technology alone is an important factor for economic growth. In this situation, even with constant level of resources but 'improvement' in the technology the p.p.c. shifts outward. The shift of the p.p.c., however, may not be parallel in this case. So, an improvement in technology and an increase in productive resources will push the p.p.c. up, *i.e.*, outward showing economic growth in the society.

In summary, what we can say is that production possibility curve or front is an important tool to understand most of the basic economic problems of a society. Further discussion on the nature and properties of the p.p.c. and its implication in the study of multiproduct firm will be provided later on in this book.

2.4 CIRCULAR FLOWS IN AN ECONOMY

It is quite interesting to see how an economic system works and how the basic problems, particularly 'What to Produce', 'How to Produce', and 'For Whom to Produce', are solved by it. For this, let us consider a simple model of a market economy. Consumers and producers are two major segments. Consumers need various types of goods and services such as food, cloth, houses, medicines, transport, etc., to satisfy their wants. They spend their incomes in acquiring these goods and services. The producers produce and supply goods to consumers. Thus, there is a link between consumers and producers. This link is not direct. It is through the commodity markets. Consumers buy goods from markets. In buying goods money flows from consumers to markets from where quantities of goods flow to consumers. Again, markets get goods from producers, *i.e.*, from factories, and pay for them. Thus, money flows from markets to producers and goods flow from producers to markets. What is the role of markets? Market not only links consumers and producers but also brings demand and supply of goods in equilibrium through the price system. By equilibrium we mean making the demand for a commodity equal to its supply. If the price system is free to operate, there will be no excess demand for goods and services. Markets will regulate these in such a situation. We have to see how this happens.

To produce goods and services producers need various types of inputs. They buy raw materials and other produced inputs from the commodity markets. They are like 'consumers' in this case. The factors of production, *i.e.*, labour, machinery, land, etc., they buy from factor markets. A factor market is just like a commodity market where factors of productions are bought and sold, labour market is an example for this. The factors of production (labour, capital, land, etc.), are owned by private individuals who are nobody but the consumers. They supply these factors to factor markets and get payments in the form of factor incomes such as wages, interest, rent and profit. This is the income of consumers which flows from the factor markets to the consumers. From factor markets the factors are bought by the producers. That is, factors of production flow to the producers and money flows from producers to the markets. Considering all flows of the economy together, we get an overall idea of the interdependence among the consumers, commodity markets, factor markets and producers. In graphical form, this is shown in Fig. 2.2.

As we see in the diagram, money or expenditure flows clockwise and flow of goods in opposite direction. The innerflow circle indicates the flow of goods and services from producers to commodity markets and from commodity markets to public *i.e.*, consumers. From consumers there is a flow of resources to factor markets from where they go to producers *i.e.*, resource users. The expenditure of producers flows from them to the factor markets and from factor markets to public in the form of factor incomes (wages, rent, interest, profit, etc.). Consumers (or public) spend their incomes on goods and services which they buy from commodity markets. From commodity markets the flow of money in revenue form goes to producers. In this way, we complete the circular flows of a market economy. Both commodity and factor markets perform the task of balancing supply and demand for goods and factors of production respectively. In a free-market economy, it is the prices

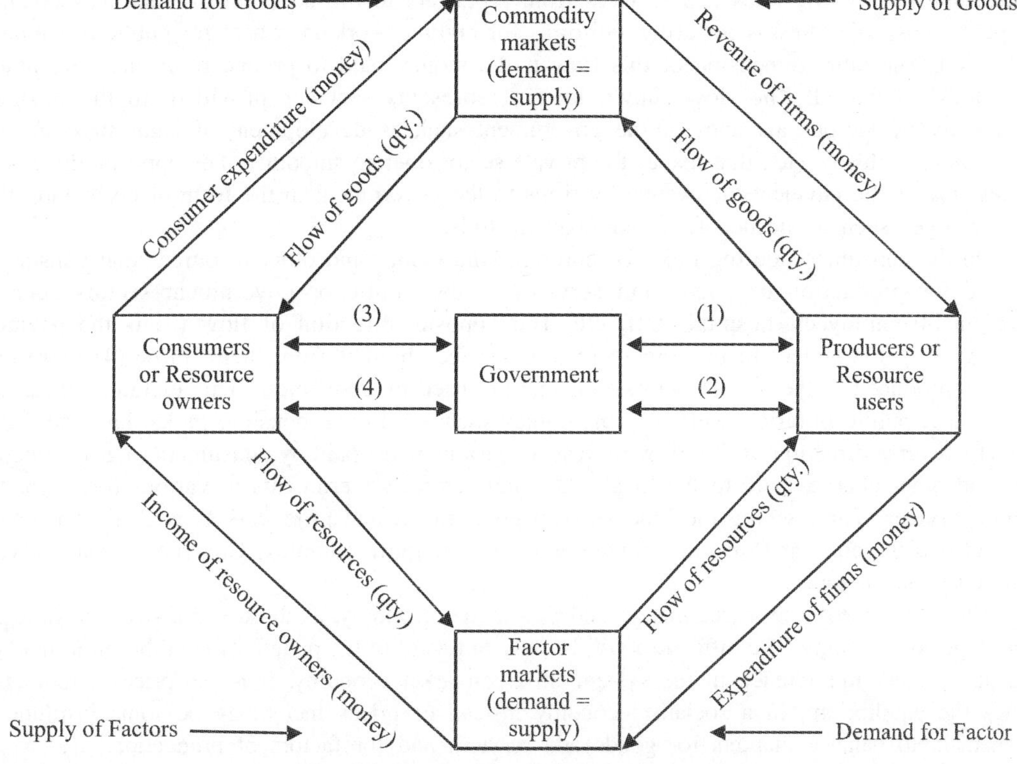

Fig. 2.2 Circular Flows in Market Economy

of goods and services and of factors of production that do this job. Prices bring equilibrium which may be defined as demand = supply for individual goods or factors and aggregate supply = aggregate demand for economy as a whole. The north-west corner of the diagram (Fig. 2.2) shows the consumer expenditure patterns. It is related to demand analysis for different goods and services and hence to the problem of 'What to Produce'. The north-eastern corner of the diagram reflects the supply side of goods and services. Similarly, the south-eastern corner relates to the demand for factors of production and hence 'How to Produce' problem of economy. The west-southern corner shows the supply of factors of production. All these basic economic problems, *i.e.*, 'What', 'How' and 'For Whom' are linked here. Once a firm decides about the use of a technology, it buys factors and inputs, pays for them and thus solves the problem of 'For Whom to Produce'.

So far, in the above discussion on the circular flows in a market economy, we have not taken government sector into consideration. We have taken the case of a capitalistic economy for discussion. Now, let us bring the government into the picture, *i.e.*, the case of a mixed economy. A government plays very crucial role in the mixed economy. It will be a producer of goods, a consumer of goods and services, a controller of the economy system and a law and order maintaining representative body of public. It will be linked directly with producers and consumers of the country. In order to show links between government and producers as well as consumers, we consider four types of flows, each of which has two dimensions. In Fig. 2.2 'Government' is shown in the centre part. The link between producers and government are shown by arrows (1) and (2) and between government and consumers by (3) and (4). The flow shown by (1) represents the flow of goods and services from producers to the government, such as medicines for public hospitals, dresses for army, uniforms for civilian workers, wheat for public distribution and so on. The other dimension of this flow is the money paid to producers by the government for goods purchased. The flow shown by (2) represents services provided. to the business community by various agencies of the government such as development of legal structure, the provision of highway, etc., that makes the private sector operate smoothly. The opposite dimension of this flow is the payment of revenue by firms to the government in the form of taxes and other users charges such as licence fees and highway tolls.

On the consumer side the link (3) represents the labour and other resources that consumers provide for production of goods and services in the public or government sectors such as government employees, hospital staff, etc. The opposite direction of flow (3) is the payment made by the government to consumers for the services bought from them. Flow (4) represents services produced in the government sector that are used by consumers. This includes education, health care, public libraries, welfare programmes such as old age pension, parks, law and order, etc. The reverse direction of this flow represents various taxes paid by consumers to governments, fees and other charges paid to the local, state and central governments in various forms for the public services. Thus, seeing the link between government and producers as well as consumers, we find that the circular flows in a mixed economy are quite complex. Government plays a very important role in this.

The circular flows in a free-market and in a mixed economy, as discussed above, are valid for other types of economy. The difference will be only in regard to the pattern of equilibrium in markets and government interference in the system. In free-market economy, it is the price system that brings the equilibrium; in a socialist economy instead of prices there may be some institutional mechanism to balance markets for goods and services and for factors of production.

In describing the circular flows, we have assumed a simple economic system in which several other flows like savings and investment, external trade and payment etc., have not been examined. One can do this but, at this stage, there is no need of going through such complexities. Our objective in this section was simply to bring the notion of the circular flows in the picture in order to understand links between the basic economic problems of 'What', 'How' and 'For Whom' to produce.

2.5 CONCLUDING REMARKS

The central theme of this chapter was to have an idea of the basic economic problems of every society. The basic problems that have been discussed were 'What', 'How' and 'For Whom' to produce, full utilisation of scarce resources, efficiency, and growth necessity for an economy. Before presenting a brief outline of each of these problems the alternative economic systems have been discussed. The notions of production possibility curve and circular flows in the economy have also been discussed in order to get a clear picture of links between various basic economic problems of societies. What we have to do now is to go through the basic laws or principles of economics that are helpful in solving the problem. This implies a thorough study of the basic economic theory. This begins from the next chapter.

SUGGESTED READINGS

Allen, G. Gruchy, *Comparative Economic System,* Houghton Mifflin Co., 1966.

Lipsey R.G.; *An Introduction to Positive Economic Analysis,* English Language Book Society, 1971, 1995.

Ralf, Eiden and Staffan Viotti, *Economic Systems,* Martin Robertson, Oxford, 1978.

Samuelson, P.A.; *Economics.* McGraw-Hill, 1964, 2005.

Wayne, A. Leeman; *Centralised and Decentralised Economic Systems,* Rand McNally Pub. Co., 1977.

REVIEW QUESTIONS

1. What are the leading alternative economic systems and how they differ from each other?
2. 'Capitalism failed to provide goods to masses that is why more and more nations are going for socialism'. Discuss and give your assessment of the performance of these two economic systems in the contemporary world.
3. What are the basic economic problems of every society? How such problems are solved under (*a*) free market mechanism, (*b*) mixed economy, and (*c*) centralised economies?
4. Full utilisation of resources, attaining economic efficiency and growth are somewhat interrelated aspects of an economy. How? Use production possibility front (PPF) diagram to elaborate your answer.
5. Through a circular flow diagram explain how price mechanism in a free market economy brings the equilibrium position of the entire economic system. If prices are controlled, does it mean that the economic system would then be in disequilibrium? Comment.
6. We find several 'isms' across the world at present; capitalism, socialism, communism, fascism, and so on. What makes the 'isms' different from each other — economics or politics? Discuss in detail. What is the exact role played by economics in differentiating the 'isms'?
7. Mixed economy is a compromise between capitalism and socialism or communism. What was the necessity of mixed economy system of economic organisation? How this system is capable of solving the basic economic problems of developing countries? Examine in full.

CHAPTER 3

Demand, Supply and Pricing: Some Elementary Concepts

In this chapter, we intend to introduce some basic concepts of economics, such as 'demand', 'supply', 'market equilibrium', elasticities, etc. These concepts frequently appear in almost every economic analysis. It will, therefore, be quite helpful to study them and related economic laws in detail right in the beginning. It is somewhat intermediate level of the economic analysis. The advanced version of that will appear at the appropriate places in other chapters of this book.

3.1 DESIRE, WANTS AND DEMAND

(*i*) *Desire*: A desire is a basic attribute of human life that induces a person to work or make efforts to fulfil that. It is that feeling or emotion which is directed to the attainment or possession of some object from which pleasure or satisfaction is expected. In other words, it is simply a wish. A person desires to have a motor car and makes efforts to get it. If a man has a desire for a wife he will get married otherwise not. We do have desires for food, cloth, houses and try to get them. A desire for better life through better things in possession is a fundamental impulse of human life. Desires may be real and/or imaginary. Desires for having goods and services for survival or better life are real while those for fantasies are unreal or imaginary. They may not be fulfilled. Man had a desire to fly in the sky. He worked for this and so today we find his desire fulfilled. If a person desires more money, he makes efforts for that, get some job or do some business and thus earns money. In the context of the economic analysis we have to take it for granted that human actions are backed by the necessary desires for that, otherwise we will be in trouble as irrationality (*i.e.*, desireless human activities) may invalidate our economic theories.

(*ii*) *Wants or Needs:* A desire for anything as a necessity to live or be happy or succeed which if not satisfied due to lack of resources is called 'Want' or 'Need'. A man desires for a house but he is not able to get it as there is no money to buy or construct the house. Since house is a necessity of life so it remains merely a want due to lack of resources. We need a number things but we may not have all of them due to lack of resources. They will, therefore, remain as wants of our lives. Each individual will have a set of wants for himself depending on his tastes, way of life, standard of living, status, etc. A doctor needs a car. In the absence of resources to buy a car, it will remain a want for him but for a labourer in a country, like India, it may not be desirable to have a car as he does not need it.

(*iii*) *Demand:* The willingness to buy a commodity or service for which necessary resources are available is called 'demand'. Both, desire and resourcefulness are essential requirements of demand. An individual or a family unit will have demand for several things like food, house, TV, clothes, medicines, transportation, education, health care and so on, to satisfy various wants. The use of such commodities and services in satisfying the needs or wants is called consumption. An individual or family performing the act of consumption is called 'consumer'. A society, as a whole, or a government buying goods or services for consumption will also be called consumers. A consumer buys a commodity or service for its own use and not for its resale.

A commodity or service may also be used in production of other commodities or services by a producer or a firm. The commodity or service is not being consumed in this situation but it is being used as an input for production of other commodities or services. Here we use the term 'input demand' indicating that there is a demand for the commodity or service as an input for production of something else.

3.2 THE CONCEPT OF DEMAND FUNCTION

What will be the factors that determine the demand for a commodity? In the case of consumption, the willingness to buy a commodity, that is the demand for that, depends on factors, such as:

(*i*) The income of the consumer.
(*ii*) The price of that commodity.
(*iii*) Prices of other goods and services on which the consumer spends his income.
(*iv*) Tastes and preferences of the consumer, size of his family, social customs, expectations and advertisement, etc.

Similarly, in the case of a firm or producer the input demand for commodity depends on factors like

(*i*) The total outlay or expenditure of the firm,
(*ii*) The price of that commodity,
(*iii*) Prices of other substitute and complementary inputs,
(*iv*) The nature of technology, etc.

For the sake of simplicity let us concentrate on consumer demand for a commodity leaving aside the producer's demand at this stage since this will be a mere repetition of consumer demand in a 'slightly changed terminology'.[1]

A consumer's demand function for a commodity specifies the relationship between quantity of the commodity that he is willing to buy and the demand factors. In other words, in a demand function, the quantity demanded is expressed as a function of the demand factors for the commodity. In mathematical form we can express the demand function for a commodity as:

$$Q_x = D_x\ [P_x, P_s, P_c, Y, T] \qquad \text{...(1)}$$

where Q_x is quantity of commodity *X* demanded, P_x is the price of the commodity, P_s denotes the price of other commodities which can be substituted for *X*, P_c is the price of a commodity which is a complement of commodity *X*, *Y* is income of the consumer and *T* represents other demand factors such as tastes, preferences, social customs, etc. D_x indicates the functional form of the relationship. There may be more than one substitute and/or complementary goods for commodity *X*. In this situation, the specification of the demand function for commodity *X* can be expanded by including their prices.

1. The concept of input demand function will be discussed later on under 'Theory of Production and Cost.'

The demand function (1) may be linear or non-linear in shape. If it is linear, it can be expressed as

$$Q_x = a_o + a_x P_x + a_s P_s + a_c P_c + bY + cT \qquad ...(2)$$

where a_o is a constant, a_x, a_s, a_c, b and c are also constant parameters called 'marginal coefficients'. These are nothing but values of partial derivatives of the function. The interpretation of these coefficients is straight forward. If P_x increases by one unit, the quantity demanded Q_x will then change by a_x units, other variables remaining unchanged. Similar interpretation can be given for a_s, a_c, b and c. Some of these coefficients may be negative like a_x, a_c and some positive like a_s and b in some cases. Why? We will find reasons for this shortly.

If the function is non-linear in shape it implies changing marginal coefficients with the levels of the concerned demand factor. For example, the coefficient of P_x may increase or decrease on increasing P_x. One standard non-linear shape of the consumer demand function is logarithmic, shown as

$$Q_x = A\, P_x^{\alpha_x} \cdot P_s^{\alpha_s} \cdot P_c^{\alpha_c} \cdot Y^{\beta} \cdot T^{\gamma} \qquad ...(3)$$

where α_x, α_s, α_c, β and γ are constant parameters (these are elasticity) coefficients which will be defined later on. Some of these parameters may be negative and some positive depending on how the quantity demanded responds to its determinants.

We cannot find the shape of the demand function appropriately. It is to be determined only on estimating or fitting the demand function.

The demand function shown either by (2) or (3) is very complex in the sense that if all determinants on right hand side change simultaneously, we will not be able to say on a-priority what will be the change in the quantity demanded unless we have estimates of the parameters. Some parameters of these functions will be negative and some positive, so the net result of a change in Q_x may be negative or positive. To know the precise nature of the effect of change in all the factors of demand on the quantity demanded of a commodity by a consumer, we have to examine the factors individually keeping others as constants. This is the assumption of "other things being equal" or "*ceteris paribus.*" Let us do this.

(a) The Relationship Between Q_x and P_x

It is a common observation that for most of the commodities the willingness to buy decreases as price of the commodity increases. Exceptions are everywhere. For certain very essential goods like medicines, however, there may not be inverse relationship between quantity demanded and price. It may be a straight line showing fixed quantity of the commodity that the consumer is willing to buy at different prices. Let us concentrate on the normal case of inverse relationship between price and quantity demanded of a commodity. If we plot the relationship using price on *x-axis* and quantity on *y*-axis the graph would be seen as following:

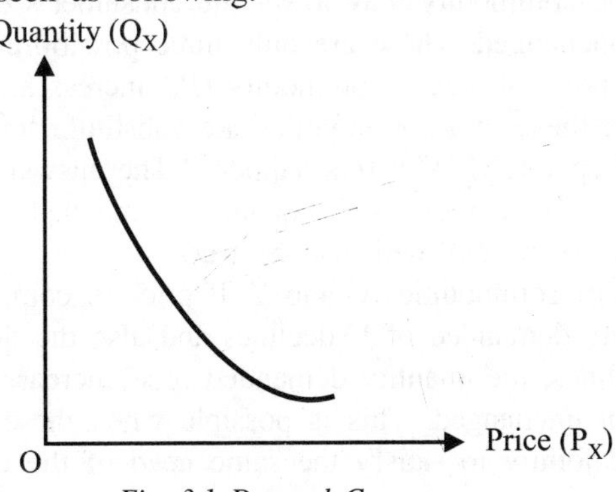

Fig. 3.1 Demand Curve

In this curve quantity demanded (Q_x) responds to price P_x. it is called 'demand curve' for the commodity. It is a convention in economics to take quantity on *x-axis* and price on *y-axis* while drawing a demand curve as shown in Fig. 3.2. This is for the sake of convenience of representing demand and other curves together to understand the process of price determination. The demand curve for a commodity shows the relationship between the price of that commodity and the quantity that a consumer is willing to buy. It is drawn on the assumption that other factors of demand remain unchanged. It is normally a downward sloping curve as we told earlier. In the form of a law we can state the relationship as under:

The Law of Demand: Other things being equal, the quantity demanded of a commodity varies inversely with its price.

Why a consumer buys more of a commodity when its price decreases and less when the price increases? Two possible explanations may be given for this at this stage:

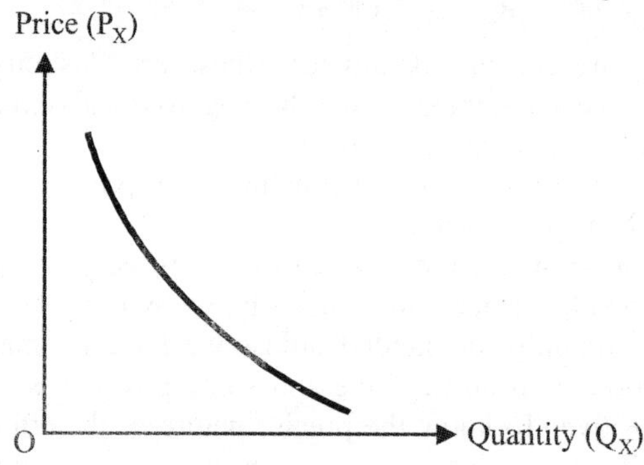

Fig. 3.2 Inverted Demand Curve

(*i*) When price declines the consumer saves some expenditure which brings him more of that commodity. We may call this as "income effect."

(*ii*) A consumer can substitute that commodity, when its price declines and other prices remain constant, for some other commodity. This is called "substitution effect".

There is a third explanation of declining marginal utility as quantity increases but we will discuss this in the chapter on the theory of consumer behaviour.

(b) The Relationship Between Quantity Demanded of a Commodity and Prices of Other Commodities

A fall in price of one commodity may lower the consumer's demand for other commodity or may raise it or leave it unchanged. These are only three possibilities. Let us take the care of two commodities *S* and *X*. If price of say, *S* commodity (P_s) increases, demand for *X* commodity goes up. This is possible when these two commodities are substitute for each other, *i.e.*, they are used to satisfy the same need separately. Why this happens? The answer is simple. An increase in price of *S*, other things being constant, reduces the quantity demanded for *S* and increases the quantity demanded for *X*. The reverse of this will also be true.

Consider another set of commodities *C* and *X*. If price of commodity *C* increases, other things being constant, the quantity demanded of *C* declines and also the quantity demanded of *X* declines and if the price of *C* declines, the quantity demanded of *C* increases but the quantity demanded of *X* may increase or remain unchanged. This is possible when these two goods are complementary goods, *i.e.*, they are used jointly to satisfy the same need of the consumer.

The third situation concerns the neutral or unrelated goods. In an increase or decrease in price of one commodity if it has no effects on quantity demanded of other commodities they are neutral or unrelated goods. The prices of other goods and services will not appear in the demand function as determinants for such commodities.

Figure 3.3 shows graphically the relationships for substitute and complementary goods as discussed above.

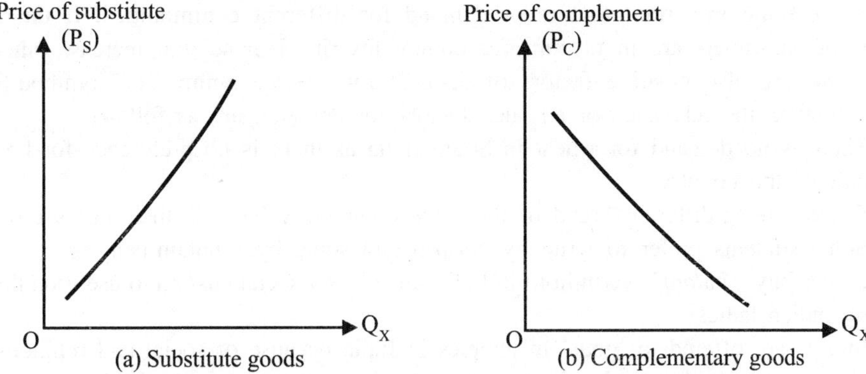

Fig. 3.3 Effects of Other Prices on Quantity Demanded of a Commodity

(c) The Relationship Between Quantity Demanded and Income

There are three possibilities for this type of relationship. An increase (decrease) in income of the consumer increases (decreases) the demand for the commodity. The commodities for which we get this type of positive relationship are called 'normal' goods. For certain commodities like foodstuff, a rise in income causes an increase in quantity demanded in the initial stage but after a certain level of the consumer's income, the quantity demanded becomes invariable with respect to the income, *i.e.*, it remains at a constant level.

For certain commodities, after a certain level of income of the consumer, the quantity demanded starts decreasing with increase in income, the commodities which depicts this type of relationship are called 'inferior' goods. Through a diagram, we can show all the three situations of the income-consumption relationship as under: (See Fig. 3.4).

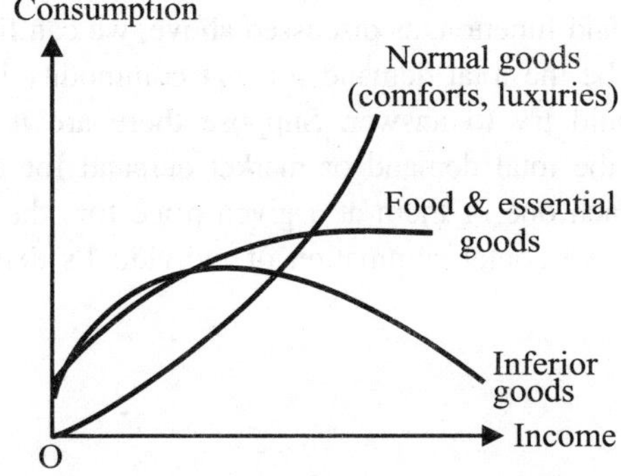

Fig. 3.4 Effects of Income on Quantity Demanded

There is a simple generalisation of the relationship between consumption of goods and income for a consumer. This is known as Engel's law. According to this law, as income increases the proportion of income spent on food declines and the proportion spent on comforts and luxuries increases. This law is quite valid as we see from our own experience as consumers.

(d) Tastes and Preferences, Social Customs and Demand

These are quite important factors of demand for different commodities. If the tastes and preferences of consumers are in favour of a commodity, its demand will increase otherwise not. Social customs are also positive factors of demand for a large number of commodities. Some examples, showing the relevance of all such factors for demand, are as follows:

(*i*) There is no demand for wheat in South India as there is no preference for bread in this part of the country.

(*ii*) People prefer different brand of the same commodity because their tastes differ.

(*iii*) Some students prefer to write by dot-pen and some by fountain-pen.

(*iv*) Ladies buy '*sindoor*' (vermilion) in India since it is a social custom to use it on the forehead by Indian ladies.

(*v*) Sweets are offered to 'gods' in temples in India because of social and religious customs.

Advertisement and other kinds of sales promotion activities are used by business units to induce consumers preferences or tastes in favour of commodities and hence an increase in their demand. From this point of view, such activities are treated as additional demand factors.

(e) Expectations and Other Factors

If prices and income are expected to increase, the quantity demanded for certain commodities may go up. In the situation of rising prices, consumers generally buy more and stock commodities for future consumption. If prices are expected to fall, they may not buy more or postpone certain type of consumption for future. Apart from expectations, there might be some other seasonal or temporary factors affecting the demand for a commodity in some way or other. Similarly, if income is expected to rise, a consumer may buy more of a commodity since he would be able to pay for this later on.

3.3 MARKET DEMAND

By estimating the demand function, as discussed above, we can find the demand for a commodity for a consumer. What will be the total demand for that commodity in the country as a whole is the next question that we should try to answer. Suppose there are n consumers or customers for a commodity in the market, the total demand or market demand for the commodity will be the sum of quantity demanded by each one of them at a given price for the commodity. In the terminology of economics we call it as horizontal summation of individual's demand to get the market demand for the commodity.

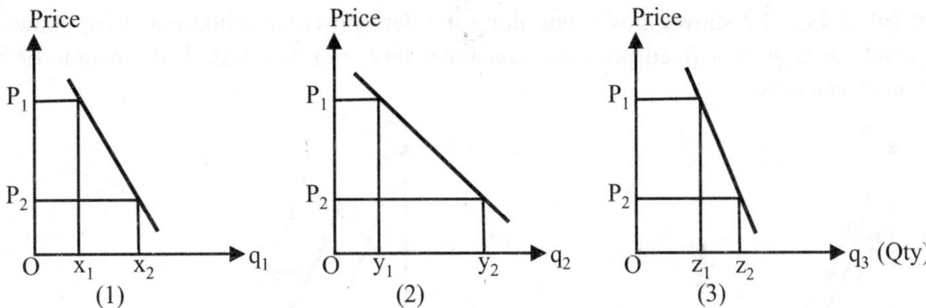

Fig. 3.5 Horizontal Summation of Demand Curves

The demand curves for three consumers—1, 2, and 3—are given in the above diagram. At P_1 price of the commodity consumer 1 buys Ox_1 units of the commodity, consumer 2 buys Oy_1 units and consumer 3 buys Oz_1 units. Total market demand for this three consumers economy would be $Ox_1 + Oy_1 + Oz_1$ units at P_1 price and, similarly, $Ox_2 + Oy_2 + Oz_2$ at P_2 price. Making such additions at different prices, we can finally find the market demand curve for the commodity as shown below:

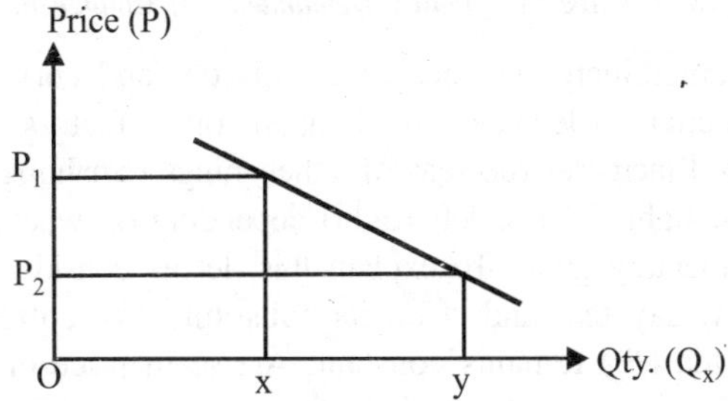

Fig. 3.6 Market Demand Curve for a Commodity

The market demand for a commodity depends on factors like (1) number of customers in the market, total population or a segment of that may be used for this depending on who uses the commodity; (2) level of income in the society and its distribution, say per capita income of the country; (3) price of the commodity; (4) prices of the substitute and complementary goods for the commodity; and (5) expectations, lags, preferences and other miscellaneous factors. All these factors may not be equally relevant for finding the market demand for a commodity. Their contributions depend on the nature of the commodity. Market demand for salt, for example, solely depends on population. Demand for writing paper depends on the number of students or literate people in the society. One has to be careful in identifying the relevant market demand factors for the concerned commodity.

3.4 SHIFT OF DEMAND CURVE AND MOVEMENT ALONG THE DEMAND CURVE

If income and other determinants of demand remain constant and only price of the commodity changes, we move along the demand curve. There will be a change in quantity demanded simply because of a change in price of the commodity. In this case, the demand curve remains unchanged. The movement along the demand curve is designated as 'change in quantity demanded'.

But, if the price of the commodity remains constant and other factors change, the demand curve shifts its position. This kind of movement of the demand curve is designated as 'change in demand'. Remember, quantity demanded do change in this case also but it is because of a shift of the demand curve.

Panel (*a*) of Fig. 3.7 shows movement along the demand curve while Panel (*b*) shows the shift of the demand curve as at a fixed price the consumer buys more or less if his income or any other relevant factor changes.

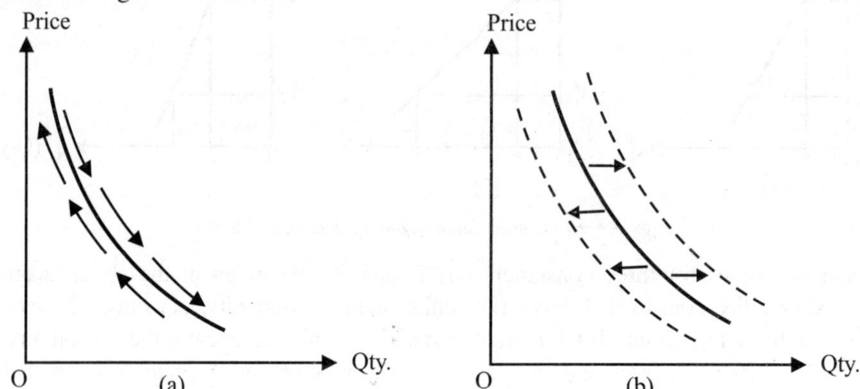

Fig. 3.7 (a) Change in Quantity Demanded, (b) Change in Demand

If income of the consumer increases (decreases) his demand curve for a commodity shifts to the right (left) indicating increase (decrease) in demand, other factors remaining the same.

If price of any other good increases (decreases), other things remaining the same, the demand curve for a commodity shifts to the right (left) or left (right) depending on whether the other commodity is a substitute good or a complementary good. To explain this, let us consider the following situations.

Let X be a commodity, say tea, and S be its substitute say coffee. Suppose price of coffee (P_s) increases and price of tea (P_x) remains constant. A rise in price of coffee means less quantify demanded of coffee and more quantity demanded of tea since people now shift to tea. This means at a given price of tea there is more demand for tea. This implies a rise or shift of the demand curve for tea to the right. The reverse sequence will take place when price of coffee decreases.

Now let us take the case of complementary goods, say tea leaves and sugar. A rise in the price of tea leaves means less quantity demanded of tea leaves. Since sugar is used in some fixed proportion with tea leaves in preparation of tea it means less demand for sugar though its price has not changed. (It is presumed here that tea without sugar is not used by people). The demand curve for sugar therefore shifts to the left showing a decrease in its demand. The demand curve of sugar shifts to the right if the price of tea leaves decline.

Now, we come to other determinants. If tastes or preferences of consumers change in favour of a commodity, its demand curve shifts to the right showing a rise in demand. Advertisement also shifts the curve to the right but expectations may shift it to the right or left depending on what is expected to change and in what direction. If price of the commodity is expected to rise the demand curve rises, *i.e.* shifts to the right and vice versa.

In conclusion, we may summarise the above discussion by saying that a rise in the demand for a commodity, *i.e.*, a shift of the demand curve to the right means more is purchased at each price of the commodity. This may be because of increase in income, increase in the price of substitute goods, decrease in the price of complementary goods, an increase in taste, preferences, etc., in favour of the commodity and expected increase in price of the commodity. The demand curve shifts to the left, *i.e.*, a fall in demand means less purchases at each price of the commodity because of decrease in income; fall in the price of substitute goods, rise in the price of complementary goods and changes in tastes, preferences against the commodity.

3.5 THE CONCEPT OF SUPPLY AND SUPPLY FUNCTION

Supply is the other side of a market for a commodity. By 'supply' we mean the quantity of that commodity that producers are willing and able to offer for sales at a certain price. It is a flow concept and measures desired quantities. Both willingness and ability to supply are its essential features.

The factors on which the supply of a commodity depends are:

(*i*) Price of that commodity.

(*ii*) Prices of substitutes and complementary goods for the commodity.

(*iii*) Prices of Factors of production.

(*iv*) Total expenditure of the producer.

(*v*) State of production technology.

(*vi*) Goal of the producer.

In a symbolic form, we can express the relationship between quantity of the commodity that a producer is willing to supply and its determinants as:

$$s_x = S\ [P_x,\ P_s,\ P_c,\ F_j,\ C,\ T,\ G] \qquad \text{...(4)}$$

where s_x is quantity of the commodity supplied, P_x is its price, P_s represents a vector of prices of substitute goods, P_c represents a vector of prices of complementary goods, F_j, $j = 1$ to k represents prices of factors of production, C is total expenditure of the producer, T represents the state of technology, and G represents goal (s) of the producer. S denotes functional shape of the relationship. This relationship is called 'supply function'. Like a demand function, it is a complex relationship. Some factors may have positive effect on quantity supplied while others negative. So the net effect of all factors, when they change simultaneously, cannot be predicted on a priori basis. The function is to be estimated first. It may be a linear function or a non-linear one. In order to find the effect of each factor on willingness to supply, we simplify the procedure by keeping the other factors unchanged and varying just one at a time.

Let us examine the effect of price of the commodity on willingness to supply keeping the other factors constant. When the price of the commodity increases, other things, particularly the cost of production, remains constant, the profit margin, *i.e.*, difference between product price and unit cost of production goes up, so the willingness to supply increases. This is quite a simple proposition which says that as profit-margin increases, producers supply larger quantity for sales. The relationship between price of the commodity and willingness to produce or sell is a positive one. We state this relationship through the *law of supply. The law of supply states that other things being equal, the quantity supplied of a commodity varies directly with the price of that commodity:*

$$s_x = S\ [P_x] \qquad \text{...(5)}$$

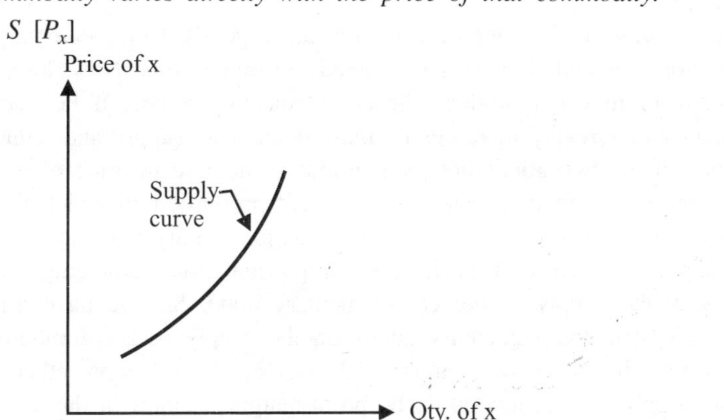

Fig. 3.8 Supply Curve

As price of the commodity increases, the quantity supplied also increases and with decline in price the quantity supplied decreases. Thus, we have movements along the supply curve. Such movements are called 'change in quantity supplied'. A shift in the position of the supply curve causing a change in quantity supplied is called simply 'change in supply'. A rise in supply, for example, means a shift of the supply curve to the right indicating producer's willingness to supply more at each price of the commodity. A fall in supply means shift of the supply curve to the left showing the willingness of the producer to supply less at each price of the commodity. The movements along the supply curve are caused by a change in the commodity price while other things being held constant while shifts of the supply curve are caused by changes in other factors, price of the commodity remaining constant.

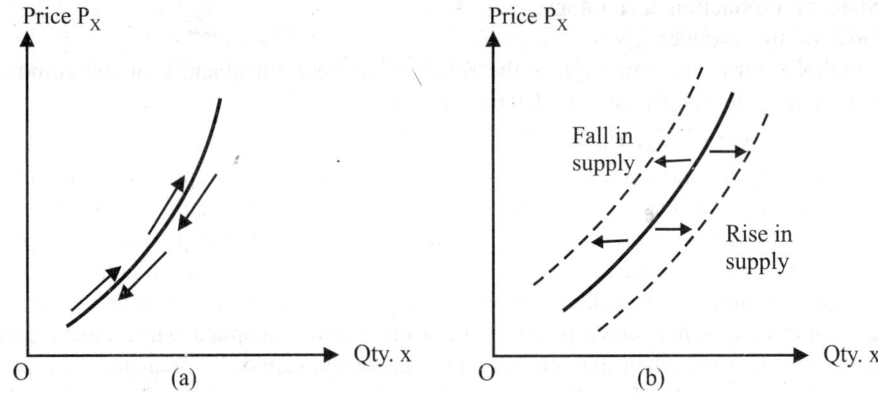

Fig. 3.9 (a) Change in Quantity Supplied, (b) Change in Supply

We have considered the effect of a change in price of the commodity on willingness to supply, other things remain constant. Now, let us consider the effects of change in the other factors on the supply of the commodity.

If prices of the substitute goods for a commodity increase, other things being constant, the willingness to supply the commodity decreases. The supply curve for the commodity shifts to the left. Why does this happen? Because of increase in its price the substitute commodity gives greater profit margin; so the producer will be tempted to increase its supply and reduce the supply of the other commodities. Even if he is not producing the substitute commodity he may switch over to it in the long-run.

We now come to the case of complementary goods. Complementary to whom—consumer or producer? From demand side we have already examined this. Now. look at it from the producer's side. He may or may not produce the complementary goods. If he does and if the price of the complementary commodity increases he may increase its supply and reduce the supply of the other commodities. If the two goods are joint products, increase in price of one of them means increase in supply for both of them because of the fixed proportion in which they are produced. There is another possibility. An increase in price of a complementary good means a rise in its supply. Since the other commodity will be used in fixed proportion to its complement so its supply may increase matching with the supply of the complementary good. So, we have different possible effects of change in prices of complementary goods on the supply of a commodity.

An increase in the prices of inputs, *i.e.*, factors of production, other things remaining constant, reduces the supply of a commodity. The profit-margin declines in this case which means a decrease in quantity of the commodity that the producer is willing to supply. The reverse of this sequence will be true in case of a fall in input prices. Any increase in the outlay of the producer means a rise in the supply and vice-versa. The state of technology is also an important supply factor. If technology is improved, supply rises otherwise it decreases with obsolete technology. The goal of the firm also affects the supply of goods that the firm makes. Supply under profit-maximizing objective and supply under sales-maximisation objective will be different. This means if the goal of the producer changes, the supply curve shifts but in what direction it cannot be said definitely unless we know the precise change in the goal of the firm. We will study these results in detail in the latter chapters of this book.

In summary, we can say that supply curve for a commodity shifts to the right because of increase in the outlay, decrease in prices of other goods, decrease in prices of factors of production, and some kind of changes in the goals of the producer. The supply curve shifts to the left showing a decrease in supply when the above factors change in opposite direction.

Market Supply: Market supply is the horizontal summation of supply curves for individual producers. That is, at a given price of the commodity, the market supply is the sum of quantities supplied by individual producers. The market supply curve depends on the same generatic factors like price of that commodity, prices of other commodities, nature of technology, goals of producers and so on as that for the supply curve for an individual producer. Apart from this, the number of producers in the market for the commodity plays a crucial role in its determination.

3.6 MARKET EQUILIBRIUM: PRICING UNDER PERFECT COMPETITION

By market equilibrium we mean the balance between supply and demand for a commodity. How this situation is achieved will be discussed in this section. Market equilibrium for a commodity gives us market price and market quantity bought or sold under perfect competition.[2] The term perfect competition is a type of market having large number of sellers, and buyers, homogeneous output of all firms, no control of any kind and perfect knowledge about the market. Under this situation, no individual seller or buyer will have any control over the price of the commodity. Before going through the analysis of market equilibrium, let us define the term 'price' and 'market'. What it costs to obtain some advantage, *i.e.*, what is given up or surrendered or foregone for the sake of something else is called 'price'. Normally, it is the money with which any thing is bought and sold in the market. One may express price of a commodity in terms of some other commodity. This is what we call as barter exchange but quoting of prices of commodities in money terms is a convenient way beside other advantages.[3] So, we take the money rates as price for exchange purposes for a commodity.

The term 'market' is an abstract concept that is used by economists to represent contacts between buyers and sellers or simply a collection or organisation of buyers and sellers. One can simply consider 'market' as a mechanism or structure that facilitates exchange among various economic units such as individuals, households, business firms, governments and non-profit organisations. One need not take a geographical area as a 'market'. Markets for commodities and services do exist without any spatial dimension attached to them. Necessary condition for existence of a market is that there must be buyers and sellers for the commodity. Buyers' side is reflected by their willingness to buy the commodity. Sellers' side is reflected by their willingness to sell the commodity. Both the demand and supply of a market for a commodity interact to determine the market price for the commodity. Along with the price we get total quantity demanded or supplied

---

2. The term 'prefect competition' will be discussed in detail later in Chapter 7.

3. One may refer a standard textbook on money to get a fairly good exposition on this aspect.

in the market for the commodity. A market gets equilibrium position when demand for the commodity is equal to its supply. Let us take a hypothetical example to explain the process of market equilibrium. The data on price, quantity demanded and quantity supplied for a commodity is given in the following table:

Table 3.1: Demand and Supply Schedules for a Commodity

Price (P)	*Qty. Demanded (Q_d)*	*Qty. Supplied (Q_s)*	*Excess Demand/Supply (Qty.)*	
(1)	*(2)*	*(3)*	*(4) = (2) – (3)*	
2	110	30	80	Shortage of Supply
3	100	40	60	
4	90	50	40	
5	80	60	20	
6	70	70	00	Equilibrium
7	60	80	– 20	Excess Supply
8	50	90	– 40	
9	40	100	– 60	

As revealed by the data given in the table, quantity demanded for the commodity declines as price increases (column 2) and quantity supplied increases with price (column 3). Column 4 of the table shows an excess demand, *i.e.*, the difference between quantity demanded and quantity supplied. Initially, we find excess demand for the commodity. At the price of 6 units, we find both quantities demanded and quantity supplied equal to one another. After this, there is an excess supply or negative excess demand. The market for the commodity will be in equilibrium at the price of 6 units showing zero excess demand. At this position, buyers are willing to buy 70 units of the commodity and sellers are also willing to sell 70 units. Graphically, we represent the equilibrium position by the point of intersection of demand and supply curves for the commodity as shown by point *E* in Fig. 3.10.

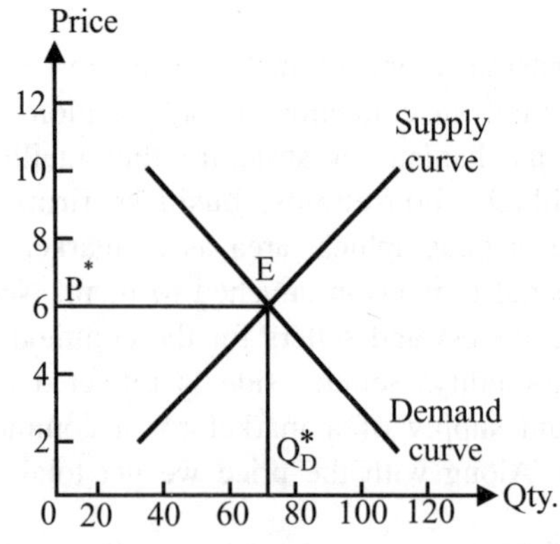

Fig. 3.10 Market Equilibrium for a Commodity

The price and quantity combination corresponding to the equilibrium point E shows the actual magnitudes as determined by the market. There will be no other combination of price and quantity of the commodity at which the willingness or intentions of buyers and sellers will be identical. Let us consider another example here. If the demand and supply curves for a commodity are given as $Q_D = 250 - 50\,P$ and $Q_S = 25 + 25\,P$ respectively, what will be the price and quantity bought and sold in the market for the commodity? What we do to answer this question is to equate demand and supply and solve the resulting equation for price. Once the price is known we can find Q_D or Q_S by substituting the price in the demand or supply function.

For equilibrium of the market

$$Q_D = Q_S$$

or $$250 - 50\,P = 25 + 25\,P$$

or $$75\,P = 225$$

or $$P = 3 \text{ units}$$

$$Q_D = 250 - 50\,(3) = 100 \text{ units}$$

$$Q_S = 25 + 25\,(3) = 100 \text{ units}$$

So $$Q_D = Q_S = 100 \text{ units and } P = 3$$

So far, we have discussed the mechanics of market equilibrium or price determination for a commodity. How is the equilibrium stage reached? Whether it will be stable or not? Let us examine these issues.

Consider the demand and supply interaction diagram as shown below:

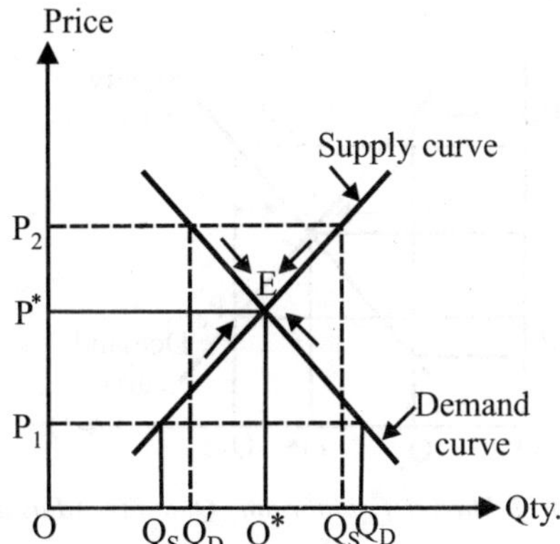

Fig. 3.11 Market Equilibrium: Price Adjustment

To explain the process of attaining the equilibrium position shown by point E, let us take the stand that market price is different than given by P^* corresponding to point E. Let it be P_1 below the equilibrium price P^*. At P_1, price at which the sellers are willing to sell Q_S units of the commodity and buyers are willing to buy Q_D units. Q_D is greater than Q_S. There is an excess demand of $Q_D - Q_S$ units because of shortage of the commodity. When there is excess demand, competition among the buyers will push the price up. There will be some customers who will buy as much as they want by paying higher price for the commodity. The price of the commodity in the market goes up. An increase in the price reduces the quantity demanded and increases the quantity supplied. Q_D tends to decline, Q_S tends to go up and the gap between Q_D and Q_S, *i.e.*, the excess demand narrows down. The upward movement of price continues till entire excess demand is eliminated. This implies attainment of point E.

Now, let us consider a situation when the market price is greater than the equilibrium price. In the figure, P_2 is Q greater than P^*. At P_2 price we find that buyers are willing to buy only Q'_D units and sellers are willing to sell Q'_S units of the commodity. There is an excess supply of $Q'_S - Q'_D$ units. The surplus or excess supply of the commodity forces the producers or sellers to sell the commodity at reduced price. That is, there will be competition among the sellers in selling the commodity. Market price will decline and, as a result quantity demanded will increase, quantity supplied will decrease and the surplus will declines. This trend with continue till the entire surplus is eliminated. Price will stabilize at P^* level and equilibrium will be attained at point E.

What we find in the above discussion is that if price deviates from its equilibrium level, competitive forces will bring it back to the equilibrium. Whenever there is some arbitrary price fixation, which is different from the equilibrium price, there will be either excess demand or excess surplus for the commodity. A change in the price will be induced by the market because of this. This change will be a function of the magnitude of excess demand or excess supply. Greater the excess demand more will be the price adjustment. Price will stop changing when excess demand or excess supply is eliminated. This type of adjustment process was conceived first by L. Walras.[4] So, it is called 'Walrasian Adjustment Process'. Market will come to equilibrium so long as demand curve slopes downward and supply curve slopes upward.

There is an alternative way of explaining the process of market equilibrium for a commodity. Consider the following figure:

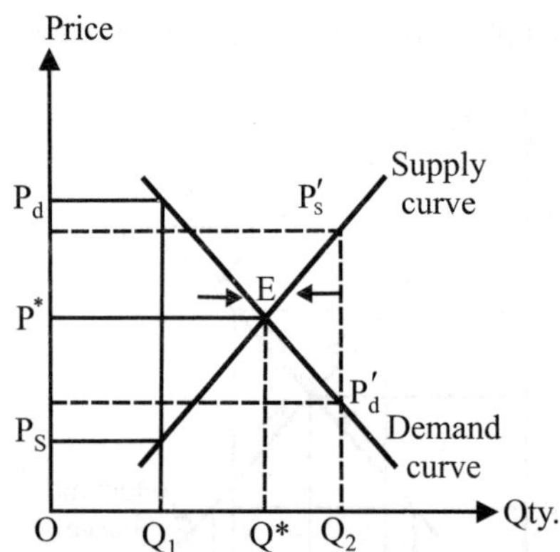

Fig. 3.12 Market Equilibrium: Quantity Adjustment

Consider a given quantity Q_1 of a commodity available for sales in the market. For this much quantity the consumers are willing to pay P_d price as shown by the demand curve. The supply curve, however, shows P_s as the price that sellers require for the quantity Q_1. There is a discrepancy between the price consumers are willing to pay and what firms wish to receive. Demand price (P_d) is greater than the supply price (P_s). The excess demand price, *i.e.*, $P_d - P_s$ induces firms to increase quantity of the commodity in the market. As quantity changes, the gap between P_d and P_s narrows down. Quantity adjustment from sellers, side continues till the excess demand price is eliminated all together. This position is attained at point E where demand price and supply price are identical. Now, take a level of quantity on the right-hand side of point E, say Q_2. For this quantity, the supply price (P'_s) is greater than the demand price (P'_d). Sellers require higher price for this quantity since this is based on its marginal cost (this is to be discussed later on).

4. L. Walras: *Elements of Pure Economics,* trans. W. Joffee, III, Richard D. Irwin Inc. 1954.

Buyers are not willing to pay this much but rather lower price. The result is that sellers suffer a loss. They reduce the quantity offered for sales. The reduction in quantity reduces the gap between sellers' price P'_s and consumers' price P'_d, P'_d goes up while P_s declines. This process of quantity adjustment continues till the price discrepancy is eliminated and equilibrium position E is attained. What we find in this process is that quantity adjusts to the price discrepancies and eventually equilibrium is attained. So long as demand is negatively sloping and supply is positively sloping the equilibrium position shown by the point E will be stable. This approach has been suggested by Marshall. So, it is called 'Marshallian Quantity Adjustment Process.[5]'

There are two further comments to be made on the market equilibrium: (1) Whenever a consumer buys anything then essentially the quantity bought is equal to the quantity sold; so one may say that the market is in equilibrium. It may not be so, because at such a point the willingness of buyers and sellers may be different and there may be unwanted exchanges between them. For equilibrium, both intention and realisation must be equal for both the sides of the market, that is, ex-ante demand = ex-post demand = ex-ante supply = ex-post supply. The term 'ex-ante' means planned and 'ex-post' means actual. (2) The equilibrium analysis, as discussed above, is valid for a market under perfect competition only when 'other things are equal'. If other demand or supply factors change the equilibrium price and quantity combination *i.e.*, the position of equilibrium shifts. In practice, it may be difficult to find all other factors constant; so markets, by and large, remain in disequilibrium position. Price rises, quantity bought or sold also rise because of changes in some other factors.

3.7 EFFECTS OF SHIFT IN THE DEMAND AND SUPPLY CURVES ON MARKET EQUILIBRIUM

We can think of a number of possibilities: demand may rise or fall, supply being constant; supply may rise or fall, demand being constant; both supply and demand rise or fall simultaneously; and supply and demand may change in opposite directions. The effects on market equilibrium in all these situations may be summarised as follows:

(*i*) A rise in demand for a commodity, *i.e.*, a shift of the demand curve to the right hand side, supply being unchanged, increases both equilibrium price and quantity of the commodity. Similarly, a fall in demand, *i.e.*, a shift of the demand curve to the left, supply being unchanged, decreases both equilibrium price and quantity of the commodity. These results hold true when the supply curve for the commodity is sloping upward but it is not a horizontal or a vertical line.

If the supply is represented by a horizontal line, there would be no effect on the equilibrium price but the equilibrium quantity increases or decreases with rise or fall in the demand. If the supply curve is a vertical line, the effect of changing demand will be on the equilibrium price only, quantity will be invariable.

Let us consider the Figure 3.13.

5. A. Marshall, *Principles of Economics,* 8th Ed. London, Macmillan & Co. Ltd., 1920, pp. 287-288.

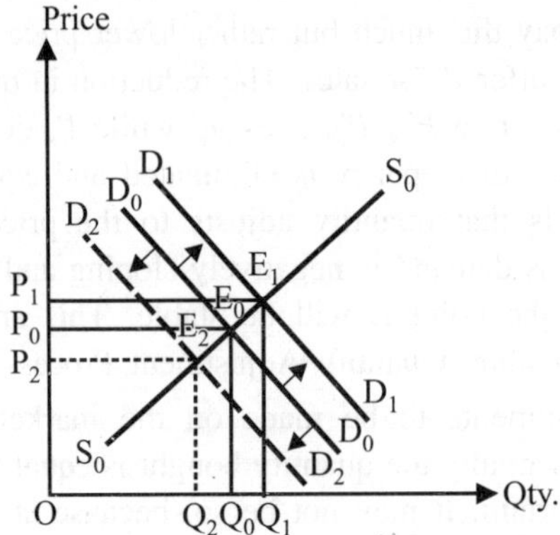

Fig. 3.13 Effects of a Shift in Demand on Market Equilibrium

D_0 and S_0 are the initial demand and supply curves which give P_0 and Q_0 as equilibrium price and quantity. When demand curve rises to D_1, the new equilibrium gives us higher price (P_1) and quantity (Q_1) than P_0, Q_0, When demand curve shifts down to D_2 level, both price and quantity at the new equilibrium decrease.

(*ii*) A rise in supply of the commodity, *i.e.,* shift of the supply curve to the right demand being unchanged, decreases the equilibrium price and increases the equilibrium quantity. A fall in supply, demand being constant, produces the opposite result: price increases, quantity demanded decreases.

The qualification for these results is that demand curve should not be a horizontal or vertical line. If it is a horizontal line, there would be no effect on price. Quantity will, of course, change, and if it is a vertical line then only price will change. Quantity remains constant when supply curve shifts up and down. Fig. 3.14 shows the effects of changing supply curves, demand curve being constant, on the market equilibrium, as discussed above.

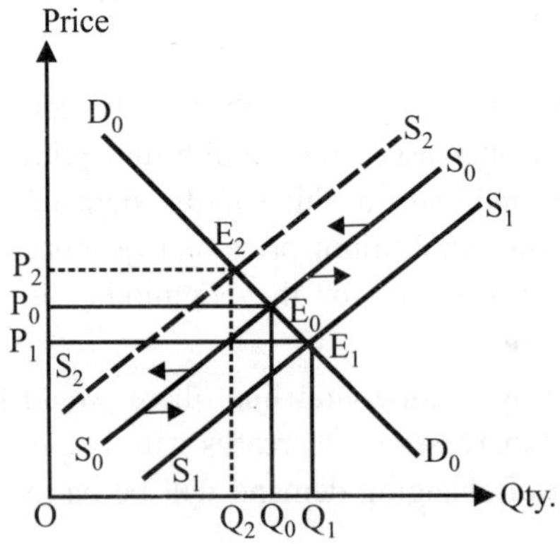

Fig. 3.14 Effects of a Shift in Supply on Market Equilibrium

(*iii*) A rise in demand curve and a fall in supply curve for a commodity increase the price of the commodity but whether equilibrium quantity demanded increases or decreases depends on the relative shifts of the demand and supply curves. In general, if the demand curve shifts more than the opposite shift of the supply curve, quantity demanded at equilibrium increases but if the supply curve shifts more than the demand curve, equilibrium quantity may decrease. The slopes of supply and demand curves also play important role for the direction of the change in quantity but we will examine this aspect later on.

When demand decreases and supply increases we get the opposite results of what we got above. The equilibrium price decreases but equilibrium quantity may increase or decrease or remain unchanged depending on the relative shifts of the demand and supply curves. (The reader may verify these results for different types of relative shifts of demand and supply curves and also with different slopes of these curves by drawing appropriate diagrams).

(*iv*) Let us now examine the case when both supply and demand increase simultaneously. In Fig. 3.15, the initial market equilibrium is given by E_0 point on the intersection of D_0 and S_0, the demand and supply curves. The price and quantity combination corresponding to this equilibrium point is given by P_0 and Q_0. Now, the demand curve shifts to D_1 position and supply curve to S_1. Demand shifts by greater magnitude than the supply. The new equilibrium is given by E_1 and the new price, quantity combination by P_1 and Q_1. Both price and quantity have increased in this case.

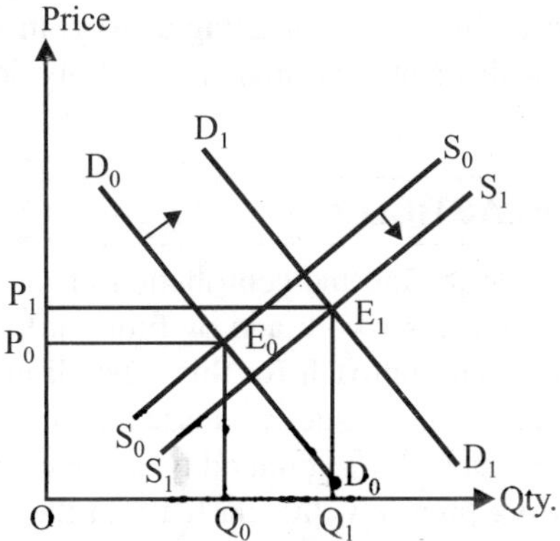

Fig. 3.15 Effects of Rising Demand and Supply on Market Equilibrium: First Situation

Now, we consider the following figure in which demand increases by lesser magnitude than the supply. The equilibrium price decreases and quantity increases as we move from point E_0 to E_1. There may be another situation when both demand and supply increase in such a way that there is no change in the price but quantity demanded increases. That is to say, in general when both demand and supply curve shift to the right, the equilibrium quantity increases but equilibrium price may increase or decrease or remain unchanged depending on the relative magnitudes of the rise in demand and supply. The reverse of this, *i.e.*, when both supply and demand decrease simultaneously, equilibrium quantity decreases but price can either increase or decrease or remain constant depending upon the relative magnitude of shifts. The reader may verify these results by plotting the diagrams on one's ohm.

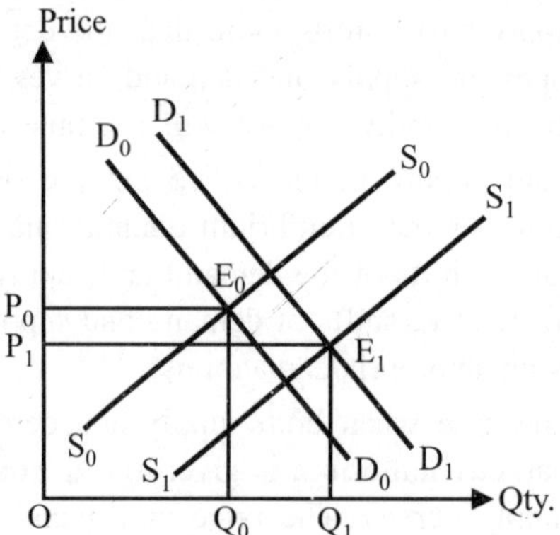

Fig. 3.16 Effects of Rising Demand and Supply on Market Equilibrium: Second Situation

An interesting property of demand and supply of a commodity is reflected by the slopes of demand and supply curves for the commodity. This is the familiar concept of elasticity. On the basis of this concept, we will be able to analyse the effects of shifting demand and supply curves on equilibrium price and quantity in a much more meaningful way. In the following section, we define the elasticity concepts and deal with their measurements and applications in economics as well as in practice.

3.8 THE CONCEPT OF ELASTICITY

A businessman may not be able to find the contribution of factors affecting the demand for its product by using the demand function framework and by fitting it to data. It may be too complicated for him. He needs a simple operational approach for this. The elasticity concept is one which meets this requirement of a businessman. The elasticity is used to measure the responsiveness of the dependent variable, say quantity demanded of a commodity, to the changes in anyone of its explanatory variables like price or income. More precisely, the elasticity in the case of demand is defined as the percentage change in quantity demanded attributable to unit percentage change in a demand factor (*i.e.*, its determinant). Symbolically, we define elasticity as:

$$\text{Elasticity Coeff.} = \frac{\%\text{ Change in Qty. Demanded}}{\%\text{ Change in any Demand factor, say } X}$$

$$= \frac{(\Delta Q/Q)\,100}{(\Delta X/X)\,100} = \frac{\Delta Q}{\Delta X}\,\frac{X}{Q} \qquad \text{...(6)}$$

This formula is applicable for discrete changes in Q and X, *i.e.*, when we move from one point to another point. Its version for continuous changes in Q and X is given as:

$$\text{Elasticity Coeff.} = \frac{dQ}{dX}\;\frac{X}{Q} = \frac{\partial\,(\log Q)}{\partial\,(\log X)} \qquad \text{...(7)}$$

This formula gives us the elasticity of demand at a point on the demand curve. It is, therefore, called 'point-elasticity'. Using the above two general specifications for finding the elasticity, we now discuss various elasticities relevant for demand analysis.

(i) Price Elasticity of Demand

This shows the responsiveness of quantity demanded of a commodity when price of that commodity changes, other factors being constant. That is,

$$\text{Price Elasticity } (e_p) = \frac{\text{\% Change in Qty. Demanded}}{\text{\% Change in Price}}$$

In place of % change we can use the term 'proportionate change' also, *i.e.*,

$$\text{Price Elasticity } (e_p) = \frac{\text{Proportionate Change in Qty. Demanded}}{\text{Proportionate Change in Price}}$$

Consider the changes in quantity demanded and price as we move from point A to point B in the following figure:

$$\text{Price Elasticity } (e_p) = \frac{(Q_2 - Q_1)/Q_1}{(P_2 - P_1)/P_1} = \frac{\Delta Q}{\Delta P}\frac{P_1}{Q_1} \quad ...(8)$$

For a downward sloping demand curve, e_p will be negative since either numerator or denominator of the above mentioned formulae will be negative. In Fig. 3.17 as we move from A to B point, $Q_2 < Q_1$, $P_2 > P_1$, so ΔQ is negative. There is a convention in economics to show price-elasticity by a positive number. For this, we simply take the module or absolute value of the right hand side of the above expression, or put a negative sign before the elasticity expression, *i.e.*,

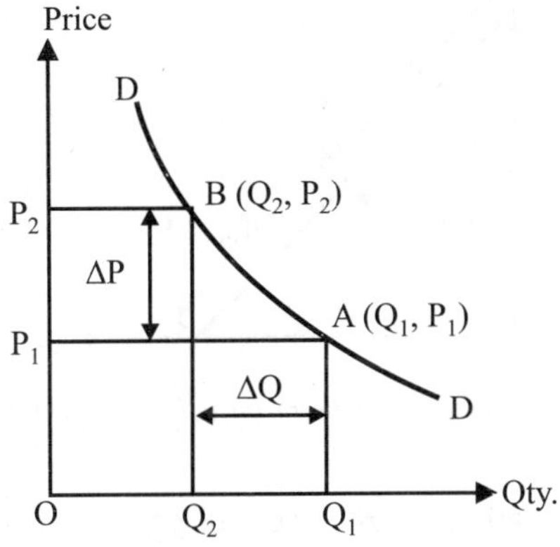

Fig. 3.17 Price Elasticity of Demand

$$e_p = \left|\frac{\Delta Q/Q_1}{\Delta P/P_1}\right| = -\left(\frac{\Delta Q/Q_1}{\Delta P/P_1}\right) \quad ...(9)$$

Two things are necessary to find the price-elasticity of demand: one the slope of the demand curve ($\Delta Q/\Delta P$) and second, the ratio P/Q. At any point on the demand curve we can find the elasticity coefficient (e_p) by using the expression:

$$e_p = \left|\frac{dQ}{dP}\cdot\frac{P}{Q}\right| \quad \text{or} \quad e_p = -\left(\frac{dQ}{dP}\cdot\frac{P}{Q}\right) \quad ...(10)$$

Whenever we move along an arc of the demand curve and use the discrete formula (Eqn. 9) to find the price-elasticity, we find some discrepancy in the values of the elasticity, when we move in different directions along the arc. In Fig. 3.17, we use point A as base to compute the price-elasticity for the movement along the segment AB. We will get some value for this. Now, suppose we change the direction of movement, *i.e.*, make B point as base and compute the elasticity for moving from *B to A* we will get another value. This discrepancy in computation of the price-elasticity arises because of either different slope of the demand curve at *B* and *A* points or different values for *P*/*Q* ratio at these points. To avoid the discrepancy in e_p it is better to take the average base for the arc *AB*. That is, we use the following expression for this:

$$e_p = \frac{\Delta Q}{\Delta P}\frac{(P_1+P_2)/2}{(Q_1+Q_2)/2} = \frac{\Delta Q}{\Delta P}\frac{P_1+P_2}{Q_1+Q_2} \qquad ...(11)$$

This is called 'Arc Elasticity of Demand'. At any point on the demand curve however, we use the expression (10) which gives us precise value for the price elasticity at the point.

Let us take the demand curve:

$q = a - bP$. From this we get $dq/dP = -b$, and therefore, price elasticity $e_p = -(-b.\ p/q)$.

Since $q = a - bP$, so $e_p = -[-b.\ P/(a - bP)]$.

In a straight line demand curve, as shown below, we can measure price-elasticity of demand at any point by taking the ratio of the distance between that point to *x-axis* to the distance between the point to *y*-axis on the demand curve. That is, if we want to measure price-elasticity at point A then we have to take the ratio of *AC/AB* for this.

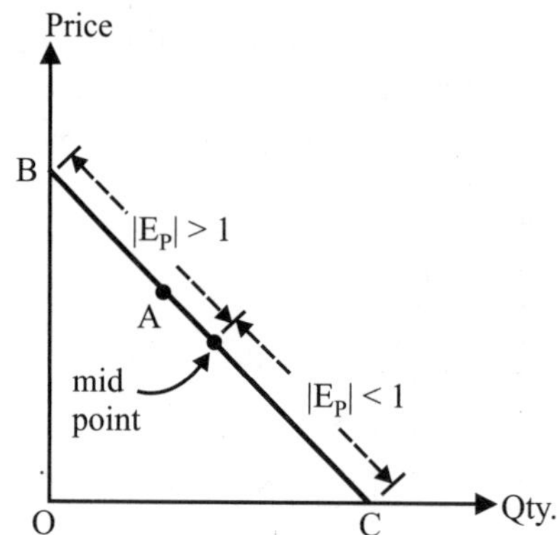

Fig. 3.18 Elasticity at a Point on a Linear Demand Curve

At point *A*, $e_p = AC/AB$.

At the mid-point of the demand curve *BC*, we will get $e_p = 1$. e_p win be less than unity on the lower-half of the demand curve and more than one on its upper half in absolute term. Using the formula $e_p = -\left(\frac{dQ}{dP}\cdot\frac{P}{q}\right)$ we can test the above results. If the demand curve for a commodity is a curve of the shape given by the equation

$$Q = A\,P^{-\alpha} \qquad ...(12)$$

This curve gives us constant price-elasticity of demand which is equal to α. We can verify this. Transforming the function into the log form we get,

$\log Q = \log A - \alpha \log P$

By taking the differentials we get,

$$\frac{dQ}{Q} = -\alpha\frac{dP}{P}$$

or

$$\frac{dQ}{dP}\frac{P}{Q} = -\alpha,\quad P \neq 0 \qquad ...(13)$$

This will be a curve like a rectangular hyperbola which never meets either P or Q axes.

Why do we take percentages or proportions instead of absolute values of P and Q while computing price-elasticity of demand? Can we write $e_p = dQ/dP$ since this also gives the response of Q when P changes. The answer to these questions is no, because by taking ratios of absolute terms of Q and P we will face the problem of units of measurements of P and Q. For one kind of measurement units of either Q or P we will get one value of the price-elasticity and for the other units we get different value for e_p. Price-elasticity of demand, like any other elasticity concept, is a number free from the dimensions of measurement of Q and P. For this purpose, we take percentage or proportionate changes in Q and P while computing the price-elasticity of demand and, in fact, any other elasticity by taking the percentage or proportionate changes of the concerned variables.

Consider a demand function as,

$$Q = A\ P_1^{\alpha_1}\ P_2^{\alpha_2}\ P_3^{\alpha_3}\ Y^{\beta} \qquad \text{...(14)}$$

Transforming in logarithmic form and taking the partial derivatives, we will get the elasticities of demand with respect to different prices P_1, P_2, P_3 and income Y as:

$$\alpha_1 = \frac{\partial\,(\log Q)}{\partial\,(\log P_1)},\ \alpha_2 = \frac{\partial\,(\log Q)}{\partial\,(\log P_2)},$$

$$\alpha_3 = \frac{\partial\,(\log Q)}{\partial\,(\log P_3)} \text{ and } \beta = \frac{\partial\,(\log Q)}{\partial\,(\log Y)} \qquad \text{...(15)}$$

This is a very convenient way to compute elasticities, provided the demand function is of the shape as given by (14).

The magnitude of price-elasticity in absolute term varies from zero to infinity. Let us consider different ranges of variation in the price-elasticity for interpretation.

(*a*) $e_p = 0$. This is defined as 'perfectly inelastic demand'. Quantity demanded will be invariable with respect to changes in price. The demand curve will be a vertical line in this case as shown by D_1 in Fig. 3.19. Some essential goods, like medicines, will have perfectly inelastic demand.

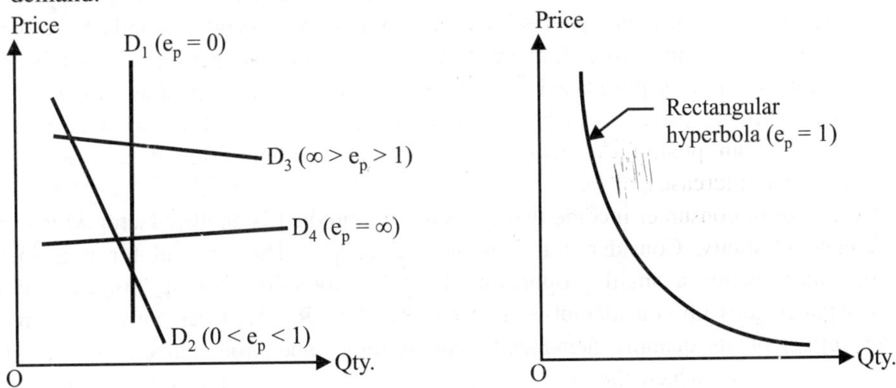

Fig. 3.19 Range of Variation of Price Elasticity of Demand

(*b*) $0 < e_p < 1$. This is the case of inelastic demand. Proportionate change in quantity demanded is less than proportionate change in price giving us $e_p < 1$. Most of the essential goods will have inelastic price-elasticity of demand. The demand curve for this will be quite steep as shown by D_2 line in Fig. 3.19.

(*c*) $\infty > e_p > 1$. Price-elasticity as greater than one but less than infinity is defined as 'elastic demand'. Proportionate change in quantity demanded will be more than proportionate change in price of the commodity. Most of the luxuries and comforts show this kind of tendency. The demand curve will be flatter in this case as shown by D_3 line in Fig. 3.19.

(*d*) Unitary price-elasticity ($e_p = 1$) implies equal proportionate change in quantity demanded and price. The shape of the demand curve will be a rectangular hyperbola in this case.

(*e*) $e_p = \infty$. This implies that one per cent change in price brings infinite change in quantity demanded. In simpler term, a consumer will buy the entire quantity of the commodity at this price and nothing else at some other price. The demand curve becomes a horizontal line parallel to quantity axis (see D_4 line in Fig. 3.19).

Why do we find such differences in price elasticity of demand? There are several factors responsible for this. We may summarize them briefly as follows:

(1) Greater the number of close substitutes of a commodity more will be the price-elasticity. Whenever there is a slight increase or decrease in the price of such a commodity it will be substituted by other close substitutes or for other substitutes making the demand quite elastic. Consider a brand of soap. It will have several close substitutes in the form of other brands of the soap; so, if price of one brand increases consumer may shift to other brands and this gives higher price-elasticity. For the entire product class of soaps, however, the price elasticity may be low as it does not have any close substitute. Price elasticity may be quite low for salt since there is no substitute for this, while for a commodity like wool, it may be high since wool has as close substitute products like cotton, man-made fibres, etc.

(2) Greater the number of uses of a commodity more will be the price-elasticity of demand for that. For example, if tennis shoes could be used only for playing tennis, not much change in sales could be expected to result from a price change, but, in practice, tennis shoes are used for general purposes which increase its overall sales significantly making the demand for it quite elastic.

(3) The nature of use of a commodity, whether it is essential or a luxury, is another important factor influencing elasticity of demand. All essential goods have a tendency of having low or in-elastic demand. Whatever be the changes in prices of such goods a certain quantity is purchased by the consumer. So, quantity does not vary much as compared to the price of such a commodity. In the case of luxuries or non-essential goods one can postpone consumption, buy more when price decreases or buy less when price increases.

(4) Percentage of consumer income that is spent on a product is another factor which influences demand elasticity. Consider, for example, newspaper. The demand for it is inelastic. A consumer spends a small proportion of one's expenditure on it. So, even if price of newspaper goes up considerably, say from Re. 1 to Rs. 1.20 per copy, there may not be any effect on its quantity demanded. Salt, writing paper, fountainpen ink, etc., are other commodities for which the above result may hold true. What we can say is that demand for those goods on which a consumer spends very small proportion of his her income will be generally inelastic as compared to the demand elasticity for goods on which the proportion of income spent is high.

(5) Another factor that influences price-elasticity is the time horizon of consumption. Demand in the short-run for some commodities may be inelastic but it may be elastic in the long-

run. Cooking gas is an example for this. In the short-run, because of the absence of its substitute its demand is inelastic but in the long-run, other thing being the same, there might be good substitutes for this, such as solar energy, electric heaters which will make the demand for cooking gas elastic.

(6) There are other miscellaneous factors, such as habitual consumption, durability of goods, etc., which affect the elasticity of demand, but they are not so important as compared to factors discussed above.

It is difficult to separate out influences of factors, as discussed above, on the price-elasticity. This is because more than one factor may operate at any given time for any particular commodity or service. They may affect the demand in the same direction or in the opposite direction. For practical purposes, it will be wise to take all factors together rather than going for the influences of individual factors.

(ii) Some Applications of Price-Elasticity of Demand

Price-elasticity of demand is a very useful concept. Apart from its uses in explanation of several economic theories, it has operational significance in decision-making. It is also an important factor which determine the shape and position of the demand curve. Some applications of price-elasticity of demand are as follows:

(*a*) If a producer wants to sell more by reducing price of his products he will be guided by the price-elasticity. To show how he will he reacting in this situation consider the following figure:

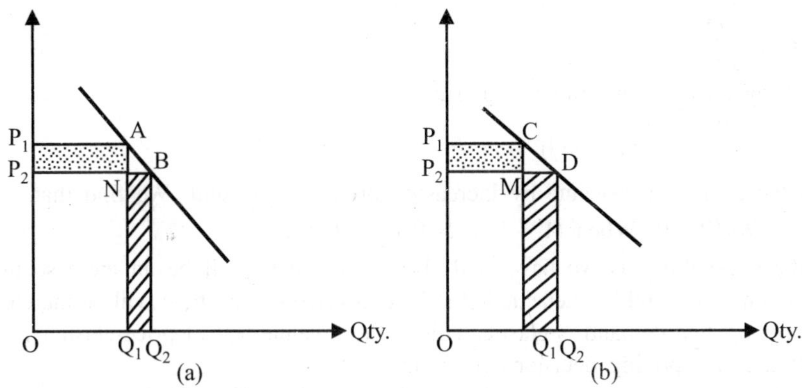

Fig. 3.20 Revenue Effects of Price Elasticity of Demand

Two demand curves are shown separately in parts (*a*) and (*b*) of this figure. The demand curve shown in part (*a*) is steeper showing inelastic demand while the demand curve in part (*b*) is elastic. Let us take uniform P_1 price that a producer charges in the two separate situations. He sells OQ_1 amount of output at this price. The revenue he gets from the sales in the situation as shown in part (*a*) is given by the area ▭ OQ_1AP_1 *i.e.,* $(OQ_1 \times OP_1)$. In the second part, he gets similarly ▭ OQ_1CP_1 revenue. Now, let there be a uniform reduction of price in both the situations. As a result of a decrease in price, quantity sold increases, so the new revenue levels in part (*a*) and part (*b*) would be ▭ OQ_2BP_2 and ▭ OQ_2DP_2 respectively, in which case he gets greater increase in revenue? The gain of revenue in part (*a*) of the figure is ▭ $Q_1Q_2\ BN$ while loss is ▭ P_2NAP_1 because of less price charged for the units OQ_1 which he was selling at higher price (P_1) earlier.

The net gain to the producer will be the difference of gain and loss, *i.e.,* ▭ Q_1Q_2 BN – ▭ P_2 NAP_1. This seems to be very low or even negative. In part (*b*), the net gain would be the difference of the area ▭ Q_1Q_2DM – ▭ P_2MCP_1. Just by seeing the diagram it is positive as ▭ Q_1Q_2DM > ▭ P_2MCP_1. What is the conclusion? We can say that a price reduction will increase revenue more if the demand is elastic. This is very important result for pricing of products. A producer will gain by price reduction when its product has elastic demand. He should not reduce price in the situation of inelastic demand because proportionate change in quantity demanded will be less than the proportionate change in price. Price is decreasing, so demand will not increase by the same proportion which means even a loss to the producer. The reverse situation is also valid, that is, if he wants to increase his revenue by increasing the price he will not gain much if the demand is elastic. Using simple calculus we can prove this as follows:

Let $$R = P.\ Q \qquad ...(16)$$

where R = Total Revenue, P = Product Price, Q = Quantity sold.

Differentiating R with respect to P, we get

$$\frac{dR}{dP} = Q + P\frac{dQ}{dP}$$

Dividing and multiplying the second term on the right hand side by Q, we have

$$\frac{dR}{dP} = Q + \frac{P}{Q}\cdot\frac{dQ}{dP}\cdot Q$$

or $$\frac{dR}{dP} = Q\ [1 + e_p] \qquad ...(17)$$

where $$(P/Q).\frac{dQ}{dP} = e_p$$

Since e_p is negative so we modify (17) as,

$$\frac{dR}{dP} = Q\ (1 - |e_p|) \qquad ...(18)$$

dR/dP is the change in revenue by increasing price by one unit. We find that,

$dR/dP > 0$. When $(1 - |e_p|) > 0$ or $|e_p| < 1$.

This is the same thing as we have said above, *i.e.,* there will be an increase in revenue by increasing price when demand is inelastic $|e_p| < 1$. Its reverse is that there will be increase in revenue by decreasing price when demand is elastic. This is the revenue test of price-elasticity. We find here how important it is for pricing decisions by a firm.

(*b*) Consider another application of price-elasticity: we know that food items will generally show inelastic demand. Suppose there is a good crop of say, wheat, then price of wheat in the market declines. Because of inelastic demand for wheat, consumers will not increase their consumption of wheat even though its price has fallen. With a decline in price and simultaneously without increase in quantity demanded of wheat, incomes of farmers decline in spite of good crop. This has policy implications. Government helps farmer in this situation by fixing higher prices than what market charges or by restricting farm output. In the familiar supply and demand interaction diagram, we can show how the government should help the farmers. The point here is that price-elasticity plays very crucial role in this respect.

(*c*) A third example showing the uses of price-elasticity is that of introduction of new technology. Suppose new technology is cost saving. The unit cost of production declines when such a technology is adopted for production. With reduction in cost, product price also declines. [It depends, however on the types of market which we will discuss later on]. If there is a decline in price, producer will gain when there is increase in sales. This depends on the price-elasticity of demand. A new cost saving technology will be feasible only if the demand for the products is elastic. If cost declines but price does not, it is a different situation. Producer gains here by increasing price-cost margin. Again, elasticity comes into picture even in this situation.

(*d*) Price-elasticity is very much useful in finding the incidence of a tax. This we will explain in detail later on in Chapter 7. Whether a commodity should be taxed or not, who bears the incidence of such a tax are obviously very important aspects of public policies. The price-elasticity of demand is a tool for formulation of such policies.

(iii) Income Elasticity of Demand

The income elasticity shows percentage change in quantity demanded when income of the consumer changes by one per cent, other things being constant.

$$e_y = \frac{\%\text{ Change in Qty. Demanded}}{\%\text{ Change in Income}} = \frac{(\Delta Q/Q).100}{(\Delta y/y)100}$$

or $$e_y = \frac{\Delta Q}{\Delta y} \cdot \frac{y}{Q} \quad \text{where } y = \text{Income} \qquad ...(19)$$

At a point, we define income-elasticity of demand as

$$e_y = \frac{dQ}{dy} \cdot \frac{y}{Q} \qquad ...(20)$$

where $\frac{dQ}{dy}$ is the slope of the income-consumption curve for the commodity

For most of the goods the income-elasticity of demand will be positive. All such goods are defined as '*normal goods*'. An increase in income increases the demand for such goods. If income-elasticity of demand is negative, it means the consumption of the commodity decreases as income increases. Such a commodity will be defined as *'inferior good'*. Among normal goods there will be certain goods for which income-elasticity of demand is greater than one. Such goods are called income-elastic as demand for them increases by greater proportion when income changes. Such goods might be called as *'luxuries'*. For certain other goods like food or other essential commodities we may have income elasticity positive but less than one. In this situation, we say that demand is income-inelastic. In between, there might be some commodities which we call *'semi-luxuries'* for which income elasticity is unity.

A knowledge of income elasticity of demand is quite useful. One can forecast demand on the basis of income changes. This kind of exercise is done both at enterprise level as well at national level. If income rises by 10 per cent and if income elasticity for a commodity is 2, the quantity demanded of the commodity would be expected to increase by 20 per cent. Under planning exercises for a country, targets for income growth are fixed for say, 3 years or 5 years. How much would be the demand for different goods and services at the end of the period would be computed exactly in the way as this example shows.

(iv) Cross-Elasticity of Demand

This is used to measure the responsiveness of quantity demanded of a commodity say *X*, when there is a change in the price of any other commodity, say Y. Two commodities may be either substitute goods or complementary goods when they are related together. The cross elasticities will tell us about their relationship as well as the interdependence.

$$\text{Cross Elasticity} \quad e_{x:y} = \frac{\Delta Q_x}{\Delta P_y} \cdot \frac{P_y}{Q_x}$$

or

$$e_{x:y} = \frac{dQ_x}{dP_y} \cdot \frac{P_y}{Q_x}$$

where Q_x = Qty. of commodity X

P_y = Price of commodity Y

For substitute goods, $e_{x:y}$ will be positive but for complementary goods it will be negative. If the two goods are unrelated then $e_{x:y} = 0$.

A knowledge of cross-elasticity is very much essential when two or more goods, or different varieties of same goods are competing among themselves. Such a knowledge will play crucial role in certain business decisions, such as pricing, investment planning, advertisement and so on. The interdependence between firms in the same or different industries can be analysed apart from other things, on the basis of cross elasticities of demand for their products.

The concept of elasticity can be applied to other factors, such as advertising and other sales promotion activities. We can find, for example, 'promotion elasticity of demand' as proportionate change in quantity demand divided by proportionate change in advertisement expenditure for the commodity. The interpretation of the magnitudes of such elasticities can be done exactly in the same way as for the price or income elasticities.

(v) The Elasticity of Supply

Just like the demand elasticities, we have the concept of supply elasticity. For example, the price elasticity of supply measures the responsiveness of quantity supplied when price of the commodity changes. That is:

$$e_s = \frac{\%\text{ Change in Qty. Supplied}}{\%\text{ Change in Price}}$$

$$e_s = \frac{\Delta Q_s}{\Delta P} \cdot \frac{P}{Q_s}$$

or

$$e_s = \frac{dQ_s}{dP} \cdot \frac{P}{Q_s} \qquad \text{...(21)}$$

where Q_s = Qty. supplied, P = Price

Price-elasticity of supply will be positive. It may vary from 0 to ∞. If $e_s = 0$, it means there is no effect of price changes on quantity supplied. The supply curve will be a vertical line parallel to price axis. On the other hand, if supply is perfectly elastic, *i.e.*, $e_s = \infty$, it will be a parallel line to the quantity axis. In elastic supply means $e_s < 1$ and elastic supply means $e_s > 1$. A unitary elastic supply curve passes through the origin as shown by S_s line in the Figure 3.21.

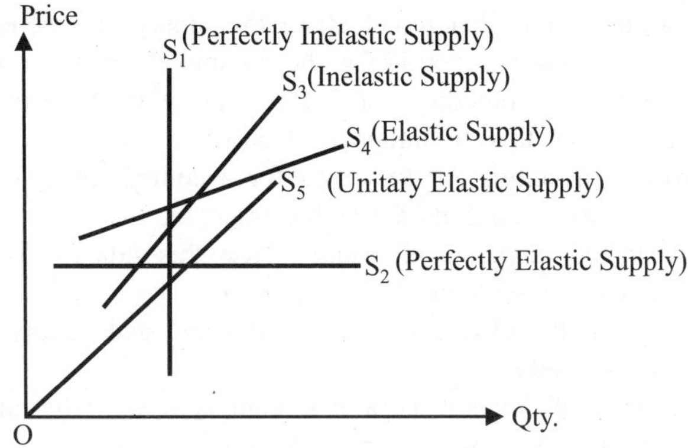

Fig. 3.21 Various Types of Supply Curve

A supply curve may be non-linear. In place of price, one may take any other determinant of supply and define the term of the elasticity accordingly.

Just like demand elasticities, supply elasticities are useful concepts for practical purposes. Through these terms we study certain aspects of producer's behaviour in the market, the effect of technological changes and the incidence of taxation. Some of these aspects will be discussed in the following chapters of this book.

3.9 CONCLUDING REMARKS

The main purpose of this chapter was to discuss some basic terms of economic science, such as 'demand', 'supply', 'price', 'market equilibrium', 'elasticities', etc. This provided us some basic understanding of economics and with this knowledge we will be able to go through slightly advance material in the following chapters:

SUGGESTED READINGS

David Begg and others, *Economics*, 8th Ed. N.Y., McGraw-Hill 2005.

Ferguson, C.E., *Microeconomic Theory*, R.D. Irwin Inc., 1966.

Kutsoyiannis, A., *Modern Microeconomics,* The Macmillan Press Ltd., 1978.

Lipsey, R.G., *An Introduction to Positive Economic Analysis,* English Language Book Society, 1971, 1995.

Marshall, A., *Principles of Economics,* 8th Ed., The Macmillan Co., 1920.

Nicholson, W. and Christopher Synder, *Microeconomic Theory: Basic Principles and Extensions,* South-Western Engage Learning, 2008.

Sher, Williams and R. Pindola, *Microeconomic Theory,* Edward Arnold, 1981.

Varian, H. R., *Microeconomic Analysis* 3rd Ed., N.Y., Norton & Co., 1992.

REVIEW QUESTIONS

1. How do you define the terms 'demand' and 'demand function' for a commodity? What are the general determinants of demand for a commodity that appear in the demand function for that? Discuss the relevance of each of the determinants of demand in details.

2. Examine the various factors that might affect the supply of a commodity and show how you can simplify the supply function for the commodity in the form of a supply law?
3. The demand curve for a commodity slopes downward while the supply curve goes upward. What are the reasons for this? Examine in details.
4. Explain the process of setting market price for a commodity under perfect competition. What are the necessary conditions for stable price for the commodity?
5. What do you mean by 'market equilibrium'? How this situation is arrived at in practice? Demonstrate your answer with graphical exposition.
6. Using graphs, explain the effects of shifting demand and supply curves on the market equilibrium for a commodity.
7. Define price-elasticity of demand. How it is computed and what are its determinants and uses in economic analysis? Give complete answers.
8. Prove that if the demand elasticity is everywhere (on the demand curve) unitary, expenditure on commodity is insensitive to price changes.
9. The demand function for a commodity is given as $q = 8/P$ where q is quantity demanded and P is the price of the commodity, other things being equal. What is the shape of the demand curve given by this function? Draw it. Also find the price elasticity at points $q = 1$, $P = 8$; and $q = 4$, $P = 2$.
10. (*a*) Explain why price elasticity of demand varies when we move along the demand curve for a commodity. What happens to the price elasticity when the demand curve shifts from its position?

    (*b*) The demand schedules for two consumers for a commodity are given as $q_1 = 10 - P$; $q_2 = 6 - 0.5\ P$.
    The market price for the commodity is Rs. 4.00. Find which one of the two consumers is consuming more of the commodity. Also find the price elasticities for the two consumers at their respective equilibrium positions.
11. The supply curve for a commodity is given as $s = a\ (P - b)^{1/2}$ where P which is greater than b, is the price of the commodity and a and b are constants. (*i*) Find the general expression of the price elasticity of supply, e_s; (*ii*) show that the price elasticity of supply decreases with increase in s and P; (*iii*) find the point on the supply curve where it takes unity value *i.e.*, $e_s = 1$.
12. Explain the concepts of 'income elasticity' and 'cross elasticity of demand'. What is the precise role of these concepts in the economic theory related to demand analysis for goods and services?

CHAPTER 4

Theory of Consumer Behaviour

The basic material relating to demand, supply, and market equilibrium has been presented in Chapter 3. The demand side of the market for a commodity's concerned with consumer behaviour. Hitherto, we have simply defined the term 'demand', identified its major determinants and examined its role in price determination, *i.e.*, in market equilibrium for a commodity without going through the analysis of consumers' bahavioural patterns upon which it is based. In this chapter, we discuss this aspect, *i.e.*, we will present the modern theory of consumer behaviour and the relation between such a theory and the theory of demand. We know that consumer is a very important actor in economic system. The goal of economic activities is ultimately to satisfy consumer needs directly and indirectly. Keeping this in mind, we will examine the principles or laws which give us tools for an analysis of consumer behaviour in the market.

4.1 THE CONCEPTS OF UTILITY AND UTILITY FUNCTION

We start our analysis of consumer behaviour by posing a simple question: Why does a consumer purchase a particular commodity? The answer is simple: using that commodity the consumer satisfies his need or want. He buys food when he is hungry. In a technical term a consumer purchases a commodity because it has utility for him. The term 'utility' is defined as the power of. a commodity or service to satisfy human want, *i.e.,* to yield a consumer some satisfaction.

Consumers' preferences of goods and services or any other thing, economic or non-economic, are formalised by the concept of utility. It is a subjective phenomenon. The feeling of satisfaction or utility derived from consumption of a commodity or use of a service may vary from person to person because each person's physiological and psychological make-up is different from each other. There will be several factors affecting an individual's feeling of satisfaction. Identification and measurement of all such factors is an extremely difficult task, if not impossible. In view of such difficulty, economists concentrate their attention on certain basic quantifiable economic variables for explaining consumers' feeling of satisfaction or utility. A number of non-quantifiable factors like aesthetics, love, friendship, security, etc., do affect human behaviour but economists treat them constant in the consumption time horizon. In other words, the utility analysis carried on by economists runs in terms of quantities of goods and services, income, and prices, keeping all other things constant.

A consumer at a time, consumes one or more commodities. He gets satisfaction or derives utility by consuming goods. The level of satisfaction or utility derived by him depends on quantities of goods consumed. This is a basic hypothesis of the consumer theory. According to this, we say that utility derived from consumption of a commodity depends exclusively on its quantity other things being constant. In symbolic form we write the relationship between the level of utility and quantity of a commodity consumed as:

$$U_i = f_i\ (q_i),\ i = 1 \text{ to } n \qquad \text{...(1)}$$

where U_i is the level of utility.

q_i is the quantity of i-th commodity, and f_i denotes the shape of the relationship. There are n commodities.

When all n commodities are consumed simultaneously, the total utility derived by the consumer will be a sum of utilities derived from consumption of individual commodities. That is:

$$U = U_1 + U_2 + \cdots + U_n$$

Substituting the right hand side of equation (1) for U_1, U_2, ..., U_n, we get:

$$U = f_1\ (q_1) + f_2\ (q_2) + \ldots + f_n\ (q_n)$$

This may be simplified as:

$$U = F\ (q_1,\ q_2,\ q_3,\ \ldots\ q_n) \qquad \text{...(2)}$$

This is called 'utility function'.

A utility function specifies the relationship between total utility derived and quantities of different goods consumed at a time.

We have used simple additive principle for getting total utility by summing up the utilities derived from consumption of different commodities. This implies that the utility derived from one good is independent of the rate of consumption of any other good. This is an assumption which might not be true in practice. However, we take consumption of all goods simultaneously and derive utility from that, which the utility function shows us. The assumption of additive utility is not necessary for this, only it simplifies the complexity of utility analysis. It is presumed that utility can be measured just like any other economic magnitude. This is a cardinal approach for utility analysis. This approach has been challenged by several economists on the ground that utility being a subjective phenomenon it cannot be measured in terms of numbers, weight or the like. They suggest a different approach by taking the stand that utility levels though non-measurable can be compared with each other. This is ordinal approach for utility analysis. In this chapter, we will study both these approaches. Initially, we will concentrate on the cardinal approach to explain the consumer behaviour.

Every consumer will have a utility function showing his preferences. This function is assumed to be single-valued and continuous. By single valued we mean that the consumer gets only one level of satisfaction and not two or more when he consumes the given quantities of different goods. If we change the quantity of anyone commodity keeping others constant or change the quantities of other goods also then of course he moves to different level of utility. By continuous function we mean that the first and second order partial derivatives of utility with respect to quantities of goods and services can be derived from it. This is a necessary requirement of the function as on its basis we derive the laws which govern consumer behaviour in practice. If the consumption activity embodied in the form of a utility function is not continuous, it may be difficult to get any kind of generalised laws or principles regarding consumer behaviour.

The level of satisfaction or utility derived from consumption depends on length of consumption period. For example, consumption of 10 cigarettes per hour or per day or per week or per month will give different levels of satisfaction. Keeping this in mind, one has to define the consumption period very clearly for which the utility function has been defined.

Let us take the first-order partial derivatives from the utility function (2).

$$\partial U/\partial q_1 = F_1\ (q_1, \ldots\ q_n)$$

$$\partial U/\partial q_2 = F_2\ (q_1, \ldots\ q_n)$$

$$\partial U/\partial q_n = F_n\ (q_1, \ldots\ q_n)$$

or

$$\partial U/\partial q_i = F_i\ (q_1,\ q_2,\ q_i, \ldots\ q_n) \qquad \ldots(3)$$

$$i = 1,\ \ldots\ n.$$

A partial derivative of the utility function is interpreted as the change in total utility by consuming one more extra unit of a commodity keeping the level of consumption of other commodities constant. In economic terminology, the partial derivatives are called 'marginal utilities' of commodities for the consumer. Marginal utility of a commodity is defined as the change (or addition) in total utility by consuming one more extra unit of the commodity, consumption of other commodities remaining the same.

If 10 units of a commodity give 100 units of utility and if 11 units give 115 units of utility, then the marginal utility of 11th unit of the commodity is 15 units.

How does marginal utility of a commodity change, if the quantity of consumption of the commodity increases? There is a basic law of economics known as the 'law of diminishing marginal utility' which shows this. According to this law:

As quantity consumed of a commodity increases, the marginal utility of that commodity tends to decline. This says that $\partial U/\partial q_i$ declines as q_i increases. It means the rate of change of marginal utility is negative. This is expressed using the second order partial derivative from the utility function as $\partial^2 U / \partial q_i^2 < 0$. One can cite several examples from real life in support of the law of diminishing marginal utility. Take the example of a smoker. The first cigarette he consumes brings considerable amount of satisfaction to him. The satisfaction derived from the second cigarette will be lower and this way succeeding units of cigarette give him less and less satisfaction. In fact, he may stop smoking cigarette after two or three which implies zero marginal utility for any more cigarettes. It may be negative if he goes beyond the level of consumption which gives him zero marginal utility. The variation in total utility and marginal utility, as quantity of consumption of a commodity increases, can be shown graphically as follows:

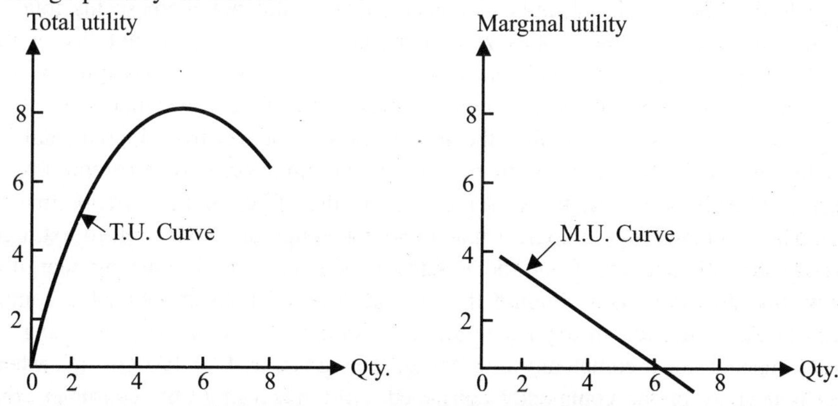

Fig. 4.1 Total and Marginal Utility Schedules

The total utility, as shown on the left hand side in the above diagram, increases at a diminishing rate and reaches at maximum level for 6 units of the commodity. The slope of tangent at any point on total utility curve gives us marginal utility. Marginal utility is declining continuously. It is zero when *TU* is maximum. After this, it is negative as *TU* declines. A rational consumer would never go beyond the zero level of marginal utility while consuming a commodity.

The law of diminishing marginal utility is valid only when: (1) there is no time-gap between consumption of successive units of the commodity. In other words, consumption is continuous; (2) tastes or preferences of the consumer remain unchanged during the process of consumption; and, (3) all units of the commodity are similar in size, quality and other attributes.

There are some exceptions to the law of diminishing marginal utility. Consumption of liquor defies the law. The more a person drinks, the more he likes it giving a positive relationship between marginal utility and quantity of liquor consumed. This may be true initially but there will come a stage when the drunkard starts taking less and less liquor and eventually stops it. Another exception to the law is that of hobbies like collection of stamps, coins, paintings, etc. A person derives satisfaction from such collection and the more he collects the relevant item the more satisfaction he gets. This is not true. We find that under hobbies people collect different varieties of the item and not the similar one. For similar varieties we find that his marginal utility declines very fast. Some economists argue that the law of diminishing marginal utility does not hold true for money. Desire for more and more money is a universal phenomenon. Money is not a commodity, rather a medium of exchange and a standard for valuation. It is not consumed but used to buy goods for consumption. So, it is unfair to apply the law of diminishing marginal utility to it. Even if we do so, we can safely say that marginal utility of money for a poor man would be more as compared to a rich man. So, we can say that marginal utility of money declines with richness and hence the law is valid even in this case.

What about marginal utility of diamond? The situation is similar to that of liquor. Initially, it may increase but eventually it will decline when there is no more scope for a man for demonstrating his wealth by having diamonds.

Why does the law of diminishing marginal utility hold good in practice? The validity of the law is an empirical fact. It is widely believed despite the absence of a generally accepted measuring rod for utilities. What we find in reality is that a consumer may not be able to satisfy all his wants but his desires or wants for individual commodities are satiable. He consumes a commodity to the extent it gives him maximum satisfaction. He stops further consumption of the commodity at this point because he feels that the additional units of consumption would not increase his total satisfaction, rather it would be reduced. This implies zero marginal utility of the commodity at the optimum consumption level and negative beyond that point. If this is not so, the consumer would never be satiated with the consumption of the commodity. We do not find any support for this. What we observe, in practice, as consumers is that the feeling of satisfaction from incremental consumption of a commodity gradually decreases with increase in consumption of the commodity. Greater the total satisfaction already achieved, the lesser would be the effect of an extra or marginal unit of consumption. Thus, our own psychological reactions or feelings of satisfaction to extra consumption of a commodity provide the proof for the validity of the law of diminishing marginal utility in practice. How this law helps us in finding the optimal level of consumption of a commodity by a consumer can be demonstrated through a numerical example. Consider the following one:

The utility function for a commodity to a consumer is given as $U = 100\,Q - Q^2$, where U is total utility and Q is quantity of the commodity consumed. How much of Q the consumer consumes? We maximise the total utility which gives us the condition for zero marginal utility and hence optimum consumption of the commodity. Differentiating U with respect to Q, we get, $MU = dU/dQ = 100 - 2Q$. For maximum utility $MU = 0$, *i.e.*, $100 - 2Q = 0$ which means $Q = 50$ units. Beyond, this level of consumption we find that MU is negative, *i.e.*, $d^2\ U/dQ^2 = -2$ so the consumer will not cross the limit of consumption of the commodity beyond 50 units.

4.2 CONSUMER EQUILIBRIUM: DERIVATION OF THE LAW OF EQUI-MARGINAL UTILITY

A consumer, at a time, needs several goods and services for consumption. His income is limited and it may not be possible for him to buy whatever he desires. He faces fixed prices of commodities in the market. In this situation, how should he decide to buy any or all the commodities? What commodity he should buy and in what amounts, that is to say how should he allocate his limited income on various goods and services so that he gets maximum satisfaction or utility? The problem here is that of maximising total utility by consuming all goods and services subject to the income constraint. The solution of this problem will give us the conditions for equilibrium for the consumer. Before taking up this problem for further discussion, let us make some assumptions to simplify the analysis.

The first assumption is that utility is measurable through cardinal scale. This is what we are assuming so far in the utility analysis. The second assumption is that goods and services are continuously divisible. The third assumption is that goods and services can be substitutes for each other. The consumer can spend money on one commodity or the other. This kind of flexibility has to be assumed for attaining equilibrium condition. The fourth assumption is that the consumer is rational. He has full knowledge about the market, *i.e.*, commodities, their attributes, prices, etc. Lastly, we assume that there is no negative consumption of any commodity.

Given the assumptions cited above, we can formalise a consumer's problem as y^0 is fixed income,

Max. $\quad U = F\ (q_1,\ q_2,\ \ldots,\ q_n)$ ...(4)

Subject to $\quad y^0 = P_1 q_1 + P_2\ q_2 + \ldots + P_n q_n$ ...(5)

$P_1,\ P_2,\ \ldots,\ P_n$ are fixed prices for $q_1,\ q_2,\ \ldots,\ q_n$ respectively. The constraint specifies consumer budget line. The right hand side of this constraint indicates consumer's expenditure on different goods and services. The total expenditure cannot exceed total income. The consumer utilises all his income; that is why we are equating total expenditure to total income. The utility function is assumed to have a maxima otherwise it may be difficult to find the consumer equilibrium position.

For solution of the constrained utility maximisation problem, as specified here, we apply the standard lagrange method.[1] The steps involved here are: (*a*) find the first order or necessary conditions for a local interior maximum: (*b*) verify the second order conditions for this; and (*c*) make sure that the conditions for global maximum are satisfied. Our interest here is in finding the global maximum for consumer's utility. Using the utility function (4) and the budget constraint (6) let us define the Lagrange function as

$$V = F\ (q_1,\ q_2,\ q_3,\ \ldots,\ q_n) + \lambda\ [y^0 - P_1\ q_1 - P_2\ q_2 - P_n\ q_n] \quad \ldots(6)$$

where λ is defined as the Lagrange Multiplier. Taking partial derivatives of V with respect to $q_1\ q_2,$ q_n and λ, we get the first order conditions for maximum utility as

1. (*a*) J.M. Henderson & R.E. Quandt, *Microeconomic Theory*, McGraw-Hill 1971, (Mathematical Appendix); pp. 404–407.
(*b*) M.D. Intriligator; *Mathematical Optimisation and Economic Theory,* Prentice Hall Inc., 1971, pp. 28-38.

$$\begin{aligned} \partial v/\partial q_1 &= F_1 - \lambda P_1 = 0 \\ \partial v/\partial q_2 &= F_2 - \lambda P_2 = 0 \\ \partial v/\partial q_n &= F_n - \lambda P_n = 0 \\ \partial v/\partial \lambda &= Y^0 - p_1q_1 - P_2q_2 \ldots P_nq_n = 0 \end{aligned} \qquad \ldots(7)$$

where $F_i = \partial U/\partial q_i$ = Marginal utility of ith commodity, $i = 1$ to n.

We have equated the first order partial derivatives of the Lagrange function to zero by assuming that the second order conditions for a local and the conditions for a global maximum are satisfied.[2]

From the first n equations of (7) we get the relations

$$F_1 = \lambda P_1, \quad F_2 = \lambda P_2, \quad \ldots, \quad F_n = \lambda P_n$$

or

$$\frac{F_1}{P_1} = \frac{F_2}{P_2} = \frac{F_3}{P_3} \cdots = \frac{F_n}{P_n} = \lambda \qquad \ldots(8)$$

or more explicitly

$$\frac{MU_1}{P_1} = \frac{MU_2}{P_2} = \frac{MU_3}{P_3} \cdots = \frac{MU_n}{P_n} = MU \text{ of Money } (= \lambda) \qquad \ldots(9)$$

This is the equilibrium condition for maximum utility with income constraint. This relationship explains that for obtaining maximum satisfaction (*i.e.*, utility) from consumption of goods and services, the consumer spends his income on these goods and services in such a way that the last unit of money spent on each good or service brings him the same marginal utility. This *is the law of equi-marginal utility or the law of commodity substitution.*

This is a very important condition for consumer equilibrium. On the basis of this, the consumer allocates his income. He must ensure that marginal utility per unit of money spent on various goods and services is identical and equal to the marginal utility of money. For any pair of commodities we can further write the equilibrium condition as

$$\frac{MU_1}{MU_2} = \frac{P_1}{P_2} \quad \text{or} \quad \frac{MU_i}{MU_j} = \frac{P_i}{P_j} \qquad \ldots(10)$$

The ratio of marginal utilities of two commodities must be equal to the ratio of their prices.

The ratio of marginal utilities of two goods defines the rate of substitution between these goods, *i.e.*,

$$\text{Rate of substitution of } X_1 \text{ for } X_2: \quad \left|\frac{dX_2}{dX_1}\right| \frac{MU_1}{MU_2} = \frac{P_1}{P_2} \qquad \ldots(11)$$

---

2. The second order conditions for constrained maximum with one constraint are that the bordered principal minors,

$$\begin{vmatrix} F_{11} & F_{12} & -P_1 \\ F_{21} & F_{22} & -P_2 \\ -P_1 & -P_2 & 0 \end{vmatrix} \begin{vmatrix} F_{11} & F_{12} & F_{13} & -P_1 \\ F_{21} & F_{22} & F_{23} & -P_2 \\ F_{31} & F_{32} & F_{33} & -P_3 \\ -P_1 & -P_2 & -P_3 & 0 \end{vmatrix}, \ldots, \begin{vmatrix} F_{11} & F_{12} & ..F_n & -P_1 \\ F_{21} & F_{22} & ..F_{2n} & -P_2 \\ F_{n1} & F_{n2} & ..F_{nn} & -P_n \\ -P_1 & -P_2 & ..P_n & 0 \end{vmatrix}$$

Where $F_{ij} = \partial^2 U/\partial q_i \partial q_j$; alternate in sign beginning with a positive sign. See for details *(1) J. M. Henderson and* R.E. Quandt, *op. cit.*, pp. 404-406 and (2) T. Apostle, Mathematical Analysis, Addison Wesley 1974, pp. 380-384.

Let us consider the two commodity case again. We have the equilibrium condition

$$\frac{MU_1}{P_1} = \frac{MU_2}{P_2}$$

Suppose $$\frac{MU_1}{P_1} > \frac{MU_2}{P_2}$$

Here the consumer is getting greater marginal utility per unit of money spent on commodity 1 than the marginal utility per unit of money spent on commodity 2. How he will react to this situation? He increases his expenditure on commodity 1, *i.e.*, buys more of it, but as his consumption of commodity 1 increases, the marginal utility derived from that decreases. It means MU_1/P_1 decreases which will be eventually equal to MU_2/P_2 ratio for the second commodity. This way he attains equilibrium.

The ratio *MU/P* must be equal to marginal utility of money. Consider just one commodity. We have the equilibrium condition for consumer in this case as

$MU_1/P_1 = \lambda$ (*i.e.*, *MU* of money)

or $$MU_1 = \lambda \ P_1 \qquad ...(12)$$

Equation (12) expresses a very useful relationship between marginal utility and price of a commodity. Using this relationship we can establish the link between marginal utility schedule and demand schedule of a commodity. This was done intuitively by Marshall.[3]

When a consumer buys a commodity he gains utility by having it. At the same time he makes a sacrifice of utility of money by paying for the commodity. A rational consumer will buy a commodity if the gain of utility to him is more or atleast equal to the loss of utility of money. The gain of utility when he buys the commodity is nothing but its marginal utility and the loss of utility of money is the product of commodity price and marginal utility of money. This is the same thing as shown by expression (12) which is the condition for the consumer equilibrium. In order to show this simple relationship between marginal utility and price of a commodity graphically, let us consider the information given in Table 4.1.

Table 4.1: Derivation of Demand Curve from *MU* curve for a Commodity

Qty. (No. of units)	*MU of successive units*	*Price per unit*	*Loss of utility of money (MU of money) × Price*
1	MU_{11}	P_{11}	$\lambda \ P_{11}$
2	MU_{12}	P_{12}	$\lambda \ P_{12}$
3	MU_{13}	P_{13}	$\lambda \ P_{13}$
4	MU_{14}	P_{14}	$\lambda \ P_{14}$
5	MU_{15}	P_{15}	$\lambda \ P_{15}$
6	MU_{16}	P_{16}	$\lambda \ P_{16}$
7	MU_{17}	P_{17}	$\lambda \ P_{17}$

3. Alfred Marshall, *Principle of Economics*, 8th Ed., Macmillan 1920, Ch. 3. (Book 3).

MU_{11}, MU_{12}, MU_{17}, represent marginal utility of successive units of commodity 1 and P_{11}, P_{12}; P_{17} represent variation in price of the commodity. λ is marginal utility of money. Total utility of money given up for buying each unit of the commodity will be λ times the price. This is shown in the last column of the table.

Let us assume that marginal utility of money is constant. From the law of diminishing marginal utility we can derive the implication as follows:

$$MU_{11} > MU_{12} > MU_{13} > \ldots > MU_{17} \quad \ldots(13)$$

Since at the equilibrium $MU = \lambda P$, so the right hand side will also show similar variation in the price of the commodity as λ is constant. Therefore, we say

$$P_{11} > P_{12} > P_{13} > \ldots. > P_{17} \quad \ldots(14)$$

By plotting (13) and (14) against quantity of the commodity, we get marginal utility and demand curves for the commodity. The two curves will show exactly similar variation. Both will be coinciding when $\lambda = 1$. Demand curve will be above the marginal utility curve when $\lambda < 1$, and it will be below the marginal utility schedule when $\lambda > 1$. This is the approach followed by Marshall to derive the demand curve from the marginal utility curve. Since marginal utility declines with increase in quantity consumed, so price of the commodity declines with increase in quantity bought. This gives us the explanation of why the demand curve slopes downward apart from the two other reasons mentioned earlier in Chapter 3.

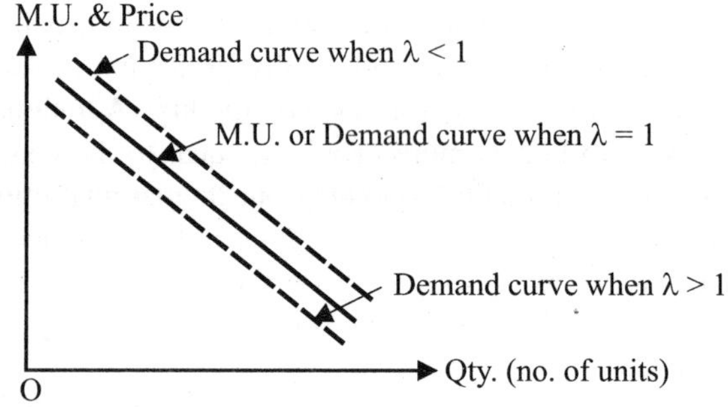

Fig. 4.2 Links Between Marginal Utility and Demand Schedules

If marginal utility is zero, equilibrium condition $MU = \lambda P$ shows that price of the commodity will be zero since marginal utility of money is not zero. This is the situation for all free goods. Such goods are freely available to consumers. They consume these goods at the level which gives them maximum total utility. At that level the marginal utility will be zero. There is no question of consuming less of them when they are freely available.

The Paradox of Value: In practice, we find several commodities like water and air which are essential for life. Without such commodities we cannot survive. Their value to life is very high but they are almost freely available. On the other hand, there are some commodities like diamond, which are quite unnecessary for human life but their price is very high in the market. There is, thus, a 'paradox of value' which is to be resolved. We know, air and water are essential goods, their 'use-value', *i.e.*, 'total utility' is very high but being almost free goods their 'exchange-value' in market is very low or zero. This is because their marginal utility is zero. The price of a commodity, *i.e.*, its 'exchange value' depends on marginal utility of that commodity and the use-value depends on its utility. Thus, there are two concepts of 'value' which must be clearly understood to resolve the 'paradox of value' seen in reality.

4.3 DERIVATION OF DEMAND FUNCTIONS: GENERALISED APPROACH

Consider the first order conditions of constrained utility maximisation as expressed by the set of equations (7). We have $n + 1$ equations in this set and the number of unknowns is also $n + 1$, *i.e.*, n commodity levels q_1, q_2 and q_n and λ, the value for the Lagrange multiplier. The system of equations is therefore solvable. The solution for the unknown would be to express their values in terms of known variables. These are:

$$\begin{aligned} q_1 &= \phi_1 (P_1, P_2, \ldots, P_n, y^\circ) \\ q_2 &= \phi_2 (P_1, P_2, \ldots, P_n, y^\circ) \qquad \ldots(15) \\ &\vdots \\ q_n &= \phi_n (P_1, P_2, \ldots, P_n, y^\circ) \end{aligned}$$

and $\lambda = \lambda^\circ (P_1, P_2, \ldots, P_n, y^\circ)$

where ϕ_1, ϕ_2, ... f_n, and λ° are functional relations.

These equations are demand functions for the different commodities. In each specification, we are expressing the quantity demanded as a function of price of the concerned commodity, prices of other commodities used by the consumer and his income level. Other things like tastes, customs, expectation, etc., mentioned as additional demand factors, are treated as constants. Intuitively, we have specified such demand function for a commodity in Chapter 3. Here we have used the consumer equilibrium theory to derive them. They are related to the utility function from which they have been deduced.

Let us consider an example with two commodities. The utility function and budget constraint for a consumer are given as

$$U = q_1 \cdot q_2 \qquad \ldots(16)$$

and $$y^\circ = P_1 q_1 + P_2 q_2 \qquad \ldots(17)$$

For maximising (16) subject to (17) as constraint, we write the Lagrange function as:

$$V = q_1\, q_2 + \lambda\, [y^\circ - P_1 q_1 - P_2 q_2]$$

By taking the partial derivatives of V with respect to q_1, q_2 and λ, and equating each one of them to zero, we get,

$$\partial V/\partial q_1 = q_2 - \lambda\, P_1 = 0 \qquad \ldots(18)$$

$$\partial V/\partial q_2 = q_1 - \lambda\, P_2 = 0 \qquad \ldots(19)$$

and $$\partial V/\partial \lambda = y^\circ - P_1 q_1 - P_2 q_2 = 0 \qquad \ldots(20)$$

From (18) and (19) we get,

$$q_2 = \lambda\, P_1,\ q_1 = \lambda\, P_2$$

and $$q_2/q_1 = P_1/P_2$$

or $$P_1 q_1 - P_2 q_2 = 0 \qquad \ldots(21)$$

Solving (20) and (21) for q_1 and q_2 we get their demand functions as:

$$q_1 = \frac{y^\circ}{2P_1},\ q_2 = \frac{y^\circ}{2P_2} \qquad \ldots(22)$$

As we have mentioned earlier, the shape of the demand curve for any commodity depends on the nature of the utility function. In this example, the utility function is such that it gives exactly similar demand function for the two commodities. Demand for each one depends directly on income (y°) and inversely with price of the commodity.

The marginal utility of money, *i.e.*, λ can also be found from the system of first order maximisation conditions. In the above example it is:

$$\lambda = \frac{y^{\circ}}{2\,P_1 P_2} \qquad \text{...(23)}$$

If the utility functions are given as $U = q_1^2\, q_2^2$, or $U = 4\, q_1 q_2$, or $U = \log(q_1, q_2)$ the solution or expressions for demand functions derived from them would be exactly similar to (22) when $U = q_1 q_2$. The value of λ, of course, will change. All these utility functions belong to the same class *i.e.*, they are monotonic transformation of each other and, therefore, represent the same preference ordering of the consumer reflecting the same behaviour.

We have defined λ as marginal utility of money. Let us show how this interpretation of λ is valid. Consider the first order conditions for constrained utility maximisation expressed by the equations set (7). We find that at the equilibrium λ is equal to marginal utility of any good divided by its price. That is,

$$F_i = \partial U/\partial q_i = \lambda\, P_i$$

or

$$\lambda = \frac{1}{P_i}\left(\frac{\partial U}{\partial q_i}\right)$$

Since P_i is constant, we can take it inside the bracket in the denominator as:

$$\lambda = \frac{\partial U}{\partial (P_i q_i)}$$

$P_i q_i$ shows the expenditure on *i*th goods. At the equilibrium, an additional unit of money spent on good *i*, (i = 1, ...n), therefore, provides the same increase in utility. [unit change in $P_i q_i$ is one unit of expenditure, *i.e.*, of money). We can, therefore, say that λ is the change in maximised value of utility as income changes.

$$\lambda = \partial U/\partial y \qquad \text{or } \lambda = \frac{1}{P_i}\frac{\partial U}{\partial q_i} \qquad \text{...(24)}$$

Further, we can show it by using some mathematical expressions.

$$U = F\,(q_1, q_2)$$

By taking total differentials of this, we have

$$dU = F_1\, dq_1 + F_2\, dq_2 \;;\quad F_1 = \partial U/\partial q_1 \;;\quad F_2 = \partial U/\partial q_2 \qquad \text{...(25)}$$

The income constraint is

$$y = P_1 q_1 + P_2 q_2$$

By taking total differentiation of this, we have

$$dy = P_1\, dq_1 + P_2\, dq_2,\ P_1 \text{ and } P_2 \text{ are constant} \qquad \text{...(26)}$$

From maximisation condition we have the equilibrium condition

$$F_1 - \lambda\, P_1 = 0, \qquad F_2 - \lambda\, P_2 = 0$$

Substituting values for F_1 and F_2 in (25), we get

$$dU = \lambda P_1\, dq_1 + \lambda\, P_2\, dq_2 \qquad \text{...(27)}$$

Dividing (27) by (26) we have

$$\frac{dU}{dy} = \lambda\left[\frac{P_1 dq_1 + P_2\, dq_2}{P_1 dq_1 + P_2\, dq_2}\right] = \lambda \qquad \text{...(28)}$$

So, marginal utility of money equals λ.

The demand functions derived above are homogeneous of degree zero in prices and income, *i.e.*, if all prices and income change in the same proportion, the consumer equilibrium position will not change and quantities demanded will also be unchanged.

Let us reformulate the budget constraint of the consumer as

$$ky° = kP_1q_1 + kP_2q_2 \quad ...(29)$$

Using the utility function $U = F(q_1, q_2)$, the Lagrange function for maximisation U will be:

$$V = F\ (q_1, q_2) + \lambda\ [ky° - kP_1q_1 - kP_2q_2]$$

From this we have:

$$\begin{aligned} \partial V/\partial q_1 &= F_1 - \lambda\ kP_1 = 0 \\ \partial V/\partial q_2 &= F_2 - \lambda\ kP_2 = 0 \\ \partial V/\partial \lambda &= ky° - kP_1q_1 - kP_2q_2 = 0 \end{aligned} \quad ...(30)$$

This gives us the equilibrium situation as,

$$F_1/F_2 = P_1/P_2 = k\lambda \quad ...(31)$$

This is same as before except a change in the marginal utility of money which is now $k\lambda$). The quantities demanded would be a function of $(kP_1, kP_2$ and $ky°)$ instead of $(P_1, P_2\ y°)$ but they will not be different in these two situations. The second order conditions will also not change and so, we can safely say that demand functions are homogeneous of zero degree. There is a practical application of this property. If income and prices are changing in the same proportion, one need not worry about inflation since real consumption of goods and services will not be affected by this.

The property of zero degree of homogeneity of the demand function is a kind of restriction. If this is so, we can use it further to derive the relationships between price-elasticity and income elasticity of demand for a commodity. For this, let us take the help of the Euler's theorem according to which a function $Z = \phi\ (x, y)$ is homogeneous of degree r if the following condition is satisfied:

$$x\frac{\partial z}{\partial x} + y\frac{\partial z}{\partial y} = rz \quad ...(32)$$

If we take a demand function for a commodity i as:

$q_i = \phi_i\ (P_1, P_2, P_3\ ...\ y)$ and apply the above theorem to it, we get,

$$P_1\frac{\partial q_i}{\partial P_1} + P_2\frac{\partial q_i}{\partial P_2} + ... + P_i\frac{\partial q_i}{\partial P_i} + ... + y\frac{\partial q_i}{\partial y} = 0 \quad ...(33)$$

Since $r = 0$ (Demand function being homogeneous of degree zero); $i = 1, ..., n$.

Dividing both the sides by q_i we have

$$\frac{P_1}{q_1}\frac{\partial q_i}{\partial P_1} + \frac{P_2}{q_i}\frac{\partial q_i}{\partial P_2} + ... + \frac{P_1}{q_i}\frac{\partial q_i}{\partial P_i} + ... = -\frac{y}{q_i}\frac{\partial q_i}{\partial y} \quad ...(34)$$

Each element in this equation is an expression for the elasticity. So, we have the sum of 'own' and cross elasticities of demand for a commodity i equal to minus of its income elasticity of demand. This is an important result which we derive from the property of zero degree of homogeneity of the demand functions for different commodities.

4.4 LIMITATIONS OF CARDINAL UTILITY ANALYSIS

The utility analysis discussed above is essentially based on cardinal approach, *i.e.*, the basic assumption for this was that utility can be measured through cardinal scale of measurement say, in terms of numbers of 'utils'. This assumption gives serious doubt about the validity of the entire analysis. Utility being a subjective phenomenon cannot be measured by numbers or weight or anything like that. If this is so, the theory of consumer analysis based on cardinal approach is not verifiable. Marshall, who was a strong supporter of the cardinal approach of utility analysis to some extent, agreed with this criticism but he pointed out that utility is measurable indirectly if not directly.[4] A person's satisfaction or utility derived from consumption of a commodity can be measured indirectly by the amount of money he is willing to pay for that. For each unit of commodity how much price he is willing to pay gives us a measurement of utility of that unit of commodity. The units of price multiplied by the marginal utility of money is equivalent to the marginal utility of the commodity at the equilibrium, ($MU = \lambda P$ as we have seen earlier). The marginal utility of money (λ) is taken to be constant by Marshall.

Even the approach of indirect measurement of utility using monetary units has been challenged by economists. The reason for this was mainly the unstable value of money. When its value is not stable how can it be used as a measuring rod for utility?

What is the need of measuring utility at all? We use this concept to understand theoretically the behaviour of a rational consumer and derive the demand functions in ex-ante sense from this. The demand functions will have all measurable variables; quantity of the commodity on one side, prices and income on the other. Using data for all such variables, we can estimate the demand functions for commodities. This is the objective of the entire utility analysis. Measurement of utility is not necessary for this although it is desirable.

There is another serious limitation of the cardinal utility analysis. We know that a demand curve slopes downward because of 'substitution effect' and 'income effect'. These two effects cannot be isolated using the above framework of utility analysis. There are some other drawbacks, such as its failure to analyse demand for indivisible goods, inferior goods, etc. But these are minor issues. By and large, the whole theory based on the cardinal approach is highly abstract in nature. It does not explain all aspects of consumer behaviour but the major issues have been tackled well by this theory.

4.5 THE INDIFFERENCE CURVE ANALYSIS

1. Concept

This is an alternative approach developed by economists like Edgeworth, Fisher, Slutsky, Hicks and Allen to analyse consumer behaviour. In this approach, the emphasis is given on comparing different utility levels instead of measuring them through some cardinal scale. In other words, this approach is based on ordinal measurement of utility. Under ordinal measurement scale, the alternatives can only be ranked such as greater or smaller, higher or lower and the like. The approach of indifference curve for analysing consumer behaviour is based on certain basic assumptions. The assumptions are as follows:

(*i*) There is complete consistency in ordering of preferences by the consumer. For example, if two alternative bundles of consumption goods, *A* and *B* are available, the consumer must state either "*I* prefer *A* to *B*" or "*I* prefer *B* to *A*" or "*A* and *B* are equally preferred". The consumer is not in the state of indecision.

(*ii*) Along with the complete consistency we expect that the consumer's preferences are not self-contradictory or conflicting with each other. This is the assumption of transitivity. This means if *A* is preferred over *B*, and *B* is preferred over *C* then *A* is preferred over *C*.

4. Alfred Marshall, *Ibid.* Chapter 3, pp. 78–85.

(*iii*) An individual's preferences are such that he prefers more to less. It means that the individual is not satiated at least not in all goods. Keeping the consumption of other goods constant and increasing consumption of at least one good is definitely a better situation.

(*iv*) The goods consumed by the consumer are substitutable. The satisfaction or utility can be maintained at the same level by consuming more of some good.

(*v*) All commodities in the consumption basket of the consumer are *divisible.*

(*vi*) Individuals are *rational* in decision-making. This is a requirement for the consumer equilibrium analysis in general and not for only the indifference curve analysis. Further, we assume that the preference scheduling of one consumer is independent of the preference schedules of other consumers. It means that there is absence of externalities as far as consumer preferences are concerned. Further, the indifference curve analysis is static in nature. It presumes certainty regarding the decision situations faced by a consumer.

Given the conditions as specified by the above assumptions, the indifference curve technique as we mentioned earlier, compares the different levels of satisfaction or utility rather than measuring them. This is the ordinal approach adopted for utility analysis. *The indifference curve is a locus of different combinations of two or more goods which yield the same level of satisfaction or utility to the consumer.* It is also called as 'iso-utility curve'.

Graphically, we can demonstrate an indifference curve as shown in Fig. 4.3.

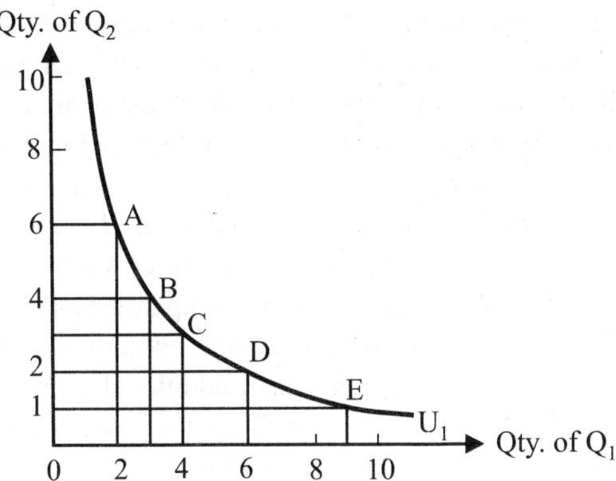

Fig. 4.3 Indifference Curve

For the sake of simplicity we take two commodities Q_1 and Q_2 into consideration for drawing the indifference curve. In practice, the number of commodities in the consumption basket will be more than two and different combinations of such goods yield some fixed level of satisfaction, but it is not possible to show it graphically. We, therefore, confine the indifference curve analysis to a case of two commodities. Points *A*, *B*, *C*, *D* and E show the different combinations of Q_1 and Q_2 commodities that yield a constant level of utility U_1. By joining these points we get the indifference curve as shown in the figure. The shape of the curve is convex towards the origin and it is downward sloping. We will be showing why it is so and what are the other possibilities for this. When we move from point *A* to point *B* the consumption of commodity Q_2 decreases by two units and consumption of commodity Q_1 increase by one unit. This rate of substitution of commodity Q_2 by commodity Q_1 is therefore – 2/1. Minus sign indicates decrease in Q_2. This is approximately the slope of the indifference curve between *A* and *B*. When we move further from point *B* to point *C* the decrease in consumption of Q_2 is only by one unit and increase in consumption of Q_1 is also by one unit. This implies that the consumer is giving up now only one unit of Q_2 for one additional unit of Q_1. The rate of substitution of Q_2 per unit of Q_1 is now –1. As we move still further to *D* or *E* we observe that the consumer gives up less and less quantity of Q_2 per additional unit of Q_1, *i.e.*, the rate of substitution of Q_2 by Q_1 declines in magnitude.

The rate of substitution of Q_2 by Q_1 is called 'Rate of Commodity Substitution (RCS)' in expanded form. It is computed at the margin (implying very small changes). So, alternatively we call it 'Marginal Rate of Commodity Substitution (MRCS)'. When we use the term RCS for this, it is implicit that it is MRCS.

The Rate of Commodity Substitution or Marginal Rate of Commodity Substitution is that amount of a commodity, say Q_2 to be given up per unit of another commodity, say Q_1 for consumption if the consumer remains on the same indifference curve.

In the consumption process, we are substituting one commodity for the other but maintaining a constant level of utility derived from them. This is precisely what the RCS or MRCS tells us. In symbolic form the RCS or MRCS is denoted by $-\dfrac{\Delta q_2}{\Delta q_1}$ or $-\dfrac{dq_2}{dq_1}$ where Δq_2 or dq_2 expresses the change in quantity of commodity Q_2 and Δq_1 or dq_1 is the change in quantity of commodity Q_1.

Why does the marginal rate of commodity substitution decline, when we move along the indifference curve? Is it because we have drawn the indifference curve as a convex line towards the origin or there is a sound economic for that? Let us examine this issue.

A consumer's marginal rate of commodity substitution between the goods (Q_2 and Q_1) for a constant level of utility will, in some way, depend on how many units of Q_2 and Q_1 he or she is currently consuming. Consider the point *A* in Fig. 4.3. At this point, the consumer consumes much more (6 units) quantity of Q_2 as compared to the quantity of Q_1 (two units). He is willing to give up two units of Q_2 for one unit of Q_1 and, thus, moves to point *B*. At this point, consumption of Q_2 decreases to 4 units and consumption of Q_1 increases to three units. He is interested in increasing consumption of Q_1 further since it is still very low as compared to the consumption of Q_2. But this time, he is willing to give up only one unit of Q_2 for one additional unit of Q_1. As he moves down further, the willingness to give up units of Q_2 for each additional unit of Q_1 decreases further. Thus, what we observe here is that the willingness to give up the commodity Q_2 in favour of the other commodity (Q_1) directly relates to the quantity of Q_2. Greater the quantity of a commodity already consumed the higher will be the willingness to give up a part of the commodity in favour of some other commodity and vice-versa. This explains why the magnitude of the marginal rate of commodity substitution of Q_2 for Q_1. declines as we decrease quantity of Q_2 and increase quantity of Q_1. The consumer prefers a balanced consumption of different goods. Too much consumption of one good induces him to substitute it for the other good in greater extent as compared to the extent of its substitution for the other when its consumption is low.

The declining tendency of the MRCS can be explained in a better way by using the marginal utility concept. From the law of diminishing marginal utility we know that there is an inverse relationship between quantity of consumption and marginal utility. When we decrease quantity of consumption of a commodity in favour of another, the marginal utility of the commodity increases. On the other hand, the marginal utility of the other commodity decreases. In the above diagram, we have the sequence of decreasing quantity of Q_2 and increasing quantity of Q_1 as we move from *A* to *E* point on the indifference curve. Decrease in the quantity of Q_2 means increase in its marginal utility and increase in the quantity of Q_1 means decrease in its marginal utility. When marginal utility of Q_1 declines then less and less quantity of Q_2 will be substituted for one unit of Q_1. To make it easier to understand we can bring the analogy of falling value of money. When the value of money falls, one rupee will fetch lesser amount of any commodity. This is the reason for diminishing rate of substitution and it is this diminishing rate of commodity substitution which makes the indifference curve convex towards the origin. Details of this property of the indifference curve are presented in the following section:

2. Properties of Indifference Curve

(*a*) An indifference curve is downward sloping and convex towards the origin. To prove this mathematically, let us consider the utility function:

$$U = F(q_1, q_2)$$

By taking total derivatives of this function we have:

$$dU = \frac{\partial U}{\partial q_1} dq_1 + \frac{\partial U}{\partial q_2} dq_2$$

By the definition of the indifference curve, utility does not change when we move along the curve. So, we can write $dU = 0$. This gives us:

$$0 = \frac{\partial U}{\partial q_1} dq_1 + \frac{\partial U}{\partial q_2} dq_2$$

or

$$-\frac{dq_2}{dq_1} = \frac{\partial U / \partial q_1}{\partial U / \partial q_2} = \frac{F_1}{F_2} \qquad ...(35)$$

dq_2/dq_1 is the slope of the indifference curve. Its negative, *i.e.*, $- dq_2/dq_1$ is the marginal rate of commodity substitution. So, equation (35) simply says that marginal rare of commodity substitution is equal to the ratio of marginal utilities of the two goods. A rational consumer will not consume a commodity beyond the level of when its marginal utility is zero. We, therefore, have $\partial U/\partial q \geq 0$ and $\partial U/\partial q_2 \geq 0$. The ratio $(\partial U/\partial q_1)/(\partial U/\partial q_2)$ is, therefore, positive. This means that the left hand side of equation (35) is also positive. That is $- dq_2/dq_1$ is positive. This is possible when there is one more negative sign attached to it. This condition is satisfied when the indifference curve is negatively sloped. So, negative of negative slope makes the MRCS positive. This proves that the indifference curve is downward sloping.

Again, as quantity q_2 decreases, its marginal utility (F_2) appearing in the denominator of the ratio $(\partial U/\partial q_1)/(\partial U/\partial q_2)$ increases, and since q_1 is being substituted for q_2, so the quantity of q_1 increases and its marginal utility (F_1) in the numerator of the marginal utility ratio decreases. A decrease in F_1 simultaneously is followed by an increase in F_2 when q_1 is substituted for q_2 meaning a fall in the magnitude of the ratio which implies a fall in the marginal rate of commodity substitution. This gives us the reason for the indifference curve being convex towards the origin.

The property of convexity of the indifference curve will be proved if we show that the rate of change of slope of the indifference curve is positive, i.e., $d^2q_2/dq_1^2 > 0$. By taking the derivative of (35) with respect to q_1. and simplifying the expressions we get the final condition for the rate of change of slope of the indifference curve as

$$\frac{d^2q_2}{dq_1^2} = -\frac{1}{F_2^3}[F_{11} F_2^2 - 2 F_1 F_2 F_{12} + F_{22} F_1^2] > 0 \qquad ...(36)$$

where $\partial U/\partial q_1 = F_1 > 0$, $\partial U/\partial q_2 = F_2 > 0$

$$\partial^2 U / \partial q_1^1 = F_{11} < 0 \text{ } (MU_1 \text{ declines with increase in } q_1)$$

$$\partial^2 U / \partial q_2^2 = F_{22} < 0 \text{ } (MU_2 \text{ declines with increase in } q_2)$$

$$\partial^2 U / \partial q_1 \, \partial q_2 = \partial^2 U / \partial q_2 \, \partial q_1 = F_{12} > 0$$

In view of such restrictions, the bracketed term in (36) is –ve so $d^2 U dq_1^2$ is positive. This implies that the indifference curve is convex towards the origin.

(*b*) The curvature of the indifference curve indicates the degree of substitution between the goods represented by it. If the goods are perfect substitutes for each other, the indifference curve will be a straight line sloping downward and intersecting the commodity axes. Such a line will show constant marginal rate of commodity substitution for the goods. The line intersects the commodity axes which means the utility level indicated by the line can be attained by consumption of one commodity alone keeping the other one at zero level. This is what perfect substitution implies. If two goods are complementary, they are required in fixed proportion. The minimum required proportion of goods will be shown by a point through which the indifference curve will pass. On either side of this point, the indifference curve will be straight line parallel to commodity axes. In other words, the indifference curve will be in the shape of a right angle at the point showing the minimum proportion of two goods. The marginal rate of substitution will be zero in this case. In Fig. 4.4, these two extreme types of indifference curve are shown in panel (*a*) and (*b*) respectively. Panel (*c*) shows the normal indifference curve.

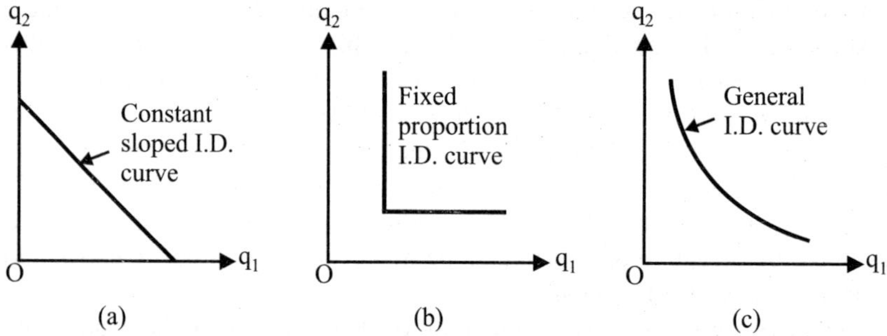

Fig. 4.4 Types of Indifference Curves

Between the two extreme cases of indifference curve we have normal curves sloping downward. Greater the curvature of the indifference curve, lesser will be the degree of substitution for the goods. This reflects low MRCS. On the other hand, if the curve is flatter, *i.e.*, of less curvature, the degree of substitution between the goods will be quite high and MRCS will tend towards constancy.

An indifference curve parallel to *X*-axis or *Y*-axis would not be possible. Suppose a consumer consumes a few units of q_2 and 0 units of q_1 to get some satisfaction U_1. Now, without reducing the amount of q_2 he increases q_1. This would give him higher level of satisfaction. So, there would not be indifference between these two situations. It implies that a parallel line to q_1 axis or a parallel line to q_2 axis cannot be called as indifference lines. The indifference curve has to be downward sloping whether it is a straight line or a curve.

(*c*) Two indifference curves cannot intersect with each other for the given pattern of preference. The reason for this can be explained by referring to Fig. 4.5.

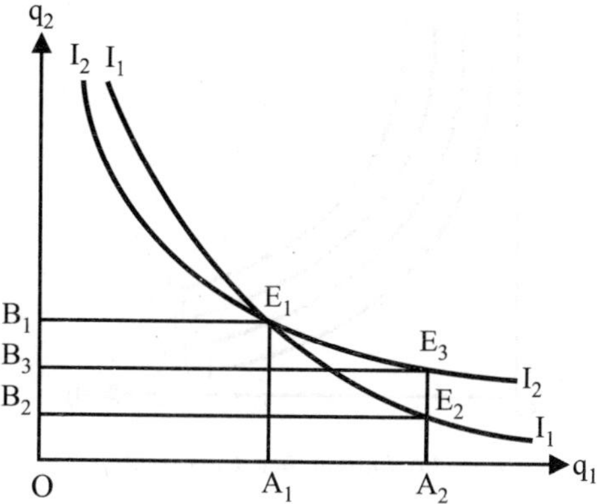

Fig. 4.5 Intersection of Two Indifference Curves

I_1 and I_2 are two indifference curves showing different levels of utility. They are intersecting at E_1 point.

By the definition of the indifference curve, a consumer would get same utility by consuming $OA_1 + OB_1$ combination of q_1 and q_2 at E_1 and $OA_2 + OB_2$ combination of the goods at E_2 point on I_1. Similarly $OA_1 + OB_1$ combination of q_1 and q_2 would give the same utility as $OA_2 + OB_3$ combination at E_3 on I_2, In other words,

Utility of E_1 bundle = utility of E_2 bundle of q_1, q_2

Utility of E_1 bundle = utility of E_3 bundle of q_1, q_2

Since the consumer is indifferent between *E*. and E_2 bundles of q_1 and q_2 and E_1 and E_3 bundles of q_1 and q_2, he would, therefore, be indifferent between E_3 and E_2 bundles of q_1 and q_2. But this is not so. The combination of q_1 and q_2 at E_2 is $(OA_2 + OB_2)$ and the combination, of these goods at E_3 is $(OA_2 + OB_3)$. OA_2 is common but $OB_3 > OB_2$. It is, therefore, clear that $OA_2 + OB_3$ is preferable over $OA_2 + OB_2$ because of greater quantity of q_2 consumed. This combination, *i.e.*, $OA_2 + OB_3$ would give more utility than $OA_2 + OB_2$ when E_3 is preferred to E_2, E_1 cannot have the same utility as shown by E_2 and E_3. What we find that it would be inconsistent to compare utility at E_1 and E_2 to utility at E_1 and E_3. It is not possible. So, we can say that intersection of two indifference curve is not possible at all given the definition of indifference curve and the assumptions behind it.

(*d*) In the non-negative consumption space, *i.e.*, positive quadrant of the graph, (see Fig. 4.6) we find a set of indifference curves each one showing a different level of utility and sequenced in orderly way. An indifference curve that lies farther from the origin represents a greater level of utility than one closer to the origin. This also follows from the assumption or observation that more is preferred to less. In Fig. 4.6, as we move up, the level of utility shown by the indifference curve increases, that is, $I_3 > I_2 > I_1 > I_0$. All combinations of q_1 and q_2 shown by I_3 are preferred over

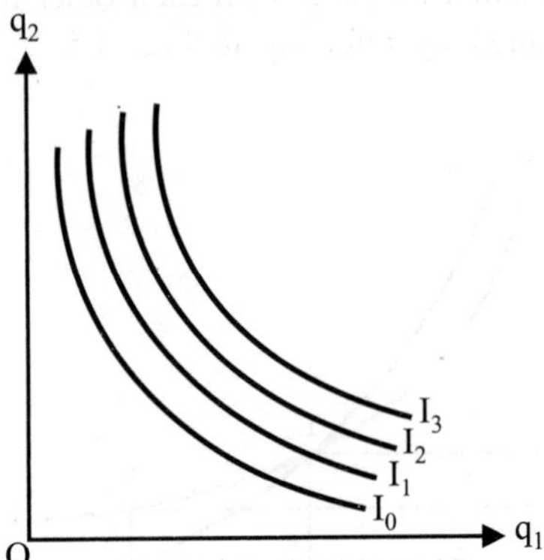

Fig. 4.6 Indifference Curves Map

the combination of q_1 and q_2 shown by I_2 and similarly we say that the combinations of q_1 and q_2 shown by I_2 are preferred to the combinations shown by I_1 and so on.

The indifference curves will be parallel for a given utility function showing constant preferences. But this is not a necessary requirement. The necessary thing is that they will never intersect each other in spite of being unparallel for some reasons. Different individuals may have different sets of indifference curves because of differences in their preferences for the same types of goods.

(*e*) The space between the consecutive indifference curves reflects the strength of diminishing marginal utility. For a given level of q_2 how much q_1 is needed to sustain one unit increment in the total utility? It will be more and more when the law of diminishing marginal utility holds true.

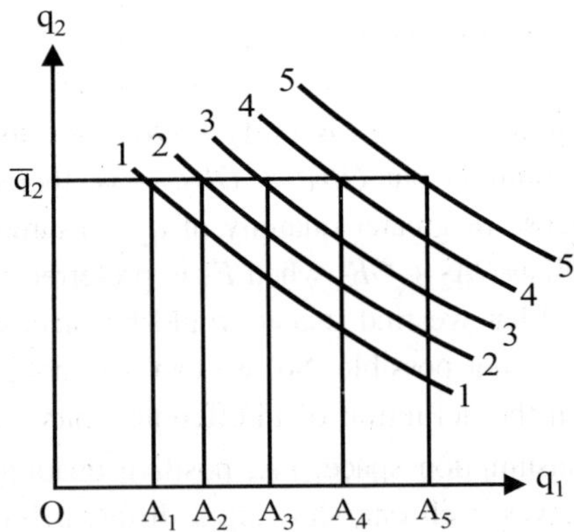

Fig. 4.7 Links between Marginal Utility and the Space between Indifference Curves

In this figure, the quantity of q_2 is kept at a constant level $\bar{q}_2$, A_1A_2 quantity of q_1 is needed to push up the total utility by one unit, *i.e.*, from level 1 to level 2 of indifference curve. Similarly, $A_2\,A_3$ units of q_1 are needed for increasing the satisfaction by one unit, say from level 2 to 3. This way, we find more and more of q_1 for the consecutive increase in the utility levels as reflected by the indifference curves of higher levels. $A_4A_5 > A_3A_4 > A_2A_3 > A_1A_2$ implies that the law of diminishing marginal utility is operating for consumption of additional units of commodity Q_1.

4.6 CONSUMER EQUILIBRIUM ON INDIFFERENCE CURVE

We have seen in the earlier sections how a consumer attains equilibrium when he spends his limited income on various goods and services. He simply follows the principle of constrained utility maximisation for this. Now, we will see how his equilibrium position can be analysed using the indifference curve. We presume that the entire set of indifference curves, *i.e.*, the indifference map, is given for the consumer. The problem is to identify that particular indifference curve showing a particular utility level on which his equilibrium position lies. Further, the indifference curve will show several plausible combinations of the goods that the consumer consumes. Which particular combination he will finally pickup? The indifference curve as such taken alone cannot help us to find the equilibrium position. For this, we need some additional information. This information is provided in the form of a budget constraint showing a fixed income and expenditure relationship. That is, the income of the consumer is fixed (y°). The prices of goods are also fixed. Let these be P_1 and P_2 for two commodities Q_1 and Q_2 respectively. In symbolic form, the budget constraint for two commodities consumption situation is,

$$y^\circ = P_1\, q_1 + P_2\, q_2$$

In the cardinal utility maximisation, we used expanded version of this budget line, *i.e.*, $y^\circ = P_1 q_1 + P_2Q_2 + ... + P_n q_n$, but in this section we confine to two commodities for which we draw the indifference curve.

A budget constraint is a locus of all combinations of two goods (or more) which can be purchased with fixed income at fixed prices. It is a boundary of consumption for both the commodities. The consumer cannot cross this boundary line since his income would not allow this. The budget constraint is a downward sloping line, its slope would be equal to $- P_1/P_2$ as we see below:

$$y^\circ = P_1q_1 + P_2q_2$$

so,
$$q_2 = \frac{y^\circ}{P_2} - \frac{P_1}{P_2} q_1 \qquad ...(37)$$

By maximising total utility $U = F(q_1, q_2)$ subject to the budget constraint $y^\circ = P_1q_1 + P_2q_2$ the equilibrium condition for the consumer would be as shown by equation (10) earlier,

$$\frac{MU_1}{MU_2} = \frac{P_1}{P_2}$$

We also have seen earlier that the marginal rate of commodity substitution equals the ratio of marginal utilities of the commodities Q_1 and Q_2, that is,

$$MRCS = -\frac{dq_2}{dq_1} = \frac{MU_1}{MU_2}$$

Combining this with the above equation, *i.e.,* (Eqn. No. 10), we have,

$$MRCS = -\frac{dq_2}{dq_1} = \frac{MU_1}{MU_2} = \frac{P_1}{P_2} \qquad ...(38)$$

MU_1/MU_2 is the slope of the indifference curve and P_1/P_2 is the slope of the budget line. At the equilibrium situation the slopes of the two curves, *i.e.*, of the indifference curve and of the budget line are equal. This implies that the budget constraint is tangent to the indifference curve. Thus, the indifference curve (and hence the utility level represented by it) which is touched by the budget line would be preferred. *The combination of goods shown by the point of tangency would give the optimum level of satisfaction to the consumer.*

The can be shown diagrammatically as follows:

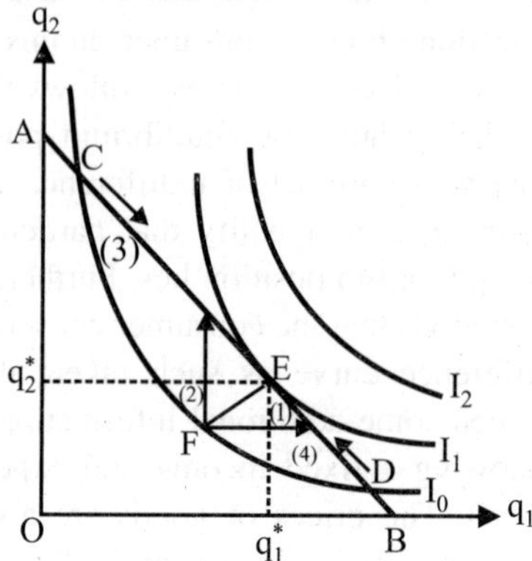

Fig. 4.8 Consumer Equilibrium on the Indifference Curve

AB is the budget line $Y^\circ = P_1 q_1 + P_2 q_2$. This line shows the various combinations of the two goods Q_1 and Q_2 that the consumer can purchase by his fixed income Y°. He may prefer any point on this line. If he buys only Q_2 then the quantity of Q_2 he can afford will be $q_2 = \frac{Y^\circ}{P_2}$ shown by the point *A*. Similarly, if he buys only Q_1 commodity, the maximum quantity of Q_1, *i.e.*, q_1 will be equal to $\frac{Y^\circ}{P_1}$ shown by the point *B*. Since his preferences are shown by the indifference curve and these curves are not intersecting the commodity axes it implies that he prefers both the commodities in some combination and the two commodities are not perfect substitutes. So, points *A* and *B* on the budget line cannot be considered for equilibrium position in this case. Any point above the budget line will also be unattainable since consumer's income is fixed, commodity prices are fixed; so the attainable boundary given by the budget line is fixed. Any indifference curve which is above the budget line but untouched by it would not be considered for examining the equilibrium position of the consumer. The points on the budget line and below this in the commodity space are, of course, feasible or attainable. For simplicity, we consider a few point, such as *F* on I_0, *C* and *D* on I_1 curve, and finally *E* point. Let us consider point *F* on the indifference curve I_0.

The combination of the two commodities Q_1 and Q_2 shown by point *F* would not yield maximum satisfaction because the consumer can move to higher indifference curves by moving either horizontally or vertically as shown by the arrows (1) and (2) respectively or between them diagonally towards the budget line. These movements from point F indicate that the consumer gets either more of q_1 or q_2 or both without decreasing the quantity of other commodity. He thus moves to a higher level of satisfaction by such movements. He has to move away from point *F* since it is far below the budget line and so the income is not utilised fully. For full utilisation of income and for maximum satisfaction the consumer has to move along the .budget line. So, all points like *F* are inefficient combinations of Q_1 and Q_2.

Now, let us consider point *C* on the budget line at which the indifference curve I_0 and the budget line (*AB*) intersect. The slope of the indifference curve is greater than the slope of the budget line at this point. That is,

$$\frac{MU_1}{MU_2} > \frac{P_1}{P_2}$$

MU_1/MU_2 is the slope of the indifference curve which is the ratio of the marginal utilities of Q_1 and Q_2 and P_1/P_2 is the price ratio for Q_1 and Q_2. This inequality can be rearranged as:

$$\frac{MU_1}{P_1} > \frac{MU_2}{P_2}$$

This shows that marginal utility per unit of money spent on commodity Q_1 is greater than marginal utility per unit of money spent on commodity Q_2. The consumer is not in equilibrium. He will increase consumption of Q_1 and reduce consumption of Q_2. This means that he moves down along the budget line to increase his utility by consuming more of q_1. As quantity q_1 increases its marginal utility decreases and since q_2 decreases so its marginal utility increases by moving down along the budget line. An adjustment process is automatically operating here through such movements and eventually we get the equilibrium position when the slope of the indifference curve and the slope of the budget line coincide at point E.

Now let us take point D. At this point, the slope of the indifference curve is less than the slope of the budget line. The indifference curve intersects the budget line from below. This means

$$\frac{MU_1}{MU_2} < \frac{P_1}{P_2}$$

or rearranging it, we have

$$\frac{MU_1}{P_1} < \frac{MU_2}{P_2}$$

The marginal utility per unit of money spent on commodity Q_2 is greater than the marginal utility per unit of money spent on Q_1. The consumer reacts to this situation by increasing his expenditure on Q_2 and hence increasing its consumption in order to increase his utility. This means that he moves on higher indifference curves by moving up along the budget line. By such movements the quantity q_2 increases and its marginal utility decreases and q_1 decreases, its marginal utility increases. The inequality $(MU_1/P_1) < MU_2/P_2$ is thus changing towards equality. The upward movement continues till the slope of the indifference curve and the slope of the budget line coincide, that is, equilibrium is reached at point E. Thus, for the consumer equilibrium eventually we find that the slopes of the indifference curve and of the budget line must be identical. This implies that the budget line must be a tangent to the indifference curve at the equilibrium position. This will be the level of maximum satisfaction attained by the consumer from his fixed income and fixed prices of commodities. q_1^* and q_2^* will be the bundles of commodities corresponding to the maximum level of satisfaction.

4.7 EFFECTS OF INCOME AND PRICE CHANGES ON CONSUMER EQUILIBRIUM

We have already seen that the quantity demanded of a commodity primarily depends on its price, prices of other commodities and services and income of the consumer. Now, let us examine the effects of income and price changes on the consumer equilibrium situation within the indifference curve framework. Through the budget line we have specified the expenditure pattern of the consumer using fixed income ($y°$), fixed prices of commodities (P_1 and P_2), and the quantities q_1 and q_2. Let us change income and prices one by one and see what happens to consumer behaviour by this.

(i) Change in Income, Price being Constant

When, for instance, income of the consumer increases, the budget line shifts upward. The shift of the budget line would be parallel as we keep prices of goods constant and so slope of the budget line does not change. Because of parallel shifts of the budget line, equilibrium position will be on higher and higher indifference curves implying increasing utility derived. This is shown in Fig. 4.9.

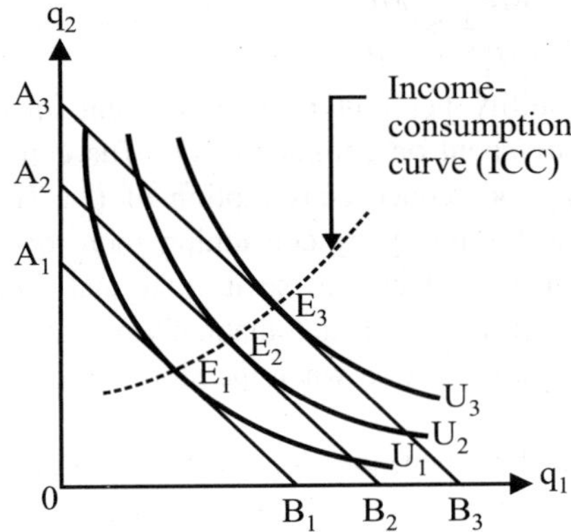

Fig 4.9 Effects of Income Changes on Consumer Equilibrium: Prices Being Constant

The line formed by joining the equilibrium points on the indifference curves, which we get by shifting the budget line up because of increasing income, other things being constant, is called 'income-consumption curve (ICC)'. This shows how a consumer will consume the goods when his income rises. The income-consumption curve need not to be a straight line. It may be a straight line or a curve depending on the consumer's preferences for the goods as reflected by the indifference curves. If the changes in quantities of goods are uniform in proportions in moving up on the indifference curves then income-consumption curve will be linear, otherwise not. A non-linear income-consumption curve will show either increasing or diminishing proportions of changes in quantities of goods. If the income-consumption curve tilts towards a commodities axis, the commodity is treated as 'superior' as compared to the other commodities. By 'superior' we mean consumer prefers that over the other as income increases. It is the case of luxury goods. If the income-consumption curve is positively sloped, both the commodities will be 'normal' goods. If it is negatively sloped, one of the commodities is 'inferior'. Th income-consumption curve may be positively sloping upward for a certain range of income shifts and then negatively sloping indicating that the commodity from whose axis it is deviated away is inferior. The other commodity is a normal one.

From the knowledge of the income-consumption curve 'ICC', we can draw the Engel curves. An Engel curve is a relationship between quantity of a commodity, say Q_1, purchased and income of the consumer, prices being constant. The name 'Engel curve' is derived after the name of Prussian economist Ernst Engel (1821–1946) who first studied the income-consumption relationship for goods. In the case of luxury goods, the demand increases proportionately more rapidly than income, while for 'necessities' the demand grows proportionately less rapidly than income. For inferior goods the Engel curve will be negatively sloped. Consider the Fig. 4.10. In part (*a*) of the figure we find the income-consumption curve 'ICC' sloping negatively and tilting towards q_2 axes. The commodity Q_2 is therefore 'superior' and the commodity Q_1 is 'inferior' because its quantity declines as income increases.

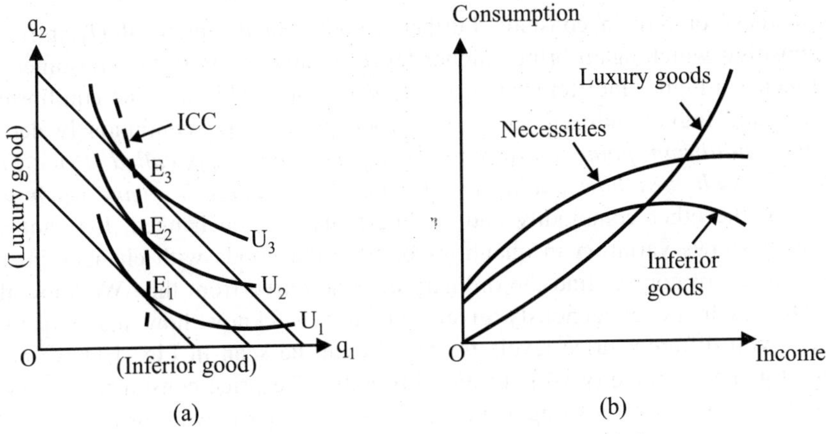

Fig. 4.10 (a) Downward Sloping 'ICC', (b) Engel Curve

In part (*b*) of the Figures 3, Engel curves have been shown, one each for a luxury good, for necessity and for an inferior goods. The trends of changes in these curves, when income increases, are self-explanatory.

(ii) Changes in a Commodity Price

We keep income of the consumer at constant level and change the prices of goods in order to find the effect of such changes on the equilibrium position. Changing both the prices simultaneously is a complex situation for analysis. Let us keep this pending for sometime and just take the price of one commodity constant and that of the other varying. Here we keep P_2 unchanged and P_1 decreasing. Because of a decrease in P_1 the slope of the budget line will also be decreasing which means it will shift to the right. Consider the following figure:

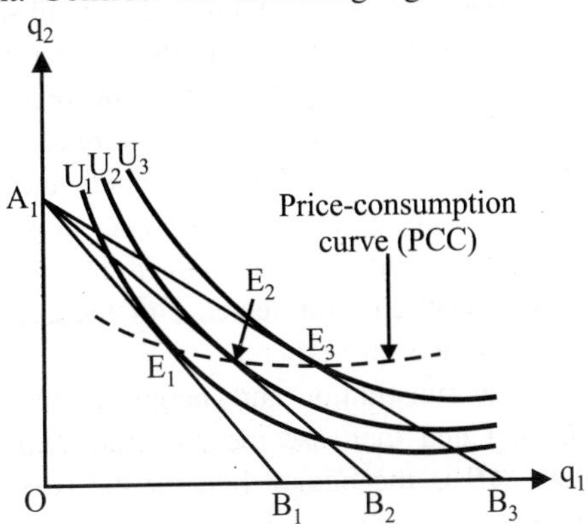

Fig. 4.11 Effect of Changing Price of a Commodity on Consumer Equilibrium: Income Being Constant

A_1B_1 is the initial budget line. When price of Q_1 decreases the consumer will be able to buy more *of* Q_1 with his fixed income when spent entirely on it. This means shifting of the line to A_1B_2 position. This new budget line will be a tangent to a higher indifference curve at E_2. The total satisfaction goes up and the quantity consumed of q_1 also goes up. Quantity of Q_2 may decrease or increase or remain constant. Further decrease in the price of Q_1 shifts the budget line to A_1B_3 position which again brings higher level of satisfaction to the consumer as this new budget line touches a higher indifference curve U_3 at E_3 point. This way the equilibrium position shifts to higher and higher indifference curves when price of Q_1 continuously decreases. *The line joining the equilibrium points on different indifference curves is called 'Price Consumption Curve (PCC)'. It indicates how quantities of both the commodities vary when price of* Q_1 changes, price of the other commodity and income remaining unchanged. It is not an ordinary demand curve. It shows variation in quantities of both the goods with changes in the price of one of them. We can of course, find the ordinary demand curve from this. We know the changes in price of Q_1 which are exogenously given and also we know how much quantity q_1 the consumer buys with different price levels for Q_1. As can be seen in Fig. 4.11 we can draw the demand curve for the commodity without any difficulty. The price-consumption curve need not to be a straight line. It may be a straight line or a curve sloping upward or downward depending on the two important effects associated with price changes which we will discuss in the following section.

(iii) Substitution and Income Effects from a Fall in Price

As we have seen in the preceding section, the effect of a price change on the quantity of a commodity is more complex to analyse than is the effect of income change. In this case, the budget line shifts and its slope also changes with changing price of the commodity. Consequently, the equilibrium shifts on a new indifference curve. The quantity demanded of the commodity changes with price changes because of 'substitution effect' and 'income effect'. These two 'effects' have been listed as reasons for downward slope of the demand curve. (Vide Chapter 3). By using the equilibrium analysis within the indifference curve framework these two effects can be isolated from each other. We will see now how this can be done.

Some clarification is needed about the precise nature of the substitution and income effects. If utility is held constant, consumer will move along an indifference curve substituting the commodity that has become relatively cheaper for the one that has become relatively more expensive because of the price change. This type of movement shows the *substitution effect.* Further, when there is a decrease in price, the consumer saves some expenditure which means his real purchasing power increases. Because of a change in purchasing power, the consumer moves on to a different indifference curve showing a different level of utility. This is *income effect.* The role of 'income effect' is to push up or down the level of satisfaction depending on decrease or increase in the price of a commodity and thus moving to different indifference curves.

The procedure for 'isolating' the substitution and income effects is quite simple. We will use graphical demonstration for this first and then use the algebraic expressions.

Consider the following figure *AB* is the budget line for the two commodities Q_1 and Q_2. The budget line touches the indifference curve for U_1 at E_1 point showing the equilibrium position for the consumer with X_1 and Y_1 quantities of Q_1 and Q_2 commodities. Now, let us consider the effect of a decrease in price P_1 for Q_1 other things remaining constant. The budget line now shifts to AB_1 position since the consumer will be able to buy more of Q_1 with fixed income if he wants to spend it entirely on Q_1.

The new budget line (AB_1) touches a higher indifference curve for U_2 level of utility at point E_2. The consumer now buys X_2 quantity of Q_1 and Y_2 quantity of Q_2 for consumption. Because of a decrease in price of Q_1 the consumer is buying more of Q_1 and less of Q_2. The total change in quantity of Q_1 is shown by X_1X_2 distance on q_1 axis. The total effect on quantity demanded of Q_1 *i.e.*, X_1X_2 is the sum of substitution effect and income effect. To isolate these two effects, we keep

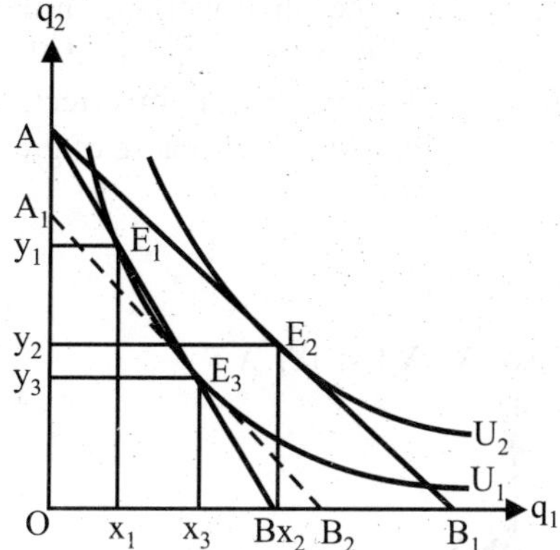

Fig. 4.12 Substitution and Income Effects: A General Case

the prices of the two commodities Q_1 and Q_2 same as shown by the new budget line AB_1 and somehow push back the consumer to his old level of satisfaction, *i.e.*, to the indifference curve marked by U_1. This type of exercise helps us to find these two effects separately.

Because of a decrease in price P_1there is increase in real income of the consumer which causes an increase in his satisfaction from U_1 to U_2 level. Suppose, we tax the consumer, *i.e.*, withdraw the increased amount of real income from him. This pushes him to the original level of satisfaction U_1. How much tax is to be imposed on the consumer? We do not know it but we can have an idea of this by shifting down the budget line AB_1 parallelly till it touches the indifference curve for U_1 level of utility. The shifted budget line A_1B_2 which is parallel to AB_1 touches the U_1 indifference curve in the diagram at E_3 level. This point (E_3) shows the equilibrium position for the consumer with substitution effect only, *i.e.*, because of a decrease in price P_1 the consumer substitutes some quantity of Q_1 for relatively costly commodity Q_2. This is substitution effect which is shown by the distance X_1X_3. The difference between total effect X_1X_2 and substitution effect X_1X_3 that is X_3X_2, is the income effect. What we are getting here is an identity showing the sum of the two effects:

Total Effect = Substitution Effect + Income Effect

$$\underset{(-)}{\overrightarrow{X_1 X_2}} = \underset{(-)}{\overrightarrow{X_1 X_3}} + \underset{(-)}{\overrightarrow{X_3 X_2}}$$

Both the effects are unidirectional. Substitution effect is always negative in the sense that an increase in price of a commodity means a decrease in the quantity of that commodity which is substituted for another commodity for maintaining constant utility level and a decrease in price means an increase in such a quantity of the commodity. The income effect may be working in the same direction or opposite to the direction of change of the substitution effect. In the above case, it is in the same direction because a change in real income increases the quantity demanded of the commodity Q_1. Total effect is thus a sum of both the effects. This is the case of a normal good. A normal good is that one whose quantity demanded increases with increase in income. For 'inferior' goods the income effect will operate in opposite direction to the substitution effect but the net effect will still be negative, *i.e.*, in the direction of the substitution effect. Let us show this through a diagram.

In this diagram (Fig. 4.13), the total effect is marked by X_1X_2. The substitution effect is X_1X_3. The income effect is, therefore, $X_2 X_3$. What we find in this case is that the total effect is less than the substitution effect but still it is negative working in the direction of substitution effect. That is, quantity bought is increasing with decrease in price of the commodity. The income effect is operating in the opposite direction of the substitution effect. The quantity demanded of the commodity decreases with increase in real income but because of greater magnitude of the substitution effect the total effect is negative.

$$\underset{(-)}{\overrightarrow{X_1 X_2}} = \underset{(-)}{\overrightarrow{X_1 X_3}} + \underset{(+)}{\overleftarrow{X_2 X_3}}$$

and $\qquad |X_1 X_3| > |X_2 X_3|$ so $|X_1 X_2| < |X_1 X_3|$

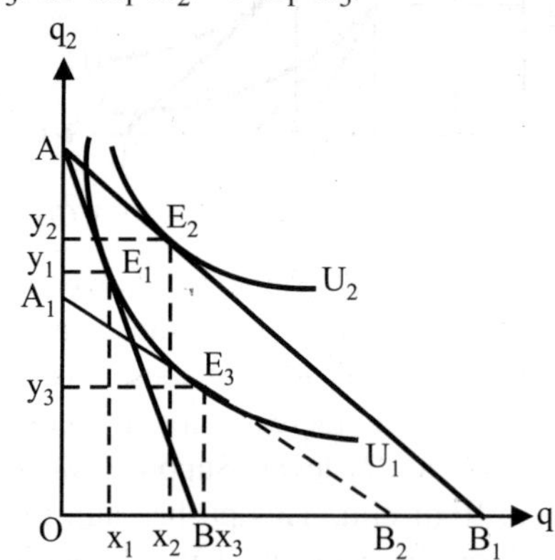

Fig. 4.13 Substitution and Income Effects for an Inferior Commodity

This result holds for an inferior commodity. There is still another possibility. There may be a decline in quantity purchased and consumed with decline in price of the commodity. This is a situation when there is positive relationship between changes in price of the commodity and quantity demanded at least for a certain range of variation in the price of the commodity. To understand this situation consider the following diagram (Fig. 4.14).

E_1 is the original equilibrium position and E_2 is the final one when price P_1 decreases. The quantity OX_2 of Q_1 corresponding to E_2 is less than the quantity of Q_1 which the consumer was buying earlier. Thus, there is a decrease in quantity of Q_1 when price of Q_1 is decreasing. The commodity

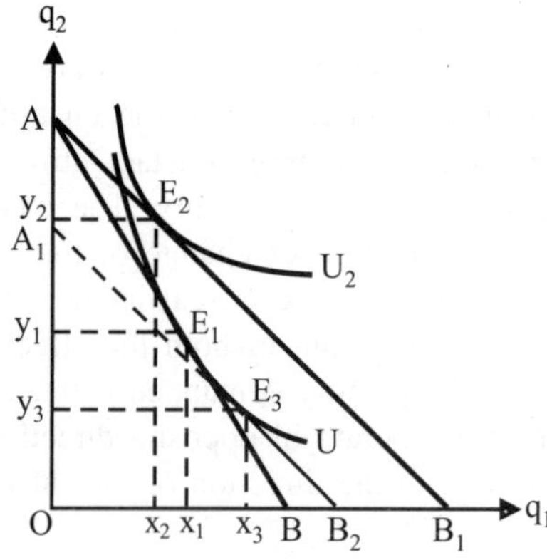

Fig. 4.14 Substitution and Inocme Effects for a 'Giffen Good'

Q_1, which is depicting this type of result, is called as "Giffen Good". This peculiar type of behaviour is called "Giffen Paradox" after the name of English economist Giffen who first observed it. 'A'Giffen good' is an inferior good for which the income effect is very strong completely out-striping the substitution effect in magnitude. This would be in opposite direction as in the case for an inferior good. A consumer spends a large proportion of his income on such a commodity and if price of the commodity declines he saves considerable amount of his expenditure from which he can buy a better substitute for the commodity. Hence, the consumer reduces its consumption and moves to the other commodity. From the diagram (Fig. 4.14) we find that

$$\underset{(+)}{\overleftarrow{X_1 X_2}} = \underset{(-)}{\overrightarrow{X_1 X_3}} + \underset{(+)}{\overleftarrow{X_3 X_2}}$$

The direction of total effect $(X_1\ X_2)$ is similar to that of income effect $(X_3\ X_2)$ and opposite to the substitution effect $(X_1 .\ X_3)$; and

$$|X_1\ X_3| < |X_3\ X_2|$$

It is difficult to find a 'Giffen good' in practice. Nevertheless, it is very useful at least conceptually to understand 'income' and 'substitution' effects in indifference curve framework.

We have gone through a graphical analysis for separation of the substitution and income effects. Let us use the algebraic expressions for this purpose now.

By maximising total utility $U = F(q_1, q_2)$ subject to the income constraint $y^0 = P_1q_1 + P_2q_2$ we got the first order conditions for maximisation as shown by the equations set (7) in section 4.2. Our objective is to find the magnitude of the effect of price and income changes on the consumer equilibrium when all variables vary simultaneously. For this we take the total differentiation of Equations (7). This gives us

$$\begin{aligned} F_{11}\ dq_1 + F_{12}\ dq_2 - P_1\ d\lambda &= \lambda\ dP_1 \\ F_{21}\ dq_1 + F_{22}\ dq_2 - P_2\ d\lambda &= \lambda\ dP_2 \\ - P_1\ dq_1 - P_2\ dq_2 &= - dy + q_1dP_1 + q_2dP_2 \end{aligned} \qquad \text{...(39)}$$

We have three equations for finding the values for three unknowns dq_1, dq_2 and $d\lambda$. The right hand side is known to us. Assuming that only P_1 price changes by dP_1 other things being constant, *i.e.*, $dP_2 = 0$, $dy = 0$, we can solve (39) using the Cramer's Rule to get the following final expression.[5]

$$\frac{\partial q_1}{\partial P_1} = \left(\frac{\partial q_1}{\partial P_1}\right)_{u=\text{constt.}} - q_1\left(\frac{\partial q_1}{\partial y}\right)_{\text{Prices = constt.}} \qquad \text{...(40)}$$

This is Slutsky Equation, named after the Russian economist E. E. Slutsky.[6] $\frac{\partial q_1}{\partial P_1}$ defines the total effect when P_1 changes, other things remaining constant. $\left(\frac{\partial q_1}{\partial P_1}\right)_{u=\text{constt.}}$ is the 'substitution effect'. The quantity demanded of Q_1 changes but utility remains at the constant level. This much quantity of Q_1 is being substituted for other commodity without moving from the indifference curve.

---

5. See Henderson J. M. and R.E. Quandt; *Micro-economic Theory:* A *Mathematical Approach,* second Ed., McGraw-Hill Tokio, 1971, pp. 31-32 for solution of the equations.
6. E. E. Slutsky: *"On the Theory of the Budget of the Consumer", Giornale degli Economisti,* Vol. 51, July 1915, pp. I–26. Also reprinted in A.E.A's Readings in Price Theory, Homewood Illinois, Irwin, 1952, pp. 27–56.

The substitution effect will be negative since with a rise in the price of the commodity less of it would be substituted for other commodities and vice-versa. The last term $q_1\left(\frac{\partial q_1}{\partial y}\right)_{\text{Prices = constt.}}$ is the income effect. It may be positive or negative depending whether the commodity is a normal good or an inferior good. We know, for a normal good $\frac{\partial q_1}{\partial y}$ is positive so $\left(q_1 \frac{\partial q_1}{\partial y}\right)$ is positive. There is a negative sign before it in the Slutsky equation that means it works in the negative direction with the substitution effect. Both have negative signs, so we add them to find the total effect. For an inferior commodity $\partial q_1 / \partial y$ is negative. So $\left(q_1 \frac{\partial q_1}{\partial y}\right)_{P=\text{constt.}}$ is negative and in the Slutsky equation, because of double negative sign, it is positive. This means that it is working in the opposite direction of the substitution effect. The net result, *i.e.*, total effect, depends on the sign of the effect which has greater magnitude. For inferior goods total effect will be negative because of greater absolute size of the substitution effect than that of income effect. For a Giffen good the total effect will be positive because of greater absolute size of the income effect as compared to the substitution effect. All these three possibilities have been shown above through graphs in Figs. 4.12 to 4.14.

Some further deductions can be made from the Slutsky equation. Multiplying both the sides of (40) by P_1/q_1 and multiplying the income-effect term on the right by y/y also, we get the Slutsky equation in terms of elasticities as:

$$E_{11} = e_{11} - \alpha_1 \eta_1 \qquad \text{...(41)}$$

where E_{11} = Price elasticity of the ordinary demand curve, e_{11} is the price elasticity of compensated demand curve, α_1 is the proportion of total expenditure spent on commodity Q_1 and η_1 is income elasticity of demand for Q_1 (The compensated demand curve shows the change in quantity Q demanded when price of the commodity changes but the utility level remains unchanged. We will derive it shortly in this chapter itself.) This equation says that ordinary demand curve will have a greater demand elasticity than the elasticity shown by the compensated demand curve, *i.e.*, e_{11}, if the income elasticity of demand is positive ($\eta_1 > 0$), and E_{11} is less than e_{11} when $\eta_1 < 0$ as in the case of inferior goods. For a Giffen good E_{11} will be positive.

The Slutsky equation (40) and its elasticity version (41) can be extended to account for changes in the demand for one commodity resulting from changes in the price of the other commodity. The expression for this, is:

$$\frac{\partial q_i}{\partial P_j} = \left(\frac{\partial q_i}{\partial P_j}\right)_{u=\text{constt.}} - q_i\left(\frac{\partial q_i}{\partial y}\right)_{\text{Prices = constt.}} \qquad \text{...(42)}$$

And $\varepsilon_{ij} = e_{ij} - \alpha_j \eta_i$ ...(43)

For $i, j = 1, 2.$

The interpretation of these equations is straightforward. If $i = j$ then we get the original Slutsky equations (40) and (41) which we have already interpreted. When $i \neq j$ then $\frac{\partial q_i}{\partial P_j}$ or $\left(\frac{\partial q_i}{\partial P_j}\right)_{u=\text{constt.}}$ will show the cross effects indicating the change in quantity demanded of *i*th commodity when price of *j*th commodity changes. The signs of cross effects are not known in general. They depend whether the commodities concerned are substitute goods or complementary goods. Consider the term

$(\partial q_i / \partial P_j)_{u\,=\,\text{constt.}}$ This shows the cross-substitution effect. The two commodities, Q_i and Q_j, are substitutes if this cross-substitute effect is positive, they are complements if it is negative. The cross-substitution effect is independent of the income effect. In other words, if Q_i and Q_j are substitute goods and if the consumer remains on the same indifference curve, an increase in price of Q_j will induce the consumer to substitute Q_i for Q_j then $\left(\frac{\partial q_i}{\partial P_j}\right)_{u=\text{constt.}}$ is greater than zero; and if Q_i and Q_j are complements then $(\partial q_i / \partial P_j)_{u\,=\,\text{constt.}}$ will be negative.

There are other uses of the generalised Slutsky equation. With the help of this equation and its elasticity version, it can be shown that (*i*) the substitution effect on the *i*th commodity resulting from a change in the *j*th price is the same as the substitution effect on the *j*th commodity resulting from a change in the *i*th price; (*ii*) the sum of compensated demand elasticities for a commodity Q_i as a result of changes in prices P_i and P_j would be zero; and (*iii*) the income elasticity of demand for a commodity equals the negative of the sum of ordinary price elasticities of demand for that commodity with respect to its own and other prices. For proof of all these results and for their generalisation to *n* variables some advance textbooks on Microeconomic Theory may be consulted.[7]

How Slutsky equation for a commodity is derived can be explained by using a specific utility function. Let the utility function be $U = q_1 q_2$ and the income constraint for this, is given as $y^{\circ} = P_1 q_1 + P_2 q_2$. Putting them together in the form of the Lagrange function we have:

$$V = q_1 q_2 + \lambda\,[y - P_1 q_1 - P_2 q_2]$$

Setting the partial derivatives equal to zero, we have,

$$\frac{\partial V}{\partial q_1} = q_2 - \lambda P_1 = 0$$

$$\frac{\partial V}{\partial q_2} = q_1 - \lambda P_2 = 0$$

$$\frac{\partial V}{\partial \lambda} = y - P\lambda q_1 - P_2 q_2 = 0$$

By taking-the total differentials for each of these first order partial derivatives we have

$$dq_2 - P_1\, d\lambda = \lambda\, dP_1$$

$$dq_1 - P_2\, d\lambda = \lambda\, dP_2$$

$$-P_1\, dq_1 - P_2 dq_2 = -\,dy + q_1\, dP_1 + q_2\, dP_2$$

The right hand side of these equations is known. Concentrating on the left-hand side, the value of the determinants of the coefficients for dq_1, dq_2 $d\lambda$ denoted by D is,

$$D = \begin{vmatrix} 0 & 1 & -P_1 \\ 1 & 0 & -P_2 \\ -P_1 & -P_2 & 0 \end{vmatrix} = 2P_1\, P_2$$

Let the cofactor of the element in the ith row and jth column be denoted as D_{ij}. So, we have,

$$D_{11} = -P_2^2;\ D_{21} = P_1 P_2\ ;\ D_{31} = -\,P_2$$

7. See Henderson & Quandt. *Ibid.*, pp. 36–39 and Russell, R. R. and Maurice Wilkinson, *Microeconomics*, John Wiley & Sons, N. Y., 1979, pp. 96–101.

Solving for dq_1 by the Cramer's rule we get

$$dq_1 = \frac{\lambda D_{11}\, dP_1 + \lambda D_{21}\, dP_{22} + D_{31}\,(-dy + q_1 dP_1 + q_2 dP_2)}{D}$$

or $$dq_1 = \frac{-P_2^2\,\lambda dP_1 + P_1 P_2\,\lambda dP_2 - P_2\,[-dy + q_1 dP_1 + q_2 dP_2]}{2\,P_1 P_2}$$

Since we assume that only P_1 changes, so

$$dP_2 = 0,\ dy = 0;\ \text{so,}$$

$$dq_1 = \frac{-P_2^2\,\lambda dP_1 - P_2\, q_1\, dP_1}{2\,P_1 P_2}$$

or $$\frac{dq_1}{dP_1} = -\frac{P_2\lambda}{2P_1} - \frac{q_1}{2P_1}$$

Substituting the value for $\lambda = \dfrac{y}{2P_1P_2}$ obtained from the first order maximisation conditions, we have,

$$\frac{dq_1}{dP_1} = \frac{-P_2 . y}{2P_1\, 2P_1\, P_2} - \frac{q_1}{2P_1}$$

or $$\frac{dq_1}{dP_1} = -\frac{y}{4P_1^2} - \frac{q_1}{2P_1}$$

Let y = Rs. 100, P_1 = Rs. 2, P_2 = Rs. 5, and q_1 = 25 at the equilibrium,

So $$\frac{dq_1}{dP_1} = -\frac{100}{4\times 4} - \frac{25}{2\times 2} = -\ 12.5 \text{ units}$$

The total effect of change in price P_1 is a reduction of demand for q_1 by 12.5 units. Out of this, the substitution effect is $-\ 6.25\left(= \dfrac{-P_2\lambda}{2P_1}\right)$ and the income effect is also $-\ 6.25\left(= \dfrac{-q}{2P_1}\right)$. The commodity q_1 is a normal good since both the effects are unidirectional.

4.8 CONSUMER EQUILIBRIUM ON EXTREME TYPES OF INDIFFERENCE CURVES

While examining the properties of the indifference curve we came across two extreme types of indifference curves; one a downward sloping straight line in the positive commodity space, *i.e.*, quadrant, and second, fixed proportion, *i.e.*, right angle type. The former one reflects perfect substitution among the commodities concerned and the later one showing only one fixed proportion for the use of the commodities together, *i.e.*, perfect complements of each other. What would be the equilibrium position for the consumer with such types of indifference curves and how to isolate the 'substitution' and 'income' effects associated with price changes in such situations? This is quite an interesting question. Let us examine this:

If the indifference curve is a downward sloping straight-line, it reflects constant slope and hence constant marginal rate of substitution between the goods. Such line, as we have said earlier, intersects the commodity axes. This implies that the level of utility for which the straight-line indifference curve stands can be achieved by consumption of either of the two commodities. This is what we mean by perfect substitution. It is not necessary that both the commodities should be consumed. The budget line for the consumer will also be a downward sloping straight-line. One straight-line cannot be a tangent to the other straight-line except when they coincide with each other. In this situation, how to find the equilibrium position for the consumer? The equilibrium will be attained at the corner point where the budget line and the indifference line meet each other on the axes of commodities. That corner point through which the indifference line showing the maximum attainable utility level passes will be the equilibrium point. Consider the following diagram (Fig. 4.15).

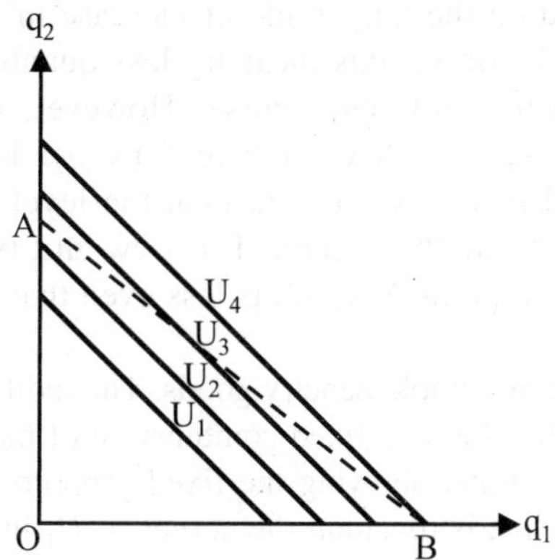

Fig. 4.15 Consumer Equilibrium on Indifference Curve for the Substitute Goods

A B is the budget line $y = p_1q_1 + P_2q_2$ and U_1, U_2, U_3 and U_4 represent the indifference curves $U_4 > U_3 > U_2 > U_1$. The equilibrium position for the consumer is shown by B point from where the highest attainable indifference curve U_4 passes. If the budget line shifts upward parallel to the origin then the equilibrium will shift outwards on q_1 axis.

To clarify the equilibrium position at either of the two corner points, let us use algebraic equations and find the solution. Let the utility function be given as:

$$U = \alpha_1 \; q_1 + \alpha_2 \; q_2$$

and budget line $y = P_1q_1 + P_2q_2$

The marginal utilities of q_1 and q_2 are α_1 and α_2 respectively.

$$\partial U/\partial q_1 = \alpha_1 \; ; \; \partial U/\partial q_2 = \alpha_2$$

An increase in q_1 by one unit gives α_1 units of utility to the consumer. The consumer spends P_1 units of money to get one unit of q_1 which means from P_1 expenditure he gets α_1 utility. Similarly, from P_2 expenditure on one unit of q_2 the consumer gets α_2 unit of utility. Simple calculation shows that from y units of money the consumer gets α_1y/P_1 units of utility when entire money is spent on Q_1 commodity, and α_2y/P_2 when y is spent on Q_2. If α_1y/P_1 (or α_1/P_1) is greater than α_2y/P_2 or (α_2/P_2) equilibrium lies on q_1 axis where budget line meets it (*e.g.*, Point B in Fig. 4.14). and if α_2y/P_2 or (α_2/P_2) is greater than α_2y/P_1 (or (α_1/P_1) it will be at A point on q_2 axis. This way, we find the corner solution for the equilibrium position when goods are perfect substitutes. If $\alpha_1y/P_1 = \alpha_2y/P_2$, the budget line and indifference curve coincide and every combination of q_1 and q_2 will be optimal $\alpha_1y/P_1 = \alpha_2y/P_2$ means

$$\frac{\alpha_1}{\alpha_2} = \frac{P_1}{P_2}$$

What will be the substitution and income effects in this case when price of a commodity changes, other things remaining constant? If $\alpha_1/P_1 > \alpha_2/P_2$ and if price of Q_1 *i.e.*, P_1 decreases further, the budget line shifts to the right on q_1 axis, this means equilibrium will be farther away on q_1 axis implying increase in utility for the consumer. If we withdraw the increased real income associated with the decrease in P_1 by taxing the consumer, he will be pushed back to the old level of utility and the equilibrium will be at B point. This means that there is only income effect when price P_1 decreases which pushes the consumer on higher indifference curve. There is no substitution effect because it is a corner case. The other commodity has already been fully substituted earlier.

Suppose P_1 increases then the budget line shifts inwards, *i.e.*, to the left on q_1 axis. The equilibrium position will depend on the magnitude of increase in P_1. If α_1/P_1 is still greater than α_2/P_2 then the equilibrium will be on q_1 axis meaning less quantity of q_1 and hence the reduced level of utility shown by a lower indifference curve. However, if $\alpha_1/P_1 < \alpha_2/P_2$, the consumer shifts to q_2 commodity. q_1 will be completely replaced by q_2. The new equilibrium on q_2 axis will, however, show lower level of utility attained than the level of utility given by the original budget line *AB*. It is obvious from the figure. The new utility level will be shown by the indifference curve passing through point A which is less even than U_3. The earlier attainable level was U_4.

Let us now examine the case of complementary goods. The indifference curve for complementary goods will be right-angle shape showing one fixed combination of the goods. The budget line touches such an indifference curve at the corner showing the fixed proportion of the commodities. In figure 4.16, AB is the budget line. This line is touching the corner of U_1 indifference curve at E_1. It is thus, the equilibrium point. If there is a decline in price of Q_1, the budget line shifts to AB_1 position touching the higher indifference curve U_2 at E_2 corner. The quantities q_1 and q_2 of Q_1 and Q_2 will change in such a way, while moving for E_1 to E_2, that the original proportion of consumption of the goods together is maintained. This means the locus of equilibrium points will be a straight-line

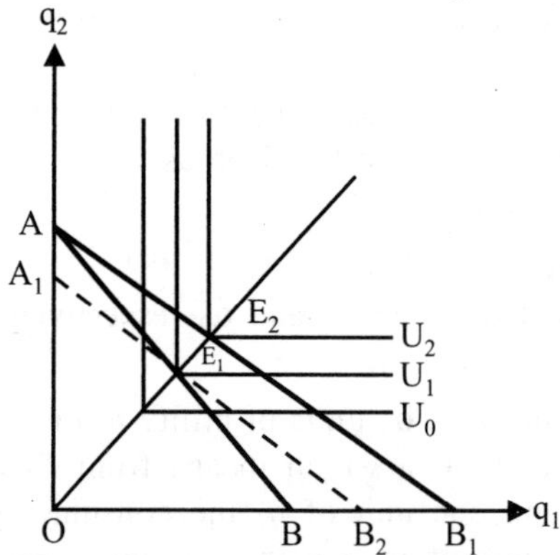

Fig. 4.16 Consumer Equilibrium on Indifference Curve for Complementary Goods

emerging from the origin. Since the two goods are complementary, there will be only 'income effect' associated with the price changes for a given level of income. This can be checked by pushing back the consumer to the original level of utility *(E_1)* by shifting down the budget line AB_1 to A_1B_2. A_1B_2 line touches the U_1 indifference curve exactly at E_1 point showing no substitution effect.

4.9 SOME APPLICATIONS OF INDIFFERENCE CURVE ANALYSIS

Indifference curve is a tool to analyse economic behaviour of a consumer. We have seen how consumer attains equilibrium position on an indifference curve and changes in prices of goods and income affect his equilibrium position. Beside this, the technique of indifference curve is applicable to solve a number of other problems related to consumer behaviour. A few of them are being discussed here.

(a) Measurement of Consumer Surplus

A consumer buys a commodity only when the gain of utility from that is greater or at least equal to the loss of utility of money spent on the commodity. Using the equilibrium concept we can show this condition by the expression:

gain of utility ≥ loss of utility of money, *i.e.*, $MU \geq \lambda P$

where λ = marginal utility of money.

When the consumer actually buys the commodity he pays uniform price for all the units of it, but we know the marginal utility of different units will be different, first unit of the commodity having higher and then declining gradually as quantity increases. It means the total gain of utility will be more than the total loss of utility by giving up the money when the commodity is purchased by the consumer. This gain of excess utility is the consumer surplus. How to measure it precisely is a problem. Marshall who first coined the concept of consumer surplus used simple demand curve to measure it. He defined consumer surplus as the difference between total amount of money the consumer would be willing to pay for a given quantity of some good and the total amount he actually pays. Here, both gain of utility and loss of utility are being assessed on the basis of money. The willingness to pay depends on the utility gained by having the commodity.

To explain how consumer surplus occurs, let us consider the following figure. In this figure, we have shown a downward sloping demand curve for the commodity. Let the market price for the commodity be Rs. 4 which is determined by the interaction of supply and demand for the commodity. At this price, the consumer buys 4 units of the commodity. According to the demand curve, the consumer is willing to pay Rs. 7 as price of the first unit of the commodity. He actually pays Rs. 4 for that. This means that there is a gain to the consumer of Rs. 3 from the first unit of the commodity. The second unit of the commodity is giving him Rs. 6 – Rs. 4 = Rs. 2 as surplus. The third unit gives Rs. 5 – Rs. 4 = Re. 1 as surplus, and last unit pays nothing (Rs. 4 – Rs. 4 = 0). Total surplus from all four units is Rs. 6.

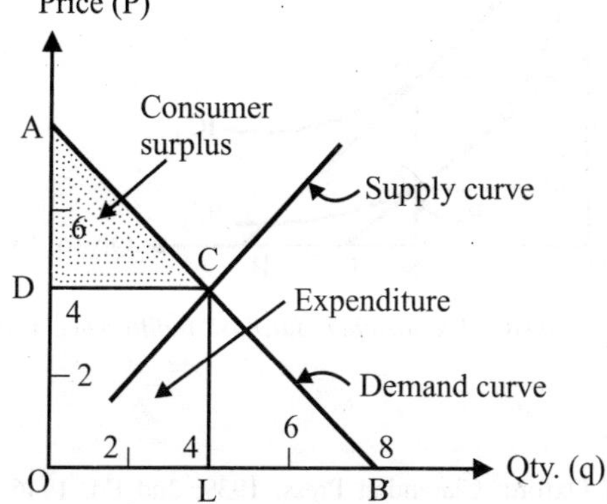

Fig. 4.17 Measurement of Consumer Surplus: Marshallian Approach

Actually, the surplus is nothing but the area of the triangle over the total expenditure rectangle. This is equal to Rs. 8 when we take continuous change in the demand rather than discrete changes. Analytically, the difference between the areas OLCA and OLCD is the consumer surplus. Using the demand equation $P = f(Q)$, and Q_1 and P_1 as given set of quantity and price for the commodity, the consumer surplus can be expressed in money term as

$$\text{C.S.} = \int_0^{Q_1} f(Q)\, dQ - P_1Q_1 \qquad \text{...(44)}$$

If the given set of quantity and price changes to q_2 and P_2, the change in consumer surplus (ΔC) would be:

$$\Delta C = \int_{Q_1}^{Q_2} f(Q)\, dQ - (P_2Q_2 - P_1Q_1), \qquad \text{...(45)}$$

This is Marshallian approach of measuring consumer surplus. Hicks in his book *Value and Capital* (1939) and later on in the *Revision of Demand Theory* (1956) has provided an alternative approach for this using the indifference curve technique.[8] A full discussion on the Hicksian approach is not intended here, rather we will go briefly through its conceptualisation within the indifference curve framework. For this, let us consider the following figure. IC_1 represents various combinations of income and a commodity, say X which yield the same level of utility to the consumer. OA is the amount of income that the consumer had. The indifference curve IC_1 originates from point A showing the stage when he retains all of his income and zero units of X for a given level of utility. He moves along the curve IC_1 down. This curve is not touching the quantity axis for X showing consumer's preference for money rather than for more of X. Suppose the price for X is known to him and so AB line shows the income-price frontier for the consumer.

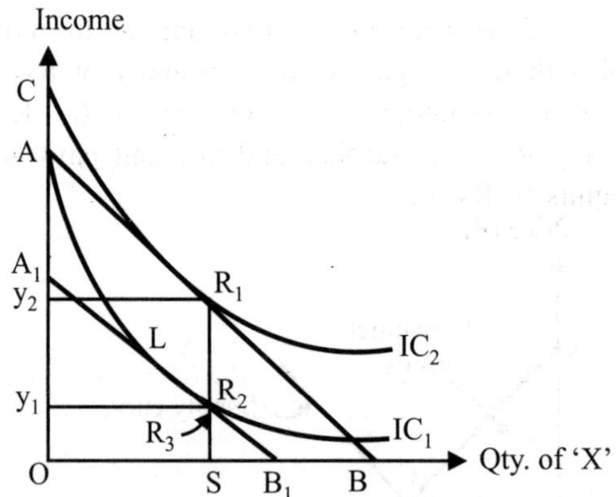

Fig. 4.18 Measurement of Consumer Surplus: Indifference Curve Approach

8. J.R. Hicks; *Value and Capital* Oxford: Clarendon Press, 1939, 2nd Ed. 1946, Chapter 2.
J.R. Hicks; "The Rehabilitation of Consumer Surplus", *Review of Economic Studies,* Vol. 8, 1941, pp. 108–116.
J.R. Hicks; *A Revision of Demand Theory,* Oxford: Clarendon Press, Ch. 10, pp. 95–108.

The income-price line touches the indifference curve IC_2 at point R_1. The consumer had OS quantity of X and OY_2 amount of income corresponding to this point. He gives up $A\ Y_2$ income to buy OS units of X. Now, suppose the consumer does not know the price of X, but plans the same quantity of X, *i.e.*, OS units to get IC_1 units of utility, he is willing to sacrifice $A\ Y_1$ amount of income for this. But having known the price of the commodity he actually spends only $A\ Y_2$ income on OS units of X. Moreover, he moves up to higher utility curve IC_2 by this. Thus, we can infer from this that $AY_1 - A\ Y_2$ *i.e.*, $Y_1\ Y_2$ is the consumer surplus because this is the difference between the amount of income the consumer was willing to spend and what he actually spends. This surplus is shifting the consumer on higher level of satisfaction from IC_1 to IC_2. This is, in fact, Marshallian concept of consumer surplus which we are measuring using the indifference curves.

The consumer moves to IC_2 curve from IC_1 because of lower price of X and hence gets consumer surplus. If we withdraw some income from him through a tax and push him to the old level of utility IC_1 by shifting down the line AB parallel, he would attain equilibrium at L point on IC_1 by this. His consumption of X decreases in this situation. However, we allow him to buy the same units 'of X as before, *i.e.*, OS units. The consumer would not be able to cross the new income-price line, so hypothetically we say that he will be in equilibrium at R_3 point on the line. The amount of income deducted from the consumer's income, *i.e.*, R_1. R_3 or AA_1 which leaves him in a position still to consume the same quantity of X, *i.e.*, OS is called *'Compensating Variation of Income'* which is also a type of consumer surplus according to Hicks. If the consumer is not buying any units of X, how much income subsidy should be given to him to move from IC_1 to IC_2. This is equal to AC. This is called *'Equivalent Variation'* of income which is yet another concept of consumer surplus. There are several other types of 'surpluses' which are associated either with a fall or a rise in price of a commodity in whose details we are not interested at this stage. They may be read from other sources.[9]

(b) Income Tax Vs. Commodity Tax

The indifference curve technique can also be used to demonstrate that taxes on purchasing power, such as income tax, are 'more efficient' than taxes imposed on commodities, *i.e.*, indirect taxes. The term 'more efficient' means that even if the two types of taxes yield the same amount of revenue to the government, income or direct taxes reduce consumer's utility by lesser magnitude as compared to commodity taxes. To show this result, let us take the budget line $Y = P_1q_1 + P_2q_2$. In Fig. 4.19, this is shown by the line AB which touches an indifference curve ICJ_3 at EJ_3 showing the equilibrium position. Corresponding to this, the optimal combination of q_1 and q_2 is $q_1{}^*$ and $q_2{}^*$. This point lies on the budget line, so we have $Y = P_1q_1^* + P_2q_2^*$.

Now, let us consider a commodity tax of t per unit of commodity Q_1. The price P_1 will now be changed to $P_1 + t$ and the budget line would be

$$Y = (P_1 + t)\ q_1 + P_2q_2$$

---

9. (*i*) Hicks, J.R., *A Revision of Demand Theory*, Oxford: Clarendon Press, 1956.
(*ii*) Ellis (Ed.), *A Survey of Contemporary Economics*, Vol. I, A.E.A. March, 1957.
(*iii*) Samuelson, P. A., *Foundations of Economic Analysis*, Cambridge University Press, 1966, pp. 197–202.

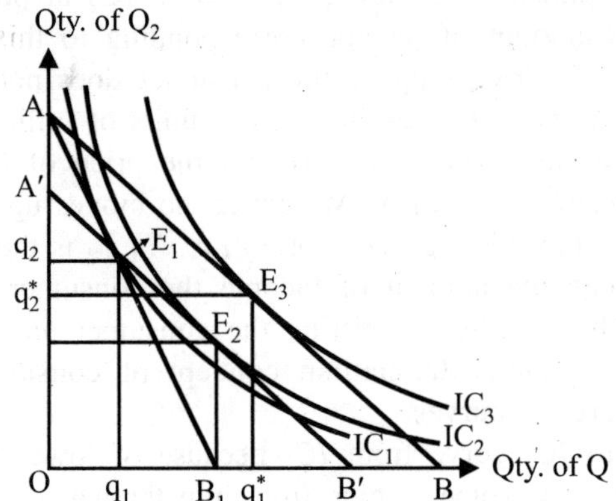

Fig. 4.19. Effects of Income and Commodity Taxes on Consumer Equilibirum

This line is shown by AB_1 and the new equilibrium at E_1 on IC_1 in the Fig. 4.19. The choice of Q_1 and Q_2 commodities would now be q_1, q_2. The satisfaction or utility derived now declines to IC_1, level. Total tax revenue would be tq_1 occurring to government.

Suppose the government collects tq_1 amount of tax in the form of income or lump-sum tax, *i.e.*, $T = tq_1$. As a result of this, the new budget line would be $Y - T = P_1q_1 + P_2q_2$. This means that the original budget line AB shifts down parallelly because of a reduction in disposable income and unchanged commodity prices. This is shown by $A'B'$. This line passes through the equilibrium point E_1 because we have to maintain the consumption level of q_1q_2 corresponding to E_1 and also $tq_1 = T$ which causes the intersection of AB_1 and A_1 B_1. Since the line A' B' is passing through point E_1, it will be a tangent to an indifference curve between IC_1 and IC_3 say to IC_2. This implies higher utility than IC_1 level. So, it is proved that direct taxes would be more efficient as compared to indirect taxes from the point of view of consumer welfare.

There are several other applications of the indifference curve technique, such as in the field of exchange between individuals or countries, rationing, subsidy programmes, product quality improvement, supply of labour, index numbers, etc. Due to paucity of space we are excluding them from the scope of this chapter.

4.10 COMPOSITE COMMODITY THEOREM

The indifference curve analysis carried on so far runs in terms of two commodities Q_1 and Q_2. In practice, a consumer, at a time, may buy several commodities and if we consider all of them together it is impossible to draw indifference curves of multiple dimensions. What then is the use of having a two commodity indifference curve analysis? The analysis is logically consistent and provides us useful insights to understand consumer's behaviour in ordinal utility framework, but because of its abstract nature it cannot be applied, in practice, to derive simultaneously the demand functions for all commodities and several related results such as income and substitution effects associated with price changes, except in the limiting case of one or two commodities. We know that price and income changes are not equiproportional, the optimal consumption bundle is generally changed then. The simple approach for this is to consider first the effect of an income change, holding all prices constant, and then the effect of a change in one price, holding all other prices and income constant. The analysis for two commodities case has been done using this approach. Now, suppose we want to consider more than two commodities to find the effect of an income change and that of a change in one price, other prices remaining constant, we can still do it using the two dimensional indifference curve diagram. For this, what we have to do is to take the commodity whose price is changing on one axis and the aggregate expenditure on all other commodities on the other axis for drawing the indifference curves and then carry on the analysis as we have done earlier. The total expenditure on all other commodities is interpreted as a "composite commodity". The results of such an analysis will give us optimal consumption of the commodity concerned and optimal expenditure on all other commodities. Hicks, in his book, *Value and Capital*, has proved this and generalised the outcome in the form of the 'composite commodity theorem'[10]. According to this theorem:

If the prices of all but the *i*th commodity are fixed, utility can be expressed as a differentiable function of the consumption of the *i*th commodity, x_i and expenditure on all other commodities, m, *i.e.*,

$$U = U\ (x_i,\ m) \qquad ...(46)$$

Moreover, the indifference cuves in x_i and m space representing U are continuous and strictly convex to the orgin. Finally, maximizing this utility function subject to

$$Y = m + P_i\ x_i \qquad ...(47)$$

yields the optimal consumption of the *i*th commodity and optimal expenditure on all commodities.[11]

4.11 THE REVEALED PREFERENCE THEORY

The theory of revealed preference was originally developed by Samuelson[12]. He tried to provide an alternative approach to study consumer behaviour free from the cardinal and ordinal concepts of utility. Samuelson has shown that significant generalisations concerning consumer choice can be derived from observing the choices that a consumer makes. The consumer's choices reveal his preferences. For a given set of prices if he prefers a combination of quantities of different goods or what we call 'consumption bundle', it means all other consumption bundles that could have been purchased with the fixed income of the consumer are inferior to him. The basic relationship of the revealed preference theory is thus the comparison of the commodity bundle that he prefers to all other commodity bundles that are rejected by him for given prices and income.

In order to develop the theory, Samuelson took help of some basic axioms regarding consumer behaviour. These are: (*i*) tastes of the consumer are unchanged during the period of analysis; (*ii*) the consumer choices are transitive; that is to say they are consistent. It means if a commodity bundle *A* is chosen from a set of alternatives that includes *B* bundle, then any set of alternatives from which *B* is chosen must not contain *A*. (*iii*) It is possible to induce a person to purchase a good if price is appropriately changed, *i.e.*, if the price is lowered sufficiently. On the basis of these assumptions or axioms, as argued by Samuelson, most of the standard results of the theory of consumer behaviour such as the existence of demand functions, their homogeneity of degree zero, and the fundamental theorems of consumption theory in its weaker form can be derived. The

---

10. *See* J. R. Hicks; *Value and Capital*, Clarendon Press (1932), Appendix, pp. 311–312 and also P. A. Samuelson; *Foundations of Economic Analysis*, Cambridge University Press, 1966, pp. 141–144.
11. For mathematical proof of the composite commodity theorem, see R. Robert Russell and M. Wilkinson; *Microeconomics*, John Wiley & Sons, 1979, pp. 55–59,.
12. P. A. Samuelson, "A Note on Pure Theory of Consumer's Behaviour", *Economica* 5, 1938, 353–54; Foundations of Economic Analysis, Harvard University Press, 1947, and 'Consumption Theory in Terms of Revealed Preferences', *Economica* 13, 1948, pp. 243–53.

fundamental theorem of consumption theory states that *if the demand for a good always increases (decreases) when income increases (decreases), then the quantity of the good demanded will always decrease (increase) when price of the good rises (falls).* In other words, this theorem means that positive income elasticity implies negative price elasticity for a good.

Let us consider two commodity diagram to explain the theory of revealed preference. As usual, we consider a given budget constraint for the consumer in the form $Y = P_1q_1 + P_2q_2$. The income and prices of the two commodities are given. In Figure 4.20, this is shown by the line *AB*.

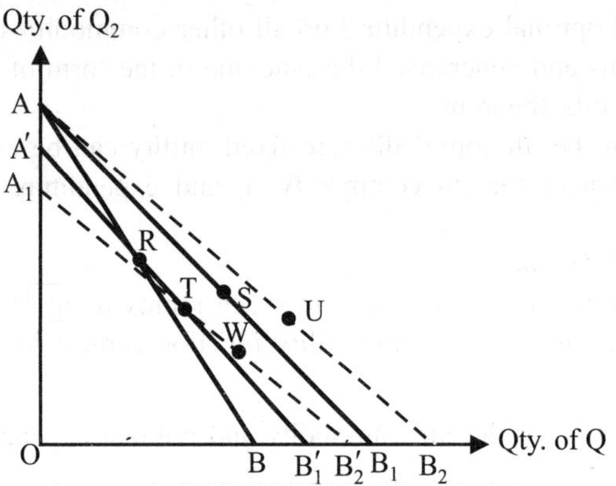

Fig. 4.20 Revealed Preference Analysis

Following the basic axiom of the revealed preference theory let us take *R* as the combination of Q_1 and Q_2 commodities chosen by the consumer. The consumer has revealed or shown his preference for this combination whatever be the reason for this, *i.e.*, either this is cheaper or he likes this, or all other combinations of Q_1 and Q_2 shown by the line *AB* or below this, inside the triangle *OAB,* are inferior to *R.* The consumer, following the axiom of consistency, will not prefer any other combination of Q_1 and Q_2 so long his income and prices of Q_1 and Q_2 are constant. He can prefer the combinations on the right hand side of *AB* but his budget line is a constraint for this. If his income increases or price of Q_1 or Q_2 declines, he must prefer some combination of Q_1 and Q_2 from this side of the line *AB* as compared to *R.* Let us consider the situation when price of commodity Q_1 decreases, price of Q_2 and income remaining unchanged. The budget line *AB* shifts to AB_1 position. The consumer responds to this new situation by shifting his preference to the combination *S* on the new budget line AB_1.

He does this because his real income, due to a fall in P_1, increases so he buys more of Q_1. The consumer is buying more of Q_1 because of positive income effect or there is a substitution effect. We cannot say anything about the substitution effect since there is no indifference curve. In order to find the substitution or quasi-substitution effect in movement from *R* to *S* let us 'eliminate' the income effect associated with purchase of Q_1 in the new situation and then evaluate the possibility of the substitution effect. This is done by reducing consumer budget in such a way that he buys the same amount of Q_1 and Q_2 as before. For this, the new budget line AB_1 is shifted down parallelly till it passes through point *R.* The effective budget line without income effect is now $A'\ B'$ is flatter than *AB* since the price of Q_1 has fallen. What will the consumer do now? He may continue to be at point *R* since it lies on the line $A'B'_1$. But, since price of Q_1 has declined, the consumer would now prefer to move from this point. He will not move to the left of *R* on *RA′* section since all such combinations fall within the triangle *OAB* which the consumer had already rejected earlier. Similarly, moving along RA was ruled out earlier because of revealed preference of combination R over others. One possibility of shifting from R is now on the line RB'_1 which gives superior combinations of Q_1 and Q_2 as compared to R. The other possibilities of shifting from R are to any point inside the triangle RBB'_1. All such possibilities including moving along RB'_1 segment of $A'B'_1$ line implies that the quasi-substitutions effect of a fall in price of Q_1 cannot reduce the quantity of Q_1 contained in R but may leave it unchanged. Assuming that the consumer acts in a rational way and utilises his full income, we may take T as the new combination which is now revealed preferred to R. So, we infer from this that the movement from R to T is because of substitution effect, *i.e.*, a decrease in price of Q_1 increases the quantity purchased of Q_1. If we give back the income 'withdrawn' from the consumer, he would move to point S implying positive income effect for the commodity, *i.e.,* an increase in quantity of Q_1 demanded with a rise in income of the consumer.

Suppose price of Q_1 decreases further. We would then have AB_2 as the new budget line and U as the revealed preferred combination of Q_1 and Q_2. As in the earlier step, we withdraw the increased income associated with further decline in price P_1, to trace the associated quasi-substitution effect. This is done by shifting AB_2 line down parallel till it passes through point T. The new effective budget line would now be A_1 B'_2. For the same reasons, as given above, the consumer would now prefer any combination on segment TB'_2 of $A_1B'_2$. Let this be W. This again implies that the substitution effect is working in negative direction implying more of Q_1 with a fall in P_1. The locus of the preferred points RTW is a convex boundary towards the origin. This is not the indifference curve since W is preferred over T and T is preferred over R. Any point on an indifference curve is equally preferred by the consumer. However, we can say that there exist points of equal preference such as R, between R and T, and T and W. The locus of all such points will be a part of the indifference curve. Now, suppose we have sufficient data on revealed preferences, we can draw an indifference curve from that. We keep income (Y) and other price (P_2) constant and vary the price (P_1) in both the side to get a convex boundary showing an indifference curve. The revealed preference theory provides empirical approach to fit an indifference curve and from this link we can argue that indifference curve analysis and revealed preference analysis are complementary to each other. Houthakkar, in fact, has demonstrated the fundamental equivalence between the utility theory and the revealed preference theory.[13]

4.12 THE DUALITY APPROACH IN UTILITY ANALYSIS

Duality is an important feature of several of modern economic theories, Consumer theory, which we have discussed so far, is one of them. Duality, in general, is defined as the existence of two logical systems characterised by certain interrelationships. The essence of a dual system is a correspondence or similarity between concepts in one system and concepts in the other which help us to derive similar results from both the systems. The dual approach in studying economic phenomena is very helpful in applied econometrics research as well as in development of economic theories. We will show its importance in this section by taking concrete examples from the consumer theory.

13. H.S. Houthakker: "Revealed Preference and the Utility Function", *Economica,* 17, 1950, pp. 159–74.

Major contribution in the duality of consumer theory came from Hetelling.[14 (a)] Following his contribution and of others we will go through indirect utility function showing dependence of utility on prices and income and the consumer expenditure function showing the minimum cost of attaining a given utility level for a given set of prices.

(a) The Indirect Utility Function

The utility function introduced in Section 4.1 is 'direct' in the sense that total utility derived by a consumer depends directly on the levels of quantities of different goods and services he consumes at a time, *i.e.*, $U = F(q_1, q_2, ...q_n)$. Through constrained maximisation of such utility function we get ordinary demand equations for the goods which are expressed in terms of prices and income. That is, reproducing the set of demand function derived earlier (see equations set (15), Section 4.3), we have:

$$q_i = \phi_i (P_1, P_2, ... P_n, y^\circ);\ i = 1, ...n.$$

Substituting the value or q_i $(i = 1, ... n)$ in the utility function we get maximum attainable utility in terms of prices and income level as:

$$U^* = F[(\phi_1 (P_1, P_2, ..., P_n, y^\circ), \phi_2 (P_1, P_2, ... P_n, y^\circ), ...\phi_n (P_1, P_2, ... P_n, y^\circ)]$$

This, on simplification, can be expressed as:

$$U^* = F^* (P_1, P_2, ... P_n, y^\circ) \qquad ...(48)$$

That is, the maximum attainable utility is a function of prices and income. This is called 'Indirect Utility Function'. U^* is the highest utility that may be obtained with given prices and income to the consumer, We have seen earlier that the demand functions obtained from the direct utility function are homogeneous of degree zero in income and prices (see Sec. 4.3). Since the indirect utility function is expressed in terms of prices and income, if these variables change in the same proportion, the optimal utility level U^* will not be changed. The price-income difference surface will be fixed, *i.e.*,

$$F^* (P_1, P_2, ..., y^\circ) = \text{constant} \qquad ...(49)$$

This surface can be represented by three dimensional graph (P_1 P_2, and y), y being on vertical axis. The shape is like a cone having its vertex at the centre. The maximum value is shown by the point of origin.

The duality between $U = F(q_1, q_2,....)$ and $U^* = F^* (P_1, P_2...., y)$ implies that both of them represent the same preference ordering. Maximisation of $U = F(q_1, q_2, ..., q_n)$ with respect to q_i $(i = 1, ..., n)$ with given income and price leads to the same demand functions as minimisation of $U^* = F^* (P_1, P_2, ..., P_n, y^\circ)$ with respect to prices and income for given quantities.

The indirect utility function can be expressed in normalized form also. For this, we have to change the constraint slightly. Let $y^\circ = P_1 q_1 + P_2 q_2 +...+ P_n q_n$ be the budget constraint. Dividing both the sides of this by y° and letting $v_i = \frac{P_i}{y^\circ}$, $i = 1, n$, we write the utility maximisation problem as:

$$\text{Max } U = f(q_1, q_2, ..., q_n) \text{ subject to } 1 = v_1 q_1 + v_2 q_2 +...+ v_n q_n \qquad ...(50)$$

By solving the first order maximisation condition from this, we find the demand relations for q_i in terms of normalized prices v_i $(i = 1, n)$ as:

---

14 (*a*). Hotelling H. Edgeworth, "Taxation Paradox and the Nature of Supply and Demand Functions", *Journal of Political Economy,* Vol. 40, 1932, pp. 557–616.

$$q_i = \varphi_i \ (v_1, v_2, ..., v_n), \ i = 1, n. \qquad ...(51)$$

By substituting (51) in the utility function we get the indirect utility function:

$$U^* = F \ [\varphi_1(v_1, v_2, ... v_n), \varphi_2(v_1, v_2, ... v_n), ..., \varphi_n(v_1, v_2, ... v_n)]$$

or $$U^* = F^{**} \ (v_1, v_2, ... v_n) \qquad ...(52)$$

That is, the maximum value of utility is a function of normalised prices $v_1, v_2, ... v_n$ F^{**} denotes the functional shape of the relationship. The properties of this function are the same as described above. The 'indirect indifference curves' generated by the utility function (51) will be very much similar to the indifference curves generated by the direct utility function, with the difference that on the axes we will have now v_1 and v_2 (for two commodity case) and the indirect indifference curve farther away from the origin will show lower level of utility and the one which is the nearest to the origin will show the highest level of utility. The optima will, of course, coincide with the origin.

(b) Derivation of Demand Function: Roy's Identity

To derive the demand functions for different commodities we minimise the indirect utility subject to the budget constraint. That is

Min $\quad U^* = F \ (P_1, P_2, ... P_n, y)$

Subject to $\quad y = P_1q_1 + P_2q_2 + P_nq_n$

Transforming the problem of minimisation in the form of the Lagrange function, we have:

$$Z = F^* \ (P_1, P_2, P_n, y) + K(y - P_1q_1 - P_2q_2, ..., P_nq_n)$$

The first order conditions for minimisation of this function are:

$$\frac{\partial F^*(.)}{\partial P_1} - K \ q_1 = 0$$

$$\frac{\partial F^*(.)}{\partial P_2} - K \ q_2 = 0$$

$$\frac{\partial F^*(.)}{\partial P_n} - K \ q_n = 0 \qquad ...(53)$$

$$\frac{\partial F^*(.)}{\partial_y} + K = 0$$

$$\frac{\partial F^*(.)}{\partial K} = y - P_1q_1 - P_2q_2 ... P_nq_n = 0$$

From the first n equations we have

$$\frac{\frac{\partial F^*(\cdot)}{\partial P_1}}{q_1} = \frac{\frac{\partial F^*(\cdot)}{\partial P_2}}{q_2} = \cdots = \frac{\frac{\partial F^*(\cdot)}{\partial P_n}}{q_n} = K = -\frac{\partial F^*(.)}{\partial y}$$

or $$\frac{\partial U^*}{\partial P_1} / q_1 = \frac{\partial U^*}{\partial P_2} / q_2 = ... = \frac{\partial U^*}{\partial P_n} / q_n = K = -\frac{\partial U^*}{\partial y} \qquad ...(54)$$

K = Lagrange Multiplier

Expression (54) implies that

$$q_1^0 = -\frac{\partial U^*/\partial P_1}{\partial U^*/\partial y}$$

$$q_2^0 = -\frac{\partial U^*/\partial P_2}{\partial U^*/\partial y} \qquad \ldots(55)$$

$$q_n^0 = -\frac{\partial U^*/\partial P_n}{\partial U^*/\partial y}$$

or

$$q_i^0 = -\frac{\partial U^*/\partial P_i}{\partial U^*/\partial y}, \; i = 1, \ldots n.$$

This defined as 'Roy's Identity' which expresses the demand functions for the commodity in the consumption bundle of the consumer.[14(b)]

Let us take a simple example for this. The indirect utility function is given as

$$U^* = a_1 \; (y/P_1)^{b_1} + a_2 \; (y/P_2)^{b_2}$$

From this, $\partial U^*/\partial P_1 = -\, a_1 b_1,\; y^{b_1}, P_1^{-b_1-1}$

$$\partial U^*/\partial P_2 = -\, a_2 b_2,\; y^{b_2}, P_2^{-b_2-1}$$

$$\partial U^*/\partial y_1 = -\, a_1 b_1,\; y^{b_1-1} + a_2 b_2 y^{b_2-1} P_2^{-b_2}$$

By using the Roy's Identity, we get

$$q_1 = -\frac{\partial U^*/\partial P_1}{\partial U^*/\partial y} = -\frac{[-a_1 b_1 y^{b_1} P_1^{-b_1-1}]}{a_1 b_1 y^{b_1-1} P_1^{-b_1} + a_2 b_2 y^{b_2-1} P_2^{-b_2}}$$

$$q_2 = -\frac{\partial U^*/\partial P_2}{\partial U^*/\partial y} = -\frac{[-a_2 b_2 y^{b_2} P_2^{-b_2-1}]}{a_1 b_1 y^{b_1-1} P_1^{-b_1} + a_2 b_2 y^{b_2-1} P_2^{-b_2}}$$

or in general form

$$q_i = \frac{a_i b_i y^{b_i} P_i^{-b_i-1}}{{}_j\Sigma_j \, a_j b_j y^{b_j-1} P_j^{-b_j}} \qquad i = 1,\, 2;\; j = 1,\, 2$$

These are the demand equations for q_1 and q_2 derived from the given utility function. In general, by solving the first order minimisation conditions (53) we will get the standard demand functions for different commodities as:

$$q_i = \phi_i\; [P_1,\, P_2,\, \ldots,\, P_n,\, y], \qquad i = 1,\, \ldots,\, n.$$

These are similar as the demand function derived from the direct utility function (Ref. Eqn. Set No. 15).

(c) The Expenditure Function and Compensated Demand Relations

A compensated demand function expresses the relationship between quantity demanded of a commodity and prices to maintain constant utility. Due to a change in price of a commodity the quantity demanded of that commodity will be affected and there may be effects on quantities

14 (*b*). R. Roy, De l'utilite, *Contribution a la Theorie des Choix; Hermann*; 1942, and R. Roy; *Analyse de la demand collectanea de Estudos*; Lisbo, 1961.

demanded of other commodities as in the case of substitute and complementary goods. The change in the quantities of the commodities, in turn, will affect the utility derived from consumption. In order to maintain the same utility level, the consumer is provided either a subsidy or taxed depending on rise or fall in the price. In this situation, the compensated demand curve plays very crucial role. This type of demand function can be derived by minimising consumer total expenditure subject to the constraint that total utility is fixed. That is:

Min. $y = P_1q_1 + P_2q_2 + ... + P_nq_n$

Subject to $U° = F(q_1, q_2,.., q_n)$

Using the Lagrange Multiplier method we write the function:

$$L = P_1q_1 + P_2q_2 + ... + P_nq_n + \mu\ [U° - F(q_1, q_2, ..., q_n)]$$

Setting the partial derivatives of this function with respect to q_1, q_2, q_n equal to zeros, we get the conditions for minimum, (provided the second order conditions are satisfied) as:

$$\frac{\partial L}{\partial q_1} = P_1 - \mu F_1 = 0$$

$$\frac{\partial L}{\partial q_2} = P_2 - \mu F_2 = 0$$

$$\frac{\partial L}{\partial q_n} = P_n - \mu F_n = 0 \qquad ...(56)$$

$$\frac{\partial L}{\partial \mu} = U° - F(q_1, q_2, ..., q_n) = 0$$

These equations on solution for $q_1, q_2, ..., q_n$ will give us the compensated demand functions for the commodities as:

$$\overset{\circ}{q_i} = h_i\ [P_1, P_2, ..., P_n, U°],\ i = 1, ..., n. \qquad ...(57)$$

$$\mu° = \mu\ [P_1, P_2, ..., P_n, U°]$$

Let us take a specific utility function $U = q_1q_2$ as we have taken earlier.

Minimising $y = P_1q_1 + P_2q_2$

Subject to $U° = q_1q_2$ we get

$$P_1 - \mu q_2 = 0$$
$$P_2 - \mu q_1 = 0$$
$$U° - q_1q_2 = 0$$

From these we have

$$q_1 = \left[\frac{P_2}{P_1} U°\right]^{1/2}$$

$$q_2 = \left[\frac{P_1}{P_2} U°\right]^{1/2}$$

It can be verified easily that the compensated demand function (57), like ordinary demand functions, is homogeneous of degree zero and at the optimum level of utility we get the familiar identity:

$$\frac{P_i}{P_n} = \frac{\partial U / \partial q_i}{\partial U / \partial q_n} \qquad ...(58)$$

Substituting the compensated demand functions for $\overset{\circ}{q_1}, \overset{\circ}{q_2} \ldots \overset{\circ}{q_n}$ in the budget equation

$$y = P_1 q_1 + P_2 q_2 + \ldots + P_n q_n, \text{ we get}$$

$$y = P_1.h_1\ (P_1, P_2, \ldots, P_n, U^\circ) + P_2.h_2\ (P_1, P_2, P_n, U^\circ) + \ldots + P_n.h_n\ (P_1, P_2, \ldots P_n\ U^\circ) \qquad \ldots(59)$$

Since we are substituting optimal values of commodities, we can write $y = y^\circ$ indicating minimal level of expenditure to attain a constant level of utility U°, the expression (59) can be now simplified as:

$$y^\circ = H\ (P^\circ, U^\circ) = \sum_i P_i,\ h_i\ [P^\circ, U^\circ]\ ; \qquad \ldots(60)$$

P° is a vector of prices, *i.e.*, $[P_1, P_2 \ldots, P_n]$.

This function is called 'Consumer's Expenditure Function'. It can be shown that this function is continuous in U° and P°, concave, homogeneous of degree zero, and non-decreasing in prices, and increasing in U°.[15]

The expenditure function has an important property which is given by the Hotelling's theorem.[16] According to this theorem. if the expenditure function is differentiable, the optimal consumption bundle is given by:

$$\overset{\circ}{q_i} = h_i\ (P, U) = \frac{\partial H\ (P, U)}{\partial P_i},\ i = 1, \ldots, n. \qquad \ldots(61)$$

P is the vector of Prices $\{P_1, P_1, P_n\}$

That is, the optimal consumption of the *i*th commodity is obtained by the partial differentiation of the expenditure function with respect to the *i*th price.

To prove the theorem, let q° be chosen at prices P° and utility U°, *i.e.*, $\overset{\circ}{q_i} = H_i\ (P^\circ, U^\circ)$.

Comparing the expenditure function and budget equation we can write $H\ (P^\circ, U^\circ) = \sum_i P_i^\circ \overset{\circ}{q_i}$.

By taking total differentiation of both the sides we get:

$$\sum_i H_i\ (P^\circ, U^\circ)\ dp_i + H_u\ (P^\circ, U^\circ)\ dU = \sum_i \overset{\circ}{q_i}\ dP_i + \sum_i P_i^\circ\ dq_i \qquad \ldots(62)$$

where $\quad H_i\ (P^\circ, U^\circ) = \partial H\ (P^\circ, U^\circ)/dP_i$

and $\quad H_u\ (P^\circ, U^\circ) = \partial H\ (P^\circ, U^\circ)/dU.$

Again, at the optimum we had the relationship

$$P_i^\circ = \mu\ \partial U / \partial q_i = \mu\ \partial F(q^\circ)/\partial q_i \qquad \ldots(63)$$

Substituting (63) in (62) and setting $dU = 0$, we get,

$$\sum_i H_i\ (P^\circ, U^\circ)\ dP_i = \sum_i \overset{\circ}{q_i}\ dP_i + \mu \sum_i F_i\ (q^\circ)\ dq_i$$

(Since $U = F\ (q_1, q_2, \ldots, q_n)$, $\partial U / \partial q_i = \partial F\ (q^\circ)/\partial q_i = F_i\ (q^\circ)$)

---

15. See C. Blackorby, D. Primont and R. R. Russell, *Duality, Separability and Functional Structure Theory of Economic Applications;* Elseveir/ North Holland 1978 (Theorem A 3).
16. H. Hotelling: Edgeworth's Taxation Paradox and the Nature of Supply and Demand Functions; *Journal of Political Economy*, 40 (1932), 557–616.

If there is a change in jth Price, all other prices being constant, *i.e.*, $dP_i = 0,\ i \neq j$ then we get

$$H_j\ (P^\circ,\ U^\circ) = \overset{\circ}{q}_j, \qquad ...(64)$$

the second term on the right hand side vanishes when utility is constant.

(d) Linear Expenditure System[17]

Let us consider a utility function of the type:

$$U = \beta_1 \log\ (q_1 - \overline{q_1}) + \beta_2 \log\ (q_2 - \overline{q_2}) + ... + \beta_n \log\ (q_n - \overline{q_n})$$

This is called Stone-Geary utility function.

q_i is the quantity of Q_i commodity purchased and $\overline{q}_i$ is a constant,

$i = 1,\ ...,\ n.$

By maxmimising this utility function subject to the budget constraint $y = P_1q_1 + P_2q_2 + \ldots + P_nq_n$, the first order maximising conditions can be written as:

$$\frac{\beta_i}{(q_i - \overline{q}_i)} - \lambda\ P_i = 0$$

or

$$\beta_i = \lambda.\ P_i(q_i - \overline{q}_i)\ i = 1,\ ...,\ n. \qquad ...(65)$$

Let us normalise the β_i's *i.e.*, $\beta_1 + \beta_2 + ... + \beta_n = 1$. This implies that

$$\sum_{i=1}^{n} \beta_i = 1 = \lambda \sum_{i=1}^{n} P_i\ (q_i - \overline{q}_i)$$

From this,

$$\lambda = \frac{1}{\sum_{i}^{n} P_i (q_1 - \overline{q}_i)} = \frac{1}{\sum_{i=1}^{n} P_i q_i - \sum_{i=1}^{n} P_i \overline{q}_i}$$

or

$$= \frac{1}{y - \sum_{i=1}^{n} P_i\, \overline{q}_i}, \text{ Since } y = P_1q_1 + P_2q_2 + ... + P_nq_n$$

Using this expression for λ and changing λ to λ° and q_i to $\overset{\circ}{q}_i$ as values for optimum, we can write

$$\beta_i = \frac{P_i\ (\overset{\circ}{q}_i - \overline{q}_i)}{y - \sum_{i}^{n} P_i\, \overline{q}_i}$$

or

$$P_i(\overset{\circ}{q}_i - \overline{q}_i) = \beta_i\ (y - \sum_{i}^{n} P_i\ \overline{q}_i)$$

17. R. Stone, "Linear Expenditure System and Demand Analysis: An Application to the British Pattern of Demand", *The Economic Journal*, Vol,. 64, 1954, pp. 511-527.

or $$P_i q_i^{\circ} = P_i \bar{q}_i + \beta_i \left(y - \sum_i^n P_i \bar{q}_i\right); \quad ...(66)$$

or $$q_i^{\circ} = \bar{q}_i + \frac{\beta_i}{P_i}\left(y - \sum_i^n P_i \bar{q}_i\right); \; i = 1, ..., n. \quad ...(67)$$

This is a linear expenditure system. This expression tells us that quantity demanded of a commodity Q_i is a function of total expenditure y and prices of all commodities in the consumption basket of the consumer. $\bar{q}_i$ is a constant interpreted as basic or committed consumption of ith commodity. $y - \sum_i^n P_i \bar{q}_i$ is defined as super-numerary income or uncommitted income, and β_i are simply the marginal propensities to consume. In terms of expenditure we interpret (66) as the expenditure $(P_1 q_1)$ on a commodity at the optimum which is a sum of committed (or essential) expenditure on that commodity $(P_i \bar{q}_i)$ and a portion of the super-numerary income $\beta_i \left(y - \sum_i^n P_i \bar{q}_i\right)$.

The linear expenditure system is based on the utility function having all properties of the conventional utility function. The system has additive property, *i.e.*, the sum of different types of expenditure equals total expenditure. The system is homogeneous of degree zero in income and prices. Stone has used this system to estimate the demand for various goods and services in the United Kingdom.

4.13 LANCASTER'S THEORY OF CONSUMER DEMAND

Kelvin Lancaster has developed a new approach to analyse consumer demand for different goods.[18] The essence of his theory is to provide a fully integrated theory of consumer choice and demand in which the characteristics of goods are taken explicitly into account. Such a theory provides a basic structure within which product variations and new products fit easily while analysing the demand. The traditional theory of demand is too abstract according to Lancaster as it is based upon preferences alone ignoring highly pertinent and obvious information about the properties of goods which play crucial role in consumer decision-making. The physical properties, for example, size, shape, colour, smell, chemical composition, ability to perform a variety of functions and so on are quite important if we look at the analysis of demand from the point of view of marketing. Some of these properties, which Lancaster termed as 'characteristics', are relevant for making choices and they must be incorporated explicitly in the demand analysis for goods and services.

Lancaster's theory is quite interesting and complex. We will not go into its details here but simply cover the basic reference model to understand its conceptual foundation. The crucial element of Lancaster's theory is the concept of the 'consumption technology' which specifies a relationship between goods and characteristics. The characteristics are assumed to be objectively measurable. The 'unit' in which a particular characteristic is measured is not important except that it must be the same for all goods possessing that characteristics. Defining b_{ij} as the quantity of ith characteristic possessed by a unit amount of jth good, and Z_i and x_j as quantities of ith characteristic and jth good, a linear relationship has been postulated by Lancaster as:

---

18. K. Lancaster: 'A New Approach to Consumer Theory', *Journal of Political Economy,* Vol. 74, 1966, pp. 132–57, and Consumer Demand: A New Approach; Columbia University Press, N.Y. 1971.

$$Z_i = b_{ij}\, x_j \quad i.e., \quad b_{ij} = \frac{Z_i}{x_j} \qquad \text{...(68)}$$

If more than one item is involved, the above relationship changes to

$$Z_i = b_{i1}\, x_1 + b_{i2}\, x_2 + ... + b_{in}\, x_n$$

This is additivity assumption for the model showing that the total amount of ith characteristic possessed by the goods collection (x_1, x_2 ..., x_n) is the sum of the amounts of the characteristic by the goods separately. Suppose there are r characteristic and n goods, we have

$$Z_i = \sum_{j=1}^{n} b_{ij}\, x_j\,;\; i = 1, ..., r. \qquad \text{...(69)}$$

In matrix form we write this as:

$$Z = Bx$$

where $Z = [Z_i]$, a vector of characteristics

$B = \{b_{ij}\}$ å matrix of coefficients relating to goods and characteristics.

It is called as "Consumption Technology Matrix."

$X = \{x_j\}$ a vector of goods.

This is a kind of input-output model. Inputs are goods and outputs are characteristics. Size of B matrix is $r \times n.$, r may be greater than n or equal to n or less than n. Nothing can be said about this at this stage. A simple example of this type of relationship can be given as that of different foods such as milk, eggs, oranges, bread having characteristics like calories, protein, vitamins in specified units. B matrix represents these characteristics possessed by the different foods.

For the sake of simplicity it was assumed that all elements b_{ij} are non-negative and all goods are non-negative. A somewhat stronger assumption made by Lancaster about the consumption-technology matrix is that it is semi-positive having at least one positive element in each row and each column. This ensures that the tabulation of the technology does not include any good which has none of the relevant characteristics or any characteristic which is not possessed by at least one of the goods (items). Further, the consumption technology is assumed to be universally valid in the sense that all consumers 'see' it in the same way. This implies that there is no difference between consumers as to what collection of characteristics is associated with any specific collection of goods.

As mentioned earlier, the consumption-technology expresses the relationship between characteristics and goods. The relationship between characteristics and people is expressed by their preferences. It is assumed that the interest of consumer is in characteristics, and not in goods *per se.* Any preference for a collection of goods is because of preferences for the characteristics. Lancasters adopted the traditional preference theory of consumer with such a modification. The assumptions of traditional consumption theory were adopted by him with modification, *e.g.*, characteristics in place of goods, preferences for characteristics rather than for goods, etc. Complete quasiordering of preferences, transitivity of preferences, completeness, convexity, non-satiation, etc., are the standard requirements of consumer theory which were applicable to Lancaster's theory also.

The behavioural assumption for the demand analysis made by Lancaster can be stated as follows:

'The consumer acts in accordance with his preferences, that is, given the opportunity to choose from some set Z of characteristics collections, the consumer will choose that collection which maximises U (Z) over Z'.[19]

---

19. K. Lancaster: *ibid:* p. 31.

The consumer's budget line can be postulated as usual $P_1x_1 + P_2 x_2 + ... + P_n x_n \leq y$ or $Px \leq y$ where P is a vector of prices, x is a vector of goods, y is income. The consumer's choice problem under the regular budget constraint will be as:

$$\begin{aligned}&\text{Max } U(Z)\\ &\text{Subject to} \quad Z = Bx\\ &\qquad\qquad\quad Px \leq y\\ &\qquad\qquad\quad x \geq 0\end{aligned} \qquad ...(70)$$

Simplifying this we can write

$$\begin{aligned}&\text{Max} \quad U(Z) = U(Bx) = v(x) \text{ since } Z = Bx\\ &\text{Subject to} \quad Px \leq y\\ &\qquad\qquad\quad x \geq 0\end{aligned} \qquad ...(71)$$

We cannot say that this is similar to the simple utility maximisation case. There will be major differences if the number of characteristics is less than the number of goods ($r < n$). In this case, the partial derivatives of v with respect to the goods (X_j) and the partial derivatives of U with respect to the characteristics Z_i are related by

$$\frac{\partial V}{\partial x_j} = \sum_{i=1}^{r} b_{ij} \frac{\partial U}{\partial Z_i}, \; j = 1, ..., n.$$

Since there are only r derivatives, $\partial U / \partial Z_i$, it follows that $n - r$: of the derivatives $\partial v / \partial x_j$ can be expressed in terms of the remaining r. Thus, all first order conditions of the traditional utility maximisation model, *i.e.*,

$$\partial v / \partial x_j = \lambda P_j$$

cannot be satisfied. The simple neo-classical optimising technique cannot be applied here. The problem can only be tackled by complex techniques of non-linear programming.

The concept of consumption-technology and its universal validity, etc., are, no doubt, simple in conception but when it is the question of application, it may create complexity, as we have seen just above. Lancaster, however, analysed the different situations arising by the inequalities between r and n and gave equilibrium position. He extended his model further and gave examples from real life indicating operational usefulness of his demand theory in terms of characteristics of goods rather than the goods *per se*. It has potential uses in industrial and managerial economics.

4.14 CONSUMER CHOICE UNDER UNCERTAINTY

The analysis of consumer behaviour through which we have gone so far is based on certainty of events. The consumer has full information or data for decision-making. Real world, however, is full of uncertainties. The consumer may not possess complete information concerning the problem he is trying to solve. He may buy a TV but whether it works satisfactorily or not is not known to him. There may be uncertainty about the earnings of the consumer itself. How should a consumer take decisions about his choices in such situations? There is no unique procedure for this. Different people may have their own individual ways of tackling uncertainties, but the one that is widely used in economics or statistics is the approach of probability and expected value maximisation. The probability of an event happening is, roughly speaking, the relative frequency with which it will occur. Consider two players, A and B, playing a game. Both 'are equally strong. What will be the chance or probability of either winning? It may be say 50 : 50, *i.e.*, 50 per cent chance for each one to win the game. Here, we say that the probability of winning the game is 0.50 for A and also

0.50 for *B*. Suppose *A* is stronger than *B, then A* may have 80 per cent or 0.80 probability of winning the game and *B* a probability of 20 per cent or 0.20. When outcome of any event is uncertain it may be guessed on the basis of probability. This helps us in finding expected value of the outcome. Let us take two possible outcomes of an event, say Z_1 and Z_2. The probability of Z_1 is P_1 and the probability of Z_2 is P_2. The expected value of the outcome in the situation of uncertainty would therefore be $E(Z)= P_1Z_1 + P_2Z_2$. If there are more than two plausible outcomes we can extend this formula to $E(Z) = P_1Z_1 + P_2Z_2 + P_3Z_3 +... + P_nZ_n$. Remember $P_1 + P_2 + P_3 +... + P_n = 1$. So under uncertainty a rational decision-maker will maximise the expected value of outcomes. We do apply this principle in the analysis of consumer behaviour also. The first major work in this direction came from *D*. Bernoulli more than 200 years ago.[20] Bernoulli argued that individuals, in deciding on their behaviour in uncertain situations, consider the expected utility of their various options rather than the expected money value of these options. It is the average utility value of a game that matters and not its monetary value. Bernoulli thought of diminishing marginal utility of income as income increases. Because of diminishing marginal utility of money or what Bernoulli called as psychic value, it is quite reasonable for an individual to refuse to pay a large amount for the right to play a game since the game is not worth very much in utility term.

The expected utility hypothesis has been applied by Von Neumann and Morgenstern[21] to construct a utility index which can be used to predict choices in uncertain situations if the consumer conforms to the following basic assumptions.[22]

(*a*) *Complete ordering:* This is transitivity assumption. According to this if the consumer prefers alternative *A* to alternative *B,* and alternative *B* to alternative C, he then prefers alternative *A* to alternative *C*.

(*b*) *Continuity Assumption:* If *A* is preferred to *B* and *B* to C, then this assumption asserts that there exists some probability *P*, $0 < P < 1$, such that the consumer is indifferent between outcome *B* with certainty and expected value of outcomes of *A* and *C* with probability *P* and $1 - P$ respectively.

(*c*) *Independence Assumption:* If one lottery ticket or investment offers outcomes *A* and *C* with probabilities *P* and $1 - P$ respectively and another the outcomes *B* and *C* with same probabilities *P* and $1 - P$, the consumer is indifferent between the lottery tickets or investment plans.

(*d*) *Unequal Probability Assumption:* The essence of this assumption is that, other things being equal, we will always prefer the investment opportunity with greater probability of favourable outcome.

(*e*) *Compound Probability Assumption:* If the individual is offered a lottery ticket whose prizes are, in turn, other lottery tickets, he will view the compound lottery ticket in the same manner as if he had gone through all the probability calculations of ultimate odds of winning and losing.

Each one of these assumptions has considerable implication for construction of the utility indices.

In construction of the utility index, Neumann and Morgenstern implicitly assumed cardinal

---

20. The article has been reprinted in 1954. See D. Bernoulli, "Exposition of A New Theory on the Measurment of Risks" *Econometrica,* 22, 1954, pp. 23–36.
21. J. Von Neumann and O. Morgenstern, *The Theory of Games and Economic Behaviour,* Princeton University Press, 1949.
22. J. M. Henderson and R. E. Quandt, op.cit., page 43, and W.J. Baumol, *Economic Theory and Operations Analysis,* Second Ed. Prentice Hall of India, 1966, pp. 524–525.

measurement for utility. There is no set origin for this type of measurement of utility in N – M (*i.e.*, Neumann and Morgenstern) framework rather it starts from some arbitrarily chosen point. Consider three events *A, B* and *C*— for which the order of the individual's preferences is to be stated. Let us take that outcomes of *A* and *C* are uncertain. Then the consumer while making the choice will use the expected utility derived from these two events jointly that is, if *P* is the probability of occurring *A* and (1 – *P*) is the probability of *C*, then expected utility from them is $PU_A + (1 - P) U_C$ and U_A and U_C are utilities derived from the event *A* and *C* respectively. Suppose an event *B* has U_B utility which is certain. If we compare between the expected utility of *A* and *C* and the utility of *B*, we may have the possibilities of $U_B \gtrless PU_A + (1 - P)U_C$. Even *B*, *i.e.*, alternative *B* is preferred if $U_B > P(U_A) + (1 - P) U_C$ and it is rejected if $U_B < PU_A + (1 - P) U_C$. There will be indifference between these alternatives if $U_B = PU_A + (1 - P) U_C$. In this situation, we can say that there exists a probability level *P* for which the consumer is indifferent between *B* with certainty and a chance between *A* and *C*. Let us now take some arbitrary values for $U_A = 100$, $U_C = 10$, and take the probability level as 0.10. This gives us $U_B = 0.10 (100) + (1 - 0.10) 10 = 19$. We were not having any idea of U_B earlier. But given *P*, and an arbitrary chosen set for U_A and U_C we got $U_B = 19$. If $U_A = 50$, $U_C = 20$, $P = 0.5$, then $U_B = 0.5 \times 50 + 0.5 \times 20 = 35$. Proceeding in this way we can find utility numbers U_A, U_B, U_C, ..., U_n, for all possible quantities and combinations of all goods and hence a complete utility index can be derived by taking two arbitrary starting points and successfully confronting the consumer with various choice situations involving probabilities or risks. Consumer choices can thus be predicted seeing the utility index numbers. Sometimes the consumer may face complicated alternatives. They can also be predicted on the basis of such utility numbers. For example, if there is a 40 : 60 chance of alternative *D* and *B* to a 50 : 50 chance of *A* and C, then alternative *B* and *D* is preferred if 0.50 (100) + 0.50 (10) < 0.4 (122.5) + (0.6)19 where $U_A = 100$, $U_C = 10$, $U_D = 122.5$, $U_B = 19$.

The N – M utilities, as described above, are useful (*a*) for complete ranking of alternatives in the situations characterised by certainty; (*b*) in comparison of utility differences in cardinal scale; and (*c*) in calculation of expected utilities, thus making it possible to deal with the consumer behaviour under uncertainty. On the basis of such utility numbers, however, it will not be possible to have interpersonal comparisons of utilities. The method suggested by Neumann and Morgenstern is fairly general, applicable to deal with uncertainties related to consumption or production or any other activity.[23]

4.15 CONCLUDING REMARKS

This is a fairly long chapter dealing with various aspects of consumer theory, starting from the conventional theory of utility to the contemporary approaches. Some of the advanced topics like duality approach of utility analysis, Lancaster theory of demand analysis, Von Neumann and Morgenstern approach of dealing with uncertainty were discussed in brief. It is expected that an interested student will cover them in full from the relevant original readings. Emphasis has been given in this chapter on understanding consumer behaviour in different decision situations. No attempt has been made to go into details of measurement or estimation of the functions. This is the task of applied economics or econometrics.

---

23. For full understanding of the N – M approach, see, Henderson and Quandt, op.cit., pp. 42–47.

SUGGESTED READINGS

Blundell, R., "Consumer Behaviour: Theory and Empirical Behaviour—A Survey"; *The Economic Journal*, Vol. 98, March 1988, pp. 16–65.

Ferber, R., "Consumer Economics: A Survey"; *Journal of Economic Literature;* Vol. 11, 1973, pp. 1303-1342.

Henderson, J.M. &: R.E. Quandt, *Micro-economic Theory,* McGraw Hill, 2nd Ed. 1971, 1980

Hicks, J. R. *A Revision of Demand Theory;* Clarendon Press, 1956.

Lancaster K., *Consumer Demand: A New Approach,* Columbia University Press, 1974.

Philips. L *Applied Consumption Analysis;* North-Holland, 1974.

Russel, R. R. and M. Wilkinson, *Micro-economics*: *A Synthesis of Modern and Neo-Classical Theory;* John Wiley and Sons, 1979.

Samuelson, P. A., *Foundation of Economic Analysis,* Harvard University Press, 1947.

Theil, H., *Theory and Measurement of Consumer Demand,* Vol. I, II, North-Holland, 1975–76.

REVIEW QUESTIONS

1. The theory of consumer behaviour rests on a set of standard assumptions. What are they and what will be the implication if each of the assumptions is violated?
2. Define the concept of utility function. Examine its properties and role in the theory of consumer behaviour?
3. A consumer has a given amount of income and faces constant commodity prices. Derive the conditions when his utility is maximised.
4. By using the cardinal approach to utility analysis, derive the demand functions for the commodities that a consumer buys. What will be the standard properties of such demand functions?
5. Define an indifference curve. How it is derived and what are its properties?
6. Explain the term 'Marginal Rate of Commodity Substitution (MRCS)'. What is the significance of this term in the theory of consumer behaviour? Also explain the implications of (*a*) decreasing MRCS, (*b*) increasing MRCS, and (*c*) constant MRCS, in the indifference curve analysis.
7. Describe the consumer equilibrium position in the framework of indifference curve analysis? What are the necessary conditions for the stability of the equilibrium position? Give reasons for this.
8. How do you get Price-Consumption Curve (PCC) and Income-Consumption Curve (ICC) by using the indifference curve analysis? What is the precise meaning of these curves and how they are useful from the point of view of understanding consumer behaviour?
9. Describe Slutsky Equation and show how it is useful to isolate the substitution and income effects for a normal good, an inferior good and a Giffen good. Use graphs to elaborate your answers?
10. What implications regarding substitution and income effects can be drawn from the extreme types of indifference curves?
11. What is the meaning of 'consumer surplus'? How do you find such surplus by using cardinal utility approach and by using the indifference curve analysis? Examine in full?
12. What is 'composite commodity theorem' and what is its precise role in consumer equilibrium analysis? Discuss.

13. Describe the revealed preference theory and show how it is helpful in understanding the behaviour of a consumer in a better way than the other theories.
14. Describe an indirect utility function. How it is useful in the study of consumer behaviour?
15. Distinguish between compensated demand function and ordinary demand function for a commodity. What is the process of deriving the compensated demand functions for different commodities? Describe in brief.
16. What is linear expenditure system and what precise result we get from this regarding consumer behaviour?
17. Give an outline of Lancaster's theory of consumer demand and its comparative advantages over the conventional demand theory.
18. Examine whether it would be possible for a consumer to be in equilibrium if (*a*) marginal utilities of some goods he consumes are zero; (*b*) the marginal utilities of some goods which he refuses to purchase are greater than the marginal utilities of some goods which he purchases, and (*c*) the marginal utilities of goods he purchases are exactly proportional to their prices?
19. The slope of indifference curve is everywhere along the curve is equal to $-y/x$ where y is the quantity of commodity Y and x is the quantity of commodity X shown along vertical and horizontal axis respectively. Given I° as income of the consumer, show that the demand for X is independent of the price of Y and the demand for Y is also independent of the price of X. Also prove that the elasticity of demand for X as well as for Y is unity.
20. Three utility functions are defined as:

$$U_1 = q_1 q_2;\ U_2 = \log q_1 + \log q_2;\ U_3 = (q_1)^2\ (q_2)^2$$

Determine whether or not these utility functions have convex indifference curves. Also explain and compare the consumer preference orderings reflected by them.

CHAPTER 5

Theory of Production and Technological Change

As we have discussed in Chapter 2, 'How to Produce' is one of the basic economic problems common to every economic system. The theory of production is concerned to deal with this question. In a broad sense, the theory of production is the theory of the firm in which the main objective is to explain the behaviour of a producer, usually in terms of a constrained optimisation model such as maximisation of output or profit subject to technological and market restrictions. In a narrower sense, the theory of production is nothing but the theory of production function concerning with the technological relations between inputs and output.. In both the situations, the realm of production theory is a producer or a firm or a factory which is a micro unit. Basically, incorporating both the meanings of the theory of production together, we study human behaviour (*i.e.*, producer's behaviour) in relation to production of goods and services in this theory. For the study of the production theory and technological change we will begin with its narrower view, *i.e.*, the concept of production function, its properties, etc. But before taking up this for discussion let us define the term 'production' first.

5.1 WHAT IS 'PRODUCTION'?

To an economist, 'production' means creation of utility for sales. The act of creating utility is done by transforming a set of inputs into some output of a good or service. The output will be having greater utility than the inputs together. The new product or output thus created is sold in the market. If it is not marketed, it is not taken as production in economic sense. Technologically, of course, it is production.

The inputs used in production may be goods either supplied by the nature and/or produced by other industries. These are called *'intermediate inputs'* or *'material inputs'* There will be another category of inputs used in production. This is defined as *'factors of production'*, such as workers, land, buildings, plant and machines, tools and equipment and managers. Such inputs are used repeatedly in the process of production. They are used to convert the material inputs into output. Such inputs are also called *'Primary inputs'*.

Some examples of production are: (*a*) production of goods in factories; (*b*) production of services, such as teaching to students; (*c*) production of agricultural goods; and (*d*) natural production of forests.

Can consumption of goods be interpreted as production? Technically, yes, since goods in the consumption basket will be transformed into some 'energy' for development of human body. But in the economic sense, it is not production since the 'output' is not sold in the market. Similarly, playing hockey will be interpreted as production when ticket is charged to see such a match, *i.e.*, it is marketed, otherwise it is not. Marketability of the output is an essential feature of production in free-market economies. The socialist economies are exception to this. Everything that is produced, whether it comes for exchange or not, is production in such economies. Since we are interested in the study of behaviour of the producer producing for the market, so we follow the concept of production relevant to the free-market economies.

The concept of production can be understood clearly with the help of a flow diagram as shown below.

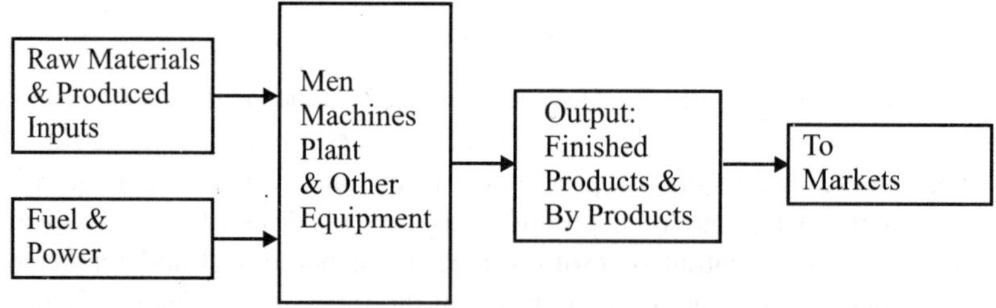

Fig. 5.1 Production Flow Diagram

The aim of production is to convert basic raw materials and other produced inputs into outputs. This is done in the 'technology box' with the help of men and machines including other equipments. To make men and machines or plant operative we need fuel and power which is also a category of inputs. From the 'technology box' we get output in the form of the desired product(s) and also get some byproducts from this.

As mentioned earlier, the realm of the production theory is a firm or a factory which is considered as the smallest technical unit of production. A firm may also be taken as an organisational unit engaged in some business activity. By organisation we mean a coalition of people having different functions but working under a single administrative set-up, duly constituted according to the law of the country. The organisation will have a common goal for all its members, such as profit maximisation or sales maximisation. For the theory of production that will be discussed here we will not go into organisational aspect of the firm, rather we take it as a technical unit of production owned by a producer. A firm means a producer in this context whose behaviour will be studied here.

5.2 THE CONCEPT OF PRODUCTION FUNCTION

The production function is a highly abstract concept that has been developed to deal with technological aspects of the theory of production. *It is an embodiment of technology which yields maximum output from the given set of inputs or specifies the way in which inputs co-operate together to produce a given level of output.* Symbolically, it is expressed as:

$$q = f(x_1, x_2, ..., x_n) \quad ...(1)$$

where q = flow of output in physical terms and x_1, x_2 ...x_n are flows of inputs in physical terms per unit of time. It is a physical relationship which is an exogenous factor in economic analysis. A producer cannot go out of the technological alternatives specified by the production function, but the one he chooses is a matter of economic consideration mainly determined by the input prices. The production function assumes that a technical maximisation problem has been solved. The inputs may or may not be substitutes for each other. The nature of the production function will reveal this possibility.

Who is responsible for developing or constructing the production function for a firm or a commodity? Since it is an engineering relationship, engineers should be given the responsibility for constructing the production function. However, they regard it as economists' concept to deal with technological aspects of production. Apart from input and output quantities, an engineer is concerned with the physical properties of material used in production, such as horse-power, tensile strength, stress and strain, etc. Economists generally abstract from such things in conceptualising the production function. However, there is no difficulty in incorporating such properties in the physical relationship specifying the link between inputs and output.[1]

There are many theoretical and empirical uses of the concept of production function. It enables economists to analyse a wide variety of problems, such as determination of relative income shares of factors of production, the factors affecting economic growth, and the nature of technological unemployment. We may have production function for a plant or a firm or an industry or it may be extended to the entire economy.

The technology embodied in a production function can be expressed in terms of four major characteristics which, taken together, may be called as 'abstract technology.'[2] The characteristics are:

(a) The Efficiency of the Technology

This reflects the quality of the technology. An increase in efficiency of technology increases the output for a given level of inputs and other characteristics of the technology and vice-versa. It may be considered as a parameter in the production function showing the overall quality of the technology. Such a parameter will have its own influence on the output. It has to be independent of the influence of changing dimensions of inputs used in production.

(b) The Capital Intensity of the Technology

This, in fact, is the factor intensity property of the technology. It shows the quantity of capital in relation to other factors normally labour. The capital labour ratio may be used as a measure of capital intensity of the technology.

(c) The Elasticity of Substitution

This indicates the ease with which capital input (or labour) can be substituted for labour (or capital) or any other set of inputs.

---

1. See for example, H. B. Chenery, "Engineering Production Functions", *Quarterly Journal of Economics*, Vol. 63, 1949, pp. 507–553.
2. Murry Brown, *On the Theory and Measurement of Technological Changes*, Cambridge University Press, 1968.

(d) The Economies of Scale

This indicates proportionate changes in output due to equiproportionate changes in all inputs. There may be increasing returns to scale or decreasing returns to scale or constant returns to scale.

Apart from these characteristics, the production function should satisfy some neo-classical properties. These are as follows:

(e) For a continuous, single valued production function the marginal products of the factors must be positive. *The marginal product of a factor is the addition in total output by employing one more unit of that factor, other factors remaining unchanged.* In the terminology of calculus, this is nothing but the partial derivative of the production function with respect to the concerned factor. So, this condition means:

$$\partial q / \partial x_i \geq 0,\ i = 1, \quad \dots n \qquad \dots(2)$$

(f) For some ranges of factors, their marginal products must eventually decline with increase in the quantities of factors; *i.e.,*

$$\partial^2 q / \partial x_i^2 < 0,\ i = 1, \quad \dots n \qquad \dots(3)$$

(g) The marginal-product of one factor increases with increase in the quantity of the other factor,

$$\partial^2 q / \partial x_i \partial x_j > 0,\ i = 1,\ n;\ j = 1,\ \dots n;\ i \neq j \qquad \dots(4)$$

(h) The production function should not specify a-priorily the degree of returns to scale. It is to be determined empirically.

All characteristics of the production function, including its neo-classical properties, are important not only from the point of view of production theory but from the practical decision-making also. We will analyse them further, as and when required, in this chapter.

There are several types of production function currently being used in the economic theory of production. Some of them are as follows:

(i) Linear Production Function

$$q = a_1 x_1 + a_2 x_2 \qquad \dots(5)$$

a_1 and a_2 are marginal physical products of the two inputs X_1 and X_2, and x_1 and x_2 their respective quantities. $a_1 \geq 0$, $a_2 \geq 0$. As we will see later on, the two inputs are perfect substitutes for each other.

(ii) Input-Output Model

$$q = \text{Min}\left(\frac{x_1^0}{c_1}, \frac{x_2^0}{c_2}\right) \qquad \dots(6)$$

x_1^0 and x_2^0 are fixed quantities of inputs X_1 and X_2, and c_1 and c_2 are the amounts of input X_1 and input X_2 respectively required per unit of output. They are positive. The two inputs are perfect complements of each other. The smaller ratio among $\frac{x_i}{c_i}$ will be the plausible output as the producer will not be able to produce more because of fixity of the concerned input.

(iii) The Cobb-Douglas Production Function[3]

$$q = B x_1^{\alpha_1} x_2^{\alpha_2} .. x_n^{\alpha_n} \quad ...(7)$$

q is output, x_1, x_n are inputs per unit of time, B is a constant α_1, α_2, α_n are output elasticities of inputs. We will see later on that if $\alpha_1 + \alpha_2 + \alpha_n > 1$ then the production function shows increasing returns to scale, and if $\sum_{i=1}^{n} \alpha_i = 1$ then constant and if $0 < \sum_{i=1}^{n} \alpha_i < 1$ then decreasing returns to scale. The elasticity of substitution for this function will be equal to unity.

(iv) The C.E.S. Production Functions[4]

$$q = \gamma \ [\delta K^{-\rho} + (1-\partial) \ L^{-\rho}]^{-1/\rho} \quad ...(8)$$

q = output, K = capital, L = Labour, γ is defined as 'efficiency' parameter, δ as 'distribution' parameter, and ρ as 'substitution' parameter. This function gives constant elasticity of substitution for capital and labour. This gives constant returns to scale but its gerneralised version reflects other types of returns also. The properties of this function will be discussed in detail later on in this chapter.

(v) Translog production Functions

$$(i) \ q = a_0 + \sum_i a_i \ x_i + \sum_i \sum_j a_{ij} \ x_i x_j, \ x_i, \ x_j = 1 \text{ to } n, \ a_{ij} = a_{ji}$$

$$(ii) \ lnq = b_0 + \sum_i b_i \ ln \ x_i + \frac{1}{2} \sum_i \sum_j b_{ij} \ ln \ x_i . ln \ x_j, \ x_i, \ x_j = 1 \text{ to } n; \ b_{ij} = b_{ji}$$

These are generalized versions of the Cobb-Douglas production functions. They are useful specifications for empirical estimation of the effects of joint variables on the dependent variables apart from other things.

5.3 DECISION PERIODS RELATED TO PRODUCTION ANALYSIS

In order to study the behaviour of producers in relation to production of goods and services, we have to take into account the time factor being called here as decision period. There are four different decision periods over which we examine the production theory. These are as follows:

(i) *Very Short-run or Momentary Period*

As the name indicates, it is a very short period of time. All inputs and hence production level is fixed. It cannot be changed at all. From the point of view of understanding producer's behaviour it is not relevant as quantity of output is invariable.

---

3. C.W. Cobb and P.H. Douglas, "A Theory of Production", *American Economic Review* (Supplement), Vol. 18, 1928, pp. 139-165.
4. K.J. Arrow, H.B. Chenery, B.S. Minhas and R.M. "Solow: Capital-Labour Substitution and Economic Efficiency", *Review of Economics & Statistics*, Vol. 63, 1961, pp. 225-250.

(ii) Short-run

It is defined as the time period over which the inputs of some factors cannot be changed. This implies that production is carried on with the help of two categories of inputs: (*a*) fixed inputs and (*b*) variable inputs. The variable inputs and fixed inputs are combined together in variable proportions. Agricultural production (fixed land and variable human labour) is an example of this kind of production. The length of short-run depends on the type of as fixed factor(s). So long it is fixed, we will be operating in the short-run, may be for a day or a week or a month or a year or even more than a year. In manufacturing, for example, it may be difficult to change the size of the plant (*i.e.*, fixed factor) even in few years. The length of short-run would be fairly long for this.

(iii) Long-run

It is the time period when all inputs, *i.e.*, the factors of production are variable but basic technology of production remains unchanged. By unchanged technology we mean a stable production function. A manufacturing firm, for example, makes necessary adjustments in the size of its plant by expanding itself in the long-run. There will be nothing like a fixed factor in this case.

(iv) Very Long-run

This is the time period over which the factors of production as well as production technology are variable. The production function changes in this case. Keeping in mind the above decision periods, we will proceed with the analysis of production by taking the following specific situations:

(*a*) Output increases in response to increase in some factors of production while other factors remain fixed. This gives us the laws of returns. This is short-run production behaviour.

(*b*) Output as well as all factors of production are changing in the same direction. This gives us the laws of returns to scale and related analysis. It is defined as long-run production behaviour.

(*c*) Output constant but inputs are changing in opposite direction, *i.e.*, they are substitutes for each other. This covers both short-run and long-run analysis of production. It is designated as iso-quant analysis of production.

(*d*) Input quantities are fixed and there are multiple products, *i.e.*, more than one product. Basically, it will be a short-run situation since in the long-run the input fixity constraint may be relaxed. This type of analysis is called 'production front analysis'.

(*e*) A generalised situation of production with several inputs and multiple outputs covering all the above four cases.

(*f*) Changing Production Functions. In this case we will study the theory of technological change.

Let us discuss these situations one by one.

5.4 SHORT-RUN BEHAVIOUR OF PRODUCTION

We have defined the short-run in previous section. For the analysis of short-run production behaviour, let us assume the production function as:

$$q = f\ (x_1, x_2^0) \qquad \text{...(9)}$$

Where q = quantity of output, x_1 = quantity of variable factor and x_2^0 = quantity of fixed factor for the production run or period. For simplicity, we consider one variable factor and one fixed factor. This production function indicates the relationship between total quantity of output and the quantity of the variable factor x_1 for a given quantity of the fixed factor x_2^0. This relationship may be called 'Total Product Curve' of the variable factor. From the production function, we derive the expressions for the average product (*AP*) and marginal product (*MP*) of the variable factor as:

$$AP_1 = \frac{q}{x_1} = \frac{f(x_1, x_2^0)}{x_1} \qquad ...(10)$$

and

$$MP_1 = \frac{\partial q}{\partial x_1} = \frac{\partial f(x_1, x_2^0)}{\partial x_1} \qquad ...(11)$$

We have already defined the marginal product of a factor while dealing with properties of the production function. It is the addition in total output by employing one more additional unit of the factor, other factors being held constant. At any point on the total product curve, the slope of its tangent (*i.e.*, $\partial q/\partial x_1$) defines the marginal product of the factor, and the slope of the line joining that point to the origin defines the average product of the factor.

There are two basic laws of the short-run production theory associated with the marginal and average products of the variable factor.

(i) The Law of Diminishing Marginal Product

According to this law, if increasing amounts of a variable factor are applied to some fixed quantity of another factor(s),the amount added to the total product by each additional unit of the variable factor, i.e., its marginal product, will eventually decline with the increasing quantity of the variable factor. This implies that the second order partial derivative of the production function (9) is eventually negative ($\partial^2 q/\partial x_1^2 < 0$).

Graphically, the relationship between the marginal product and quantity of the variable factor can be described as:

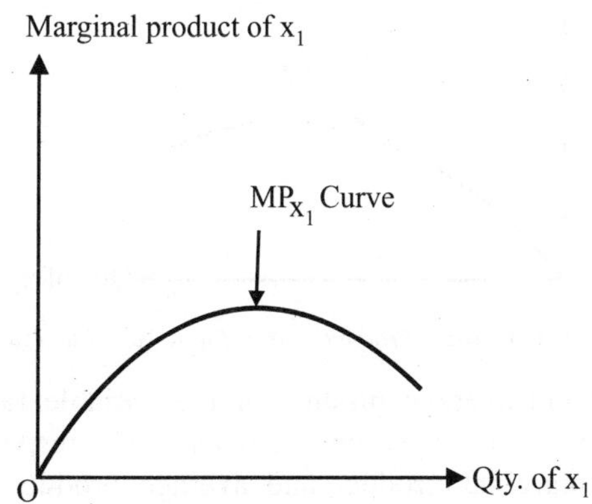

Fig. 5.2 Marginal Product Curve for a Variable Factor

Initially, the relationship is positive but later on it is negative, as shown in the above figure. We may denote this behaviour by writing $\partial^2 q/\partial x_1^2 \gtrless 0$. This is a general relationship; exceptions to this are possible.

The law of diminishing marginal product is valid when the following conditions are satisfied:

(*a*) the technology of production is fixed;

(*b*) there is, at least, one fixed factor used in production;

(*c*) the fixed factor and the variable factor combine together in variable proportions in the process of production.

The last condition is essential for the law. Because of this condition, the law is also known as *the law of variable proportion.* This is more general in scope in the sense that the law of diminishing return becomes universally valid even in the situation when the combining factors vary at different rates thus giving us their variable proportions which, in turn, affect the total, average and marginal products of the variable factors.

(ii) The Law of Diminishing Average Product

The statement of this law is similar to the law of diminishing marginal product except the use of average product in place of the marginal product. *That is, if increasing quantity of a .variable factor is applied to a fixed quantity of some other factor(s), the average product of the variable factor eventually declines with increase in the quantity of the variable factor.* Graphically, this relationship can be represented as follows:

Using the expression (10) the law of diminishing average product of X_1 means eventually $\frac{\partial(AP_1)}{\partial x_1} < 0$.* The conditions for the validity of this law are the same as for the law of diminishing marginal product.

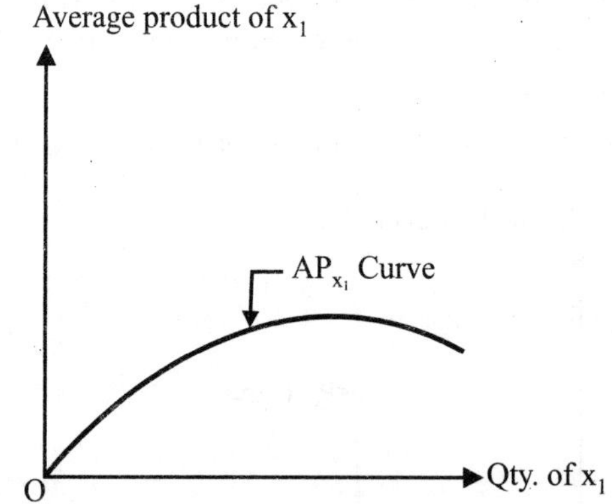

Fig. 5.3 Average Product Curve for a Variable Factor

Both marginal product and average product of the variable factor are derived from total product of the factor as we see in equations (10) and (11) respectively. The three types of retruns, *i.e.*, total product, marginal product and average product are thus inter-related. The inter-relatedness among them can be shown with the help of a diagram. For this, consider the following data.

---

* Initially $\partial(AP_1)/\partial x_1$ may be greater than zero as the curve in Figure 5.3 shows.

Table 5.1: Total, Average, and Marginal Products for a Variable Factor (x_1): Labour

Capital (x_2)	*Labour (x_1)*	*Capital/Labour Ratio x_2/x_1*	*Total Product of Labour*	*Marginal Product of Labour*	*Average Product of Labour*	*Stages of Production*
1	2	3	4	5	6	7
1	1	1/1	10	10	10.0	
1	2	1/2	28	18	14.0	Stage 1
1	3	1/3	51	23	17.0	
1	4	1/4	76	25	19.0	
1	5	1/5	95	19	19.0	
1	6	1/6	105	10	17.5	Stage 2
1	7	1/7	105	0	15.0	
1	8	1/8	95	– 10	11.9	
1	9	1/9	75	– 20	8.3	Stage 3
1	10	1/10	53	– 22	5.3	

In column (1) of the table, one fixed unit of capital is given. It may be, for example, land in area. Column (2) contains variable factor, say labour in numbers. Column (3) gives capital/labour ratios. The next three columns contain Total, Marginal and Average Products for labour in appropriate units. All these schedules are shown graphically in Fig. 5.4.

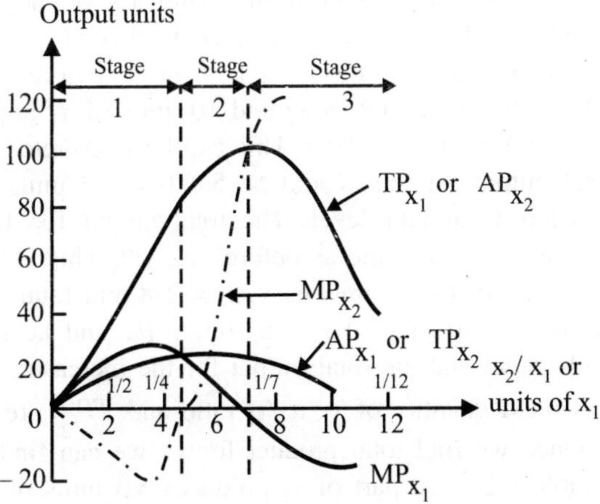

Fig. 5.4 Stages of Production: Total, Average, and Marginal Products of Fixed and Variable Factors

As shown in this figure, the total product curve for X_1 *i.e.*, TP_{x_1} starts from the origin, rises smoothly, reaches at the top at the 7th unit of X_1 showing maximum output of 105 units for labour, and then declines. The rate of growth of TP_{x_1} is faster upto 4th unit of X_1 showing maximum marginal product of 25 units. The rate of change of TP_{x_1}, *i.e.*, MP of X_1 then declines. MP_{x_1} is zero *when*. TP_{x_1} is at the maximum, after that it is negative which means a decline in TP_{x_1}. The average product curve AP_{x_1} also rises first and then declines. Its top is 19 units for 4th and 5th units of X_1. There is very important link between MP_{x_1} *,and* APx_1. As long as MP_{x_1} is greater than AP_{x_1}, the AP_{x_1} rises with rise in MP_{x_1} and if MP_{x_1} is less than AP_{x_1} then AP_{x_1} declines with MP_{x_1}. The Marginal Product curve MP_{x_1} passes through the top of AP_{x_1}. This is a mathematical property of the relationship between marginal and average magnitudes. Average product curve cannot cross the horizontal axis, i.e., AP_{x_1} can't be negative since negative output is ruled out in production. TP_{x_1} and hence AP_{x_1} can only be zero at the limiting end.

It is conventional to divide production into three stages based on the relationship between average product, marginal product and total product for the variable factor. Stage 1 indicates rising average product (AP_{x_1}) for the variable factor. With fixed output and input prices, the producer would find it profitable to expand its output in this stage. Stage 2 of production begins when average product curve starts declining and ends when marginal product becomes zero or total product reaches its maximum level. After this, we have the Stage 3 in which total product curve declines because of negative marginal product for the variable factor. It would be irrational for any producer to produce output in this stage. The only stage where production can take place is Stage 2 where both marginal and average product curves are declining but they are showing positive values for AP_{x_1} and MP_{x_1}.

We have shown the three stages of production for the variable factor (x_1), Further, we can also show that these stages are symmetric for the fixed and variable factors in the two input case. That is Stage 1 for x_1 (Labour) is Stage 3 for x_2 (Capital) and Stage 3 for x_1 is Stage 1 for x_2. Stage 2 is common for both the factors. In order to show the symmetry of the stages, let us generate the required data series from Table 5.1. For this, we keep x_1 at fixed label say 1 unit and keep the second factor x_2 variable in such a way' that the ratio x_2/x_1 is same as before as quantity of x_2 increases. Consider the last row of Table 5.1. One unit of x_2 and 10 units of x_1 implies $x_2/x_1 = 1/10$, i.e., the amount of fixed factor (x_2) per unit of x_1 is 1/10. This can be interpreted as if 1/10 of x_1 combines with 1 unit of x_1. The total output for this would be 53/10 = 5.3 units. Now, let us increase the amount of x_2 to 1/9 and keep x_1 at unit level. The total output for 1/9th part of x_2 would be 75/9 = 8.3 units. x_2/x_1 ratio remains the same as before *i.e.*, 1/9. This is given in row 9th of Table 5.2. Further increase in x_2 from 1/9 to 1/8 implies $x_2/x_1 = 1/8$ and total-out 95/8 = 11.9 for 1/8 of x_2. In this way, by increasing x_2 further to 1/7, 1/6, 1/5,.., 1/1 and keeping $x_1 = 1$, we get same x_2/x_1 ratio as for the variable input and the total output for the increasing quantity of x_2. The series of increasing quantity of x_2 fixed quantity of x_1, x_2/x_1 ratio and TP_{x_2} are shown in columns 1 to 4 respectively of Table 5.2. Once we find total product for x_2, we can find average product for this. Consider the last row of Table 5.2. 1/10 part of x_2 produces 5.3 units of output, so one unit, of x_2 would produce 5.3 ÷ 1/10 = 53 units. Similarly, 1/9 x_2 produces 8.3 units so 1 unit of x_2 will produce 75 units of output. What we are getting through such calculations is that average product of x_1 (APx_1) is total product for x_2 (TP_{x_2}) and total product for x_2 is average product for x_1. The TP_{x_2} and APx_2 series are shown in columns 4 and 6 respectively of Table 5.2.

We have to compute MP_{x_2} now. For this, we have to divide the increment in total output of X_2 by the increment in the amount of X_2. Consider rows (1) and (2) in Table 5.2. Increment in x_2 is 1/2 – 1/1 = – 1/2, and increment in TP_{x_2} is 14 – 10 = 4, so MP_{x_2} = 4.0 ÷ (–1/2) = – 8 units. Moving down to row 3, we have increment in x_2 as 1/3 – 1/2 = – 1/6, and increment in TP_{x_2} as 17 – 14 = 3 and so MP_{x_2} = 3.0 ÷ (–1/6) = – 18.0. Proceeding further in this way, we get the MP_{x_2} series which is shown in column 5 of Table 5.2. The last two rows gives us MP_{x_2} = 270.0. For identification of the stages of production, we have to start from the bottom of Table 5.2. First stage of production corresponding to x_2 will be upto the point when APx_2 is maximum, *i.e.*, for 1/7 unit of x_2. The MP_{x_2} passes through the top of APx_2 for this level of the input uses. The Stage 2 for x_2 then begins and ends up to the level, of x_2 = 1/5. The TP_{x_2} is maximum for this level of x_2 and its marginal product (MP_{x_2}) will be zero. After this, we get Stage 3 for x_2 which ends at the origin. Remember, while showing

Table 5.2: Total, Average and Marginal Products for Fixed factor x_2: Symmetry of Stages

Capital *(x_2)*	*Labour* *(x_1)*	*Capital/ Labour Ratio* *x_2/x_1*	*Total Product of* *x_2*	*Marginal Product of* *x_2*	*Average Product of* *x_2*	*Stages of Production*
1/1	2	3	4	5	6	7
1/1	1	1/1:1	10.0	–	10.0	Stage
1/2	1	1/2:1	14.0	– 8.0	28.0	3 for x_2
1/3	1	1/3:1	17.0	– 18.0	51.0	
1/4	1	1/4:1	19.0	– 24.0	76.0	
1/5	1	1/5:1	19.0	0.0	95.0	Stage 2
1/6	1	1/6:1	17.5	45.0	105.0	
1/7	1	1/7:1	15.0	105.0	105.0	
1/8	1	1/8:1	11.9	173.6	95	Stage 1
1/9	1	1/9:1	8.3	259.2	75	
1/10	1	1/10:1	5.3	270.0	53	

the stages for variable factor x_1 we move from the origin to the right in the increasing order of x_1, but for the other factor (x_2) the stages begin from that point on *x-axis* where the use of variable input x_1 is so much that its total product is zero (conceptually it is possible since the TPx_1 is downward sloping after it reaches the optimum) in its Third stage towards left showing increasing amount of x_2. This point, of course, we have not shown in Fig. 5.3. The stages of x_1 and x_2 are thus opposite to each other in direction. The Stage 1 for x_1 is the Stage 3 for x_2 and Stage 3 for X_1 is the Stage 1 for x_2. Stage 2 is common for both. From the point of view of x_2, production takes place only in Stage 2 where both its MPx_2 and APx_2 are positive but declining. This stage is the feasible zone of product using both the factors. No other stage of production will give us equilibrium level of production except Stage 2. The reversibility of stages is shown in Fig 5.4 using the same scale as for x_1. Mathematically, we can further elaborate this phenomenon as follows:

Let us consider the production function

$$q = f(x_1, x_2)$$

using the Euler's theorem, this function can be written in transformed form as:

$$Kq = (\partial q_1 / \partial x_1)\, x_1 + (\partial q / \partial x_2)\, x_2$$

where K is constant to be defined later on.

For simplicity, we assume $K = 1$ and so we have

$$q = (\partial q / \partial x_1)\, x_1 + (\partial q / \partial x_2)\, x_2 \qquad \text{...(12)}$$

Dividing both sides of this equation by x_1, we get

$$\frac{q}{x_1} = \partial q / \partial x_1 + (\partial q / \partial x_2)\, \frac{x_2}{x_1} \qquad \text{...(13)}$$

q/x_1 is APx_1, $\partial q / \partial x_1$ is MP_{x_1}, $\partial q / \partial x_2$ is MP_{x_2}.

If $q/x_1 = \partial q / \partial x_1$, then $(\partial q / \partial x_2)\, \frac{x_2}{x_1} = 0$.

Since x_2/x_1 cannot be zero, this implies that $\partial q / \partial x_2 = 0$. Further, if $\partial q / \partial x_1 > q/x_1$ *i.e.*, $MP_{x_1} > APx_1$ then $\partial q / \partial x_2$ (*i.e.*, MP_{x_2}) is – ve. The Stage 1 for x_1 shows these relations.

Similarly, dividing (12) on both sides by x_2 we have

$$q/x_2 = (\partial q / \partial x_1)\, \frac{x_1}{x_2} + \partial q / \partial x_2 \qquad \text{...(14)}$$

In this equation, if $q/x_2 = \partial q / \partial x_2$ *i.e.*, $APx_2 = MP_{x_2}$ then $\partial q / \partial x_1 = 0$ since $x_1/x_2 \neq 0$, and if $\partial q / \partial x_2 > q / x_2$ then $\partial q / \partial x_1 < 0$. This is reflected by the Stage 3 for X_1 or Stage 1 for X_2.

All these relations are proving the reversibility of stages for the two factors X_1 and X_2 which are combining together in variable proportions in the process of production.

As we have seen in the above analysis of stages of production, the marginal product curve in its declining course passes through the maxima of the average product curve for each factor. We can show this result mathematically.

Given $q = f(x_1, x_2^0)$, the average product for X_1 would be (keeping X_2 fixed)

$$q/x_1 = \frac{f(x_1, x_2^o)}{x_1}$$

The first order maximization condition for the average product of x_1 is,

$$\frac{d(q/x_1)}{dx_1} = \frac{x_1 f(x_1, x_2^o) - 1 \times f(x_1, x_2^o)}{x_1^2} = 0$$

Provided $\frac{d^2(q/x_1)}{dx_1^2} < 0.$

This gives us,

$$x_1 f^1(x_1, x_2^o) = f(x_1, x_2^o)$$

or $$f^1(x_1, x_2^o) = \frac{f(x_1, x_2^o)}{x_1}$$

or $$MP_{x_1} = APx_1 \qquad ...(15)$$

This shows that MP_{x_1} is equal to AP_{x_1} when AP_{x_1} is maximum. If AP_{x_1} is constant, *i.e.*, invariable then MP_{x_1} would also be invariable. Both will be identical. The total product curve and associated marginal and average product curves, as described above, give us a general picture of production behaviour in the short-run. The curves are showing the variations in the marginal and average products for the variable factor according to the laws of returns. Constant marginal and average products are special cases for them. Now, an important question to answer is: why does short-run production behave as described by the product curves of the shape as shown above? We have to find the economic interpretation for this.

The shapes of the total, average, and marginal product curves are determined by the operation of the law of diminishing return. For this, an essential assumption is that there is at least one fixed factor with which the variable factor cooperates in production. The fixed factor is indivisible. Because of indivisibility of the fixed factor, initially the output from combination of fixed and variable factors will be quite low since the fixed factor cannot be utilised efficiently. As the amount of variable factor increases, utilisation of the fixed factor improves and so output goes up. Further increase in the amount of the variable factor continues to improve the utilisation of the fixed factor and hence an increase in output till we reach maximum marginal product for the variable factor. After this point, the law of diminishing return starts operating. Average product of the variable factor continues to rise because of greater marginal product ($MP_{x_1} > AP_{x_1}$) though MP_{x_1} curve is declining. Soon, we find the average product declining, *i.e.*, the end of Stage 1 of production. The point where Stage 1 ends, *i.e.*, top of AP_{x_1} curve, is called 'Point of Extensive Margin'. The direction of the average product curve changes after this point. It starts declining. The total product curve still rises because of positive marginal product for the variable factor. The stage 2 has both diminishing marginal and average product curves. The producer's actual equilibrium position will be somewhere in this stage. By merely seeing the product curves we cannot decide about the exact location of the most efficient level of input proportions. It requires some more information, particularly about the prices of factors. However, if output maximisation is a goal and there are no constraints for this then the end of Stage 2, *i.e.*, the point where marginal product curve cuts the horizontal axis ($MP_{x_1} = 0$) will be the most efficient level of input proportion. This gives maximum output. This point is called 'Point of Intensive Margin'. Beyond this, we have the Third Stage of production where input proportions are not favourable showing a continuous decline in total output. So, we conclude that it is the indivisibility of the fixed factor that is the root cause of diminishing returns. Another reason for variable returns can be attributed to specialisation or division of labour. As the amount of the variable factor labour is increased, it would be possible to assign specific work to each individual rather than assigning all work related to production to him. This type of work organisation helps in increasing productivity initially but later on because of too much labour, the gains of specialisation may be surpassed by diminishing returns. Both these reasons, *i.e.*, indivisibility of fixed factor, and specialisation of labour, together generate conditions—for operation of the law of diminishing returns in the production process.

Suppose we increase the amount of fixed factor, what happens then? The product curves shift from their respective positions. For total product curve the situation may be as reflected by Fig. 5.5.

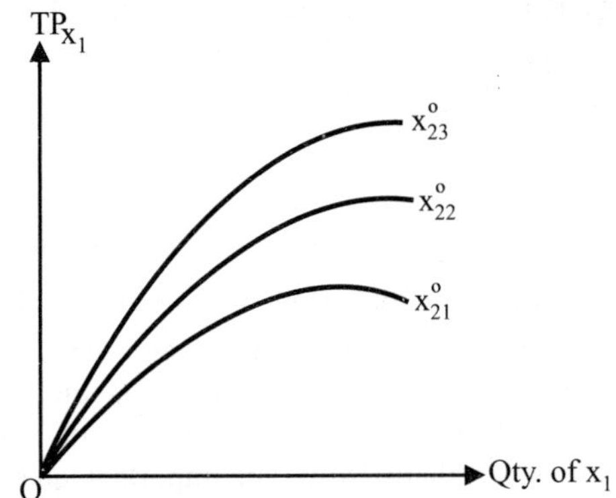

Fig. 5.5 Shift of Total Product Curve

x^0_{21} is the initial level of the fixed factor. When it is increased to x^0_{22} level, the corresponding total product curve for the variable factor (X_1) will be below the old product curve initially, *i.e.*; in Stage 1 of production but later on it will be on the higher side, *i.e.*, above the old curve. This is because, in the early stage the fixed factor is too much as compared to the variable factor which contributes very little output. Now, if the fixed factor is increased further for the same units of the variable factor, the factor proportion will become much worse causing inefficiency and hence lower output. Later on however, because of increased amount of the fixed factor and increasing amount of the variable factor, there may be increase in the efficiency and hence increase in output; partly however, this may be due to increasing returns to scale. This type of shift in the total product curve continues for greater and greater amounts of the fixed factor as shown for x^0_{21} , x^0_{22}, x^0_{23}. The variation in the corresponding marginal and average product curves can be explained in the same way as for the total product curve.

For certain types of production functions which are homogeneous in nature, the pattern of shifts may be different than what we 'have mentioned above. Let us consider an example for this. The production function is given as,

$$Q = 10\,x_1^{1/2} . x_2^{1/2}$$

Let[5] $\quad x_2^0 = 4$, then $Q = 10 \times 2\,x_1^{1/2}$

5. These are to be defined in the next section.

$x_2^0 = 9$, then $Q = 10 \times 3\,x_1^{1/2}$

$x_2^0 = 16$, then $Q = 10 \times 4\,x_1^{1/2}$

For these different levels of fixed factor and varying amounts of the variable factor x_1 > the total, marginal and average schedules of products computed from the above mentioned short-run functions are given as follows:

Table 5.3: Total Product, Marginal Product and Average Product Schedules for X_1 with Varying Fixed Factor

Variable Amount of x_1	$x_2^0 = 4$			$x_2^0 = 9$			$x_2^0 = 16$		
	TP_{x_1}	MP_{x_1}	APx_1	TP_{x_1}	MP_{x_1}	APx_1	TP_{x_1}	MP_{x_1}	APx_1
1	20.0	–	20.0	30.0	–	30.0	40.0	–	40.0
2	28.3	8.3	14.2	42.4	12.4	21.2	56.6	16.6	28.3
3	34.6	6.3	11.5	52.0	9.6	17.3	69.2	12.6	23.0
4	40.0	5.4	10.0	60.0	8.0	15.0	80.0	10.8	20.0
5	44.7	4.7	8.9	67.1	7.1	13.4	89.4	9.4	17.8
6	49.0	4.3	8.2	73.5	6.4	12.3	98.0	8.6	16.3
7	52.9	3.9	7.6	79.4	5.9	11.3	105.8	7.8	15.1
8	56.5	3.7	7.1	84.8	5.4	10.6	113.2	7.4	14.2
9	60.0	3.4	6.7	90.0	5.2	10.0	120.0	6.8	13.3
10	63.2	3.2	6.3	94.9	4.9	9.5	126.4	6.4	12.6

Comparing TP_{x_1}, AP_{x_1} and MP_{x_1} for different levels of the fixed factor X_2^0, we find upward shifts of all the three curves for X_1, *i.e.*, total product, marginal product and average product of the variable factor increase with increase in the fixed factor for homogeneous production functions. This is a general result of the theory of production which will be valid for a production function showing positive and downward sloping marginal products for inputs.

Thus, in conclusion. we can say that product curves for a variable factor in the short-run reflect the variation in output when the variable factor changes, the other factors (*e.g.*, fixed factors) being constant. If the fixed factor(s) increases in quantity, the product curves would move to new positions. For example, if a farmer doubles the land under cultivation and the use of machinery, we would expect both *MP* and *AP* curves of labour to shift to the right. With increased levels of complementary inputs, more labour can be used before the diminishing returns begin to appear.

5.5 LONG-RUN BEHAVIOUR OF PRODUCTION

We now come to the second type of production behaviour in which output and all inputs vary in the same direction. There will be no fixed factor in this situation. The inputs vary together giving us variation in the output. Conventionally, it is defined as long-run behaviour of production. Such behaviour is explained in terms of the laws of returns to scale and related theorems. The laws of returns and the laws of returns to scale are different things. In the case of the laws of returns, we study the behaviour of production when only one input changes others remaining fixed (or the inputs change with different rates) but under the laws of returns to scale, all inputs change in the same direction and we examine the effect of such changes on the level of output.

The law of returns to scale is a basic law of the production theory. This law *says that successive uniform increments in all inputs will eventually lead to less than proportionate increment in output.* This is, in fact, the law of diminishing returns to scale. In the initial stage of inputs variation, we may get more than proportionate increment in output. This is the stage of *increasing returns to scale.* If the proportion of increase in inputs and the proportion of increase in output are the same it is the stage of *constant returns to scale,* and if the proportionate increase in output is less than the proportionate increase in inputs then it is *decreasing returns to scale.* There will be some production functions which reflect all these three types of returns to scale in sequence. Such functions are called non-homogeneous production functions. There will be another category of production functions which reflect either increasing or constant or decreasing returns to scale. These are called homogeneous production functions.

In order to understand the laws of returns to scale, let us take a numerical example: In the following table, we have shown variation in total output for changing scale of utilisation of two inputs X_1 (labour) and X_2 (capital).

Table 5.4: Returns to Scale

Labour x_1	*Capital* x_2	*Total output* q	**Increment in output* q	*Nature of Returns to scale*
1	2	3	4	5
0	0	0	0	0
1	1	4	4	Increasing
2	2	10	6	
3	3	18	8	
4	4	28	10	
5	5	38	10	
6	6	48	10	Constant
7	7	58	10	
8	8	65	7	
9	9	70	05	Decreasing
10	10	74	04	

For simplicity, we have taken 1 unit of X_1 and 1 unit of X_2 as their combination for production. In column (1) this combination is being increased by adding one unit of each input every time. Initially, when input proportion is changing, the output is changing by a greater proportion. This reflects the increasing returns to scale upto the doze 4 : 4 of x_1 and x_2. After this, the output increment is constant at 10 unit level up to the doze 7 : 7 of the inputs. It then declines showing the decreasing returns to scale. Graphically, the incremental output, as inputs are increased proportinoally, can be shown as under:

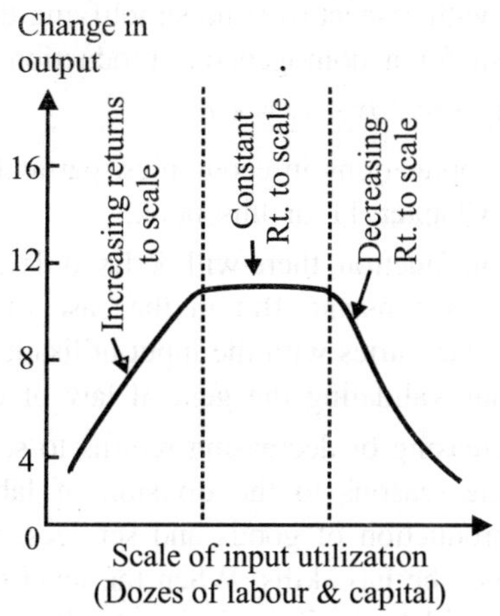

Fig. 5.6 Stages of Returns to Scale

The law of returns to scale can be explained in a better way by using a homogeneous production function. Given the production function $q = f(x_1, x_2)$. This function is said to be homogeneous if the following result holds for it.

$$f(tx_1, tx_2) = t^k f(x_1, x_2) \qquad \text{...(16)}$$

where t shows the identical change in all inputs, k is a constant defined as 'the degree of homogeneity' of the production function. This result shows that if both (or more) inputs are changed to 't'th scale, then output changes by t^k, (t is a positive real number). For increasing returns to scale $k > 1$; for constant returns to scale $k = 1$, and for decreasing returns to scale $k < 1$. Consider a Cobb-Douglas production function: $q = A\ x_1^{\alpha}\ x_2^{\beta}$. Let both the inputs are changed by 10%, so using (16) we have new level of output q^1 as

$$q^1 = A\ (1.10\ x_1)^{\alpha}\ (1.10\ x_2)^{b}$$

or $$q^1 = A\ (1.10\ )^{\alpha + \beta}\ A\ x_1^{\alpha}\ x_2^{\beta}$$

or $$q^1 = A\ (1.10)^{\alpha + \beta}\ q.$$

If $\alpha + \beta > 1$ it is increasing returns to scale, $(\alpha + \beta) = 1$ then constant returns to scale, and $(\alpha + \beta) < 1$ then decreasing returns to scale. Here $k = \alpha + \beta$.

Consider another function: $q = f(x_1, x_2) = 5x_1 + 3x_2$. By using the above result (*i.e.*, 16) to a homogeneous production function we have:

$$q^1 = 5\,(t\,x_1) + 3\,(t\,x_2)$$

or $$q^1 = t\,(5\,x_1 + 3\,x_2)$$

or $$q^1 = t\,q.$$

This function is homogeneous of degree 1 showing the constant returns to scale.

Differentiating (16) partially with respect to t and simplifying the resulting expression by putting $t = 1$ we get the Euler's theorem for a homogeneous production function of degree k as:

$$\partial q/\partial x_1 \,.\, x_1 + \partial q/\partial x_2 \,.\, x_2 = k\,q \qquad ...(17)$$

This theorem has important applications in economics, particularly in the theory of distribution which we will study later on in Chapter 11 of this book.

For a homogeneous production function, there will be fixed degree of returns to scale; increasing, or constant or decreasing, *i.e.*, k is constant. But in the case of a non-homogeneous production function the degree of returns to scale varies with the input utilisation—first increasing, then constant and eventually decreasing and thus validating the general law of decreasing returns to scale.

What are the reasons for increasing or decreasing returns to scale in the process of production? Economists normally attribute the reasons to the division of labour or specialisation and other technological factors related to production of goods and services. Specialisation means assigning a particular job to a worker for which he has skills. When the level of production is very small, there cannot be any scope for division of labour. One man or machine has to do several jobs and there may be a considerable amount of loss of efficiency in such a situation. When the scale of production goes up, the scope for division of labour increases which brings economies of scale. There are three basic advantages from division of labour: (*a*) increase in skills of workers; (*b*) saving of time and tools in switching over from one job to another; and (*c*) increase in innovation, *i.e.*, technological progress. Because of such advantages, we find increasing returns to scale from increasing specialisation in production.

The other factor, *i.e.*, technological dimensions of production also contribute to increasing returns to scale. Larger machines may be employed when scale of production increases. Such machines normally bring economies of big machines. Apart from this, economies of linked processes, better utilisation of by-products, etc., provide considerable scope for increasing returns to scale. One might argue for indivisibility of fixed factor as a factor for low return initially. This is true. But it is relevant for short-run analysis of production. When we talk of returns to scale, there is no fixed factor. If all factors are utilised fully, we can argue for the above mentioned reasons for increasing returns to scale otherwise existence of indivisibility may neutralise gains from division of labour.

The stage of increasing returns to scale would not be continuing for a long time as we increase the dozes of inputs further and further. The size of production will be unmanageable and so inefficiency creeps in causing decreasing returns to scale. Moreover, it may be difficult to get certain critical inputs in the same proportion as others. This will create conditions for operation of the law of variable proportion which reinforce the operation of the law of decreasing returns to scale. The stage when decreasing returns to scale begins is very much significant from the point of view of production. Entrepreneurs would be avoiding this. They must know what is causing the decreasing returns to scale. We will return to this issue again while going through the long-run cost of production theory in Chapter 6.

In this context, there are some important terms which we would like to summarise now.

(i) Output Elasticity of an Input

This is a ratio of proportionate change in output to the proportionate change in the amount of an input. That is, given $q = f\ (z_1, x_2)$, the output elasticity for X_1 and X_2 would be as:

$$\varepsilon_{x_1} = \frac{dq}{dx_1} \times \frac{x_1}{q} = \frac{MP_{x_1}}{AP_{x_1}}\ ;\ \varepsilon_{x_2} = \frac{dq}{dx_2} \cdot \frac{x_2}{q} = \frac{MP_{x_2}}{AP_{x_2}}$$

For ith input we have,

$$\varepsilon_{x_i} = \frac{dq}{dx_i} \times \frac{x_i}{q} = \frac{MP_{x_i}}{AP_{x_i}},\ i = 1;\ n. \qquad ...(18)$$

(ii) Function Coefficient

The sum of output elasticities of different inputs, *i.e.*, factors of production is called 'function coefficient' (E), *i.e.*,

$$E = \varepsilon_{x_1} + \varepsilon_{x_2} + ... + \varepsilon_{x_n} \qquad ...(19)$$

For increasing returns to scale 'function coefficient' would be greater than one, and for decreasing returns to scale, it would be less than one. For constant returns to scale $E = 1$. 'Function coefficient' is nothing but the degree of homogeneity of the production function.

5.6 ISO-QUANT ANALYSIS OF PRODUCTION

This is the third important situation of production theory. The basic assumptions for this type of production behaviour are: (*a*) level of output remains constant, and (*b*) the inputs used in its production vary in opposite direction. In other words, the inputs can be substituted for each other. For simplicity, we take one output and two inputs for the iso-quant analysis in the familiar production function framework $q = f\ (x_1, x_2)$.

An iso-quant is the firm's counterpart of the consumer's indifference curve. It is the locus of all possible combinations of the inputs which yield a specific' level of output. 'Iso'—means equal and 'quant' means quantity; so, an iso-quant specifies a constant quantity of output.

The relationship between output (q) and two inputs (x_1 and x_2) can be shown through a three dimensional figure as shown in Part (*a*) of the following diagram. From this part of the diagram we draw cross-sections for different levels of output which, when represented in a two dimensional graph with x_1 and x_2 as axes, we get the iso-quants as shown in Part (*b*). Iso-quants are contour-lines. They are convex towards the origin. An isoquant near the origin shows smaller output and the one which is farther away from the origin shows higher level of output. The entire set of iso-quants together is called 'iso-quant map'. We have shown the convex iso-quants but they may be straight-lines or right-angled-shapes which we will discuss very shortly. Before this, let us define the rate at which one input will be substituted for the other since this is a crucial aspect of the isoquant theory of production.

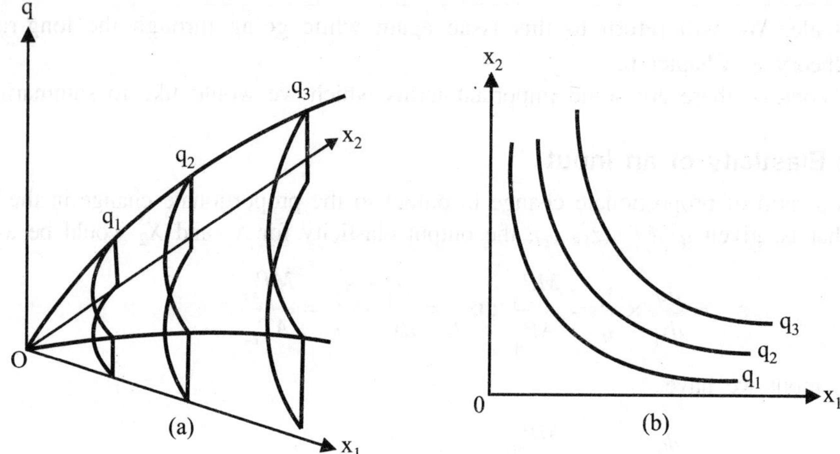

Fig. 5.7 Iso-quant Picture

(i) Marginal Rate of Technical Substitution

Consider Figure 5.8. Let us take point *A* on the iso-quant which defines the combination of x_1 and x_2 used in production of $q°$. Suppose a new situation develops and the producer shifts to the

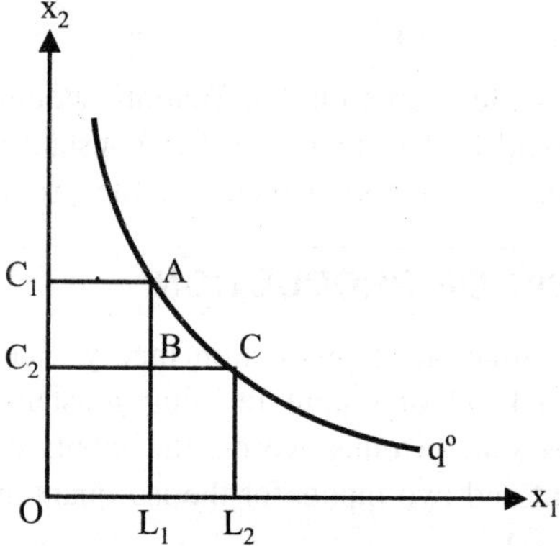

Fig. 5.8 The M.R.T.S. Derived from an Iso-quant

combination of x_1 and x_2 as defined by point *C* on the iso-quant for production of $q°$. What is the rate of substitution between the two inputs? Clearly, we see that quantity, of x_2 has decreased from OC_1 to OC_2 and quantity of x_1 has increased from OL_1 to OL_2. The rate at which x_2 has been substituted by x_1 would be the ratio of change in quantities of these inputs. That is,

$$RTS = \frac{OC_2 - OC_1}{OL_2 - OL_1} = -\frac{AB}{BC}.$$

It is negative since we have drawn the iso-quant as a downward sloping curve. In fact, we have to prove that it will be definitely negative. The ratio $-AB/BC$ shows the slope of the iso-quant between the segment *AC*. If we take a point on the iso-quant and find its slope at that point it would give us the rate of substitution for the inputs. That is,

$$RTS = -dx_2/dx_1 \qquad ...(20)$$

Since the rate of technical substitution for the inputs is computed at the margin, it is normally known as *'marginal rate of technical substitution'* or *MRTS* in short.

The marginal rate of technical substitution (or RTS) of x_1 for x_2 is the amount by which x_2 can be reduced per unit increase of x_1 for maintaining a constant level of output ($q°$).

How to find *MRTS?* For this, we have to derive an expression linking the *RTS* with the ratio of the marginal products of the concerned inputs. Let the production function be as:

$$q = f\ (x_1,\ x_2)$$

The total derivatives for this function would be

$$dq = (\partial q / \partial x_1)\ dx_1\ + (\partial q / \partial x_2) dx_2$$

when we move along an iso-quant there will be no change in the output since by definition of the iso-quant itself $dq = 0$. Therefore, we have:

$$0 = (\partial q / \partial x_1)\ dx_1\ + (\partial q / \partial x_2) dx_2$$

From this we get:

$$MRTS = \frac{-dx_2}{dx_1} = \frac{\partial q / \partial x_1}{\partial q / \partial x_2} = \frac{f_1}{f_2} \quad ...(21)$$

For simplicity we write $\partial q / \partial x_1 = f_1$, $\partial q / \partial x_2 = f_2$. If $f_1 = 0$, then $MRTS = 0$. This means the input x_1 will not be substituted for x_2, and if $f_2 = 0$, then $MRTS = \infty$ (infinite), *i.e.*, one additional unit of x_1 is substituted for unlimited amount of x_2. Thus, the limits or extreme points between which the inputs are substitutable are defined as

$$0 \leq \text{MRTS}\left(\frac{-dx_2}{dx_1} = \frac{f_1}{f_2}\right) \leq \infty \quad ...(22)$$

In the following Figure *OA* and *OB* are the lines joining all those points at which or beyond which the rate of technical substitution between the factors is infinite and zero respectively for different iso-quants. The segments of the iso-quants bounded by these lines are relevant to us for the study of the theory of production. These segments correspond to the Stage 2 of production which we have shown in Fig. 5.3 where marginal products of both the factors are positive and which defines the zone of production. The lines *OA* and *OB* are called 'Ridge Lines'. Along *OA* we have infinite *MRTS* and along *OB* we have zero *MRTS*. Between these ridge lines one may draw several other lines originating from the starting point and showing constant rate of technical substitution. These are called 'Isoclines'. In fact, the ridge-lines are also 'isoclines'.

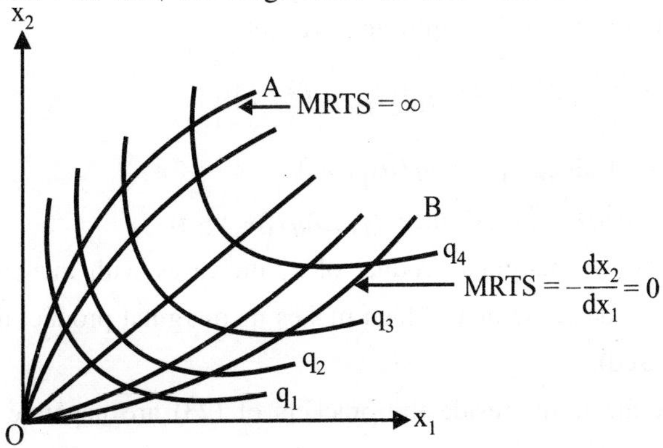

Fig. 5.9 Ridge Lines and Isoclines

(ii) Properties of Iso-quant

(*a*) Iso-quants are downward sloping curves, convex towards the origin showing decreasing rate of technical substitution as one factor is substituted for the other.

We have $MRTS = \frac{-dx_2}{dx_1} = \frac{MP_{x_1}}{MP_{x_2}} = \frac{f_1}{f_2}$. The ratio f_1/f_2 is positive since $f_1 > 0$, $f_2 > 0$. Therefore, $-dx_2/dx_1$ must be positive. It ımplies that to make $-dx_2/dx_1$ positive there must be one more negative sign attahced to it. This is possible when the iso-quant is sloping downward. We confine ourselves to the segment of an iso-quant bounded by the ridge line, *i.e.*, in the economic zone of production. If either of f_1 or f_2 is negative the iso-quant will be sloping upward and this violates the law of diminishing returns. So long f_1 and f_2 are positive and declining with increase in the relevant input (x_1 and x_2) the iso-quants will be sloping downward. This can be shown using the above expression for the *MRTS*. As x_1 increases f_1 decreases, and an increase in x_1 implies a decrease in x_2 and with a decrease in x_2 its marginal product (f_2) increases. So, when we move in the direction of x_1, *i.e.*, substitute x_1 for x_2, the marginal product of x_1 decreases and the marginal product of x_2 increases. The ratio f_1/f_2, therefore, decreases. This is the economic interpretation of the decreasing rate of technical substitution. We can derive the same conclusion by proving the convexity property for the iso-quant.

Let $$\frac{-dx_2}{dx_1} = \frac{\partial q/\partial x_1}{\partial q/\partial x_2}$$

or $$\frac{dx_2}{dx_1} = -\frac{\partial q/\partial x_1}{\partial q/\partial x_2} \qquad ...(i)$$

By taking the second order partial derives of this we have,

$$\frac{d^2x_2}{dx_1^2} = \frac{d\dfrac{-\partial q/\partial x_1}{\partial q/\partial x_2}}{dx_1}$$

or $$\frac{d^2x_2}{dx_1^2} = \frac{-\left[\frac{\partial q}{\partial x_2}\left(\frac{\partial^2 q}{\partial x_1^2} + \frac{\partial^2 q}{\partial x_1 \partial x_2}\cdot\frac{dx_2}{dx_1}\right) - \frac{\partial q}{\partial x_1}\left(\frac{\partial^2 q}{\partial x_2 \partial x_1} + \frac{\partial^2 q}{\partial x_2^2}\cdot\frac{dx_2}{dx_1}\right)\right]}{(dq/dx_2)^2}$$

Substituting (*i*) for dx_2/dx_1 and simplifying we get,

$$\frac{d^2x_2}{dx_1} = \frac{-1}{f_2^3}[f_2^2\, f_{11} - 2f_1 f_2 f_{12} + f_1^2 f_{22}] \qquad ...(23)$$

where $f_{11}\ (= \partial^2 q/\partial x_1^2) < 0$ since $f_1\ (= \partial q/\partial x_1) > 0$.

$$f_{22}(= \partial^2 q/dx_2^2) < 0 \text{ since } f_2(= \partial q/\partial x_2) > 0$$

$f_{12} = f_{21} \geq 0$, this shows marginal product of x_1 increases with increase in x_2 and vice versa. (An increase in x_1 means a decrease in x_2 which makes its marginal product to rise and similar results holds when x_2 is increased).

Thus, we find that the terms inside the brackets of (23) are negative and there is a negative sign before it. Therefore, $\frac{d^2x_2}{dx_1^2} > 0$, that is, the rate of change of *MRTS* is + ve. This shows that the iso-quant is convex towards the origin. Positive rate of change of *MRTS* implies that the *MRTS* showing substitution of x_2 by x_1, *declines with increase in* x_1 and vice-versa.

(*b*) The curvature of an iso-quant reflects the ease with which one factor can be substituted for the other while moving along the iso-quant. The ease of substitution between the factors of production is measured through the elasticity of substitution.[6] When we move along an isoquant, the factor proportion, say x_2/x_1 (which are normally capital and labout inputs) changes and, at the same time, *RTS* also changes. A formal definition of the elasticity of substitution given by Mrs. John Robinson is as follows.[7]

The elasticity of substitution (σ) is a measure of the responsiveness of a change in the factor proportion (x_2/x_1) as a result of a change in the rate of technical substitution (R). Symbolically, we express this as:

$$\sigma = \frac{d(x_2/x_1)}{x_2/x_1} \div \frac{d(R)}{R}, \text{ where } R = RTS \qquad ...(24)$$

Since $\quad R = RTS = -\dfrac{dx_2}{dx_1} = f_1/f_2$, therefore, we can also write,

$$\sigma = \frac{d(x_2/x_1)}{x_2/x_1} \div \frac{d\,(f_1/f_2)}{f_1/f_2} \qquad ..(25)$$

Also, as we will find later on,

$f_1/f_2 = r_1/r_2$ where r_1 = Price of X_1,

r_2 = Price of X_2. Therefore,

$$\sigma = \frac{d(x_2/x_1)}{x_2/x_1} \div \frac{d\,(r_1/r_2)}{r_1/r_2} \qquad ...(26)$$

Now, let us derive the precise expression to compute the elasticity of substitution (σ) and to show its relevance for the slope of the iso-quant.

For simplification, we write R for *MRTS*, or as,

$$R = -\frac{dx_2}{dx_1} = \frac{f_1}{f_2}; \text{and let } y = x_2/x_1$$

Therefore, $\quad \sigma = \dfrac{dy}{y} \div \dfrac{dR}{R} \qquad ...(27)$

The variation in y and R indicate the movement along the iso-quant showing constant level of output. We have defined $y = x_2/x_1$. From this we have,

$$dy = \frac{x_1 dx_2 - x_2 dx_1}{x_1^2} \qquad ...(28)$$

6. Originally this concept was given by J. R. Hicks in his *Theory of Wages,* Macmillan (1932), pp. 117, 245.

7. J. Robinson, *The Economics of Imperfect Competition,* Macmillan 1933, pp. 256, 330.

By using the Euler's theorem we can write,

$$dR = \frac{\partial R}{\partial x_1} dx_1 + \frac{\partial R}{\partial x_2} dx_2 \qquad ...(29)$$

Also we have,

$$dx_2 = \frac{-f_1}{f_2} dx_1 = -R\ dx_1 \text{ (Since } R = \frac{f_1}{f_2}) \qquad ...(30)$$

By substituting (30) in (28) we have,

$$dy = \frac{x_1(-Rdx_1) - x_2 dx_1}{x_1^2}$$

or

$$dy = \frac{-(Rx_1 + x_2)\ dx_1}{x_1^2} \qquad ...(31)$$

Similarly, substituting (30) in (29) we have,

$$dR = \frac{\partial R}{\partial x_1} dx_1 + \frac{\partial R}{\partial x_2}(-\ Rdx_1)$$

or

$$dR = -\left(R\frac{\partial R}{\partial x_2} - \frac{\partial R}{\partial x_1}\right) dx_1 \qquad ...(32)$$

Now, we have

$$\frac{\partial R}{\partial x_1} = \frac{\partial(f_1/f_2)}{\partial x_1} = (f_2 f_{11} - f_1 f_{12})/f_2^2 \qquad ...(33)$$

$$\frac{\partial R}{\partial x_2} = \frac{\partial(f_1/f_2)}{\partial x_2} = (f_2 f_{12} - f_1 f_{22})/f_2^2 \qquad ...(34)$$

Now, substituting (31) to (34) in (27), and simplifying we have,

$$\sigma = \frac{-f_1 f_2\ (x_1 f_1 + f_2 x_2)}{x_1 x_2\ (f_{11} f_2^2 - 2 f_1 f_2 f_{12} + f_{22} f_1^2)} \qquad ...(35)$$

σ will be + ve since bracketed term in the denominator is – ve. It is a number independent of dimensions of measurement of the inputs and output.

By putting the values for dy and dR obtained from (31) and (32) in (27) we can express σ as:

$$\sigma = \frac{R}{x_1 x_2} \frac{x_1 R + x_2}{R\left(\frac{\partial R}{\partial x_2}\right) - \frac{\partial R}{\partial x_1}} \qquad ..(36)$$

Since $R = -\ dx_2/dx_1$, therefore, the rate of change of slope of the isoquant

$$= \frac{d^2 x_2}{dx_1^2} = \frac{-dR}{dx_1} = R\frac{\partial R}{\partial x_2} - \frac{\partial R}{\partial x_1} \text{ from (32)} \qquad ...(37)$$

Substituting (37) in (36) we have

$$\sigma = \frac{R}{x_1 x_2}, \frac{x_1 R + x_2}{(d^2 x_2/dx_1^2)} \qquad ...(38)$$

This shows that the elasticity of substitutes σ is inversely related to the rate of change of the slope of the iso-quant $(d^2 x_2/dx_1^2)$. We know from the convexity property of the iso-quant that $d^2 x_2/dx_1^2 > 0$, this implies $\sigma > 0$, since R, x_1, and x_2 are all positive.

Also, as reflected by (35), the elasticity of substitution is symmetric, *i.e.*, the elasticity of substitution of x_1 for x_2 is same as the elasticity of substitution of x_2 for x_1.

A simpler expression for the elasticity of substitution, which can be derived from the above relation, is:

$$\sigma = \frac{f_1 f_2}{q f_{12}} \quad \text{where } q = f(x_1, x_2) \qquad \text{...(39)}$$

This is applicable to the homogeneous production functions.

If the factors of production are perfect substitutes then R (*i.e.*, *MRTS*) is constant and therefore $\frac{dR}{dx_1} = \frac{d^2x_2}{dx_1^2} = 0$. This means that the elasticity of substitution would be infinite, *i.e.*, $\sigma = \frac{R}{x_1, x_2} \cdot \frac{x_1 R + x_2}{0} = \infty$ by using (38).

On the other hand, if one input (x_1) cannot be substituted for the other (x_2), that is, they are used in fixed proportion then $d^2x_2/dx_1^2 = \infty$ and therefore (38) gives us $\sigma = 0$

These two extremes shapes are shown in Fig. 5.10.

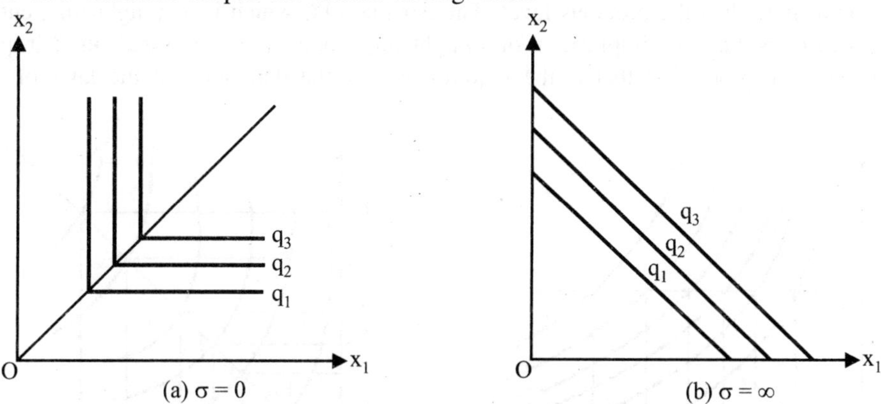

Fig. 5.10 Extreme Shapes of Iso-quant

Between these two extremes, we find the normal isoquants. We have already seen above that the elasticity of substitution varies inversely with curvature of the iso-quant. Greater the curvature lesser will be the elasticity of substitution and vice-versa.

For two inputs case, *i.e.*, capital and labour we can find the elasticity of substitution as described above. If there are more than two inputs in the production function, the interpretation of the elasticity of substitution becomes quite complex and unclear. Allen has given the concept of 'partial elasticity of substitution' to analyse such a situation but that also lacks generalisation and economic interpretation.[8]

There is practical usefulness of the elasticity of substitution particularly in examining employment potential in an industry. If σ is high, one can think of creating more jobs without capital, *i.e.*, physical equipment, but if σ is low one can create jobs only by increasing capital stock. This may be difficult for poor countries.

8. R. G. D. Allen, *Mathematical Analysis for Economists,* Macmillan, 1938, pp. 503–505.

(*c*) Two isoquants cannot intersect each other. If they intersect, the very foundation of the isoquant theory will become invalid. We can apply here same logic as we have used in the case of indifference curves. (Ref. Ch. 4).

(*d*) The space between successive isoquants showing unit increase in output reflects the strength of the diminishing returns as well as returns to scale. The following diagram (Fig. 5.11 (*a*) makes this point clear.

Keeping x_2 at a constant level $\bar{x}_2$ say x_2, we find less and less amount of x_1 to produce one more additional unit of output (q being increased by one unit each time) but eventually more and more amount of x_1 is needed for this. This means increasing returns initially upto D level of x_1 (or q_4 level of output) and then diminishing returns. Less of x_1 per unit output means increasing marginal product for x_1 and more of x_1 per unit output means decreasing marginal product for x_1. From the diagram (Part a) we conclude that $CD < BC < AB$: this reflects increasing returns and $FE > DE$ which shows decreasing returns.

We will obtain similar results if we keep x_1 at constant level and vary x_2 to produce more and more units of output.

To show the operation of the laws of returns to scale we have to draw an isocline which intersects the iso-quants. In Fig 5.11 (*b*), we have shown iso-quants q_1 to q_6, each one representing one unit output more than the previous level. The isocline OX, which is a straight line, cuts the iso-quants at E_1 to E_6 points. The implication of straight line isoquants is that inputs used in production change in the same proportion that is the requirement for the derivation of the laws of returns to scale.

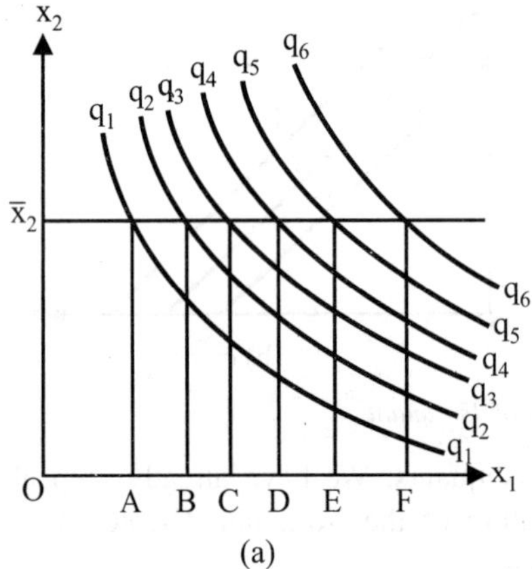

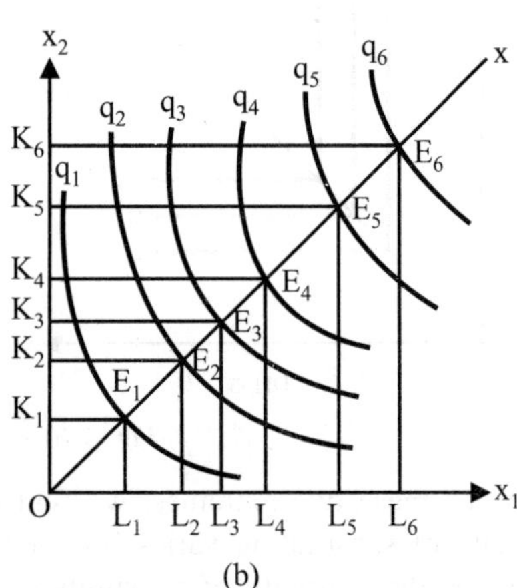

Fig. 5.11 Derivation of the Laws of Returns and Returns to Scale from Iso-quants

As we move from q_1 to q_2 iso-quant (*i.e.*, one unit increment in output) the inputs required for this change from $(L_1\ K_1)$ to (L_2, K_2), and similarly, from (L_2, K_2) to (L_3, K_3) when we move from q_2 to q_3 iso-quant. From the Figure 5 .11 (*b*) we find that

$$L_1\ L_2 > L_2\ L_3 > L_3\ L_4 \text{ and } K_1\ K_2 > K_2\ K_3 > K_3\ K_4$$

This means, as we increase output further and further by unit level, the inputs (x_1, x_2) are required in lesser and lesser quantities, but in constant proportion for this. This means increasing returns to scale. From (L_4, K_4) or q_4 level of output we have opposite pattern, that is, $L_4\ L_5 < L_5\ L_6$ and $K_4\ K_5 < K_5\ K_6$. This means decreasing returns to scale. If all successive iso-quants are uniformally spaced, we will get constant returns to scale by varying the inputs in equiproportion.

(iii) Producer's Equilibrium on Isoquants: The Optimal Choice of Inputs

We have identified the economic zone of isoquants, *i.e.*, the area bounded by the ridge-lines from which a producer chooses the isoquant and the actual combination of the inputs to be used for the concerned output. We cannot take such decision without additional information about total outlay, the producer is capable of making and the input prices. Let us assume that the producer has C^o units of money for expenditure on inputs. We consider C^o as fixed. Let the input prices be given as r_1 and r_2 for X_1 and X_2 inputs respectively. These input prices are also fixed. With this information, we can define a boundary for utilisation of inputs which we call as 'iso-cost line.' This is given as:

$$C^\circ = r_1x_1 + r_2x_2 \qquad ...(40)$$

where x_1 and x_2 are quantities of two inputs X_1 and X_2. The iso-cost line is, in fact, producer's budget equation or resource line. *It is a locus of all combinations of two (or more) inputs which the producer can buy using his fixed outlay (C°) at fixed input prices.* The line reflects constant cost of production (C°); that is why it is called 'iso-cost line'. We see that this is downward sloping line.

The slope of this line will be equal to $-\frac{r_1}{r_2}$ *i.e.*, minus of the input price ratio.

$$x_2 = \frac{C^\circ}{r_2} - \frac{r_1}{r_2}x_1 \qquad ...(41)$$

Graphically, the line can be shown as follows:

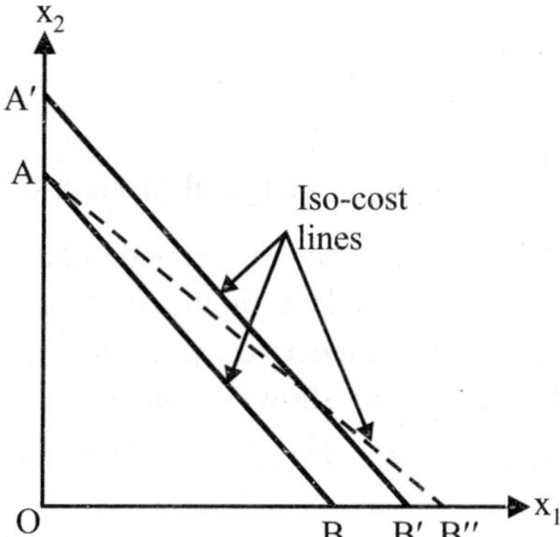

Fig. 5.12 Iso-cost Line

A producer cannot cross the iso-cost line because of fixed outlay (C°). If outlay (C°) increases, input price being constant, the iso-cost line shifts parallelly upward as shown by the line *A′B′*. If price of one input decreases, other things being equal, the iso-cost line expands horizontal intercept on the quantity axis of the inputs whose price had decreased. This implies greater quantity of the concerned input that the producer will be able to buy if he spends the entire outlay (C°) on that. The slope of the budget line will also change. *A B*" is one such changed iso-cost line when r_1 decreases, other things being constant.

If the input prices are variable, the iso-cost line would not be a straight line. With increasing input prices, it would be a concave curve towards the origin.[9] For the basic exposition of the production theory, however, we take input prices as fixed throughout in this analysis.

9. See C. E. Ferguson; the Neoclassical Theory of Production and Distribution, Cambridge University Press, 1968, pp. 171-172.

Given the iso-cost line, a producer would be able to select the optimum (or best) combination of inputs. For this, we have two approaches—one is constrained output maximisation and the other is constrained cost minimisation. Both the approaches produce the same equilibrium state for the producer and, therefore, they are dual of each other. Let us consider them one by one.

(a) Constrained Output Maximisation

In this, we assume output maximisation subject to the budget constraint as goal of the producer. The optimisation problem is defined as:

Max. $q = f(x_1, x_2)$

Subject to $C^\circ = r_1x_1 + r_2x_2$

This problem can be analysed further using the Lagrange Multiplier method. Combining these two expressions together the Lagrange function be defined as:

$$V = f(x_1, x_2) + \mu\, [C^\circ - r_1x_1 - r_2x_2]$$

where μ is the Lagrange multiplier.

Taking the partial derivatives of V for x_1 and x_2 and μ, the first order maximum conditions are:

$$\frac{\partial V}{\partial x_1} = f_1 - \mu\, r_1 = 0$$
$$\frac{\partial V}{\partial x_2} = f_2 - \mu\, r_2 = 0 \qquad ...(42)$$
$$\frac{\partial V}{\partial \mu} = C^\circ - r_1x_1 - r_2x_2 = 0$$

where $f_1 = \dfrac{\partial f(.)}{\partial x_1}$ and $f_2 = \dfrac{\partial f(.)}{\partial x_2}$, defined as marginal product of the input x_1 and x_2 respectively.

The equations-set (42) would be valid provided the second order conditions for output maximisation are satisfied. Such conditions are normally taken in the form of boarder Hessian determinant of second order partial derivatives of V with respect to x_1, x_2 and μ whose value should be positive, *i.e.*, what the second order conditions has to show is that the rate of change of the slope of the tangent to an isoquant must be positive, *i.e.*, $d^2x_2 / dx_1^2 > 0$ at the point of tangency with the iso-cost line.

In expanded form, we write the second order condition as:

$$\begin{vmatrix} f_{11} & f_{12} & -r_1 \\ f_{21} & f_{22} & -r_2 \\ -r_1 & -r_2 & 0 \end{vmatrix} > 0.$$

From the first two equations of (42) we have

$$\frac{f_1}{r_1} = \frac{f_2}{r_2} = \mu \qquad ...(43)$$

'μ' is a constant defined as '*marginal contribution of expenditure* (dq/dc°) *or marginal product of money*. Equation (43) gives us the equilibrium condition for the producer. According to this, *the contribution to output of the last unit of money spent upon each input must be equal and identical to the marginal contribution of money* (μ).

From (43), we get the expression,

$$\frac{f_1}{f_2} = \frac{r_1}{r_2} \qquad \text{...(44)}$$

We know $\frac{-dx_2}{dx_1} = MRTS = \frac{f_1}{f_2}$ (*i.e.*, ratio of MP_{x_1} to MP_{x_2})

Therefore, we have

$$MRTS = \frac{-dx_2}{dx_1} = \frac{f_1}{f_2} = \frac{r_1}{r_2} \qquad \text{...(45)}$$

f_1/f_2 is the slope of the iso-quant, and r_1/r_2 is the slope of the iso-cost line. At the equilibrium situation we have the slope of the iso-quant equal to the slope of the iso-cost line. In other words, the iso-cost line is tangent to the iso-quant. The second order condition for such tangency situation is that d^2x_2/dx_1^2, *i.e.*, the rate of change of the slope of the iso-quant is positive as we have mentioned above. The convexity property of the iso-quant automatically satisfies this. The maximisation problem of the producer is thus 'solved'. With a given outlay ($C°$) and input prices (r_1, r_2), the producer chooses that particular isoquant (*i.e.*, produces the level of output given by the iso-quant) which is touched by the iso-cost line. Once we find such equilibrium position on the iso-quant, corresponding levels of x_1 and x_2 inputs will be optimal or least cost combination.

Let us consider the geometry of the producer's equilibrium.

AB is the iso-cost line touching the isoquant q_3 at *E* point and thus giving us the equilibrium position. We have to give economic reasons for *E* being the equilibrium point. By definition, *AB* line sets the upper boundary for purchase of inputs when outlay ($C°$) and input prices are fixed. The

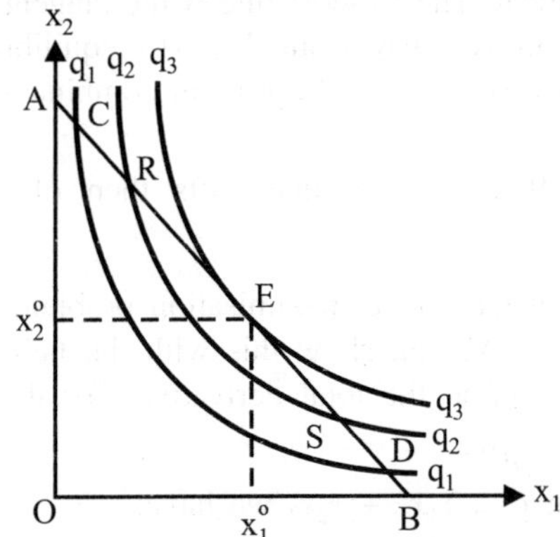

Fig. 5.13 Producer's Equilibrium on Iso-quant

segments of iso-quants lying above this line would not be considered for examining the equilibrium position of the producer since the combinations of inputs cannot be purchased at all. Outlay is not sufficient for that. Similarly, the segments of iso-quants falling below the iso-cost line would not be considered since in that case the producer would not be utilising his outlay fully. Rationality, on the part of the producer requires full utilisation of resources for optimisation of output. This leaves us the possibility of having producer's equilibrium on the iso-cost line itself where either the isoquants intersect it such as points *C, R, S, D* or where the line touches a particular iso-quant such as *E*. Let us consider point *C* where iso-quant q_1 intersects the iso-cost line from above. At this point, the slope of the isoquant is greater than the slope of the iso-cost line. That is:

$$\frac{f_1}{f_2} > \frac{r_1}{r_2}$$

This means $\frac{f_1}{r_1} > \frac{f_2}{r_2}$, *i.e.*, the marginal product per unit of expenditure on x_1 is more than the marginal product per unit expenditure on x_2. In other words, x_1 is more productive than x_2. Since the objective of the producer is to maximise output, he would, therefore, increase the amount of x_1 and reduce the amount of x_2 in production. For this the producer would be moving along the iso-cost line downwards since if he moves down along the isoquant q_1 he would not be utilising his outlay fully. So, the only choice for him is to shift down along the isocost line which means on higher iso-quant, such as q_2. Suppose he moves to position *R*. Here also the isoquailt q_2 is cutting the iso-cost line from above which means $\frac{f_1}{r_1} > \frac{f_2}{r_2}$. So, producer would be again in disequilibrium. He will continue to move downward along the iso-cost line, *i.e.*, increase x_1 and decrease x_2 till he reaches point *E*.

Now, consider the downside (*i.e.*, below *E*) of the isocost line. At point *D* iso-quant q_1 intersects the iso-cost line from below. This point shows the slope of iso-cost line greater than the slope of the iso-quant, *i.e.*, $\frac{r_1}{r_2} > \frac{f_1}{f_2}$. This means $\frac{f_2}{r_2} > \frac{f_1}{r_1}$. In this situation, x_2 is more productive than x_1. The producer increases x_2 and decreases x_1, *i.e.*, he moves up along the iso-cost line. His upward movement will continue so long as the slope of the iso-cost line is greater than the slope of the isoquant. He will finally stop at point *E*. At this point, the slopes of both the curves, *i.e.*, iso-quant (q_3) and the isocost line are identical. The iso-cost line is the tangent to the iso-quant (q_3) and there is no scope for the producer to move away from this. His equilibrium position has reached, *i.e.*, optimum output as reflected by q_3 iso-quant and optimum combination of inputs given by the point *E i.e.*, (x_1^o, x_2^o) and $\frac{f_1}{r_1} = \frac{f_2}{r_2} = \mu$. If the iso-cost line shifts, then, of course, the equilibrium position will be changed accordingly.

The Lagrange multiplier μ in the above maximisation problem has been defined as 'marginal product of money or expenditure'. We can show this with the help of the following derivation.

Given $q_1 = f(x_1, x_2)$, we can find the total derivatives for this as

$$dq = f_1 dx_1 + f_2 dx_2 \qquad ...(i)$$

Also from the cost equation $C = r_1x_1 + r_2x_2$ we have:

$$dC = r_1 dx_1 + r_2 dx_2 \qquad ...(ii)$$

Then optimum conditions for output maximisation, as derived above, [see (43)] are:

$$\frac{f_1}{r_1} = \mu; \frac{f_2}{r_2} = \mu; \qquad ...(iii)$$

Substituting the values for r_1 and r_2 from (*iii*) in (*i*) and dividing dq by dC we have

$$\frac{dq}{dC} = \mu\left[\frac{f_1 dx_1 + f_2 dx_2}{f_1 dx_1 + f_2 dx_2}\right]$$

or

$$\frac{dq}{dC} = \mu \qquad ...(46)$$

Thus, we have shown that μ is the marginal product or marginal physical contribution of money or expenditure.

(b) Constrained Cost Minimisation

This is the dual problem of output maximisation. In this, we find the conditions for minimum cost of production for a given level of output. We define our problem as

Minimise $C = r_1x_1 + r_2x_2$

Subject to $q° = f(x_1, x_2)$

Using the Lagrange Multiplier method, we write the new function for minimisation as:

$$Z = r_1x_1 + r_2x_2 + \lambda\,[q° - f(x_1, x_2)]$$

Taking partial derivatives of Z with respect to x_1, x_2 and λ, we have the first order conditions for minimisation of C as:

$$\frac{\partial Z}{\partial x_1} = r_1 - \lambda f_1 = 0$$

$$\frac{\partial Z}{\partial x_2} = r_2 - \lambda f_2 = 0 \qquad ...(47)$$

$$\frac{\partial Z}{\partial \lambda} = q° - f(x_1, x_2) = 0$$

The second order conditions for this would be the same as that for the constrained output maximisation. That is

$$\begin{vmatrix} f_{11} & f_{12} & -r_1 \\ f_{21} & f_{22} & -r_2 \\ -r_1 & -r_2 & 0 \end{vmatrix} > 0$$

which implies that $d^2x_2/dx_1^2 > 0$, *i.e.*, the rate of change of slope of the iso-quant at the point of tangency is positive. The convexity property of the isoquant ensures this.

From (47) we have

$$\lambda f_1 = r_1 \; \lambda f_2 = r_2$$

or
$$\frac{f_1}{r_1} = \frac{f_2}{r_2} = \frac{1}{\lambda} \qquad ...(48)$$

This is the same condition as expressed by (43) except that in place of μ we have now $\frac{1}{\lambda}$, λ is defined as 'marginal cost of output', *i.e.*, increment in total cost of production (C) in real terms to produce one more extra unit of output $\left(i.e., \frac{dC}{dq}\right)$. It is inverse of μ. Therefore, $\frac{1}{\lambda}$ is nothing but dq/dC. Expression (48) shows the same tangency condition as (43). Here what we do is to select that cost equation which minimises total cost of production of a given level of output q^o. Consider Figure 5.14.

Let us consider $A'B'$ and AB as two iso-cost lines showing two possible levels of costs to produce q^o output. The combinations of x_1 and x_2 required to produce $q°$ output must lie on the isoquant of $q°$ as well as on the isocost line. This rules out the section of the isoquant above R and beyond T and along the segment RT of the iso-cost line $A'B'$. At point R and T the slopes of the isoquant and iso-cost line are different. They are not the equilibrium points. Commonsense shows that the combinations of x_1 and x_2 shown by R and T points are costly as compared to the combinations shown by the arc RT of the isoquant below the line RT. It is possible to produce q°

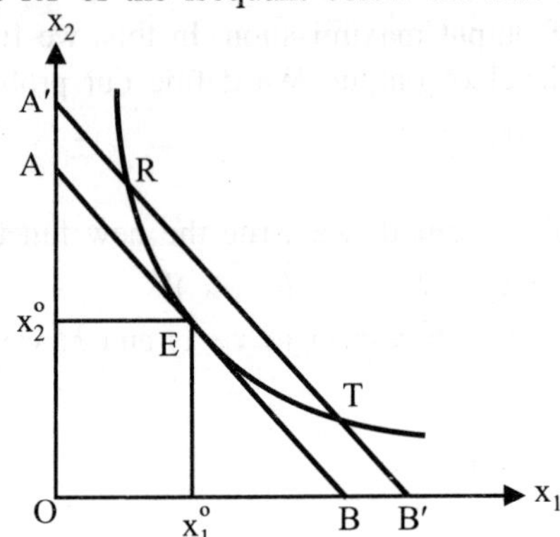

Fig. 5.14 Constrained Cost Minimisation

by shifting down the line $A'B'$ to eventually AB line. The AB line represents lowest cost for production of q°. It is tangent to the isoquant q° at E point showing the equilibrium situation and optimum, *i.e.*, least cost combination of x_1 and x_2 which is (x_1^o, x_2^o).

λ is defined as 'marginal cost of production' of q. Let us prove this. We have already expressed above the two relations:

$$dc = r_1 dx_1 + r_2 dx_2$$

and

$$dq = f_1 dx_1 + f_2 dx_2.$$

Further, the equilibrium conditions (47) show

$$r_1 = \lambda f_1, \; r_2 = \lambda f_2$$

Substituting these in the expression for dc, we have

$$dc = \lambda f_1 dx_1 + \lambda f_2 dx_2$$

and now taking dc/dq ratio we have:

$$\frac{dc}{dq} = \lambda \left[\frac{f_1 dx_1 + f_2 dx_2}{f_1 dx_1 + f_2 dx_2} \right]$$

or

$$\frac{dc}{dq} = \lambda \qquad \text{...(49)}$$

We have found earlier that $\mu = dq/dC$, μ and λ are thus inverse of each other.

(c) Profit Maximisation

Using isoquant approach, let us derive the conditions for profit maximisation.

The profit equation can be written as:

$$\pi = P.q - C$$

π is total profit, $P.q$ is total revenue and C total cost. Let us assume P as constant (This will be the case under perfect competition which we will discuss later on in Chapter 7).

Substituting $q = f(x_1, x_2)$ and $C = r_1x_1 + r_2x_2$ we have the changed profit equation as:

$$\pi = P\, f(x_1, x_2) - r_1x_1 - r_2x_2$$

Taking partial derivative with respect to x_1 and x_2 and equating them to zero, the first order profit maximising conditions are:

$$\partial\pi / \partial x_1 = P\, f_1 - r_1 = 0$$

$$\partial\pi / \partial x_2 = P\, f_2 - r_2 = 0$$

The second order conditions for these are,

$$\partial^2\pi / \partial x_1^2 < 0, \quad \partial^2\pi / \partial x_2^2 < 0$$

From the first order conditions of profit maximisation we have

$$Pf_1 = r_1;\ P\, f_2 = r_2 \qquad \text{...(50)}$$

that is, the value of marginal product of an input must be equal to its price for profit maximisation under perfect competition.

We can also say, by interpreting (50), that the value of the marginal product of an input is the rate at which the revenue of the firm increases with increase in the quantity of the input in production of a commodity. A firm continues to employ an input so long as the condition $P\, f_1 \geq r_1$ *and* $P\, f_2 \geq r_2$. These are very important results for factor employment decisions of a firm. They reflect the demand side for inputs. We will discuss this aspect further under the theory of distribution.

(d) Effect of Changes in Outlay on Equilibrium Position

Let us take input prices (r_1 and r_2) as fixed and assume that total money available, *i.e.*, outlay (C) to be spent on inputs increases. The iso-cost line in such a situation shifts parallelly upward which touches a higher isoquant. The shift of the iso-cost line continues further with increase in outlay (C) and thus producer's equilibrium will be on higher and higher iso-quants. If we join the equilibrium points through a line or curve passing through the origin, such curve or line is called 'expansion path'. *An expansion path is the locus of all equilibrium points when input prices remain constant and expenditure on inputs increases. The producer moves on higher and higher level of output in this type of change.*

The expansion path is a very useful concept. It gives an idea of how input proportion changes with increase in expenditure of the producer, input prices being constant. For a homogeneous production function, the expansion path will be a ray (straight line) originating from the origin showing constant proportion of the inputs used while increasing the level of output. For a non-homogeneous production function, it will be a curve showing different proportions of inputs at different stages of production. An expansion path is one of the isoclines. We can derive it just by taking the equilibrium condition for output maximisation or cost minimisation. Consider a Cobb-Douglas production function: $q = A\ x_1^{\alpha}\ x_2^{\beta}$. The marginal products of x_1 and x_2 derived from this function are:

$$\partial q / \partial x_1 = \alpha \frac{A x_1^{\alpha}\ x_2^{\beta}}{x_1} = \alpha \frac{q}{x_1}$$

and
$$\partial q / \partial x_2 = \frac{\beta A x_1^{\alpha}\ x_2^{\beta}}{x_2} = \beta \frac{q}{x_2}$$

For equilibrium we have the condition:

$$\frac{\partial q / dx_1}{\partial q / dx_2} = \frac{r_1}{r_2}$$

So, we have:

$$\frac{\partial q / \partial x_1}{\partial q / \partial x_2} = \frac{\alpha q / x_1}{\beta q / x_2} = \frac{r_1}{r_2}$$

or
$$\frac{\alpha x_2}{\beta x_1} = \frac{r_1}{r_2}$$

or
$$\alpha\, x_2\, r_2 - \beta\, r_1\, x_1 = 0 \qquad ...(51)$$

In general, we can write the expression for the expansion path as

$$g\ (x_1,\ x_2) = 0 \qquad ...(52)$$

that is, it is a function of x_1 and x_2 at the equilibrium. The expansion path helps us in deriving the elasticity of substitution as well as the cost function apart from other things as we will show in the following sections of this chapter.

(e) Effect of a Change in Price of One Input, Other Things Being Constant

Here we assume that only one input price is changing, the other prices and outlay (C) remain constant. What will happen to the equilibrium situation then? We take that r_1 decreases. The iso-cost line will now have greater intersection on the quantity axis for x_1, *i.e.*, with reduced price the producer is able to buy more of x_1 if he spends his entire outlay on x_1. In Fig. 5.15, this is shown by the line AB_1, while the original iso-cost line by AB.

With AB as the iso-cost line the producer is in equilibrium at point E_1 on the isoquant q_1. The optimal quantities of the two inputs corresponding to E_1 point are ox_1 and oy_1 for X_1 and X_2 respectively. The new iso-cost line AB_1 resulting from a decrease in the price of X_1 is tangent to a higher iso-quant q_2 at point E_2. The new optimal combination of X_1 and X_2 would now be Ox_2 and Oy_2 respectively. As a result of a decrease in the price, the producer is employing more of x_1 input in production. The change in the input usage for X_1 is $Ox_2 - Ox_1 = x_1x_2$ in the figure and for X_2 it is $Oy_2 - Oy_1 = y_1y_2$.

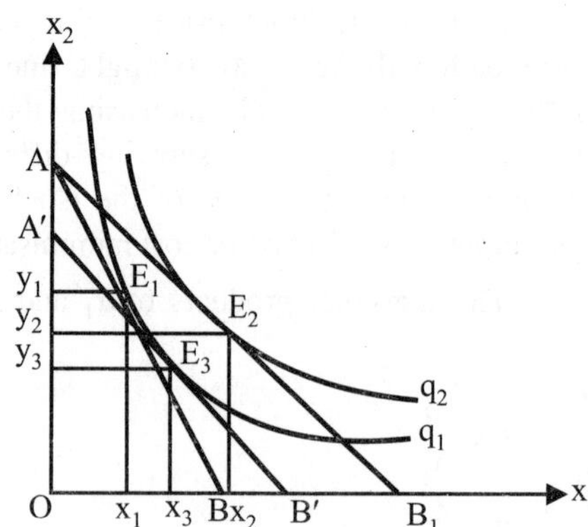

Fig. 5.15 Substitution and Output Effect of an Input Price Change

Because of a decrease in the price of X_1 there is an increase in quantity demanded for it which is shown of x_1x_2. This is the total effect of a change (*i.e.*, decrease here) in the price of the input

X_1. This effect may be decomposed into two components—'substitution effect' and 'output effect.'[10] The substitution effect shows the change in input usage attributable exclusively to the changes in relative prices of inputs, output remaining constant. This effect is always negative in the sense that a rise in the price of the input leads to a fall in its use and a fall in its price increases its use in production. The movement in this situation will be along the isoquant.

The output effect shows the change in input use attributable exclusively to a change in the level of output, input prices remaining the same. This effect is normally positive but there may be a situation when increase in output leads to a reduction in the demand for an input. Such an input is called 'inferior input' as we know of an inferior commodity in the consumer theory.

To isolate the substitution and output effects associated with a change in the price of an input we follow the same approach as adopted in the indifference curve analysis to separate the substitution and income effects. As mentioned above, with a decrease in the price of an input, other things being equal, the iso-cost line shifts outward having greater intersection on the quantity axis of the input whose price declines and thus touches a higher isoquant such as q_2 in Fig. 5.15. A decrease in the price of the input implies a saving in outlay of the producer. This saved outlay, when spent on the inputs, brings more output. This is the basic logic of the output effect. If we withdraw the saved outlay from the producer, either through taxation or otherwise, so that he moves back to the original output level, we will be able to find precisely the magnitude of the output effect. This is done by shifting the new iso-cost line (AB_1 in Fig. 5.15) parallelly downward till it touches the old isoquant. This new equilibrium situation as compared with the old equilibrium situation when price of the input was not changed defines the substitution effect and when compared with the equilibrium situation on the higher isoquant when price of the input changes, defines the output effect. To be explicit, let us go back to Fig. 5.15. The line $A'B'$, which is parallel to AB_1, touches q_1 isoquant at E_3 point. The substitution effect in this case is $Ox_3 - Ox_1$ *i.e.*, $x_1\, x_3$ distance. The output effect is $Ox_2 - Ox_3 = x_3x_2$ distance on x_1 axis. Thus, the total effect $x_1\, x_2$ is a sum of the substitution effect ($x_1\, x_3$) and the output effect ($x_3\, x_2$). Both these effects are unidirectional. In the case of an inferior input they will vary in opposite direction and so the net effect depends on the absolute values of the substitution and output effects. We may have a producer's Slutsky Equation to explain this. The producer's Slutsky equation may be written as:

$$\frac{dx_1}{dr_1} = \left(\frac{\partial x_1}{\partial r_1}\right)_{q\,=\,\text{constt.}} - x_1 \left(\frac{\partial x_1}{\partial C}\right)_{\text{Input Prices = constt.}} \quad ...(53)$$

$\dfrac{dx_1}{dr_1}$ is the total effect $\left(\dfrac{\partial x_1}{\partial r_1}\right)_{q\,=\,\text{constt.}}$ is the substitution effect, and $x_1\left(\dfrac{\partial x_1}{\partial C}\right)$ is the output effect.

$\dfrac{\partial x_1}{\partial C}$ is positive for a normal input, *i.e.*, an increase in outlay (C) increases the demand for the input, prices being constant. Since there is a negative sign before this, so the two effects will be unidirectional working negatively. However, if $\dfrac{\partial x_1}{\partial C}$ is negative (inferior input) then $- x_1\left(\dfrac{\partial x_1}{\partial C}\right)$ will be positive and

10. C.E. Ferguson, *Microeconomic Theory,* R.D. Irwin Inc., 1971, pp. 197–201.

so the two effects will be opposite to each other. The total effect $\left(\frac{dx_1}{dr_1}\right)$ in this situation will be negative if the absolute value of the substitution effect is greater than the absolute value of the output effect, and it will be positive when we have absolute value of the output effect greater than the absolute value of the substitution effect (*i.e.*, a 'Giffen' input situation).[11] In order to substantiate the case for inferiority of an input let us consider an example. If output level is low a firm may use more labour as compared to machines to produce it. But as output level increases there may be greater and greater use of machines. That is, the degree of automation goes up with increase in output. This implies that labour gradually becomes inferior as compared to machines at higher level of output. Ultimately, there might be a situation when a plant used in production is fully automatic displacing the labour input altogether. We may interpret labour as inferior input as compared to machines in such a situation.

5.7 PRODUCTION POSSIBILITY FRONT ANALYSIS

(a) Concepts and Properties

This is the fourth situation for the study of the production theory. In this case, input quantities are fixed and there are more than one product to be produced. For this, let us consider the simplest case in which an entrepreneur uses. a single input (X) for production of two commodities Q_1 and Q_2. Let x be the quantity of the input and q_1 and q_2 are quantities of the two commodities Q_1 and Q_2 respectively, we can express the relationship between the input quantity and output quantities through a production function as:

$$x = h\ [q_1,\ q_2] \qquad \text{...(54)}$$

h defines the functional shape of the relationship. This function is expressing the cost of production in terms of x as a function of the quantities of the two products, that is, q_1 and q_2. Suppose x is fixed, *i.e.*, let $x = x^\circ$, then the production function will be

$$x^\circ = h\ [q_1,\ q_2] \qquad \text{...(55)}$$

This gives us a boundary for full utilisation of the input. This boundary is called as 'Production

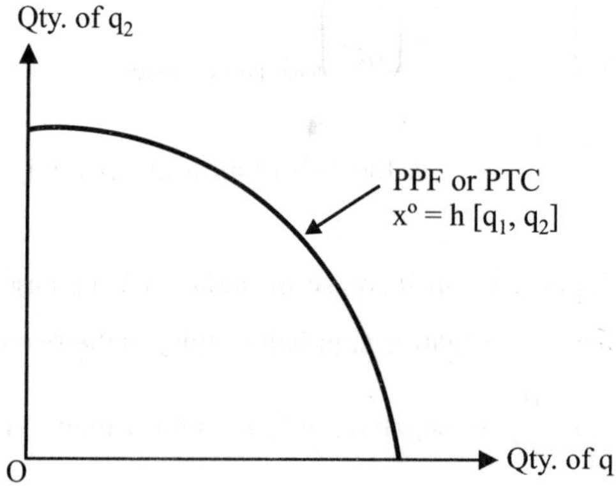

Fig. 5.16 Production Possibility Front (PPF)

11. The analysis to isolate 'substitution' and 'output' effects in the isoquant analysis is exactly similar as followed for the separation of the substitution and income effects in the indifference curve analysis. Only terminology is different.

Possibility Front' or 'Product Transformation Curve.'[12] A 'Production Possibility Front (*PPF*) or Product Transformation Curve (*PTC*)' is defined as the locus of output combinations that can be produced from a given input or given set of inputs. Its normal shape is a concave surface towards the origin as shown in Fig. 5.16.

If the resource quantity (x°) increases the *PPF* shifts outwards showing more output of both the products.

The shape of the *PPF* at any point (shown by the slope of its tangent at that point) is the rate at which one output, say Q_2, must be sacrificed to obtain one more additional unit of the other output (Q_1) without varying the input quantity. The negative of the slope is defined as the rate of product transformation (*RPT*).

Let us take

$$x = h\,[q_1, q_2]$$

Taking total derivatives of this we have

$$dx = \frac{\partial x}{\partial q_1} dq_1 + \frac{\partial x}{\partial q_2} dq_2$$

when we move along the *PPF*, there will be no change in the input quantity.This means $dx = 0$. Therefore, we have

$$0 = \frac{\partial x}{\partial q_1} dq_1 + \frac{\partial x}{\partial q_2} dq_2$$

or $$-\frac{\partial q_2}{\partial q_1} = \frac{\partial x / \partial q_1}{\partial x / \partial q_2} = \frac{h_1}{h_2} \qquad ...(56)$$

$\partial x / \partial q_1$ is the marginal cost of q_1, *i.e.* increase in cost (x) by producing one more unit of q_1 and similarly, $\partial x / \partial q_2$ is the marginal cost of q_2. The above relationship simply says that the rate of product transformation is equal to the ratio of the marginal costs for production of q_1 and q_2.

For simplicity, we write $h_1 = \frac{\partial x}{\partial q_1}$ and $h_2 = \frac{\partial x}{\partial q_2}$, *i.e.* these are first order derivatives of the production possibility front (54) with respect to q_1 and q_2 respectively.

The term h_1/h_2 on the right-hand side of (56) is positive (marginal cost of production for either of q_1 and q_2 cannot be negative); this implies that $-\,dq_2/dq_1$ is positive. This is possible when there is another minus sign attached with it which will be the situation when the *PPF* is a downward sloping curve. So, we have an important property of the *PPF* here. It is a downward sloping curve.

We can express the relationship shown by (56) in terms of marginal products of x for q_1 and q_2. We have defined $h_1 = \partial x / \partial q_1$. Inverting this we get $1/h_1 = \partial q_1 / \partial x$, *i.e.*, the marginal product of x when it is used for production of q_1. Similarly, $1/h_2 = \partial q_2 / \partial x$. Therefore, we have

$$RPT = -\,dq_2/dq_1 = \frac{h_1}{h_2} = \frac{\partial q_2 / \partial x}{\partial q_1 / \partial x} \qquad ...(57)$$

Marginal cost of output and marginal products of input are inversely related to each other, and so we are getting the new relationship for RPT as shown by (57).

12. This curve has already been introduced in Chapter 2. Here the analysis is being extended further.

The slope of the *PPF* is determined by the pattern of variation of the rate of product transformation (*RPT*). When we move from Q_2 axis towards Q_1, we produce more of Q_1 and less of Q_2. To produce an extra unit of Q_1 we have to spend more quantity of the input as implied by the law of diminishing return. This means an increase in $\partial x/\partial q_1$. At the same time, we are producing less of Q_2 so $\partial x/\partial q_2$ declines. The ratio $\frac{\partial x/\partial q_1}{\partial x/\partial q_2}$ therefore increases as we move towards q_1 axis. To be more specific, we have $-\, dq_2/dq_1 = \frac{h_1}{h_2}$. Since q_1 increases so h_1 increases and q_2 decreases so h_2 decreases. This gives us an increasing h_1/h_2 for the *PPF.* This proves that the *PPF* is a concave boundary towards the origin. Using the second order condition to prove this we have:

$$\frac{-d^2q_2}{dq_1^2} = \frac{1}{h_2^3}[h_{11}h_2^2 - 2h_{12}h_1h_2 + h_{22}h_1^2] \qquad ...(58)$$

Here $h_{11} > 0$, $h_{22} > 0$ as implied by rising marginal costs and $h_{12} < 0$. *i.e.*, increase in q_1 means a decrease in marginal cost of q_2. The bracketed term on the right hand side is positive. Therefore; we have $-d^2q_2/dq_1^2 > 0$. This implies that the *PPF* is a concave curve.

As an example, let us have $x = q_1^2 + q_2^2$. $\partial x/\partial q_1 = 2q_1$, $\partial x/\partial q_2 = 2q_2$.

$RPT = -\, dq_2/dq_1 = (\partial x/\partial q_1)/(\partial x/\partial q_2) = 2q_1/2q_2 = q_1/q_2$. The rate of change of *RPT* using (58) comes out to be equal to $(q_1^2 + q_2^2)/q_2^3$ which is positive.

If the two commodities, Q_1 and Q_2, are strictly joint-products, they will be shown by the corner point of the inverted right angles as shown by point E_1 in Part (*a*) of the following diagram:

If resources are increasing, greater levels of output of the joint products are possible as shown by E_2 and E_3 points. The ray $O\ E_3$ will be the locus of all such points.

If the two products are perfect substitutes from production point of view, the *PPF* would be a downward sloping straight-line showing constant rate of product transformation (See Fig. 5.17 (*b*)). Between these two extreme shapes, we will be having the normal concave *ppfs*.

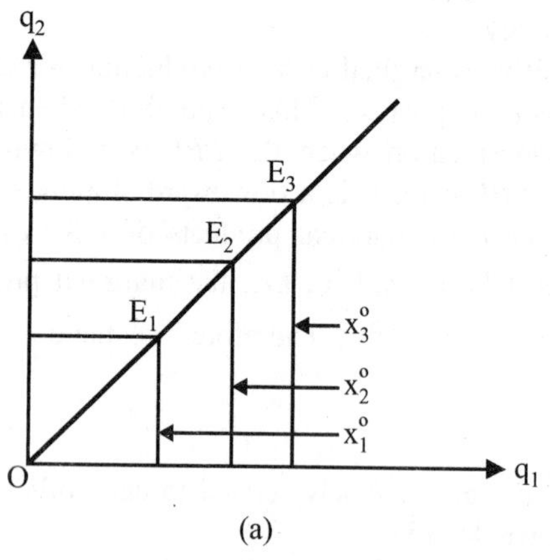

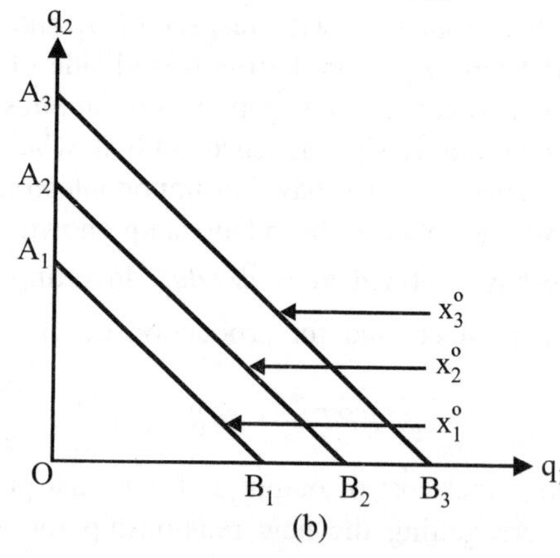

Fig. 5.17 Production Possibility Fronts for Joint Products and Substitute Goods

(b) Optimising Behaviour in PPF Framework

An important issue related to the *PPF* analysis is to find the optimal combination of the two products that can be produced from the given amount of the resource(s). To find this, we need the objective function for the producer. Let us assume that the objective of the producer is revenue or sales maximisation. We can define a revenue line for him as

$$R = P_1 q_1 + P_2 q_2 \qquad \text{...(59)}$$

P_1 and P_2 are prices for Q_1 and Q_2 and q_1 and q_2 are quantities. This line is defined as 'iso-revenue line'. *It is the locus of all combinations of the quantities of the two products that yield a given level of revenue at constant product prices.* There will be a system of iso-revenue lines parallel to each other showing different levels of revenue at constant product prices. The slope of the iso-revenue line would be equal to $-P_1/P_2$.

Given the iso-revenue line, we can define the optimising behaviour of the producer as:

Max. $R = P_1 q_1 + P_2 q_2$

Subject to $x^\circ = h\,[q_1, q_2]$ ...(60)

Using the Lagrange Method, we have

$$W = P_1 q_1 + P_2 q_2 + \gamma\,[x^\circ - h\,(q_1, q_2)]$$

The first order maximum conditions for this are:

$$\frac{\partial W}{\partial q_1} = P_1 - \gamma h_1 = 0$$

$$\frac{\partial W}{\partial q_2} = P_2 - \gamma h_2 = 0 \qquad \text{...(61)}$$

$$\frac{\partial W}{\partial \gamma} = x^\circ - h\,[q_1, q_2] = 0$$

where $h_1 = \dfrac{\partial h(.)}{\partial q_1}$ and $h_2 = \dfrac{\partial h(.)}{\partial q_2}$ defined earlier as marginal cost for q_1 and q_2 respectively.

From the first two first order maximum conditions we have,

$$\frac{P_1}{h_1} = \frac{P_2}{h_2} = \gamma \qquad \text{...(62)}$$

The price of product divided by the marginal cost must be identical for all products and equal to γ which is defined as marginal revenue product of the resource (dR/dx). In fact, P_1/h_1 and P_2/h_2 are nothing but price-cost margins for the two products which must be equal at the optimum revenue level. Also, we have $h_1 = \partial x/\partial q_1 = \dfrac{1}{\partial q_1/\partial x}$ and $h_2 = \partial x/\partial q_2 = \dfrac{1}{\partial q_2/\partial x}$, therefore,

$$\gamma = P_1 \frac{\partial q_1}{\partial x} = P_2 \frac{\partial q_2}{\partial x} \qquad \text{...(63)}$$

The value of the marginal product of x in production of each output must be equal to γ, the derivative of total revenue with respect to x when prices are constant $\left(\gamma = \dfrac{\partial q}{\partial x}\right)$.

Again, from (62) we have the expression for the rate of product transformation as

$$RPT = -\frac{dq_2}{dq_1} = \frac{P_1}{P_2} = \frac{\partial x/\partial q_1}{\partial x \partial q_2} = \frac{h_1}{h_2} \qquad \text{...(64)}$$

or $$RPT = \frac{P_1}{P_2} = \frac{\partial q_2 / \partial x}{\partial q_1 / \partial x} \qquad \text{...(65)}$$

condition (64) shows that for maximum revenue the iso-revenue line must be a tangent to the production possibility front. The point of tangency shows the optimum combination of the two products that the producer should produce.

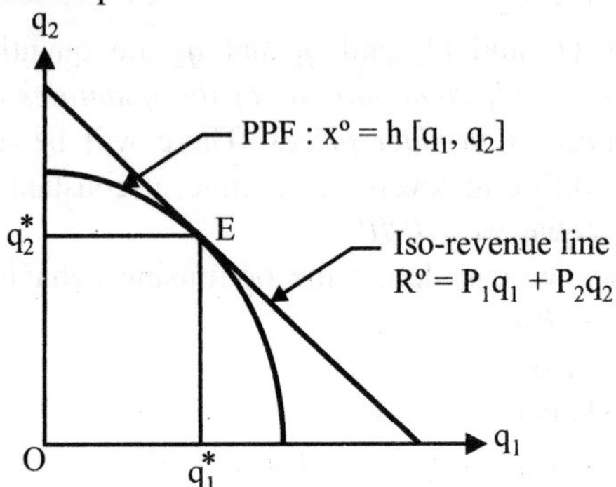

Fig. 5.18 Producer's Equilibrium on a Production Possibility Front

We have derived the above optimality conditions on the assumption that the second order optimum condition is satisfied. Such condition is $[h_{11}h_2^2 - 2h_{12}h_1h_2 + h_{22}h_1^2] > 0$. All terms in this expression have already been defined earlier. The concavity of the *PPF* ensures this condition.

To show that $\gamma = dR/dx$, we use same line of arguments as done for μ in the case of constrained output maximisation.

$$R = P_1q_1 + P_2q_2$$

so, $$dR = P_1dq_1 + P_2dq_2$$

Also from (62) we have,

$$P_1 = \gamma\, h_1,\ P_2 = \gamma\, h_2$$

Therefore, we can write

$$dR = \gamma h_1\, dq_1 + \gamma h_2 dq_2 \qquad \text{...(66)}$$

From the *PPF* expression we have

$$dx = h_1dq_1 + h_2dq_2 \qquad \text{...(67)}$$

Dividing (66) by (67) we have

$$\frac{dR}{dx} = \gamma\left[\frac{h_1dq_1 + h_2dq_2}{h_1dq_1 + h_2dq_2}\right] = \gamma \qquad \text{...(68)}$$

This is, γ is equal to the marginal revenue product of x.

If the production possibility front is a downward sloping straight line showing constant *RPT*, the tangency solution for optimum revenue will not be possible. In this case, we will have the corner solution, *i.e.* the choice of only one of the two perfect substitute products which yields higher revenue to the producer.

We have taken revenue maximisation as the goal for the producer. Let us now shift to the profit maximisation alternative. For this we write the profit function as

$$\pi = (P_1q_1 + P_2q_2) - rx^\circ$$

Since $x° = h\ [q_1, q_2]$, so substituting this for $x°$ we have

$$\pi = P_1q_1 + P_2q_2 - r\ h\ [q_1, q_2] \qquad ...(69)$$

r is the price for the input and $rx°$ is the cost of production.

Setting the partial derivatives equal to zero, We have:

$$\frac{\partial\pi}{\partial q_1} = P_1 - rh_1 = 0$$

$$\frac{\partial\pi}{\partial q_2} = P_2 - rh_2 = 0 \qquad ...(70)$$

From these conditions we are getting

$$r = \frac{P_1}{\partial x/\partial q_1} = \frac{P_2}{\partial x/\partial q_2} \qquad ...(71)$$

or

$$r = P_1\partial q_1/\partial x = P_2\partial q_2/\partial x \qquad ...(72)$$

The value of the marginal product of X in production of each output must be equal to the price of the input X for maximum profit. For profit maximisation we have the same equilibrium condition ($P_1/h_1 = P_2/h_2$) which is for the revenue maximisation. By comparing the two optimum situations we have $r = \gamma$ that is the input price r is equal to the marginal revenue product of X at the equilibrium. This is a very important result having its implications for the theory of distribution which we will explain later on in this book.

Why revenue maximisation and profit maximisation yield the same equilibrium, *i.e.*, same combination of the two (or more) products in the *p.p.f.* analysis? The reason is simple. Since resource quantity $x°$ is fixed so the cost of production $rx°$ is fixed; it means that profit will be maximum when revenue is maximum.

The second order condition for profit maximisation are $h_{11} > 0$; $[h_{11}\ h_{22} - (h_{12})^2] > 0$; and $h_{22} > 0$. That is the marginal cost of each product in terms of x must be increasing and the *ppf* must be strictly concave.[13]

(c) Multiple Inputs PPF and Linear Programming

So far we have assumed a single input (X) used for production of two commodities. If we have more than one fixed input, then for each input we will have a production possibility front. See the following diagram (Fig. 5.19) in which labour *(L)* and Capital (K) are two inputs and so two *PPFs* have been plotted. The common area of the two boundaries will be the Production Possibility Front feasible from production point of view. *PPF* for labour is $L° = L\ [q_1, q_2]$ shown by the curve A_1CB_1 and for capital, $K° = K\ [q_1, q_2]$ which is shown by $A\ C\ B$. The common area $A\ C\ B_1$ is the feasible boundary of production for the producer. This boundary cannot be crossed because of input constraints. Where will be the equilibrium position of the producer on such a boundary? It is difficult to say on an a-priori basis. This depends on the slope of the iso-revenue line. The line may touch the *ppf* on the arc AC or B_1C or it may touch it at the point C.

13. See Henderson J.M. and R.E. Quandt, *Microeconomic Theory,* McGraw-Hill, 1971, pp. 94-95 for derivation of the second order conditions for profit maximisation.

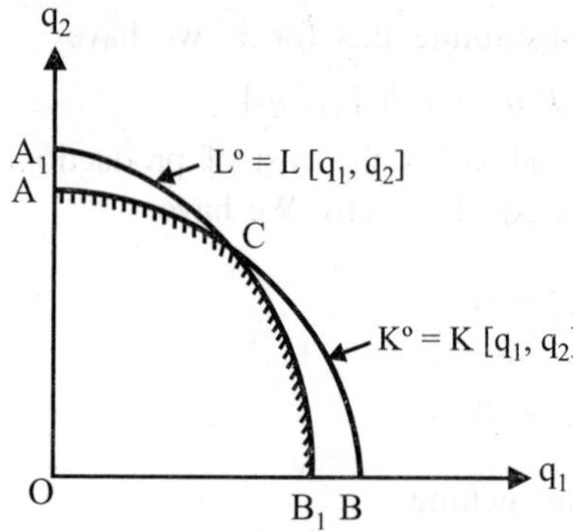

Fig. 5.19 Multiple Inputs Production Possibility Front

Suppose we have straight line *ppfs* for the inputs, as shown in Fig. 5.20. In this case, the equilibrium position of the producer lies at one of the corners of the feasible *ppf* since the isorevenue line cannot be tangent on the linear segments of the *ppf*. This is a very useful property of the feasible production possibility front formed by several linear production possibility fronts for different inputs. This is the foundation on which the entire linear programming approach is based. It will be worthwhile for us here to go through an example of the linear programming to show that it is nothing but the production possibility front analysis with multiple inputs.

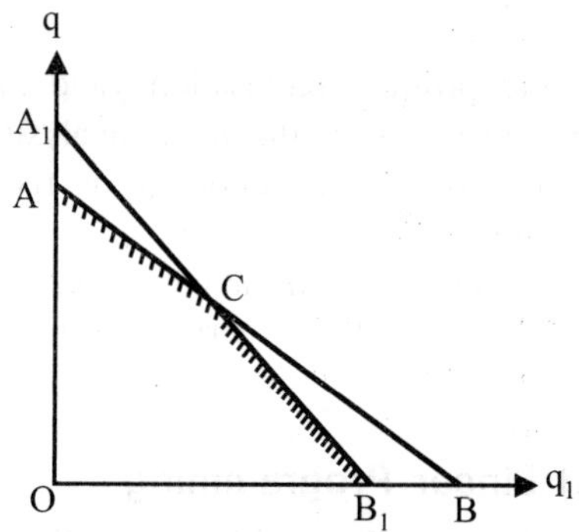

Fig. 5.20 Linear Production Possibility Fronts

Linear programming is a mathematical tool used for resource allocation. It is an optimising technique in which the objective function and the constraints for that are expressed in the form of linear equations. That is why it is called linear programming. To specify a linear programming problem and to solve it, let us consider the following data:

> A firm produces two products, *A* and *B*. Each unit of product *A* requires one man-hour of labour, three machine-hours, and five units of a raw material. Similarly, each unit of product *B* requires two manhours, one machine-hour, and four units of the raw material. Total availability of resources at the disposal of the firm is given as 720 manhours, 900 machine hours and 1800 units of the raw material. The price of product *A* in the market is Rs. 4000 and that of product *B* is Rs. 5000. What should be the optimum combination of products *A* and *B* that the firm should produce?

Clearly the objective of the firm in this example is to maximise total revenue. The revenue function for the firm would be

R = ₹ 4000 q_1 + ₹ 5000 q_2 where q_1 and q_2 are the output levels which we have to find. To maximise total revenue, there are constraints because of fixity of resources. These constraints can be specified as follows:

Total demand for manhours of labour for production of q_1 and q_2 output levels of product *A* and product *B* respectively would be $1q_1 + 2q_2$. This cannot exceed the total availability of labour. Therefore, we have

$1q_1 + 2q_2 \leq 720$: Labour constraint

Similarly, the demand and supply balance equation for machine-hours would be,

$3q_1 + 1q_2 \leq 900$: machine-hour constraints and for raw material, we have,

$5q_1 + 4q_2 \leq 1800$: raw material constraints.

Apart from these constraints, there is another set of constraints for this problem, that is, neither of the two products should be negative ($q_1 \geq 0$, $q_2 \geq 0$). as there is no economic sense of any negative output.

This problem can be solved through an algebraic method but a simpler way for this is to use the graphic technique. The first step of the graphic technique is to plot the resource constraints using *X* and *Y* axes for the two products. For our example, the manhours, the machinehours, and the raw material constraints have been plotted as shown in Fig. 5.21. While plotting the constraints we take the equality sign for each one of them.

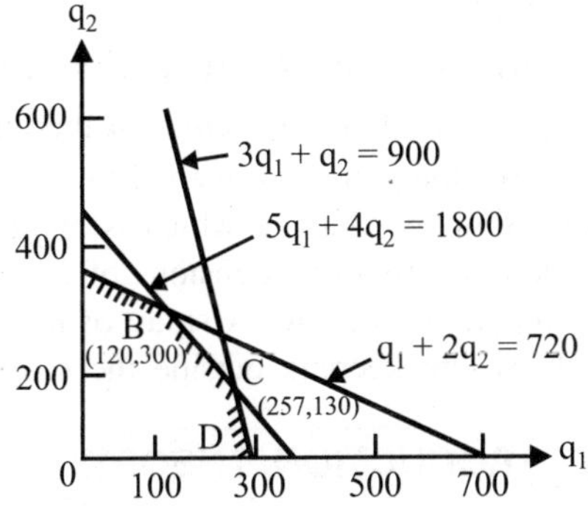

Fig. 5.21 Graphical Solution of a Linear Programming Problem

In this diagram, the boundary, where all constraints are satisfied is shown, by *A B C D.* It is, therefore, the production possibility front for the linear programming problem under solution. To find the optimum set of the outputs of product *A* and product *B,* the isorevenue line $R = 4000q_1 + 5000q_1$ has to be a tangent to the *PPF* shown by *A B C D.* The *PPF* is not a continuous boundary. It. has linear segments so that isorevenue line can only be the tangent at one of the vertices, *i.e.*, corners of the *PPF.* We accept that particular position of the isorevenue line when it touches a corner point yielding maximum revenue. To find this point, what we have to do is to substitute the coordinates of the corner points in the isorevenue line to compute total revenue. One of the corner points will give us the maximum revenue which defines the optimum combination of the two products: For the problem under study, we find total revenue at different corners of the *PPF* as follows.

	Point $(q_1\ q_2)$	Revenue (Rs) $(R = 4000q_1 + 5000q_2)$
0	(0,0)	0
A	(0, 360)	18, 00, 000
B	(120, 300)	19,80,000←Best computation of q_1 and q_2.
C	(257, 130)	16, 78, 000
D	(300, 0)	12, 00, 000

From these calculations, we find the best combination of the two products given by point *B*. Accordingly, the firm should produce 120 units of product *A* and 300 units of product *B* for maximum revenue of Rs. 19, 80, 000.

This is a simple linear programming problem. A producer may face a situation in which there are several products (*i.e.*, more than two) to be produced with given quantities of different resources. It will be impossible to use the graphic technique to get the solution of such a linear programming problem. We have to use algebraic technique. Consider, for example, the general specification of a linear programming problem in which there are *n* products and *m* constraints such as:

$$\text{Maximise } R = P_1q_1 + P_2q_2 + ... + P_nq_n$$

$$\text{subject to } \left.\begin{aligned} a_{11}q_1 + a_{12}q_2 + ...a_{1n}q_n &\leq X_1^0 \\ a_{21}q_1 + a_{22}q_2 + ...a_{2n}q_n &\leq X_2^0 \\ a_{m1}q_1 + a_{m2}q_2 + ...a_{mn}q_n &\leq X_n^0 \end{aligned}\right\} \text{Input constraints}$$

and $q_1 \geq 0$; $i = 1, n$. Non-negativity constraint. Where a_{ij} $(i = 1, m, j = 1, n)$ are input *i* required to produce one unit of product. X_1^0, X_m^0 are fixed quantities of the inputs and q_1, q_n are output levels. As we see, it will not be easy to apply the graphical method to solve such a complex problem. There is an algebraic method, known as Simplex Method, which is applied to solve this type of complex linear programming problems. There are further extensions of linear programming analysis such as integer programming, non-linear programming, etc. A study of this branch of knowledge is covered under Operations Analysis which we are keeping outside the scope of this book.[14]

5.8 THE GENERALISED PRODUCTION THEORY

In this production theory we take into consideration production of multiple outputs with the help of several inputs. This case is a generalisation of all the four cases of production described in the preceding sections of this chapter.

In order to conduct this type of analysis, we have to conceive a production function which links, say *M*, outputs with *N* inputs. Let q_1, q_2, q_M be the amounts of each output which could be produced during a period and let x_1, x_2, ...x_N be the quantities of each input used in production of all output. The outputs as well as the inputs are not negative, *i.e.*, $q_1 \geq 0$, $i = 1,...M$, and, $x_j \geq 0$, $j = 1, N$. The firm's production function, showing the transformation of all inputs into outputs, can be expressed in a general form as:

$$F\ (q_1, q_2,..., q_M) = G\ (x_1, x_2,..., x_N) \quad ...(73)$$

---

14. For details of programming techniques one may refer to (a) Boumol, W. J., *Economic Theory and Operations Analysis,* Prentice-Hall, 1961, Ch. 5, Ch. 18; (b) Dorfman, R.,P. A. Samuelson and R.M. Solow, *Linear Programming and Economic Analysis,* McGraw-Hill 1958, (c) Hadley, G., Linear Programming, Addison-Wesley 1962.

This production function is assumed to be continuous with first and second order partial derivatives (F and G are functional forms for the two sides of the PF).

For the optimal production decision, we make the assumption that the goal of the firm is profit maximisation. The profit equation for the firm can be written as,

$$\pi = \sum_{i=1}^{M} P_i q_i - \sum_{j=1}^{N} r_j x_j - b \qquad \text{...(74)}$$

P_i (i = 1, M) and r_j, (j = 1, N) are output and input prices respectively. They are assumed to be fixed. b is the level of fixed cost, if any.

For optimal choice of the outputs and inputs combinations we define our maximisation problem as

$$\text{Max.} \qquad \pi = \sum_{i=1}^{M} P_i q_i - \sum_{j=1}^{N} r_j x_j - b \qquad \text{...(75)}$$

Subject to $F(q_1, q_2, ..q_M) = G(x_1, x_2, ...x_N)$

Using the Lagrange Multipliers Method we have

$$L = \sum_{i=1}^{M} P_i q_i - \sum_{j=1}^{N} r_j x_j - b - \lambda [F(q_1, q_2, ..q_M) - G(x_1, x_2, ...x_N)] \qquad \text{...(76)}$$

Differentiating this with respect to q_i and x_j and equating them to zeros we have:

$$\frac{\partial L}{\partial q_i} = P_i - \lambda \frac{\partial F}{\partial q_i} = 0; \; i = 1, ...M \qquad \text{...(77)}$$

$$\frac{\partial L}{\partial x_j} = -r_j + \lambda \frac{\partial G}{\partial x_j} = 0; \; j = 1, ...N \qquad \text{...(78)}$$

$$\frac{\partial L}{\partial \lambda} = -[F(q_1, q_2, ..q_M) - G(x_1, x_2, ...x_N)] \qquad \text{...(79)}$$

From the set of equations (77) and (78), we get the equilibrium situation for the firm as:

$$\frac{\partial F/\partial q_1}{P_1} = \frac{\partial F/\partial q_2}{P_2} \cdots = \frac{\partial F/\partial q_M}{P_M} = \frac{1}{\lambda}$$

$$\frac{\partial G/\partial x_1}{r_1} = \frac{\partial G/\partial x_2}{r_2} \cdots = \frac{\partial G/\partial x_N}{r_N} = \frac{1}{\lambda} \qquad \text{...(80)}$$

Each of the partial derivatives may contain all or some of the q_is. The system of equations for the partial derivatives (77 to 79) contains $M + N + 1$ equations for $M + N + 1$ unknowns (M of q_is, N of x_js and λ). We can therefore solve them. How to interpret the partial derivatives?

Let us take $\frac{\partial G}{\partial x_j}$; ($j$ = 1,..N) first. These are marginal products of inputs, (j = 1, ..N). A marginal increase in input j, all other being constants, may result in an increase in all outputs rather than just one output as we see in the conventional one output case of production analysis. In a way, we may interpret it as an index of marginal increase in all outputs from a unit increment in jth input. For simplicity, we still call it as marginal product of input. If there is only one output we write the pf for that as $q = G(x_1, x_2)$ and therefore $\partial q/\partial x_1 = \frac{\partial G}{\partial x_1} = MP$ of X_1 and $\partial q/\partial x_2 = \frac{\partial G}{\partial x_2} = MP$ of X_2.

Similarly, $\frac{\partial F}{\partial q_i}$, ($i$ = 1, ...M) is defined as marginal input requirement to produce one more extra unit of *ith* product. We have N inputs; so, to produce one more extra unit of q_i, other outputs being constant, we may require an increase in all inputs. We may interpret it, *i.e.*, $\frac{\partial F}{\partial q_i}$, ($i$ = 1, ...M) as an index of the marginal increase in resource requirement to produce an additional unit of q_i. However, for simplicity, we use the term marginal input requirement of *ith* product.

The economic interpretation of the equilibrium conditions summarised by (80) can be carried on in terms of following statements or theorems.

(*i*) The marginal product of the last unit or money spent on purchasing an input must be equal for all inputs. This is shown by $\frac{\partial G/\partial x_j}{r_j} = \frac{1}{\lambda}$, ($j$ = 1,..N).

(*ii*) λ $(\partial G/\partial x_j)$ is equal to the value of the marginal product resulting from a change in any one input. That is, $\lambda\ \partial G/\partial x_j = dR/dx_j$, j = 1,...N. where the right hand side is the value of the marginal product of input x_j, *i.e.*, it is the incremental revenue obtained by selling the extra output-mix produced when a small additional amount of x_j input is used.

(*iii*) Any input will be utilised in such a manner that its market price equals the value of its marginal product.

From (80) we have $\lambda(\partial G/\partial x_j) = r_j$.

(*iv*) The marginal revenue received from the last unit of input must be equal for every output.

This implies that $\frac{P_1}{\partial F/\partial x_1} = \frac{P_2}{\partial F/\partial x_2} = .. = \frac{P_n}{\partial F/\partial x_N}$

(*v*) $\lambda(\partial q/\partial x_i)$ is equal to the marginal cost resulting from a change in anyone output. This is proved when

$$\lambda(\partial F/\partial q_i) = \frac{dC}{dq_i};\ (i = 1,..M).$$

(*vi*) Any output will be produced in such a way that its selling price is equal to its marginal cost.

This is proved as we have $\frac{\partial F/\partial q_i}{P_i} = \frac{1}{\lambda}$, therefore, $\lambda(\partial F/\partial q_i) = P_i$, i = 1,..M.

Also from (v), we have $[\partial F/\partial q_i] = \frac{dC}{dq_i} = P_i$, i = 1..,M.

(*vii*) The rate of product transformation *(RPT)* between any pair of output, holding all other outputs and inputs constant, must be equal to their price ratio and also be equal to their marginal cost ratio.

$$RPT = -\frac{dq_k}{dq_i} = \frac{\partial F/\partial q_i}{\partial F/\partial q_K} = \frac{P_i}{P_K} \quad i, K, = 1,...M \quad i \neq K.$$

(*viii*) The rate of technical substitution between every pair of inputs holding all other inputs and outputs constant is equal to the ratio of their prices.

$$RTS = -\frac{dx_K}{dx_j} = r_j/r_k,\ d,\ K = 1,\ ..\ N,\ i \neq K.$$

(*ix*) The rate at which any input can be transformed into any output, holding all other inputs and outputs constant, is equal to their prices.

$$\frac{dq_i}{dx_j} = \frac{r_j}{P_i} = i = 1,\ M,\ j = 1,.N.$$

This means $r_j = P_i \frac{dq_i}{dx_j}$, *i.e.*, the value of the marginal product of each input with respect to each output is equated to the input price.

All the above mentioned conclusions have been derived from (80). Some of them require further proofs but we are not going' into this at this stage.[15]

Further, while deriving these results from the first order profit maximisation conditions (77 to 79 or 80) we assumed that the second order maximisation conditions are satisfied.[16]

These results are applicable to both the isoquant (one output, two input case) and Production Possibility Front analysis (one input, two outputs as special cases).

5.9 SOME STANDARD PRODUCTION FUNCTIONS

We have discussed a few types of production function earlier in this chapter. We now discuss their properties and uses in the production theory.

(i) The Cobb-Douglas Production Function

This is perhaps the simplest and the most widely used production function in the economic theory. It was originally given by C.W. Cobb and P.H. Douglas.[17] The general form of this function, as we have mentioned earlier, is given as:

$$q = \beta x_1^{\alpha_1} . x_2^{\alpha_2} .. x_n^{\alpha_n} \qquad ...(81)$$

where q is the flow of output, and x_1, x_2,...x_n are flows of input quantities, all are time rates. β, and α_1 to α_n are parameters. Confining to two inputs case and converting it in logarithms we get,

$$\log q = \log \beta + \alpha_1 \log x_1 + \alpha_2 \log x_2 \qquad ...(82)$$

This gives us

$$\frac{\partial(\log q)}{\partial(\log x_1)} = \alpha_1$$

and,
$$\frac{\partial(\log q)}{\partial(\log x_2)} = \alpha_2$$

That is, α_1 and α_2 are output elasticities of the two inputs X_1 and X_2 respectively. We can extend this to any number of inputs for finding their output elasticities. As we have mentioned earlier,

---

15. For detail proofs, etc., of these conclusions, see K. J. Cohen and R.M. Cyert, *Theory of the Firm:* Resource *Allocation in A Market Economy*, Prentice-Hall of India, 1976.
16. For the second order conditions, see Henderson and Quandt *Microeconomic Theory* (1971), pp. 96-97.
17. C.W. Cobb and P. H. Douglas, *op.cit.*

if $(\alpha_1 + \alpha_2) > 1$ then the function shows increasing returns to scale and if $(\alpha_1 + \alpha_2) < 1$ then decreasing returns to scale. For constant returns to scale, we have $\alpha_1 + \alpha_2 = 1$. The sum of output elasticities, thus, gives us the degree of homogeneity of the production function and the degree of return to scale.

Taking partial derivatives of q with respect to x_1 and x_2 we have

$$\partial q/\partial x_1 = \alpha_1 \beta x_1^{\alpha_1 - 1} x_2^{\alpha_2} = \alpha_1 \frac{\beta x_1^{\alpha_1} x_2^{\alpha_2}}{x_1} = \alpha_1 \frac{q}{x_1}$$

and
$$\partial q/\partial x_2 = \alpha_2 \beta x_1^{\alpha_1} x_2^{\alpha_2 - 1} = \alpha_2 \frac{\beta x_1^{\alpha_1} x_2^{\alpha_2}}{x_1} = \alpha_2 \frac{q}{x_2} \quad ...(83)$$

From these, we find

$$\frac{\partial q/\partial x_1}{q/x_1} = \alpha_1 \text{ and } \frac{\partial q/\alpha x_2}{q/x_2} = \alpha_2$$

That is, the ratio of marginal product and average product of an input equals to its output elasticity.

The equilibrium condition for optimum combination of the inputs using the Cobb-Douglas production function is:

$$\frac{\partial q/\partial x_1}{\partial q/\partial x_2} = \frac{\alpha_1 q/x_1}{\alpha_2 q/x_2} = \frac{r_1}{r_2}$$

or
$$\frac{\alpha_1 x_2}{\alpha_2 x_1} = \frac{r_1}{r_2} \quad ...(83)$$

This gives us the expansion path as

$$r_2\alpha_1 x_2 - r_1\alpha_2 x_1 = 0 \quad ...(84)$$

This is a straight line emerging from the origin in the isoquant plane.

From (83) we have

$$\frac{\alpha_1}{\alpha_2} = \frac{r_1 x_1}{r_2 x_2} \quad ...(85)$$

The ratio of output elasticities of the two inputs is equal to the ratio of their shares in output value.

By taking the log of (83) we get

$$\log\left(\frac{\alpha_1}{\alpha_2}\right) + \log\left(\frac{x_2}{x_1}\right) = \log\left(\frac{r_1}{r_2}\right)$$

By using the definition of the elasticity of substitution and applying it to this equation we have

$$\frac{\partial \log (x_2/x_1)}{\partial \log (r_1/r_2)} = 1 \quad ...(86)$$

Thus, we find that the elasticity of substitution for x_2 and x_1 derived from the Cobb-Douglas *pf.* is always equal to one. This is a serious limitation of this function which forced the economists to search for an alternative production function where the elasticity of substitution needs not to be restricted to unity but it varies depending on the nature of the technology.

(ii) The CES Production Function

The constant elasticity of substitution production function, briefly called *CES* Production Function, is a generalisation of the Cobb-Douglas production function. This function specifies constant elasticity of substitution between capital and labour but not necessarily at unit level. Constancy of the elasticity of substitution implies that changes in the factor proportion, *i.e.*, *K*/*L* ratio, and their relative prices do not alter it. The value of the elasticity of substitution is determined by the technology embodied in the production function. So long ago this technology is constant the elasticity of substitution remains constant.

The *CES* production function has been derived independently by two groups of economists: Arrow, Chenery, Minhas and Solow (1961) and Murry Brown and John, S. deCani (1963).[18] The form of the *CES pf* using Brown's version is given as

$$q = \gamma\ [\delta\ K^{-\rho} + (1 - \delta)\ L^{-\rho}]^{-v/\rho} \qquad ...(87)$$

where q is the level of output, K. is capital and L is labour input per unit time; γ, δ, ρ and v are parameters. The four parameters of this function have special significance for the production theory.

'γ' is a scale parameter showing the efficiency of the technology; 'δ' is defined as input intensity parameter. It denotes the extent to which technology is capital intensive. It is also known as 'distributional parameter'. The limit of variation of δ is $0 < \delta < 1$.

'v' represents the degree of homogeneity of the function and therefore the degree of returns to scale. $v \gtrless 1$ for increasing and decreasing returns to scale. 'ρ' is the substitution parameter. It is a transformation of the elasticity of substitution parameter (σ) in the form:

$$\sigma = \frac{1}{1+\rho}, \qquad ...(88)$$

The range of variation of ρ is $\infty \geq \rho \geq -1$ for which $\sigma \geq 0$.

The *ACMS* Version of the *CES pf* shows constant returns to scale ($v = 1$). It is written as,

$$q = \gamma\ [\delta\ K^{-\rho} + (1 - \delta)\ L^{-\rho}]^{1/\rho} \qquad ...(89)$$

It can be easily shown that the *CES pf* is homogeneous of degree v

The marginal products of K and L from the *ACMS* version of the *CES pf* are:

$$\frac{\partial q}{\partial K} = \delta\gamma^{-\rho}\left(\frac{q}{K}\right)^{1+\rho} \qquad ...(90)$$

and
$$\frac{\partial q}{\partial L}\ (1-\delta)\gamma^{-\rho}\left(\frac{q}{L}\right)^{1+\rho}$$

Both the marginal products are positive for non-zero values of inputs. They depend on the input intensity (δ), efficiency of the technology (γ), and the elasticity of substitution $\left((1-\rho) = \frac{1}{\sigma}\right)$. Further, by taking the second order derivatives $(\partial^2 q/\partial K^2)$ and $(\partial^2 q/\partial L^2)$ we can show that marginal product of K and L decline as K and L increase.

---

18 (*a*) K. J. Arrow, H. B. Chenery, B.S. Minhas and R.M. Solow, "Capital Labour Substitution and Economic Efficiency", *Review of Eco and Stat,* Vol 43, 1961, pp. 228–232.

(*b*) Murry Brown and John Decani, "Technological Change and the Distribution of Income," *International Economic Review,* Vol 4, 1963.

The rate of technical substitution between the inputs K and L would be:

$$RTS = \frac{\partial q/\partial K}{\partial q/\partial L} = \frac{\delta}{1-\delta}\left(\frac{L}{K}\right)^{1+\rho} \quad ...(91)$$

$$= \frac{\delta}{1-\delta}\left(\frac{L}{K}\right)^{1/\sigma} \quad ...(92)$$

Since $1/(1 + \rho = \sigma)$, so $1 + \rho = \frac{1}{\sigma}$

At the equilibrium position (ref. the isoquant analysis, we have

$RTS = \frac{\partial q/\partial K}{\partial q/\partial L} = \frac{r_1}{r_2}$ where r_1 = Price of Capital and r_2 = Price of Labour, *i.e.*, the wage rate. Therefore, we can write:

$$RTS = \frac{\partial q/\partial K}{\partial q/\partial L} = \frac{r_1}{r_2} = \left(\frac{\delta}{1-\delta}\right)\left(\frac{L}{K}\right)^{1/\sigma} \quad ...(93)$$

This gives us the equation of expansion path. Now, simplifying it further, we have

$$\left(\frac{r_1}{r_2}\right)^{\sigma} = \left[\frac{\delta}{(1-\delta)}\right]^{\sigma}\left(\frac{L}{K}\right)$$

or $$\sigma \log\left(\frac{r_1}{r_2}\right) = \log A + \log\left(\frac{L}{K}\right) \text{where} \left(\frac{\delta}{1-\delta}\right)^{\sigma} = A.$$

From this, we have $\frac{\partial \log (L/K)}{\partial \log (r_1/r_2)} = \sigma$ ...(94)

The elasticity of substitution is thus a constant in the *CES pf.*

Further, we have $\sigma = \frac{1}{1+\rho}$.

If $\rho = -1$ then $\sigma = \infty$, and if $\rho = 0$ then $\sigma = 1$.

For $\rho = \infty$ we have $\sigma = 0$.

The Cobb-Douglas and the fixed factor production-functions are special cases of the *CES* production function. For Cobb-Douglas production function $\rho = 0$, so $\sigma = 1$, and for fixed factor Leontief production function we have $\sigma = 0$, *i.e.*, when $\rho = \infty$. Mathematically we can prove these results but that is not required here.

Major application of the *CES* production function is in estimation of the elasticity of substitution. For this we simply use the marginal product equation for labour. By equating marginal product of Labour to wage-rate we have,

$$\frac{\partial q}{\partial L} = W = (1-\delta)_{\gamma}^{-\rho}\left(\frac{q}{L}\right)^{1+\rho} \quad ...(95)$$

or $$W = Z\left(\frac{q}{L}\right)^{1/\sigma} \text{ where } Z = (1 - \delta)\gamma \text{ and } (1 + \rho) = \frac{1}{\sigma}$$

or $$W^{\sigma} = Z^{\sigma}\frac{q}{L}$$

or $$\log \frac{q}{L} = \text{constant} + \sigma \log W. \quad ...(96)$$

By regressing log of $\frac{q}{L}$ on log of W we find σ directly as the regression coefficient of log W.

The elasticity of substitution is an important property of the technology. If it is high, say greater than one, the factors of production resemble each other from the technology point of view. In this situation, if one factor increases indefinitely, the other being constant, the technology permits substitution of the growing factor for the constant factor. This makes both the factors growing indefinitely and so output grows subject to the degree of returns to scale. On the other hand, if $\sigma < 1$, the two factors would be relatively dis-similar from the point of view of the technology, and it would not be easy to substitute the expanding factor for the constant factor. This will result in the disproportionate growth of factors which may restrict the growth of the output.

The *CES* production function has been generalised further by a number of economists, particularly by Lu and Fletcher.[19] They developed a new-type of production function of which the *CES pf* is a special case. This function is called *VES* (Variable Elasticity of Substitution) production function. It is expressed as:

$$q = \gamma\ [\delta K^{-\rho} + (1 - \delta)\ \eta\ (K/L)^{\sigma\ (1 + \rho)}\ L^{-\rho}]^{-1/\rho} \quad ...(97)$$

where $\eta = (1 - b)/(1 - b - c)$

and $\rho = \frac{1}{b} - 1$

'b' and 'c' are the regression coefficients of the equation,

$$\log \left(\frac{q}{L}\right) = \log a + b \log w + c \log \frac{K}{L} + e.$$

If $c = 0$ then $\eta = 1$ and, therefore, the *VES* production function (97) reduces to the *ACMS* version of the *CES* production function. The expression for the elasticity of substitution is given by the *VES* production function as

$$\sigma = \frac{b}{1 - c\left(1 + \frac{wL}{rK}\right)} \quad ...(98)$$

σ the relative factor share (wL/rK) of capital and labour varies. Again, if $c = 0$, then s $= b$, i.e., the regression coefficient of log W as we have in the *CES* production function.

(iii) Fixed Coefficients Types of Production Function

By fixed coefficients we mean that the inputs are required in production of output in fixed quantities. It means, they cannot be substituted for each other and the iso-quants will be right angled as shown in Fig. 5.10 Part a. Let us take a simple case of one output (q) and multiple inputs x_1 ($i = 1,..., n$) to explain this type of production function. Earlier, however, we have already explained this briefly.

We define a_i as the requirement of input i to produce one unit of output (q). Let x_1^0, x_2^0, x_n^0 be the fixed levels of inputs. How much output the firm can produce? For each input we have the relationship.

19. Y. C. La and L. Fletcher, "A Generalisation of the CES Production Function," *Review of Economic and statistics*, Vol 50, 1968, pp. 449–452.

$$x_i^0 = a_i\, q \;;\; i = 1,...,n \qquad ...(99)$$

Comparing these relations, the maximum output that can be produced from the fixed input quantities would be,

$$q = \text{minimum}\left[\frac{x_i^0}{a_i^0}\right], a_i > 0,\; i = 1,...,\; n \qquad ...(100)$$

This means the smallest $\frac{x_i^0}{a_i}$ determines the maximum level of output. It is limiting input. The other inputs in this situation will be partly unused. Let us take an example for this. If $a_1 = 2$, $a_2 = 4$, Let $x_1^0 = 20$, and $x_2^0 = 80$. Total output possible from x_1^0 is $20/2 = 10$ units and from $x_2^0 = 80/4 = 20$ units. Thus, the firms would be able to produce only 10 units of output because the first input x_1^0 is limiting it. The firm has to maintain fixed input proportions which means that it moves along an expansion path showing this fixed proportion while moving on higher and higher right-angled isoquants.

Now, let us extend this case of production to a different situation in which a single output can be produced by m different production activities. Each activity represents a technology. Let a_{ij} $(i = 1,..,n$, and $j = 1,..m)$ be the quantity of ith inputs required to produce one unit of output by jth activity. The output can be produced partly by all different activities and the sum of their outputs would be equal to total output.

$q = \sum_{j=1}^{m} q_j$, where q_j is output produced by jth activity. The inputs used for this would be given as

$$x_i^0 = \sum_{j}^{m} a_{ij}\, q_j,\; i = 1,..n. \qquad ...(101)$$

The output q can be produced by a new activity showing weighted average of the coefficients of the individual activities. Such weighted coefficients are called 'composite' input which may be defined as

$$\alpha_i = \sum_{j=1}^{m} \lambda_j\, a_{ij},\; i = 1,...n. \qquad ...(102)$$

where $0 < \lambda_i < 1$, $j \sum_{j=1}^{m} \lambda j = 1$ and $\lambda j = \frac{q_i}{q}$, *i.e.*, the proportion of total output produced by jth activity. The maximum output that can be produced from a given set of input quantities would be now.

$$q = \min\left(\frac{x_i^0}{\alpha_i}\right),\; \alpha_i > 0 \qquad ...(103)$$

The minimum ratio $\frac{x_i^0}{\alpha_i}$ is limiting but λ_j are selected in such a way as to maximise the minimum ratio.

Let us take an example.

A commodity Q can be produced with three different activities given as $a_{11} = 2$, $a_{21} = 4$; $a_{12} = 3$, $a_{22} = 2$; $a_{13} = 6$, $a_{23} = 1$. As mentioned above, these are requirements of the inputs 1 and 2 per unit output for different activities. By plotting the activities on x_1 and x_2 axes we get the isoquants for different units of the commodity, such as shown for $q = 1$ and $q = 2$. The expansion paths for different activities are OE_1 OE_2, and OE_3. How these three activities will be used to produce a given level of output, say $q = 2$? From the diagram, we find that at point A only activity

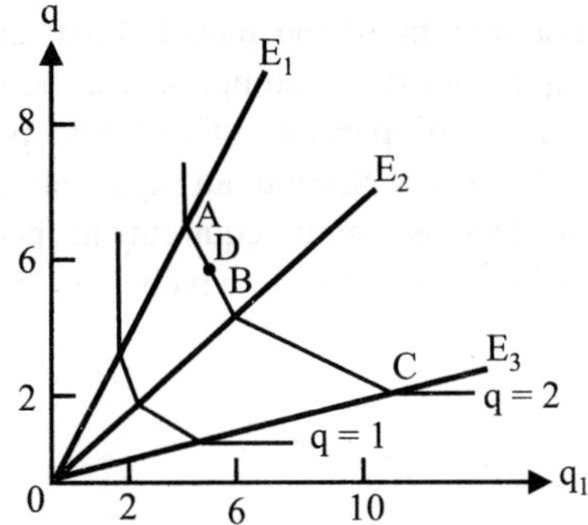

Fig. 5.22 Linear Production Activities and formation of Isoquants

1 will be used to produce 2 units of output. Similarly, at point B only activity 2 and at point C only activity, 3 will be used for this. Between AB segment of the isoquant. we will have composite activities formed by activity 1 and 2. and between BC segment, we have composite activities formed by activity 2 and activity 3 to produce the output. The input requirement for two units of output using a composite activity on AB segment of the isoquant would be:

$$x_1 = 2\alpha_1 = 2[2\lambda + 3\ (1 - \lambda)]$$
$$x_2 = 2\alpha_2 = 2[4\lambda + 2\ (1 - \lambda)]$$

λ varies from 0 at point B to 1 at point. A. Similar computation for a composite activity formed by activity 2 and activity 3 can be made for the isoquant segment BC. Input substitution with composite activities is not possible to the left of OE_1 line, only activity 1 will be used in this region and there may be some unutilised x_2. Similarly, to the right of OE_3 only activity 3 will be used and some x_1 may be left unused.

How to find λ to form the composite activity? We defined $\lambda = q_j/q$, *i.e.*, the proportion of output produced by activity j. We have mentioned that at point say B, $\lambda = 0$ and at point A, $\lambda = 1$. At any point between them, say D, the value of λ would be DB/BA. If the point lies near A then more output will be produced by activity 1 and if it is near point B, more output comes from activity 2. If D is at the mid point of AB, each activity will produce 50% of the total required output. Similar arguments hold for any point between BC segment of the isoquant.

The isoquants shown by the linear activities, as shown above, are of normal shape, convex towards the origin. They are, however, not continuous but discrete. This is a general result for all linear activities. Any activity which is not giving convex isoquants will be inefficient and hence out of the perview of the analysis.

(iv) The Input-Ouput Model

This is also called Leontief's Model after the name of its originator W.W. Leontief. The model is essentially a general equilibrium empirical analysis of production. Demand theory plays no role in it as consumption in the basic input-output model is treated as exogenous. Basically, the model is technological in nature. The production function forming the crux of the model is fixed factors type. Several industries or production sectors of the economy are linked together by this model.

There are two sets of input coefficients of an input-output model. One is that of produced inputs which are outputs of other sectors and second is that of primary factors like labour, capital, etc. In the context of production theory, we will focus on the input-output relations using the produced inputs.

There are two fundamental assumptions of the model. First, each industry or sector produces one and only one homogeneous output; but this assumption can be relaxed by using the concept of composite commodity representing fixed proportions of different products. This assumption is not necessary if output is measured in value terms. Second, all inputs are used strictly in fixed proportions to produce a given level of output. That is, input requirements per unit of output are fixed. The relationship between inputs and output is thus linear which may be specified as,

$$q_{ij} = a_{ij}\, q_j \qquad i = 1,\dots n \qquad \text{...(104)}$$

or

$$a_{ij} = \frac{q_{ij}}{q_j}$$

where q_{ij} is output of ith industry used as input to produce q_j level of output of jth industry a_{ij} known as technological coefficient or input coefficient defines the requirement of output of ith industry to produce one unit output of jth product. All are in physical terms but they may also be expressed in value terms at constant prices.

Now, let us take q_i as total output of ith industry. Part of this output goes to other industries as input to produce their outputs and another part goes to exogenous uses like consumption, export, etc. We may show this type of distribution of q_i as:

$$q_i = q_{i1} + q_{i2} + q_{i3} + .. + q_{in} + y_i,\ i = 1,..n \qquad \text{...(105)}$$

where q_{ij} $(i = 1, n, j = 1,..n)$ represents flow of output of ith industry as input in jth industry, and y_i represents all exogenous uses.

Using (104), we can convert at q_{ij} into $a_{ij}\, q_j$ and therefore rewrite (105) as

$$q = q_{i1}q_1 + a_{i2}q_2 + .. + q_{in}q_m + y_i,\ i = 1,..n. \qquad \text{...(106)}$$

or expanding this we have,

$$\begin{aligned}
(1 - a_{11})\, q_1 - a_{12}q_2 - a_{13}q_3.. - a_{1n}\, q_n &= y_1 \\
- a_{21}q_1 + (1 - a_{22})q_2 - a_{23}q_3.. - a_{2n}q_n &= y_2 \\
- a_{31}q_1 - a_{32}q_2 + (1 - a_{33})q_3.. - a_{3n}q_n &= y_3 \\
- a_{n1}q_1 - a_{n2}q_2 - a_{n3}q_3.. + (1 - a_{nn})q_n &= y_n
\end{aligned} \qquad \text{...(107)}$$

There are n equations for n unknowns (q_1, q_n) since all y_s are known, a_{ij} are known; so, we can solve the system of equations to get:

$$\begin{aligned}
q_1 &= \alpha_{11}y_1 + \alpha_{12}y_2 + ...+ \alpha_{1n}y_n \\
q_2 &= \alpha_{21}y_1 + \alpha_{12}y_2 + ...+ \alpha_{2n}y_n \\
q_n &= \alpha_{n_1}y_1 + \alpha_{22}y_2 + ...+ \alpha_{nn}y_n
\end{aligned} \qquad \text{...(108)}$$

where α_{ij} represents direct and indirect requirement of output q_i to provide one unit of jth output for exogenous uses, *i.e.*, for final demand $(y_j = 1)$. This way, given $y_1,...y_n$, we are able to find $q_1, q_2,..q_n$. Once output levels for different industries are known, the total requirements of primary inputs like labour, capital etc., can be calculated since per unit factor requirements are known.

The input-output model has several extensions, such as dynamic input-output model, regional input-output model, open input-output models and so on.[20] It is applicable to industry level, regional level, national level or even global level of an economy. It is also applicable to a factory level producing many outputs with several inputs. The model has wide applications in resource allocation, planning, pricing, and so on. A detailed study of this technique is out of the scope of this book as it requires a separate volume because of its coverage. Our purpose here was only to demonstrate its nature of being based on fixed input coefficients.

(v) Engineering Production Functions

The conventional specification of the production function is done in terms of the economic factors like land, labour, capital and material. This approach, though widely used in the neo-classical economic theory, has been criticised by some economists like Mrs. John Robinson and also by engineers who considered such production function somewhat hypothetical. This led to the search of an alternative approach for specification of the production function. Engineering production function is an outcome of such an attempt. In engineering production function, the physical properties of inputs are taken into consideration while specifying it and not merely the quantities of inputs. How to do it? The basic approach for this has been suggested by Chenery in his pioneering work on engineering production function.[21] According to him, if the production function is

$$q = f\ (x_1,\ x_2, \ldots x_n)$$

where x_1, $x_2, \ldots x_n$ are quantities of inputs. Suppose each input is expressed in terms of certain physical properties like $\upsilon_1, \upsilon_2 .., \upsilon_m$, we can then have:

$$x_1 = x_i\ (\upsilon_1, \upsilon_2 .., \upsilon_m);\ i = 1,..n$$

Substituting for x_i in the p.f., we, therefore, get

$$q = \phi\ (\upsilon_1, \upsilon_2 .., \upsilon_m) \qquad \ldots(109)$$

Here output of the commodity is a function of certain physical properties of inputs. This is nothing but a general specification for the engineering production function.

For input prices also we may have the specification

$$P_i = P_i\ [\upsilon_1, \upsilon_2 .., \upsilon_m];\ i = 1,..,\ n$$

The cost of production is specified as

$$C = \sum_i^n P_i\ x_i\ ;\ i = 1,..n.$$

Making the substitution for P_i and simplifying the expression, we get a cost function as,

$$C = \pi\ (\upsilon_1, \upsilon_2 .., \upsilon_m) \qquad \ldots(110)$$

that is, the cost of production is a function of the physical properties of inputs.

Suppose we minimise C for a given level of output $q°$, we have the Lagrange function for this as,

$$Z = \pi\ (\upsilon_1, \upsilon_2 .., \upsilon_m) - \lambda\ [\phi\ (\upsilon_1, \upsilon_2 .., \upsilon_m) - q°]$$

---

20. These books provide a good description of the input-output model: (a) W.W. Leontief, *The Structure of American Economy*, 1919-1939, 2nd Ed. Oxford University Press, 1951, (b) H.B. Chenery, *Inter-industry Economics,* John Wiley and Sons 1959.
21. H. B. Chenery, "Engineering Production Functions," *Quarterly Journal of Economics,* Vol. 63, 1949, pp. 507–53.

Equating the partial derivatives of $\upsilon_1, \upsilon_2.., \upsilon_m$ to zeros assuming that the second order condition for this are satisfied we get.

$$\frac{\partial Z}{\partial \vartheta_i} = \pi_i' - \lambda \phi_i' = 0, \; i = 1,..m \qquad ...(111)$$

where π'_i and ϕ'_i are derivatives of cost and output with respect to the properties v_i ... The equilibrium condition that emerge now is:

$$\frac{\phi_1'}{\pi_1'} = \frac{\phi_2'}{\pi_2'} = ... = \frac{\phi_n'}{\pi_n'} = \frac{1}{\lambda} \qquad ...(112)$$

Using (112) and (109), we can determine the values for all m physical properties of the system.

In order to provide an example for this approach, Chenery, has taken up the problem of gas transportation through pipeline. The production function used for this was $X = K_i \; D^{5/3}$. $T\left(1 - \frac{I}{R^2}\right)^{1/2}$ where D stands for inside diameter of the pipe and T is thickness of pipe, R is compression ratio and K_1 is constant. This production function was an outcome of several intermediate steps of linking the concerned physical attributes of pipeline gas transportation, *e.g.*, pressure, temperature, etc. The cost function has also been specified similarly and the genesis of the approach suggested by Chenery has been explained further.

The approach of specifying and using engineering production function looks quite simple but it is difficult as it involves a thorough understanding of concerned engineering problem.

The emphasis on engineering production function is very much similar to the Lancaster's approach of specifying the utility function for a consumer in terms of certain attributes of goods consumed by him rather than the quantities of the goods (See Ch. 4). Both approaches are in the initial stages of development with potentiality for becoming popular in future.

5.10 TECHNOLOGICAL CHANGE: SHIFTS IN PRODUCTION FUNCTION

The entire production theory presented so far in the preceding sections is based on the assumption that production technology does not change; in other words, the production function remains unchanged. Over time, of course, productive techniques do change. The development and application of scientific knowledge leads to both more efficient methods of production and utilisation of better quality inputs. Not only better machines and inputs, there may be improvement in the training and overall quality of workers and in the organisational structure of production. Economists put all such changes overtime under the title of 'technical progress'. This causes a shift of the production function. A shift in the production function is identified through a change in some of its parameters. For example, for a given level of factors, there may be an improvement in the efficiency of the technology or the elasticity of substitution or factor intensity may change. All such changes shift the production function from its original position implying a change in the overall production technology. Consider the following diagram (Fig. 5.23).

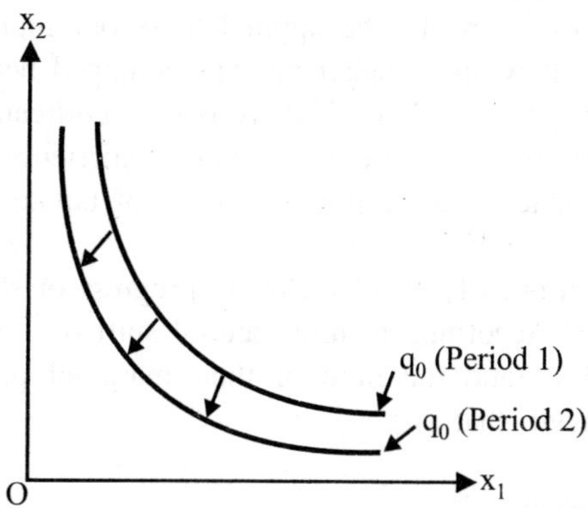

Fig. 5.23 Shift of an Isoquant showing Technical Progress

The isoquant q_o in period 1 has shifted towards the origin in period 2. This means less of inputs x_1 and x_2 are required now to produce q_o level of output of the commodity. This is the effect of the technical progress. In order to understand the process of technical progress in depth let us write the production function for a firm or an economy as:

$$q = A\ (t)\ f\ (K,\ L) \qquad ...(113)$$

Capital (K) and labour (L) are the two inputs, q is the level of output and $A\ (t)$ represents shifts of the production function overtime due to technical progress. If K and L remain unchanged and $A(t)$ grows at the rate of one per cent per year, output also grows at the rate of one per cent per year. It means, from the same amount of the two inputs K and L the firm would be producing more output because of technical progress. This is the same thing as saying that to produce a given level of output lesser amount of K and L is needed as reflected by the inward shift of the isoquant q_o in Fig. 5.23.

Technological change may be *capital augmenting* or *labour augmenting* or *neutral.* To explain these terms let us modify the production function (113) slightly as:

$$q = A(t)\ f\ [a(t)\ K,\ b(t)\ L] \qquad ...(114)$$

where $a(t)$ and $b(t)$ show the efficiency growth of capital and labour inputs respectively overtime. Changes in $A(t)$, K and L being unchanged, bring 'neutral' technological change over time. On the other hand if $a(t)$ is increasing, other things being equal, it is *capital augmenting* or *capital using* or *labour saving.* If $b(t)$ changes, other things being constant, it is *labour augmenting* or *capital saving.* Disproportionate changes in $a(t)$ and $b(t)$ will be generating non-neutral technological changes.

Changes in capital input provide an interesting case (or technological change which is commonly described by the *embodiment hypothesis* of technical progress. As we know, the capital stock used in production at any time constitute a collection of machines and equipment of different ages. Some are old and some new. Under the argument of capital augmentation, it is assumed that all capital equipment, old and new, become more productive over time, thus causing technical progress. The supporter of embodiment hypothesis, however, object to this. In their opinion, technical progress is brought only by new or latest machines and the productivity of old machines remain more or less constant. New machines are embodiments of new or better technology which brings technical progress. There is a weight to this assertion and empirically it has been verified by economists like Solow and others.[22]

---

22. R. M. Solow, *Capital Theory and the Rate of Return,* Amsterdam; North-Holland Pub. Co., 1964, Ch. 3.

The embodiment hypothesis can also be applied to labour input. As old workers retire, new workers join the labour force, they are younger persons equipped better with training and skill and hence are sources of technical progress. Even if there is no significant addition of new workers, the workers in the existing labour force get more and more experience over time and thus get more skilled. This gaining of experience is an important source of labour augmenting technical progress over time.[23]

A test for the above mentioned types of technical progress or shifts in the production function has been provided by Hicks.[24] According to him, neutral shift (*i.e.*, a neutral technical progress) is the one when for a given *K/L* ratio the ratio of their marginal products (*i.e.*, Rate of technical Substitution) remains unchanged, that is,

$$\frac{\partial q / \partial K}{\partial q / \partial L} = \text{Constant}$$

The shape of isoquants remains unchanged and so does the capital intensity as shown in Fig. 5.23.

For labour-saving or capital-using technical progress (*i.e.*, non-neutral shift of the pf) the ratio $\frac{\partial q / \partial K}{\partial q / \partial L}$ increases with a constant *K/L* ratio.

The capital intensity of the technology increases in this case.

In the case of labour-using or capital-saving change in the technology, for a given *K/L* ratio, the ratio $\frac{\partial q / \partial K}{\partial q / \partial L}$ decreases.

Labour intensity of the technology increases in this case.

Using the specific types of production function, such as a Cobb-Douglas or *CES* production function we can derive the conditions of neutral and non-neutral technological changes for the firm or the economy.[25] Technological progress is a comprehensive concept itself. It has three steps linked together in a sequence. The first step is invention. By invention we mean creation of new technology and by technology we mean any tool or technique, any product or process, any physical equipment or method of doing or making, by which human capability is extended. Inventions are made by individuals or corporate bodies like business firms, universities, government institutions and voluntary organisations. Most of the inventions are goal-oriented but some time they may be random or by-products of some other research activities. Innovation is the second stage of technological progress. In this stage, the invention is put on commercial use and it is this stage which is concerned to us in our analysis of shifting the production function for a firm. The last stage is defined as diffusion of the new technology across the economy. From social point of view, this will be beneficial to make improvements in human well-being. There are economic models which analyse the process of technological innovation and diffusion but it is out of the context of this book to go into their detail.[26]

---

23. K. J. Arrow, "The Economic Implications of Learning by Doing," *Review of Economics & Statistics*, Vol. 29, 1962, 155–173.
24. J. R. Hicks, *Theory of Wages,* 2nd Edition, London, 1963, p. 121.
25. For this one may refer to Murry Brown, *On Theory and Measurement of Technological Change,* N.Y., Cambridge University Press, 1968.
26. If interest, one may go through E. Mansfield, *The Economics of Technical Change,* N.Y., W. W. Norton and Co., 1968, for detailed study of this subject.

We have given the types of technical progress and the reasons for them. It will be quite useful to go briefly through measurement of technical progress. Normally, growth in any activity, say X, is measured through percentage or proportionate change in that, *i.e.*,

$$G_x = \frac{\Delta X}{X} \text{ or } \frac{100.\Delta X}{X}$$

ΔX is the change in the activity level over the period defined, say one year. The growth rate of the product of two variables, say X and Y, would be the sum of each variable's growth rate, *i.e.*, $G_{x.y}$, $= G_x + G_y$. Similarly, growth rate of the ratio of two variables is given by the difference of the growth rates of variables, *i.e.*, $G_{x/y} = G_x - G_y$. Growth of per capita income, for example, is defined simply as growth rate of national income minus growth rate of population over the time. Let us apply these rules for measuring the growth rate of technology. We have the production function $q = A(t)$ $f(K,L)$. This function gives us the growth equation for output q as:

$$G_q = G_A + e_{q.l}\, G_L + e_{q.k}\, G_K \qquad ...(115)$$

where $e_{q.l}$ and $e_{q.k}$ are output elasticities with respect to labour (L) and capital (K). Our interest is to find the growth rate of technology, *i.e.*, G_A, given the growth rate of output (G_q) and growth rates for Labour (G_L) and capital (G_K) inputs and the output elasticities for the inputs. R.M. Solow in his pioneering study on technical progress measured G_A for the American economy using the above expression.[27] For the output elasticities, he used the shares of income accruing to labour and capital inputs separately. His study indicated the technology growing at a rate of 1.50 per cent over the period 1909 to 1949 for the American economy. The real output was growing at the rate of 2.75 per cent per year over the same period for the economy. It implies that more than 50 per cent growth in real output was attributed to the technological progress alone. The rest was attributed to the growth of the physical inputs K and L.

This is quite simple approach to measure technical change. It is confined to the measurement of neutral technical change. There are several other ways to measure neutral as well as non-neutral technological progress. These may be read for advance understanding of the subject from other sources.[28]

5.11 CONCLUDING REMARKS

An elementary exposition of the static production theory in the neoclassical framework has been given in this chapter. Emphasis has been given, on understanding producer's behaviour and hence on the concerned equilibrium conditions.

There is another side of the production theory which is its dual and commonly known as the theory of cost. In the next chapter, we will go through this theory, to complete our understanding of production.

27. R. M. Solow, "Technical Progress and the Aggregate Production Function." *Review of Economic and Statistics*, Vol. 39, 1957, pp. 312–320.

28. The following sources provide useful guidance for this:
    (*a*) C. Kennedy and A. P. Tirwell, "Surveys in Applied Economics, Technical Progress," *Economic Journal,* Vol. 82, 1972, pp. 11–72,
    (*b*) Lester, B. Lave, *Technological Change: Its Conception and Measurement,* Englewood Clif: Prentice Hall, 1966.

SUGGESTED READINGS

Baumol, W. J., *Economic Theory and Operations Analysis,* Prentice-Hall of India, N.D., 1978. 2002.

Brown, M., *On the Theory and Measurement of Technological Change,* Cambridge University Press, N.Y., 1968.

Doll, J. P. and Frank Orazen, *Production Economics: Theory with Application,* John Wiley, 1978.

Ferguson, C. E., *Neo-classical Theory of Production and Distribution,* Cambridge University Press, 1968.

Henderson, J. M. and R. E., Quandt, *Microeconomic Theory: A Mathematical Approach,* McGraw-Hill, 1971, 1980.

Shephard, R.W., *Theory of Cost and Production Functions,* Princeton University Press, 1981.

Sher, W. and R. Pindola, *Microeconomic Theory*: Edward Arnold, 1981.

Steven, T. Hackman, *Production Economics,* Springer-Verlag Berlin, 2008.

Varian, H. R., *Microeconomic Analysis,* N.Y., Norton & Co., 3rd Ed., 1992.

REVIEW QUESTIONS

1. Define the concept of 'production' and show how it is different from 'consumption'? Give four different types of examples of 'production' in economic sense.
2. If a variable and a fixed factor cooperate together in production of a commodity, what general pattern of behaviour of total product, marginal product and average product of the variable factor can be conceived in this case? Explain and show the results graphically.
3. In the short-run, it is argued that production occurs only in the stage II. What is the stage II and why it is so important? Explain.
4. Define a production function and show its general properties which are useful from the point of view of theoretical as well as empirical analyses.
5. What is the law of diminishing return? Why do economists consider it as one of the fundamental laws to understand production behaviour?
6. Describe what is meant by the terms 'increasing returns to scale', 'decreasing returns to scale' and constant returns to scale'?
   Is there a law of diminishing returns to scale? To what factors one may attribute reasons for increasing and decreasing returns to scale? Explain in detail.
7. It is said that the marginal product *(MP)* curve of a variable factor always intersects the average product *(AP)* curve of the factor at its top. Is this a true statement? Give an explanation for your answer.
8. Define an 'isoquant' and show its general properties and significance in production theory.
9. Explain the meaning of 'Marginal Rate of Technical Substitution *(MRTS)* and show why and when *MRTS* decreases?
10. An output maximising firm is said to be in equilibrium when for a given cost and input prices the *MRTS* is equal to the ratio of corresponding input prices. Explain why it is so? Same type of equilibrium condition is obtained when we minimise' the cost (or a given level of output. What is the reason for this?
11. Suppose two inputs are required to produce a product. Would it be correct to say that if the prices of the inputs are equal, optimal behaviour on the part of producers will be such that the inputs are used in equal quantities? Explain in full.
12. Define the term 'expansion path'. How it is derived and describe its uses in production theory?

13. What is the meaning of 'production possibility front'? Normally, it is a concave curve towards the origin. Why it is so? Give full explanation for this and also show the practical utility of the *P.P.F.*
14. The production for a commodity is given as
$Q = \alpha K^2L^2 - \beta K^3 L^3$, where L and K are labour and capital quantities, Q is quantity of output and α and β are constants. Show that the marginal product curve passes through the top of the average production curve for each of the two inputs. How much capital and how much labour is employed when average product for each one of them is maximum? Also find the limit of labour utilisation for a given amount of capital, and the limit of capital utilisation for a given amount of labour.
15. What is the definition of a homogeneous production function? What are the properties of such a function? Is Cobb-Douglas production function a homogeneous one? Give reasons for the answer you give.
16. It is argued that shifts in the production function are caused by technological change. Do you agree with this or not? What causes a shift in the production function? Are there other ways of defining technological change? Discuss all these aspects.
17. If we have a situation when m outputs are being produced simultaneously with n inputs. What are the general profit-maximising conditions for this? Give brief deductions of the conditions.
18. 'The Theory of multi-product firm has not been given much importance in microeconomics as it was considered as a straight-forward extension of the theory of single product firm'. Discuss.
19. The production possibility front and the indifference curve for two commodities are linear in shape and downward sloping. Should both of them, in this situation, explain the same phenomenon or different? Explain.
20. (*a*) Explain how elasticity of substitution is a useful concept for examining employment potential in an industry.
(*b*) The production function and iso-cost line for an industry are given as $q = 8L^{0.5} + 20 K^{0.5}$, and $100 = 1\ L + 5\ K$ respectively where q = output, L = Labour and K = Capital. If the price of capital decreases to Rs. 4.0 per unit, find the elasticity of substitution for the industry.
21. A manufacturer has facilities to produce two products. Each product requires a blend of three ingredients. Two of the three ingredients are used in both products. The available quantities of the ingredients X_1, X_2, X_3 and X_4 in pounds (1bs) are 6000, 4000, 350, and 800 respectively. One hundred 1bs of product Y_1 requires 70 1bs of X_1, 25 1bs of X_2, and 5 1bs of X_3. Similarly, one hundred 1bs of product Y_2 requires 35 1bs of X_1, 25 1bs of X_2 and 13 1bs of X_4.
(*a*) Draw the production possibility front for the manufacturer.
(*b*) How much of Y_1 and Y_2 should be produced for maximum net return when the net price of product Y_1 is Rs. 3.20 per 1b, and that of product Y_2 is Rs. 2.40 per 1b?
22. For a Cobb-Douglas production function homogeneous of degree one, show that the rate of technological substitution can be expressed as a function of the input ratio independent of the output level, *i.e.*,

$$RTS_{1:2}\ (x_1,\ x_2) = g\left(\frac{x_1}{x_2}\right).$$

Also derive the expression that can be used to compute the elasticity of substitution between the inputs.

CHAPTER 6

Theory of Cost and Supply

Production and cost are interrelated terms. There cannot be any production without cost and cost without production is economically meaningless. One may argue for a free good for which there will be no cost and hence no price but such goods are excluded from the realm of economic analysis. We have gone through the technical and economic theory of production in the previous chapter. In this theory, we have taken cost of production in the form of either physical quantities of inputs or their values for deriving the equilibrium conditions or production. No attempt has been made to examine the complexities associated with the definition of the term cost, its relationship with the level of output, and its role in the supply of output in the market. All these aspects will now be examined in detail in this chapter.

6.1 WHAT IS 'COST'?

(i) Money Cost

Normally, cost of production means the expenditure or outlay in money terms made on production of a commodity. This is called *'money cost of production'* or *simply cost of production.* This will have components like value of raw materials, total wages and salaries, rent, insurance, taxes, interest on borrowed money, etc. More explicitly, we can say that everything that is used up in production, when expressed in money terms, is called money cost or simply cost of production.

(ii) Real Cost

The cost of production can also be expressed in real terms, *i.e.*, in physical terms. It is the sum of quantities of different inputs used up in production of a commodity. In the production function $q = f(x_1, x_2, \ldots, x_n)$, the right hand side expresses the cost of production in real or physical terms.

It is not possible to sum up the diverse physical units of inputs, including services, into a single unit in order to find the total physical or real cost of production. So, the normal practice for this is to express total physical or real cost still in value terms but at constant input prices. When prices of inputs are constant, variation in total cost in money units will reflect variation in physical cost of production. To be more clear, we have the link between real cost and money cost of production.

(Physical Qty. of Input) × (Input Price) = (Money cost of Input)

If input price is constant, money cost and real (physical) costs are directly proportioned to each other. When cost of production is expressed in money units at constant input prices it is called deflated cost. The process of converting cost of any input at current prices into its cost at constant price is called deflation. This is quite simple. The current cost is divided by the price index of the input and then multiplied by 100 in order to have the cost expressed in terms of base year price of the input.

There is another interpretation of the real cost of production. Economists conceptualize it as the sum of disutilities or discomforts or pains associated in production of a commodity. A worker provides his services in production of the commodity. He is sacrificing his comforts for this. Further, there is sacrifice of consumption, *i.e.*, abstinence, when a producer or any body else saves money for use in production of the commodity. The raw materials, as such, do not give any (or provide less) utility to the producer but certainly more when they are converted in the form of some other produced commodity. Wheats, as such, is useless from consumption point of view but when it is converted in flour, then into bread and then its utility is quite high. So, there is a point when we say that disutilities, abstinence and pains associated in production of a commodity constitute its real cost of production. Compensation is paid in money terms or otherwise for all such pains or discomforts which we may call explicitly as cost of production.

There is a problem with this concept of real cost. We know a sweeper gets very little compensation for the work he does although the disutility or pains for the work done by him is very high. Why this is so? The concept of real cost is inadequate to explain this discrepancy.

(iii) Opportunity Cost

As we know, the resources are generally limited and they can be put into alternative uses. When we choose to produce a commodity or bundle of commodities, say *A* from the given amount of resources we make a sacrifice of another alternative commodity or bundle of commodities, say *B*, which could alternatively be produced with the given resources. Thus, we can express the cost of production of the commodity (or commodities) which we are making in terms of alternatives foregone. This is called opportunity cost. Consider the following production possibility front. If we produce only *OA* quantity of *B* from a given amount of resource X^0, its opportunity cost would be the sacrifice of the alternative *OB* quantity of commodity *A* that could be produced from X^0. If we operate at *R* point, *OC* of commodity *B* and *OD* of commodity *A* would be produced. The opportunity cost of *OC* units of *B* would be *DB* units of commodity *A*, and the opportunity cost of *OD* units of commodity *A* would be *CA* units of commodity *B*.

The opportunity cost can be defined from the points of view of a society as a whole as well as an individual producer. How many hospitals can be constructed instead of buying a jet fighter aircraft? How much sacrifice of agricultural output will be there if the land on which it is grown is put under construction of houses? What is the opportunity cost of a worker in India? Clearly, we can find answers for such questions in terms of the opportunity costs. A private investor can put his money on real estate business or a manufacturing business. What will be the opportunity cost of either of these two investment alternatives? It is the sacrifice of the return from the one when the other investment alternative is chosen. When a worker is given a wage, the principle of opportunity cost will be in operation in taking such a decision. He will not be paid less than what he can get elsewhere. A sweeper is given low wage rate because his opportunity cost is very low. A worker

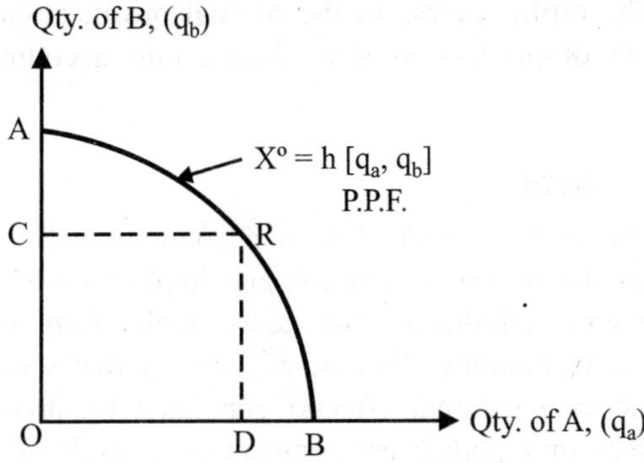

Fig. 6.1 The Concept of Opportunity Cost

in India, in general, is paid a low wage because his opportunity cost is low due to high unemployment in the country.

(iv) Economic Cost

We may now define economic cost. Let us first define it from the view point of a producer. Given the notion of opportunity cost, we can say that economic costs are the payments a producer must make or income he must yield, to the resource suppliers in order to attract the resources used by him away from the alternative lines of production. By the alternative lines of production we mean diversion of resources either to production of a different commodity or to a different producer altogether.

Payments may be made either explicitly or implicitly. That is, total cost is the sum of the explicit payments and implicit payments to the resource suppliers. The monetary payments, that is, cash outlays, which a producer makes to those outsiders who supply inputs to him are called 'explicit costs'. But a producer may use certain resources for which he does not pay to outsiders. The costs of self owned and self employed resources are called 'implicit costs'. The opportunity costs of self owned resources, including self employment, will be in implicit form.

(v) Accounting Costs

Accountants do not take into consideration non-expenditure items of cost while recording them in their books. For them total cost of production will be just the sum of all explicit costs. Several implicit costs for which there is no precise way of measurement are not included in the accounting costs. The concept of opportunity cost is of little help for this to accountants. Thus, we find a basic difference in conceptualization of cost of production by economists and accountants. For an accountant, it is the sacrifice of money or expenditure made on purchase of inputs in connection with the business. For an economist, on the other hand, cost means sacrifice of alternatives that have been foregone in production of a commodity.

(vi) The Concept of Normal Profit

This is the opportunity cost of the entrepreneur if there is no explicit payment made to him in the form of salary or otherwise. That is, in this case, the implicit cost of the producer will be called 'normal profit'. This is the wage or salary assigned to him when he is engaged in his own business. Normal profit is thus an item of cost. If there is no normal profit, no one will be tempted to start his own business. The profit, excess to the normal profit, is called economic profit. It is a surplus over the total cost of production after taking into account all explicit and implicit payments.

(vii) Social and Private Costs

All private costs, *i.e.*, the cost of production of a commodity from the point of view of its producer, will be expressed as the sum of all explicit and implicit costs. From the point of view of society there may be some more additional cost items in the form of adverse external effects generated by production of the commodity. That is, we can say that social cost is a sum of private costs and disutilities (*i.e.*, adverse external effects) generated by production of the commodity. Smoke coming out of a factory may pollute environment as a result of which people may be sick and therefore spend more money on treatment which will be an item of social cost. Similar example is that of external effects generated by disposing factory waste in river. Several other such examples can be cited.

Sometimes a government provides subsidy for production of an essential commodity, such as fertiliser. The subsidy will be a part of social cost. Taxes paid by a private manufacturer will be included in private cost but excluded from the social cost as they are mere transfers.

Private cost of a commodity is expressed in terms of market prices of inputs but social cost will be expressed in terms of opportunity prices or imputed costs of the inputs. A private manufacturer will not bother regarding external effects of its business but from the point of view of society we have to examine them very carefully.

From the above brief description of various concepts of cost we may now be able to answer the question: what is cost? We may define it in terms of money cost, real cost, accounting cost, private cost or social depending on whose view point we are taking into account. The term 'economic cost' takes care of all such view points since it is based on the principle of opportunity cost and also uses money as accounting unit. Therefore, when we try to answer the question 'what is cost', we have to express it in terms of economic cost.

6.2 SOME SPECIFIC TYPES OF COSTS

Some kinds of costs have already been discussed above. There are some more categories which we would like to discuss here.

(i) Establishment *Vs.* Operating Costs

The expenditure made on construction of a factory or business unit is called 'establishment' or 'construction cost.' It is also called as 'First Cost' or 'Phase I' cost in the terminology of cost-benefit analysis or project appraisal. Items of expenditure included in the establishment cost will be such as initial cost of preparing feasibility reports for the establishment of the factory; expenditure on getting licences, etc.; land and site development expenditure; cost of plant and equipment; furniture, etc., including their installation; buildings and other constructions; expenditure on training of personnel; royalties for seeking rights; cost of raising finance; and stock of raw material, tools, etc., for initial run of the plant.

Once the plant is ready for operation, it will function and production begins. To produce goods we have to spend money on wages and salaries of workers and other personnel, raw materials including fuel and power, maintenance and repair works, rent, interest, insurance, taxes, depreciation, etc. All this is called 'operating cost' or 'running cost' or 'phase 2 cost'. There will be two types of operating costs, one is 'fixed cost' or overhead cost or 'indirect cost.' These cost items do not vary with the volume of output. They have to be met whether output is low or high. Items like salaries of certain administrative staff, interest on borrowed money, depreciation charges, certain royalties and taxes, etc., will be included in the fixed cost. The second part of the operating cost is the cost on labour, fuel and power, raw material packaging, etc., which vary with the volume of output. These are called 'variable costs' or 'direct costs' or 'prime costs'. All operating cost is shown itemwise in the profit and loss account of the producer. The establishment cost, on the other hand, is shown on the time-profile of the project. A time profile is the statement showing the benefit and cost accruing from a project over its life time. The profit and loss account, on the other hand, is concerned with the annual operation of the business giving the account of its sales revenue and cost and hence profit occuring to the producer.

(ii) Short-run and Long-run Costs

This classification of cost is based on time element. We have already defined a short-run as a period during which there will be at least one input which cannot be varied in size (or quantity). Normally, it is the plant and machinery used in production. Production has to be carried on with the fixed size of the plant. The cost of production, *i.e.*, operating cost of output with the given or fixed size of the plant is called 'short-run cost' which will constitute both 'fixed costs' and 'variable costs' as defined above. So long as the fixed size of the plant continues, the short run continues. It may be one week, or one month, or few months, or few years depending on the nature of the technology, construction period, etc. For some types of production, the size of plant can be changed easily but for others it may take long time, such as in capital-intensive plants like steel mills, oil refineries, shipbuilding, etc.

The long-run is defined as the time period during which all inputs, including size of the plant, are variable. The cost of production related to this period will be called long-run cost. There will be no fixed cost in the long-run, since every input is variable. Therefore, all long-run costs will be variable.

Both short-run and long-run costs are vital for business decision-making. Short-run costs will be useful for taking decisions regarding operation of the plant while long-run costs will be useful to decide optimum size of the plant, *i.e.*, in taking decisions whether the plant size is to be changed or not.

(iii) Historical and Replacement Costs

The historical cost, of an asset (*i.e.*, property used in production) is the expenditure made on it when it was purchased. The replacement cost, on the other hand, will be the outlay or expenditure on the asset if it is to be purchased now. The difference between these two costs of the asset will be because of price variation over time. Most of the financial accounting of capital stock in business firms is done in terms of historical cost, a cumulative total of which is called 'book value'. This will be a poor indicator of the true value of capital stock if variation in prices of assets over time is significant. Replacement cost, however, reflects the true value of assets in the market at the time of their replacement.

(iv) Separable and Common Costs

Costs, which can be attributed exclusively, to a product are called separable costs. On the other hand, common costs are those which cannot be attributed exclusively to any product. They are joint costs in the sense that different products share them. For example, it may be difficult to separate electricity cost product-wise in a multi-product case but raw material and labour costs can be separated product-wise without any difficulty. Fixed cost items are, by and large, common costs. There is no exact method to allocate such costs product-wise. Only approximations are made for this, such as in the proportion of turnover of each product, one can allocate the common costs. Non-separation of common costs or fixed costs creates a problem in pricing decisions for the products in a multiproduct situation.

Apart from the types of costs mentioned above there are some more cost terms, such as marginal cost, average cost, etc. These costs will be discussed in the following section.

6.3 THE COST-OUTPUT RELATIONSHIP: DERIVATION OF COST FUNCTION

Henceforth, we will be studying different aspects of operating cost only. An important aspect of this is to trace out the plausible relationship between volume of output and its total cost of production. *A mathematical expression, showing the relationship between volume of output and its total cost of production, is called 'cost-function'*. The objective of this section is to go through the procedure of derivation of the cost-function for a producer or for a commodity as one may prefer to call it.

To derive the cost-function we require essentially two things: the production function for the commodity which we have specified in Ch. 5 as $q = F(x_1, x_2, \ldots, x_n)$, and the isocost line $C = r_1x_1 + r_2x_2 + \ldots + r_nx_n$, where x_i $(i = 1, \ldots n)$ are input quantities and r_i $(i = 1, \ldots, n)$ their respective prices. Given this information, we can maximise total output for a given cost or minimise total cost for a given level of output to get the optimum (*i.e.*, least cost) combination of inputs. Once we find the input demand function, we can substitute them in the production function to get the desired cost-output relationship. To explain the procedure let us take a two input production function:

$$q = F(x_1, x_2) \qquad \ldots(1)$$

The iso-cost line for this is given as:

$$C = r_1x_1 + r_2x_2 + b \qquad \ldots(2)$$

The isocost line is being changed slightly by adding 'b' to it. 'b' is fixed cost while other component $r_1x_1 + r_2x_2$ reflects the variable cost. It is being done for the derivation of the cost function in the standard notation, otherwise there is no need for this. We may assume some x_i as fixed and get the cost function without putting 'b' separately.

In Chapter 5, while discussing the equilibrium on isoquants we have mentioned two approaches, one is constrained output maximisation and the other is constrained cost minimisation. Both the approaches give the same equilibrium condition for the producer. Let us follow one of them here. We specify our problem as

Max. $\quad q = F(x_1, x_2)$

Subject to $\quad C^0 = r_1x_1 + r_2x_2 + b \qquad \ldots(3)$

Using the Lagrange multiplier method, we have:

$$V = F(x_1, x_2) + \mu\,[C^0 - r_1x_1 - r_2x_2 - b]$$

By taking the partial derivatives and equating them to zeros, the first order maximisation conditions for this, assuming fulfilment of the second order conditions, are:

$$\partial V/\partial x_1 = F_1 - \mu r_1 = 0$$

$$\partial V/\partial x_2 = F_2 - \mu r_2 = 0 \qquad \ldots(4)$$

$$\partial V / \partial x_{\mu} = C^0 - r_1 x_1 - r_2 x_2 - b = 0$$

We have three unknown here x_1, x_2 and $\mu(x_1$ and x_2 will be in F_1 and $F_2)$ and there are three equations. We can, therefore solve the system. This solution will give us the input demand functions in terms of known magnitudes r_1, r_2 and $C - b$. Essentially, we have

$$x_1 = x_1 \; [r_1, r_2, C - b] \qquad ...(5)$$
$$x_2 = x_2 \; [r_1, r_2, C - b]$$

The demand for each input is a function of its price, the price of other input(s) and the amount of outlay available for spending on the inputs $(C - b)$.

By substituting these input demand functions in the production function (1) we have,

$$q = F \; [(r_1, r_2, C - b), (r_1, r_2, C - b)]$$

This function on simplification produces

$$C^0 = \phi \; [q, r_1, r_2] + b$$

At every equilibrium, we get this relationship for varying C and q we would thus be getting;

$$C = \phi \; (q, r_1, r_2) + b \qquad ...(6)$$

The total cost of production thus constitutes two components: $\phi(q_1, r_1, r_2)$ and b. The first one $\phi \; (q_1, r_1, r_2)$ is called variable cost, which depends on the level of output, and input prices. The second component 'b' is the fixed cost. The expression (6) thus reflects the short-run cost-function. If input prices are constant, q alone will be the determinant of the variable cost and hence of total cost of production. The cost-function (6) is a reduced form of the production function (1). It reflects the same characteristics in a different way which are shown by the production function. Both the functions are thus interrelated.

Let us take some specific examples for derivation of the cost function. We first take the Cobb-Douglas production function for this. We have

$$q = A \; x_1^{\alpha} . x_2^{\beta}$$

and
$$C = r_1 x_1 + r_2 x_2 + b.$$

The marginal products for x_1 and x_2 from the Cobb-Douglas pf are:

$$\frac{\partial q}{\partial x_1} = \alpha A \; x_1^{\alpha - 1} . x_2^{\beta} = \alpha \frac{q}{x_1}$$

and
$$\frac{\partial q}{\partial x_2} = A\beta = x_1^{\alpha} . x_2^{\beta - 1} = \beta \frac{q}{x_2} \qquad ...(7)$$

The equilibrium condition for optimum combination of the inputs is given as:

$$\frac{\partial q / \partial x_1}{\partial q / \partial x_2} = \frac{\alpha q / x_1}{\beta q / x_2} = \frac{\alpha x_2}{\beta x_1} = \frac{r_1}{r_2} \qquad ...(8)$$

On simplification, this yields the equation of the expansion path as,

$$\alpha x_2 r_2 - b x_1 r_1 = 0 \qquad ...(9)$$

From the isocost equation we have,

$$r_1 x_1 = C - r_2 x_2 - b.$$

Substituting this in (9), we have

$$\alpha \; x_2 r_2 - \beta \; [C - r_2 x_2 - b] = 0$$

or
$$x_2 = \frac{\beta}{\alpha+\beta}\left[\frac{C-b}{r_2}\right] \quad ...(10)$$

Similarly, substituting $r_2x_2 = C - r_1x_1 - b$ from the isocost line in (9) and simplifying, we get

$$x_1 = \frac{\alpha}{\alpha+\beta}\left[\frac{C-b}{r_1}\right] \quad ...(11)$$

(10) and (11) are the input demand equations

We now substitute them in the production function (1) which gives us,

$$q = A\left[\frac{\alpha}{\alpha+\beta}\frac{(C-b)}{r_1}\right]^{\alpha}\left[\frac{\beta}{\alpha+\beta}\left(\frac{C-b}{r_2}\right)\right]^{\beta}$$

or
$$q = A\left(\frac{\alpha}{\alpha+\beta}\right)^{\alpha}\left(\frac{\beta}{\alpha+\beta}\right)^{\beta}\left(\frac{1}{r_1}\right)^{\alpha}\left(\frac{1}{r_2}\right)^{\beta}[C-b]^{\alpha+\beta}$$

By taking the $(\alpha + \beta)$th root of this we have,

$$q^{1/(\alpha+\beta)} = \left[A\left(\frac{\alpha}{\alpha+\beta}\right)^{\alpha}\left(\frac{\beta}{\alpha+\beta}\right)^{\beta}\left(\frac{1}{r_1}\right)^{\alpha}\left(\frac{1}{r_2}\right)^{\beta}\right]^{\frac{1}{\alpha+\beta}}(C-b)$$

or
$$C = \left[A\left(\frac{\alpha}{\alpha+\beta}\right)^{\alpha}\left(\frac{\beta}{\alpha+\beta}\right)^{\beta}\left(\frac{1}{r_1}\right)^{\alpha}\left(\frac{1}{r_2}\right)^{\beta}\right]^{-1/(\alpha+\beta)}.q1/(\alpha+\beta)+b$$

or
$$C = (\alpha + \beta)\ [A\ \alpha^{\alpha}\beta^{\beta}]^{-1/(\alpha+\beta)}.q^{1/(\alpha+\beta)}.r_1^{-\alpha/(\alpha+\beta)}.r_2^{-\beta/(\alpha+\beta)} + b$$

Let $\alpha + \beta = R$ (*i.e.*, the degree of returns to scale), so we have,

$$C = R\ [A\ \alpha^{\alpha}\beta^{\beta}]^{-1/R}.q^{1/R}.r_1^{\alpha/R}.r_2^{\beta/R} + b$$

Let $\quad K = R\ [A\ \alpha^{\alpha}\beta^{\beta}]^{-1/R}$

Therefore,

$$C = K\ q^{1/R}\ .\ r_1^{\alpha/R}\ r_2^{\beta/R} + b \quad ...(12)$$

If there are n inputs $x_1, x_2, ..., x_n$ we expand this as

$$C = K\ q^{1/R}\ .\ r_1^{\alpha/R}\ .\ r_2^{\beta/R}\ .\ r_3^{\gamma/R}\ ... + b. \quad ...(13)$$

Where $\quad K = R\ [A\alpha^{\alpha}\beta^{\beta}\gamma^{\gamma}...]^{-1/R}$

and $\quad R = (\alpha + \beta + \gamma + ...)$

Equation (13) provides the cost function derived from the Cobb-Douglas p.f.

In a general form, we are getting:

$$C = \phi\ (q, r_1, r_2... r_n) + b$$

which is the same as given by equation (6)

The equation (13) indicates that total cost of production depends on

(*a*) level of output (q)

(*b*) input prices (r_1, r_2... r_n)

(*c*) type of production function

(*d*) period of decision: short-run or long-run

If input prices are constant, we have

$$C = \phi(q) + b \qquad ...(14)$$

where C = total deflated' (*i.e.*, at constant prices) cost

$\phi(q)$ = total variable cost

and b = fixed cost

Output level is the sole determinant of the cost in this case.

In the long-run, all costs will be variable. Even 'b' varies with the size of the plant and hence with the level of output. We will, therefore, get,

$$C = \psi(q) \qquad ...(15)$$

When input prices are constant, and

$$C = \psi(q_1, r_1, r_2 ... r_n) \qquad ...(16)$$

When input prices are variable.

The derivation of the cost function from the *CES* production function is done in the same way as we derive it from the Cobb-Douglas production function. It is, of course, slightly complicated exercise from mathematical point of view. The final shape of the cost function comes out as follows.[1]

Given the *CES* p.f. as $q = \gamma\ [\delta x_1^{-\rho} + (1-\delta)x_2^{-\rho}]^{-1/\rho}$ and the isocost line $C = r_1x_1 + r_2x_2$, the cost function from this would be

$$C = \left(\frac{1-\delta}{r_2}\right)^{\sigma/(1-\sigma)} \left[r_1 \left(\frac{\delta}{1-\delta}\right)^{\sigma} \left(\frac{r_2}{r_1}\right)^{\sigma} + r_2 \right]^{1/(1-\sigma)} \cdot \frac{q}{\gamma}$$

which, on simplification, can be written as

$$C = \frac{K}{\gamma} \cdot q \qquad ...(17)$$

where K = constant shown, by the product of the bracketed terms. γ is the efficiency parameter of the *CES* pf. If efficiency goes up, total cost decreases. That is an obvious result from (17). The cost function (17) indicates constant return to scale. It can be generalized further for any degree of returns to scale by taking $1/v$ as exponential of q, where v is the degree of returns to scale.

For further analysis, let us take the cost function $C = \phi(q) + b$ into consideration. As we mentioned earlier, since input prices are not appearing in $\phi(q)$, which means output level is the sole determinant of C which is now interpreted as real cost (*i.e.*, physical cost).

Dividing both sides of this function by the level of output q we get

$$\frac{C}{q} = \frac{\phi(q)}{q} + \frac{b}{q} \qquad ...(18)$$

where C/q is average total cost of production and $\phi(q)/q$ is average variable cost of production; and b/q is average fixed cost of production. The average total cost is thus a sum of average variable cost and average fixed cost.

1. For derivation of the cost function, see C. E. Fergusion, *Neo-classical Theory of Production and Distribution;* Cambridge University Press, 1968, pp. 166-167.

By taking the derivative of $C = \phi(q) + b$, we have

$$dC/dq = \phi'(q) \qquad \text{...(19)}$$

dC/dq is defined as marginal cost of production which is equal to the derivative of $\phi(q)$ with respect to q as shown by $\phi'(q)$.

Marginal cost of production is the addition in total cost of production by producing one more additional unit of output. That is, $TC_{n+1} - TC_n = MC_{n+1}$ where TC_{n+1} is total cost of $n + 1$ units of q and TC_n is total cost of n units of q. The slope of total cost function or the slope of total variable cost function defines the marginal cost at a point on the *TC* or *TVC* curve. The average cost, however, would be given by the slope of the line joining that point to the origin. Fixed cost plays no role in defining the marginal cost of a commodity.

How total cost of production varies with the level of output depends on the type of technology shown by the production function for the commodity. A fairly general picture, as emerged from the observations and empirical work on cost-output relationship for various industries, is presented in Fig. 6.2.

In part (*a*) of this diagram, we see variation in total cost and its components, *TVC* and *TFC*, with the level of output. Fixed cost does not vary; so, it is a straight line showing *OA* level for all output levels. The total variable cost *(TVC)* starts from the origin. It is shown initially increasing at a slower proportion than the output but later on increases at a greater proportion than the output. This means the slope of the *TVC* decreases first but later on increases. The total cost curve (*TC*) shows similar variation as the *TVC* and starts from point *A* on *y*-axis.

Figure 6.2(*b*) shows variations in the average and marginal costs with the level of output. Since total fixed cost is constant, so average fixed cost (*AFC*) declines continuously as output increases forming a rectangular hyperbola. It meets the quantity axis only at the infinity. The average variable cost (*AVC*) declines first, reaching the lowest level for *qv* output and then starts rising showing '*U*' shape with changes in output. This is a very important form of the *AVC* since this, together with the *AFC*, determines the shape of the *ATC* curve which is also showing '*U*' shape showing the lowest average total cost for q_T level of output. q_T is greater than q_v and we see that *ATC* = *AVC* + *AFC*. The marginal cost (*i.e.*, slope of *TC* or *TVC*) declines first, reaching the lowest level for q_m output and then rises. It passes through the lowest points of the *AVC* and *ATC* curves.

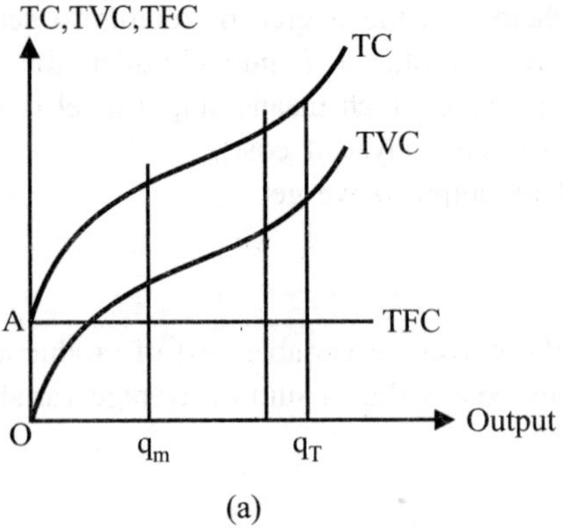

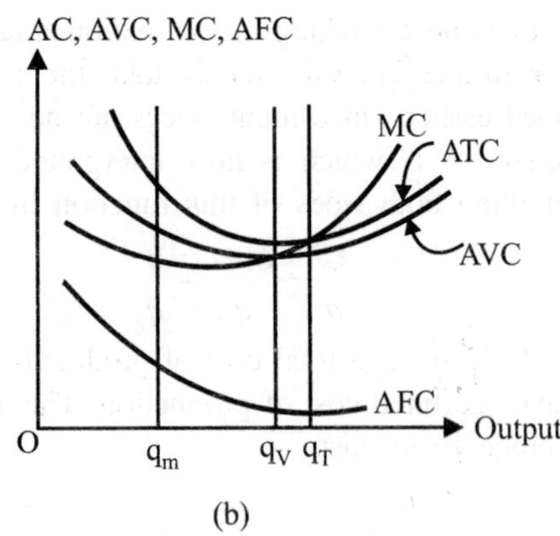

Fig. 6.2 Short-run Cost-Output Relations

So long as *MC* is less than *AVC, AVC* declines and if *MC* is greater than *AVC, AVC* rises. Similarly, when *MC* is less than *AC, AC* declines and when *MC* is greater than *AC, AC* rises. These trends are reflected In Fig. 6.2(b).

As mentioned above, *AVC* curve and the pattern of its variation is very important from the point of view of the cost theory. The *AVC* curve declines initially as output goes up. This means we are getting increasing returns in production of the commodity initially. After reaching a lowest point *AVC* starts rising. A rise in *AVC* means decreasing returns. So, it is the effect of increasing and decreasing returns that causes the *AVC* to decline first and then increasing forming '*U*' shape. Since *AC* is a sum of *AVC* and *AFC*, the shape of the *AVC* curve determines the shape of the *AC* curve. The variation in the *MC* is also reflecting increasing marginal return initially and then decreasing marginal return for the factors in production. Marginal cost and marginal product of a variable factor are inversely related to each other and so is the situation for the average cost and average product for the factor. These relations will also be shown through algebra shortly in this section itself.

As mentioned earlier, there are some important factors which cause increasing returns initially and hence decreasing average variable or average total cost as output increases. The most important one is the greater utilisation of the indivisible fixed factor(s). As capacity utilization (increase in output) increases, the average cost declines. Thus, we find increasing returns to the variable inputs in this stage. Later on, however, the cost rises because of either capacity constraint or some other factors responsible for this. Another factor that is responsible for the increasing returns is the increasing scope for division of labour. We know at lower level of output, one may not sustain the process of division of labour since work for each specialist may not be adequate. When output level goes up it is quite possible to have the division of labour implemented in the work and so efficiency increases leading thereby increasing returns and decreasing costs. The division of labour may be applicable to all categories of labour including. management and supervision, and lines of processing. Further, with increase in output, a firm may think of having better machines, better inputs and proper utilization of by-products which also give increasing returns. Thus, the technological factors supported by the organisational changes make production efficient which reduces the cost of production.

If we take into consideration the current cost of production rather than deflated, then, of course, there will be factors like economies of bulk marketing, economies of financing and a host of other economic factors responsible for decreasing costs. However, the average total and variable costs do not decline continuously, after reaching a minimum point they start rising. This is the situation when the stage of decreasing returns sets in the process of production. Probably, the most important factor for this is the difficulty in coordinating the production properly. There will be disproportionate growth of certain critical inputs and overall internal organisation becomes inefficient; so cost rises. Thus, in general, we observe '*U*' shaped average cost curves *(AVC* and *AC*) for a firm producing a commodity. Exceptions, such as linear *AVC* and *AC*, and *'L'* shapes *AVC* or *AC* are quite possible. This depends on the technology which is expressed by the production and cost functions for the commodity as we have seen earlier.

By using the average total cost curve, we can define the optimum capacity of production for a firm. It is that level of output for which the average total cost of production is minimum. In Fig. 6.2, q_T is the optimum capacity of production since it is showing the least average total cost. The optimum capacity of output, by and large, depends on the technological factors which are eventually represented by the cost-output relationship for the commodity.

We find from above, marginal and average products are inversely related to marginal and average costs. Let us show these relations in precise quantitative forms. We define short-run marginal cost as:

$$SMC = \frac{\Delta TC}{\Delta q} = \frac{\Delta TC}{\Delta X}\frac{\Delta X}{\Delta q} \qquad ...(20)$$

where ΔX is the change in quantity of the variable factor, Δq is the change in quantity of output and ΔTC is the change in total cost.

$\frac{\Delta TC}{\Delta X} = r_x$, since the change in total cost is brought only by the change in the quantity of the variable factor. The expression (20) can now be written as:

$$SMC = \frac{r_x}{MP_x} \qquad ...(21)$$

MP_x is the marginal product of x.

If there are several variable factors we can still show the inverse relation between marginal cost and marginal products of the variable factors. The constrained cost minimization in the isoquant framework as discussed in Chapter 5 provided the equilibrium condition for optimal factor combination as:

$$\frac{f_1}{r_1} = \frac{J_2}{r_2} = ... = \frac{1}{\lambda}$$

when λ is defined as marginal cost $\left(\frac{dC}{dq}\right)$. Inversing this, we directly get,

$$\frac{r_1}{f_1} = \frac{r_2}{f_2} = \lambda \qquad ...(22)$$

That is, for each input we have inverse relationship between marginal product and marginal cost. Whenever marginal product increases, the marginal cost decreases and vice versa.

For average variable cost (*AVC*) we have the expression:

$$AVC = \frac{TVC}{q}$$

Also $TVC = r_x \cdot x$; r_x is the price of the factor and x its quantity.

Therefore, we have

$$AVC = \frac{r_x x}{q} = \frac{r_x}{q/x} = \frac{r_x}{AP_x} \qquad ...(23)$$

This defines the inverse relationship between average variable cost and average product of a factor.

If there are more than one variable factor, we have:

$$AVC = \frac{TVC}{q} = \frac{r_1x_1 + r_2x_2}{q} = \frac{r_1}{q/x_1} + \frac{r_2}{q/x_2}$$

or

$$AVC = \frac{r_1}{AP_1} + \frac{r_2}{AP_2} \qquad ...(24)$$

AP_1 = Average product of x_1, AP_2 = Average product of x_2

To show that marginal cost curve passes through the minimum point of *AVC* and *AC* curves, let us take the relationship,

$$AVC = \frac{TVC}{q}$$

$$\frac{d(AVC)}{dq} = \frac{d(TVC/q)}{dq} = \frac{q.\frac{d(TVC)}{dq} - TVC}{q^2} = 0$$

Subject to satisfaction of the second order condition for this.

This gives us $q\ \frac{d(TVC)}{dq} - TVC = 0$

or $$\frac{d(TVC)}{dq} = \frac{TVC}{q} \quad ...(25)$$

i.e., $$MC = AVC$$

So when *AVC* is minimum, *MC* is equal to *AVC*. Similarly, for minimum of *ATC*, we have

$$\frac{d(TC/q)}{dq} = \frac{q\,d(TC)/dq - TC}{q^2} = 0$$

That is, $qd(TC)/dq - TC = 0$

or $$\frac{d(TC)}{dq} = \frac{TC}{q}$$

or $$MC = ATC \quad ...(26)$$

Since $d(TC)/dq = d(TVC/dq) = MC$

This means the marginal cost curve passes through the lowest point of the average total cost.

6.4 THE DERIVATION AND ANALYSIS OF LONG-RUN COST FUNCTION

In the long-run, as we have said earlier, all inputs are variable but the production technology remains unchanged. The time period corresponding to the long-run will be such that the producer can make necessary changes in the size of his plant. If one particular size of the plant turns out to be inadequate to produce a given level of output the firm or producer can switch over to the bigger plant. If plants of different sizes are available, the producer will face the problem of choice from them. For every size of plant there exists one level of fixed cost. Now, since size of plant is variable, fixed cost will also be variable. It varies with the size of plant. The size of a plant is expressed in terms of output units; so, when we say that fixed cost varies with size of the plant, it means it varies with the level of output in the long-run and behaves in the same way as the other components of the variable cost. For simplicity, we may express fixed cost '*b*' as

$$b = b(k) \quad ...(27)$$

where *k* is a measure of the size of plant.

Let us take a simple example of production to explain how the problem of choice of sizes of plant arises in the long-run.

A manufacturer plans to produce 10,000 units of a product per month. Three different sizes of the plant are available from which he can make the choice *i.e.*, 5,000 units, 10,000 units, and 20,000 units of plant capacity. Which one he should pick-up? It is not simple to decide on this unless we know the cost of production for the required units of product to be manufactured.

He will select that particular size of the plant which gives minimum total cost for the planned output level.

In general, let us consider plants of three sizes for which cost functions are given by STC_1, STC_2, and STC_3 in the following figure. If the producer wants to produce q_1 level of output, he should select the size of plant which shows the cost curve STC_1 since the other two cost curves are above to it, so it will be costly to produce by the other two plants. Similarly, if the producer wants to produce q_2 level of output, STC_2 *i.e.*, the plant of size 2 will be chosen and for q_3 it will be the plant of size 3, *i.e.*, STC_3 will be chosen since it shows lower total cost for this level of

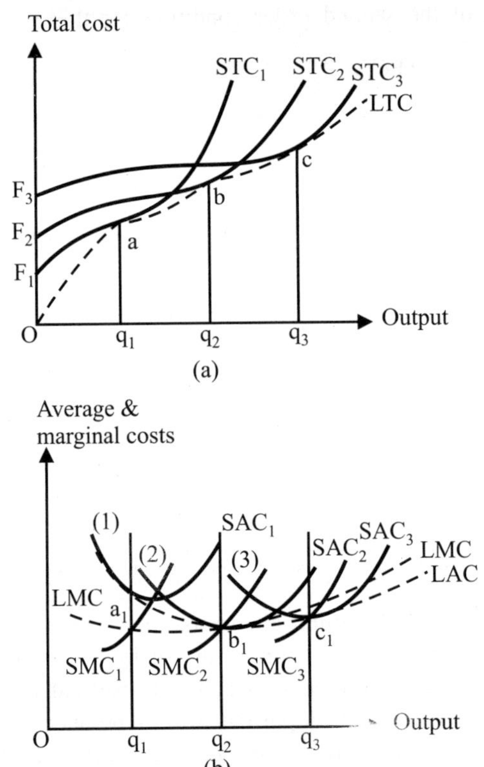

Fig. 6.3 Long-run Cost Curves

output. Now, we have to identify the long-run total cost function. Since there is no fixed cost, so when output $q = 0$ the LTC will be zero. It means that it passes through the origin. The LTC, as we have conceptualised it, shows the lowest cost of producing any given level of output because when alternative plants are available and all costs are variable the firm is free to choose the most economical combination of inputs to produce its output. This means the lowest cost of production for the output. If we assume an infinite number of short-run total cost curves, we can define a long-run total cost curve as the locus of all those points on the short-run total cost curves which show least cost of production for production of each possible level of output. At every point of the long-run, total cost curve, will fmd a short-run total cost curve touching it. Thus, we can say that the LTC curve is a locus of the points of tangency of all short-run total cost curves with it. In Figure 6.3, we have shown only three STCs, and identified the LTC for three levels of output q_1, q_2 and q_3. The LTC, in this case, is shown by the dotted curve marked as 'LTC' which is being touched by the short-run TCs at (*a*), (*b*) and (*c*) points for q_1, q_2, and q_3 output respectively. This curve passes through the origin. It is not a straight line since the returns to scale are not uniform in this case. If there are constant returns to scale the LTC will be a straight line passing through the origin. LTC is an envelope of the short-run TCs in the sense that it contains all of them as they are above the LTC.

Now, let us define the long-run average and long-run marginal costs. For this, we consider the lower part of Figure 6.3. For every short-run total cost curve, we have one short-run variable cost curve, SAC_1 for STC_1, SAC_2 for STC_2, and SAC_3 for STC_3 and like that. If we join the minimum points of all short-run average cost curves we get the long-run average cost curve or 'envelope curve' for the producer. This will be valid when we have infinite number of short-run total cost curves and hence infinite number of short-run average cost curves. In the discrete situation, when there are a few short-run total cost curves or average cost curves we have to find the lowest unit cost for producing a given level of output which will be the 'lower envelope' of the SRAC curves. The long-run average cost is touched by the short-run average cost curves for the same levels of output where STCs touched the LTC. From this we infer that the LAC curve is the locus of all such points of tangency on the SAC curves. In Figure 6.3 (lower part) we have a_1 b_1 and c_1 as the points where SAC_1 SAC_2 and SAC_3 touch the LAC. The LAC curve, thus identified, shows the behaviour of cost with output in the long-run. On the basis of this curve the producer can choose the optimal (least cost) size of plant in the long-run. The long-run average cost will be downward sloping if there are increasing returns to scale. It will be upward sloping for decreasing returns to scale and a straight line parallel to quantity axis for constant returns to scale. The shape of the LAC is, therefore, very important from the point of view of planning for expansion of the plant. It is, therefore, called alternatively as "planning curve". In general, LAC is expected to be 'U' shaped but empirical evidence, apart from supporting 'U' shaped LAC curve also supported L shape for it in several other cases. In the long-run, a firm will choose that particular size of plant which shows lowest average cost, such as the plant showing SAC_2.

In order to explain the shape of the LAC in terms of the degree of returns to scale, let us consider the cost function derived from the Cobb-Dougls p.f. (see Eqns. 13 to 15).

$$C = K\, q^{1/R}.$$

input prices are treated as constant in this function.

$$\frac{C}{q} = K\, q^{1/R\,-1} = K\, q^{(1\,-\,R)/R} \qquad \text{...(28)}$$

If $R > 1$ (increasing returns to scale) then C/q *i.e.*, LAC declines with increase in output since $(1 - R)/R$ is negative. For $R < 1$ we get increasing C/q with increase in q and C/q will be constant equal to K when $R =$ (*i.e.*, for constant returns to scale).

Now, let us examine the long-run marginal cost and its relationship with short-run marginal costs. In Fig. 6.3 (upper part), the LTC is given. The slope of this curve gives us the long-run marginal cost. Also the slope of the short-run total cost curve gives us, similarly, the short-run marginal cost. For q_1 level of output both short-run total cost curve STC_1 and LTC touch each other at point *a*. It means their slopes are identical for q_1 level of output. Further, at q_i output both short-run average cost and long-run average costs are the same as shown by point a_1 in Fig. 6.3 (lower part). This means the LMC and SMC_1 intersect each other vertically just below the point where SAC_1 = LAC (Point a_1). This shows q_1 level of output. Similarly, the SMC_2 is equal to LMC just at the point b_1 when SAC_2 = LAC for q_2 level of output and SMC_3 = LMC above point c_1

where SAC_3 = LAC for q_3 level of output. To the left of q_1 level of output, *i.e.*, to the left of the point of intersection of SMC_1 and LMC and SMC_1 is below LMC, but to the right of the point of intersection LMC is below the SMC_1. Why this is so? As we see in the upper part of Fig. 6.3, the LTC is below the STC_1 to the left of q_1 and both STC_1 and LTC are rising. The LTC touches the STC_1 from below. It means LTC is rising at a faster rate than the STC_1. Since the rate of increase of LTC is LMC and the rate of increase of STC_1 is SMC_1, it means to the left of q_1 LMC > SMC_1. To the right of q_l the LTC rises at a slower rate than the STC_1 which means LMC < SMC_1. This way, the two marginal costs are linked. Similar logic holds true for the other levels of output, such as q_2 and q_3 for STC_2 and STC_3 curves. As we find in the case of the short-run, the long-run MC curve passes through the minimum level of the long-run average cost. The long-run minimum average cost is also a short-run minimum cost for the optimal size of the plant. It means, at that point, the SMC = SAC such as $SMC_2 = SAC_2$ in Fig. 6.3. Thus, for long-run optimum choice of the size of plant we have LMC = LAC and SMC = SAC for that size of q. It means, LMC = LAC = SMC = SAC. In our example here, q_2 shows the optimal size of the plant in the long-run since it is showing the lowest LAC.

We have to keep in mind that SMC intersects LMC from below for every level of output. The LMC would, therefore, be less steep in slope as compared to the SMCs. The reason for this is that in the short-run there is a fixed factor (*i.e.*, capital). The very existence of the fixed factor will be a source of diminishing return eventually causing the cost to rise. In the long-run nothing is fixed; and the scope of diminishing return will be quite low. So, long run marginal cost rises at a slower rate than the short-run marginal cost. This is important relationship as it plays a vital role in the identification or distinguishing of the short-run and long-run supply functions for a firm under perfect competition, as we will see later on.

How to derive a long-run total cost curve mathematically? For this we have to follow the same procedure of derivation initially as for the short-run cost function with the addition that size of plant expressed by K appears in the production function and the fixed cost for a given size of plant is changed as $b = \psi(K)$. The logic of having K as a variable in the production function is quite simple. It is not only production of a given level of output which is important but also which size of plant is used for this. So, keeping this in mind, we modify our constrained output maximisation problem as:

Max $\quad q = f(x_1, x_2, K)$

Subject to $\quad C = r_1x_1 + r_2x_2 + y(K)$

This will give us the equilibrium condition shown by the expansion path as:

$$g(x_1, x_2, K) = 0$$

K is appearing in the expansion path also.

Using the above information, *i.e.*, a production p.f., an isocost line, and the expansion path, we get the cost function as,

$$C = \phi(q, K) + \psi(K) \qquad ...(29)$$

This gives a family of short-run cost functions for different sizes of K (*i.e.*, of the plant), such as STC_1, STC_2 and STC_3 in Fig. 6.3.

By writing (29) in implicit form we have;

$$C - \phi(q, K) - \psi(K) = 0$$

or

$$G(C, q, K) = 0 \qquad ...(30)$$

G expresses the functional form of (30).

For the optimal choice of the plant size we take partial derivative of (30) with respect to K and equate it with zero. That is,

$$\frac{d\,G\,(C, q, K)}{dK} = G_k\,(C,\ q,\ K) = 0 \qquad \text{...(31)}$$

By solving this, we find K in terms of q, and substituting for K in (29) we find the long-run total cost function as:

$$C = \phi(q) \qquad \text{...(32)}$$

From this, we find the LAC and LMC curves.

Let us take an example for this. Suppose the derived version for the function (29) is given as:

$$C = q^3 - 2q^2 + (1 - 2K)\,q + K^2 \qquad \text{...(33)}$$

where K is the size of the fixed factor.

By taking the partial derivative of C with respect to K, we get

$$\frac{\partial C}{\partial K} = 2\text{K} - 2\text{q} = 0$$

This gives us $K = q$

Substituting $K = q$ in (33) the long-run total cost curve would be:

$$LTC = C = q^3 - 3q^2 + q \qquad \text{...(34)}$$

The long-run average cost would then be

$$LAC = \frac{C}{q} = q^2 - 3q + 1 \qquad \text{...(35)}$$

and

$$LMC = \frac{dC}{dq} = 3q^2 - 6q + 1 \qquad \text{...(36)}$$

6.5 SHIFTS IN COST CURVES

As we have seen above, the total cost curve or function for a firm is derived through cost minimisation or output maximisation process using the production function and isocost line. The crucial relationship in the process of derivation of the cost function is the expansion path indicating the equilibrium situation for the firm. Suppose there is a change in the economic environment that affects the expansion path, the shape and position of the cost curve will change. Normally, there are two possibilities for this changes in the input prices, and changes in the production function.

The input prices appear in the expansion path and hence in the cost curves through the isocost line. If such prices are changed, the isocost line changes and hence there would be new equilibrium position on the isoquants. The factor proportion changes and thereby the cost curve changes. As we know, in the general expression derived for the cost function, input prices appear as determinants along with the output (Ref. Equation 6). So, it is obvious that when either of the input price changes cost curve shifts from its position, say with a rise in input prices it moves up. Even if we treat cost in real term, the input prices appearing as parameters will change. So the cost curve will shift accordingly. To be more explicit, let us assume that wages are rising. This may force the firm to 'use more capital if permitted by the technology. The expansion path of the firm will rotate towards the capital axis. This, in turn, implies a set of new cost curves for the firm.

What will be the shape of cost curves when input prices change is difficult to perceive. It is an empirical question, but shifting up of the cost curve is expected with a rise in all or some input prices, the cost curve shifts down with a decline in the input prices.

The second factor that causes the cost curves to shift is the technological progress. A change in the technology is reflected by a change in the production function. The change in the production function means changes in its parameters related to efficiency, returns to scale, elasticity of substitution and factor intensity. All such parameters are also appearing in the cost function in its constant term. In fact, the constant term of the cost function ('*K*' in equations (13) and (17)) is nothing but a complex in mathematical term formed by the interaction of the parameter of the production function. If anyone of its parameters changes, *K* changes and so the total cost curve shifts its position and therefore the average and marginal cost curves shift. In general, any technological improvement means either a change in the product quality or a reduction in the cost of production, *i.e.*, downward shift of the cost function, or both. One can cite the example of introduction of powerlooms in place of handlooms which has reduced the cost of production in textile production significantly in India during the last few years.

Apart from changes in input 'prices and technology', one can argue for a number of other factors such as accelerating rate of output, changes in the output-mix of the firm, changes in internal organisation of production, which do affect the shape and position of the cost curves. The effects of all such factors on the cost can be analysed in the framework of the dynamic cost function in which along with the volume of output some other variable appears in the form of a time rate. Consider, for example, the rate of output. If the volume of output q and the rate of output change $\frac{dq}{dt}$ are taken as determinants of the cost, the cost curves are quite likely to change in shape and even in position. According to Alchian and Allen, the average cost per unit of output decreases with larger volume of output when the rate or speed of output is kept constant. But the average cost increases with larger rate of output, volume of output being constant. However, when volume and rate of output increase in proportion, average cost per unit of output first falls and then, after an interval of constant average cost, begins to increase as a function of the size of output and its rate.[2] The inclusion of output rate as a determinant of the cost, and hence of the dynamic cost curves has been recognized as far back as 1934 by Charles Frederick Roos in his Dynamic Economics,[3] but it is rather surprising to see that bulk of the cost analysis is done even today in the static framework keeping all dynamic elements likely to enter a cost function as constant. Even very little attention is paid to analyse the impact of changing input prices on current cost of production using the generalized cost function specification. The analysis of the cost of production at constant input prices is not so much exciting as its analysis in terms of current prices of inputs. A profit maximising producer will naturally be interested in the analysis of current cost of production for its output rather than the real cost. When we examine the variation of real cost (*i.e.*, physical cost) of production with volume of output, we merely get the information apout the technical side of production, such as optimum size of plant, technical efficiency rather than the profits or economic efficiency of the business.

6.6 ESTIMATION OF COST FUNCTION

To estimate a cost function there are two main methods: one is the engineering method and the second, statistical method. For a given level of output engineers will be able to specify the requirements

2. A. A. Alchian and W. R. Allen, *Exchange and Production Theory in Use,* Belmont, Wordsworth Pub. Co. 1969, Ch. 14.
3. Charles Frederick Roos, *Dynamic Economics: Monograph of the Cowles Commission for Research in Economics,* No.1; The Principia Press Ltd., Bloomington 1934, Ch. 9, pp. 148–173 especially, pp. 152–156.

of various physical inputs including services. The value of all such inputs will provide us the total cost of production for the given level of output. By repeating such an exercise for different levels of output or rated capacity we will be knowing the cost function for the firm. Once we find the total cost and output relationship we will be able to find the average and marginal cost curves from that.

This method is quite simple. It is not necessary that the requirements of inputs always vary in proportion of the output level and so there is linear relationship between cost of production and output of the commodity. Technologically, only few inputs may be required to change when output goes up. This will provide the basis for non-linear cost curves, such as the ones we discussed above. For example, in engineering design, the capital cost and expansion of capacity of production is governed by the so-called '0.6' rule of thumb. According to this rule, on an average a 100% increase in capacity needs only 60% increase in the capital cost. A more general relationship for this may be assumed as

$$C_c = \alpha\ Q^{\beta} \qquad ...(37)$$

where C_c = construction cost of plant and machinery

Q = level of output (*i.e.*, machine or plant capacity)

α and β are parameters. If $\beta < 1$, this implies economies in the use of bigger plant or machine. One Q can cite several such examples of engineering cost function.[4] From the knowledge of such functions one can estimate' the total cost function in ex-ante sense for production.

In statistical method, past data on the level of output and total cost of production is collected from the records of the firm. On availability of such data for a number of years or a number of production-run different sizes, a statistical curve is fitted using the least-squares method. The fitted curve, whether it is a straight line or a non-linear function, provides us the estimate of the cost function $C = f(q)$. Once we get the total cost function estimated the average and marginal cost functions can be derived from that easily.[5]

6.7 PROFIT MAXIMISATION IN TERMS OF COST FUNCTION

Profit maximisation is a popular goal of business firms. In this section, we will see how the cost function is useful in derivation of the equilibrium condition for profit maximisation. Let us define profit as

$$\pi = p \cdot q - C \qquad ...(38)$$

We assume that in a single product case, P is the price of the product and q its quantity, and C represents total cost of production. P is assumed to be fixed. This is the case of perfect competition as we will see later on. By taking the first and second order conditions for profit maximisation with respect to q, we have,

$$\frac{d\pi}{dq} = P - \frac{dC}{dq} = 0 \qquad ...(39)$$

and

$$\frac{d^2\pi}{dq^2} = -\frac{d^2C}{dq^2} < 0 \text{ or } \frac{d^2C}{dq^2} > 0$$

4. See for some examples T.V.S. Ramamohan Rao, *Theory of Firm: Economic & Managerial Aspects,* Affiliated East-West Press, New Delhi 1985, pp. 28–31.
5. Estimation of functions is not the theme of this book. Any one interested in fitting a curve or function statistically may consult any book on econometrics, such as J. Johnston, *Econometric Methods,* McGraw-Hill 1981, For cost functions, see J. Johnston, *Statistical Cost Analysis,* McGraw Hill, 1960 and Dean Joel, *Statistical Cost Estimations,* Indiana University Press, 1976.

The first condition for profit maximisation is that the price of the commodity must be equal to the marginal cost of production, (P = MC).

The second condition is that the rate of change of marginal cost is positive. This implies that the marginal cost curve is rising and intersects the price line from below. This is because the demand curve is a straight line. Therefore, a rising marginal cost curve intersects it from below. Even the price line (or demand curve) slopes downward the marginal cost curve and must intersect it from below, otherwise profit will not be maximum. In the following diagram, price is equal to marginal cost at points *A* and *B*.

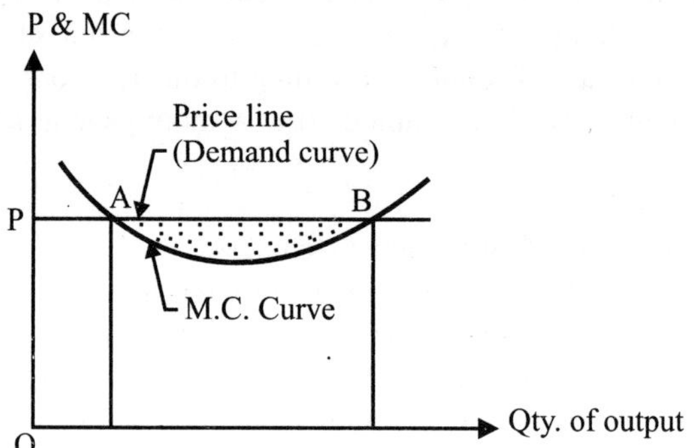

Fig. 6.4 Equilibrium Condition for Maximum Profit with Constant Output Price

At point *A*, the *MC* curve intersects the price line from above. It is not the equilibrium position for profit rnaximisation since by expanding the output further the firm gets addition in profit as shown by the dotted area. For this region $P > MC$, and so long $P >$ MC a fmn expands its level of output. The expansion of output will be stopped at point *B* where *MC* curve intersects the price line from below. As we see, beyond this point $MC > P$ and so there will not be any addition in the profit; rather it will be declining if the firm expands its output further. Point *B* is thus the equilibrium point for profit maximisation.

6.8 THE DERIVATION OF SUPPLY CURVE FOR A FIRM

As we have discussed in Chapter 3, the supply curve shows the willingness of a firm to supply a commodity in the market when its price is changing, other things being constant. In other words, we express this symbolically as,

$$s = s(P)$$

where $s =$ quantity of the commodity offered for sale

$P =$ price of that commodity.

Under perfect competition or, say, in a situation when price is an exogenous variable, price of the product must be equal to its marginal cost for profit maximisation. This is what we have seen just above in section 6.6. For profit maximisation, we do have a relationship between the marginal cost and quantity of output. This relationship can be obtained from the total cost function for the product. We have the first condition from profit maximisation as $P = MC$. So, by putting *P* in place of *MC* in the marginal cost expression we get a relationship between price and quantity of output of the product which is nothing but the supply curve for the firm on simplification. *It means, the marginal cost curve of a firm represents its supply curve.* However, the whole of the marginal cost curve may not be relevant from the point of view of the supply of the commodity. Falling *MC* curve cannot be taken as a part of the supply curve for the firm since the second order profit maximisation condition rules out this. For profit maximisation the *MC* curve must be rising. So, *the supply curve of the firm will be only a portion of the rising marginal cost curve.* We have to identify that portion. For this, let us proceed first graphically and then algebraically.

Consider the following diagram in which we have shown the various cost curves for a firm.

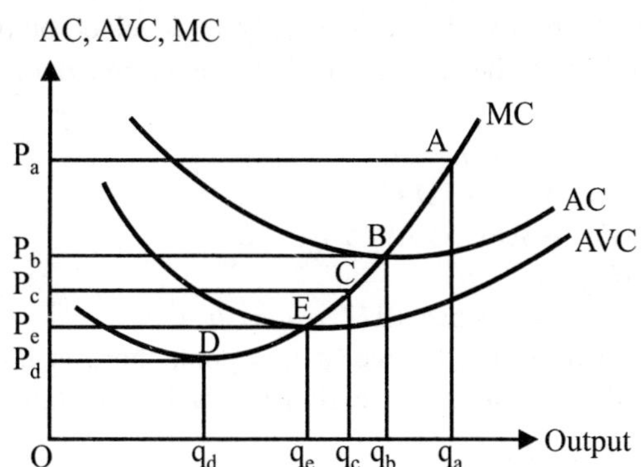

Fig. 6.5 Derivation of Supply Curve (Graphical Analysis)

We have the profit equation for the firm as

$$\pi = P \cdot q - C$$

writing $C = (AVC)\ q + b$

We have

$$\pi = P \cdot q - (AVC)\ q - b$$

where all the terms have already been defined earlier.

If the firm produces zero level of output, the profit of the firm would be equal to $-b$. That is, $\pi = P(0) - (AVC)\ (0) - b = -b$. This is the maximum loss to the firm. A firm has to pay the same fixed cost whatever be the level of output. So, with zero output, loss is equal to b.

Now consider very low price of the product, such as P_d corresponding to the lowest point of the marginal cost curve q_d is the quantity of output for this. For this level of output and price we have

$$\pi = (P_d - AVC)\ q_d - b$$

Since $P_d < AVC$ so $(P_d - AVC) = -x$

Therefore $\pi = -xq_d - b.$

What we find here is that the loss of the firm is increasing if price of its product is less than average variable cost. With such a low price the firm is unable to recover its variable cost; so the loss increases. At such a low price, there will be no supply by the firm.

Now, take point E on the marginal cost curve. At this point, we. have P_e = minimum AVC. The profit would be

$$\pi = (P_e - AVC)\ q_e - b$$

Since $P_e = AVC$

Therefore $\pi = 0 - b = -b$

The loss is equal to the fixed cost if price of the product equals to the minimum *AVC*. This will be the starting point for supply by the firm since after this level, as we see below, the loss of the firm declines and eventually it gets positive profit.

Now, consider point C on the MC curve, The price P_c of the commodity is greater than min. AVC but less than AC. The profit would be

$$\pi = (P - AVC)\ q_c - b$$

or $$\pi = xq_c - b \text{ since } P_c > AVC, \text{ so } P - AVC = x.$$

The loss of the firm declines by xq_c. Part of the fixed cost is being recovered by production of q_c amount of output. The firm would like to supply q_c level of output in the short-run.

If price of product is equal to the minimum of AC as corresponding to point B, the profit of the firm would be

$$\pi = (P_b - AVC)\ q_b - b$$

and $$P_b = AC = AVC + AFC$$

Therefore $$\pi = (AVC + AFC - AVC)\ q_b - b$$
$$= (AFC)\ q_b - b$$
$$= b - b = 0 \text{ since } (AFC)\ q_b = b$$

Point B is called 'break-even point', since at this point there is no profit-no loss. Firm starts getting positive profit beyond this point, as we find below in Fig. 6.6.

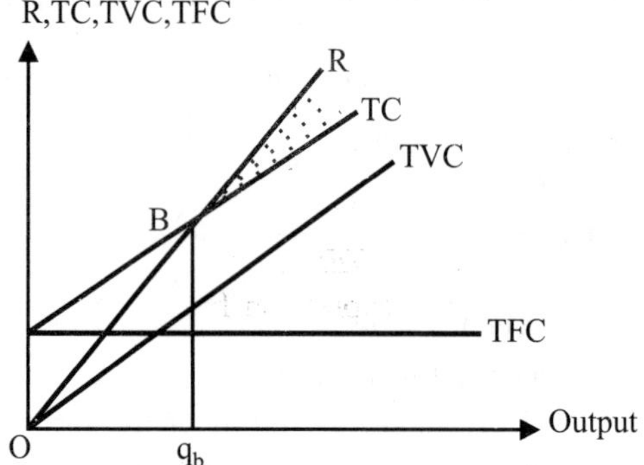

Fig. 6.6 Break-even Point

For break-even $R = TC$ and $\pi = 0$.

If the price (*i.e., MC*) is greater than ATC the firm gets positive profit.

Consider point A in Fig. 6.5.

$$P_a > ATC \text{ Let } P - ATC = y.$$

$$ATC = AVC + AFC$$

$$AVC = ATC - AFC$$

$$\pi = (P_a - AVC)\ q_a - b$$

Substituting for $AVC = ATC - AFC$

$$\pi = (P_a - (ATC - AFC))\ q_a - b$$

or $$r = y \cdot q_a, \text{ since } (AFC)\ q_a = b.$$

There will be positive profit when price is more than minimum of ATC.

From the above analysis we find that a firm starts supplying its product when its price is greater or equal to minimum of average variable cost. *This means the rising portion of the marginal cost curve above the minima of average variable cost will be the supply curve for the firm under perfect competition.*

If $P <$ Min AVC, the firm will be closed down. The point $P =$ min AVC is therefore called as "Shut-down Point".

Now, we specify the rules for algebraic derivation of the supply curve.

(*a*) From the total cost function find the expression (or equation) for the marginal cost.

(*b*) Substitute P for MC in that expression to get a relationship between price and quantity of output.

(*c*) Solve the expression for q in terms of P.

(*d*) Put 's' for quantity variable in order to get the supply curve in the standard notation: $s = f(P)$.

(*e*) Find the expression for AVC.

(*f*) Get the minima of AVC by taking the derivative

$$\frac{d(AVC)}{dq} = 0 \text{ and solve it for } q \text{ and hence for } P.$$

or find q when $MC = AVC$ and then substitute it in MC expression to find P.

(*g*) Supply curve for the firm would be:

$s = (P)$ when $P \geq$ min AVC

$s = 0$ when $P <$ min AVC

(*h*) If there are several firms, get supply curve for each one of them, say s_1, s_2, s_n. The market supply would then be equal to the horizontal summation of individual supply curves.

$$S = s_1 + s_2 + \ldots, s_n \text{ for all prices}$$

If all firms are identical then

$$S = ns \text{ where } n = \text{no. of firms.}$$

Let us take a worked example for this.

The cost function is given as

$$C = 0.04\, q^3 - 0.9\, q^2 + 10\, q + 5$$

$$\therefore \quad MC = 0.12\, q^2 - 1.8\, q + 10$$

Setting $\quad P = MC$ we get

$$P = 0.12\, q^2 - 1.8\, q + 10$$

or $\quad 0.12\, q^2 - 1.8\, q + 10 - P = 0$

Solving for q in terms of P we have

$$q = s = \frac{1.8 + \sqrt{0.48P - 1.56}}{0.24}$$

Negative side of $\sqrt{0.48\,P - 1.56}$ is not considered as it reflects the declining side of the MC curve.

Total variable cost for the firm is

$$TVC = 0.04\, q^3 - 0.9\, q^2 + 10\, q$$

$$AVC = \frac{TVC}{q} = 0.04\, q^2 - 0.9\, q + 10$$

For minima

$$\frac{d\,(AVC)}{dq} = 0.08\ q - 0.9 = 0, \text{ since } \frac{d^2(AVC)}{dq^2} = 0.08 > 0$$

This gives us $q = 11.25$

For $q = 11.25$, $AVC = 4.94$.

The supply function will, therefore, be valid for all prices greater than minimum AVC which is equal to 4.94.

Therefore, we have the supply function for the firm as

$$s = \frac{1.8 + \sqrt{0.48P - 1.56}}{0.24} \quad \text{if } P \geq 4.94.$$

and $s = 0$ if $P < 4.94$.

If there are 100 firms in the industry, all having similar cost functions, then the market supply would be

$$S = 100s = 100 \times \frac{1.8 + \sqrt{0.48P - 1.56}}{0.24} \cdot P \geq 4 \cdot 94$$

and $S = 0$ if $P < 4.94$.

The relevance of supply curve for economic analysis has already been discussed in Chapter 3. This reflects one side of the market for a commodity or factor of production which, in relation to the demand for that commodity or factor of production, determines the price for that in the market under competitive environment. The basic assumption behind the derivation of the supply curve for a firm is that market is under perfect competition and therefore the price of the commodity for the firm is exogenous. Given this, the firm maximises its total profit. The profit maximisation process gives price equal to marginal cost and hence rising portion of the *MC* curve above the lowest point of the *AVC* curve becomes the supply curve for the firm. In the next chapter, we will see how the supply curve along with the demand curve for a commodity determines its price both in the short-run and long-run under perfect competition.

6.9 CONCLUDING REMARKS

This chapter was concerned with the analysis of cost of production. Initially, various concepts related to the definition of the cost have been discussed and then the cost-output relationship has been derived which gave us the cost function. From the cost function we have derived the average and marginal costs for short-run and long-run decision situations. The cost function is a reduced form of the production function. It reflects the technological side of the supply, *i.e.*, production of a commodity but can be easily extended to the study of the economic side of production in terms of current cost of production which is an important aspect for determining the profit of the firm. We found that in the short-run with fixity of certain factors of production the laws of returns govern the shape of the cost curves, such as the familiar '*U*' shaped *AVC* and *ATC* curves. In the long-run, on the other hand, when all inputs are variable, the laws of returns to scale determine the shape of long-run cost curves. A brief mention has been made about the conditions which shift the cost curves from their positions and change their shapes. Finally, we have outlined the process of derivation of the supply curve for a commodity from the cost function under profit maximisation, goal of the firm. In the next chapter, we will use the supply curve for the analysis of price determination under perfect competition.

SUGGESTED READINGS

Baumol, W. J., *Economic Theory and Operation Analysis,* Prentice-Hall of India, 1978.

Dean, Joel. *Statistical Cost Estimation;* Bloomington, Indiana University Press, 1976.

Ferguson, C. E., *Microeconomic Theory,* R.D. Irwin Inc., 1971.

Henderson, J.M. and R.E. Quandt., *Microeconomic Theory: A Mathematical Approach,* McGraw-Hill, 1971.

Koutsoyiannis, A., *Modern Microeconomics,* The Macmillan Press, 1978.

Shephard, R.W., *Cost and Production Functions,* Princeton University Press, 1971.

Sher, W. and R. Pindola. *Microeconomic Theory: A Synthesis of Classical and the Modern Approach,* Edward Arnold, 1981.

Viner, Jacob, "Cost Curves and Supply Curves" in K. E. Boulding and G. J. Stigler (Ed.) A.E.A., *Readings in Price Theory,* R. D. Irwin Inc., 1952.

REVIEW QUESTIONS

1. Explain how economists define the term 'cost'. Also, using suitable examples bring out the distinction between 'social cost' and 'private cost'.
2. What do you mean by the term 'cost function'? Give an outline of its derivation, and also of its uses in economic analysis and business decision-making.
3. Using graphical representation, show how variation in average variable cost, average total cost and marginal cost with the level of output can be explained? Give reasons for the pattern of variations of these costs as you conceive.
4. It is argued that a short-run total cost curve is always above the long-run total cost curve, except at one point. Also, economists say that a long-run average cost curve is an envelope to the short-run average cost curves. Why these relations hold in practice? Give full justification.
5. Explain the pattern of variation in the long-run marginal cost vis-a-vis short-run marginal cost. What is the relationship between these two costs?
6. Average product, average cost, marginal product, marginal cost, are all interrelated terms. Explain how?
7. Give an outline of deriving a supply curve from the cost curve for a competitive firm as well as the market of which the firm is a part.
8. The short-run total cost curve for a firm is given as $C = 10 + 6q - 2q^2 + 1/3q^3$. Derive the supply function for the firm from this. If there are n identical firms operating in the market for the commodity produced by the firms, find the market supply function for that.
9. Review your understanding of the following cost and profit concepts: Opportunity Cost, Real Cost, Establishment Cost, Separable and Common Cost, Replacement Cost, Normal Profit, Economic Profit.
10. A producer owns two plants. Both have constant marginal costs. However, the fixed Cost and the marginal cost of one plant differ from those of the other. Will the producer ever operate both the plants simultaneously? Give explanation for your answer.
11. The production function for a commodity is given as $Q = 8L^{1/2} + 20\,K^{1/2}$. The prices for labour (L) and capital (K) inputs are given as Rs. 1.00 and Rs. 5.00 respectively. Find the expansion path and supply function for the commodity.

CHAPTER 7

Price and Output Determination Under Perfect Competition

As mentioned in Chapter 3, price determination for a commodity under perfect competition is done by the market itself through interaction of supply and demand for the commodity. We have gone through demand and supply sides of the market and hence its equilibrium using, by and large, the graphic analysis in the chapter. Chapter 4 is devoted to the on understanding of consumer behaviour in depth which provide the theoretical basis for the demand analysis for goods. Similarly, Chapters 5 and 6 deal with the production and cost sides of the market and hence to the supply side of a commodity market. The relevant theories have been discussed in these chapters in order to get finally a supply curve required for pricing decision. Now, the task for us is to see how demand and supply curves determine market price for a commodity; how a firm under competitive situation gets equilibrium both in the short-run and in the long-run. Apart from this, we will examine the stability of market equilibrium from various angles. Since we are going through a particular type of market situation called, 'perfect competition', it is necessary for us to define this and then proceed with the intended economic analysis of price and output determination.

7.1 THE CONCEPT OF PERFECT COMPETITION

An industry or market is said to be operating under perfect competition if the following conditions are satisfied:

(*a*) There is a large number of sellers, *i.e.*, producers (individual proprietors or partners or corporations coming in the real *m* of 'firm' or enterprise) in the industry producing a commodity. Each of the firms or sellers is too small as compared with the size of the industry and, therefore, it will not have any perceptible or significant influence on the market price of the commodity and its total supply. The producers or suppliers in this situation will be 'price-takers', *i.e.*, the price of the commodity for them is determined exogenously. They take it as given.

(*b*) There is a large number of buyers In the market for a commodity. Individual buyer will not have any significant influence on the market price or quantity of the commodity demanded. Like producers, they will also be 'price-takers' in the market for the commodity.

(*c*) All firms or producers are producing exactly similar product. This is product homogeneity condition. The implication of this is that buyers will be indifferent in choice of the seller from whom they buy it.

(*d*) There is freedom for entry and exit. Both, firms and customers, are free to join the market for a product or to depart or leave it. There will be no licensing, no control and no government interference in that market.

(*e*) There is perfect information about the market. Both buyers and sellers have full knowledge about the product quality and its nature, price and other attributes. There is complete absence of advertisement and other sales promotion activities.

(*f*) There is no collusion among buyers and sellers or sellers and buyers. The trade and manufacturing associations as well as consumer associations are not existing in the market. Each customer and each seller is independent in taking the decision himself.

If only first four conditions are satisfied, the market would be under 'pure competition' and if all six conditions are satisfied, it is 'perfect competition'.

If any one or more of the above conditions are not satisfied, the industry or market would be operating under 'imperfect competition'. Some important cases of imperfect competition are as follows:

(*i*) Monopoly: In this case, there is only *one* producer in the industry and the product manufactured by that firm has no substitutes supplied by other firms.

(*ii*) Duopoly: When there are only *two* producers competing in the industry.

(*iii*) Oligopoly: This is the market situation when there are *few* firms dominating the industry, the other firms being too small or insignificant as compared to them.

(*iv*) Monopolistic competition: This is the market situation when number of firms is quite large but their products are not exactly similar. Brands or different qualities of products exist in this type of market.

(*v*) Monopsony: This is the case when the market is having only one buyer, such as defence ministry for military hardwares.

(*vi*) Bilateral monopoly: A market with one buyer and one seller is defined as 'bilateral monopoly'.

In this chapter, we are going through the market analysis under perfect competition leaving the imperfect markets for the next few chapters.

A careful observation of the conditions of perfect competition reveals that it is now more or less a hypothetical market situation since it is extremely difficult to satisfy all the conditions. In spite of this, we study this type of market in the economic theory mainly because of the following reasons:

(*i*) It provides a simplified model to understand the complex economic system.

(*ii*) It provides crude and approximate estimates of economic variables.

(*iii*) It provides strong base for political ideology and welfare maximisation.

(*iv*) It helps in developing norms for desirable performance applicable to an industry.

The relevance of the competitive market situation for all these accounts will be known to us clearly later on when we complete the study of the perfect and imperfect markets and the welfare economics.

Historically, the study of perfect competition preceded any other type of market because in the initial stage of the development of the economic science (second-half of the 18th century) most of the economists concentrated on products like corn, textiles, etc., where almost perfect competition was prevailing. There were no major industries at that time and the market as well as technological complexities, as we find today, were absent. The shift from the perfect competition to the imperfect competition in economic systems was a gradual process and this has been noticed even in the economic theories. Although imperfect markets are ruling the economic scene today yet economists are busy in studying perfect competition. It is not a paradox. The complex markets, *i.e.*, those having several imperfections, can be studied in a meaningful way when we compare them with perfect markets both from the point of view of the structure of the price theory and the policy implication of that. This is the reason why we are also beginning our study of the price theory with the analysis of the perfect competition in this chapter.

7.2 DETERMINATION OF PRICE UNDER PERFECT COMPETITION

As mentioned in Chapter 3, to determine the market price of a commodity we need essentially:

(*a*) the market demand curve, and

(*b*) the market supply curve for the commodity.

The interaction of supply and demand curves defines the market equilibrium for the commodity giving us the market price and the total market demand or supply of the commodity. The logic for such interaction of supply and demand for price determination and the stability of the equilibrium point have been discussed in detail in Section 3.6 of Chapter 3, we will therefore not go through it again.

There are three different situations of market equilibrium for a commodity: (*a*) very short-run, (b) short-run and (*c*) long-run.

(*a*) Equilibrium in very short-run or what we call as 'momentary equilibrium' or market period equilibrium is based on the assumption that supply of the commodity is fixed, all other adjustments are instantaneous, and holding of inventories are ruled out because either the commodity is perishable and the inventory costs for that are too much and/or the sellers are in dire need for money so they want to sell their product. Now, given the fixed supply, which means a vertical supply curve, the price of the commodity depends solely on the demand for that commodity. If demand is high, price will be high and if it is low, price will be low as can be seen from the following diagram:

When quantity of the commodity is absolutely fixed in supply at q^* level, price P_1, will be the equilibrium one with D_1 as demand curve, and if the demand curve shifts to D_2 position, P_2 will be the equilibrium price. The basic principle of market equilibrium, *i.e.*, demand is equal to supply is in operation here. Price of the commodity is acting as a device to ration demand for that.

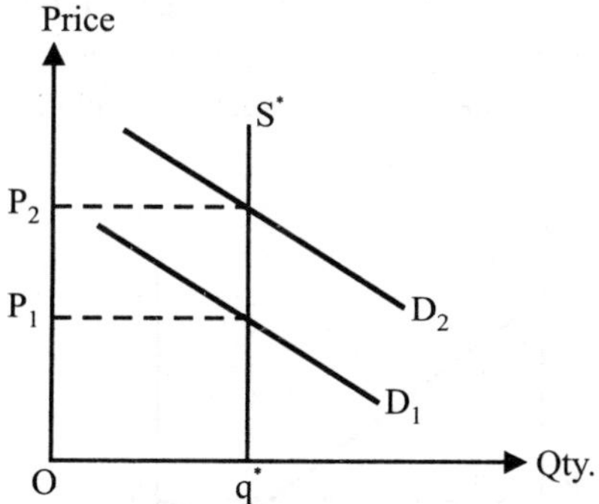

Fig. 7.1 Very Short-run Market Equilibrium with Fixed Supply

If the supply is too much as compared to the demand, the intersection of the supply and demand curves is not taking place in the positive quadrant. How the market equilibrium is established then? Figure 7.2 shows such a situation.

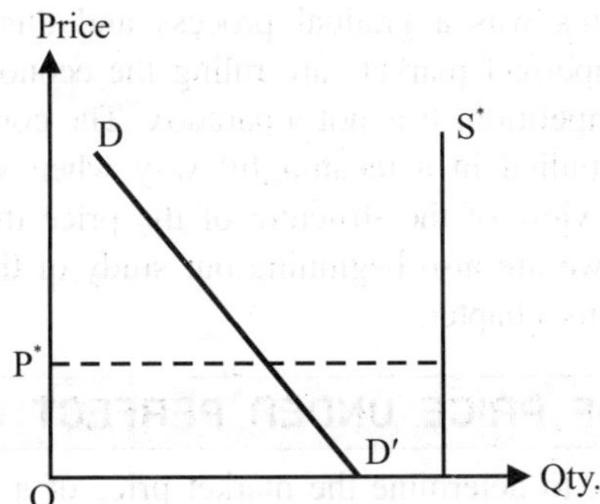

Fig. 7.2 Very Short-run Market Equilibrium with Excess Supply

We have assumed that the sellers are having full information about the market which means they know the demand curve. If this is so why should they bring more output for sales as shown by S^* line? Clearly such a situation is unlikely. The supply-demand interaction mechanism, even if there is the situation as shown in Fig. 7.2, fails to bring the market equilibrium. The suppliers will be adopting some other strategy for price fixation in this situation. For example, they may collude together and fix a minimum price for the market as shown by P^*. If the price offered by buyers is less than P^* then sellers offer no output for sales, and at a price greater than P^* they sell all output. The price P^* will be fixed in such a way that it covers the average cost of production for the output though it may not give maximum revenue to them.

Sometimes the sellers' supply curve is not perfectly in-elastic in spite of given fixed supply of the commodity. Sellers may not wish to offer the entire stock of the commodity at any price that may be had. This may be possible when the commodity can be stored temporarily, the storage costs are reasonable and there is no crisis sales in the market or sellers are not under financial pressure to get their output sold. Under such situations, they may offer only a part of their stock of the commodity at a price lower than a certain limit. The quantity offered for sale increases with increase in price up to that limit but after that the entire output is offered for sales. This means the supply curve in this case would be seen like SRS^* as shown in Fig. 7.3. Sellers retaining a part of the stock of their commodity at prices less than P_1 are said to have reservation price. When a seller has reservation price he expects of more favourable price later. The expected future price must be such that the seller is able to cover the additional costs such as storage expenses incurred in holding the stock of the commodity.

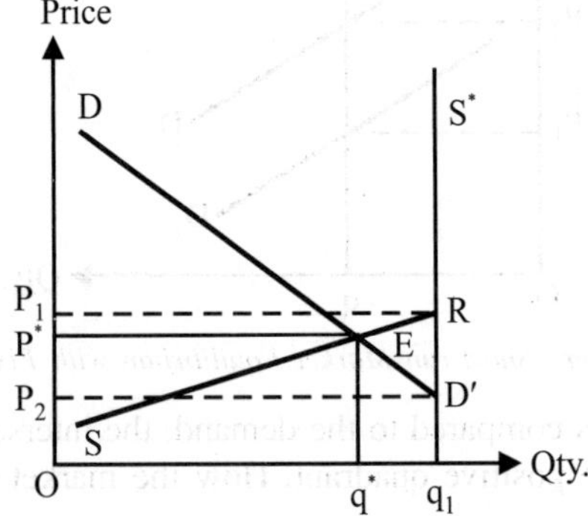

Fig. 7.3 Very Short-run Market Equilibrium with Reservation Price

The equilibrium situation in the above figure is shown by point *E*, where the demand curve *DD* and the supply curve *SRS** intersect. The equilibrium price is P^* and equilibrium quantity demanded or supplied is q^*. The seller is willing to sell more if price is greater than P^*, say at P_1, price or more than this, he is willing to sell q_1 quantity, *i.e.*, the entire stock at his disposal, but buyers are willing to buy it only at P_2 price.

This type of analysis is applicable to some agricultural products which can be stored and sold in phases but are to be sold fully before the next crop comes in the market. The analysis is also applicable to products like bread and other food preparations for markets since they can be stored for some time only. If the product is totally perishable, it cannot be stored, then the earlier type of equilibrium, *i.e.*, as shown in Figs. 7.1 or 7.2 prevails.

(*b*) Short-run equilibrium under perfect competition is determined by the intersection of the demand and supply curves for a commodity. The supply curves for a firm is given by the rising portion of the marginal cost curve above the minima of the AVC curve. We have already derived it in the preceding chapter. Horizontal summation of the supply curves for all firms gives us the market supply for the commodity. Now, let us have:

$$D = D\ (P)$$

and $$S = S\ (P) \qquad \ldots(i)$$

as supply and demand curves for the commodity, the market equilibrium would then be, as discussed in Chapter 3, $D(P) = S(P)$, which is possible at the intersection of these two curves. Consider $D = 250 - 50P$ and $S = 25 + 25P$ as the demand and supply curves. For equilibrium we equate them, so $250 - 50P = 25 + 25P$. This gives us $P = 3$, $D = S = 100$ units as price and quantity for the commodity at the equilibrium situation of the market. In other words, we have determined the price and equilibrium quantity bought and sold. of the commodity.

The short-run supply curve for a firm will not be a vertical line, neither will it be a horizontal one. It will, however, show low elasticity of supply than the long-run supply curve. Supply in the short-run is constrained by the existence of the fixed factor(s) which is, of course, the size of the plant. In the short-run, firms may be getting profit or loss in the industry. There is no restriction for that since $P = MC$, which is the first condition for profit maximisation, may be well above the average cost or below this. We will see this situation shortly in this section itself.

(*c*) The long-run equilibrium of a market is also determined by the intersection of the demand and supply curves. But there is another condition for this, *i.e.*, the profit of the industry in the long-run must be zero. We may show the long-run market equilibrium as:

$$\begin{aligned} D &= D\ (P) \\ S &= S\ (P) \\ D &= S \qquad \ldots(ii) \\ \pi &= P.S. - C = 0 \end{aligned}$$

where *P* is the long-run equilibrium price, *S* is supply, *D* is demand and *C* is total cost of production of the industry. Let us define *n* as the optimum number of firms in the industry and c_i as the cost of production for *i*th firm, then we can write

$$C = n \times c_i = n\ \phi\left(\frac{S}{n}\right) \qquad \ldots(iii)$$

where $\frac{S}{n}$ is the output of one firm in the industry in the long-run. All firms are identical; so they have similar cost function and the same level of output. The long-run market equilibrium model gives the long-run price for the commodity, equilibrium quantity demanded or sold and the optimum number of firms in the industry.

How the long-run equilibrium situation will come under perfect competition is an interesting issue for examination. For this, let us consider the process of attaining equilibrium condition by a firm under this type of market in the long-run since this will tell us how zero profit market equilibrium will be eventually established in the industry in which firms operate. Fig. 7.4(*a*) shows the short-run market equilibrium for an industry. The price P_1 for the industry is determined through intersection of its demand and supply curves at *E* point which gives us Q_1 as the total quantity of the commodity demanded or sold in the market. Since price is the exogenous factor for a firm in

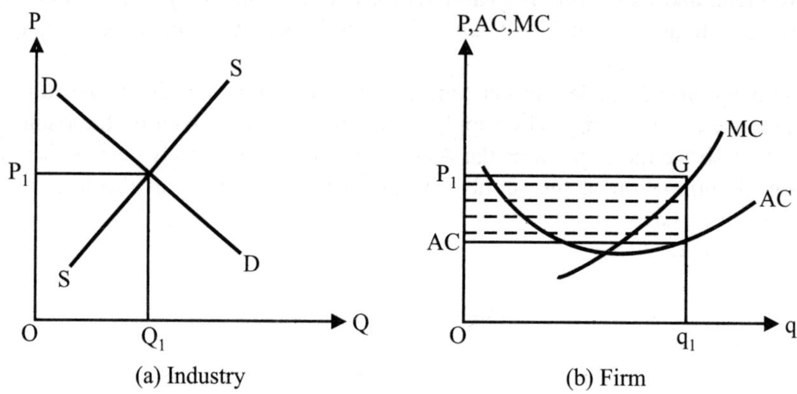

Fig. 7.4 Short-run Equilibrium for an Industry and for a Firm under Perfect Competition

the industry, so it (*i.e.* the firm) will adjust its level of output in such a way as to maximise total profit and thus attains short-run equilibrium. Such an equilibrium for a representative firm (not in Marshallian sense) is given in part (*b*) of Fig. 7.4. Conditions for the equilibrium of the firm for profit maximisation are, as we have seen earlier, $P = MC$ and the *MC* curve intersects the price line from below. This situation is shown by the point *G* in the figure. The profit maximising level of output or, what is called as the equilibrium output corresponding to, *G* point, is q_1. What the firm is doing here is just to adjust its output in order to get maximum profit for the given price of its product. The maximum profit that the firm gets is shown by the dotted area which is equal to $(P - AC)q_1$. All other firms in the industry may also be getting this much profit since all of them are assumed to be similar. Even if they are not similar we can take it for sure that there is positive profit in the short-run in the industry.

Since the entry of new firms in the industry is free, *i.e.*, there is no restriction for that, they are-attracted to join the industry because of short-run positive profit. When new firms join the industry, the number of suppliers thus goes up. The industry's supply increases. This means the market supply curve shifts towards the right and becomes more elastic. An increase in market supply, market demand being same, means a decrease in market price of the commodity. This will affect the equilibrium position of firms. The representative firm, therefore, will have equilibrium at a lower level of output on its marginal cost curve. This reduces profits of the firm. The entry of new firms in the industry will continue till the entire positive profit-margin is eliminated. At that stage, the market supply curve will be such that when it intersects with the market demand curve, the market price thus given would be equal to the minimum average cost of the firm. At that point, *i.e.*, at the minima of the *AC* curve we have $P = MC = AC$ and profit will be zero. Figure 7.5, part (*b*) shows this situation.

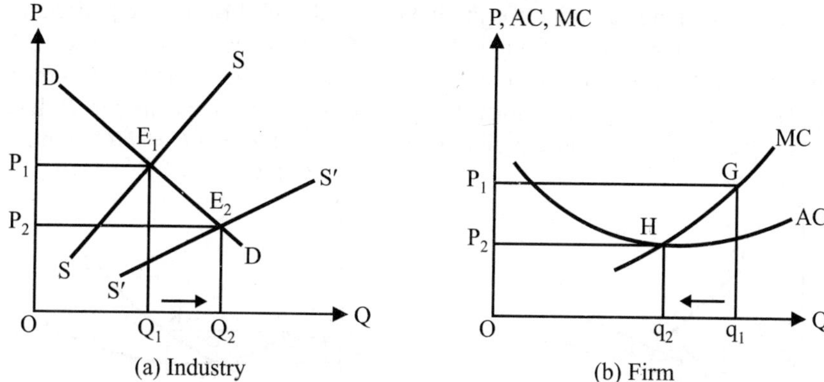

Fig. 7.5 Long-run Equilibrium of an Industry vis-a-vis a Firm under Perfect Competition

The reverse situation can also be explained in the same way as we have done above. Suppose market price in the short-run is very low, it is showing negative profit, *i.e.*, loss to the firms, then some marginal firms will leave the industry. This reduces the number of firms in the industry and hence a reduction in market supply, *i.e.*, shift of the supply curve to the left. The market price goes up which eliminates the loss of firms. This process continues till the entire loss is eliminated and market price equals average cost of the firm establishing the equilibrium when $P = MC = AC$. This is the long-run equilibrium condition. In the long-run, the equilibrium quantity of each firm decreases ($q_2 < q_1$) but the equilibrium quantity for the industry increases ($Q_2 > Q_1$).

As mentioned above, a firm under perfect competition is a 'price-taker', that is, the price is an exogenous factor for it, its demand curve would therefore be a horizontal line parallel to the quantity axis. This is what has been shown above in the part (*b*) of figures where $P = MC$. Also one should keep in mind that profit is zero in the long-run means zero economic profit. The normal profit being a part of the cost of production would be occuring to the firms. If normal profit is zero, producers would not be staying in the business. For survival of business units occurrence of the normal profit is a necessary condition.

7.3 EFFECTS OF THE SHIFT IN DEMAND AND COST CURVES ON THE EQUILIBRIUM OF THE FIRM

Let us conduct this analysis in two phases: first, we examine the effect of changing market demand, cost being constant, on the equilibrium position of the firm and, later on, we examine the effects of changing demand as well as of the cost on the equilibrium.

A favourable shift in demand, say from D_1D_1 to D_2D_2 in Fig. 7.6, will upset the market equilibrium. The price of the product increases. With increase in the price, the firms which were in the long-run equilibrium (or even in short-run equilibrium) will earn now more economic profit because of higher price and intersection of the price line and marginal cost at the higher level of output. (It is assumed that the rise of *AC* for greater level of output is not steep and so it does not neutralize the effect of rising price on the profit of the firm). Increased positive profit attracts new firms to join the industry. As a result of this, as market supply increases, the supply curve shifts to the right which causes a decline in the price of the product and hence a decrease in profits of firms. This process continues till the entire excess profit is eliminated and equilibrium is restored at the original level of the minimum point of the *AC* curve. The effect of a rise in the demand is neutralized by the increased number of sellers in the industry.

In Fig. 7.6 P_2 is the long-run price for the industry and each firm is in equilibrium at the point $P = AC = MC$. Now, demand shifts from D_1D_1 to D_2D_2. This increases the price of the product to P_3 giving positive profit to firms shown by the crossed area in Fig. 7.6(*b*). This attracts new firms in the industry. Eventually, supply curve shifts to S_2S_2 position and price comes to P_2 level and profit is eliminated and, therefore, long-run equilibrium is restored at $P = AC = MC$ point.

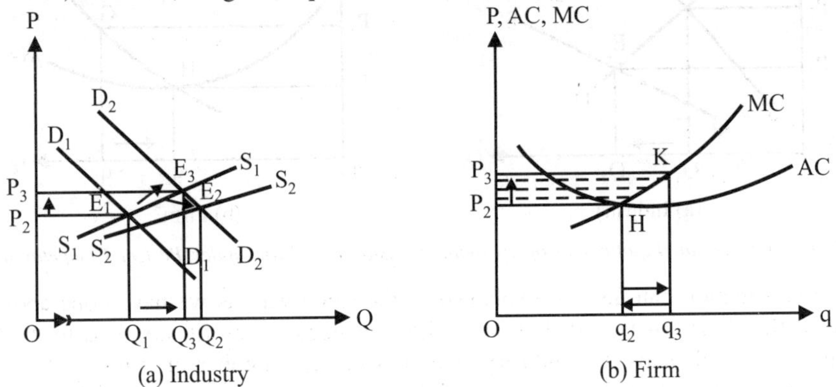

Fig. 7.6 Effect of a Change (Rise) in Demand On Firm's Equilibrium

Suppose demand decreases, its immediate effect would be a decline in price of the commodity. Because of lower price, the long-run equilibrium position of the firm is disturbed. Firms in the industry will now earn negative profits. The negative profit will push some firms out of the industry. This means a reduction in market supply, that is, a shift of the supply curve to the left. This pushes the price of the product up. This process continues till entire negative profit is eliminated and the firm gets back its original long-run zero profit equilibrium at the lowest point of the *AC* curve.

Now, let us examine the effect of changing cost as well as of changing demand on the equilibrium positions of the market and of the firm. There are three possibilities for a change in cost of production of a commodity. The first is that overtime the average cost of production increases. This may be because of a rise in input prices and/or a decrease in the efficiency of the technology overtime. It may become obsolete. There might be other factors also. The long-run equilibrium of the firm, which was originally on lower *AC* curve, will now be at the lowest point of a higher *AC* curve. If this happens, the industry is called' *increasing cost industry.'* The case of increasing cost industry is shown graphically in Fig. 7.7.

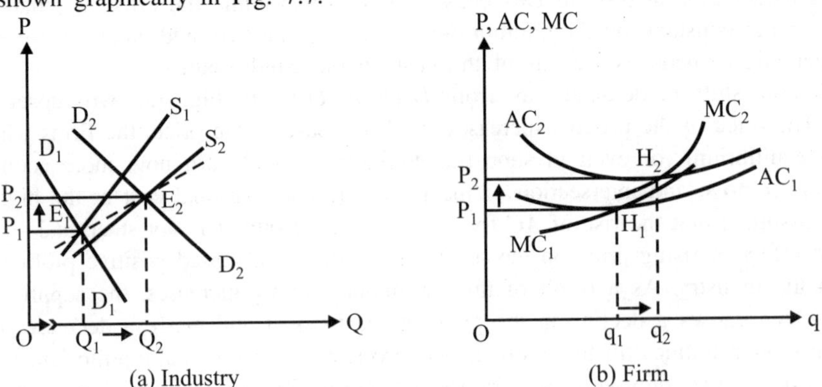

Fig. 7.7 Increasing Cost Industry

The locus of the market equilibrium points (E_1 and E_2) in this figure has been shown as a rising line which is the implication of the rising cost industry. The output of the industry and of the firm is rising but this is not a necessary implication of the rising cost industry. The important implication is that price of the product over time is increasing.

The second possibility of a change is that of decreasing average cost over time. There may be a decrease in input prices as result of new sources of raw materials; the technology may improve and several other factors may lead to a decrease in average cost of production over time. The price of the product also declines and the locus of the market equilibrium points (E_1, E_2) is declining over time as one can see in Fig. 7.8. This happens in a *'decreasing cost industry'*.

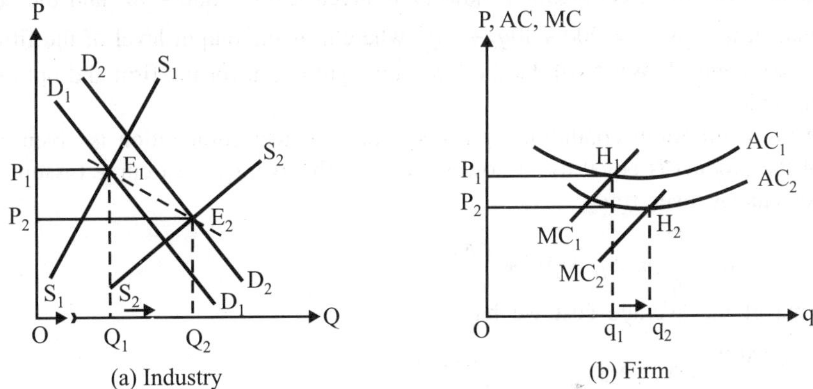

Fig. 7.8 Decreasing Cost Industry

The third possibility of cost variation is that of the *'constant cost industry'*. In this case, the average cost of production does not vary over time. The price of the product does not change. The locus of the market equilibrium point will be a horizontal line in this case. Why cost of production does not change over time? We know that factors that change the cost are several, basically falling into two categories: (*i*) the input prices, and (*ii*) technological factors. There might be some internal changes in the organisation of firms. The configuration of changes in all such factors will be such that the average cost curve does not change though it may shift horizontally from its position.

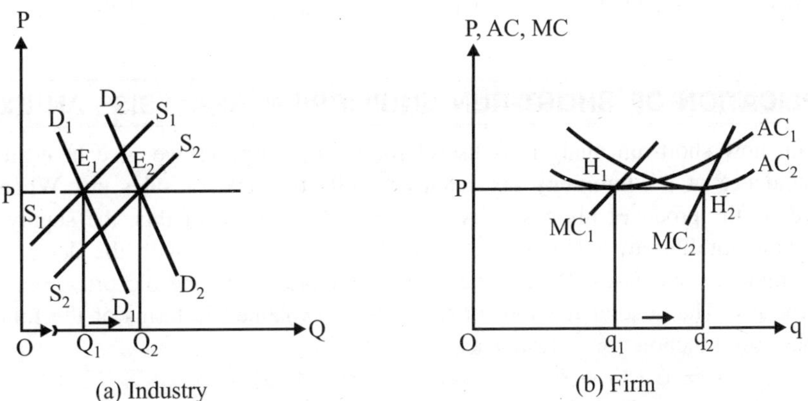

Fig. 7.9 Constant Cost Industry

The identification of the increasing, decreasing and constant cost industries is useful not only from the point of view of understanding the equilibrium of firms under the competitive condition but from the point of view of the economic policy of price regulation also. Costs and hence prices of the increasing cost industries over time are to be checked from rising in the interest of consumers. This can only be done when we identify such industries and reasons for the price rise over time, and the degree of competition prevailing in them.

We have described the process of achieving long-run equilibrium for an industry (*i.e.*, the market) and for an individual firm operating therein. Let us support this analysis by a numerical example.

The demand curve for a competitive industry is given as $Q = 800 - 8P$ and the cost function for an individual firm '*i*' is $C_i = 200 + 10q_i + 2q_i^2$ where q_i is the output level of the firm. All firms in the industry are identical. What will be the long-run equilibrium for the firm and optimum number of firms in the industry?

The long-run equilibrium condition for a firm under perfect competition is given by the point where price of the product is equal to the lowest point of the average cost curve (assuming that cost curve does not change over time).

$$AC = \frac{C_i}{q_i} = 2q_i + 10 + \frac{200}{q_i}$$

For minima of the average cost we have,

$$\frac{d(AC)}{dq_i} = 2 - 200\, q_i^{-2} = 0, \frac{d^2(AC)}{dq_i^2} > 0$$

or $\quad q_i^2 = 100$ giving us $q_i = \pm\, 10$ units.

The negative root is ruled out, so maximum output the firm would produce in the long-run is equal to 10 units of the commodity.

The price of the commodity when $q_i = 10$, is equal to AC and $AC = \frac{200}{10} + 10 + 2 \times 10 = 50$ units.

Total market demand when $P = 50$ is equal to $Q = 800 - 8 \times 50 = 400$ units.

Since all firms in the industry are identical and each one produces 10 units of output, therefore, the total number of firms operating in the industry to produce 400 units of the commodity will be 400/10 = 40.

7.4 APPLICATION OF SHORT-RUN EQUILIBRIUM ANALYSIS—AN EXAMPLE

To explain how short-run analysis is useful for policy purposes we give here an example of finding the incidence of a commodity tax, such as production tax, or sales tax. Whenever such a tax is imposed on the producer his cost curves change. As a result of this, the supply curve shifts which brings new equilibrium position for the market on interaction with the demand curve. The price of the commodity increases. By comparing the new price with the old price, one can find the incidence of the tax. The general method for this can be explained in terms of the following steps:

Given the cost function for a firm i as,

$$C_i = \phi\,(q_i) + b.$$

Let '*t*' be the tax per unit of the commodity produced or sold, the cost function then changes as,

$$C_i = \phi(q_i) + b + tq.$$

Differentiating C_i with respect to q_i we get the new level of mc as,

$$mc = \phi'(q_i) + t$$

By putting $P = mc$, we have,

$$P = \phi'(q) + t$$

or $$\phi'(q) = P - t$$

Solving this, we get the supply curve for the firm as,

$$q_i = s_i = s_i\ (P - t).$$

Summing up for all firms, the market supply curve would then be given as,

$$S = \sum_i^n s_i = \sum_i^n s_i(P - t)$$

Let the demand curve for the commodity be given as

$$D = D\ (P)$$

The Supply Curve and Demand Curve together give us the new price of the commodity on solving $D(P) - S(P - t) = 0$.

This equilibrium situation, when compared with the earlier one, *i.e.*, when there is no tax, tells us about the incidence of the tax on consumers and on producers.

Let us take a numerical example for this.

The cost function for a firm is given as

$C = 4q^2 + 10q + 5$. There are 10 similar firms operating in the industry. The market demand curve for the commodity is given as $Q = 87.5 - 1.5\ P$.

If a production tax of Rs. 2 is imposed on the commodity, find the incidence of this tax.

Given the cost function, $C = 4q^2 + 10q + 5$, so $P = MC = 8q + 10$. The Supply Curve for the firm is then,

$$P = 8q + 10$$

or $$q = -\frac{10}{8} + \frac{P}{8}$$

or $$s = q = -\ 1.25 + 0.125\ P$$

There are 10 similar firms in the industry. The market supply curve would, therefore, be:

$$S = 10q = -10\ (1.25) + 10\ (0.125)\ P$$

or $$S = -\ 12.5 + 1.25\ P$$

The demand curve is $Q = 87.5 - 0.75\ P$.

On solving these two functions, the equilibrium price and quantity are coming as $P = 50$, $Q = 50$.

Now, on imposing the tax, the cost curve for the firm changes to:

$$C = 4q^2 + 10q + 5 + 2q$$

or $$C = 4q^2 + 12q + 5$$

$$MC = 8q + 12 = P,\ (P \text{ is new price})$$

or $$s = q = -\ 1.5 + 0.125\ P$$

is the Supply Curve for one firm. Total Market Supply function is therefore,

$$S = 10s = -15 + 1.25\ P$$

The new supply function $S = -\ 15 + 1.25\ P$ and the demand function $Q = 87.5 - 0.75\ P$ on solution give the new equilibrium price and quantity as $P = 51.25$ and $Q = 49.06$ units. Change in the market price $= 51.25 - 50.0 = 1.25$. So, the incidence of the tax (Rs. 2) on consumer will be Rs. 1.25 and on the producer Rs. 0.75.

How to find the incidence of tax on the producer? Although it is quite simple to find as whatever is the incidence of the tax on the consumers the rest of that will fall on the producers. We may understand it in a better way by comparing the net price received by the producers in the two situations. The net price received by the producer will be the difference between the market price and the amount of the tax. Now, when there is no tax the net price received by the producer is Rs. 50 – 0 = Rs. 50, and when there is a tax of Rs. 2, it is Rs. 51.25 – Rs. 2 = Rs. 49.25. The decrease of the net price, which is due to the incidence of the tax on the producer, is Rs. 50 – Rs. 49.25 = Re. 0.75.

In this example, consumers are having greater incidence of the tax as compared to producers. This is because the demand is relatively inelastic as compared to the supply (compare the slopes of the demand and supply curves for this). Elasticities of demand and supply play crucial role in shifting the incidence of a commodity tax. If the demand is relatively inelastic, as compared to the elasticity of supply, the major incidence of the tax will be borne by consumers. On the other hand, if the demand is relatively elastic than the supply, producers will have greater incidence of the tax.

In a more general sense the link between elasticities and incidence of the commodity tax can be summarised as follows:

(*a*) For a given supply, the higher the price elasticity of demand, the less will be the consumers' share of a commodity (sales or production) tax and the greater will be the producers' share. Conversely, the more inelastic the demand the greater will be the buyers' share of the tax and less will be the producers' share.

(*b*) For a given demand, the higher the price elasticity of supply, the less will be the producers' share of the tax and the greater will be the buyers' share. Conversely, the more inelastic the supply, the greater will be the producers' share of the tax and lesser will be the buyers' share.

All these statements can be validated using the graphical presentation. A representative diagram for this is shown by Fig. 7.10. Why these results hold can be explained through the implication of elasticities in terms of their definitions. *DD* is the demand curve, *SS* is the original supply curve. The original market equilibrium is shown by E_1 which gives us q_1, P_1 as the equilibrium output and price combination. S' S' is the new supply curve after the tax. The vertical shift of the supply curve is exactly equal to the amount of tax 't' imposed on the commodity. New equilibrium with new supply curve, and the demand curve is shown by E_2 giving us (q_2, P_2) as the combination of

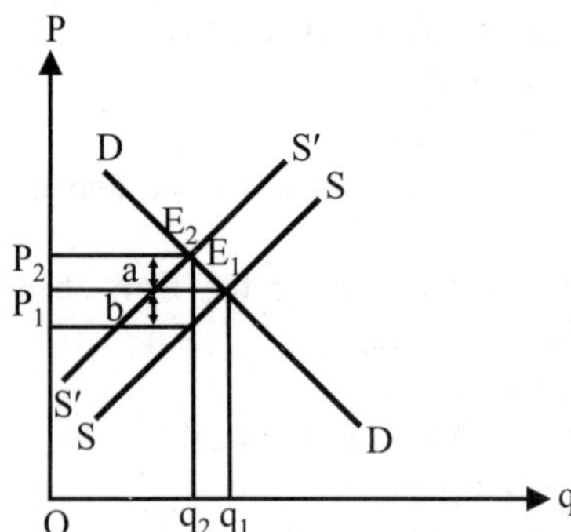

Fig. 7.10 Incidence of a Production or Sales Tax under Perfect Competition

equilibrium quantity and price. The increase in price $P_2 - P_1$ is the incidence of the tax on buyers which is equal to the distance 'a' and rest as shown by the distance 'b' goes to sellers, $a + b = t$.

Sometimes, a government supports its producers by giving them cost subsidy on commodity unit basis. This may be interpreted as negative commodity tax. It pushes down the marginal cost or the supply curve giving a new equilibrium with the demand curve for the market. The price decreases and hence buyers gain from the subsidy. The entire subsidy, however, will not be 'passed' to the buyers. Producers will also get a part of this so long as the supply and demand curves are not of the extreme shapes, *i.e.*, vertical, or horizontal lines. (Show this result graphically).

The analytical procedure of finding the incidence of a tax or subsidy by using the cost curve change has been described above. If the demand curve and the supply curve along with the tax or subsidy rate are given, the simpler technique of finding the incidence of the tax or subsidy, more or less based on the above procedure, is as follows.

Let P_b is the demand price that buyers are willing to pay and P_s be the supply price that sellers get in the market for a commodity. With these prices the demand and supply curves for the commodity would be as:

Demand curve $Q_d = f_d\ (P_d)$ ...(1)

Supply curve $Q_s = f_s\ (P_s)$ ...(2)

'f_d' and 'f_s' are functional forms of the demand and supply curves respectively. When a tax of Rs 't' is imposed on per unit of the commodity, then there would be a deviation between the demand and supply prices. Let this be given as

$P_b - P_s =$ 't', 't' is the taxrate. ...(3)

By substituting $P_b = P_s + t$ in the demand equation, we solve (1) and (2) for market equilibrium. This gives us P_s and so P_b, *i.e.*, $P_b = P_s + t$.

By comparing the new set of prices with those obtained by solving (1) and (2) without tax, we get the incidence of the tax on buyers and sellers.

In the case of subsidy, the supply prices P_s would be greater than the demand price, *i.e.*, $P_s = P_d +$'s' where 's' is the rate of subsidy per unit of output. The market equilibrium solutions, with and without subsidy, would then give us the incidence of subsidy on buyers and sellers.

Let the demand and supply curves be as:

$$Q_d = 87.5 - 0.75\ P_d,$$

$$Q_s = -12.5 + 1.25\ P_s.$$

By solving these two equations, when there is no tax, *i.e.*, $P_d = P_s$, we get price as Rs. 50, and $Q_d = Q_s = 50$ units.

When there is a tax of Rs. 2 per unit output of the commodity, then $P_d = P_s + 2.0$

By substituting $P_s + 2.0 = P_d$ in the demand curve and solving the model ($Q_d = Q_s$) we get new market equilibrium as $P_s = 49.25$, and $P_d = 49.25 + 2.0 = 51.25$.

The incidence of tax on consumer is Rs. 51.25 – Rs. 50 = Rs. 1.25, and on producer 50.0 – 49.25 = Re. 0.75.

If the tax is not related to the commodity units, it is lumpsum then the marginal cost will not change. There will not be a shift of the supply curve and the quantity: price combination remains unchanged. Producers will be having less profit now. They will bear the entire tax and consumers' price will be unaffected by this.

Normally, a government does not tax essential goods since they show inelastic demand and when demand is inelastic the greater incidence of the tax passes to the consumers. To protect the interest of consumers, therefore, essential commodities are left untaxed by the public authorities. Luxuries, on the other hand, are taxed heavily.

7.5 MARKET EQUILIBRIUM WITH LAGGED RESPONSES

The analysis of commodity market equilibrium under perfect competition presented so far is static in nature because the supply and demand responses relate to the quantity of output and its price of the same time period, that is $D_{(t)} = D(P_{(t)})$ and $S_{(t)} = S(P_{(t)})$. The market equilibrium given by such functions will be quite stable so long as the demand curve slopes downward and the supply curve upward, and they intersect in the positive quadrant. This, we have seen in Chapter 3. There are, however, some situations in the market when we come across dynamic or lagged responses which cannot be explained by static analysis. The equilibrium process of the market in such a situation can only be examined in the dynamic framework. Such equilibrium may be stable or unstable depending on the type of relationships of the model and their parameters. To explain this, we take here the case of the Cobweb model.

In many production systems of an economy, we do find considerable time-lag between production planning arid product sales. The best example of this is the agricultural sector. Wheat price in one harvest season, for example, will influence area under wheat cultivation and supply of wheat for the next season. In this situation, we specify the supply function with a lagged adjustment of the price. That is the supply in the current season; $S_{(t)}$ is a function of the price for the commodity prevailing in the previous season $(P_{(t-1)})$. The demand function on the other hand does not change, it will be $D_t = D(P_t)$. Let us take linear relationships into consideration. The dynamic model now before us for examination is:

$$D_{(t)} = a + b\, P_{(t)}$$
$$S_{(t)} = \alpha + \beta\, P_{(t-A)} \quad \text{...(4)}$$

For market equilibrium we have $D_{(t)} = S_{(t)}$

i.e., $$a + b\, P_{(t)} = \alpha + \beta\, P_{(t-1)} \quad \text{...(5)}$$

or $$P_{(t)} = \frac{\alpha - a}{b} + \frac{\beta}{b}\, P_{(t-1)}$$

This is a simple difference equation. Let $P_{(o)}$ be the initial condition when $t = 0$, the solution of this difference equation would then be,

$$P_{(t)} = \left(P_{(o)} - \frac{\alpha - a}{b - \beta}\right)\left(\frac{\beta}{b}\right)^t + \frac{\alpha - a}{b - \beta} \quad \text{...(6)}$$

The general condition for market equilibrium, as we find in the static case, is given by the equation $P_e = (\alpha - a)/(b - \beta)$. Let us call this as the equilibrium price. In the dynamic case, which is under discussion, it implies that the market will be in equilibrium when $P_t = P_{t-1} = P_e$. Will the equation (6) be giving this kind of dynamic equilibrium, *i.e.*, stable one or unstable?

Let us substitute $P_e = (\alpha - a)/(b - \beta)$ in (6) in order to get its simplified form as

$$P_{(t)} = (P_{(o)} - P_e)\left(\frac{\beta}{b}\right)^t + P_e \quad \text{...(7)}$$

If $|\beta/b| < 1$ or $|\beta| < |b|$ that is the absolute value of the slope of the demand curve is greater than the absolute value of slope of the supply curve (demand more elastic than the supply), then oscillations given by the above equation, around the equilibrium price P_e will decrease as t tends to infinity. This means the market will be dynamically in stable equilibrium. Through a graph this situation is shown by Panel (*a*) of the following diagram:

Let initial price P_o prevail in the market. This induces to supply S_1 quantity in period 1 but for S_1 quantity buyers are willing to pay P_1 price in period 1. P_1 price again induces the supplies to supply S_2 quantity in period 2 but for that buyers pay only P_2 price. This sequence goes on. That is $P_0 \rightarrow S_1 \rightarrow P_1 \rightarrow S_2 \rightarrow P_2 \rightarrow S_3 \rightarrow P_3 ... \rightarrow P_e$. The convergence of this price is achieved at the intersection point of the demand and supply curve corresponding to which P_e is the equilibrium price. This will be stable equilibrium.

In Panel (*b*) we are not getting converging oscillations. It is diverging situation. Price P_t increasingly oscillates around the equilibrium price P_e. There will be no equilibrium at point *e*. This is the situation when $|\beta/b| > 1$ or $|\beta| > |b|$ that is, the slope of the supply curve is more than the slope of the demand curve (supply curve more elastic than the demand curve). The graph of price changes vs time period clearly indicates the divergence of the market price away from the equilibrium price in greater and greater magnitudes. This is quite unstable situation.

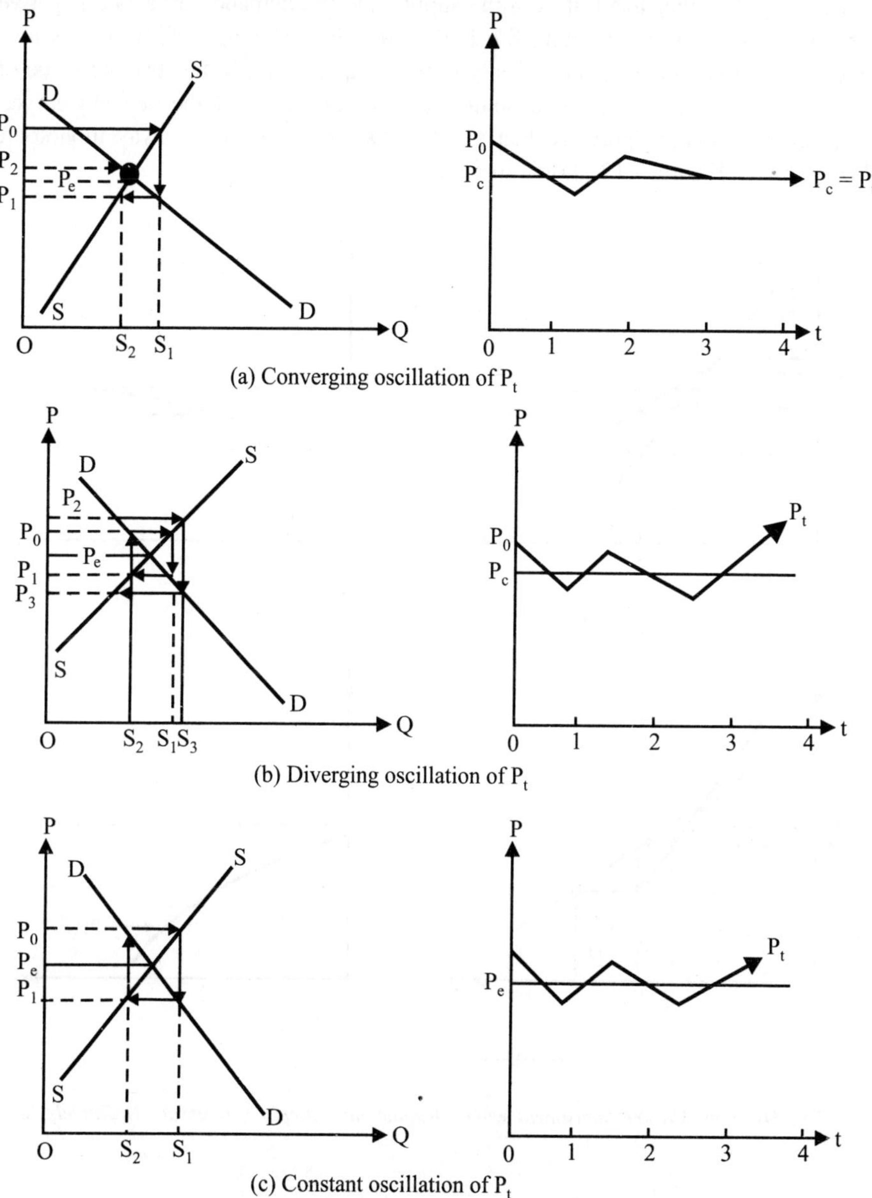

Fig. 7.11 Dynamic Equilibrium of a Commodity Market (The Cobweb Model)

Between these two market situations, *i.e.* the convergent situation and the divergent situation of the market price, we have a third possibility when the actual price of the commodity fluctuates around the equilibrium price by a constant amplitude. Panel (*c*) of Fig. 7.11 shows this case. In this case, both the supply and demand curves are having identical slopes $|\beta| = |b|$. This is 'quasi-stable' situation of the market.

If the demand curve slopes downward and supply curve upward, *i.e.*, $b < 0$, $\beta > 0$, $(\beta/b)^+$ alternates in sign as t increases and so the price (P_t) oscillates around the equilibrium price P_e, as Fig. 7.11 shows. On the other hand, if both the supply and the demand curves are negatively sloped, *i.e.* b as well as β are negative, the ratio β/b is then positive. The sign of (β/b) does not vary with time; this means the price moves monotonically towards equilibrium if the absolute value of the slope of the supply curve is greater than the absolute value of the slope of the demand curve, *i.e.*, $|\beta| > |b|$ and if the reverse situation prevails, that is, $|\beta| < |b|$ the price moves away monotonically from the equilibrium price. Figure 7.12 shows these two situations.

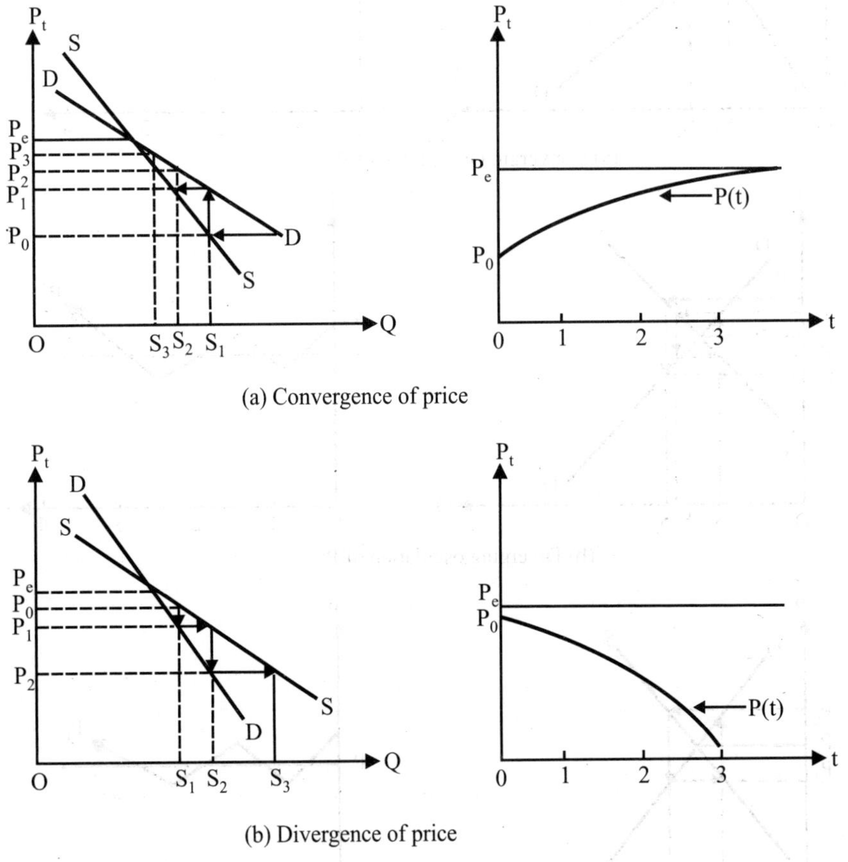

Fig. 7.12 Dynamic Market Adjustment when Demand and Supply Curves are Negatively Sloped

The dynamic adjustment process, described above, is known as the Cobweb model because the shape of the equilibrium process resembles like a Cobweb in Fig. 7.11. The situation, showing convergence or quasi-convergence of price, is quite realistic in practice but exploding price situation is unlikely.

7.6 THE EQUILIBRIUM OF A FIRM: GENERAL CONDITIONS

In this section, we will go through some general conditions for the equilibrium of a firm of which the equilibrium under perfect competition for the firm will be a special case. For the conditions of equilibrium, which we are going to discuss, let us first clear the meaning of the basic terms involved therein.

(*a*) *Total Revenue or Gross Revenue:* This is the total amount of money that a firm gets from the sales of its products. For a single output firm, total revenue (TR) will be simply a product of the price and quantity sold. That is, $TR = P.q$. If the price changes, quantity being constant, then TR changes and similarly if the price is constant and quantity sold changes, TR changes. Normally, price and quantity are linked through the demand function. The change in price means a change in quantity also since $q = f(P)$, so, we express TR in terms of either price or quantity and call it as 'revenue function' for the firm.

$$\left.\begin{aligned} TR &= P \cdot q = R(q) \\ \text{or} \quad TR &= P \cdot q = R(P) \end{aligned}\right\} \text{Revenue Function} \qquad ...(8)$$

(*b*) *Average Revenue* (*AR*)*:* It is the amount of money received per unit of output which is obviously the price of the product.

$$AR = TR/q = P \cdot q/q = P \qquad ...(9)$$

(*c*) *Marginal Revenue* (*MR*)*:* It is defined as addition to total revenue by selling one more extra unit of output. Say, if TR_n is the total revenue accruing from the sales of n units of output and TR_{n+1} is the total revenue from $n + 1$ units of output, marginal revenue (MR) of the (n + l)th unit is simply the difference $TR_{n+1} - TR_n$. If the revenue function is given in terms of q, MR will be the first derivative of that with respect to q.

That is

$$R = R\ (q)$$

$$\frac{dR}{dq} = R'\ (q) = MR \qquad ...(10)$$

More explicitly $R = P \cdot q$.

Therefore $$\frac{dR}{dq} = P + q\frac{dP}{dq} \qquad ...(11)$$

For a normal downward sloping demand curve we have $\frac{dP}{dq} < 0$; so the term $q\ dP/dq$ in (11) is negative. This negative term is a loss to the firm on all units of its output sold earlier because, an increase in q means a decrease in price which means less revenue from units sold earlier. Therefore, net addition in total revenue by producing and selling one more unit of output would be equal to the price minus the loss on previously sold units as a result of the reduced price. This is the interpretation of equation (11). In Fig. 7.13 the areas showing 'loss' and 'gain' are shown clearly. Whether net increase in *TR* is positive or negative depends on the difference between gain and loss.

On simplification, we can express the *MR* for the firm in terms of *AR* or *P* and price elasticity of demand (e_d). We know:

$$e_d = \frac{dq}{dP}\frac{P}{q}$$

Therefore, $$\frac{dq}{dP} = e_d \cdot \frac{q}{P}$$

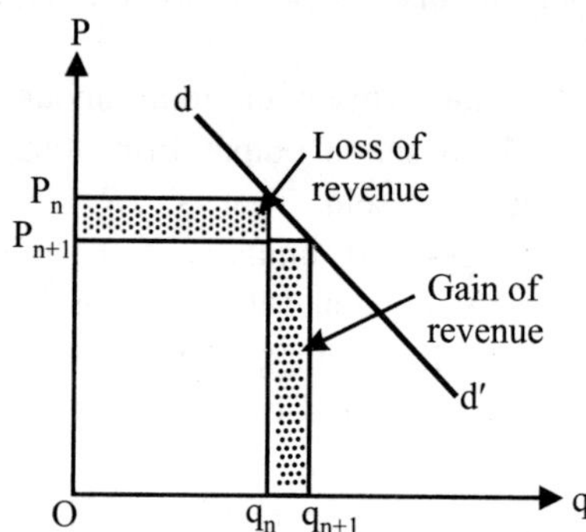

Fig. 7.13 The Concept of Marginal Revenue

On inverting it, we have

$$\frac{dP}{dq} = \frac{P}{e_d \cdot q}$$

Substituting this in equation (11), we get

$$MR = P + q \cdot \frac{P}{e_d \cdot q}$$

or $$MR = P + \frac{P}{e_d} = P\left[1 + \frac{1}{e_d}\right]$$

For a downward sloping demand curve e_d will be negative. Taking this into account, we modify the above expression as:

$$MR = P\left[1 - \frac{1}{|e_d|}\right]$$

Since $P = AR$, therefore,

$$MR = AR\left[1 - \frac{1}{|e_d|}\right] \qquad ...(12)$$

We have seen that the demand curve for a firm under perfect competition is a horizontal line parallel to the quantity axis showing infinite price elasticity of demand. That is,

$$e_d = \infty, \qquad \text{so } MR = P.$$

If $|e_d| > 1$, then MR is positive and if

$|e_d| < 1$, then MR is negative.

Now let us take a linear demand function as

$$P = a - bq. \quad \text{...(13)}$$

Therefore $$R = P \cdot q = (a - bq)\, q = aq - bq^2$$

and $$MR = \frac{dR}{dq} = a - 2bq. \quad \text{...(14)}$$

Comparing the slopes of the demand curve and MR curve we find *that the rate of decline of MR is twice of the rate of decline of AR, i.e., Price.* This result is valid only for straight line AR and MR schedules or when the total revenue function is quadratic.

(*d*) *Equilibrium Condition for Maximum Revenue:* The condition for revenue maximisation is quite simple to derive. Consider the revenue function for the firm as:

$$R = R(q)$$

The first and second order maximisation conditions for this are:

$$dR/dq = R'(q) = 0$$

and $$d^2R/dq^2 < 0 \quad \text{...(15)}$$

Let $P = 85 - 3q$ be the demand curve for a commodity. The total revenue would then be $R = P \cdot q = (85 - 3q)q$

or $$R = 85q - 3q^2.$$

$$\frac{dR}{dq} = 85 - 6q = 0$$

$$d^2R/dq^2 = -6.$$

The firm gets maximum revenue when its output is equal to 14.17 units and charging a price of 42.5 for that.

(*e*) *Profit Maximisation Conditions:* The profit is the difference between total revenue and total cost of production of the firm. We define the profit function for the firm as:

$$\pi = R(a) - (C(a) - b) \quad \text{...(16)}$$

where $R(q)$ is the total revenue, $C(q)$ is total variable cost and b is total fixed cost. Differentiating this function with respect to q, the first order condition for maximum profit is,

$$d\pi/dq = R'(q) - C'(q) = 0 \quad \text{...(17)}$$

and the second order condition for this is,

$$d^2\pi/dq^2 = \left(\frac{d(R'(q))}{dq} - \frac{d(C'(q))}{dq} \right) < 0$$

or $$\frac{d^2R}{dq^2} - \frac{d^2C}{dq^2} < 0$$

or $$\frac{d^2C}{dq^2} > \frac{d^2R}{dq^2} \quad \text{...(18)}$$

The first order condition states that for maximum profit the marginal revenue must be equal to the marginal cost of the output.

The second order condition states that the rate of change of the marginal cost must be greater than the rate of change of the marginal revenue. This implies that the marginal cost curve intersects the marginal revenue curve from below. Normally, this condition is satisfied when *MR* curve is downward sloping and *MC* curve is upward sloping.

Graphically, the implication of the second order condition can be explained as follows.

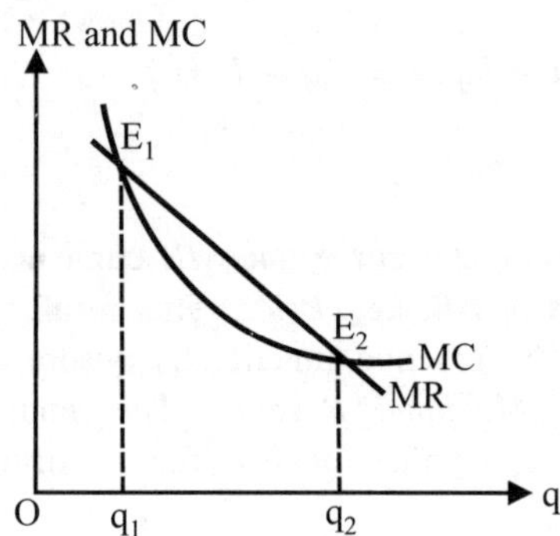

Fig. 7.14 Equilibrium Condition for Profit Maximisation

At E_1 point $MR = MC$ but the *MC* curve intersects the *MR* curve from above. It is, therefore, not an equilibrium point since as output increases marginal cost decreases more than the marginal revenue which means a surplus $(MR - MC) > 0$. The dotted area shows this surplus which will be the profit. At E_2 point, however, $MR = MC$ but *MC* curve intersects the *MR* curve from below. If the output is increased further marginal cost will be more than the marginal revenue, so there will be a loss to the firm. The firm would not be producing more than q_2 level of output. So, E_2 point defines the equilibrium condition for the firm while E_1 point defines the condition for the minimum profit.

There is a third condition for profit maximisation according to which the price of the product must be more than the average variable cost. This means $R > TVC$. The rationale for this has been given in Chapter 6 while deriving a supply curve from the cost function for the firm. A general picture of the profit maximisation conditions is presented below. Figure 7.15 has three parts — Part (*a*) deals with the representation of conditions in terms of averages, Part (*b*) shows them in terms of total, and Part (*c*) shows the profit function having the optima.

If *AR* (*i.e. P*) = *AC*, then profit will be zero. Points *X* and *Y* in part (*a*) of the figure show this, consequently q_1 and q_2 are zero profit levels of output. q_m is the level of output which gives maximum profit since for this $MR = MC$ and *MC* curve intersects the *MR* curve from below. The maximum profit is shown by the area of the rectangle *PQVZ*. In part (*b*), profit is zero when $TR = TC$ exactly for the same levels of the output *i.e.*, q_1 and q_2. The maximum profit is given by the distance *MN* since at this point the slope of *TR* is equal to the slope of *TC* curve, *i.e.*, the two tangents at *M* and *N* points on *TR* and *TC* curves respectively are parallel lines which means $MR = MC$. In part (*c*), total profit is shown as a function of output. Profit is maximum for q_m output and zero for q_1 and q_2 levels of output.

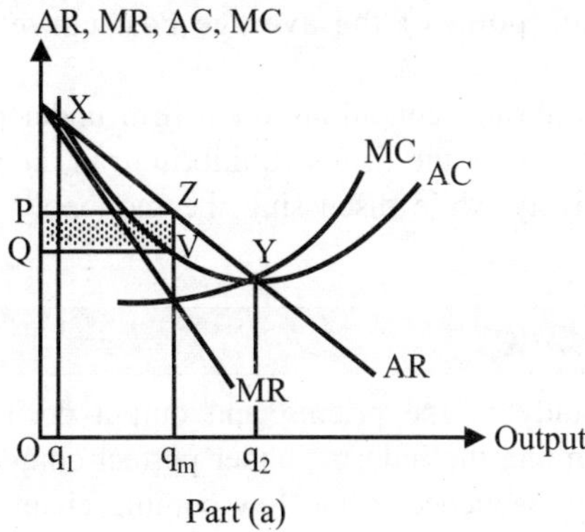

Part (a)

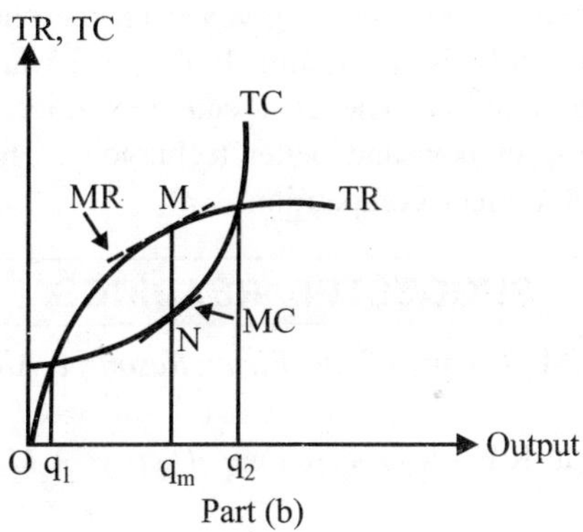

Part (b)

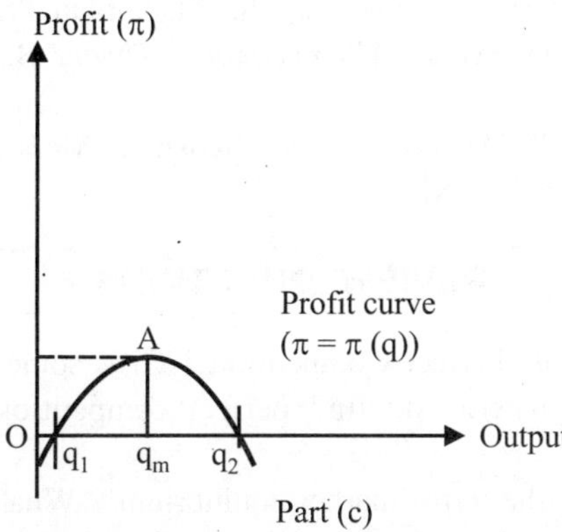

Part (c)

Fig. 7.15 Profit Maximisation Equilibrium for a Firm

Suppose a firm is operating under perfect competition, then $\frac{dp}{dq} = 0$ and the *AR* curve will be a horizontal line. That is, $AR = MR$. The profit maximum condition would now be $P = AR = MC$ and *MC* intersects the price line from below. We have already defined these conditions for the firm under perfect competition. In the short-run, the firm may be getting positive or negative profit but in the long-run its profit will be zero and, therefore the long-run equilibrium condition for the firm under perfect competition would be $P = MR = AC$

= *MC*. This gives the minimum point of the average cost curve as the equilibrium point for the firm in the long-run.

Thus, we find that the equilibrium conditions for a firm under perfect competition are special cases of the more general conditions for the firm's equilibrium. In the next chapters, we will be using these general conditions extensively while discussing the monopoly, monopolistic competition and other types of markets.

7.7 CONCLUDING REMARKS

We have completed the study of the pricing and output decision-making and hence of the equilibrium conditions for a firm and the industry under perfect competition. More complex markets will be taken up for the study in sequence in the few coming chapters. Under perfect competition, as we have seen in this chapter, the firm is a price-taker. In this situation, it has no control over the price of its product. The price is exogenously given from the outside. The flrm can only adjust its output in such a way that its profit is maximum. If the firm wants to increase its proflt further it has to reduce the cost of production. The cost can be reduced through improvement in the efflciency or through introduction of new and better technology. This is the message we get from an analysis of the market under perfect competition.

SUGGESTED READINGS

Cohen, K.J.; and Cyert, R.M, *Theory of the Firm: Resource Allocation in a Market Economy,* Prentice-Hall of India, 1976.

Henderson, J.M. and Quandt, R.E., *Microeconomic Theory: A Mathematical Approach,* McGraw Hill, 1971, 1980.

Koutsoyiannis, A., *Modern Microeconomics,* The Macmillan Press, 1978.

Nicholson, W. and Christopher Synder, *Microeconomic Theory,* South-western Cengage Learning, Canada, 10th Edn. 2008.

Sher, William and Pindola, R., *Microeconomic Theory. A Synthesis of Classical Theory and the Modern Approach,* Edward Arnold, 1981.

REVIEW QUESTIONS

1. What is the meaning of 'Perfect Competition'? Give some examples with explanation of industries or markets where you find perfect competition or near perfect competition prevailing in practice.
2. What do you mean by the term 'market equilibrium'? What are the essential requirements for short-run and long-run equilibrium of a market?
3. Give Marshallian and Walrassian explanations of how a market reaches equilibrium position under perfect competition. Under what situation, these two approaches give conflicting conclusions regarding market equilibrium for a commodity? Discuss.
4. What are the conditions for short-run and long-run equilibrium of a firm under perfect competition? Do you think that a competitive firm would be able to get excess profit, *i.e.*, more than the normal, in the short-run and in the long-run? Give reasons for your answers. Use graphical representation to support your explanation.

5. Explain the momentary or market period equilibrium for a commodity market. In this context, what is the meaning and role of the reservation price? Examine with the help of suitable diagrams.
6. What do you mean by 'increasing', 'decreasing' and 'constant' cost industries? How such classification of industries is practically useful?
7. By using the demand and supply interaction diagram, identify those situations when the incidence of a production or sales tax would be relatively more on producers and on consumers.
8. What do you mean by lagged adjustment in the market equilibrium? In this context, describe the Cobweb model and show when this model leads to stable and unstable market equilibrium?
9. By using the revenue and cost concepts what are the general equilibrium conditions for a profit-maximising firm? Also, show how such conditions would be different from the conditions for revenue maximisation?
10. The demand curve for a commodity is given as $q_d = 13.5 - 1.5P$. The supply curve for the commodity is $q_s = -4.5 + 3P$. What will be the effects on the market equilibrium for the commodity if (*a*) a tax of Rs. 1.50 per unit of the commodity is imposed, (*b*) a subsidy of Rs. 1.00 per unit of the commodity is given to the supplier?
11. An industry has 100 firms, 50 of which are located at one place and the other 50 at second place. All firms at each place possess identical cost functions. For a representative firm at each place the cost functions are given as $C_1 = 0.5q_1^2 + 6q_1$; and $C_2 = 0.5q_2^2 + 10q_2$ where q_1 and q_2 are output levels and C_1 and C_2 are total costs at place 1 and place 2 respectively of the representative firm. Derive the market supply function for the commodity and find the equilibrium price and quantity supplied if the market demand curve for the commodity is $D = 1600 - 20P$.
12. A perfectly competitive market has 1000 producers, each with the variable cost function defined as $VC = 20q + 0.5q^2$. The market demand function is defined as $Q = D(P) = 105{,}000 - 500P$.
    (*a*) Derive the short-run supply curve for a producer.
    (*b*) Find the short-run market supply curve.
    (*c*) Find the equilibrium price for producers and total quantity of output sold.
    (d) What will be the output of each producer?
    (*e*) If each producer has a fixed cost of Rs. 200, what will be the profit accruing to him?
13. (*a*) Show that the relative (differential) incidence of (a differential change in) an excise tax depends upon the relative slopes (and hence the relative elasticities) of the demand and supply functions at the equilibrium point.

    (*b*) If the principal purpose of an excise tax is the procurement of government revenue, a given tax rate will be more effective as demand is less elastic. If the principal purpose of the tax is to reduce consumption of the commodity, a given tax rate is more effective as demand is more elastic. Illustrate these results by diagrams.

CHAPTER 8

Pricing and Output Decisions Under Monopoly

We have gone through pricing and output decisions in one extreme type of market, that is, perfect competition. In this chapter, we take up another extreme for the study of such decisions which is called monopoly. Like perfect competition, a pure monopoly may not be existing in reality as it is defined in economic theory. Yet, a study of pure monopoly provides us guidelines and approach to study the market which is monopolistic in nature. The first thing we will do in this chapter is to define the monopoly and go through conditions of a market which perpetuate the existence of monopoly. Later on, we will take up for discussion topics like monopoly equilibrium, price discrimination, and regulation of monopoly.

8.1 DEFINITION OF PURE MONOPOLY[1]

Like perfect competition, pure monopoly can be defined in terms of certain conditions prevailing in the market which we take here as assumptions.

(*a*) There is only one seller (*i.e.*, producer) in the market but the number of buyers is large.

(*b*) The product of the seller may be homogeneous or there may be differentiated products but there are no close substitutes in the market for the product or products of the seller: When substitutes are not available it implies that the cross-elasticity of demand between the product of a monopolist and every other product of other firms is zero or very low.

(*c*) There is no free entry to the market.

(*d*) Perfect information or knowledge. This is available to the seller and buyers free of cost.

If all these conditions are satisfied, we call it pure monopoly. However, in practice, some of them may not be met precisely and that is why we are saying that pure monopoly, like the perfect competition, is more or less a hypothetical market situation.

1. Mohopoly is an important form of market imperfection, the pioneering analysis of which was conducted by Mrs. J. Robinson in her book, *The Theory of Imperfect Competition,* London, Macmillan, 1933.

8.2 EMERGENCE OF MONOPOLY: THE BARRIERS TO ENTRY IN THE MARKET

A monopoly perpetuates in the market if rivals are not allowed to join, it, *i.e.*, the entry to the market is prohibited by certain factors which we call as barriers to entry. We may call all such barriers as sources of monopoly power. There are two general types of barriers to entry: technical barriers and legal barriers.

(*a*) *Technical Barriers to Entry:* The most important one in this category is the efficiency of large scale production which is materialised through economies of large-scale production. If there are economies of large scale production, an existing firm continuously expands its level of output and gains from the cost reduction advantages. New firms may find it extremely difficult to compete with such a large firm. Even several, existing firms producing low level of output at a relatively high level of cost would not be able to compete with the bigger one in the situation of economies of scale, so they may be eventually thrown out of the market and thus perpetuating the monopoly of the large firm. It is a natural factor for existence of the monopoly.

A large firm may be having access to the better technology because of its capability of having or buying of that. And if such a technology is in use, it is quite natural that the firm would be more efficient than others and this difference in efficiency may be eventually a source of monopoly.

Another important technical factor causing monopoly is seen in the situation when supply from more than one firm is inconvenient and costly. Most of the public utilities come in this category.

(*b*) *Legal Barriers to Entry:* In many situations we find legal factors leading to the growth of monopolies. Permits and other legal rights granted by any government do restrict the entry. of others in the business. Patent rights to protect productive techniques or products are best examples of the legal factors. In many situations, legally awarding of an exclusive franchise to serve a market leads to monopoly. Several examples may be cited for this, such as gas and electric services, communication services, airline routes, railways, and like that. Monopoly also tends to develop when a single firm manages to acquire control over all or most strategic raw material sources for production. Control over bauxite mines for production of aluminium is an example for this.

(*c*) There are some other barriers to entry, such as product differentiation and economies of being established. If the monopoly firm itself differentiates its products internally, it will be extremely difficult for rivals to compete with the firm in this situation. Further, if the firm is already in business it will be having several advantages over the potentially new firms. It will be having established markets, access to the sources of raw material and other inputs, including finance, which a new firm can get only at a higher cost and so the cost differences will be the sources of perpetuation of the monopoly power of the existing firms.

Some times unfair means adopted by some firm are responsible for development of monopolies. Product disparagement tactics, disturbing the supply-line of rivals, bribing of government officials for some favours, etc., are a few examples of this which may have positive implications for growth of monopolies.

The list of barriers to entry is not exhaustive. All these factors or some of them interacting jointly cause monopolies in markets. Such monopolies may not be in the pure form as we have defined above but certainly in some approximate form with considerable market power to influence the price and output decisions in the industry. Under public sector, for example, we do find monopolies in pure form. The Indian Railways, which is a public monopoly, can be cited as an example for this.

8.3 SHORT-RUN EQUILIBRIUM OF A MONOPOLY FIRM

To find the short-run equilibrium, we need information regarding the demand and cost functions for the firm and its goal. As far as the demand curve is concerned, it will be a downward sloping curve or line as we find for the industry under perfect competition. Since a monopoly means one firm industry, so a downward sloping demand curve is a logical conclusion for it. A firm under perfect competition will have a horizontal demand curve -but a monopoly firm will have a negatively sloping demand curve. Whether the demand curve for the product of the monopoly is elastic or inelastic: depends on the nature of the product from consumer's utility point of view. Once we know the demand curve for the monopoly we can specify its total revenue function as $R = P{\cdot}q = R(q)$.

The total cost function and hence the average and marginal cost curves for the monopoly firm will be similar to that of a firm under perfect competition. The cost function, as usual, is specified as $C = C(q) + b$.

Now, we may take the stand that the goal of the monopoly firm is profit maximisation. Therefore, the general equilibrium conditions for a firm, which we have presented in the previous chapter, will be applicable to the monopoly firm. That is, given;

$$\pi = R(q) - C(q) - b$$

$$d\pi/dq = R'(q) - C'(q) = 0 \qquad ...(1)$$

and

$$d^2\pi/dq^2 = R''(q) - C''(q) < 0$$

For equilibrium of a monopoly, we have two conditions: (*a*) the *MR* of the firm is equal to its *MC*, and (*b*) the *MC* curve intersects the *MR* curve from below.

Graphically, we can represent the monopoly equilibrium in the short-run as follows:

A monopoly firm, with given *AR* and *AC* curve would be fulfilling the equilibrium conditions at point *E* where *MC* = *MR* and MC curve intersects the *MR* curve from below. Consequently, q_m is the monopoly output and P_m is its price and the optimum profit is shown by the dotted area, *i.e.*,

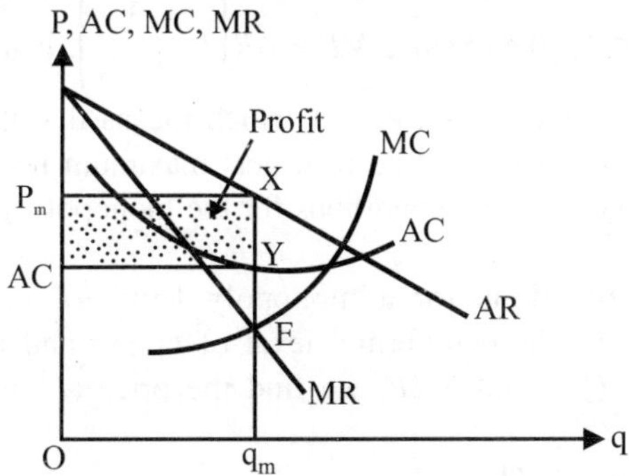

Fig. 8.1 Short-run Monopoly Equilibrium

$(P_m - AC)\ q_m = \pi$. So long as the *AR* and *AC* curves are fixed there will be only one equilibrium point for the firm. The equilibrium position of the monopoly changes if there is a shift of the demand and cost curves. The monopoly firm will not have a supply curve since $P \neq MC$. The supply by the monopoly firm, of course, depends on the shift or change of the demand and/ or cost curves.

We have shown the equilibrium position for the monopoly firm using average revenue, average cost and marginal cost curves. It may be shown using total revenue and total cost curves as we have done in Fig. 7.16 of Chapter 7 where q_e indicates the equilibrium level of output since, for this level, the slope of *TR* (*i.e.*, *MR*) and the slope of *TC* (*i.e.*, *MC*) are identical.

It is not necessary that the equilibrium conditions always yield positive profit to the monopoly. Consider, for example, the following figure in which the *AC* curve is above the demand curve for the equilibrium conditions: *MR* = *MC* and *MC* curve intersecting *MR* curve from below. The profit is negative, shown by the shaded area.

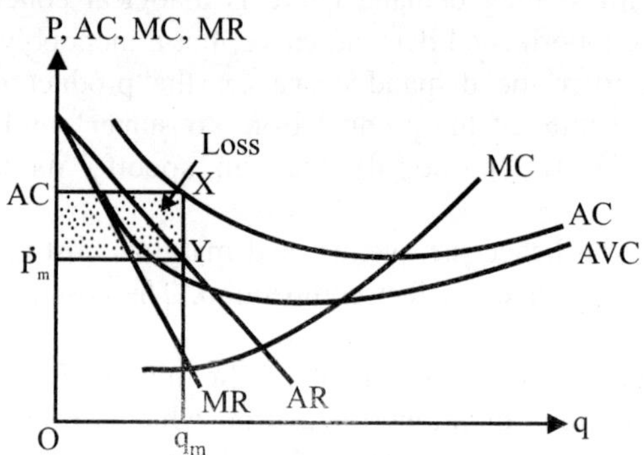

Fig. 8.2 Monopoly Equilibrium with Negative Profit

A monopoly firm in such a situation, *i.e.*, with negative profit at the equilibrium, will go out of the business in the long-run unless it switches over to an appropriate sized plant matching with the demand for its product. For short-run stay in the business with negative profits the condition is that it must be able to cover its variable cost. If the equilibrium price is less than the average variable cost, the monopoly firm will close down its plant even in the short-run just like a competitive firm.

There is another important phenomenon to the equilibrium of a monopoly firm. It always operates in the elastic range of its demand curve for profit maximisation. To show this, we take the equilibrium condition $MR = MC > 0$ and since $MR = AR\left(1 - \frac{1}{|e_d|}\right)$, which implies that $AR\left(1 - \frac{1}{|e_d|}\right) = MC > 0$ *MR*, will be positive only when $e_d > 1$ which means that the firm operates in the elastic range of its demand curve. When $MR = 0$, the firm gets maximum revenue and at that level $e_d = 1$.

In order to elaborate the equilibrium conditions for the monopoly, as described above, let us take a numerical example.

The demand and cost functions for a monopoly firm are given as $Q = 160 - 2P$ and $C = 5Q + 0.5\ Q^2$. What will be the equilibrium level of output and price for the firm?

From the demand curve $Q = 160 - 2P$, we find the price (*P*) in terms of *Q* by inverting it. That is,

$$P = 80 - 0.5\ Q$$

Total revenue for the firm would then be,

$$R = P \cdot Q = (80 - 0.5\ Q)\ Q = 80Q - 0.5\ Q^2$$

and the profit is the difference between *TR* and *TC*, *i.e.*,

$$\pi = 80Q - 0.5Q^2 - 5Q - 0.5\ Q^2$$

or

$$\pi = 75Q - Q^2$$

Maximising *n* with respect to *Q*, we get

$$\frac{d\pi}{dQ} = 75 - 2Q = 0 \qquad ...(i)$$

$$d^2\pi/dQ^2 = -2 < 0 \qquad ...(ii)$$

From (*i*) we get $2Q = 75$, $Q = 75/2 = 37.5$ units. The monopoly price can be obtained now from its demand curve $P = 80 - 0.5Q = 80 - 0.5 \times 37.5$ which is equal to Rs. 61.25.

Total Profit of the firm is Rs. 1406.25.

Suppose the monopoly firm is regulated, it has to follow norms of profit-maximisation as a firm does under perfect competition. The profit maximising output would be given by the condition $P = MC$ and MC curve intersecting the price line from below.

From the cost function $C = 5Q + 0.5Q^2$ we get the marginal cost as $dC/dQ = 5 + Q$. Equating this to the price, we get

$$P = MC \text{ or } 80 - 0.5Q = 5 + Q.$$

or $$1.5Q = 75, \text{ or } Q = 75/1.5 = 50 \text{ units}$$

and price of the commodity, $80 - 0.5 \times 50 =$ Rs. 55; total profit would be Rs. 1250.

The competitive output is more than the monopoly output, but the competitive price is less than the monopoly price.

This is a general property of the monopoly, that is, for any given price monopoly output will be less than the competitive output, and for a given output monopoly price will be greater than the competitive price.

For a competitive firm $P = MC$ and for a monopoly $MR = MC$ and $MR < P$ (= AR) which means $P > MC$. The deviation of price from the marginal cost in the case of monopoly is attributed to the exploitation of consumers by the monopoly by charging higher price. This property of the monopoly firm has been used by Lerner to measure its monopoly power.[2]

According to him,

$$\frac{P - MC}{P} = I \qquad ...(2)$$

where '*I*' shows the monopoly power. Since $MC = MR = AR\left(1 - \frac{1}{|e_d|}\right)$ which implies that,

$$\frac{P - MC}{P} = I = \frac{1}{|e_d|} \text{ since } AR = P. \qquad ...(3)$$

The Lerner's index will be zero when $e_d = \infty$ *i.e.*, $P = MC$, the firm operates under perfect competition. Further, we know that the monopoly firm operates only in the elastic region of its demand curve. So, if $e_d < 1$, $MR < 0$. Therefore, the limiting maximum value for '*I*' is 1 when e_d approaches to unity.

8.4 LONG-RUN EQUILIBRIUM OF A MONOPOLY FIRM

In the long-run, a profit-maximising monopoly will be in equilibrium at that level of output for which long-run *MC* is equal to *MR* and the *LMC* intersects the *MR* curve from below. Such a long-run equilibrium for the firm must also imply short-run equilibrium. In the long-run, all factors of

2. A.P. Lerner, "The Concept of Monopoly and the Measurement of Monopoly Power". *Review of Economic Studies,* Vol. 1, 1934, pp. 157-175.

production, including the plant size, will be variable. The firm, therefore, makes the choice of the size of its plant in such a way that it gets positive profit or at least zero profit. Negative profit is ruled out in the long-run. In the following figure, the long-run equilibrium situation for the monopoly is given by Q^* for which $LMC = SMC = MR$ and both LMC and SMC curves intersects the MR curve from below. The profit of the firm is given by the dotted area of P^*ABC and P^* is the equilibrium price for the firm in the long-run. We find that there is a short-run equilibrium at Q^* level of output. However, the plant associated with the SAC curve is not utilised fully as the equilibrium output Q^* is less than its optimum output capacity Q_s. The optimum level of output for the firm in the long-run is given by Q_L where LAC is minimum. This level of output is also not as profitable as Q^*; so it will not be produced. The firm can produce Q_L output only when demand is so high that the MR curve intersects the LMC at the lowest point of the LAC, *i.e.*, at E point.

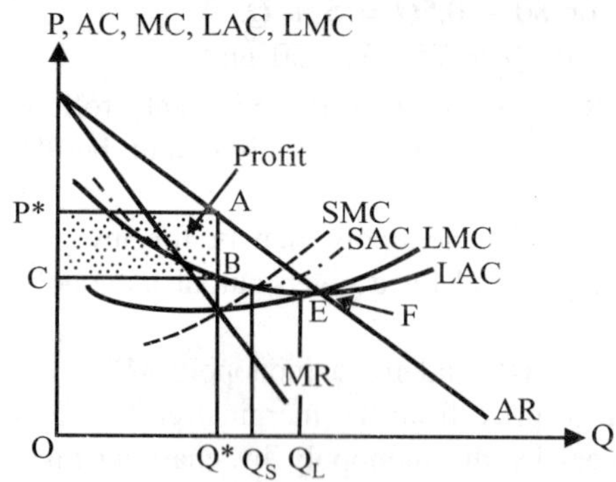

Fig. 8.3 Long-run Equilibrium of a Monopoly Firm

The above analysis of the long-run equilibrium of a monopoly firm is valid when the firm maintains its monopoly status, that is, there is no effective threat of entry in the industry of the potential firm. The equilibrium position of the firm, in this case, will be stable. However, if there is a plausibility of the entry of new firms in the market, there are two options for the firm for its courses of action. First, allow the entry of new firms and share the market for the product with them. The market power of the monopoly firm reduces by this and eventually this would lead to a change in market structure, *i.e.*, from monopoly to perfect competition. The second course of action is to block the entry of rivals in the industry through temporary price cut or unfair means or in some other way. If the price reduction strategy is adopted, the profit of the monopoly firm declines and output increases. A decline in profit means disincentive to the potential firms; so they would not join the industry. The limit of price reduction will be set at that point on the AR curve when price equals average cost, *i.e.*, the point when LAC curve intersects the AR curve from below. Such a situation is given by the point F in Fig. 8.3. The price corresponding to $AR = LAC$ is called 'Limit Price'. The firm gets no-profit no-loss at this point. No specific equilibrium situation can be given before the limit price situation for the monopoly firm in the long-run. It depends on how strong is the threat of potential entry in the industry.

8.5 MARKET PERIOD EQUILIBRIUM OF A MONOPOLY

The equilibrium in a very short period is called 'market period equilibrium' or 'momentary equilibrium'. The period is very short and there cannot be any adjustment in the production and supply of the product. The supply is fixed as shown by a vertical line *SE* in Fig. 8.4. The demand curve or average revenue curve for the firm is given by the line *AX,* and *AY* is the marginal revenue curve associated with this. *OE* is the fixed supply. The firm can choose any quantity that it wishes to sell in the market up to *OE* level. If the choice of the quantity is made, the firm can find the price for that from the demand curve, and if the price is fixed, the firm can find the quantity to be sold for that using the demand curve. The question here is: what should be the optimum combination of price and quantity for the firm?

In this case, since supply is fixed, the cost is fixed. Therefore, maximisation of profits means maximisation of revenue. So, the firm follows exclusively the principle of revenue maximisation to find its equilibrium position. The condition for revenue maximisation is that $MR = 0$ and the rate of change of the total revenue curve is negative after this.

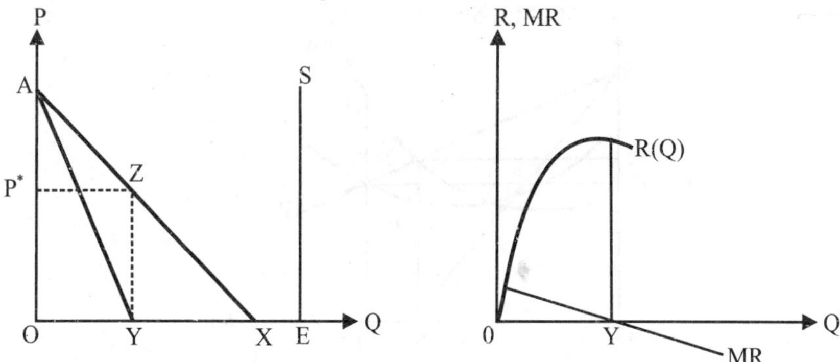

Fig. 8.4 Equilibrium of a Monopoly Firm in the Market Period

$$\pi = P \cdot d - C^* \quad \text{...(4)}$$

$$d\pi/dq = P + q\frac{dP}{dq} = 0 \text{ since } C^* = \text{Constant}$$

$$d^2\pi/dq^2 = d^2R/dq^2 < 0.$$

In the above figure, *MR* is zero at point *Y* on the quantity axis. The firm gets maximum revenue and hence maximum profit when it sells *OY* output and charges *P** price for that. If the supply exceeds *OY*, as we find in the diagram, the excess over *OY*, *i.e.*, *YE* quantity will be destroyed by the firm. If the supply is less than the level when $MR = 0$, the entire quantity will be sold at the corresponding price on the demand curve. There is no question of talking of maximisation of revenue for such a level of output since *MR* is not zero.

8.6 EQUILIBRIUM OF A PUBLIC MONOPOLY FIRM

Public monopolies are operating in several key sectors of economies in different countries, particularly in mixed economies and socialistic countries. Such firms are owned by the government to control industries in the interest of the people. The objective of a public monopoly firm will be to provide more output and charge less price for that in order to increase the welfare of the people. They are not supposed to work for economic surplus or greater revenue. Absence of the profit maximisation or sales maximisation motives and pursuance of the welfare maximisation principle for the working of public monopolies creates some difficulty in optimal pricing and output decisions by such undertakings. Theoretically, we may examine some simple norms for such decision-making as follows.

(i) Capacity Constrained Situation

In this case, we postulate that the demand for the product of the firm is quite high as compared to the capacity of production. This situation is shown in the following figure where *AR* curve intersects the *A* curve on its rising side. As we have mentioned above, a public monopoly will not be working for profits. Its aim is to provide maximum possible quantity of output at the lowest possible price. There are two plausible situations for this. One is given by the points on the *AR* curve. At this point, $AR = AC$ which gives P_1 as the equilibrium price and q_1 as the equilibrium quantity of output.

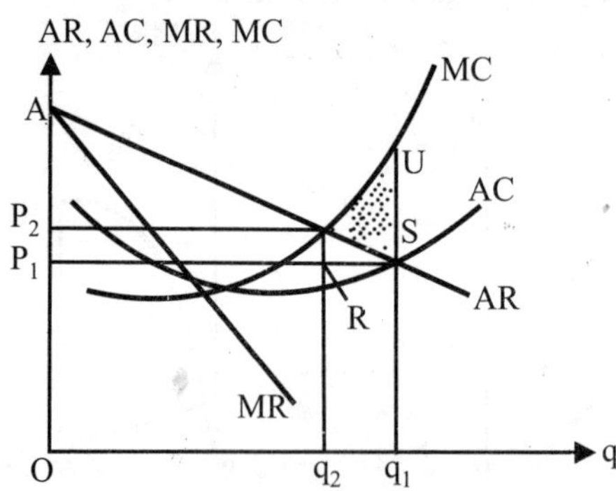

Fig. 8.5 Equilibrium of a Public Monopoly Firm : Capacity Constrained Case

Point *S* shows no profit no loss situation; when we say no profit, it means there is no economic profit, the normal profit which is a part of the cost is included in the *AC*.. The consumer surplus, which may be taken as a measure of welfare, is shown by the area of the triangle AP_1S.

The other possibility for the equilibrium of the firm is given by point *T* on the *AR* curve. At this point, we find *AR* (*i.e.*, *P*) = *MC* and the *MC* curve intersecting the *AR* curve from below. This is the situation for maximum profit for a competitive firm. The public monopoly firm corresponding to this point produces q_2 output which is less than q_1 and charges P_2 price which is more than P_1, The consumer surplus is now shown by the area AP_2T, and the profit transferred to the firm is P_2TRP_1 which was earlier a part of the consumer surplus.

The two situations for the possible equilibrium for a public monopoly firm are before us now for evaluation. Which one is to be chosen? Point *S* on the *AR* curve is giving us 'average cost pricing' norm while point *T* is giving the 'marginal cost pricing' norm. If we accept the average cost pricing norm for the firm, there is greater consumer surplus but there is no surplus for the firm itself. If the firm wants to expand in view of high demand for its output, it has to depend on others, *i.e.*, the government for funds. Moreover, it is not having adequate financial support to meet risks and uncertainties. The marginal cost pricing norm, on the other hand, is having lower consumer surplus because of marginally lower output and higher price but it is giving some surplus in the form of profit transferred from consumers to the firm. This makes the firm, financially strong internally which is a desirable situation. From this point of view, marginal cost pricing principle or norm is better than the average cost-pricing norm.

The superiority of the marginal-cost pricing over the average cost pricing can best be explained in terms of total surplus accruing to the society. By total surplus we mean the sum of consumers' surplus and producers' surplus, *i.e.*, profit since the public monopoly firm is a state enterprise; so whatever profit goes to it that is the state profit or public profit. When price equals to marginal cost (refer q_2 level of output) the total surplus is the area given by AP_1 RTA which is the sum of the consumer surplus shown by the area of the triangle AP_2T and the area of rectangle P_2 TRP_1. Let us denote the area of the triangle AP_2T by α, and the area P_2TRP_1 by β, so,

$$(\text{Total surplus})_{q_2} = \alpha + \beta.$$

Now, suppose we move to the average cost pricing $P = AR = AC$ (refer to q_1 level of output), there is consumer surplus shown by the area of the triangle AP_1S, which is a sum of α, β and γ, where γ is the area of the small triangle TRS. We know, for output greater than q_2, marginal cost exceeds the price of the product. The price is nothing but 'marginal willingness to pay'. Since MC is greater than P, it implies that there is an efficiency loss from the producer's point of view by increasing the output beyond q_2. The efficiency loss is given by the area $UTRS$ which is a sum of the area TRS and TSU. This is the producer's loss, that is, the negative surplus accruing to the public monopoly firm. If we represent the area TSU by δ, loss of surplus to the firm is equal to γ + δ and, therefore, total surplus accruing to the society at q_1 level of output is

$$(\text{Total surplus})_{q_1} = \alpha + \beta + \gamma - \gamma - \delta = \alpha + \beta - \delta \qquad \text{...(5)}$$

Comparing (4) and (5), we find that the total surplus at the marginal cost pricing situation is greater than the total surplus at the average-cost pricing situation. Therefore, the public monopoly should follow the principle of marginal-cost pricing to define its equilibrium.

(ii) Excess Capacity Situation

Let us examine a different situation for the equilibrium of the public monopoly firm in which the demand curve intersects the average cost curve on its declining side, that is, there is excess capacity of production than the demand for the product. Figure 8.6 shows this situation.

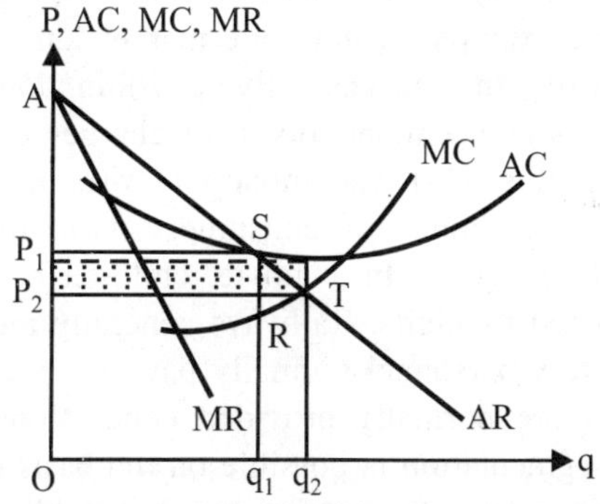

Fig. 8.6 Equilibrium of a Public Monopoly Firm: Excess Capacity Case

At point S on the AR curve, we have $AR = AC$, that is, P_1 price which gives no profit no loss to the firm, the output level is q_1. If we equate AR to MC, the equilibrium price P_2, is lower than P_1 and output q_2 is more than q_1. There is more output and less price and therefore the consumer surplus is more when we decide the price according to the marginal-cost pricing principle but there is a direct loss to the firm as AC is more than P_2 for q_2 output. Like the earlier case, we can show that the surplus accruing to the society in the case of marginal cost pricing will be more than the average cost pricing situation, so the firm should produce q_2 level of output and charge P_2 price. Further, the firm should be compensated by the government for the direct loss it is having at this level of output.

8.7 MONOPOLY PRICE DISCRIMINATION: MULTIPLE PRICES AND SINGLE PRODUCT

A monopoly firm, being the only one seller in the market, is free to charge different prices to different markets or buyers when conditions are appropriate for this. If the firm follows such a policy in practice we call it price discrimination. Instead of selling all output at a single price the monopoly firm charges higher price for a part of its output and thus increases its revenue. The profit of the monopoly will also go up since in the situation of discriminating prices, its cost of production does not change. Increase in profit is the eventual aim of the price discrimination by a monopoly firm. If there is no such possibility, price discrimination is not feasible.

There are two necessary conditions for price discrimination: (1) The market for the product of the monopoly firm is segmented, that is, there are different segments of the market having different price elasticities of demand. The firm is able to identify such submarkets. (2) Different segments of the market are insulated from each other. That is, it is difficult and costly for customers to buy the product from one market and resell it in the other market. If resale of the product is possible, speculators will buy it from the 'low price' market and sell it to 'high price' market and thus gain from this, making the price discrimination activity of the monopoly quite unsuccessful.

Market segmentation or separation depends on certain factors: (*i*) The nature of the product may permit segmentation and obviate resale possibilities. For example, a doctor may adopt the policy of price discrimination since he provides his services to customers one by one and his services cannot be subjected to resale. In the case of electricity supply, water supply, telephone services, and like that, we find a physical connection between the producer and the consumers and therefore it is not possible to have resale of such services. (*ii*) Geography plays important role in market segmentation. Take the example of domestic markets and foreign markets for a product. Resale practice will be too costly in this case. Even within domestic markets we may have geographically separate regions where a monopoly firm charges different prices for its product. Zone-pricing is an example for this. (*iii*) The monopoly firm may identify submarkets for its product on the basis of certain attributes of consumers with minimal resale possibility. For example, age may be a separation device. In a movie, children below a certain age are charged lower price for tickets as compared to adults. Railways generally reduce fare by 50% for children below the age of 10 years. Military personnel normally pay less prices for several commodities as compared to civilians. Students are normally provided concessions when they travel by public transport systems. (*iv*) Market segmentation is possible on the basis of time also. Price of a dinner may be more than of a lunch in a five-star hotel, Fresh vegetables may have higher prices than the stock of old vegetables. First few runs of a movie may be priced higher as compared to the later ones.

There may be other factors responsible for market segmentation by a monopoly firm. We need not go into any further details of the identification of such factors. Rather, we conclude here that a monopoly firm is able to segment the market for its product and charge different prices for them as the situations command.

Depending on the extent of price discrimination, economists classify it into three types: 'First Degree', 'Second Degree' and the 'Third Degree' price-discrimination. For simplicity of understanding these types of price discrimination, let us consider the third degree price discrimination first. We begin with a simple case of two markets, each one showing different pattern of demand for the product of the firm and both the markets are insulated from each other. Let P_1 and P_2 be the prices charged by the monopoly firm and q_1 and q_2 are the quantities sold in the respective markets. The total output produced and sold by the firm is $q_1 + q_2$ which is assumed to be produced at a single plant. The total profit accruing to the firm in this situation of multiple pricing or price discrimination would be:

$$\pi = P_1q_1 + P_2q_2 - C(q) \qquad \text{...(5a)}$$

where $\quad q = q_1 + q_2.$

By deducing the conditions for profit maximisation, we get

$$\frac{\partial \pi}{\partial q_1} = \frac{\partial (P_1q_1)}{\partial q_1} - \frac{\partial C(q)}{\partial q}\frac{dq}{dq_1} = 0$$

or
$$\frac{\partial R_1}{\partial q_1} - \frac{\partial C(q)}{\partial q} = 0 \qquad \text{...(6)}$$

Since $dq/dq_1 = 1$ as one unit sale of output in market 1 means production of one more unit of output.

Similarly, we have

$$\partial \pi / \partial q_2 = \frac{\partial (P_2q_2)}{\partial q_2} - \frac{\partial C(q)}{\partial q}\frac{dq}{dq_2} = 0$$

or
$$\frac{\partial R_2}{\partial q_2} - \frac{\partial C(q)}{\partial q} = 0 \qquad \text{...(7)}$$

where $dq/dq_2 = 1$ by using the same argument as for dq/dq_1.

$$\frac{\partial C(q)}{\partial q} = \frac{dC(q)}{dq} = MC, \text{ since there is only one plant.}$$

The equations (6) and (7) yield the equilibrium condition for optimal price discrimination as,

$$\frac{\partial R_1}{\partial q_1} = \frac{\partial R_2}{\partial q_2} = \frac{dC(q)}{dq} \qquad \text{...(8)}$$

That is,

$$MR_1 = MR_2 = MR = MC \qquad \text{...(9)}$$

Marginal revenue accruing from both the markets must be identical and equal to marginal cost of production. This result can be safely extended to more than two markets.

The second order conditions for the above equilibrium condition would be that the marginal revenue in each market must be increasing less rapidly than the marginal cost for the output as a whole.

We know $\quad MR_1 = P_1\left(1 - \frac{1}{|e_1|}\right)$

and $\quad MR_2 = P_2\left(1 - \frac{1}{|e_2|}\right)$

For $MR_1 = MR_2$ we then have

$$P_1 = \left(1 - \frac{1}{|e_1|}\right) = P_2\left(1 - \frac{1}{|e_2|}\right)$$

If $|e_1| > |e_2|$ then $P_1 < P_2$. ...(10)

The monopoly firm will fix lower price in the market which is showing more elastic demand for its product. Price and price elasticity of demand are showing inverse link in this regard. Using a diagram, the equilibrium for a discriminating monopoly firm can be shown as follows:

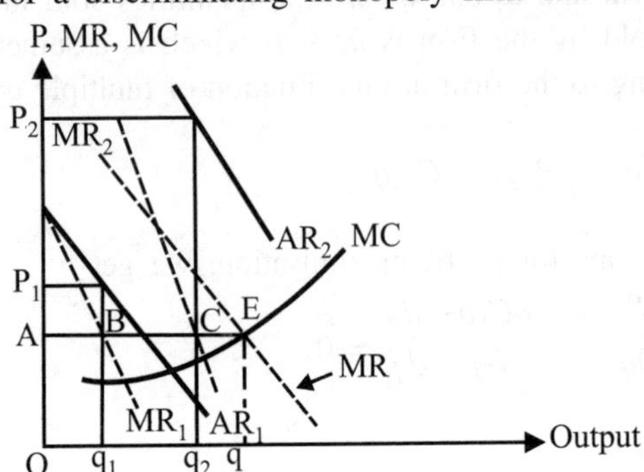

Fig. 8.7 Equilibrium of a Discriminating Monopoly

AR_1 and AR_2 are the demand curves for the two markets. Corresponding to them, MR_1 and MR_2 are the marginal revenue curves. The combined marginal revenue for the monopoly is given by MR line. The monopoly will be in equilibrium when MR is equal to MC at point E. The line AE indicates constant' marginal revenues for both the markets. At point B, we have $MR_1.= MR$, at point C we have $MR_2 = MR$. The line AE, therefore, shows the equilibrium MR as $MR_1. = MR_2 = MR = MC$. The output sold in market 1 is q_1 and price for that is P_1 and for market 2 it is q_2 with P_2 price. Total output sold is $q = q_1 + q_2$. With different prices the monopoly will get higher profit as compared to the single non-discriminating price (profits are not shown in the diagram but one can do it very easily). From the figure we find that higher the price lesser the price elasticity of demand and vice versa. $P_1 < P_2$ since $|e_1| > |e_2|$ as we have seen in equation (10).

Let us take a numerical example to explain the logic of price discrimination. The demand curves for the two markets are given as:

$$q = 55 - P_1 \text{ or } P_1 = 55 - q_1 \text{ for Market 1}$$

and $$q_2 =. 70 - 2P_2 \text{ or } P_2 = 35 - 0.5\, q_2 \text{ for Market 2.}$$

The cost function is given as $C = 25 + 5\,q$ where $q = q_1 + q_2$.

The total revenue for separate markets would be

$$R_1 = p_1 q_1 = (55 - q_1)\, q_1 = 55q_1 - q_1^2$$

and $$R_2 = P_2 q_2 = (35 - 0.5\, q_2)\, q_2 = 35\, q_2 - 0.5\, q_2^2$$

$$MR_1 = \frac{dR_1}{dq_1} = 55 - 2q_1$$

$$MR_2 = \frac{dR_2}{dq_2} = 35 - q_2$$

$$MC = \frac{dC}{dq} = 5$$

Taking the equilibrium condition

$MR_1 = MR_2 = MC$, we have

$$55 - 2q_1 = 35 - q_2 = 5$$

That is, $55 - 2q_1 = 5$ or $q_1 = 25$ units

and $35 - q_2 = 5$ or $q_2 = 30$ units

For $q_1 = 25$, we have P_1 = Rs. 30, Profit (π_1) = Rs. 600

For $q_2 = 30$, we have P_2 = Rs. 20, Profit (π_2) = Rs. 425

Total profit of the firm is Rs. 600 + Rs. 425 = Rs. 1025.

If the firm is not discriminating, its aggregate demand curve would be

$$q_1 + q_2 = q = 55 - P + 70 - 2P$$

or
$$q = 125 - 3P \cdot \text{ or } P = \frac{125}{3} - \frac{1}{3}q$$

Total revenue $= P \cdot q = (125/3 - 1/3\ q)q$

$= (125/3)q - 1/3.q^2$

$$MR = \frac{125}{3} - \frac{2}{3}q$$

For equilibrium, $MR = MC$, so $\frac{125}{3} - \frac{2}{3}q = 5$

or $125 - 2q = 15$, this gives $q = 55$ units which is exactly the same as the total output sold in the discriminating situation (30 + 25 = 55)

The undiscriminated price is then = Rs. 23.33

The total profit in this case would be

$= (70/3)\ 55 - 25 - 5(55) =$ Rs. 983.33

Thus, we find that discriminating strategy provides more profit to the monopoly than the non-discriminating strategy by a margin of Rs. 1025 – Rs. 983.34 = Rs. 42.66.

In the above analysis, we have considered only two markets to elaborate the theory of price discrimination. Suppose a monopoly firm is able to subdivide its market to such a degree that it sells each successive infinitesimal unit of its commodity for the maximum price that consumers are willing to pay then we call it 'perfect price discrimination' or 'price discrimination of the first degree'. The monopoly firm extracts the entire consumer surplus in this type of price discrimination. For this, the firm operates on its demand curve by which the total revenue extracted by the monopoly will be given by the area under the demand curve. It chooses the level of output for supply in such a way that its profit is maximum. In mathematical form, we may show the profit equation for the monopoly as:

$$\pi = \int_0^{q_0} F(q)\,dq - C(q) \qquad ...(11)$$

where $P = F(q)$ is the inverse of the demand equation. For maximum profit we have the condition.

$$\frac{d\pi}{dq} = F(q) - C'(q) = 0 \qquad ...(12)$$

and
$$\frac{d^2\pi}{dq^2} = F'(q) - C''(q) < 0$$

The first order condition says that for maximum profit under perfect discrimination, the marginal price must be equal to the marginal cost of the output. The *AR* curve acts as a marginal revenue curve for the monopolist in this case.

The second order condition says that the rate of change of price must be less than the rate of change of the marginal cost or the marginal cost curve intersects the *AR* curve from below at the equilibrium. Figure 8.8 shows these conditions.

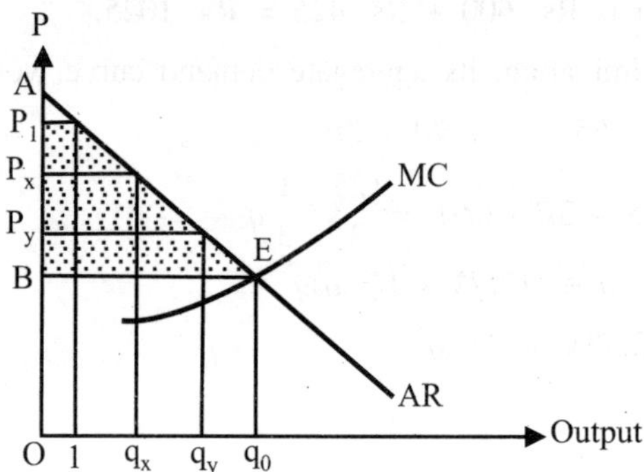

Fig. 8.8 Perfect Price-Discrimination

The monopoly takes away the entire consumer surplus shown by the area of ΔABE by charging maximum price for each unit that consumers are willing to pay. Indivisibility of units of the commodity however, may leave a very little surplus for consumers but that is negligible. The monopoly will not supply more than q_0 output since beyond this point *MC* is greater than price which implies a loss to the firm.

Let $q = 125 - 3P$ be the demand curve for the monopoly firm and $C = 25 + 5q$ the cost curve. We have,

$$P = 125/3 - (1/3)\ q$$

and

$$\pi = \int_0^{q_0} (125/3 - (1/3)q)\, dq - (25 + 5q)$$

$$d\pi/dq = 125/3 - 1/3.\ q - 5 = 0$$

$$d^2\pi/dq^2 = -1/3 < 0$$

The solution is $q_0 = 110$ units, and Profit = Rs. 2016.66

Thus, with perfect price discrimination a monopoly firm produces and sells more output and gets much higher profits than the non-price discrimination or less than perfect price-discriminating output and profits.

Between the first and the third degree types of price discrimination lies the second degree price discrimination. In this situation, the monopoly firm sells the consumer several units or a block of output, at one price and the additional block of output units at a lower price and like that. In the following figure, the firm, for example, sells OX_1 *i.e.*, q_1 output at P_1 price, the next block X_1X_2, *i.e.*, q_2 at P_2 price, and the next one X_2X_3 *i.e.*, q_3 at P_3 price; $P_1 > P_2 > P_3$.

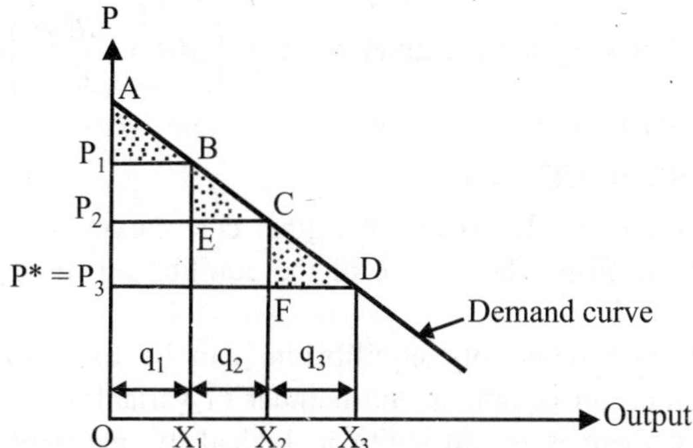

Fig. 8.9 Second Degree Price-Discrimination

It stops at P_3 which may be the marginal price for the monopoly. What the firm is doing here is to apply the *multiple part pricing strategy*. It provides incentive to buyers to buy additional units of output at a lower price. The firm is not extracting the entire consumer surplus from consumers. The dotted area of the small triangles shows the surplus left with consumers. The revenue of the firm is indicated by the rectangles $OP_1\ BX_1 + X_1ECX_2 + X_2FDX_3$ (*i.e.*, $OP_1 \cdot q_1 + OP_2 \cdot q_2 + OP_3.q_3$), which is more than what the firm would be getting if it sells all its output OX_3 (= $q_1 + q_2 + q_3$) at a lower price, say P_3. This type of price discrimination is seen in practice quite often. In the limiting case, *i.e.*, with infinite multiple parts, this type of price discrimination leaves surplus with consumers and it becomes perfect price discrimination.

Among the three types of price discrimination strategies, the third degree price discrimination is more popular than the other two. The first degree price discrimination, on the other hand, is a rare phenomenon. It may be too costly for the monopoly firm to monitor it. There are, of course, some examples of this type of price discrimination in practice. A lone doctor, for example, in a village or locality may adopt it.

8.8 EQUILIBRIUM OF A MULTI-PLANT MONOPOLY

The monopoly firm may produce its output at more than one plant in different places. It will then face different cost curves pertaining to the different plants. Assuming that the firm sells in a single market, the profit equation for the firm would be as:

$$\pi = R(q) - C_1(q_1) - C_2(q_2) \qquad ...(13)$$

where q_1 is the level of output produced at Plant 1 and q_2 at Plant 2, $C_1(q_1)$ and $C_2(q_2)$ are cost functions for the plants respectively. $R(q)$ is the total revenue accruing to the firm and $q = q_1 + q_2$. On taking the partial derivatives of profit (π) with respect to q_1 and q_2 and equating them to zeros for derivation of the maximum conditions, we get

$$\partial\pi/\partial q_1 = \frac{\partial R(q)}{\partial q} \cdot \frac{dq}{dq_1} - \frac{\partial C_1(q_1)}{\partial q_1} = 0 \qquad ...(14)$$

$$\partial\pi/\partial q_2 = \frac{\partial R(q)}{\partial q} \cdot \frac{dq}{dq_2} - \frac{\partial C_2(q_2)}{\partial q_2} = 0$$

where $\frac{dq}{dq_1} = \frac{dq}{dq_2} = 1$, since production of one more additional unit of output, either at Plant 1 or Plant 2, means selling of one more unit of output in the market.

The equation-set (14) shows us that marginal revenue $\left(MR = \frac{dR(q)}{dq}\right)$ of the firm must be equal to the marginal cost of production at each plant for maximum profit. That is,

$$MR = MC_1 = MC_2 = MC \qquad ...(15)$$

The second order condition for this is that marginal cost curves must be rising faster than the marginal revenue curve for the firm. The picture of the equilibrium for the multiplant monopoly is shown in Fig. 8.10.

The analysis of multiplant monopoly equilibrium can be extended easily to multi-market multiplant situation. The number of equations and number of variables to be determined in this case will be more, of course, but there is no difficulty in logical extension of the analysis to it.

8.9 MONOPSONY

We have examined monopoly from the supply side but there may be monopoly from the demand side also. Just like existence of one and only one firm in the industry is defined as a monopoly, in

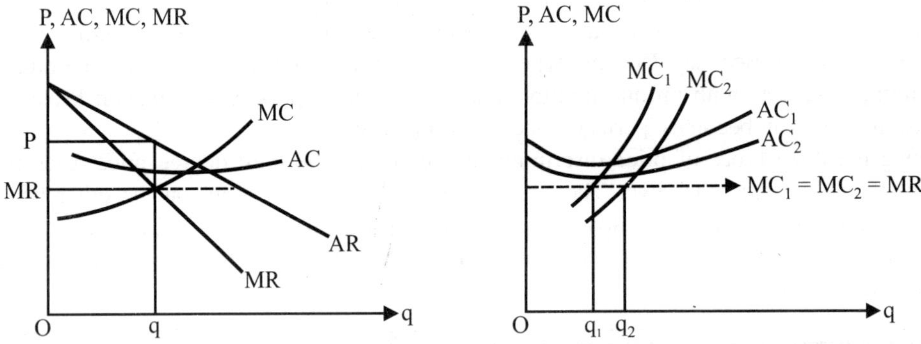

Fig. 8.10 Multiplant Monopoly Equilibrium

the same way existence of only one buyer in the market is called *monopsony.* A monopsonist will be in a position to affect the market price of the good. When a monopsonist buys any quantity of a commodity he pays a price shown on the supply curve for the commodity. In contrast, when a monopoly sells the commodity he receives a price shown by the demand curve for the commodity. For a monopsonist the supply curve will be upward sloping. He will not assume it, as a purchaser under perfect competition assumes, that the supply curve is perfectly elastic. The monopsonist takes the industry's supply curve relevant for his decision-making. Why the supply curve slopes upward we have seen it while deriving the supply curve from the cost curves for maximum profit in Chapter 6. At any point on the supply curve the monopsonist pays uniform price for the units of the commodity he buys. We define such price as '*average supply price*' for the commodity. So, the supply curve for a supplier of the commodity is 'average supply price (*ASP*)' curve for the monopsonist. Associated with this curve there will be a '*marginal supply cost*' (*MSC*) curve for the monopsonist. How the *MSC* curve comes into picture and where will be the position of the curve, let us examine this.

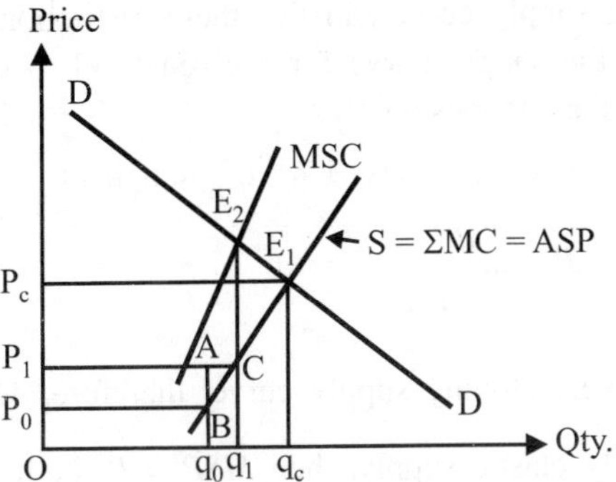

Fig. 8.11 Equilibrium of a Monopoly Market

Let us take that initially the monopsonist purchases q_0 units of output. The sellers are willing to sell this at P_0 price; so the monopsonist pays P_0 price for this. Total expenditure of the monopsonist in buying q_0 output is $TC_1 = P_0q_0$. This is shown by the area of the rectangle Oq_0BP_0. Now, let the monopsonist purchase a larger quantity of output say q_1 for which he pays the average price P_1. His total expenditure on buying q_1 output is P_1q_1 which is represented by the area of the rectangle Oq_1CP_1. The change in total expenditure by increasing the purchase from q_0 to q_1 is the difference of the area of the two rectangles. That is,

$$\Delta TC = TC_2 - TC_1 = \square\ Oq_1\ CP_1 - \square\ Oq_0\ BP_0.$$

which is equal to the sum of areas $\square\ q_0\ q_1\ CA$ and $\square\ P_0\ BAP_1$. As a result of an increase in the average supply price from P_0 to P_1, the units of output q_0 which were being purchased at a lower price P_0 are now costly. The monopsonist is paying higher price for them and hence incurring more expenditure on them. The second part of the increase in total expenditure is on the additional units $q_0 - q_0$ for which P_1 price is paid. What we find here is that purchase of additional units of output pushes up the expenditure of the monopsonist on all units of output previously purchased at a lower price. The increase in the expenditure of the monopsonist from purchasing a larger rather than a smaller quantity of output (q_{n+1} over q_n) is called the marginal supply cost which is greater than the price. Let us prove this.

We have $TC_0 = P_0q_0$

and
$$\begin{aligned} TC_1 &= P_1q_1 = (P_0 + \Delta P)\ (q_0 + \Delta q) \\ &= P_0q_0 + \Delta P.q_0 + P_0 \cdot \Delta q + \Delta P \cdot \Delta q \\ &= P_0q_0 + \Delta P \cdot q_0 + \Delta q \cdot (P_0\ \Delta P) \\ &= P_0 \cdot q_0 + \Delta P \cdot q_0 + \Delta q \cdot (P_1) \end{aligned}$$

We define the marginal supply cost as:

$$MSC = \frac{\Delta TC}{\Delta q} = \frac{TC_1 - TC_0}{\Delta q} = \frac{P_0q_0 + \Delta P \cdot q_0 + \Delta q(P_1) - P_0q_0}{\Delta q}$$

or
$$MSC = P_1 + q_0\frac{\Delta P}{\Delta q} \qquad ...(16)$$

$MSC > P_1$ when $\Delta P > 0,\ \Delta q > 0$ or $\Delta P < 0,\ \Delta q < 0$.

A normal upward sloping supply curve satisfies these restrictions. Therefore, we can say that the *MSC* curve will be above the supply curve for a given level of output. For a continuous case, we define the expenditure of the monopsonist as,

$TC = P \cdot q$, which is the revenue received by the suppliers,

$$MSC = \frac{dTC}{dq} = P + q.\frac{dP}{dq} \qquad ...(17)$$

Since $\frac{dP}{dq} > 0$ for a positively sloping supply curve, therefore, $MSC > P$.

If $dP/dq = 0$, *i.e.*, perfectly elastic supply, then $MSP = P$, both the *ASP* and *MSC* curve will coincide in this case.

Now, let us examine the equilibrium situation for the monopsonist. In making his purchase decision, the monopsonist, being a consumer, selects that price quantity combination which gives him maximum satisfaction or utility or welfare. For him price is not an exogenous factor as for a competitive consumer who adjusts his purchases according to the given prices. The monopsonist is a 'price-maker'. The monopsonist knows the *MSC* curve, *ASP* curve and also his demand curve. The demand curve shows the willingness to pay for a given quantity of output. This reflects the value of the marginal units of output to the monopsonist as in the case of general consumers which we have examined in terms of marginal utility earlier in Chapter 3. The decision-making problem faced by the monopsonist is now very simple to evaluate. He continues to buy additional units of the commodity so long as his willingness to pay exceeds the marginal supply cost of the commodity. He will be in equilibrium when willingness to pay is equal to the *MSC* of the commodity. In other words, when the *MSC* curve intersects the demand curve from below. E_2 is such a point in Fig. 8.11. Correspondingly, P_1 will be the supply price paid by him for q_1 output. The consumer surplus accruing to the monopsonist will be shown by the area DE_2CP_1. If there is competitive equilibrium, *i.e.*, no monopsony, then price will be P_c and output supplied q_c. Thus, existence of monopsony means less price to sellers as well as less quantity sold by them as compared to the competitive situation.

Monopsony is a quite prevalent phenomenon in input markets. We will, therefore, examine its application in detail while discussing the factor prices under the theory of distribution. Here we have examined it from the point of view of a buyer in the commodity market.

8.10 BILATERAL MONOPOLY

A market in which there is only one seller and only one buyer is called *'bilateral monopoly'*. In this situation, a monopolistic producer sells to a monopsonistic buyer. It may be quite rare to have a market situation like this. It is most likely to occur in factor markets. The process of attaining equilibrium in a bilateral monopoly is not well established. The price that finally sets in depends on the bargaining skill and power of the two parties in the market. Consider *AD* as the demand curve for the monopsonist consumer which is the *AR* curve for the monopolist supplier. The *MR* curve corresponding to the *AR* curve lies below it as shown in Fig. 8.12.

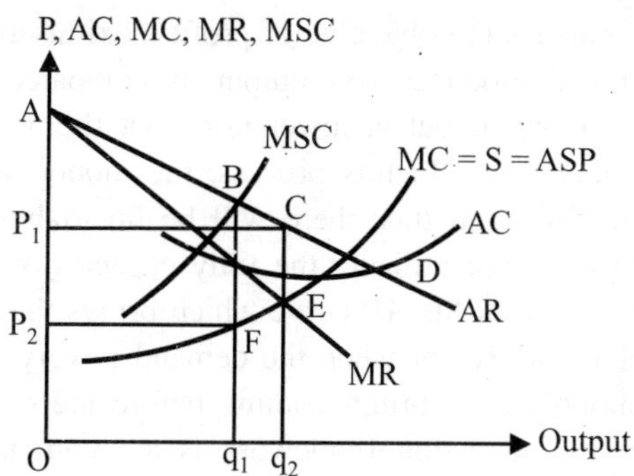

Fig. 8.12 Bilateral Monopoly

The average and marginal cost curves for the monopolist are shown by *AC* and *MC* curves respectively. The marginal cost curve is the supply curve, *i.e.*, *ASP* curve for the monopsonist. Following the analysis of the monopsony as carried on in Section 8.9, the marginal supply cost (*MSC*) curve for the monopsonist lies above the *ASP* curve as shown in the diagram. The monopoly firm fixes the price of the product through usual profit maximisation criterion $MR = MC$. This gives P_1 and q_2 as optimum price-quantity combination for him. The monopsonist has also the power of fixing the price of the product. He uses for this the *ASP* and *MSC* curves. He would choose q_1 output and P_2 price on the basis of the equality of marginal supply cost and the price of the product he is willing to pay, *i.e.*, the intersection of the *MSC* and demand curves. We have two different price quantity sets P_1, q_2 and P_2, q_1 based on the price setting criteria of the monopolist and the monopsonist. There is no unique price and quantity set for the market. Both the parties are not having alternatives for price setting. There is no way to get a price and quantity set for the participants in the market. As we have said earlier, probably the bargaining process may help to settle down the price. If the monopolist is strong enough as compared to the monopsonist, price may be quite high but less than P_1. On the other hand, if the monopsonist is strong in bargaining skill, price may be settled down quite low but more than P_2. There is, thus, in-determinacy of the price in the situation of the bilateral monopoly through the conventional tools of the economic analysis. May be the game theory or some advance modern techniques are helpful in this respect.

8.11 REGULATION OF MONOPOLIES

The regulation of monopolies is an important subject in theoretical and applied economic analysis. Obviously, there must be some undesirable aspects of the monopoly market which pave the way for its regulation. We do find in reality public utilities and several other industries of basic nature coming under the purview of government regulation all over the world. The arguments which go against a private monopoly and hence its regulation are as follows:

(*i*) Private monopolisation of industries means concentration of economic power which is against the spirit of equity and equality in the society. A society prefers diffusion of economic power so that the benefits of industrial profits accrue to a greater number of people. Concentration of economic power is a source of feudalism and political dictatorship. So, from the point of view of distribution of wealth and its creation a private monopoly is certainly an evil.

(*ii*) A private monopoly often charges discriminatory prices and, this way, extracts major portion of consumer surplus from consumers and thus reduces their welfare.

(*iii*) A private monopolist pursues the objective of profit maximisation. For this he charges high price for his product and produces less output as compared to a competitive producer. What society wants is more output at lower price but the action of the monopolist leads to less output and higher price. In this process, the monopolist never bothers to use his capacity of production fully and thus there will be invariably wastage of resources from the social point of view by not utilising the fully capacity of production. The monopolist operates on the elastic range of his *AR* curve which brings the equilibrium normally on the falling side of the *AC* curve except when the demand is very very high for the product of the firm. So, the monopoly equilibrium coming before the competitive equilibrium in the demand and cost curves interaction framework is a common phenomenon.

(*iv*) Monopoly is an inefficient type of market structure. In order to elaborate this, let us consider the following diagram (Fig. 8.13). The *AR* and *MR* curves along with the *MC* curve are shown in the diagram for the monopolist. The equilibrium price and quantity for the monopolist are given by P_m and q_m respectively. In the diagram, we have shown the competitive equilibrium also. This is the point where *MC* intersects the demand curve from below, *i.e.*, the point *C*. As we know, under perfect competition, the rising portion of the *MC* curve above the minima of the *AVC* curve is the supply curve for the firm. The competitive price is P_c and output, q_c. We find that $q_c > q_m$ and $P_m > P_c$. Further, the consumer surplus with the competitive equilibrium is the area of the triangle above the P_c

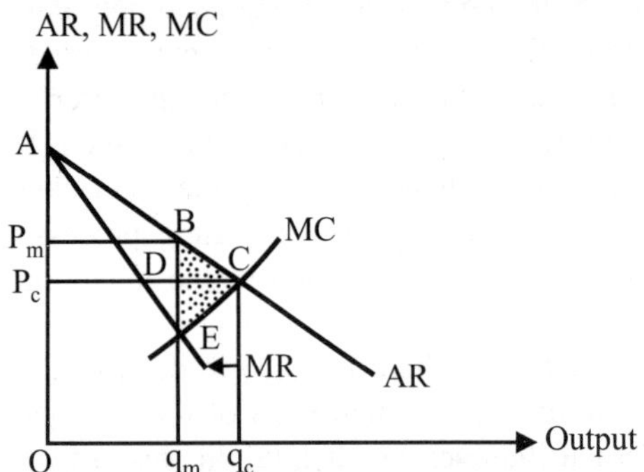

Fig. 8.13 Efficiency Loss Due to Monopoly

line, *i.e.*, ΔAP_cC, while with the monopoly equilibrium it is the area of the triangle AP_mB. So, consumers get less surplus in the case of the monopoly as compared to the competition. There is a transfer of the surplus shown by the rectangle P_mBDP_c from consumers to the monopolist if the market becomes monopolistic as against competitive. Apart from this, there is a dead loss of the consumer surplus in the case of monopoly shown by the area of the triangle *BDC*. Further, it is not only the consumers who lose their surplus because of the monopoly, the producer also loses. Producer's loss of the surplus is shown by the area *DEC* where *MC* curve falls below the competitive price line P_c. By expanding the output level from q_m to q_c the producer could have gained this surplus. So, apart from the transfer of the surplus from consumers to the monopolist, there is a dead loss of the surplus (consumer surplus + producers' surplus) in the case of monopoly which is shown by the area *BEC*. This shows that monopolistic market is inefficient from the point of view of society as a whole.

(*v*) A monopoly firm may not bother for improvement of the technology and hence in the productivity since there will not be a pressure for this. Even if it does so, the benefits of such changes will not be passed on the consumers. Further, the monopoly firm may exploit workers by paying them less wages, particularly when it is a monopsony in the factor market.

So, on account of all of the above reasons, a private monopoly is an undesirable economic entity and that is why it is put under severe public control in all countries. One may argue for positive benefits of private monopolies, such as economies of scale, growth in productive capacities in the economy through expansion of such companies. But growth with exploitation or distributional inequalities is something which is also an undesirable symptom of an economy. So, we cannot argue strongly in favour of monopolies in this regard.

How to check monopolies? There are several measures for this, such as (*i*) through regulation of prices and output levels by the government; (*ii*) by creating anti-monopoly legislations and thus restricting the growth of such firms; (*iii*) by putting taxes on monopolies; and (*iv*) through nationalisation of such companies altogether.

If the price and quantity of output of the monopoly firm are regulated, the question arises as what should be the criterion for this. Economists argue that a monopolist should be asked to operate at the level of output for which marginal cost is equal to the price. That is, to adopt the norm_of competitive equilibrium as it gives maximum welfare to consumers and the firm is left with some positive profit provided the capacity of production is not greater than the demand for the commodity. In that case, it should be compensated by the state. Graphically, we have demonstrated these possibilities while discussing the equilibrium of a public monopoly in Section 8.6. The equilibrium analysis for a public monopoly should be applied for the regulation of the private monopoly. One thing we should keep in mind is that normal profit is included in the cost of production; so, when we talk of profit accruing to the firm, this means economic profit which may be positive or negative.

There are some problems in the regulation of monopolies through price and quantity controls. The market demand curve for the firm may not be known correctly and similarly the cost curves might be estimated incorrectly. If this is so, the price and quantity regulations may not bring the desired results about the control of monopolies.

Suppose, monopolies are regulated by using instruments of taxation then an immediate problem arises regarding the type of the tax, whether it should be a lump-sum tax or a commodity tax or a profit tax or some other tax. While taking the decision about the type of the tax to be imposed on the monopoly, we have to keep in mind, (*a*) profits and growth of the monopoly should be restricted, and (*b*) there should not be a reduction in the output and hence a rise in the price of the product supplied by the monopolist. If this happens, the very purpose of the tax will be defeated and the monopolist would be able to shift the incidence of the tax to consumers.

Let us take the case of a lump-sum tax. Such a tax will be just like an increase in the fixed cost. The equilibrium level of profit of the monopoly decreases by this type of tax while the quantity and price of the product do not change. We may show this by using the following expressions and diagram.

$$\pi = R(q) - C(q) - T \qquad ...(18)$$

where T is the lump-sum tax.

The equilibrium conditions for the profit maximisation would be

$$R'(q) = C'(q) \text{ i.e., } MR = MC$$

and $$R''(q) < C''(q) \qquad ...(19)$$

There is no change in the market equilibrium. *T,* being fixed, does not alter it. The monopoly price and quantity do not change but the profit declines by the amount of *T.*

A decrease in profit means a check on the growth of the monopoly and on its economic power.

In the diagram, the monopoly equilibrium is given by the intersection of the *MR* and *MC* curves at *E* point, corresponding to which P_m is the price and q_m is the quantity supplied by the monopolist. The monopoly profit is shown by the rectangle P_m *CBA.* Now, on imposition of the lump-sum tax *T,* the average cost curve shifts to AC_2 position ($AC_2 = AC_1 + T/q$). The marginal cost curve does not change since *T* is fixed. Therefore, *MR* = *MC* equilibrium is undisturbed. Only the monopoly profit reduces to the rectangle P_m *AXD* shown by the dotted area.

If the tax is in some fixed proportion of the monopoly profit then also there will be no change in the price-quantity equilibrium but the monopoly profit will be decreasing by the proportion of the tax on it.

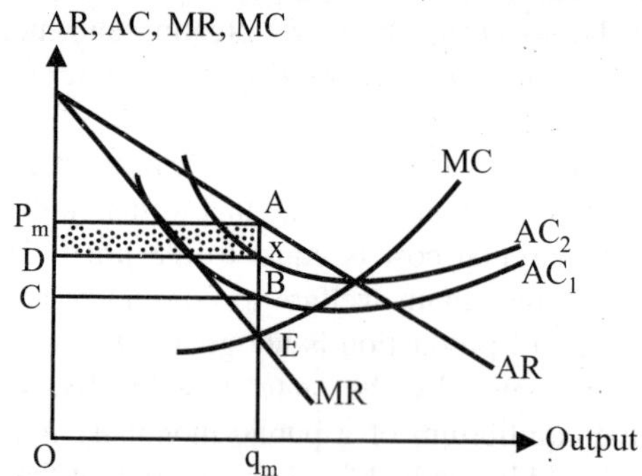

Fig. 8.14 The Effect of Lump-sum Tax on Monopoly

Suppose a commodity tax, at the rate of '*t*' per unit of output, is imposed on the monopoly. In this situation, the total cost will go up by *tq* units and average and marginal cost by *t* units. The equilibrium position of the monopoly is disturbed now. There will be lesser output and higher price. The profit of the monopoly may or may not decrease depending on the elasticity of demand. Quantitatively, we have

$$\pi = R(q) - C(q) - t(q) \qquad ...(20)$$

Profit maximisation now yields

$$MR = MC + t$$

The *MC* curve rises and the equilibrium point shifts to the left giving us higher price and lesser output as shown in Fig. 8.15.

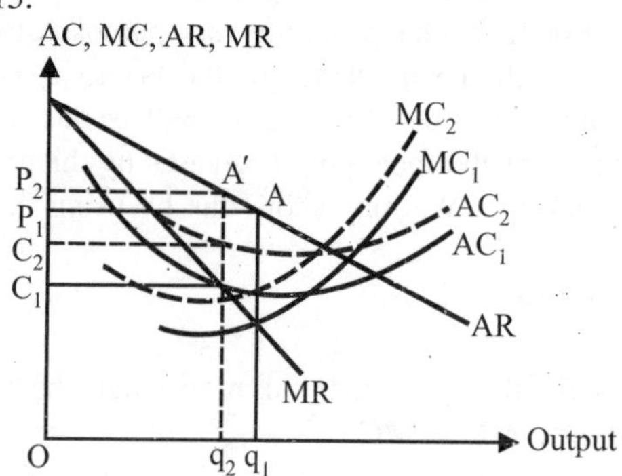

Fig. 8.15 Effect of a Commodity Tax on Monopoly

The initial equilibrium of the monopoly gives P_1 price and q_1 output. On imposition of the commodity tax at the rate 't' per unit of q, the AC_1 and MC_1 curves shift to AC_2 and MC_2 positions parallelly by the amount of t. The new equilibrium price is P_2 which is more than P_1 and new equilibrium quantity q_2 which is less than q_1. The original profit is $(P_1 - C_1)q_1$ and the new profit is $(P_2 - C_2)q_2$. Profit has also declined in this case. So, the conclusion here is that it is not desirable to impose a commodity tax on the monopoly. Consumers will get less output and pay higher price by this and, thus, their welfare comes down. If the rate of tax 't' increases, there will be a further decrease in the quantity of output and increase in its price. Similar effect on market equilibrium will be observed if the tax is ad-valorem, *i.e.*, a fixed proportion of the revenue accruing to the monopolist. This kind of tax is also not feasible to regulate the monopoly.

The conclusion we draw from the above analysis is that only lump-sum tax or a tax on profit will be feasible to regulate the monopoly and not the commodity tax or ad-valorem tax on it.

8.12 CONCLUDING REMARKS

We have gone through the theory of monopoly, monopsony and bilateral monopoly in this chapter. Major coverage was, of course, of the monopoly market. The concept of monopoly, sources of monopoly, short-run and long-run equilibrium of a monopoly, public monopoly, monopoly price discrimination and regulation of private monopolies, etc., were discussed with a view to provide a comprehensive theoretical understanding of this type of market.

SUGGESTED READINGS

Henderson, J.M. and R.E. Quandt, *Microeconomic Theory: A Mathematical Approach,* McGraw-Hill, 1971.

Koutsoyiannis, A., *Modern Microeconomics,* The Macmillan Press, 1978.

Robinson, Joan, *The Economics of Imperfect Competition,* Macmillan, 1933.

Sher, W. and R. Pindola, *Microeconomic Theory: A Synthesis of Classical Theory and the Modern Approach:* Edward Arnold, 1981.

Stigler, G.J., *The Theory of Price,* Macmillan, 1966.

REVIEW QUESTIONS

1. Discuss the concept of 'monopoly'. What are the major determinants of monopoly power of a firm? Give adequate explanation for this with suitable examples.
2. Compare the short-run and long-run equilibrium of a monopoly firm with the equilibrium conditions of a firm operating under perfect competition.
3. What do you mean by price discrimination? How a monopoly firm is able to charge discriminating prices from its customers? Give explanation in terms of graphical exposition.
4. In what respect a public monopoly is different from a private monopoly? How does a public monopoly firm make pricing and output decisions under excess capacity of production and under capacity constrained situations?
5. Define monopsony and show the equilibrium conditions for a monopsony buyer in a factor market.
6. Examine why there is, in general, indeterminacy of price in the situation of bilateral monopoly?
7. Why monopolies are regarded as 'evils' in an economy? What are the conventional ways of regulating monopolies? Examine their potential effectiveness for this.

8. The demand and cost functions for a monopoly firm are given as $Q = 50 - 0.5P$ and $C = 50 + 40\,Q$ where Q is the output-level, P is the product price and C is the total cost of production. Find the level of output and price charged by the firm at which it gets maximum profit. Also, find the level of output and price at which its revenue is maximum. What will be the price elasticity of demand when revenue is maximum?
9. The monopolist demand curve is given as $Q = 200 - 2P$. It has two plants operation having the total cost function for each one of them as $C_1 = 10\,Q_1$; and $C_2 = 0.25\,Q_2^2$; where Q_1 and Q_2 are the output levels for the two plants respectively and $Q = Q_1 + Q_2$. Determine the equilibrium profit maximising situation for the monopolist.
10. A discriminating monopoly firm is having two distinct markets for which the demand curves are given as $Q_1 = 32 - 0.4P_1$; $Q_2 = 18 - 0.1P_2$, where Q_1 and Q_2 are output quantities sold in the two markets at P_1 and P_2 prices respectively. The firm produces at a single plant with the cost function given as $C = 50 + 40\,Q$. Determine the profit maximising equilibrium position of the firm. Also, find the price elasticity of demand for each of the two markets.
11. A monopoly firm produces two goods for which the demand functions are given as: $P_1 = 36 - 3q_1$, and $P_2 = 40 - 5q_2$. The joint cost function for production of these goods is given as $C = q_1^2 + 2q_1q_2 + 3\,q_2^2$. Determine the quantities of goods and their prices that maximise the profit of the firm and find the optimum profit.
12. Given the demand function for a monopoly firm as $P = 20 - q$, and the cost function as $C = q^2 + 8q + 2$.
    (*a*) What output level maximises total profit and what are the corresponding values of price, profit and total revenue?
    (*b*) What output level maximises sales in value and what are the corresponding values of price, profit and total revenue?
    (*c*) What output level maximises sales in Rs. subject to the constraint: Profit ≥ 8? Find the corresponding values of price, profit and revenue.
    (*d*) How much will be the incidence of a tax of Rs. 1.0 per unit of the product on its consumers?
13. A supply function is regarded as a one-to-one relationship between price and quantity, that is, associated with each price is a unique quantity of output supplied. With the use of a diagram illustrate that it makes no sense to speak of the "supply function of a monopolist."

CHAPTER 9

Theory of Monopolistic Competition

In the preceding two chapters we have gone through the pricing and output decisions under two simplified models of market structure: perfect competition on one extreme and monopoly on the other. Both of them are abstract concepts of the market somewhat far from the reality as some of their assumptions are hardly met in practice. Between these two opposite extremes of the market mechanism we encounter various other forms which are less abstract and more realistic in nature. Monopolistic competition is one of them which we intend to study in this chapter. The theory of monopolistic competition which has been developed originally by E.H. Chamberlin[1] combines the elements of perfect competition and pure monopoly for a realistic market setting for pricing and output decisions, apart from the other important aspects related to business conduct policies, such as advertising and sales promotion, product development, and quality variation of products.

As usual, the first thing we have to do here is to define the concept of 'monopolistic competition' and to identify its base. After this, we will go through the equilibrium conditions relevant to the monopolistic competition, both in the short-run as well as in the long-run. This will be followed by a section of the chapter on non-price competition for this type of market.

9.1 MONOPOLISTIC COMPETITION: ITS CONCEPT AND BASE

A market is said to be operating under monopolistic competition if the following assumptions are satisfied by it.

(i) Differentiated Products that are Close Substitutes for Each Other

The output of sellers under monopolistic competition is not homogeneous, that is, they produce differentiated products which are close substitutes for each other. By product differentiation we mean production of different varieties or brands of the same product in the industry which buyers purchase according to their preferences. Each firm produces a product which is different from varieties of

1. E.H. Chamberlin: The Theory of Monopolistic Competition; Harvard University Press, 1934.

the same product produced by other firms in the market. Since the products of the firms are varieties of the same product they are therefore close substitutes for each other. We do see varieties for almost every product the markets. Some products show a large variety while others have a low one. Why different varieties of a product exist in the market? This is a very important question. We know, goods are ultimately produced to satisfy consumers' needs. Consumers' preferences of the goods will not be uniform rather than varying in terms of some quantifiable attributes such as size, colour, shape. taste, durability, and weight, etc. The market response in such a situation will be to provide a combination of varieties of the products to consumers.

(ii) Large Number of Sellers and Buyers

This is second important characteristic of the monopolistic competition. The market constitutes a large number of producers and a large number of customers. This is similar requirement of the market as that of perfect competition.

(iii) Free Entry and Exit from the Market

There are no restrictions on potential sellers in joining the market. They are free for this. Similarly existing firms if find the market unfavourable can leave it without any restriction.

(iv) Perfect Knowledge or Information

Firms under monopolistic competition have reasonably complete knowledge about all aspects of the industry. Each firm has a good feel for prices that rival firms pay for inputs or charge for outputs. All of them are having similar access to the existing technological base, government liaison and other types of market information.

All characteristics except (*i*) create the conditions for perfect competition in the market but, in spite of this, the first characteristic or assumption *i.e.*, product heterogeneity or product differentiation provides monopoly power to the firms especially in the short-run. Thus, both monopolistic and competitive elements together generate a new type of market structure called '*monopolistic competition*'.

In the short-run because of product differentiation the firms are free to set prices for their respective products. They are, therefore, monopolistic in nature as well as in action. In the long-run, however; substitutability of different products for each other and large number of buyers and sellers create almost perfect competition in the market and the monopoly power of the firm fritters away because of this.

Products of sellers are said to be differentiated if consumers treat them dissimilar while making their purchases. There may be both real and spurious causes for this. The most important reason of product differentiation, as we have said earlier, is that the physical characteristics of goods offered by different sellers are not alike. The technological composition of products such as design, workmanship, ingredients, colour, etc., may be quite different and so the quality of products, will be different and hence they are differentiated by their consumers. Functionally, the products are similar but from the point of the view of consumer preferences they are not alike. The second reason for product differentiation is the location of the seller. A consumer prefers to buy from a shop located near his residence so that he saves time and transportation cost in going elsewhere although that particular shop may not sell different varieties of the product the consumer can choose from them. Because of locational advantages many small retail shops survive while competing with large units.

The third factor that creates considerable scope for product differentiation is dissimilarities in the kind of services offered by sellers of a particular product. Qualities like promptness, courtesy, good delivery service, and favourable credit terms together are sources of product differentiation. Although the product in this case may be the same but buyers differentiate it because of all such qualities of the seller. The next source of product differentiation is attributed to the physical attractiveness of the seller's place of business. One may cite cleanliness, carpeting, lighting and internal general decoration for this. This may be a spurious factor but we do find it quite prevalent in reality. Another category of sources for product differentiation is the type of brand or brand names, packaging and advertisement. The product may not be significantly different across the sellers but all such factors make it somewhat different from the point of view of buyers. Lastly, personal considerations, say, friendship, relationship, religious and other such interests, may also contribute in product differentiation though it will be spurious.

All the above reasons, for product differentiation are not independent while in operation. All of them or their subsets reinforce each other and thus create conditions for the existence of the monopolistic competition as a viable market structure.

The existence of product differentiation creates a conceptual difficulty in the analysis of price and output determination under monopolistic competition, particularly for the industry as a whole. This is, because, the concept of 'industry' itself is not valid for such a market. An 'industry' in abstract sense is a group of the firm or even a firm alone producing a homogeneous product. This concept is not applicable to the monopolistically competitive markets since the products produced by the firms are not alike but close substitutes. Chamberlin suggested an alternative name for 'industry' as 'product group'. However, in a narrow sense, some economists still use the word 'industry' for the group of the firm producing differentiated products. Under monopolistic competition, it is not possible to identify the industry supply since supplies of the individual firms are not additive because of product variation. The normal practice is, therefore, to examine the behaviour of a single firm and then the implications are drawn from this for the group of the firms as a whole. This approach we will follow in this chapter also.

9.2 THE NATURE OF DEMAND CURVE FOR A FIRM UNDER MONOPOLISTIC COMPETITION

The demand curve for a firm under perfect competition is a horizontal line showing infinite price-elasticity. The output of one firm is a perfect substitute for the output of the other firms. Under monopoly, on the other hand, the demand curve for the output of the firm is the demand curve for the industry and it is downward sloping which show low elasticity of demand, as no substitute is available for the commodity. Under monopolistic competition, the demand curve for the firm will stand somewhere in between the demand curves of the extreme situations. It will not be perfectly elastic as the output of the firm is not similar to outputs of other firms but they are however substitutes for each other to some extent for certain range of price differentials. If price difference of outputs of two firms is within the tolerable limit, consumers do not bother for substituting one variety for the other and stick to their preferences. However, if there is 'too much' difference in the prices of rival varieties, the consumer may resort to the substitution of low price variety for the higher price variety making the demand curve more elastic. This might cause non-linearity in the demand function. Normally, the demand curve for a firm under monopolistic competition will be downward sloping showing higher elasticity as compared to the monopoly firm.

A firm under monopolistic competition faces two demand curves. One demand curve is based on the assumption that the firm's pricing decisions do not make any impact on its rival's prices. That is, it can change the price of its product in order to get increased sales but other firms do not make any change in their prices. This demand curve is called 'anticipated' or 'expected' demand curve. It is shown by the line *dd′* in Fig. 9.1. The other demand curve that the firm faces is based on the assumption that other firms, *i.e.*, rivals also make similar changes in their prices. The expected sales of the firm, while reducing its price, will be lower as compared to the earlier situation. This type of demand curve is called 'proportional' or 'actual' demand curve. It is also 'called as 'effective' demand curve. It is shown by the line *DD′* in Fig. 9.1. This demand curve is, in fact, the market

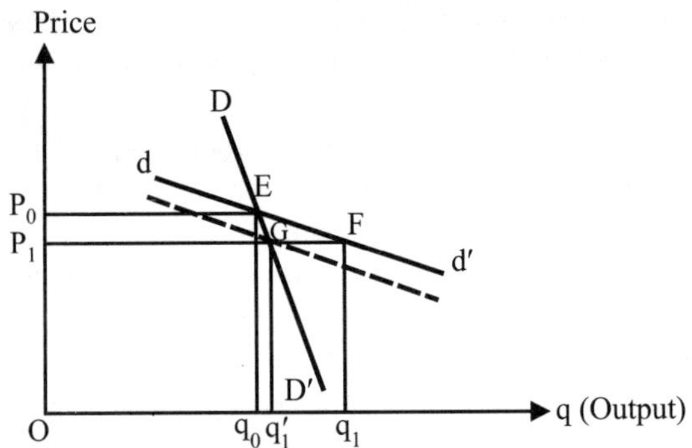

Fig. 9.1 Demand Curves for a Monopolistically Competitive Firm

share curve for the firm in the sense that when prices of all firms are changing uniformly, there will not be a change in their market share on this account alone. That is, the price changes will not alter the market shares of firms.

The proportional demand curve will be less elastic as compared to the anticipated demand curve. When we express it in inverse form, *i.e.*, $P = f(q)$, it shows steeper slope than the anticipated demand curve. In Fig. 9.1, consider *E* as the initial equilibrium point which gives P_0, q_0 as price-quantity combination. Both anticipated and proportional demand curves pass through this point which implies that along the equilibrium the firm maintains its market share in the industry. Now, let the firm reduce its price from P_0 to P_1. It anticipated an increase in sales from $0q_0$ to $0q_1$ level by moving down along *dd'* provided other firms do not make similar reduction in their prices. So, *dd′* is the relevant demand curve for the firm. On the other hand, if other firms also reduce their prices proportionally, the individual firm will not be able to sell more as indicated by its anticipated demand curve but less than that such as $0q_1'$ instead of $0q_1$. It means the price line P_1 *F* and a vertical line showing $0q_1'$ output meet at *G* point on *DD′*. In this case, the firm moves down along the proportional demand curve. If the firm moves up from the point *E* by increasing its price, there will be more reduction in its sales as some of its buyers move to the alternative cheap varieties when their prices are unchanged. The movement in this case will be on the *dd′*curve. However, if all other firms, are increasing their prices, the reduction in sales of one firm will be less and the relevant demand curve for this will be *DD′*. Any point on the proportional demand shows the equilibrium position for all the firms, *i.e.*, it will indicate group equilibrium. At a point *E*, we have equilibrium corresponding to the anticipated demand curve *dd′* as well as corresponding to the proportional demand curve. Through use of these two curves we will be getting the same price-quantity combination. Same will be the situation at other points on the *DD′* where anticipated demand curve cuts it.

In order to elaborate the concepts of the two demand functions for a firm under monopolistic competition, let us assume that P_1, P_2, P_3 .... P_n are the prices charged by the firm 1, 2, 3,..., n respectively and the quantities produced by them are q_1, q_2,..., q_n. Prices charged by all firms may be uniform or different. We then specify the demand function for a representative firm, say Firm 1 as:

$$q_1 = q(P_1, P_2, ..., P_n) \qquad ...(1)$$

That is, the quantity produced by the firm 1 is a function of prices charged by all firms in the product-group because their products are substitutes. For simplicity, let us concentrate with linear form of the demand function with a few firms, say 3. The demand function for this would be as:

$$q_1 = a_0 + a_1 P_1 + a_2P_2 + a_3P_3 \qquad ...(2)$$

a_0, a_1, a_2, and a_3 are constants $\partial q_1/\partial P_1 = a_1 < 0$ since quantity q_1 is inversely related to its price.

$\partial q_1/\partial P_2 = a_2 > 0$ and $\partial q_1/\partial P_3 = a_3 > 0$ since both P_1 and P_2 are prices of the substitute varieties of the good, so a rise in them means more demand for commodity 1.

In Fig. 9.1, we consider point E as the original equilibrium for the representative firm. At this point, both anticipated and proportional demand curves of the firm intersect. Further, we have assumed that all firms under monopolistic competition have identical demand and cost curves. This implies that if E is the equilibrium situation for one firm, it is the equilibrium situation for all firms, *i.e.*, it is the group equilibrium under monopolistic competition. So, the equilibrium price P_0 is uniformly identical for all firms. In this case, the demand curve (9.2) reduces to,

$$q_0 = a_0 + (a_1 + a_2 + a_3) P_0 \qquad ...(3)$$

This is the situation reflected by point E in the figure. Now, if the representative firm 1 reduces its price to P_1 level, the other firms keeping their prices at P_0 level, the firm 1 moves along its anticipated demand curve which will be as,

$$q_1 = a_0 + [(a_2 + a_3) P_0] + a_1P_1 \qquad ...(4)$$

It is downward sloping since $\partial q_1/\partial P_1 = a_1 < 0$, other thing being constant including P_0.

The price-quantity combination is shown by the point F on the *dd'* curve.

If the other firms also alter their prices to P_1 level, the representative firm (1) moves along the proportional demand curve DD' and price-quantity combination will be shown by point G. At G point, the anticipated and proportional demand curves must intersect each other. This implies that the dd' curve slides down along the DD' curve as shown by the dotted anticipated demand curve in Fig. 9.1. At point G, we have the equilibrium for the group as a whole which means

$$q_1 = a_0 + (a_1 + a_2 + a_3) P_1 \qquad ...(5)$$

We have followed Chamberlin's original assumption of uniformity of price across firms for their differentiated products under monopolistic competition. This is somewhat too restrictive assumption as all varieties of the product produced by the different firms are unlikely to have the same price in the market. A better approach is to assume the prices of different varieties proportional rather than identical. Say $P_1 = \alpha P_2 = \beta P_3$. With such a change, the Chamberlin's analysis of the two demand curves under monopolistic competition can be modified which results in exactly the same findings as the original Chamberlin's analysis.[2]

---

2. See W. Sher and R. Pindola; *Microeconomic Theory,* London, Edward Arnold Pub., 1981, pp. 456-458 for this:

9.3 SHORT-RUN EQUILIBRIUM OF A FIRM UNDER MONOPOLISTIC COMPETITION

The short-run condition prevails under monopolistic market when the plant size for each firm is fixed and the total number of firms in the market is also fixed. The output of each firm varies with changing variable inputs. Apart from prices, the demand for the product of a firm under monopolistic competition is affected by factors like quality changes, advertisement, and other types of non-price competition. For short-run equilibrium of the firm in the market under study all such factors are assumed to be constant and so prices are the only relevant variables for that. In other words, we will study the short-run equilibrium of a monopolistically competitive firm using the price competition in this section.

In the short-run, as we have said earlier, a firm acts as a monopoly for its product since it is different from products of all other firms. A firm follows the conditions of a monopoly market to decide its equilibrium price and quantity combination. It operates on its anticipated demand curve with the assumption that its actions will not be followed by the other firms. Consider Fig. 9.2 in which we have shown the two demand curves *dd′* and *DD′* and the *AC* and *MC* curves for a representative firm. The *MR* curves corresponding to the demand curves are also shown. The equilibrium situation of the firm under the assumption that rival firms do not change their prices and quantities, is given by point E_1 where *MC* and MR_d curves intersect which gives P_1 and q_1 as price-output combination for the firm. The proportional demand curve is not playing any role in determining this equilibrium of the firm. If the firm is quite small, almost insignificant as compared to the market as a whole, much this kind of equilibrium may be stable in the short-run as rival firms will not be affected by this. However, as per the concept of the monopolistic competition itself, there is competition in the market along with the monopoly. Therefore, it is too restricted assumption that rival firms are not reacting when an individual firm reduces its price or increases its quantity. By assumption, all firms are identical under the monopolistic competition. All of them react almost in

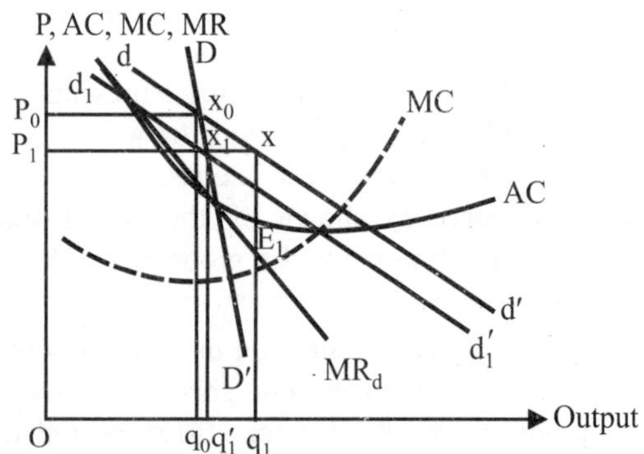

Fig. 9.2 Short-run Equilibrium Under Monopolistic Competition : Initial Adjustment

the same way. Therefore, a better way of analysing short-run equilibrium under monopolistic competition is to take into account the 'group-equilibrium' rather than equilibrium of an individual firm alone. By group-equilibrium we mean equilibrium of the representative firm when other firms are also in the equilibrium with similar kind of action of all firms. It is not the equilibrium of all firms in the form of a cartel, as there is little scope for this under the monopolistic competition because of product differentiation.

For the group equilibrium under monopolistic competition both the demand curves anticipated and proportional (or market share curve), play important role. Let us see how such equilibrium is attained in the market.

Consider an arbitrary point X_0 in Fig. 9.2, where the two demand curves for the representative firm intersect. Let this point define the initial situation for group-equilibrium position for the firm giving P_0 and q_0 as price-quantity combination. The firm is not satisfied with this price-quantity combination as it is not giving maximum profit to it. The anticipated *MR* curve and *MC* curve intersect at point E_1. Consequently, the price-quantity combination for the firm is P_1 and q_1 for maximum profit. In order to get the maximum profit, the firm, therefore, reduces its price P_0 to P_1 level for which the anticipated increase in sales is $q_1 - q_0$. Other firms in the industry, which are also in the same position as the representative firm, also find P_0 as a price higher than the profit maximising price. To get maximum profit they also reduce their prices accordingly although not necessarily by the same amount. The implication of this kind of move by other firms is that the representative firm will not be able to sell q_1 level of output at P_1 price but less than this as there will not be diversion of buyers of other firms to this firm since they have also reduced their prices. Let us say that in this new situation, sales of the firm increases to q_1' level and the point X_1 where the P_1 and q_1' lines meet defines its new position for the interaction of the anticipated and proportional demand curves. This point will be on the proportional demand curve and the anticipated demand curve also passes through this which means *dd* slides down to this position (d_1 d_1') from its original position. When *dd* slides down along the *DD′* the marginal revenue curve corresponding to the *dd'* also shifts downward. The proportional demand curve *DD′* will not shift from its position since the number of firms in the product group is constant. Now, from Fig. 9.2, we come to Fig. 9.3. d_1d_1' is the new position for the anticipated demand curve after the first round of price adjustment across the group. X_1 defines the equilibrium with P_1, q_1' as price-quantity combination. This price-quantity combination is also not giving maximum profit to the firm as its new anticipated marginal revenue curve MR_{d_1} and the *MC* curves intersect at E_2 showing a greater level of output (q_2) and lesser price than P_1. Consequently, the firm reduces its price to P_2 level and anticipates an increase in sales of its output by $q_2 - q_1'$ amount. Other firms also act in the similar fashion. They also reduce their prices proportionally and stop the representative firm to get greater increase in its sales. This move reduces the anticipated demand to q_2' corresponding to the X_3 on the *DD′* curve. Again, the

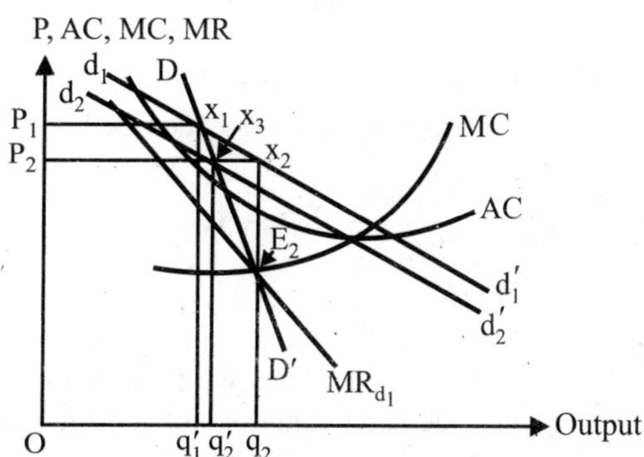

Fig. 9.3 Short-run Equilibrium Under Monopolistic Competition: Second Adjustment

anticipated demand curve d_1d_1' slides down along the *DD′* curve and passes through the point X_3. Now, P_2 and q_2' defines the new price-quantity combination for the firm when other firms are also in the similar equilibrium situation.

The adjustment process and hence search for the group equilibrium in the market continues further in the way as described above. The process comes to the end when the *MR* and *MC* intersection level output is the same which corresponds with the intersection of the proportional (*DD*′) and anticipated demand curve (d_3d_3'), as shown in Fig. 9.4. The short-run equilibrium for the firm along with the group equilibrium is now established with P^* and q^* as price-quantity combination. There is no reason and, in fact, the scope for changing this so long the *DD*′, *AC* and *MC* curves are fixed. Whether firms make profit in this situation depends on the position of the *ATC* curve. If the *ATC* curve is above the point *G*, there will be negative profit; if the *ATC* curve passes through *G* point, profit will be zero and if it lies below *G*, there will be positive profit. By profit we mean economic profit since normal profit is a part of the cost of production which is included in the *ATC*.

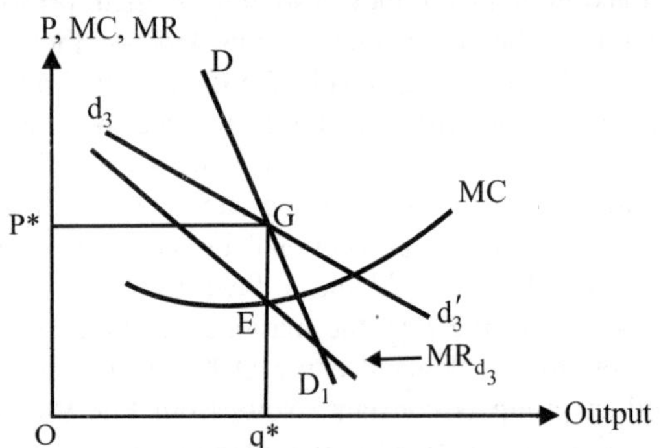

Fig. 9.4 Group Equilibrium Under Monopolistic Competition

Using the algebraic format, the short-run equilibrium condition for firms under monopolistic competition can be specified as follows:

We have seen that the demand function for a firm under monopolistic competition is a function of prices charged by all firms, *i.e.*, $q_i = d\ (P_1\ P_2, \ldots, P_n)$. Prices of firms are themselves functions of quantities. The inverse of the demand function for *i*th firm will give us its price in terms of quantities of output of all firms, *i.e.*, $P_i = P(q_1\ q_2, \ldots, q_n)$. It involves all the *n* quantities of output. Now, given the cost curve for the *i*th firm ($C = C_i\ (q_i)$) we have the profit function for the *i*th firm as

$$\pi_i = q_iP_i - C_i(q_i);\ i = 1, \ldots, n. \qquad \ldots(6)$$

The first order profit maximisation condition would then be

$$\partial\pi_i / \partial q_i = P_i + q_i \frac{\partial P_i}{\partial q_i} - \frac{\partial C_i(q_i)}{\partial q_i} = 0,\ i = 1,\ \ldots,\ n. \qquad \ldots(7)$$

That is, for each firm its $MR = MC$.

The second order condition for this will be as usual the *MC* curve must intersect the *MR* curve for each firm from below. Solving all these *n* equations we find short-run equilibrium conditions for all firms in the market. Let the inverse demand function for a firm *i* is given as

$$P_i = a_{0i} - a_iq_i - \sum_{\substack{j \\ j \neq i}}^{n} b_{ji}\ q_j;\ \ i = 1,\ \ldots,\ n. \qquad \ldots(8)$$

where b_{ji} shows the effect of unit increase in the quantity of jth output on the price of ith output $(\partial P_i/\partial q_j = - b_{ji})$.

It is negative and quite small when n is large enough. If all firms are having identical demand and cost functions, we can simplify the above expression as

$$P_i = a_0 - aq_i - b\sum_{\substack{j=1 \\ j \neq i}}^{n} q_j; \; i = 1, ..., n \qquad ...(9)$$

where $a_i = a$, $b_{ji} = b$, *i.e.* uniform for all q_j and $a_{0i} = a_0$. The cost function for the firm can be shown as

$$C_i = C(q_i) \qquad ...(10)$$

The profit function then comes as

$$\pi_i = q_i \left(a_0 - aq_i - b\sum_{\substack{j=1 \\ j \neq i}}^{n} q_j\right) - C(q_i), \; i = 1, ..., n \qquad ...(11)$$

From this the $MR = MC$ condition for profit maximisation, assuming that the second order condition for profit maximisation is satisfied;

$$a_0 - 2aq_i - b\sum_{\substack{j=1 \\ j \neq i}}^{n} q_j = C'(q_i), \; i = 1, ..., n \qquad ...(12)$$

This can be solved for all n firms. For effective demand curve we substitute,

$q_j = q_i$, therefore

$$P_i = a_0 - [a + (n - 1)\, b]\, q_i \qquad ...(13)$$

and the $MR = MC$ condition for this is

$$a_0 - [2a + (n - 1)\, b]\, q_i = C'(q_i) \qquad ...(14)$$

If n is fixed and all parameters are known, we can find q_i. This q_i is identical for all firms which we got on the basis of the proportional demand curve under assumption of $q_i = q_j$.

9.4 LONG-RUN EQUILIBRIUM OF A FIRM UNDER MONOPOLISTIC COMPETITION

In the long-run, the plant size for each firm in the market can change. There will be nothing like a fixed factor. Apart from this, the number of firms competing in the product group changes. If the existing firms in the product group earn positive profit, new firms are attracted by this to join the group since the entry is free and unrestricted. This reduces the profit of the firms in the long-run. If there is a loss in the short-run, some firms will leave the group, causing a reduction in the loss for the other firms. The entry of new firms in the product group or exit of some existing firms, as the case may be, continues till zero profit condition equilibrium is achieved in the long-run. The surplus profit, positive or negative, is eliminated through the process of entry and exit of firms. Along with this, firms also make appropriate changes in their plant sizes in the long-run.

Figure 9.5 shows the long-run equilibrium for a representative firm under monopolistic competition. According to this, the long-run equilibrium is given by the point L on the LAC curve at which the anticipated demand curve is a tangent to the LAC curve and the proportional demand curve passes

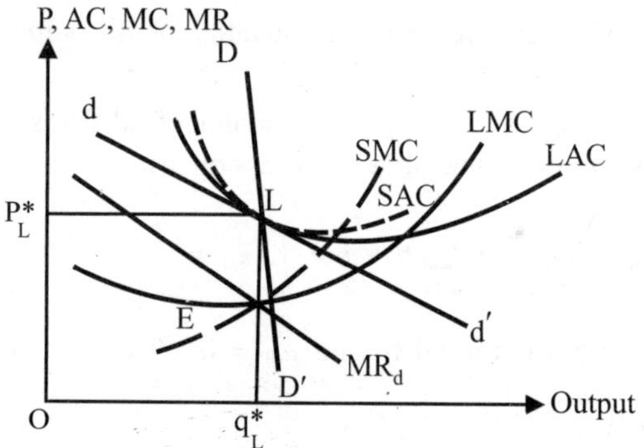

Fig. 9.5 Long-run Equilibrium for a Firm Under Monopolistic Competition: Fixed Number of Firms

through this point. There is a *SAC* curve which is also touched by the anticipated demand curve at this point. Just below this point, on the vertical line the *LMC* and MR_d curves intersect each other. The *SMC* also intersects the MR_d curve at that point. Both, *LMC* and *SMC*, intersect the MR_d curve from below ensuring no scope for positive profit beyond that level of output. The maximum possible profit is, of course, zero in the long-run equilibrium. All firms in the product-group get similar long-run equilibrium with zero profit.

For the purpose of the long-run equilibrium we may take the demand curve for the firm as

$$q_i = D(P_1, P_2, ..., P_n, n), \; i = 1, ..., n, \qquad ...(15)$$

where *n* is the number of the firms which appear as variable in the demand function. The profit for the *i*th firm would be:

$$\pi_i = q_i P_i - C_i(q_i) = 0, \; i = 1, ..., n^* \qquad ...(16)$$

and

$$\sum_{i=1}^{n^*} q_i P_i - \sum_{i=1}^{n^*} C_i(q_i) = 0 \qquad ...(17)$$

where n^* is the equilibrium number of the firm in the product group.

The long-run equilibrium situation is a short-run equilibrium situation also as we have shown in the figure, the condition of equilibrium, as shown by equation (7), will also be valid in the long-run. The system of equations (16) and (17) can be solved to find n^*, and n^* output levels. Consider the simplified example as revealed by equations (8) to (14) in the preceding section. We have taken all firms identical in the industry and so equation (14) gives us the $MR = MC$ condition valid for all firms. The equation is

$$a_0 - [2a + (n - 1) b] \, q_i = C' (q_i) \qquad ...(18)$$

$C'(q)$ is now interpreted as *LMC*.

The profit equation for the long-run equilibrium can be written as

$$\pi_i = a_0 \, q_i - [a + (n - 1)b] \, q_i^2 - C(q_i) = 0 \qquad ...(19)$$

Equations (14) and (18) have two unknowns q_i and *n*, which can be found out on their solution. Since q_i is identical for all firms, so long-run equilibrium gives us *n* uniform output levels and the optimum number of firms in the product-group.

How is the long-run equilibrium position attained under monopolistic competition? We take an initial short-run in which the number of competing firm is quite small, each one making high profits. This position is shown by the D_0D_0' and d_0d_0' curves and their intersection point G_0 in Fig. 9.6.

The excessive positive profit in this initial short-run group-equilibrium situation attracts new firms to join the product-group since there is no restriction for this. With their joining the group, the number of firms increase, market share of firms declines which means a shift of the proportional demand curve to the left. The anticipated demand curve also shifts to the left along with the proportional demand curve.

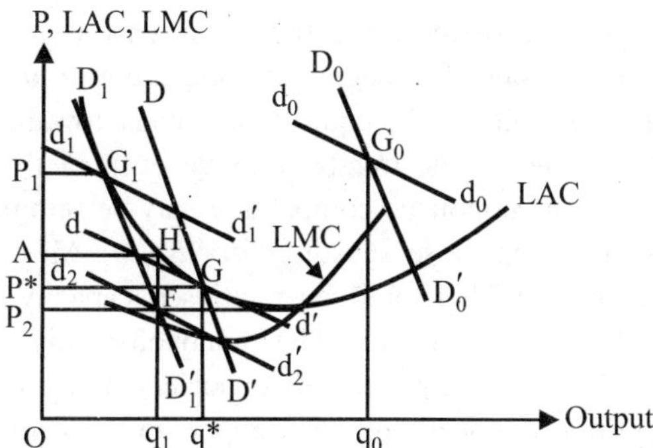

Fig. 9.6 Long-run Equilibrium for a Firm Under Monopolistic Competition: The Case of Changing Number of Firms

The increase in the number of firms in the product-group, and hence contraction of the demand curves continues till the economic profit is eliminated. This position is shown by point G_1 where the proportional demand curve (D_1D_1') touches the *LAC* curve and the anticipated demand curve d_1d_1' passes through this point. At G_1 point, there is no-profit and no-loss but it cannot be considered as the equilibrium point since the second order conditions for profit maximisation are not satisfied. The firm can increase its profit by increasing its output level and decreasing its price because its anticipated demand curve is above the *LAC* on the right of point G_1. The limit of price reduction is given by P_2 which corresponds to the minimum point of the *LAC* and $P_2 = LMC = LAC$. For P_2 price, the equilibrium position for the group has to be at point *F*, and therefore the anticipated demand curve d_1d_1' slides down to the position d_2d_2' and intersects the D_1D_1' at *F* point. At P_2 price, q_1 is the quantity of output. This cannot be taken as the equilibrium situation since the firm is getting negative profit shown by the area $FHAP_2$. Other firms in the product group also react to the market as the representative firm does. This implies that at P_2 price they will be having loss. Some marginal firm may not bear this loss; so, they will leave the product group. The number of firms declines which pushes the proportional demand curve D_1D_1' to shift to the right. The d_2d_2' curve starts rising up and the price also increases along with the output. This process continues till the loss accruing to firms is completely eliminated. This is possible when anticipated demand curve touches the *LAC* curve and the proportional or effective demand curve passes through that point of tangency as shown by *G*. This gives us *DD'* and *dd'* as the two demand curves for the firm and the long-run equilibrium position for it. q^* and P^* are the long-run quantity and price for the firm and identically for other firms also when demand and cost curves for all of them are similar. The condition $MR_d = LMC$ will also be satisfied at the q^* level of output. Along with the equilibrium price and quantity, we get the optimum number of firms in the product group in this situation. There cannot be any other equilibrium situation for the firm except the one (*G* here) where the anticipated demand curve is tangent to the *LAC* curve and proportional demand curve passing through that point. Zero profit condition is not merely sufficient. Beyond such equilibrium situation there must not be further scope for positive profit and before that for a loss.

The anticipated demand curve (*dd*′) for the firm is downward sloping. It is not perfectly elastic. So, the point of tangency *G* will always be on the declining side of the *LAC*. This, implies that in the long-run equilibrium under monopolistic competition firms will produce less than their capacity of production. Existence of un-utilised capacity is a phenomenon of the monopolistically competitive markets. The position of the equilibrium depends on the price elasticity of demand. If it is high, the equilibrium will be near the minima of the *LAC*. If the elasticity is low, it will be away from the minima of the *LAC* on its declining side. The degree of competition in the market will also determine the equilibrium position. If it is quite high, equilibrium tends towards the minima of the *LAC*, otherwise away from it when monopolistic trends continue even in the long-run.

The long-run situation under monopolistic competition may be summarised below: (*a*) There will be a large number of firms providing close substitute goods. (*b*) All of them will be having zero economic profit in the long-run. (*c*) There will be unutilised capacity of production and hence a wastage of resources under this type of market. The monopolistically competitive market is, thus, certainly bad from the point of view of firms as well as society. What should be done to avoid such a situation? The price competition is not giving any support to the firm because of competition. Its alternative is to resort to non-price competition in order to maintain profitable equilibrium for the firms.

To support the long-run equilibrium condition let us consider the following numerical examples.

The demand curve in inverse form for a firm is given as $P = 165 - 20q$. The average cost curve is given as $AC = 215 - 40q + 2q^2$, and the market share curve (*i.e.*, proportional demand curve) is $P = 180 - 23\,q$. The problem for solution is to find the equilibrium position for the firm.

The profit of the firm is $\pi = P.q - C$, that is, $\pi = (165 - 20q)\,q - q(215 - 40q + 2q^2)$

or $$\pi = -\,2q^3 - 50q + 20q^2$$

$$d\pi/dq = -\,6q^2 - 50 + 40q = 0$$

or $$q = 5 \text{ or } 5/3$$

For max. profit, $q = 5$ since $5/3 = q$ corresponds to the lowest profit.

For $q = 5,\ d^2\pi/dq^2 = -\,12(5) + 40 = -\,20$

So, the second order condition for profit maximisation is satisfied.

For $q = 5,\ \pi = 0$

This implies that at the equilibrium position the firm produces 5 units of output which gives maximum profit of 0 units to it. This is checked by the $MR = MC$ condition. This is, therefore, the long-run equilibrium condition for the firm.

To check whether the anticipated demand curve is a tangent to the *LAC*, we equate their slopes at the point of the tangency. This is,

$$\frac{d(AC)}{dq} = \frac{dP}{dq} \text{ or } 4q - 40 = -\,20 \text{ or } q = 5$$

which is the same level of output as we got above. Further, we find that the proportional demand curve (*i.e.*, market share curve) and the anticipated demand curve for the firm intersect when $q = 5$.

$$165 - 20q = 180 - 23q \text{ or } q = 5.$$

This is confirmed that the firm attains long-run equilibrium position when $q = 5$.

9.5 NON-PRICE COMPETITION UNDER MONOPOLISTIC COMPETITION

As we know; price competition may not be successful under monopolistic competition. In fact, it seems to be a very minor aspect of the competitive rivalry among the firms in the market, the major aspect of which, as we find in practice, is the non-price competition. There are five important ways for non-price competition: advertisement, quality variations, product development, locational changes, and provision of supplementary services. In fact, the whole of marketing strategies minus price variations constitute together the structure of non-price competition in business circles.

The very purpose of advertisement is to shift the demand curve for the firm upward or to the right showing an increase in sales at the given price of the product. The cost of sales also goes up because of advertisement expenditure. This shifts the average cost curve and the marginal cost curve up. The net result of advertisement depends on the relative shifts of these two curves. If demand shifts by larger magnitude than the cost, then the firm will gain; on the other hand if the cost curve shifts by greater magnitude, there would be a loss to the firm. In practice, a firm would be undertaking advertisement when it is beneficial in some way or other.

There are some different types of advertisements, such as informative advertisement and competitive advertisement. The objective of informative advertisement is to inform the buyers about new products and their attributes, while the competitive advertisement is aimed at inincreasing the market power of the firm. The firm competes on the basis of such advertisements. If successful, this type of advertisement leads to an increase in the market share of the firm. The informative advertisement reinforces this to some extent.

Competitive advertisement may be 'offensive' or 'defensive'. If a firm starts advertising first, it is 'offensive' type. Other firms are forced to follow it; so, it is then defensive since if they do not advertise, they will be adversely affected by the offensive advertisement of some other firm. Advertisement may be useful for new industries but when all firms in an established industry advertise, perhaps its gains are neutralized by this. Advertisement beyond a certain limit is considered as a social waste but it is now functioning as an industry itself, providing jobs to people and revenue to governments. Consumers might be paying high prices for products under monopolistically competitive markets for which there is excessive advertisement.

Product variation and product development are important aspects of non-price competition. Once a firm gets positive profit, it can be maintained for longer period through the strategy of product variation. The quality of the product is to be changed by changing some of its attributes or design. The firm has to create the impression that the product is different than what it used to be earlier. Product development is a part of product variation. Initiation of new varieties certainly helps the firm in pushing up its demand curve and maintaining its profitable equilibrium. Automobile firms do change their models frequently and similar is the situation in several other industries. Product variation may be real or spurious but the impression created by it would be that it is different from the earlier one.

Location strategies are other important dimensions of non-price competition. Having a shop near the entrance of a shopping centre, taking the products to the consumer's house, locating service centres for various things in residential colonies, etc., are a few examples for non-price competition based on locational strategies.

Other aspects of non-price competition are such as credit facilities, hire-purchase facilities, carpeting and airconditioning of the shop, free carry home services, developing friendship with consumers and so on. Such strategies do help in sales promotion and hence maintaining profitable equilibrium under monopolistic competition otherwise the competitive forces in the market will force the firm to the situation of the long-run equilibrium with zero profits and wastage of productive capacity by not utilising it.

How to incorporate elements of non-price competition in the equilibrium analysis for a firm under monopolistic competition? We will present a simple model for this. To develop this model, we assume that the firm simultaneously chooses optimum strategy for price, quality and advertisement. Other aspects of non-price competition are ignored at this stage. Further, for simplicity, we assume that quality can be represented by a quantifiable variable G and similarly, advertisement and sales promotion can be represented by a variable A. The demand for the product of firms can then be expressed as a function of price, quality and advertisement. We take only the price charged by the firm assuming rivals' prices as insignificant demand factors for it. The demand function is specified as,

$$q = D(P, G, A) \quad \text{...(20)}$$

The cost of the firm will also be a function of G and A apart from q, the level of output,

$$C = C(q, G, A) \quad \text{...(21)}$$

The profit of the firm can now be expressed as

$$\pi = Pq - C(q, G, A) \quad \text{...(22)}$$

We assume that the inverse of the demand function (20) exists; so we can express price as:

$$P = D^{-1}(q, G, A) \quad \text{...(23)}$$

By taking the partial derivatives of (22) with respect to q, G, and A, and equating them to zeros, the first order profit maximising conditions for the firm are:

$$\partial\pi/\partial q = P + q\frac{dP}{dq} - \frac{\partial C}{\partial q} = 0$$

$$\partial\pi/\partial G = P\frac{\partial q}{\partial G} + q\frac{\partial P}{\partial G} - \frac{\partial C}{\partial G} = 0 \quad \text{...(24)}$$

$$\partial\pi/\partial A = P\partial q/\partial A + q\partial P/\partial A - \partial C/\partial A = 0$$

Assuming that the second order conditions for profit maximisation are satisfied, we can solve the above set of equations for three unknowns q, G, and A. Let the optimal values for them are q^*, G^* and A^*. Substituting these values for q, G, and A in the demand equation (23) we can find the optimal price for the firm as,

$$P^* = D^{-1}(Q^*, G^*, A^*) \quad \text{...(25)}$$

Similarly, from the profit equation (22) the optimum profit for the firm would be

$$\pi^* = q^* P^* - C(q^*, G^*, A^*) \quad \text{...(26)}$$

The number of firms has been taken as fixed here. If it is variable, the above system of equations (24) can be supplemented by having $\pi^* = 0$ for long-run equilibrium which gives us the optimal number of firms in the industry.

9.6 CONCLUDING REMARKS

This is rather a small chapter on a very important type of market structure. The emphasis in this chapter was to understand the behaviour of firms from the view point of short-run and long-run equilibrium under profit maximisation objective. Along with the price competition, emphasis has been given on non-price competition since this is the aspect which is very important in the context of market conduct policies of firms in the real life situation.

SUGGESTED READINGS

Chamberlin, E.H. *The Theory of Monopolistic Competition,* Harvard University Press, 1933, (6th Ed. 1950).

Fergusion, C.E., *Microeconomic Theory,* R.D. Irwin, 1966.

Koutsoyiannis, A., *Modern Microeconomics,* The Macmillan Press, 1978.

Machlup, F., *The Economics of Sellers' Competition;* Johns Hopkins Press, 1952.

Nicholson, W. and Chrispher Synder, *Microeconomic Theory: Basic Principles and Extensions*; South-Western. Cengage Learning, Canada.

Stigler, G.J., *Monopolistic Competition in Retrospect in Five Lectures on Economic Problems,* Longmans, Green, 1949.

Sher, W. and R. Pindola, *Microeconomic Theory: A Synthesis of Classical and the Modern Approach;* Edward Arnold, 1981.

REVIEW QUESTIONS

1. Distinguish between monopolistic competition and perfect competition. Why the condition for monopolistic competition is created in the market? Examine in detail.
2. It is argued that the demand curve for the product of a monopolistically competitive firm is quite different than the demand curve for the output of a perfectly competitive firm. Why it is so? What are the special features of the demand curve faced by the monopolistically competitive firm? Use diagrams to elaborate your answer.
3. Describe how long-run equilibrium situation of a monopolistically competitive firm is reached under assumption of (*a*) group equilibrium with constant number of firms, (*b*) changing number of rival firms.
4. It is argued that price competition is not fruitful under monopolistic competition and so the firms have to go for non-price competition. Why it is so? What are the various ways for non-price competition. Examine in details.
5. How does a firm under monopolistic competition attains equilibrium position when product quality and selling costs are changed simultaneously? Elaborate in full details.
6. The average cost curve for a firm under monopolistic competition is given as $AC = 210 - 40q + 2q^2$ and its demand curve as $P = 160 - 20q$.
   (*a*) Show that the firm will produce 5 units of output when it is in group equilibrium with market share curve given as $P = 175 - 23q$.
   (*b*) Will the firm be in group equilibrium when it incurs a cost of Rs. 15 per unit of output on advertisement as a result of which its demand curve changes to $P = 165 - 19q$, market share curve being unchanged?
7. Do you consider monopolistically competitive industry better than pure monopoly and perfect competitive industries? Give your assessment of this from the view point of attaining economic efficiency.

SUGGESTED READINGS

Chamberlin, E.H., *The Theory of Monopolistic Competition*, Harvard University Press, 1933 [illegible]

Ferguson, C.E., *Microeconomic Theory*, R.D. Irwin, 1969.

Koutsoyiannis, A., *Modern Microeconomics*, The Macmillan Press, [illegible]

Machlup, F., *The Economics of Sellers' Competition*, Johns Hopkins Press, [illegible]

Nicholson, W. and Christopher Snyder, *Microeconomic Theory: Basic Principles and Extensions*, [illegible]

Stigler, G., *Monopolistic Competition in Retrospect*, in *Five Lectures on Economic Problems*, Longmans, Green [illegible]

[illegible] Edward Arnold [illegible]

REVIEW QUESTIONS

[illegible]

CHAPTER 10

Theory of Oligopolistic Markets

Between the two extreme types of market—perfect competition and monopoly—we find oligopoly as an important intermediate type of market structure. This chapter deals with the analysis of oligopoly and its limiting form called duopoly. First, we will define these types of markets and then present the various models which have been developed to study them. At the end, we will present the mark-up pricing system applicable to the oligopolistic markets.

10.1 THE CONCEPT OF OLIGOPOLY

Like other types of market structures, we define oligopoly in terms of a few characteristics as follows:

(i) Few Sellers and Many Buyers

An oligopoly, as it is commonly understood, is a market structure where a few firms dominate the industry. It is not a necessary condition that there should be only a few firms to constitute the industry. The number of firms may be quite large but the major portion of the industry's productive capacity is accounted for only by a few firms, others will be insignificant as far as the market is concerned. The number of buyers in the oligopolist markets will be quite large.

(ii) Homogeneous or Differentiated Products

Firms in the industry produce either a homogeneous product or differentiated products. If the product of all the firms is identical or homogeneous, it is 'pure oligopoly' and if their products are differentiated, it would be called 'differentiated oligopoly'.

(iii) Restricted Entry

Legally, the entry in an oligopolistic market is free but there will be several barriers to entry which make it quite difficult for the new firms to join the industry or market. From this account we call it as limited or restricted entry in the industry.

(iv) There is Perfect Knowledge or Information about the Market

Firms in the oligopolistic markets are having full knowledge about the market, particularly about the rival firms.

Characteristics of (iii) and (iv) reveal a very important behavioural feature of an oligopoly market. The few dominating firms having full knowledge about the market will be *interdependent* in decision making. The interdependence of firms in decision-making under oligopoly is the essential feature which makes it different from perfect competition or monopolistic competition. If one firm under oligopoly reduces its product price in order to increase sales, other firms will not ignore it since their sales and hence profits will be adversely affected by this. So, they will react to the first firm's price reduction decision. There is another aspect of the interdependency hypothesis. If the influence of one firm's quantity or price decision upon the profit or sales of other firms is zero or imperceptible, *i.e.*, $\partial\pi_i/\partial q_j = 0$, $ij = 1,...n$, $i \neq j$, firms are independent and the industry satisfies the requirements of perfect competition or monopolistic competition. On the other hand, if such an effect is not zero, that is, $\partial\pi_i/\partial q_j \neq 0$, they are interdependent and this is the situation in oligopoly.

The interdependence among firms under the oligopoly depends on their number. Greater the number of firms higher may be the degree of interdependence. However, mere number of firms is not the sole determinant for this. The size distribution of firms also plays an important role in determining their interdependence. Consider a simple case of three firms oligopoly. If one firm is large enough accounting, say 80% of sales in the industry, the other two sharing the rest of it (20%). The large firm may consider the other two firms too small as compared to itself and so it can ignore their reactions while taking decisions. That is, the large firm acts independently. But the other firms act as if interdependence existed. So, here we have only one way interdependence pattern. There is another factor affecting the degree of interdependence of firms under the oligopoly. If products of firms are homogeneous, the feeling of interdependence will tend to be strong because of the perfect substitutability of products of firms. On the other hand, if products of firms are differentiated the degree of interdependence is weakened. Each firm in this situation will have more freedom to act independently because its products are not perfect substitutes for each other. The nature of the product, homogeneous or differentiated produced by the oligopolistic firms thus affects the mutual interdependency of firms in the industry.

The mutual interdependency of the oligopolistic firms is an attribute which acts as a restraint upon the decision that a firm takes. The outcome of the decision and action taken will normally be less certain to be favourable. This depends on the reaction of other firms which are not always predictable. Moreover, the reaction of firms may not be uniform in type.

10.2 ECONOMIC MODELS OF OLIGOPOLISTIC MARKETS

The economic theory of oligopoly and its special form duopoly concerning pricing and output decisions has not yet been standardised. The difficulty in this connection lies in conceptualisation of the form or type of the conjectural variation or how rivals react when any firm in the oligopolistic market takes such decisions. There is no unique behavioural assumption for this. Several economic models have been developed for duopoly and oligopoly, each one based on different assumptions. Because of such a diversity in approach, models differ in solution. The restrictive and, in some cases, inconsistent assumptions of models make them less useful in practice. However, economists study them since they are part of the modern oligopoly theory and an understanding of models helps in better appreciation of problems associated in modeling the behaviour of oligopolistic firms. A brief review of the economic models of oligopoly and duopoly is presented here. We begin with models of duopoly since it is the simplest form of the oligopoly in which only two firms exist in the market and an extension of models covers the oligopoly in general.

(i) The Cournot Model[1]

As far back as 1839, Cournot, a French economist, developed a simple model for duopoly. He considered two firms engaged in the business of selling mineral water from two springs located adjacent to one another, with one owned by each firm. Customers came to springs with their own buckets to draw the water, and firms having only the fixed cost of digging wells, sold water at zero marginal cost. The market price of the water was determined by the total quantity of the water demanded by customers. Each firm was taken to sell that quantity of water which maximised its profit under the assumption that the output of other firm remaining constant. This kind of assumption generated a reaction sequence in the market for the water, which eventually converged at a point giving the solution for the output levels of firms and the market price for the water.

To explain the model, let us consider a general situation with non-zero marginal costs for the duopolists. Let us assume that the two firms supply a homogeneous product to the same market. The price of the product is uniform for both the firms in the market. Let it be P, and q_1 and q_2 as quantities of the output supplied by firm 1 and firm 2 respectively. By taking the inverse demand function for the product, the expression for the price P can be written as:

$$P = f(q_1 + q_2) = f(q) \qquad ...(1)$$

This demand curve is downward sloping, *i.e.*,

$$f' < 0; \; q = q_1 + q_2$$

The revenue of each firm would be,

$$R_1 = P \cdot q_1 = f(q_1 + q_2) \cdot q_1 = R_1 \, (q_1, q_2) \qquad ...(2)$$

$$R_2 = P \cdot q_2 = f(q_1 + q_2) \cdot q_2 = R_2 \, (q_1, q_2)$$

That is, each firm's revenue depends on the level of the output of both the firms. The profit earned by firm 1 and firm 2, would be,

$$\pi_1 = R_1(q_1, q_2) - C_1(q_1) \qquad ...(3)$$

$$\pi_2 = R_2(q_1, q_2) - C_2(q_2)$$

$C_1(q_1)$ and $C_2(q_2)$ show total cost of production for the two firms respectively.

Differentiating each firm's profit with respect to its own output level the profit maximisation conditions can be expressed as:

$$\frac{\partial \pi_1}{\partial q_1} = \frac{\partial R_1(q_1, q_2)}{\partial q_1} + \frac{\partial R_1(q_1, q_2)}{\partial q_2} \cdot \frac{dq_2}{dq_1} - \frac{dC_1(q_1)}{dq_1} = 0 \qquad ...(4)$$

$$\frac{\partial \pi_2}{\partial q_2} = \frac{\partial R_1(q_1, q_2)}{\partial q_1} \cdot \frac{dq_1}{dq_2} + \frac{\partial R_2(q_1, q_2)}{\partial q_2} - \frac{dC_2(q_2)}{dq_2} = 0$$

In order to find the solution of these two equations we must know dq_2/dq_1 and dq_1/dq_2. These two derivatives are called 'conjectural variations'. They show one firm's conjecture or expectation of how other firm's output will change when there is a change in its own output. To solve the first order, profit maximisation condition, as shown by (4) Cournot, assumed that both the conjectural variation terms dq_2/dq_1 and dq_1/dq_2 are zeros, that is, while maximising the profit by changing the level of output, each firm assumes its rival's output unchanged. Thus, putting $dq_2/dq_1 = 0$, $dq_1/dq_2 = 0$ in (4), we get

1. Augustin, A. Cournot, *Researches into the Mathematical Principles of the Theory of Wealth* (1839) (Translated by N. Bacon, Macmillan, N.Y., 1927.

$$\frac{\partial R_1(q_1, q_2)}{\partial q_1} = \frac{dC_1(q_1)}{dq_1} \text{ or } MR_1 = MC_1 \quad ...(5)$$

$$\frac{\partial R_2(q_1, q_2)}{\partial q_2} = \frac{dC_2(q_2)}{dq_2} \text{ or } MR_2 = MC_2$$

Each firm is equating its own *MR* and *MC*. The second order's condition would be, as usual, the rate of change of marginal cost must be greater than the rate of change of marginal revenue at the equilibrium.

We have $P = f(q)$, and therefore,

$$R_1 = P \cdot q_1 \text{ and } R_2 = P \cdot q_2$$

so,

$$\frac{dR_1}{dq} \cdot \frac{dq}{dq_1} = P + q_1 \frac{dP}{dq} = MR_1 \quad ...(6)$$

$$\frac{dR_2}{dq} \cdot \frac{dq}{dq_2} = P + q_2 \frac{dP}{dq} = MR_2$$

$\frac{dq}{dq_1} = \frac{dq}{dq_2} = 1$ since unit increase in output of either firm means unit increase in supply of that commodity in the market.

The equation set (6), therefore, indicates the marginal revenue for each firm. Since $\frac{dP}{dq} < 0$, because of downward sloping demand curve, it implies that marginal revenue for the duopolist depends on their level of output. A firm having greater output will have smaller marginal revenue.

The duopoly firms will be in equilibrium when values of q_1 and q_2 are such that each firm maximises its profit. These values can be obtained by solving the two equations, one for q_1 in terms of q_2, and other for q_2 in terms of q_1 obtained from the first and second equations of (5). Specifically, we get $q_1 = \Psi_1(q_2)$. and $q_2 = \Psi_2(q_1)$. These are called reaction functions. On solving them, we get optimal values for q_1 and q_2. Once we know q_1 and q_2, we can sum them and find the market price and profits for each firm in the duopoly.

The two reaction functions, $q_1 = \Psi_1(q_2)$ and $q_2 = \Psi_2(q_1)$, for the duopoly firms are shown in Fig. 10.1 by the lines *AB* and *CD* respectively. At *E* point, they intersect which gives the equilibrium solution for q_1 and q_2.

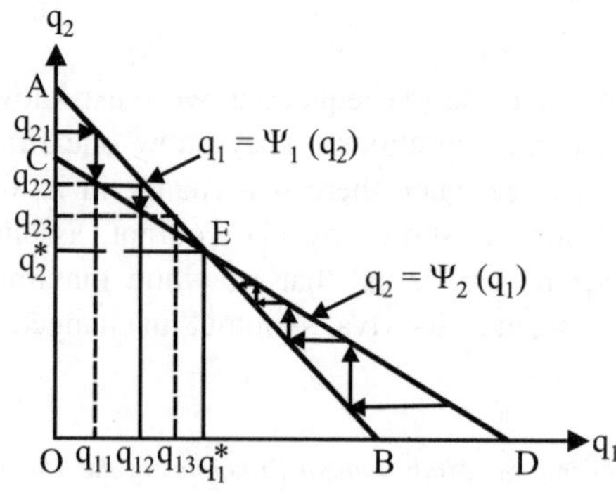

Fig. 10.1 Cournot Duopoly Solution

Let q_{21} be some arbitrary level of output of firm 2. Firm 1 feels that when q_{21} is fixed, its optimum level of output is q_{11} as given by its reaction function. But for q_{11} level of output of firm 1, firm 2 feels that its optimum output level is q_{22} as given by its reaction function. For q_{22} level of output, however, firm's 1 optimum output level is q_{12}.Thus, there is a chain of adjustment process which finally converges at E point where both the firms, attain equilibrium level of output (q_1^* and q_2^*). Same kind of chain reaction process starts from the right side of the equilibrium point E. This point will be a stable one giving the quantity solution for the duopoly. Once we find quantities q_1^* and q_2^*, the market price and profits of firms can then be found easily.

To explain the solution let us have a numerical example. Consider the two firms for which the cost functions are given as $C_1 = 50 + 20q_1$ and $C_2 = 45 + 24q_2$ respectively. The inverse form of the market demand curve for their products is given as $P = 100 - 4(q_1 + q_2)$ where $q_1 + q_2 = q$. Using this information, we express the profit equations for the firms as

$$\pi_1 = [100 - 4(q_1 + q_2)]\, q_1 - 50 - 20q_1 = -4q_1^2 - 4q_1q_2 + 80q_1 - 50$$

and $$\pi_2 = [100 - 4(q_1 + q_2)]\, q_2 - 45 - 24q_2 = -4q_1^2 - 4q_1q_2 + 76q_2 - 45$$

The first order conditions for profit maximisation for firms, are therefore, as

$$\partial\pi_1/\partial q_1 = -8q_1 - 4q_2 + 80 = 0 \text{ or } q_1 = 10 - 0.5q_2$$
$$\partial\pi_2/\partial q_2 = -8q_2 - 4q_1 + 76 = 0 \text{ or } q_2 = 9.5 - 0.5q_1$$

Solving these two reaction functions, we get

$$q_1^* = 7 \text{ units}, \; q_2^* = 6 \text{ units}$$

The market price = 100 – 4(7 + 6) = Rs. 48.

π_1 = Rs. 146; and π_2 = Rs. 103, are profit levels for the firms.

(ii) The Edgeworth's Model

The Cournot duopoly model was a pioneering one though somewhat naive and inconsistent because of its restrictive assumption of constant output of the rival firm. Joseph Bertrand, while reviewing Cournot's model in 1883, suggested a modification in the model by dropping the assumption of constant output and replacing it by the assumption of constant price of the rival firm.[2] Based on this suggestion, Edgeworth, in 1897, developed a duopoly model which was named after him.[3] Edgeworth has taken the same set of initial conditions as did the Cournot model, *i.e.*, zero marginal cost and the same mineral water supply business. In addition to this, two different suggestions were made by him: (*i*) each firm had a maximum but equal rate of output, and (*ii*) each firm assumed that the other would maintain a constant price rather than constant output.

In order to see the process of equilibrium in the Edgeworth model, let us consider the following figure. The two firms share the market for a homogeneous product evenly. Their demand curves are similar, as shown by DD_1 and DD_2, at each price, both having half of the total quantity available for the market. The maximum output that firms can sell individually is shown by OA_1 for firm 1 and OB_1 for firm 2. Neither of the two firms sell the commodity at zero price. Now, let us assume that firm 1 enters the market first. Since it will be the only firm in the market initially, therefore, it

---

2. Joseph Bertrand, "Thoeric Mathematique de la Richesse Sociale," Journal des Savants, Paris, 1803, pp. 499-508.
3. F.Y. Edgeworth, "The Pure Theory of Monopoly" in Edgeworths, Papers Relating to Political Economy, London Macmillan & Co. Ltd., 1925, Vol. 1, pp. 111-42 (Reprint of the original article).

acts as a monopoly and sets its price following the norm of revenue maximisation (*i.e.*, $MR = 0$ since MC is assumed to be zero). The output level supplied by the firm in this case is shown by OA_2 and the price for that P_1, Firm 2 then comes in the picture. This firm assumes that firm 1 will not change its price; so, it reduces its own price slightly below P_1, say at P_2, selling OB_2 output in its own market and $OB_1 - OB_2$ output extra in firm's 1 market. Firm 1 then retaliates by cutting down its price from P_1 to below P_2, say at P_3 level assuming that P_2 remains unchanged.

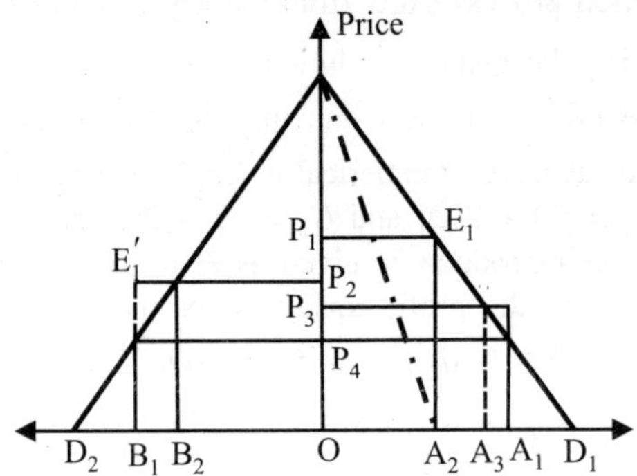

Fig. 10.2 Edgeworth's Duopoly Model

At P_3 price, firm A sells OA_3 output of its own plus $OA_1 - OA_3$ in firm 2's market. The price cutting sequence continues till the price level P_4 is established at which both the firms sell their maximum outputs, OA_1 and OB_1 respectively for firm 1 and firm 2. Their profits or revenue would be $P_4 \cdot OA_1$ and $P_4 \cdot OB_1$ respectively. According to Edgeworth, it is unlikely that the market will be in equilibrium at this stage. One of the two firms recognises that it could increase its profit by raising its price to P_1 because the other firm would not change its price from P_4 and would be selling its maximum output at this price. The other firm also thinks like that. So, it raises its price to P_2 slightly below P_1. From this stage, the price cutting sequence starts again and this type of movements in prices, up and down, continue, and the market never attains stability in the Edgeworth model. We may not find this kind of situation in practice for a duopoly market; so, Edgeworth's assumption of rival firm's constant price maintenance seems to be quite naive and unrealistic.

As a numerical example for the Edgeworth's model, let us take two firm case, Firm 1 and Firm 2, with the following demand functions,

$$Q_1 = 60 - 4P_1 + 2.5P_2$$
$$Q_2 = 50 - 5P_2 + 2P_1$$

where Q_1 and Q_2 are the demand levels for a commodity of two firms respectively and P_1 and P_2 their market prices.

Total demand for the commodity in the market would be

$$Q = Q_1 + Q_2 = 60 - 4P_1 + 2.5P_2 + 50 - 5P_2 + 2P_1 = 110 - 2P_1 - 2.5P_2$$

Let the marginal costs for the firm be given as Rs. 5 and Rs. 4 respectively. There are no fixed costs, so $MC = AC$ for each firm.

Profit functions for the firms would be

$$\pi_1 = (P_1 - AC_1)\ Q_1 = (P_1 - 5)\ (60 - 4P_1 + 2.5P_2)$$
$$= 80\ P_1 - 4P_1^2 + 2.5\ P_1P_2 - 300 - 12.5P_2$$

and

$$\pi_2 = (P_2 - AC_2)\ Q_2 = (P_2 - 4)\ (50 - 5P_2 + 2P_1)$$
$$\pi_2 = 70P_2 - 5P_2^2 + 2P_2P_1 - 200 + 8P_1$$

For maximum profit of firms, we have,

$$\partial\pi_1/\partial P_1 = 80 - 8P_1 + 2.5P_2 = 0 \quad ...(i)$$

and

$$\partial\pi/\partial P_2 = 70 - 10P_2 + 2P_1 = 0 \quad ...(ii)$$

The second order conditions for profit maximisation are satisfied for (i) & (ii)

Equations (i) & (ii) on simplification would be

$$P_1 = 10 + 0.3125P_2$$

$$P_2 = 7 + 0.20P_1$$

These are price reaction functions for firms. Solving them, we get

$$P_1 = \text{Rs. } 13, \; P_2 = \text{Rs. } 9.60$$

The output levels Q_1 and Q_2 for firms can now be found out through the demand functions.

The reaction functions are positively sloping, which means that higher the price that one firm thinks the other firm will charge the higher price it will itself charge.

(iii) Hotelling's Model

As we have seen above, the Edgeworth's model of duopoly, based on price rather output as the decision variable for firms, leads to indeterminacy of the equilibrium price and quantity for the market. The duopoly and oligopoly markets are often found to be quite stable in practice in spite of temporary price wars. Hotelling has developed a model which, in fact, has shown the stability of equilibrium for both duopoly and oligopoly markets.[4] It was an important model which has introduced spatial dimension in the theory of market having far reaching significance.

In order to explain Hotelling model, let us consider A and B as two firms producing a physically identical product at zero marginal cost. Firms are located at different places; so, their products are differentiated by buyers because of such locational difference. Each firm has a region as its market area where it is in quasi-monopolistic status. According to Hotelling, buyers are uniformly distributed along a line 'L' showing the total market distance, say a market street. This is shown in Fig. 10.3. A and B are the points on the line where Firm A and Firm B are located. To the left of point A firm A will have its 'sheltered' market and similarly to the right of B, firm B will have its 'sheltered' market. The market area between A and B points will be shared by the two firms. How to find the boundary for their markets in this area? For this, let us introduce the concept of delivered price which includes the price charged at the location plus a transportation cost for the product at the rate say Rs. 't' per unit product per unit distance. For example, a buyer at x distance from A pays a price $P_A + tx$ per unit of output and at a distance y from point B it will be, $P_B + ty$.

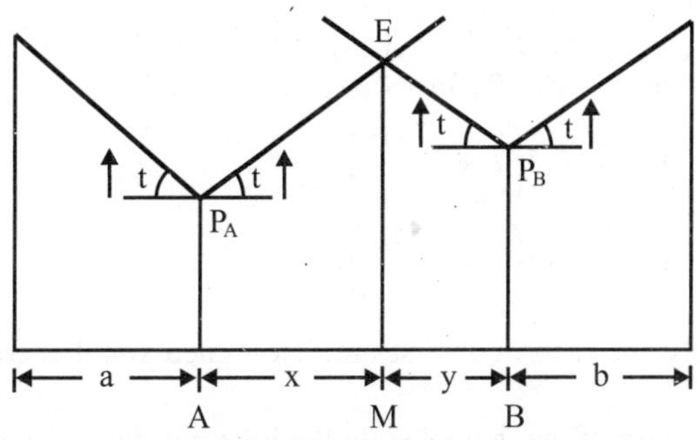

Fig. 10.3 Hotelling Duopoly Model

4. H. Hotelling, "Stability in Competition", *Economic Journal,* Vol. 39, 1929, pp. 41-57.

To simplify his analysis, Hotelling assumed demand for the product completely inelastic, the market as 'L' units in length, one buyer living at each unit of the length and in each unit of time each buyer purchasing one unit of output. The purpose of all this was to make total number of buyers equal to L. Let the number of buyers to the left of A be 'a' and to the right of B be 'b', and the distance between AB is shared by the firms in $x : y$ proportion. Then, $(a + x) + (y + b) = L$. Also, to find the market boundary between A and B for firms, we equate their delivered prices, that is $P_A + tx = P_B + ty$. This is the situation shown by point M. Now, we have two equations: $a + x + y + b = \text{L}$ and $P_A + tx = P_B + ty$ for two unknowns x and y which we get on solution. Once we find x and y, we find the quantity sold by each firm. Firm A sells $x + a$ units and Firm B sells $y + b$ units (Remember by the assumption of each buyer located at each unit length along L buying one unit of output we got this). The profit or revenue of the firm would be $\pi_A = P_A \cdot (a + x) - F_1$ and $\pi_B = P_B\,(b + y) - F_2$, F_1 and F_2 being fixed costs for the firms, marginal costs are zeros by assumption. These profits can be maximised which yield stable solution for the duopoly firms.

We have $$a + x + y + b = L \qquad ...(7)$$

and $$P_A + tx = P_B + ty$$

By solving them

$$x = \frac{1}{2}[L - a - b + (P_B - P_A)/t] \qquad ...(8)$$

$$y = \frac{1}{2}[L - a - b + (P_A - P_B)/t]$$

$$\pi_A = P_A\,(x + a) = \frac{1}{2}(L + a - b)P_A - \frac{P_A^2}{2t} + \frac{P_A P_B}{2t} - F_1 \qquad ...(9)$$

$$\pi_B = P_B\,(y + b) = \frac{1}{2}(L - a + b)P_B - \frac{P_B^2}{2t} + \frac{P_A P_B}{2t} - F_2$$

For profit maximisation

$$\frac{\partial \pi_A}{\partial P_A} = 1/2\,(L + a - b) - \frac{P_A}{t} + \frac{P_B}{2t} = 0 \qquad ...(10)$$

$$\frac{\partial \pi_B}{\partial P_B} = 1/2\,(L - a + b) - \frac{P_B}{t} + \frac{P_A}{2t} = 0$$

Solving (10) we get

$$P_A = t\left(L + \frac{a-b}{3}\right); \; P_B = t\left(L - \frac{a-b}{3}\right) \qquad ...(11)$$

By substituting values of P_A and P_B in (8) we find

$$q_A = a + x = 1/2\left(L + \frac{a-b}{3}\right) \qquad ...(12)$$

and $$q_B = b + y = 1/2\left(L - \frac{a-b}{3}\right)$$

Both, price and quantity for each duopolist are determined simultaneously. The solution is quite stable.

This is short-run equilibrium of the duopolist. In the long-run, Firm A will have an incentive to shift its location towards B point and thus to increase its 'sheltered' market to its left. Similarly Firm B has incentive to move to point A and thus to increase its 'sheltered' market to its right. As a consequence of this tendency, they may be eventually located at the centre of the market in the .long-run. If this is so, the spatial dimension of the analysis becomes irrelevant in the long-run for the duopoly firms.

(iv) Chamberlin's Model[5]

E.H. Chamberlin, in the 1930s, proposed an improved model in which each duopoly firm recognised its inter-dependence on its rival in the market place.

The model in its basic framework is similar to that of Cournot's model except for a more realistic assumption regarding the awareness of firms that they can do better by sharing the monopoly profit than by any other action.

The Chamberlin model can be explained using Fig. 10.4. Let us assume that Firm A enters the market first. The demand curve for Firm A is shown by D_A and correspondingly its marginal revenue is MR_A. The firm initially is a monopoly, producing Q_A level of output for maximum profit. ($MR_A = 0$ since $MC = 0$, we are having same mineral water problem as a reference here). The profit of the firm is the area OQ_AEP_A. With P_A as its price Firm B now enters the market. The demand for the output of Firm B will be total market demand minus the quantity sold by Firm A. The market demand coincides with D_A since initially Firm A was the only one selling in the market. Firm B would not come to the picture if market demand falls below Q_A. If market demand is more than Q_A at a price less than P_A, Q_A part of that will be supplied by Firm A and rest by Firm B. At P_A price Firm B supplies zero output. Its demand curve starts from this point and is shown by D_B. For Firm B we set the equilibrium by equating $MR_B = MC = 0$, which gives Q_B output at P_B price.

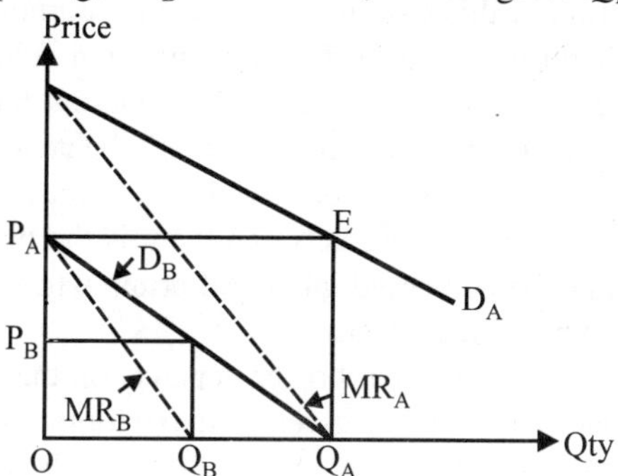

Fig. 10.4 Chamberlin's Duopoly Solution

At this stage, Firm A finds that Firm B's decision is based on the same strategy as its own (both maximising profits on the basis of $MR = MC = 0$ criterion) and recognising the market interdependence, cuts its output by 50 per cent, *i.e.*, 1/2 of Q_A equal to Q_B. Firm B, recognising the market interdependence, maintains its output at Q_B level but increases its price to P_A level. Both firms are mutually cooperating to each other. One reduces its output, other increases its price. Both are producing equal output, charging equal price and sharing the monopoly profit OQ_AEP_A by equal proportion.

The approach adopted by Chamberlin is definitely better than Cournot but to call it realistic, is again quite doubtful. The duopoly firms may not behave as conceived here.

5. E.H. Chamberlin, *The Theory of Monopolistic Competition,* Cambridge, Harvard University Press, 1933, pp. 46-51.

(v) The Stackelberg Model[6]

This model is based on the assumption of leadership and followership. A firm which is a follower bahaves like the one in the Cournot model. A leader takes the advantage of this. Specifically, we may say that if Firm 1 is a follower, it will choose q_1 in such a way as to maximise its objective function $\pi_1 = \pi_1(q_1, q_2)$ on the assumption that $dq_2/dq_1 = 0$. Similarly, if Firm 2 is a follower it chooses its output q_2 for maximising its profit $\pi_2 = \pi_2(q_1, q_2)$ on the assumption that $dq_1/dq_2 = 0$. But if Firm 1 is a leader, it chooses q_1 in order to maximise $\pi_1 = \pi_1(q_1, \Psi_2(q_1)$ where $q_2 = \Psi_2(q_1)$ is the reaction function of the second firm which is supposed to be a follower and therefore $q_2 = \Psi_2(q_1)$ shows its optimal value. This implies that Firm 1 assumes:

$$\frac{dq_2}{dq_1} = \frac{d\Psi_2(q_1)}{dq_1} \qquad \text{...(13)}$$

Similarly, if Firm 2 is a leader, it chooses q_2 for maximisation of $\pi_2(\Psi_1(q_2), q_2)$ where $q_1 = \Psi_1(q_2)$ is the reaction function for Firm 1. It means the second firm as a leader believes,

$$\frac{dq_1}{dq_2} = \frac{d(\Psi_1(q_2))}{dq_2} \qquad \text{...(14)}$$

In both the situations, that is, if Firm 1 is a leader it does not obey its reaction function and similarly if Firm 2 is a leader, it does not obey its reaction function. Only a follower firm obeys its reaction function.

There are four possible outcomes that arise in the Stackelberg duopoly analysis: (*i*) both the firms act as followers, the solution in this case is given by the Cournot model; (*ii*) Firm 1 is a leader and Firm 2 as a follower; (*iii*) Firm 2 is a leader and Firm 1 a follower; and (*iv*) both the firms are leaders. Situations under (*ii*) and (*iii*) provide stable solutions but (*iv*) is the case of unstable equilibrium. In this situation, each firm thinks that its rival's behaviour is governed by its reaction function but neither of the reaction functions is observed. There may not be any solution when both the duopolist are leaders; the economic warfare between them is the likely end. This is 'Stackelberg's disequilibrium' situation. This may be converted into equilibrium when both the firms collude together or one firm succumbs to the other's leadership.

Whether a firm prefers to be a leader or follower depends on the level of profit it earns in these situations. The firm prefers that status which gives it maximum profit.

Consider the numerical example which is given for the duopoly solution. The reaction functions derived for the firms were:

$$q_1 = 10 - 0.5q_2 \text{ for Firm 1.}$$
$$q_2 = 10 - 0.5q_1 \text{ for Firm 2.}$$

Substituting Firm 2's reaction function in the expression for π_1 and simplifying it we get,

$$\pi_1 = -\ 4P_1^2 - 4q_1\ (9.5 - 0.5q_1) + 80q_1 - 50$$

or

$$\pi_1 = -\ 2P_1^2 + 42q_1 - 50$$

$$d\pi_1/dq_1 = -\ 4q_1 + 42 = 0 \text{ for which } d^2\pi_1/dq_1^2 = -\ 4 < 0$$

This gives $q_1 = 10.5$ units

Firm 1 as Leader

and $\pi_1 =$ ₹ 170.50

6. H. Von Stackelberg: *The Theory of the Market Economy;* Translation by Alan T. Peacock, Oxford University Press, 1952.

Similarly, substituting Firm 1's reaction function in the expression for π_2 we get,

$$\pi_2 = -4q_2^2 - 4q_2 (10 - 0.5q_2) + 76q_2 - 45$$

or

$$\pi_2 = -2q_2^2 + 36q_2 - 45$$

$$d\pi_2/dq_2 = -4q_2 + 36 = 0 \text{ for which } d^2\pi_2/dq_2 = -4 < 0$$

This gives $q_2 = 9$ units

Firm 2 as leader.

and $\pi_1 =$ Rs. 117

Let us now examine how much profit Firm 2 gets as follower when firm 1 is the leader. Substituting Firm 1's leadership output in the reaction function for Firm 2 we have

$$q_2 = 9.5 - 0.5(10.5) = 4.25 \text{ units}$$

Firm 2 as follower

and $\pi_2 =$ Rs. 44.20

Similarly, the output of Firm 1 as a follower can be found by substituting Firm 2 leadership output in its reaction function, we then have:

and $q_1 = 10 - 0.5(9) = 5.5$ units,

Firm 1 as Follower

$\pi_1 =$ Rs. 71.

What we find here is that both the firms get higher profit when they are leaders than followers. This is Stackelberg's disequilibrium situation. In the Cournot model, we, of course, got equilibrium solution for the problem. A change of the duopoly behaviour assumption, makes all the difference in the solution by the two models.

(vi) The Product Differentiation Model

So far we have considered a duopoly market for a homogeneous product. Let us now take up the case for a duopoly with product differentiation. As we know, the quantity demanded for the product of a firm under product differentiation depends on the price of that product as well as on prices of other varieties of the product. That is,

$$q_i = f_i(P_1, P_2, ..., P_n), \; i = 1,..., n. \quad ...(15)$$

where $\dfrac{\partial q_i}{\partial P_i} < 0, \dfrac{\partial q_i}{\partial P_j} > 0$, for all, $i \neq j$.

The interpretation of all such partial derivatives is straight-forward as we have gone through them under the theory of monopolistic competition. Individual sellers under duopoly or oligopoly can set either price or quantity. Let us take price as the decision variable. The demand function in inverse form will be:

$$P_i = F(q_1, q_2, ..., q_n), \; i = 1, ..., n. \quad ...(16)$$

All partial derivatives of this equation are negative. If quantity of ith product goes up, its price declines. Similarly, quantity of jth product goes up, its price P_j falls and the price P_i will also decline otherwise the ith firm will lose its market. Now let us concentrate on the duopoly market only. Prices for the two firms will be,

$$P_1 = F_1(q_1, q_2) \text{ and } P_2 = F_2(q_1, q_2), \quad ...(17)$$

From (15) we have,

$$q_1 = f_1(P_1, P_2) \text{ and } q_2 = f_2(P_1, P_2)$$

The expression for the profits of the firms would be

$$\pi_1 = P_1q_1 - C_1(q_1);\ \pi_2 = P_2q_2 - C_2(q_2)$$

or
$$\pi_1 = P_1\, f_1(P_1,\ P_2) - C_1(f_1\ (P_1,\ P_2)) = H_1(P_1,\ P_2) \qquad ...(18)$$

and
$$\pi_2 = P_2\, f_2(P_1,\ P_2) - C_2(f_2\ (P_1,\ P_2)) = H_2(P_1,\ P_2)$$

Equating the partial derivatives of profits with respect to prices to zero, and solving the corresponding equations we find the equilibrium solution for the duopolists. This will be the Cournot solution for the differentiated duopoly market.

Consider an example for this. Given the information $q_1 = 88 - 4P_1 + 2P_2$ and $C_1 = 10q_1$ for Firm 1, and $q_2 = 56 + 2P_1 - 4P_2$ and $C_2 = 8q_2$ for Firm 2, we can write the profit equations for them as:

$$\pi_1 = P_1q_1 - C_1$$

or
$$\pi_1 = P_1q_1 - 10q_1 = q_1(P_1 - 10)$$

or
$$\pi_1 = (88 - 4P_1 + 2P_2)\ (P_1 - 10)$$

or
$$\pi_1 = -\ 4\,P_1^2 + 128P_1 + 2P_1P_2 - 20P_2 - 880,$$

and
$$\pi_2 = P_2q_2 - C_2 = P_2q_2 - 8q_2 = q_2(P_2 - 8)$$

or
$$\pi_2 = (56 + 2P_1 - 4P_2)\ (P_2 - 8)$$

or
$$\pi_2 = -\ 4\,P_2^2 + 88P_2 + 2P_1P_2 - 16P_1 - 448$$

Now, for maximum profits we have

$$\partial\pi_1/\partial P_1 = -\ 8P_1 + 128 + 2P_2 = 0$$

$$\therefore \quad P_1 = 16 + 0.25P_2 \qquad ...(i)$$

$$\partial\pi_2/\partial P_2 = -\ 8P_2 + 88 + 2P_1 = 0$$

$$\therefore \quad P_2 = 11 + 0.25P_1 \qquad ...(ii)$$

(*i*) and (*ii*) are price-reaction function for Firm 1 and Firm 2 respectively. Solving them we have,

$$P_1 = \text{Rs. } 20 \qquad P_2 = \text{Rs. } 16 \qquad \pi_1 = \text{Rs. } 400$$

$$q_1 = 40 \text{ units}, \quad q_2 = 32 \text{ units} \qquad \pi_2 = \text{Rs. } 256.$$

(vii) The Market Share Model

In this model, firms are assumed to maintain their market shares in the industry. This strategy is quite relevant from the point of view of long-run advantages to the firms. Let us take the two duopolist firms into account and define the market share of one of them, say Firm 2 as:

$$\frac{q_2}{q_1 + q_2} = K \qquad ...(18a)$$

where K is a fixed proportion. This gives the relationship between the outputs of the two firms as

$$q_2 = (K\ q_1)/(1 - K) \qquad ...(19)$$

If q_1 changes, Firm 2 makes appropriate changes in its output to make its market share intact. This means Firm 1 is treated as a leader by Firm 2 in determining its own output. It implies that $dq_1/dq_2 = 0$. Firm 1 in maximising its profits, keeps in mind the strategy of Firm 2 of maintaining its market share. Its profit function would be $\pi_1(q_1,\ q_2) = \pi_1\left(q_1, \frac{Kq_1}{1-K}\right)$ which can be maximised. The conjectural variation for the Firm would be $dq_2/dq_1 = K/(1 - K)$.

The market share model gives stable equilibrium provided the sum of market shares of firms is unity.

Consider the market price given as:

$$P = 200 - q_1 - q_2.$$

This is uniform for both the firms.

The cost curves for the two firms are

$$C_1 = 10q_1 \text{ and } C_2 = q_2^2.$$

The profit function for Firm 1 would be,

$$\pi_1 = q_1(200 - q_1 - q_2) - 10q_1$$

Let $K = 0.5$, therefore, $q_2 = \frac{0.5}{1-0.5} q_1$ or $q_2 = q_1$

Substituting $q_2 = q_1$ in the profit equation for Firm 1

$$\pi_1 = q_1(200 - q_1 - q_1) - 10q_1$$

or $$\pi_1 = 190q_1 - 2q_1^2$$

$$d\pi_1/dq_1 = 190 - 4q_1 = 0$$

$$d^2\pi_1/dq_1^2 = -4 < 0$$

Solution is:

$q_1 = 47.5$, $\pi_1 = 4512.5$

$q_2 = 47.5$, $\pi_2 = 2731.4$

$P = 105.$

(viii) The Kinked Demand Curve Model[7]

This model was developed by Paul Sweezy as an attempt to explain the phenomenon of price rigidity in oligopolistic industries. To develop the model, the author used the two demand-curves concepts as used to explain the equilibrium of a firm under monopolistic competition. Let us consider these curves once again for an oligopolist firm as shown in Fig. 10.5. *dd* is the anticipated demand curve for a representative oligopolistic firm and *DD* is the market share or proportional demand curve. As under monopolistic competition, let us consider the initial equilibrium for the firm under oligopoly at a point *K* where the two demand curves intersect. Suppose the oligopoly firm for which we have shown the demand curves, because of some reason, decides to increase its price from P_o level. It is free to do so, the other firms in the market need not follow it. It implies that the firm operates in the increasing price situation on the *Kd* segment of its anticipated demand curve. Now,

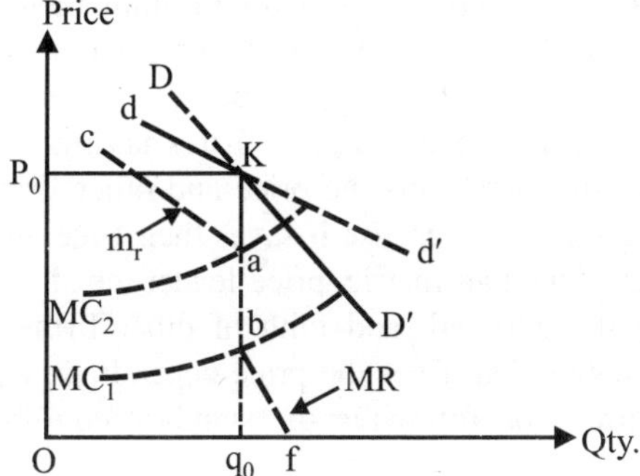

Fig. 10.5 Kinked Demand Curve Equilibrium for a Firm under Oligopoly

7. (*a*) Paul Sweezy: "Demand Under Conditions of Oligopoly," *Journal of Political Economy,* Vol. 47, 1939, pp. 568-73.
(*b*) R.L. Hall and C.J. Hitch (1939); *Price Theory and Business Behaviour*; Oxford Economic Papers, Vol. 2, pp. 12-45.
(*c*) G.J. Stigler, "The Kinky Oligopoly Demand Curve and Rigid Prices", *Journal of Political Economy*, Vol. 55, 1947.

suppose the firm lowers its price from P_o in order to increase its sales, the other firms in the market would quickly match the price reduction in order to maintain their market shares. The movement in this case will be along the *KD′* segment of the proportional demand curve and not along the *Kd′* segment of the anticipated demand curve for the representative firm. Thus, under oligopoly the effective demand curve would be *dKD′* which is not a straight line but a combination of two such lines (*dK* and *D′K*) meeting at the point *K*, *i.e.*, the demand curve *dKD′* is having a kink at the point *K* which was originally the equilibrium point for the firm.

The marginal revenue curve for the effective oligopoly demand curve *dKD′* is given by *cabf* curve. It is having two segments: one *mr* line associated with *dK* part of the demand curve and the other *MR* associated with *KD′* part of the demand curve. Thus, the entire marginal revenue curve is *c a b f*. It is having a vertical portion *a b*. As long as the marginal cost curve, such as MC_1 or MC_2, intersects, the marginal revenue curve in this region, the price and quantity, *i.e.*, the equilibrium position would not change. It means, if marginal cost changes from MC_1 to MC_2 there is no change in the equilibrium price and quantity of the firm. This shows that at least for this range of a change in the marginal cost the equilibrium price in oligopoly will be unchanged. The phenomenon of price stickiness under oligopoly is, thus, being explained by the discontinuity of the marginal revenue curve for the firm.

The kinked demand curve model explains an important feature of price rigidity in oligopoly. Stigler, however, questioned the validity of this model itself. In his study of seven oligopolistic industries, he did not find any support for the kinked demand curve. According to him, "There is little historical basis for a firm to believe that price increase will not be matched by rivals and the price decrease will be matched."[8]

A major limitation of the model is that it is not able to explain how original equilibrium, such as (P_o, q_o), has been established in the market. Like other models of duopoly and oligopoly, this particular model is not explaining the behaviour of oligopolistic markets adequately. Therefore, we cannot call it as a general model of oligopoly markets.

(ix) Price Leadership Models

By 'price leadership' we mean one firm in the market assuming the responsibility of fixing the price and others just accepting it for their products. Such a practice is quite prevalent under oligopolistic markets such as steel, automobiles, agricultural implements, tyres, and a number of other industries. Three types of price leadership arrangements are popular in practice: (*a*) barometric-firm price leadership; (*b*) low-cost firm price leadership; and (*c*) dominant-firm price leadership.

In the case of barometric price leadership, a firm, having a proven record of successful business operations and pricing strategies, sets the price and other firms accept the leadership of the firm in pricing decision-making for them because it saves their time and cost and reduces the friction and uncertainty in the market. The barometric price-leader need not be the largest firm in the industry. Rather, it must have the goodwill and faith of other firms apart from its own record of success in pricing policies. How this firm fixes the price depends on its own objective, such as profit maximisation or revenue maximisation following the standard equilibrium analysis in terms of the demand and the cost curves.

The low-cost firm price-leadership emerges in a situation under oligopoly when cost conditions across the firms are different. A firm may have a comparative cost advantage and thus a lower profit maximising price as compared to other firms. In this situation, other firms accept the price charged

8. G.J. Stigler, *Ibid.*

by the low-cost firm. In doing so, they will not get the optimum profits. Let us explain the low-cost firm price-leadership with the help of a diagram. Let us consider a homogeneous commodity produced by a few oligopolist firms. This implies that the demand curves for the firms are identical. In Fig. 10.6, dd' is the line showing the demand for each of the oligopolist firms. The associated marginal revenue curve is shown by MR. AC_1 and AC_2 are average cost curves for Firm 1 and Firm 2

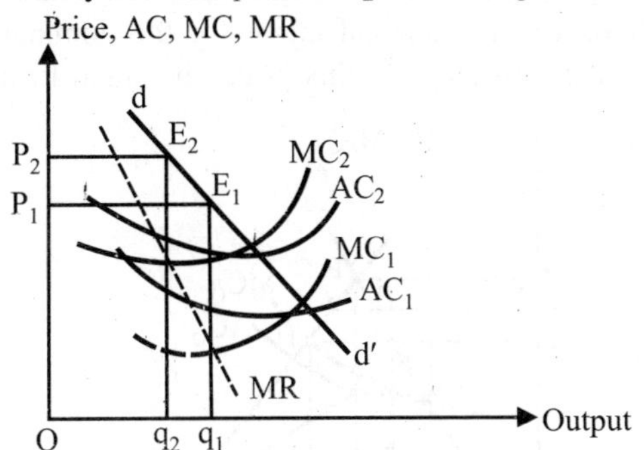

Fig. 10.6 Low-cost Firm Price Leadership Model

respectively and MC_1 and MC_2 the associated marginal cost curves for them. We are taking duopoly case for consideration in this figure which can be easily extended for oligopoly by drawing more AC_s and MC_s. The optimum profit situation for Firm 1 is given by P_1 and q_1 price-quantity combination based on the equality of $MC_1 = MR$ and similarly for Firm 2 it is P_2 and q_2 combination. Firm 1 is the low-cost firm. It is the price leader if P_1 is the price accepted by Firm 2 for its output. Thus, under low-cost firm price leadership P_1 is the equilibrium price for other firms also which are having higher cost of production than the low-cost firm.

The process of price fixation through low-cost price leadership seems to be quite simple but it has several ramifications depending upon the total size of market, number of firms in the market, market shares of firms and product differentiation, apart from cost differences. For a duopoly market when both the firms are of equal size, the low-cost price leadership model fits well. But if the market is oligopolistic and the low-cost firm is relatively small as compared with some other large firms, the model may not be applicable.

The third type of price leadership in an oligopolistic industry is provided by a dominating firm after which it is known as dominant-firm price-leadership model.[9] The setting for this type of model is that the industry has a large firm and others too small as compared to that. The large firm being dominant in the industry fixes the price and allows small firms to sell their output at that price. Small firms are thus price-takers and so they behave like firms under perfect competition. Each one of them supplies that level of output for which price equals marginal cost, and the marginal cost curve intersecting the price line from below. This is what we call as equilibrium conditions for profit maximisation under perfect competition. The marginal cost curve for each firm above the minima of the average cost curve defines the supply curve for such a firm. Their aggregate supply will be the sum of supplies by the individual firms. In Fig. 10.7 this is shown by the line SS. Total market demand for the industry output is shown by DD^1 line. The dominant firm knows the total market supply curve of the small firms which it uses in conjunction with the market demand to derive the demand curve for its own output. The demand curve for the dominating firm is shown in the figure

9. Fritz Machlup, *The Economics of Sellers Competition*, 1952, pp. 496-498.

by the line P_1d. It shows the total amount of the output that will be purchased at each price in excess of what the small firms offer for sales. To derive this curve let us consider the intersection point E of the supply curve of the small firms (SS') and the market demand curve DD'. This gives P_1 and q_1 as price and quantity combination for the industry. That is, at P_1 price the small firms are willing to supply q_1 which is equal to the amount demanded. The additional amount demanded from the dominant firm is zero. It means the demand curve for the dominant firm starts from P_1 point on the vertical axis. Now, consider price P_2. At this price, the small firms are willing to supply only

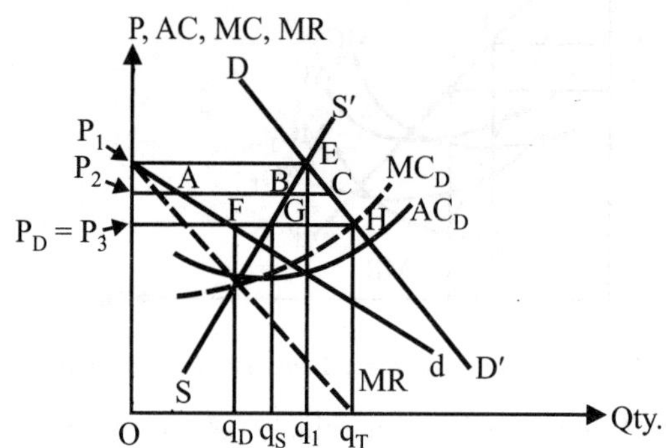

Fig. 10.7 Dominant Firm Price Leadership Model

P_2B quantity while the market demand is P_2C. It means the excess quantity over the willingness of small firms to supply will be met by the dominating firm. This is BC which is equivalent to P_2A. Similarly, at P_3 price, the excess demand for the output shown by GH will be met by the dominating firm. Taking GH equal to P_3F we get another point for constructing the demand curve for the dominant firm. By joining P_1AF we get the line showing the demand curve for the dominant firm. The line designated by MR is the associated marginal revenue curve for the firm. AC_D and MC_D are the average and marginal cost curves for the dominating firm. It is presumed that the dominating firm is a profit maximiser. It sets the price of its product on the basis of the equality of its marginal revenue and marginal cost. Corresponding to this, P_3 is the price and q_D is the equilibrium quantity for the dominant firm. Total market demand at P_3 price is q_T, so the difference $q_T - q_D = q_s$ will be supplied by the small firms according to their supply curve, $q_s = P_3G$.. Small firms, thus, take P_3 as price for their output and sell q_s quantity of output in the market.

We have examined the case of one dominant firm and several small firms in the industry. If there are two equally dominating firms, what will be the situation of pricing? Nothing can be said with confidence in this case. Both the firms may collude together to fix the price or react in a different way as several duopoly models suggest.

(x) The Collusion Model

As we know, firms under oligopoly are independent in decision-making. However, their actions are not unnoticed by rivals and, in this sense, they are interdependent. In this situation, best interest of firms can be served through mutual cooperation rather than competition. Cooperation in the market by the competing firms is called collusion. There is no unique way for collusion. Sellers might form professional or trade associations. Such organisations set norms for the market behaviour of their members. The price is set jointly through mutual agreement of members and several other related business decisions are made with the concurrence of members of associations. Although all such associations will be voluntary in nature yet they are powerful devices for reducing market competition and strengthening mutual cooperation among their members.

The most effective form of collusion, as seen in practice, is that of a cartel. A cartel is defined as a group of sellers, *i.e.*, producers, who agree upon certain rules concerning the price and/or allocation of market according to some well-defined basis, such as location, size and similar characteristics. For example, OPEC is a cartel of petroleum producing countries. Similar cartels exist in international air transportation business and even in manufacturing and service industries.

Formation of a cartel by firms means creation of a single body to take pricing and output decisions for firms. This body acts like a monopoly in the market. Its objective will be to maximise joint profit of all firms in the industry. The solution of this would be the same as the monopoly equilibrium with multi-plants and single market. The market demand curve would be the *AR* curve for the cartel and the horizontal sum of marginal cost curves of all firms as its *MC* curve. By equating *MR* to *MC* the solution is obtained for the price of the commodity, and output levels for firms.

A necessary condition of profit maximisation under cartel arrangement is that the marginal cost of all firms, according to their relative share of market, must be equal, otherwise the cartel could increase its profit by reducing the production of high marginal cost firms and, at the same time, increasing the production of low marginal cost firms by the same amount. This may create a rift among members of the cartel endangering its very existence.

Further, a cartel would be feasible when firms get more profit by joining it rather than acting independently or there might be some other threat for survival if firms do not join the cartel.

Consider a numerical example for a profit maximising cartel. The inverse of the market demand curve for a homogeneous product is given as $P = 200 - (q_1 + q_2)$ where q_1 and q_2 are the output levels of two firms in the market. Let the cost curve for Firm 1 be given as $C_1 = 10q_1$ and for Firm 2 it is $C_2 = q_2^2$. With this information, the total profit for the two firms can be expressed as:

$$\pi_1 = q_1(200 - q_1 - q_2) - 10q_1 = 190q_1 - q_1^2 - q_1q_2$$

$$\pi_2 = q_2(200 - q_1 - q_2) - q_2^2 = 200q_2 - 2q_2^2 - q_1q_2$$

For the Cournot solution of this problem, we get

$$d\pi_1/dq_1 = 190 - 2q_1 - q_2 = 0 \text{ when } q_2 \text{ is constant.}$$

and

$$d\pi_2/dq_2 = 200 - 4q_2 - q_1 = 0 \text{ when } q_1 \text{ is constant.}$$

Solving these two reaction functions we get:

$$q_1 = 80 \text{ units, } q_2 = 30 \text{ units, } P = \text{Rs. } 90, \ \pi_1 = \text{Rs. } 6400;$$

and

$$\pi_2 = \text{Rs. } 1800; \ \pi_1 + \pi_2 = \text{Rs. } 8200.$$

Now, suppose the two firms collude, their joint profit function would be:

$$\pi = \pi_1 + \pi_2 = 190q_1 + 200q_2 - q_1^2 - 2q_2^2 - 2q_1q_2$$

For maximum joint profit we have

$$\partial \pi_1/\partial q_1 = 190 - 2q_1 - 2q_2 = 0$$

$$\partial \pi_2/\partial q_2 = 200 - 4q_2 - 2q_1 = 0$$

Solving these we get

$$q_1 = 90 \text{ units; } q_2 = 5 \text{ units; } P = \text{Rs. } 105;$$

$$\pi_1 = \text{Rs. } 8550; \ \pi_2 = \text{Rs. } 500; \text{ and } \pi = \pi_1 + \pi_2 = \text{Rs. } 9050.$$

On comparing the two solutions, we find that

(*i*) there is a decrease in total output and hence an increase in price in collusion;

(*ii*) Collusion provides higher profits,

(*iii*) Firm 1, which has lower marginal cost, increases its output, and the output of the second firm decreases under collusion.

(*iv*) Profit of Firm 1 increases while there is a decline in the profit of Firm 2 by Rs. 1300. Firm 2 has to be paid at least Rs. 1300 in order to induce it to join the collusion. This payment will be made by Firm 2 who will be still getting higher profit after compensating the loss of profit of Firm 2 by joining the collusion.

10.3 NON-PRICE COMPETITION IN OLIGOPOLISTIC MARKETS

As we have mentioned under the kinked demand curve model, there is a general tendency of price stickiness under oligopoly. Firms maintain their prices in spite of rise in the marginal cost to some extent. As in the case of monopolistic competition, firms under oligopoly will be unable to compete with themselves on the basis of price changes because of their interdependency nature. The alternative to this, particularly under differentiated oligopoly, is the non-price competition. There is no unique way for non-price competition. It may be adopted in different forms. The most important one is advertisement for our products. Advertising is now an established practice in business circles and huge amount of money is being spent on this type of non-price competition.

The other type of non-price competition is to introduce quality differentiation for the product. It may be bonafide or spurious. Sometime, price differentials for the same product in different markets may be used as indicators of quality differentiation but, by and large, firms make changes in the quality of their products by changing the physical attributes of products including design differences. Introduction of new and improved varieties of products, new methods of production and changes in the organisational structure of the firm, etc., are some ways on the basis of which firms do compete under oligopolistic markets. Oligopolistic industries are branded as 'concentrated industries'. Such industries put several barriers to entry for the potential firms and thus keep them away from the market. The existing few firms in such industries maintain their monopoly status through non-price competition which includes, apart from the elements mentioned above, the unfair practices in the market.

10.4 GAME THEORY AND ITS APPLICATIONS TO OLIGOPOLY

An important contribution in the development of methods for economic analysis has been made by Von Neumann and Oscar Morgenstern which is known as the game theory.[10] This theory has been applied to the analysis of market situations in which the outcome depends upon the actions of participants with conflicting interests, such as duopoly, bilateral monopoly and oligopoly. In this section, we will go through the elementary exposition of the game theory and see how it can be applied to the equilibrium analysis of oligopolistic markets.

A 'game' is any situation in which two or more persons compete. The 'game' is played through a sequence of 'moves' as in chess or it may consist of a single move on the part of its players. A specific sequence of successive moves is called 'strategy'. The simplest type of game is a single move game in which 'move' and 'strategy' have similar meaning. For example, reducing price or

10. J. Von Neumann and O. Morgestern, *The Theory of Games and Economic Behaviour*, Princeton University Press, 1949.

increasing advertisement expenditure may be alternative strategies for a duopoly firm to increase its market share.

Games may be classified either on the basis of the number of participants, such as one person, two person and n person games, or on the basis of the net outcome of the game, such as zero-sum and non-zero-sum games. A zero-sum game is that one in which the algebraic sum of outcomes for the participants is zero, say the gain of profit to one firm plus the loss of profit to the other equals zero. If the algebraic sum of outcomes of the game is not zero, it is non-zero-sum game. Both these criterion of classifying games can be combined together, such as one person zero-sum game, two persons zero-sum games or n persons zero-sum or n persons non-zero-sum games. The simplest meaningful case for study is the two person zero-sum game which is applicable to a duopoly market. We will use this type of game for illustration in this section.

To start with the formal structure of the game theory model, let us make some crucial assumptions: (1) Each participant has a finite number of strategies in a game. It implies that there is no continuous variation of the action variable defining the strategies. (2) The outcome of the game in the context of a duopoly study is shown by the profit which is determined by the relevant cost and demand relations, once each of the firms (*i.e.*, participants) has selected a strategy.

For a two person zero-sum game, let us name the two participants as Firm 1 and Firm 2. Firm 1 has m strategies while Firm 2 has n strategies. The possible outcomes of all such strategies in combination are expressed by a_{ij} $(i = 1,\dots m;\ j = 1,\dots n)$ as shown below:

Firm 2's Strategies

Firm 1's Strategies	1	2	3	..	n
1	a_{11}	a_{12}	a_{13}	..	a_{1n}
2	a_{21}	a_{22}	a_{23}	..	a_{2n}
3	a_{31}	a_{32}	a_{33}	..	a_{3n}
m	: a_{m1}	: a_{m2}	: a_{m3}	:· ..	a_{mn}

a_{ij} shows Firm 1's profit or gain when it employs its *ith* strategy and Firm 2 employs its *j*th strategy. Since the 'sum' of the game is 'zero', the profit or gain of the second Firm would be $-\ a_{ij}$. The matrix of a_{ij}, that is $(a_{ij})_{m \times n}$, is called 'Pay-off Matrix'. The elements of this matrix are to be carefully interpreted. Suppose some of the a_{ij}'s are negative which means First firm's gain is negative while the gain of the second firm is positive. For all strategies the pay-off matrix is assumed to be known to firms.

Let us consider some numbers as an example for the pay-off matrix. The two firms have three common strategies S_1 – 'Do Nothing', S_2 – 'Reduction in Price' and S_3 – 'Advertisement'. The gain or loss of, say profit, when they play with different combinations of these strategies is given as:

Firm 3's Strategies

Firm 1's Strategies	S_1	S_2	S_3	Row Minimum
S_1	0	– 10	– 8	–10
S_2	10	6	5	5
S_3	9	5	2	2
Column Maximum	10	6	5	

Each number in this matrix represents gain or loss to firms in appropriate unit. Positive numbers indicate gain to Firm 1 and equivalent amount of loss to Firm 2 while negative numbers show gain from Firm 1 to Firm 2. The best strategy for Firm 1 is S_2, when it gets 10 units of gain, Firm 2 does nothing. However, Firm 2 cannot afford this. It also moves with S_2 and gains 10 units from Firm 1. Which strategy is best for each of these firms and how they reach equilibrium situation if there is any possibility for this? As mentioned earlier, both the firms are aware of the pay-off matrix. While playing the game, the firms adopt a cautious approach by assuming the worst and act accordingly. If Firm 1 employs S_1 strategy, it assumes that Firm 2 will employ S_2 strategy and thus reduce its gain to a minimum level of –10 units. For S_2 strategy, Firm 1 assumes that Firm 2 adopts S_3 strategy since that gives minimum gain of 5 units to it. Similarly, for S_3 strategy of Firm 1, Firm 2 will have S_3 strategy where gain is minimum of 2 units. Thus, Firm 1 has identified moves of Firm 2 on the basis of the minimum pay-off value for its own strategies. The final choice of the strategy by Firm 1 is postulated to be that one which maximises the minimum pay-offs. That is, the firm selects the strategy i for which $\min_j$, a_{ij} is maximum. In the pay-off matrix shown above, this means maximum value of the row minimum which is 5. So, Firm 1 selects S_2 strategy. This is the principle of $\underset{i}{\text{mix}}\ \underset{j}{\text{min}}\ a_{ij}$ for selecting the strategy by Firm 1.

Now, as we have explained above, Firm 1's gain is the loss of Firm 2. Firm 2 would like to hold down Firm 1's gain as much as possible. This firm also tries to guard itself against the worst. The worst situation for Firm 2 is that one when its loss or Firm 1's gain is quite large. Now, consider Firm 2's S_1 strategy. The worst situation for it is when firm 1 moves with S_2 strategy. The quantum of pay-off to Firm 1 is maximum in this case. If Firm 2 adopts S_2 strategy, its worst situation (*i.e.*, maximum loss to it) is shown again by S_2 strategy of Firm 1. Similarly, S_2 strategy of Firm 1 introduces worst situation for Firm 2 when it adopts S_3 strategy. Firm 2 is aware of all such possibilities. What will be the best strategy for Firm 2? This is that one which gives minimum loss to it, *i.e.*, the firm selects the strategy on the basis of minimum or maximum pay-offs accruing to the rival firm. This implies minimum value for column maximum. The pay off matrix shown above indicates S_3 is the best strategy for Firm 2. This firm selects the strategy j (j = 3) that minimise the column maximum. It is, thus, following $\min_j \max_i a_{ij}$ approach to select its best strategy.

If decisions of both the firms are consistent and they reach the equilibrium situation, the conditions

$$\max_i \min_j (a_{ij}) = \min_j \max_i (a_{ij}) \quad ...(20)$$

must be satisfied. For two-person-zero-sum game this is known as 'max-min' or 'min-max' theorem. The min-max criterion is called as 'value of the game'. It is zero here. This approach is also called as 'Saddle Point Solution'.

There might be situations when participants playing the game with one strategy at a time, as those indicated above, may not attain equilibrium, *i.e.*,

$$\max_i \min_j (a_{ij}) \neq \min_j \max_i (a_{ij}) \quad ...(21)$$

If this is so, the equilibrium of the game or saddle point solution for two person-zero-sum games is possible with mixed strategies. The concept of mixed strategies is nothing but an assignment of probabilities to the feasible pure strategies in such a manner that the sum of probabilities is unity for each participant. Say, for m strategies of Firm 1 the P_i is the probability assigned to ith strategy, $0 \leq P_i \leq 1$ and $\sum_{i=1}^{m} P_i = 1$. Similarly, to each of the n strategies of Firm 2, q_j is the probability assigned to jth strategy, $0 \leq q_j \leq 1$ and $\sum_{j=1}^{m} q_j = 1$. Keeping in mind the definition of mixed strategy, we should note that it does not mean a mixture of different strategies in each play of the game. The participants still move with one strategy at a time as before, but the difference is that in mixed strategy move every single strategy is given a chance according to its assigned probability. Elements of the pay-off matrix are now probabilistic in nature. The objective of each participant of the game will no longer be simple maximisation or minimisation of a particular value. It will be rather the expected value of the game in which they will be interested. The crucial aspect of mixed strategies is to select that set of probabilities that will either maximise the expected gain or minimise the expected loss in terms of mathematical expectation for the participants.

The expected gain, say for Firm 1, if Firm 2 employs its jth strategy can be expressed as

$$\sum_{i}^{m} a_{ij} P_i \quad ...(22)$$

The value of this mathematical expectation depends on the probabilities P_i selected by Firm 1 as well as the strategy selected by Firm 2. But Firm 1 has control only over the selection of its probabilities P_i. The criterion for selection of optimal P_i by Firm 1 would be:

$$\sum_{i=1}^{m} a_{ij} P_i \geq V, \; j = 1, 2, ..., n. \quad ...(23)$$

where V is the value of the game. Since Firm 1 gains, it means Firm 2 loses. The expected loss for Firm 2, when Firm 1 employs its ith strategy, would be as,

$$\sum_{j}^{n} a_{ij}\, q_j \qquad \text{...(24)}$$

Firm 2 tries to hold down Firm 1's gain as much as possible. It will select its probabilities q_j in such a way that minimise (24). For optimal selection of $q_j s$ Firm 2 would meet the condition:

$$\sum_{j}^{n} a_{ij}\, q_j \leq V,\ i = 1, 2, ..., m. \qquad \text{...(25)}$$

It means that Firm 2's expected loss cannot be larger than V whatever pure strategy Firm 1 employs.

Von Neumann and Morgenstern have shown that there always exists a set of probabilities P_i for Firm 1 and a set of probabilities q_j for Firm 2 so that both expressions (23) and (25) are satisfied and V is unique.

This result can be verified as follows:

The expected gain E_1 for the Firm 1 given the probabilities P_i and q_j can be derived from (23) as:

$$E_1 = \sum_{j=1}^{n} q_j \left(\sum_{i=1}^{m} a_{ij}\, P_i\right) \geq \sum_{j=1}^{n} q_j\, V$$

or

$$E_1 = \sum_{j=1}^{n} \sum_{i=1}^{m} a_{ij}\, P_i q_j \geq V \qquad \text{...(26)}$$

Since $\sum_{j}^{n} q_j\, V = V \sum_{j}^{n} q_j = V$ because $\sum_{j}^{n} q_j = 1.$

Similarly, the expected gain (*i.e.*, loss in this case) of Firm 2 can be derived from (25) as:

$$E_2 = \sum_{i=1}^{n} P_i \left(\sum_{j=1}^{n} a_{ij}\, q_j\right) \leq \sum_{i=1}^{m} P_i\, V$$

or

$$E_2 = \sum_{j=1}^{n} \sum_{i=1}^{m} a_{ij}\, P_i q_j \leq V \quad \text{Since} \sum_{i=1}^{m} P_i = 1 \qquad \text{...(27)}$$

Comparing (26) and (27) we have,

$$V \leq E_1 = E_2 \leq V \qquad \text{...(28)}$$

Because the expected gain of Firm 1 is equal to the expected loss of Firm 2 as the zero-sum implies. This proves that.

$$E_1 = E_2 = V \qquad \text{...(29)}$$

This shows the saddle point equilibrium for participants of the game under mixed strategies for two-person-zero-sum games.

Conceptually, it is easy to show the uniqueness of the saddle point equilibrium under mixed strategies. In practice, it is quite difficult to compute the set of probabilities both $P_{i's}$ and $q_{j's}$ when m and n are quite large. With known pay-off matrix, the technique of linear programming is used to find the optimal sets of probabilities for participants in the game.[11]

---

11. For further details regarding the technique of game theory, and methods of solution see Neumann and Morgenstern (1949) *opcit.*, and W.J. Baumol, *Economic Theory and Operations Analysis,* Prentice-Hall of India, 2nd Ed. 1966, Chapter 23, pp. 529-549.

The theory of games is an important contribution in mathematical economics. It helps to understand the behaviour of not only the oligopolistic markets but rivalry in general, whether it is business or anything else. The theory is, however, under severe criticism on several grounds by economists. The basis for acting in the game, as the theory postulates, is that a player always must guard against the worst. It is a pessimistic approach which cannot be realistic either in business or in every day life decisions where adventurous or risk taking spirit would be conducive. The game theory may be quite useful in developing military strategy on a large scale but it is hardly applicable to day-to-day decisions in business and everyday life.

The game theory may not be easily applicable to the complicated market situations. If every participant of the game moves with single strategy (pure or mixed) at a time they may get the saddle point equilibrium. But suppose the situation is complicated as at a time a participant may play with multiple strategies like reduction in price, advertisement, change in product and so on, in order to increase its market share; how the game theory will tackle such situations is not clear. Further, it is assumed that the pay-off matrix is known to players, they have precise idea of one another's moves but in practice it is not possible to know in advance the counter-moves of rivals. Considering all such possibilities we may say that the game theory has not yet been developed fully to analyse the complicated market situations. The whole approach of the game theory is static in nature. It is not permitting even comparative static analysis. May be we have to wait for some more time till this theory develops further.

10.5 OPERATIONAL PRICING MODELS

The approach to price determination discussed so far for various types of markets is essentially a theoretical one. In this approach, we assume that the price makers know their demand and cost functions and other relevant information such as reaction functions, etc., for price fixation. In most of the cases, we have used the profit maximising conditions, such as price = marginal cost or marginal revenue = marginal cost and thus determined the price and quantity combination for firms. This is what we call marginal cost pricing technique. Theoretically, it is quite logical but when the question of its adoption in practice arises, we find several difficulties with it. For example, the marginal cost-pricing system is based on the pursuance of a single objective like profit or sales maximisation. If a firm pursues multiple objectives at a time, this system of pricing is inapplicable. If the firm produces multiproducts and there are common costs, the application of marginal cost pricing is quite difficult. Further, this system of pricing does not take into account the internal organisational aspects of price fixation. There are several prices, such as wholesale price, retail price, intermediate price, final price, etc., which are never heard in the marginal cost pricing systems. The price which is considered in this system is received by the producer and paid by consumers. In practice, we have intermediate stages in sales of products for which different prices are fixed. The theoretical pricing system assumes that demand and cost curves are known to firms but a large number of businessmen may not be knowing such curves and, therefore, the question of applying marginal cost-pricing technique by such firms does not arise.

Considering all such limitations of the theoretical pricing models, business circles have devised much simpler and operational methods of price fixation. The technique of mark-up pricing is one of them. This technique is also called as 'cost plus' or 'full-cost' pricing technique.

The mark-up pricing procedure is a cost oriented technique. The approach in this procedure is to estimate the average cost of production for a normal, *i.e.*, chosen level of output and then add to it a profit margin to arrive at the selling price. The average cost of production may be the actual one in the current or most recent past period, or one may take the estimated average cost for the required level of capacity utilisation. There are two variations of this method, in one as mentioned just now, we take average cost of production and then add the fixed proportion of that as mark-up to cover the profit margin, and the second one is to estimate or to take only the average variable cost and then add the fixed proportion of this for profit-margin and average fixed cost. The mark-up in the second case will be higher than that of the first case.

The profit-margin or mark-up over the average cost or average variable cost of the product may be fixed by a rule of thumb what firms individually are considered to be a 'fair' or 'just' percentage for this. It may be rigid or flexible depending upon factors, such as: (*a*) the nature of product; (*b*) the objective of the firm; (*c*) the market situation; (*d*) the age of the product; (*e*) the scope for price discrimination, and (*f*) the governments controls over prices, output, etc.

Most of these points are self-explanatory. Yet, we would like to mention briefly that mark-up may be quite high under monopoly and low under competition and even zero as in the case of perfect competition in the long-run. A new product may have low mark-up as compared to an established one. Profit maximisation captures higher mark-up than the revenue maximisation level of output and similarly we can interpret other factors influencing the mark-up.

Although marginal revenue and marginal costs are not considered while fixing the mark-up but a firm does consider the demand for the product and then selects the level of output to be produced by taking into account the other relevant factors also. The firm will be considering the above mentioned factors also while fixing the mark-up for pricing. Mark-up fixation is not an arbitrary choice. While fixing it, the firm keeps in mind its objective and, in an operational way acts for its achievement. We may show that mark-up pricing and theoretical marginal cost pricing are quite consistent with each other although in the case of mark-up pricing firms do take into account several other factors to achieve their goals.

We know, the general equilibrium condition for profit maximisation is

$$MR = MC.$$

The expression for *MR*, as we have derived earlier, is:

$$MR = P\left(1 + \frac{1}{e_d}\right),$$

where e_d = price-elasticity of demand. Substituting it in the $MR = MC$ equation, we get

$$P\left(1 + \frac{1}{e_d}\right) = MC.$$

or
$$P = MC\left(\frac{e_d}{e_d + 1}\right) \qquad \text{...(30)}$$

If we assume average cost (*AC*) as constant, $AC = MC$. Therefore,

$$P = AC\left(\frac{e_d}{e_d + 1}\right) \qquad \text{...(31)}$$

If we have the magnitude for e_d say, let it be –2, then,

$$P = AC\left(\frac{-2}{-2 + 1}\right) = 2AC. \qquad \text{...(32)}$$

In this case, we have 100 per cent mark-up, which equates *MR* and *MC* under assumption of constant average cost. If the price elasticity is –4, the mark-up would come down to 33.33% ($P = 1.333AC$ or $P = AC + 0.333AC$). From this we can conclude that greater the price elasticity of demand (in absolute terms) lesser will be the mark-up and vice versa (Provided $|e_d| > 1$ and therefore $MR > 0$).

The mark-up can also be expressed as a percentage of price, such as:

$$K = (P - AC)/P. \qquad ...(33)$$

The difference between price and average cost is expressed as a proportion of the price. If $K = 0.25$, it means the difference between price and average cost of the product is 25 per cent of its price. In other words, price is 1.33 (= 1.00/0.75) times of the average cost of production.

Suppose we define the mark-up on the basis of marginal cost rather than average cost, we would have

$$K = (P - MC)/P \qquad ...(34)$$

We know that for profit maximisation $MR = MC$, we write:

$$K = (P - MR)/P = -\frac{1}{e_d} \text{ (as shown earlier)}$$

This result says that the mark-up of a profit-maximising firm varies inversely with the price-elasticity of demand. Firms with highly elastic demand will fix low mark-up. For products showing low price elasticity of demand the mark-up would be higher.

The mark-up pricing procedure, as discussed above, is a cost oriented technique, *i.e.*, cost of production is the base for price fixation whether it is average total cost or average variable cost or marginal cost. In making the cost of production as the base for price fixation the producer makes it sure that he is not selling his product at a loss provided he realises his expected sales. Apart from this, the mark-up pricing producer is quite simple to follow. It takes care of market situations including uncertainties though not through some mathematical functions but by intuition or experience in the business. This technique suits all price makers including oligopolistic firm. The mark-up may be fixed or flexible depending on the market situations. Normally, firms maintain the mark-up level and adjust their prices with changes in cost conditions because of changing input prices and/or increasing utilisation of their production capacities. One may question the theoretical soundness of the mark-up pricing system on the basis of its weaknesses, such as less emphasis on demand side of pricing, inadequate treatment of market competition, arbitrariness in fixing the mark-up and so on, but, by and large, it is a popular operational technique of price fixation in business circles.

There is another variant of mark-up pricing procedure which is called as 'Target Rate of Return Pricing'. The basic procedure for fixing the price of a product is similar to that of full-cost pricing. The only difference between the two approaches is about the setting of the mark-up. The target-rate of return procedure considers the desired rate of return on initial investment made by the firm in setting the mark-up. Consider '*K*' as the investment made by the firm and let π be the target rate of return on this. Total expected profit of the firm would be πK. Now, let 'α' be the mark-up on total cost. So, we have the equality $\alpha(TC) = \pi K$. This means $\alpha = \pi K/TC$. If investment K = ₹ 10 crores, and $\pi = 0.20$, *i.e.*, 20% of *K*, and let *TC* = ₹ 15 crores, $\alpha = (0.20 \times 10)/15 = 0.1333$ or 13.33%. The mark-up showing the profit-margin over the cost for achieving the target rate of return on the investment made by the firm is 13.33%. If the average cost of firm in this case is ₹ 30, the price of product should, therefore, be ₹ 30 + 0.1333 (30) = ₹ 33.99.

This technique is better than fixing the mark-up arbitrarily. It takes into account the short-term as well as long-term interests of the firm in fixing the price.

10.6 CONCLUDING REMARKS

The models developed to explain the behaviour of the oligopolistic markets, including its limiting form duopoly, have been discussed in this chapter. In spite of such a variety of models none of them can be accepted as a standard model which explains the behaviour of oligopolistic markets adequately. The reason for this is that there is no unique way of conceptualising reactions of the rival firms in the oligopolistic market setting. Each model has a different assumption about the rivals' reactions in the market. Because of such a diversity in approach, models differ in solution. Nevertheless, they throw considerable light on the behaviour of the firm and, thus, are quite useful in understanding the theory of oligopoly.

SUGGESTED READINGS

Baumol, W.J., *Economic Theory and Operations Analysis,* New Delhi, Prentice-Hall of India, EEE Edition, 1978, 2002.

Baumol, W.J., *Business Behaviour, Value and Growth;* N.Y. Harcourt, Brace & The World, 1967.

Cohen, R.J. and R.M. Cyert, *Theory of Firm: Resource Allocation in a Market Economy,* Prentice Hall of India, N.D., 1976.

Fellner, W.J., *Competition Among Few: Oligopoly and Similar Market Structures;* A.M. Kelly, 1965.

Fergusion, C.E., *Micro-economic Theory:* R.D. Irwin Ind., 1966.

Friedman, J.W., *Oligopoly Theory:* Cambridge University Press, 1983.

Friedman, J.W., *Oligopoly and the Theory of Games;* North-Holland Pub. Co., 1977.

Henderson, J.M. and R.E. Quandt, *Microeconomic Theory: A Mathematical Approach;* McGraw-Hill, Japan, 1971, 1980.

Neumann, J.V. and Oskar Morgenstern; *Theory of Games and Economic Behaviour*, Princeton University Press, 1953.

REVIEW QUESTIONS

1. It is argued that oligopoly market is more difficult to analyse than monopoly and competitive markets. Explain why it is so? Why are there so many different oligopoly models in microeconomics as compared to other types of markets?
2. Give a brief outline of Cournot, Chamberlin and Edgeworth models of duopoly and highlight the essential differences between them.
3. Describe the Kinked demand curve model of oligopoly and show how this model is able to explain the phenomenon of price rigidity under oligopoly.
4. What do you mean by 'Price leadership'? What are the various models of oligopoly based on price-leadership phenomenon?
5. Define a Cartel and analyse the applicability of Cartel model to study the behaviour of oligopolistic market. Support your answer with some examples of Cartel-based business operations in real life.

6. Discuss the essential feature of game theory and show how it is applicable to study the behaviour of firms under oligopoly.
7. What do you mean by 'mark-up pricing'? How this type of pricing technique is applicable to oligopoly markets? What are the merits and demerits of mark-up pricing procedure and find out whether it is consistent with the traditional marginal cost pricing procedure based on profit maximisation assumption?
8. Describe Stackelberg's duopoly model and identify the situation when it fails to give the equilibrium solution for duopoly.
9. Consider a duopoly with product differentiation in which the demand and cost functions are given as
   $q_1 = 88 - 4P_1 + 2P_2$, $C_1 = 10q_1$, and $q_2 = 56 + 2P_1 - 2P_2$, $C_2 = 8q_2$ for Firm 1 and Firm 2 respectively. Derive the price-reaction functions for the firms on the assumption that each firm maximises its own profit with respect to its own price. Determine the equilibrium values of price, quantity and profit for each firm.
10. The duopoly firms selling slightly differentiated commodities have demand functions as $D_1\ (P_1, P_2) = a - bP_1 + cP_2$ and $D_2\ (P_1, P_2) = \alpha - \beta P_2 + \gamma P_1$ where P_1 and P_2 are the prices of duopolists 1 and 2 respectively, and *a, b, c*, α, β and γ are positive parameters. There is no marginal cost for either of the duopolists.
    (*a*) Find the Bertrand equilibrium *i.e.*, assuming that each duopolist maximises profit subject to the price of the other, calculate the equilibrium prices in terms of parameters).
    (*b*) Find the leadership equilibrium, *i.e.*, suppose that duopolist 1 wishes to maximise his profit subject to the reaction function of duopolist 2.
    (*c*) Find the solution for joint-profit maximisation for duopolisis and compare it with solutions for (*a*) and (*b*).

CHAPTER 11

Theory of Distribution: Factor Pricing Analysis

As mentioned in Chapter 2, one of the basic economic problems faced by every society is 'for whom' to produce. The query 'for whom' to produce connotes the sense of distribution of net product among its claimants. What is the problem of distribution, how the problem of distribution is solved in the economic system, and an idea of the general and specific theories concerning the study of the problem of distribution from the points of view of different factors of production are the major issues which are being discussed in this chapter.

11.1 THE PROBLEM OF DISTRIBUTION

A firm employs various factors of production, such as land, buildings, plant and machinery, labour, including managerial supervision, to convert a set of material inputs into some output. From the sales of the output the firm gets revenue. The total revenue is the value of goods and services produced by the firm which is realized when the output is sold in the market.

Who actually gets this revenue? One may say that it is the firm or the producer. But actually it is not so. If we examine the distributio.n of total revenue among its claimants we will find the answer to the above question. As per accounting practices, total value of output, including work done for others and work in progress and other miscellaneous receipts, is always equal to the total expenditure of the firm plus a residual amount called profits. Total expenditure of the firm constitutes the value of material inputs used in the business plus the expenses on wages and salaries, rent, interest, taxes, etc. If we write TR = Total Revenue (*i.e.*, total value of products plus other incomes), M = total value of material inputs used in production, W = wages and salaries including other monetary benefits to persons employed, R = Rental Payments, I = interest on capital employed, D = depreciation amount, T = taxes, and Π = residual surplus defined as profits, we have the identity:

$$TR = M + W + R + I + D + T + \Pi$$

or $$TR - M = W + R + I + D + T + \Pi \qquad ...(1)$$

The difference between TR and M is called 'Gross Value Added'. Further, if we remove the amount of depreciation (D) from this, it is 'Net Value Added', *i.e.*, Gross Value Added minus Depreciation = Net Valued Added.

$$NVA = \text{Net Value Added} = W + R + I + T + \Pi \qquad ...(2)$$

The Net Value Added is the income generated by production. This has components like wages and salaries, rent, interest and profits. The value of materials consumed in production is not an addition in income or income creation at all. It is merely recovery of whatever has gone in production of the product as raw materials. A person can get income in different forms, say through his earnings as well as in the form of rent from his property and/or through interest earned on his capital. In general, persons employed get their incomes in the form of wages and salaries, landlords in the form of rents, capitalists in the form of interest and entrepreneurs in the form of profits. Taxes will be simply transfers from producers to the government. When we classify value-added or income according to the factor incomes we call it 'functional distribution' or income.

The problem of distribution in microeconomics relates to this aspect. It is not the distribution of output among buyers or total income among families or population. These are other types of distribution problems which we study elsewhere and not in the price theory or microeconomics.

The traditional economic theory states that functional distribution of income is simply a case of price theory. The income of any factor of production (and hence the amount of national income that it is able to command) depends upon the price that is paid to the factor of production and the quantity of that factor used in production:

Factor Income = Factor Price × Factor Quantity ...(3)

To develop a theory of distribution we thus need a theory of factor-prices determination. As in the case of a commodity market under perfect competition, if we know the demand and supply curves for a factor of production, we can find the equilibrium factor price-quantity combination and thus find out the factor income. Consider Fig. 11.1. D_f line shows the demand for a factor and S_f line shows the supply in the traditional price and quantity axes for the factor.

The equilibrium factor price is OP_f and quantity OQ_f. The factor income is therefore $OP_f \times OQ_f$. If the demand for the factor goes up, the factor income also goes up if the supply of the factor is not changed. Effects of changes in the demand and supply on the factor market equilibrium and hence on the factor income can be analyzed analogously as in the case of a commodity. Thus, in a free market economy for both, commodities and factors, the problem of distribution reduces to the demand and supply analysis and thus to the analysis of the market equilibrium for the factors of production. Such analysis is then extended further to cover imperfect factor markets as we do for commodity markets.

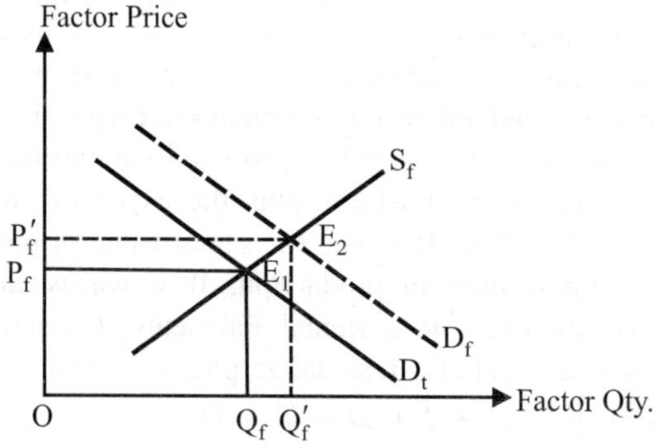

Fig. 11.1 Supply and Demand Interaction of a Factor Market

11.2 THE CONCEPT OF DERIVED DEMAND

The factors of production like land, labour, machines and raw material, etc., are used in production of goods and services for markets. The demand for them depends on the demand for the goods in whose production they are used. In other words, the factors of production including raw materials, have no intrinsic economic value of their own. They contribute to the output of a firm. Because of this function, they or their services acquire economic value since the output for which they are used has a value. That is, the factors of production derive their values from the values of goods and services to whose production they contribute. If the demand for a product increases then the demand for the factors used in its production will also increase. We can say that the demand for a factor of production is the *derived demand* since it is derived from the demand for the product in whose production it is used. For example, there will be demand for school teachers if there is a demand for the school education. As far as the link between the product demand and the demand for factors used in its production is concerned there is no doubt about it, but a deeper question is to examine how this kind of link is established precisely. That is, which is the relevant variable through which the link is established. For this we have to find the determinants of the factor demand. Let us examine this.

We know whenever a firm takes decisions about factor employment, it has to keep in mind its equilibrium position. Normally, we take into account the profit-maximising goal of a producer but it may be something else also such as revenue maximisation. For simplicity, let us consider a simple case of production where a firm is using a single variable input, producing a single product and pursuing the goal of profit maximisation. The variable input is labour and there is a fixed factor with which it cooperates in production of the product. The total cost of production for the firm in this case can be expressed as:

$$C = b + wL, \text{ where } b = \text{Fixed cost; } w = \text{Wage rate.} \qquad ...(4)$$

The total output of the firm is given by the production function

$$q = f(L) \text{ for a given level of the fixed factor} \qquad ...(5)$$

Let us assume that the firm is operating under perfect competition in the product market, *i.e.*, it is a price taker. The product price (P) is therefore exogenously given and constant. The revenue of the firm when it produces q units of output would be

$$R = Pq = P{\cdot}f(L) \qquad ...(6)$$

and profit of the firm would be,

$$\pi = P{\cdot}f(L) - b - w{\cdot}L \qquad ...(7)$$

For maximum profit we have the conditions,

$$d\pi/dL = P{\cdot}f'(L) - w = 0 \qquad ...(8)$$

and

$$d^2\pi/dL^2 = Pf''(L) < 0 \qquad ...(9)$$

$f'(L)$ is defined as marginal product of labour; and $f''(L)$ is the rate of change of marginal product. The equilibrium conditions for profit maximisation expressed by (8) and (9) can also be expressed as

$$d\pi = Pdf(L) - wdL \geq 0 \text{ for } L^* \qquad ...(10)$$

$$d\pi = Pdf(L) - wdL \leq 0 \text{ for } L^* + 1$$

Where L^* is the optimum level of employment. For continuous case, of course, we have,

$$d\pi = P\,df(L) - wdL = 0 \qquad ...(11)$$

Now, coming back to equation (8) we have the equilibrium, condition for factor employment as,

$$P\,f'(L) = w \qquad ...(12)$$

w is the wage rate. It is fixed which means the firm has no control over it. It is exogenously given to it. It implies that the firm operates under perfect competitive market in this example. The left hand side of (12) *i.e.*, $P{\cdot}f'(L)$ is the value of marginal product of labour. The equilibrium condition (8) is simply telling us that the firm employs the variable factor (L) upto a level say L^* at which the value of marginal product (*VMP*) is equal to its price (w).

While discussing the short-run behaviour of production in Chapter 5, we have explicitly shown the relationship between marginal product of a variable input and its quantity. This relationship in a formal terminology is nothing but the law of diminishing marginal product. Initially, the marginal product of the factor increases but eventually it declines with increase in the factor quantity. Since we are multiplying the marginal product of the factor by product price (*P*), which is fixed, the VMP would, therefore, show exactly the same pattern of behaviour as the marginal product when the factor quantity increases. This relationship is shown below in Figure 11.2.

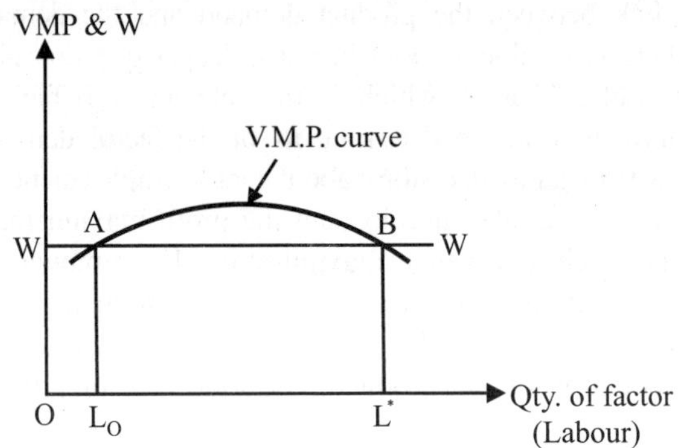

Fig. 11.2 Equilibrium of a Profit Maximising Firm with Single Variable Factor

The firm will not attain equilibrium at point *A* where *VMP* is equal to wage rate (*w*) because the second order condition for profit-maximization is not satisfied. As long as the marginal physical product increases, the firm would have the tendency to employ more and more quantity of the variable input. The equilibrium can only be established at the point where the *VMP* is equal to the factor price and beyond that point there is no possibility of *VMP* being greater to the factor price. *B* is the point in the above figure where these conditions are met. That is, apart from $VMP = w$, the *VMP* curve is downward sloping since marginal product of the factor is downward sloping. The optimal quantity of the factor employment is, therefore, L^* in the above example.

An important implication of the above analysis is that we are getting the demand curve for the variable factor. It is the declining portion of the *VMP* curve. This has conformity with the Stage II of production where a firm gets equilibrium in the short-run. Other stages of production, as we have seen in Chapter 5, are not feasible from the point of view of a rational profit maximising firm. Summarising in brief, we can say that under perfect competition in both products and the factor market, where there is only one variable factor, the downward sloping portion of the value of the marginal product curve is the firm's demand curve for the variable factor.

Figure 11.3 shows the *VMP* and the demand curves for the variable factor *L* separately which are, in fact, identical since *VMP* = wage rate. Each and every point on the *VMP* or the demand curve for labour (*L*) indicates profit maximising factor employment for different exogenously given wage rate.

The *VMP* is a product of the price of a unit of output and the marginal physical product of the variable factor (*L*). If the output price changes, the position of the *VMP* and the factor demand curves will change. They will shift to the right when there is an increase in the output price and to the left when there is a decline in it *i.e.*, in the product price. The quantity demanded of labour thus changes positively with a change in the output price. This is the precise meaning of the derived demand. It is via the product price effect on the quantity of the factor demanded that

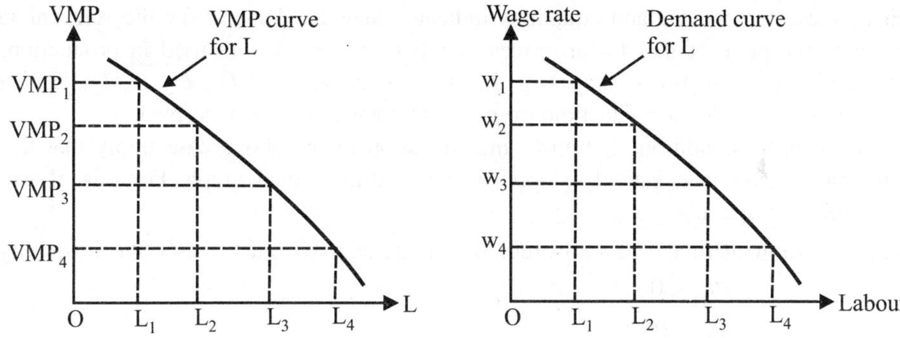

Fig. 11.3 Demand Curve for a Variable Factor

the two demand curves, *i.e.*, product demand curve and the factor demand curve are linked together. The marginal physical product varies inversely with the amount of the variable factor used in production. This gives an explanation of the downward sloping demand curve for the factor.

The marginal physical product curve of a variable factor and hence its *VMP* curve, however, shifts from its position when there is a change in the technology. But, so long as the production technology is fixed we will move along the marginal physical product curve with the changing amount of the factor quantity. The position of the marginal product curve does not change in this case.

Two important demand factors for the variable factor identified in the above analysis are: the product price (*P*), and the technology reflected by the marginal product *(MP)* of the factor. There are some more which we will find in the following analysis of the derivation of a general demand function for a variable input.

We have derived the demand curve for a factor when there is only one variable factor used in production along with some fixed factor(s). Let us now consider a general case in which there are several variable factors used in production of a commodity. The method of derivation of the factor demand functions in this situation is exactly similar as outlined above.

Let the n variable factors be written as $X_1, X_2, ..., X_n$. The production function expressed in terms of these variable factors will be

$$q = f(x_1, x_2, ..., x_n) \quad ...(13)$$

where q = output quantity, $x_1, x_2, ..., x_n$ are the factor quantities for the production period.

The cost equation for the firm would be:

$$C = b + r_1x_1 + r_2x_2 + ... + r_nx_n \quad ...(14)$$

where as usual, b is fixed cost, $r_1, r_2, ..., r_n$ are exogenously given fixed input prices,

We define the profit function for the firm as:

$$\pi = P{\cdot}f(x_1, x_2, ..., x_n) - b - r_1x_1 - r_2x_2 .. - r_nx_n \quad ...(15)$$

By equating the partial derivatives of π with respect to x_i $(i = 1,..., n)$, the first order profit maximizing conditions are:

$$\partial\pi/\partial x_i = Pf_i - r_i = 0, \; i = 1, 2, ..., n \quad ...(16)$$

where P = Product price,$f_i = \partial q/\partial x_i$ is the marginal physical product for ith variable factor. The system of equations in (16) contains n unknowns $x_1, x_2, ..., x_n$ and there are n equations in it. The exogenous variables in this system of equations are P, and r_i $(i = 1, 2, ..., n)$. The solution of the system provides us n factor demand functions as,

$$\begin{aligned} x_1 &= D_1(r_1, r_2, ..., r_n, P) \\ x_2 &= D_2(r_1, r_2, ..., r_n, P) \\ x_n &= D_n(r_1, r_2, ..., r_n, P) \end{aligned} \quad ...(17)$$

Each of these factors demand equations indicates that the demand for the relevant factor (x_i) is a function of the price of that factor, prices of other variable factors used in production, and the product price (P). The functional shapes of the demand curves *i.e.*, D_1, D_2, ..., D_n, depend on the shape and nature of production function from which they have been derived.

The second order conditions for profit maximisation in the above case imply that the demand function for each factor is negatively sloped in a two dimensional graph. For this, if we express,

$$\partial^2\pi/\partial x_i \, \partial x_j = f_{ij}, \; i, j = 1, 2, ..., n \qquad ...(18)$$

the Hessian Determinant of the second order partial derivatives must satisfy the inequality,

$$Pf_{11} < 0$$

$$\begin{vmatrix} Pf_{11} & Pf_{12} \\ Pf_{21} & Pf_{22} \end{vmatrix} > 0$$

$$\begin{vmatrix} Pf_{11} & Pf_{12} & Pf_{13} \\ Pf_{21} & Pf_{22} & Pf_{23} \\ Pf_{31} & Pf_{32} & Pf_{33} \end{vmatrix} < 0$$

and in this way,

$$(-1)^n \begin{vmatrix} Pf_{11} & Pf_{12} & \cdots & Pf_{1n} \\ Pf_{21} & Pf_{22} & \cdots & Pf_{2n} \\ Pf_{n1} & Pf_{n2} & \cdots & Pf_{nn} \end{vmatrix} > 0 \qquad ...(19)$$

Further, by taking the total differentials of the first order conditions under assumption that only price of a factor changes, prices of other factors and product price are unchanged, *i.e.*, $dr_j = dP = 0 \; (i \neq j)$ then

$$dx_j/dr_j \quad < 0 \qquad ...(20)$$

That is, the demand curve for the factor j is negatively sloped. In a simpler way, the downward f_{ij} curve ensures this.

Now, let us come to the interpretation of the demand functions for x_i s as shown by (17). In each of the demand functions for the factors we find $n + 1$ determinant; n factor prices (r_j, $j = 1, n$) and one product price (P). Prices of different factors appearing in the demand functions for each and every factor link them together. A change in the price of one factor leads to changes in the rates of utilisation of that factor as well as other factors. It means that the *VMP* curve will no longer be interpreted as a demand curve for a factor when more than one variable factors are involved in production. Let us explain this phenomenon a bit more. We know when there are several variable factors, some of them may be complementary and some substitutes, apart from some being independent. When there is a decline in the price of one factor, other factor prices being constant, we come across two types of effects associated with the use of that factor as well as the other; one is the substitution effect and the other is the output effect. Reasons for these effects and their interpretation have already been discussed in Chapter 5 under isoquant analysis. We simply reiterate here that the factor whose price changes either will be substituted for the other(s) or will be substituted by others to produce a given level of output, depending on decrease or increase in its price. Further, since the price of the factor has changed, which means some saving of resources, positive or negative depending on decrease or increase in the price which pushes the firm on higher or lower isoquant. This is what we call as the output effect. The factor proportions change when we have these types of effects in operations. Because of changing quantities of factors associated with the change in the price of one factor, the *VMP* curve for the factor as well as for others shift their positions. A shifting *VMP* curve means a shifting equilibrium position of the firm on different curve with different levels of factor prices. The locus of all such equilibrium points will be, in fact, the demand curve for the factor and not a single *VMP* curve, as it was in the earlier case. Let us explain this with the help of a diagram.

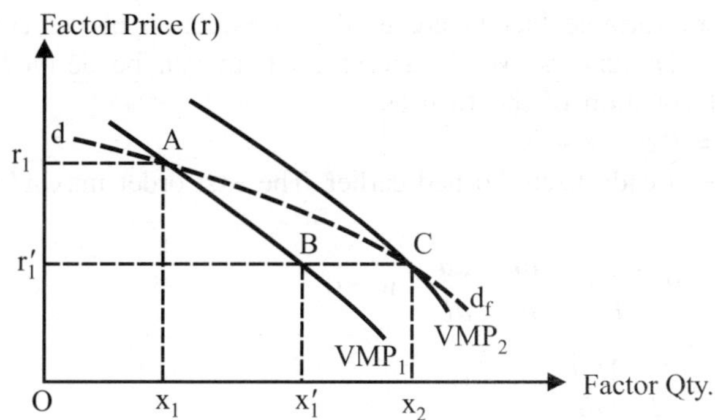

Fig. 11.4 The Shifting VMP Curve and the Demand Curve for a Factor of Production

Let the initial price for a factor *(X)* is given as r_1. At this price, the profit maximising level of factor use is ox_1. Showing the equilibrium point at *A* on the curve VMP_1, now suppose the factor price declines to r_1', prices of other factors being constant, the factor becomes relatively cheaper than the other factors. The firm, therefore, substitutes the factor (*X*) for the other factors. Apart from this there might be some complementary inputs for the factor whose quantities might also change with the reduction in the price of the factor. With changes in the quantities of the cooperating factors the marginal product curve and hence the value of marginal product curve for the factor shifts from its present position of VMP_1. Let us take VMP_2 as its new position. The new equilibrium for profit maximisation with r_1' price of the factor would therefore be at point *C* on the VMP_2 curve. If there would not have been more than one variable factor, the equilibrium position for the firm would be given by *B* point on the VMP_1 curve itself but the presence of the other variable factors because of their being complements and/or substitutes for the factor shifts the equilibrium to *C* point on VMP_2 giving ox_2 as the optimum quantity of the factor (*X*) at r_1' price. In this way, we can generate other equilibrium points on shifting *VMP* curves for *X* for different price levels. By joining all such equilibrium points (*A* and *C* in the above figure) we get the demand curve for the variable factor. This is dd_f in the above figure.

We have derived the demand curve for a factor *X* in the situation of using multiple variable factors in production of a product. The demand curve for other factors can be derived in the similar way.

11.3 THE DEMAND CURVES FOR VARIABLE FACTORS UNDER MONOPOLISTIC CONDITIONS IN THE PRODUCT MARKET

To derive the demand curve for a variable factor so far we have assumed the product price as constant, that is, perfect competition prevailing in the product market. If there are imperfections or say monopolistic conditions prevailing in the product market, the commodity demand curve for a firm will be downward sloping and the price of the commodity, which appears in the derived demand for the factors will no longer be constant but varies with respect to changing output level, and, as a consequence, with changing factor utilization level. With variable price, the *VMP* curve will not represent the demand curve for the factor. Instead, there will be a *marginal revenue product curve* (*MRP*) which will be the relevant demand curve for a single variable factor, and the locus of equilibrium points on the shifting marginal revenue product curves will be the demand curve for the factor when two or more variable factors are used in production of the commodity. For a single variable factor case (*i.e.*, labour) the *MRP* curve for labour can be derived as under:

Consider the profit equation of the firm as:

$$\pi = P \cdot q - b - wL$$

where the variables have already been defined earlier. The first order maximization condition for the profit of the firm is:

$$\frac{d\pi}{dL} = P \cdot \frac{dq}{dL} + q\,\frac{dP}{dq} \cdot \frac{dq}{dL} - w = 0$$

or

$$\left(P + q\,\frac{dP}{dq}\right)\frac{dq}{dL} - w = 0 \qquad \text{...(21)}$$

Since $R = P \cdot q$

Therefore, $MR = \dfrac{dR}{dq} = P + q\,\dfrac{dP}{dq}$, so substituting this in (21) we have:

$$MR \cdot MP_L = w \qquad \text{...(22)}$$

The term $MR \cdot MP_L$ is a product of the marginal revenue, and marginal physical product of labour. It is called *Marginal Revenue Product (MRP)* of labour. So, under imperfect competition in the product market, the price of the factor, *i.e.*, wage rate, will be equal to the marginal revenue product of the factor (L).

i.e.,

$$MRP = \frac{dR}{dL} = \frac{dR}{dq}\,\frac{dq}{dL} = MR \cdot MP_L \qquad \text{...(23)}$$

The production function for q will provide us MP_L, and the demand curve for the product provides MR; so, we can find the optimum employment level for which $MR \cdot MP_L$ = wage rate (w). This condition provides us the demand curve for labour, as shown below, in Fig. 11.5.

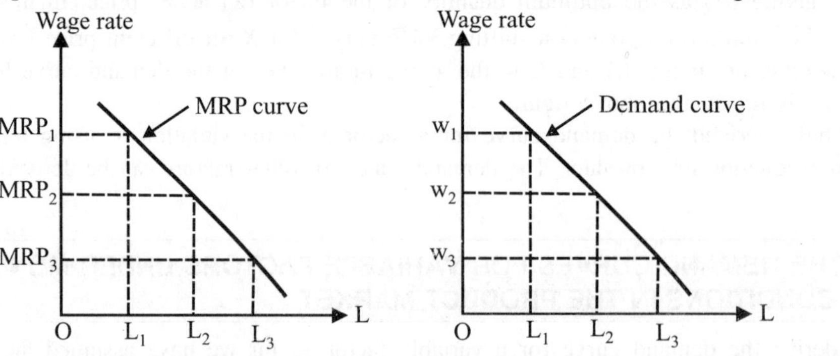

Fig. 11.5 Derivation of Factor Demand Curve: Imperfect Product Market, Single Variable Factor

The *MRP* and Demand curve for labour input are shown separately. Since ,*MRP* = wage rate, therefore, both the curves are identical. Every point on the *MRP* curve for labour indicates profit maximising employment level for exogenously given wage rates in monopolistic commodity market. The downward sloping *MRP* curve is the demand curve for the factor, (*i.e.*, labour). Summarizing in brief, under perfect competition in the product market the *VMP* curve is the factor demand curve for a single variable factor production case, while under the same production situation but imperfect competition in the product market, the *MRP* curve will be the factor demand curve.

The single variable factor case can be generalized for multiple variable factor case for determination of the factor demand curves under the monopolistic conditions in the product market. For this, we define the profit function for the firm as:

$$\pi = P \cdot q - r_1x_1 - r_2x_2 - r_3x_3, \ldots, - r_nx_n - b \qquad \ldots(24)$$

Since $\quad q = f(x_1, x_2, \ldots, x_n)$

We have,

$$\pi = P \cdot f(x_1, x_2, \ldots, x_n) - r_1x_1 - r_2x_2 - r_3x_3, \ldots, r_nx_n - b$$

Taking the first order profit maximisation conditions for this we have, when P is not constant,

$$\partial\pi/dx_1 = P \cdot \frac{dq}{dx_1} + q \cdot \frac{dp}{dq} \cdot \frac{dq}{dx_1} - r_1 = 0$$

$$= \left(P + q\frac{dP}{dq}\right)\frac{dq}{dx_1} - r_1 = 0$$

$$\partial\pi/dx_2 = \left(P + q\frac{dP}{dq}\right)\frac{dq}{dx_2} - r_2 = 0$$

$$\partial\pi/dx_n = \left(P + q\frac{dP}{dq}\right)\frac{dq}{dx_n} - r_n = 0$$

Provided the second order condition for profit maximisation similar to (18), (19) and (20), are satisfied for this.

The equilibrium conditions for profit maximisation show the equality of *MRP* and factor price for each and every factor. Solving (24) for n unknown quantities of $x_1, \ldots, x_n$ we get:

$$\begin{aligned} x_1 &= D_1\ (MR, r_1, r_2, \ldots, r_n) \\ x_2 &= D_2\ (MR, r_1, r_2, \ldots, r_n) \\ x_n &= D_n\ (MR, r_1, r_2, \ldots, r_n) \end{aligned} \qquad \ldots(25)$$

As compared to the solution expressed by (17), we have *MR* in place of *P* in equations (25). When the factor employment increases, output increases, price of product decreases. The net gain, when output goes up by one unit, is not the price but the marginal revenue. Therefore, under monopolistic condition in the product market, marginal revenue is the relevant variable which 'derives' the factor demand and not the product price.

Again, as in the case of multiple variable factors with fixed product price, where the locus of equilibrium points define the factor demand curves, in the same way the locus of the equilibrium points on the shifting marginal revenue product curves for each and every factor defines the demand curve for them in monopolistic product markets. The logic for this is exactly the same as we have presented before. The complementarily and/or substitution possibilities among the variable factors shift the marginal revenue product curves when price of anyone variable factor changes. This makes a single *MRP* curve for a factor irrelevant for being called as its demand curve. The demand curve will be the locus of the equilibrium points on the shifting *MRP* curve as shown by the line *AC* in the following figure.

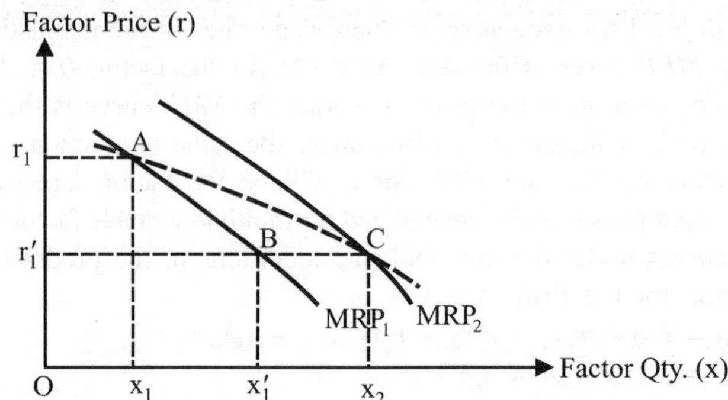

Fig. 11.6 Derivation of a Factor Demand Curve: Multiple Factors, Monopolistic Product Market

11.4 MARKET DEMAND FOR FACTORS OF PRODUCTION

The market demand for factors of production will be the horizontal sum of the demands of various firms employing them if all those firms behave like pure monopolists, *i.e.*, there are no external effects because of the summation, the product price remains unchanged. But this is unlikely to happen. If the output markets are not completely monopolised, rather they are monopolistically competitive or oligopolistic, expansion of output by one firm because of reduced factor cost reduces the price of the product. The proportional demand curve as well as the marginal revenue product curves of firms shift to the left. So, in this case, the shifting marginal revenue product curves, when horizontally aggregated, will provide the market demand for the concerned factor of production. To explain this process let us consider Fig. 11.7.

The left hand side panel of Fig. 11.7 is concerned with a representative firm employing a factor of production, say labour $d_1 d_1'$, is the demand curve for the firm in the initial stage. When market wage rate is w_1, the firm employs ol_1 units of labour. All firms operating in the industry will have similar initial equilibrium position for employing labour units. The sum of labour units employed by all the firms in the industry at w_1 wage rate is given by OL_1 units in panel (*B*) of Fig. 11.7. Thus, M_1, in this part of the figure, shows one point on the market demand curve for labour.

Suppose the market wage rate declines to w_2. If other things are equal, say product price is unchanged, the firm will move to point *C* on $d_1 d_1'$ showing ol_2' units of labour in this situation. But, with a decline in the market wage rate, the firm employs more labour and output expands. This reduces the price of the commodity because of a shift in the supply curve to the right as a result of the reduced input cost. With decline in the product price, the *VMP* or *MRP* curve for the factor falls. The new demand curve for the factor is shown by d_2d_2' in panel (*A*) of the above figure. With w_2 as wage rate, the equilibrium position would now be at point *B* on d_2d_2' demand curve. The optimum units of labour now would be Ol_2. Aggregating for all firms, the market demand for labour is given by OL_2 in panel (*B*) of the figure. This corresponds to point M_2. This way, for varying wage

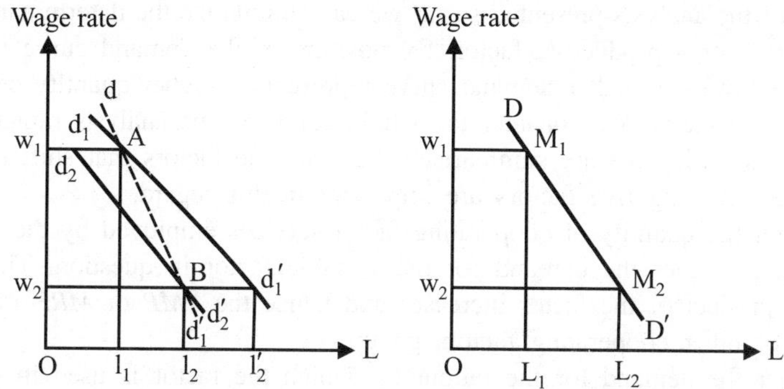

Fig. 11.7 Derivation of Market Demand Curve for a Variable Factor

rate we can find the different points for derivation of the market demand for the factor. By joining all such points such as M_1 and M_2 in Fig. 11.7, we get the market demand for labour. Similar approach is followed for derivation of the market demand curves for other variable factors employed by the firms for the individual firms, if we join points *A* and *B* which would give us long-run demand curve for the concerned factor. How the process of shifting demand curves takes place can be summarised as below.

Given initial equilibrium for optimum employment of the factor, a fall in the factor price increases the quantity demanded of labour which reduces its marginal product and hence *VMP* in the case of single variable input or shifts the marginal revenue product to right in the case of multiple inputs used in production. This, in sequence, increases the output of all firms and a decline in the product price. With a decline in product price the *VMP* or *MRP* curve shifts downward. By joining the equilibrium points on such shifting demand curves for the factor, we get its long-run demand curve, and by summing the units of the factor employed by firms corresponding to different equilibrium situations on varying factor prices, we get the market demand for the factor.

11.5 THE DETERMINANTS OF THE DEMAND FOR A PRODUCTIVE FACTOR: SUMMARY RESULTS

The earlier sections have thrown enough light on the determinants of the demand for a productive factor. In this section, we will briefly summarize them; but before doing this we would like to say a few words regarding the determinants of the price elasticity for a factor.

The price elasticity of demand for a factor depends on the variables like number of substitutes for the factor, the elasticity of substitution, the product price in whose production the factor is used, and the time period. (*i*) The more easily other factors can be substituted for a certain factor, the higher the price elasticity of demand for that factor. If firms cannot substitute other factors readily for the given factor, its price elasticity will be low. (*ii*) The higher the price elasticity of demand for the product in whose production the factor is used, more is the price elasticity of demand for the factor. (*iii*) The price elasticity of demand for a factor is usually higher in the long-run than in the short-run. This is because in the short-run the factor substitution may not take place as readily as in the long-run.[1]

1. For mathematical derivation of some of these results, particularly the elasticity of derived demand, see J. R. Hicks, *Theory of Wages*; Macmillan, 1963 (Edn.), pp. 241–243, and Martin Bronfebbrenner, *Income Distribution Theory*, Macmillan 1971, pp. 140–150, 166–171.

On the basis of the analysis presented so far we can summarize the determinants of the position of the demand curve for a productive factor. By position of the demand curve we mean whether it will be higher or lower. A higher demand curve represents a higher quantity demanded for each and every price of the factor. We consider the whole curve in this analysis rather than a point on the curve. In this way, what we are summarising here are the factors that shift the demand curve for the factor. The following five factors are important in this regard.

1. The greater the quantity of cooperating factor services employed by the firm, other things being equal, higher the demand for the variable factor in question. This is because the marginal product of the factor increases and hence the *VMP* or *MRP* increases when the quantity of other cooperating factors go up.
2. The higher the demand for the output for which the factor is used in production, better is the demand for the factor, other things being equal. When the demand for the product is high it will fetch higher price in the market, which, in turn, pushes the *VMP* or *MRP* of the factor to higher level.
3. The demand for a factor is inversely related to its current level of usage. That is, the more of the factor currently in use, other things being equal, the lower the demand for it and vice-versa. This is because of diminishing marginal product of the factor if its quantity is increased further and further.
4. The demand for a factor (or input) depends on the technology. The isoquant analysis presented in Chapter 5 has already thrown enough light on this aspect.
5. The market demand for a factor depends on the number of firms. Larger the number of firms using the factor, other things being equal, the higher the demand for it.

11.6 THE SUPPLY OF FACTORS OF PRODUCTION

The demand side of a factor market has been analyzed so far in this chapter. Let us now examine its supply side. We know that the market price of a commodity is determined by its supply and demand under perfect competition. However, under conditions of imperfect competition in the commodity market, the concept of market supply for price determination does not have much meaning. In such conditions the market price of the commodity is determined through demand and cost considerations. The situation of the factor markets is also similar to some extent but in certain respect it is quite different.

The market price of a factor under perfect competition in the factor market is determined through the interaction of the demand and supply curves, very much similar to a commodity market-price under perfect competition. The supply curve for a commodity shows the willingness of its producers to offer the commodity for sale in the market as price of the commodity changes. It is a positively sloping curve derived by summing the rising marginal cost curves above the minima of the average variable cost for different firms. (See Ch. 6 for this). Conceptually, the supply curve for a factor is very much similar to the supply curve or function for a commodity. It shows the willingness of the factor owners to supply the factor in the market as price of the factor increases. By and large, it is also a positively sloping curve with the factor price. However, the derivation of the factor supply curve is quite complicated as the factor owners in the market are not solely concerned with profit maximising. In fact, it is difficult to define the profit derived from selling of a productive factor. For example, a worker sells his labour, he gets a wage for that but what is his profit is quite difficult to define. In view of this difficulty, the approach followed in derivation of the supply curve for a factor of production is different from the one used in derivation of the supply curve for a commodity. The major factors of production, *e.g.*, land, labour and capital, have their unique characteristics as a result of which different sets of conditions are applied to the derivation of their supply curves. We will come across such conditions very soon in the following sections of this chapter itself.

(i) Derivation of Labour Supply Curve

Since labour is an important factor of production, the factor supply analysis can best be explained by taking it as an example. However, it does not mean that whatever is true for labour is true for other factors also. We have already made it clear that each factor has its unique features which are considered to derive its supply curve.

The supply of labour offered by an individual can be determined, in principle, by the indifference curve analysis. For this, we need the utility function and budget constraint for the worker. A worker's satisfaction or utility depends on the income he gets from his work and the leisure time available to him to enjoy. The income of the worker, in turn, depends on the wage-rate and the number of hours he devotes to work. If he is devoting more hours for work, lesser time will be available for leisure. For a given wage rate, there is thus a trade-off between work-hours and leisure-time which we represent through an indifference curve for him. The budget constraint is not with respect to fixed income as it is in the case of a consumer but it is with respect to the total time at his disposal, say, 24 hours a day. The utility function and the time constraint for the worker can be specified as:

$$U = U(S, M) \qquad ...(26)$$

and

$$T = S + L \qquad ...(27)$$

where S = Leisure time, M = Income, T = Total hours, and L = No. of hours worked.

The money income of the worker will be:

$$M = wL \text{ where } w = \text{wage rate (hourly)} \qquad ...(28)$$

Substituting (27) and (28) in (26) the utility function can be modified as:

$$U = U(T - L, wL) \qquad ...(29)$$

where T and w are constants and L is variable. By taking the total differentiation of (26) we have

$$dU = \partial U/\partial S \cdot dS + \partial U/\partial M \cdot dM \qquad ...(30)$$

For moving along the indifference curve $dU = 0$, so

$$0 = \partial U/\partial S \cdot dS + \partial U/\partial M \cdot dM \qquad ...(31)$$

and therefore,

$$-\frac{dM}{dS} = \frac{\partial U}{\partial S} \Big/ \frac{\partial U}{\partial M} \qquad ...(32)$$

where $-\dfrac{dM}{dS}$ = Marginal rate of substitution of income by leisure. It is the slope of the indifference curve (26). At the equilibrium position the slope of the indifference curve would be equal to the slope of the 'budget line' for the worker. Substituting (28) in (27) we have

$$T = S + M/w$$

or

$$M = wT - wS \qquad ...(33)$$

$$\frac{dM}{dS} = -w \qquad ...(34)$$

This is the slope of the 'budget line' for the worker. Equating (32) and (34) we have the equilibrium condition for the worker as

$$MRS = -\frac{dM}{dS} = \frac{\partial U / \partial S}{\partial U / \partial M} = w \qquad ...(35)$$

This equilibrium condition can be derived directly from (29). The first order conditions for utility maximization can be written as:

$$dU/dL = -\partial U/\partial S + \partial U/M \cdot w = 0$$

Therefore, $\frac{\partial U / \partial S}{\partial U / \partial M} = w$

The second order condition for the utility maximisation would be

$$d^2U/dL^2 = U_{ss} - 2wU_{SM} + w^2U_{MM} < 0 \qquad ...(36)$$

where $U_{SS} = \partial^2\partial/\partial S^2$; $U_{SM} = \partial^2U/\partial S\partial M = \partial^2U/\partial M\partial S = U_{MS}$,

and $U_{MM} = \partial^2U/\partial M^2$.

In the equilibrium condition (35), both $\partial U/\partial S$ and $\partial U/\partial M$ are functions of *L, T,* and *W* of which *L* is the only variable, we can therefore solve the equation for *L* in terms of *W* and *T.* The solution can be written as

$$L = s(w) \qquad ...(37)$$

This is the supply function for labour. The quantity of *L* (in terms of hours) in a function of wage rate, *T* being constant.

The worker's equilibrium position on the indifference curve for the choice of *S* and *M* can be analyzed graphically as follows.

In Fig. 11.8, the horizontal axis represents *S*, *i.e.*, the leisure time and the vertical axis shows *M*, *i.e.*, the income of the worker. The maximum time at the disposal of the worker per day is 24 hours shown by point *B*. The budget line starts from point *B*, since, if the entire time at the disposal of the worker is devoted to leisure, his or her income would be zero. On the other hand, if all 24 hours are devoted to work at a given hourly wage rate, say ₹ 10 per hour, the worker will get maximum income shown by point *A* on *y*-axis. The line *AB* is, therefore, the budget line for the worker. If the wage rate increases, the budget line shifts up on *y*-axis as shown by A_1B, and in the case of a decreasing wage rate, the line shifts downward on *y*-axis as shown by A_2B.

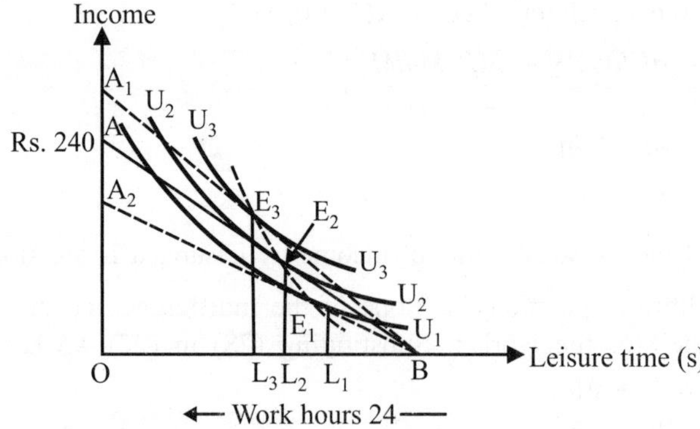

Fig. 11.8 Worker's Indifference Curve: Work.Vs Leisure and Equilibrium Position

The slope of the budget line is thus determined solely by the wage rate, the price of money as assumed to be unity. Higher the wage rate, steeper is the slope is of the budget line and vice-versa.

The worker's equilibrium position is reflected by the point of tangency, *i.e.*, when the budget line is tangent to the indifference curve. For the three budget lines in the figure the worker is in equilibrium at points E_1, E_2 and E_3 on the three indifference curves U_1, U_2 and U_3 respectively. The line joining E_1, E_2 and E_3, *i.e.*, the equilibrium points shows the labour hours vis-a-vis leisure time for the workers when wage-rate differs. BL_1 is the work time in the first case while BL_2 and BL_3 for the other two indifference curves. The reverse situation, *i.e.*, OL_1, OL_2 and OL_3 would be the leisure time for the worker. If we draw the work-hours against the wage-rate, the supply curve for the labour would be as follows:

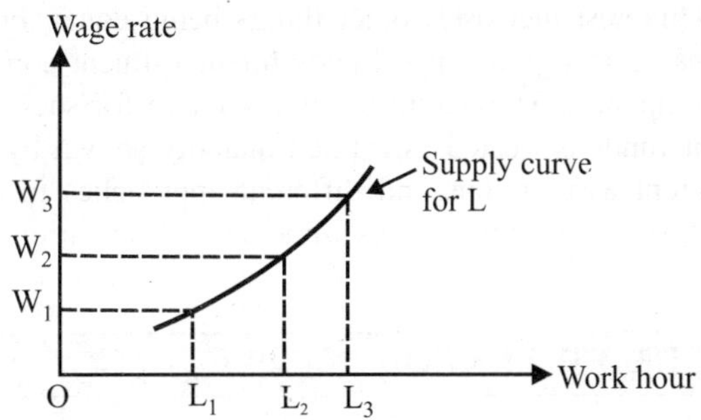

Fig. 11.9 Supply Curve for Labour

The supply curve is positively sloped in this case. In general, the labour supply curve will be positively sloped. However, there might be a wage rate so high that the quantity of labour supplied reaches a maximum level and after that it might decline with further increase in the wage rate. This would give us the backward bending supply curve for labour in such a situation. When wage rate goes up, the worker's income increases for the same number of hours worked. With a higher income the worker consumes more of every normal good. The leisure time is considered to be an item of comfort. At the higher income, the worker opts for more leisure time and less work-time. This is what we call as income effect that causes the backward bending supply curve for the worker's labour.

The market supply curve for labour can be obtained by horizontal aggregation of the individual supply curves under the assumption that each worker's supply curve is independent of those of other workers. This assumption is quite reasonable. This is, in fact, the basis of the utility analysis from which we have derived the supply curve for the worker. It ensures that there are no externalities associated in summing up the individual supply curves for workers. Methodologically, the procedure of horizontal summation of the supply curves for individual workers is identical with the summation of the supply curves for a commodity of the individual firms. There is no need of repeating the procedure here. The market supply curve for labour will be normally positively sloping upward, but may be negatively sloped at a very high wage rate. The negatively sloping supply curve for labour, of course, will have implication for the stability of the labour market equilibrium similar to that of a commodity market with negatively sloping supply and demand curves.

(ii) Derivation of Supply Curves for Land and Capital Factors

Capital and land are other two important factors of production. As we have said earlier, each factor of production has its unique characteristics which make the process of derivation of the supply curve for each one of them somewhat different and difficult. For labour input we have already derived the supply curve. In the case of land, the supply curve is considered as a fixed vertical line since the size of the earth is constant. Some economists, however, argue that land can be created by drainage or fertility of land can be increased by using soil nutrients and thus the supply side of the land can be changed. This is true for agricultural land. On the whole, if we look at the availability of land from the point of view of society, it is fixed but from individual's point of view it may be variable, particularly in the long-run. In the context of fixing the rent, *i.e.*, the price of land services, the supply curve of land is taken as a vertical line since it is the nearest approach to its real situation.

The supply of capital funds depends on factors like interest and income. The incentive to save will be more if the rate of interest increases, other things being equal. Further, a rich man may be able to save more as compared to a poor man. Funds for investment come from other sources also like retained earnings of companies. The nature of supply curve for such funds will be different. In some theories the supply of funds is treated as a fixed quantity shown by a vertical line. The point here is that there are different assumptions and different approaches to derive a supply curve for capital. We will briefly go through such approaches while discussing various theories for determination of the rate of interest.

11.7 FACTOR PRICE DETERMINATION

The demand and supply curves are two important sides of a market to determine price whether it is a commodity price or a factor price. For factors of production we have developed the concepts and procedures for derivation of their demand and supply curves in the preceding sections of this chapter. We will use these curves to find out prices of different factors of production, *e.g.*, wage-rate, rent, and interest rate for labour, land and capital inputs respectively.

(i) Determination of Wage Rate

Keeping in mind the importance of labour as a factor of production, we will go through the exercise of wage-rate determination somewhat in detail. We will examine this under three different situations: (*a*) competitive demand and supply for labour; (*b*) monopsony in hiring labour services; and (*c*) bilateral monopoly in which there is a single buyer of labour and a single supplier, such as a trade union acting as a representative body for collective bargaining on behalf of workers.

The situation of competitive demand and supply of labour is the simplest case for the analysis. The market demand curve for labour is given as D_LD_L in the following figure. It is negatively sloping curve representing either *VMP* or *MRP* for the factor. The market supply curve is shown by S_LS_L which is a positively sloping curve. The possibility of backward sloping supply curve for labour is not taken into account since we are concerned with the most general case of wage rate determination. Both the demand and the supply curves are shown in inverse forms.

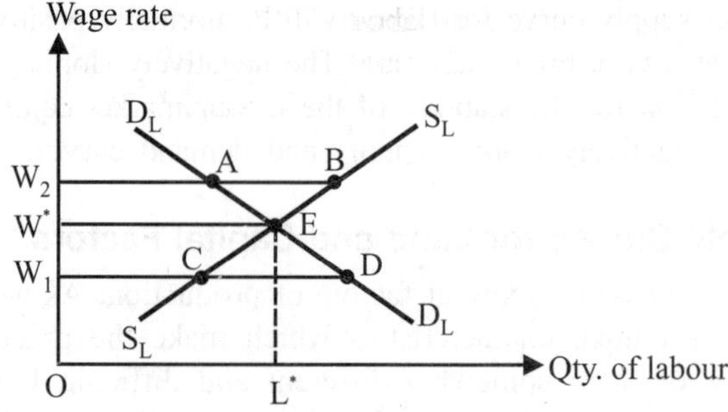

Fig. 11.10 Determination of Wage Rate: Competitive Case

The demand and supply curves for labour intersect at point *E*, which implies that the quantity of labour demanded is equal to the quantity of labour supplied. This is the equilibrium condition for the competitive labour market. The equilibrium market wage-rate is W^* and the equilibrium market quantity of labour employed L^*. If the actual wage-rate is less than the equilibrium wage-rate then there will be excess demand for labour. This is shown by *CD* segment on W_1 wage line in the figure. The excess demand for labour will generate competition among users of labour for additional workers. The wage-rate will be pushed up and this sequence continues till the entire excess demand is eliminated and wage-rate takes its equilibrium value.

Suppose there is excess supply of labour, such as at W_2 wage-rate, shown by the line segment *AB*. The excess supply of labour means a competition among workers to sell their services. Wage rate declines. The declining trend continues till the entire excess supply is eliminated and equilibrium is established at point *E*.

If the demand or the supply curve shifts from its present position, the equilibrium of the labour market will be disturbed and both the wage-rate and the market quantity of demand or supply of labour will change in the analogous ways as for a competitive commodity market discussed in chapter 3. This is for the entire labour market. The individual users of labour will take wage-rate as given and determine their optimum requirements of labour on the basis of VMP = Wage rate or MRP = Wage rate as discussed earlier.

Now let us examine the second situation where monopsonic condition prevails in the labour market. There is only one firm *i.e.*, buyer of labour in the market. The demand curve for labour for the firm is its *MRP* or *VMP* curve shown by DD_L in Fig. 11.11. As we have argued under monopsony analysis in Chapter 8, the firm, being a single buyer of the factor, views the market supply curve of labour as its average resource cost (*ARC*) curve. This is positively sloping upward and associated with this there will be marginal resource cost (*MRC*) curve for the firm (see Monopsony section in Chapter 8 for its derivation). The *MRC* curve lies above the *ARC* curve.

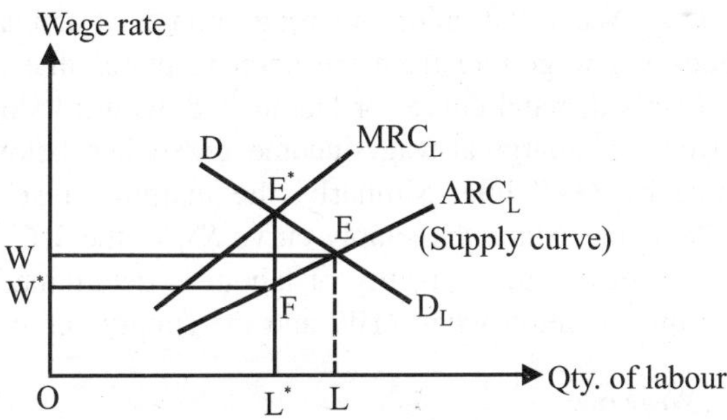

Fig. 11.11 Determination of Wage Rate: Monopsony Case

If there is no monopsony in the market then the factor market equilibrium is given by *E* point corresponding to which *W* is the wage-rate and *L* is the labour employment. However, the presence of monopsony shifts the market equilibrium from *E* to E^* point where *MRP* or *VMP* of the firm is equal to the marginal resource cost (MRC_L) of labour. The basis for this equality is exactly similar as to that of a monopoly firm where $MR = MC$ is the rule to determine the profit maximising output and price for a commodity. In the same manner, the profit maximising factor employment is given for the monopsonist when $MRC_L = MRP$ or VMP. Corresponding to point E^*, the optimum employment of labour for the monopsonist is L^*. The optimum wage-rate is given by the point

F where the quantity line $E^* L^*$ intersects the supply curve, *i.e.*, Average Resource Cost Curve for the monopsonist. This gives us W^* as the equilibrium wage rate.

We find that the market-wage and quantity of labour demanded under monopsony are lower than the corresponding figures for a competitive labour market. It may be interpreted as a situation of exploitation of labour by the monopsonist. From the point of view of workers as well as society as a whole, a higher wage-rate and higher level of employment is desirable. For this, the competitive market setting for labour is preferable than the monopsonistic.

Let us now examine the third situation for wage-rate determination in which the labour union comes in the picture as a representative body of the worker, *i.e.*, a collusion of labour suppliers. Theoretically, we may argue for determining wages through interaction of demand and supply forces in the labour market under competitive conditions or through monopsonist $MRP_L = MSC_L$ equilibrium condition. In practice wages are more often determined by the trade union leaders and management or government representatives as the bargaining table. The economic theory is capable of explaining this kind of wage determination process through the use of a bilateral monopoly model.

Bilateral monopoly prevails when there is only one buyer and only one seller in the market, *i.e.*, the case of a monopolist and a monopsonist interacting in the market. The trade union of workers acts as a sole seller of labour services and thus would have monopoly power. As we have seen in Chapter 8, bilateral monopoly, if left free of its own, is unable to give a stable market equilibrium. In fact, both, market-price and equilibrium quantity of a commodity or factor are indeterminate under bilateral monopoly. To determine the market-price of the factor under bilateral monopoly, we need a system which is not solely based on the market forces. The collective bargaining model is one such systems. Let us see how this works.

In Fig. 11.12, the competitive market supply curve for labour is given by SS_L curve. This is nothing but the horizontal sum of the marginal cost for supply of labour. Also this is the average resource cost curve (*ARC*) for the monopsonist as argued earlier. The trade union of workers is assumed to be aware of this curve. The union also knows the demand curve of monopsonist for labour which is shown by DD_L. When the union is strong enough, it acts as a monopolist in supply of labour services, and chooses a wage-rate from the demand prices that the monopsonist, *i.e.*, the firm is willing to pay. The firm's demand curve for labour is downward sloping. So when additional units of labour are employed, the marginal-wage-income curve lies below the demand curve for labour. This curve is shown by *MWI* line. Similarly, the marginal resource cost (*MRC*) for the monopsonist is given by MRC_L line. Since the supply curve SS_L is the *MC* curve for the monopolist, *i.e.*, the trade union, the profit maximizing quantity of labour is determined by the equality of *MWI* and the *MC*. Point *Y* shows this situation when *MWI* and the supply curve intersect. As a result, L_U

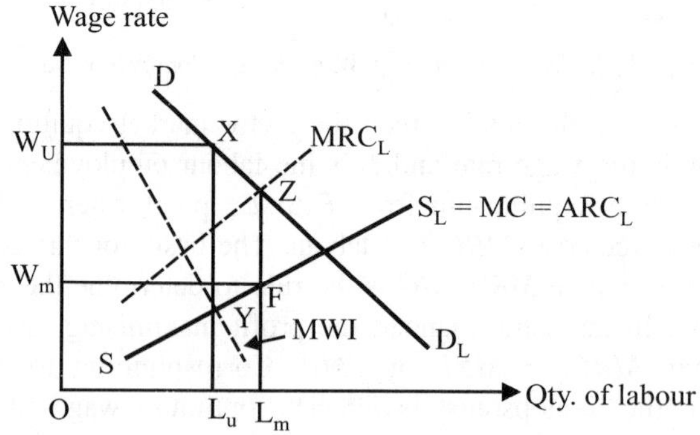

Fig. 11.12 Determination of Wage Rate: Bilateral Monopoly Model

is the optimum supply of labour that the trade union makes. The wage-rate corresponding to L_U is given by point X on the demand curve for the labour. The wage-rate that the trade union fixes is therefore W_U. If the buyer of labour is one of the several in the labour market the wage-rate W_U and employment level will prevail in the market. But, there is only one buyer. As we are examining the case of bilateral monopoly, we have a monopsonist. His profit will be maximised when the marginal resource cost (*MRC*) of labour is equal to the marginal valuation of labour, *i.e.*, marginal revenue product of labour, that is, at the point Z where the MRC_L line intersects the demand curve for labour (DD_L). Correspondingly, the optimum amount of labour is L_m and the actual wage-rate (from his point of view) given by the ARC_L line matching to L_m is W_m. Thus, we have now two typical situations for wage-rate and employment combination. One is the pair W_U and L_U which the monopolist (*i.e.*, the trade union) expects to prevail in the labour market under the assumption of the buyer of labour being a small competitor, and second, the pair W_m and L_m which the monopsonist expect to prevail in the market under the assumption that the supplier of labour is a small competitor in the market. But the reality is that neither of them is a small competitor; rather they are quite dominating market-powers in their own activities. In such a situation, there is no unique solution for either wage-rate or the quantity of labour in the market. This is what we mean by the theoretical indeterminacy of wage rate under bilateral monopoly. But it does not mean that there is no exchange between the employer and the employee. It only implies that market forces themselves cannot produce a consistent solution for the bilateral monopoly in the factor market. What is determined theoretically is a range in which the actual wage rate lies, *i.e.*, between W_m and W_U. The actual wage-rate would come out of negotiation between the trade-union leaders and the management's representatives. The employer, *i.e.*, the monopsonist would try to convince the union that his demand curve for labour is highly elastic at the wage-rate W_m, the union on the other hand would attempt to argue that its supply curve for labour is highly elastic at the wage-rate W_U. The net outcome of the negotiation depends on the relative bargaining strength of parties concerned. If the monopsonist's demand curve for labour is relatively more elastic as compared with the monopolist's (*i.e.*, trade-unions) supply curve for labour, the monopsonist's optimum employment (L_m) will be less than the trade-union's determined supply of labour (L_U). The sequence of the employment levels will be reversed, *i.e.*, $L_m > L_U$ if the supply curve is relatively elastic as compared with the demand curve for labour. The union determined wage-rate, W_U, will, however, be always greater than the monopsonist's wage-rate. The competitive wage-rate lies between the monopoly wage-rate (W_U) and the monopsonist's wage-rate W_m. If the collective bargaining results in an increase in the wage, rate the employment goes up so long as the new wage-rate is equal or less to the competitive wage-rate. Any further increase in the wage rate may leave the employment constant or decrease it.

In most of the organized oligopolistic industries we find the bilateral monopoly model in operation. The manufactures' association in such industries acts on behalf of its members as a monopsonist and the trade-union as a monopolist in the wage bargaining. If the bargaining is not successful, a strike or arbitration will be the result. The economic theory cannot provide any guidance in such a situation. So, practically the institutional forces, *i.e.*, management, trade-unions and government officials play crucial role in fixing the final wage-rate under bilateral monopolies.

The wage-determination exercise can be demonstrated with the help of a numerical example. Let us assume that monopsony prevails in the labour market and monopoly in the product market (Remember, it is not bilateral monopoly). Labour is the only variable and independent factor. The profit function for the firm can be written as;

$$\pi = f(L)\ D\ [f(L)] - b - wL \qquad \text{...(38)}$$

where the first term on the right hand side is the revenue and rest are elements of total cost.

The production function for the firm is

$$Q = f(L) \qquad ...(39)$$

where Q is the output. The inverse of the demand curve is given as

$$P = D(Q) \qquad ...(40)$$

Using (39) and (40), the total revenue comes out as

$$R = f(L) \cdot D[f(L)]$$

The wage rate w is a function of the quantity of labour along the labour supply curve. Therefore,

$$W = S(L). \qquad ...(41)$$

The total cost is therefore,

$$C = b + S(L).\ L$$

By substitution of the expressions for total revenue and total cost, we define the profit function as expressed by the equation (38).

The first order for profit maximisation, using labour as the only variable factor, is

$$\frac{d\pi}{dL} = \left[P + Q \cdot \frac{dP}{dQ}\right]\frac{dQ}{dL} - \left[W + L\frac{dW}{dL}\right] = 0 \qquad ...(42)$$

or

$$\left[P + Q\frac{dP}{dQ}\right] \cdot \frac{dQ}{dL} = W + L\frac{dW}{dL} \qquad ...(43)$$

that is, marginal revenue product equals marginal expense of the firm. If perfect competition prevails in the product market, then $dP/dQ = 0$. In this case, P is constant and therefore *VMP* will be equal to the marginal expense of the firm. Again, if $dW/dL = 0$, *i.e.*, perfect competitions prevails in the factor market, $VMP = W$ which is the standard result for the competitive product and labour market.

Assuming that the second order profit maximisation condition is satisfied, so (43) can be solved for the equilibrium quantity of labour.

The above analysis can be extended to n variable factor's case. In this case, the production function of the monopoly firm would be,

$$Q = f(x_1, x_2, ..., x_n) \qquad ...(44)$$

and so the revenue function would be modified as

$$R = f(x_1, x_2, ..., x_n) \cdot D[f\{x_1, x_2, ..., x_n)] \qquad ...(45)$$

$x_1, x_2, ..., x_n$ are factor quantities used by the firm. The cost production will be including prices and quantities of all factors that the firm uses in production. The quantity of each and every factor will be a function of all prices of factors (Ref. Eqn. 25). The inverse supply function for factors would, therefore, be,

$$r_i = S_i\ [x_1, x_2, ..., x_n],\ i = 1, ..., n \qquad ...(46)$$

The profit function for the firm can then be expressed as

$$\pi = f(x_1, x_2, ..., x_n)D[f(x_1), x_2, ..., x_n)] - b - \sum_{i=1}^{n} x_i \cdot S_i[x_1, ..., x_n] \qquad ...(47)$$

For short-run $b > 0$, and for long-run $b = 0$;

The first order maximization conditions are now:

$$\partial\pi/\partial x_i \left(P + Q\frac{dP}{dQ}\right)\frac{dQ}{dx_i} - r_i - \sum_{j=1}^{n} x_j\ \partial\pi/\partial x_i \frac{\partial r_j}{\partial x_i} = 0,\ i = 1,\ ...,\ n \qquad ...(48)$$

or

$$\left(P + Q\frac{dP}{dQ}\right)\cdot\frac{dQ}{dx_i} = r_i + \sum_{j=1}^{n} x_j \cdot \frac{\partial r_j}{\partial x_i} = 0,\ i = 1,\ ...,\ n \qquad ...(49)$$

Provided the second order conditions for profit maximisation are satisfied. The interpretation of (49) is straight-forward, marginal revenue product for each factor must be equal to marginal expense of that factor. The marginal expense takes care of inter-factor substitution effects of factor price. The first order profit maximisation conditions provide us n equations for n unknowns $(x_1, x_2, ..., x_n)$ which can be solved. By substituting the equilibrium values of x_i, $i = 1, ..., n$ in the factor supply equation we would get factor prices.

(ii) Determination of Economic Rent

In ordinary sense, the term 'rent' means a payment made for hiring of any particular thing, such as a machine, a house, a vehicle and like that to its owner. However, in economics by 'rent', we mean the payment made by farmers or land users to landlord for the use of the land which is a free gift of nature. The phenomenon of rent is now no longer confined to land. Rent is any payment which is in excess of the minimum amount necessary to keep a factor of production in its present occupation in an industry under equilibrium state. This is what we call as 'pure economic rent'. It is applicable to any factor of production which has an inelastic supply curve. In a simple way, we may define rent as the amount paid for having a temporary ownership of any factor of production or property.

How rent is determined? The earlier explanation for this was given by David Ricardo, according to him rent is "that portion of the produce of the earth which is paid to the landlord for the use of the original and indestructible powers of the soil."[2] According to him, rent is the differential surplus that emerges because of differences in the fertility of different plots of land. If equal amounts of inputs are used to, say, two plots of land of equal size, one plot yields, say 80 quintal of a crop, say, wheat, and the other yields 100 quintals, excess output of the second plot over the output of the first one, *i.e.*, 100 – 80 = 20 quintal is the rent of that plot.

As mentioned above, Ricardo attributed occurrence of rent to fertility differences of different grades of land. His contention was that it was the result of the niggardliness of nature. With increase in demand for food because of rising population and scarcity, of fertile land, more and more of less fertile land had to be brought under cultivation. Consequently, the return, in terms of output of corn, for additional units of land or which may also be interpreted as for additional dozes of labour and capital to the land, tends to decline. It is not because of operation of the law of diminishing marginal return but due to declining fertility of additional units of land. Ricardo considered the cost of production of corn similar for the plots of land of equal dimensions. The profit (*i.e.*, return to capital) was also treated as similar for the plots. The only thing that varied was a surplus earned on the superior land over the marginal land mainly due to fertility variation and this was defined as rent by Ricardo.

Although Ricardo's theory of rent is very crude, yet it provided ingredients for the modern theory of rent which is fairly general and applicable to any factor of production with fixed or inelastic supply. The marginal product of a factor which enters in as an aspect of determining the demand for the factor takes care of the superior skills or talents and hence more payment to the factor when its supply is fixed or highly inelastic. Such payments may be interpreted as rent of

2. David Ricardo, *The Principles of Political Economy and Taxation,* (1817).

the factor in the Ricardian line. For a fixed factor in the short-run it is difficult to generate its marginal product since the quantity of the factor is not varying for this. The return or income accruing to a short-run fixed factor therefore needs a different explanation for which Marshall suggested the concept of 'quasi rent'. Marshall in his book, *Principles of Economics* (Book VI. Ch. 3), explained this point by saying, "If the supply of any factor of production is limited and incapable of much increase by man's effort in any given period of time, the income to be derived from it is to be regarded as of the nature of rent rather than profit in enquiries as to the action of economic causes during that period."

The term quasy-rent may be defined formally as the payment to any input in temporarily fixed supply or, more specifically, the earnings of a productive factor which are economic rent in the short-run, but which are converted into necessary payments required to bring forth the services of the factor in the long-run.

There is a distinction between price of a factor service and the rent. Rent is the return to a factor when its quantity is fixed while price is the return to that factor when its quantity is variable. In the long-run, all factors are variables. Therefore, earnings of a productive factor, which we interpret as economic rent becomes price of that factor service in the long-run although such a price may contain some element of rent because of productivity differentials of the factor units.

A factor of production captures rent when its supply is fixed. We may call it as 'scarcity rent'. Another source of rent to the factor is the productivity differences among its different units, call this as 'differential rent'. Scarcity rent can be earned even when all units of the factor, say land, are homogeneous provided their supply is fixed. The differential rents are earned only when there are productivity differences among the different units of the factor. In both the cases, rent will increase with growing population or growing demand for goods because it will induce producers to increase production with the use of inferior units of factors and/or encourage them to offer higher factor prices because of their fixed quantities. This is applicable to all factors of production and not only to land.

Quasi-rent is, in fact, a difference between total revenue and total variable cost of production. Consider Fig. 11.13 in which we have shown average total cost (*AC*), average variable cost (*AVC*) and the marginal cost of production (*MC*) with respect to output of a commodity *X*.

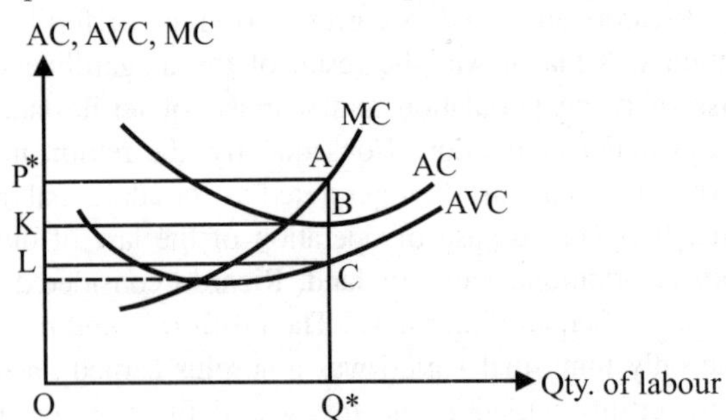

Fig. 11.13 The Economic Rent of a Fixed Factor

The output market is assumed to be perfectly competitive. The profit maximising short-run equilibrium for the firm is given by the price *OP** and quantity *OQ** corresponding to point *A* where price equals the marginal cost and the marginal cost intersects the price line from below. The total revenue accruing to the firm will be *OP*·OQ**, *i.e.*, the area of the rectangle *OP* AQ**. Out of this revenue, a portion shown by the area *OLCQ** will be paid as variable cost for production of *OQ** units of the output. The remaining revenue shown by the area *LP*AC* is attributable to the fixed factors and thus called the economic rent. A portion of this rent shown by the area *KP*AB* is the pure economic profit and the rest shown by the area *LK BC* is the return to the fixed factor in an opportunity cost sense. If the price of the commodity is equal to the minimum of average variable cost, the payment to the fixed factor or rent would be zero but for prices more than this there will be positive rent to the fixed factors.

We have shown rent or quasi-rent as the return or payment for services of the fixed factors particularly of land. Obviously, rent is a part of the cost of production; so we expect it to affect the price of the commodity in whose production the concerned fixed factor was used. There has been a controversy on this aspect which is now more or less revolved. In the early 19th century, corn was a staple food for people as it is today in most parts of the world. Whenever prices of corn went up, people attributed it to the high price of land and the related high rent. David Ricardo, however, provided a different explanation for this. According to him, "it is not really true that the price of corn is high because the price of corn land is high. Actually, the reverse is more nearly the truth; the price of cornland is high because the price of corn is high. Total land being inelastic in supply, it will always be used whatever is paid to it as price. Thus, the value of land is completely derived from the value of product and not vice versa."

This explanation is true when we consider the relationship between price of corn and rent from the point of view of society as a whole. The value of land increases and rent goes up whenever there is increase in the demand for food reflected by the rising price of the corn (Price of food may go up because of failure of crop but that is a different aspect). For an individual producer land under a particular crop may be variable. In this case, rent will be a part of the cost of production of the crop and hence a determinant of its price.

We may now summarise the rent-price relationship by simply quoting Samuelson's view-point on this.

> To a small industry using relatively little of a factor, the factor price is an important determiner of the industry's commodity price, and not vice versa. At the same time, to an economy as a whole, the rent of a factor whose total quantity is inelastic can still be said to be more the result than the cause of the values of the various final products.[3]

(iii) Determination of the Price of Capital Services

Among factors of production one may consider capital as the most important one and perhaps more complicated than others for pricing analysis. The span of the economic theory dealing with capital factor is quite vast covering microeconomics, macroeconomics, development economics, growth economics, financial management, project analysis and other similar areas of study. Our objective here is not to go through the entire capital theory but to present a few of its basic aspects concerned with its price determination in the microeconomic context.

Capital is a productive factor. It consists of produced goods that are used in producing other goods. We may cite some examples of such goods like machines, factory buildings, trucks, tools, office equipment, coal, natural gas, minerals, and so on. All such goods are tangible goods. Some of them are durable, used repeatedly in the process of production, and some are non-durable, used in production once for all. All tangible goods that can be changed into other forms and which are used to make certain other goods, are called circulating capital or working capital. Items like raw material, cash in hand, work in progress, inventories of inputs and finished products, etc., come in this category. The tangible durable goods, which are used repeatedly in the process of production

---

3. P. A. Samuelson, *Economics*, McGraw-Hill, 6th Ed., p. 540.

because of their long life are called Fixed Capital goods. These goods are not meant for sales. Their function is similar to that of labour, *i.e.*, to convert the raw materials into some finished product according to the technological prescription. Machines and fixtures, buildings, tools and equipment, etc., are a few of such items. All capital goods will be inanimate and tangible. Workers are also providers of productive services. They provide similar services as capital does. Because of such similarity of work, we put them in the category of human capital. However, workers cannot be bought and sold like tangible capital assets. One can buy or hire their services only.

Land is also a productive factor or asset. Its function is exactly similar as that of fixed capital. But land is not a produced asset; rather, it is a free gift of nature to mankind. It is non-augmentable and undiminishable gift. In view of such characteristics, land is treated as a different type of productive factor than capital.

Being highly heterogeneous in composition, as defined above, capital creates considerable difficulty in measurement. In fact, there is no single physical unit in which the aggregate capital can be measured. For specific type of capital, when taken into consideration individually, there exists a physical unit for measurement such as machine-hours, square-feet of floor area of a building, number of tools or tables or type-writers and so on. The aggregate capital can only be measured in value terms at constant prices. When prices of capital items are kept constant, variation in the aggregate capital in value term reflects changes in its physical magnitudes. Capital accumulates over time. Additions in capital stock in different years are converted first in terms of constant prices and then summed together to get the aggregate capital at constant prices. This method of measuring capital stock is called perpetual inventory method.

The durable capital, *i.e.*, the fixed capital, is used repeatedly in the process of production over its life time. There will be a gradual loss in its physical efficiency or even in value over time because of wear and tear or obsolescence. This loss is called depreciation. There are several methods in practice to measure depreciation of physical capital.[4] Gross value of fixed capital minus depreciation is called 'net fixed capital'.

A capital good, or say capital in general, will be productive over its life-time. It produces a net-output over the amount needed for its maintenance and replacement. Let us say that the gross-output expected from the capital annually over its life-time is ₹ 1000. This is gross marginal contribution of the capital to the producer. If the annual depreciation of the capital is ₹ 500, let ₹ 100 be the maintenance charges. The annual net marginal contribution of the capital would then be ₹ 1000 – ₹ 600 = ₹ 400 in the revenue. The cumulative depreciation returns back the cost of capital at the end of its life. It is thus a provision for the replacement of the capital. The net marginal value product of capital is the surplus created by it. This must be positive, and greater the value of net marginal product higher will be the demand for the capital. We have seen this earlier while dealing with the derivation of the demand for a factor of production. However, we have to go again through this aspect in order to outline a method of deriving, returns from capital over its life time and not just in one year.

We know, capital is a source of productive service through which income is generated. There is a price of the capital service in the market which we define as the rate of interest. The rate of interest is conceptualized simply as a ratio between the annual value of capital service and the value of the capital stock itself. This is proportionate yield on the stock of capital used in production. Consider land as a capital asset. If an acre of land is valued as ₹ 1000 and generates real income of 50 quintals of wheat. If the price of wheat is ₹ 2, the value of wheat in the market is

4. See R. R. Barthwal: *Industrial Economics,* Wiley Eastern, New Delhi, 1984, pp. 254–56.

₹ 2.0 × 50 = ₹ 100. This is income generated. The rate of interest earned on the investment of ₹1000 in land would therefore be ₹ 100/₹ 1000 = ₹ 0.10 or 10% per annum.

We may simply say that

$$\text{Rate of Interest} = \frac{\text{Annual Income from capital}}{\text{Value of Capital Stock}}$$

In computing the income, both positive and negative sides must be taken into account. Say for example the loss due to depreciation of capital stock must be taken into account as an offset in calculating the net income from capital services.

In the market, we do find several types of capital assets, each one of them having a yield rate or rate of interest. Under perfect capital market, the proportionate yield or rate of interest tends to be equal because of inter assets substitution or what we call as perfect malleability of capital. Based on this phenomenon, we can define market-rate of interest or equilibrium rate of interest as,

> The market rate of interest is that percentage return per year which has to be paid on any safe loan of money, which has to be yielded by any safe bond or other types of security, and which has to be earned on the value of any capital asset (such as a machine, a hotel building, a patent right) in any competitive market where there are no risks or where all risk factors have already been taken care of by special premium payments to protect against risks.[5]

An ideal capital market, perfect in competition, free from risks and uncertainties, has been conceived in this definition. The forces that interact in such a market to determine the rate of interest are that of supply and demand for capital as usual, the case of price determination for a product or a factor services in production. The supply side of capital deals with the availability of funds for investment and the demand side relates with the net productivity, *i.e.*, the return on capital investment. The market rate of interest plays vital roles on both the sides of the capital market. It provides inducement to curtail current consumption and save more for future gains, and ration out the uses of capital on the basis of its net productivity. Imperfections in the capital market, either on its demand or supply side, affect the market-rate of interest and so risks and uncertainties, and future expectations also exert their influence on the rate of interest. There are some abstract theories used in the determination of market-rate of interest, and also there are practical approaches to find the specific rates of interest applicable to different types of capital assets, such as bank loans, bonds, equity, retained earnings, etc.

We have already discussed the process of derivation of the demand curve for a factor of production. Conceptually, the value of marginal product under the competitive conditions in the product and capital market and the marginal revenue product under imperfect product market where capital is used, or locus of the shifting equilibrium points on different *VMP* or *MRP* curves for more than one variable factors of production technology, defines the demand curve for capital services (see Section 11.2). In the context of the interest rate determination this is not adequate since returns on capital throughout its life time have not been taken explicitly into account. We have to enlarge the concept of demand curve for capital by considering such returns. Let us do this starting with the definition of a very fundamental notion called net productivity of capital.

As we know, capital goods produced by the economic system itself are used as productive inputs for production of future consumption and other goods and services. The use of capital makes the productive process indirect or roundabout. This requires some explanation. Direct production is the use or conversion of a given stock of resources directly to a consumer good. However, if resources are first employed into production of a capital good and then the capital good is used in

5. P. A. Samuelson; *Economics*, McGraw-Hill 1964 (6th Ed.), *p*. 580.

production of the consumer good, it is indirect or sequential or roundabout process. There might be several sequential steps and not just one or two. If there are more roundabout methods in the production process, the time involved from the start of the activity of production to the output of the first unit of the required consumer good will be lengthened by the time spent on the production of capital goods. Thus, the period of production tends to increase as production becomes more and more roundabout. There will be a gain if capital does have a positive net productivity so that over the life-span of the capital goods, the total output becomes greater and greater than it would have been otherwise. In other words, we can say that there exist, roundabout processes of production which take time to get started and which are more productive than direct processes. This is a technological fact from which we can draw the conclusion that after allowing for all depreciation requirements, capital has a net productivity that can be expressed in the form of a percentage yield per annum. The net productivity of capital, in a formal way, can be defined as follows:

> A capital or investment project's net productivity is that annual percentage yield which you could earn by tying up your money in it. What is the same thing, the project's net productivity is that market-rate of interest at which it would just pay to undertake it.[6]

In the terminology of investment analysis or project appraisal, the net productivity of capital as defined above, is called 'internal rate of return'. The concept of internal rate of return or net productivity of capital can be understood in a better way by examining the process of compounding of interest and hence a change in the value of capital overtime and its inverse process called discounting of future incomes. The value of money over time changes because of interest and, changes in its purchasing power. For simplicity, we consider interest as the relevant factor for changing the value of money (*i.e.*, capital in the present context) overtime. Let us consider C_0 as initial amount of capital which is given on loan at an annual interest rate of i per unit of money (normally interest rate is expressed in percentage term but here we have to consider it in unit term). The interest is compounded annually. At the end of first year, C_0 becomes the sum of the principal (C_0) plus the interest income on it which is iC_0. Let us denote this by C_1, we then have the identity:

$$C_1 = C_0 + iC_0 = C_0\ (1 + i) \qquad \text{...(50)}$$

At the end of second year, C_1 becomes $C_1 + iC_1$, *i.e.*,

$$C_2 = C_1 + iC_1 = C_1\ (1 + i)$$

Substituting $C_1 = C_0\ (1 + i)$ we have,

$$C_2 = C_0\ (1 + i)\ (1 + i) = C_0(1 + i)^2 \qquad \text{...(51)}$$

Similarly, the value of C_0 at the end of third year becomes

$$C_3 = C_0\ (1 + i)^3 \qquad \text{...(52)}$$

This way, we can get values of C_0 at the end of the successive years. A general expression for this at the end of the year t is:

$$C_t = C_0\ (1 + i)^t \qquad \text{...(53)}$$

If C_0 = ₹ 100, $i = 0.05$ (*i.e.*, 5% per annum) and t = 10 year, then $C_{10} = 100\ (1 + .05)^{10}$ = ₹ 162.89. Tabulated values of $(1 + i)^t$ for different years at different rates of interest are available in books on financial accounting. The term $(1 + i)$ is called 'single payment future worth' factor For continuous (instantaneous) compounding we use the formula

$$C_t = C_0\ e^{it}. \qquad \text{...(54)}$$

6. P.A. Samuelson; *Economics*, *Ibid.*; p. 579.

where $e = 2.71828$ is the base of natural logarithms. The interest is normally compounded annually. If it is compounded quarterly or half yearly, suitable modifications are made in the interest rate and interest period. For example, if interest is to be compounded quarterly, the interest rate for this would be $i/4$ where i is the annual rate and the interest periods would be $4t$. This gives the future value of C_0 as $C_t = C_0 (1 + i/4)^{4t}$.

By using the equation (53) or (54), we can find the future value of the present sum at a given interest rate i per annum. Suppose, the future value of money say C_t is known, we can find its present value through discounting. The basic equation for this is the same, *i.e.* (53) or (54). From (53) we get

$$C_0 = C_t/(1 + i)^t \qquad ...(55)$$

The interest rate is now interpreted as the discount rate and $1/(1 + i)^t$ is the 'single payment present worth' factor or simply the discount factor. Tabulated values for this at different rates of interest for different years are available.

Now, let us say that C_0 is the initial investment at the period 0 by a firm and let R_1, R_2, R_3 ..., R_n be the annual return from this upto the life-span of the project or capital investment. R_n includes the salvage value of the capital at the end of its life. The present value of the stream of earnings R_1, R_2, ..., R_n can be expressed as:

$$V = R_1/(1 + i) + R_2/(1 + i)^2 + R_3/(1 + i)^3 + ... + R_n/(1 + i)^n \qquad ...(56)$$

We have defined the net productivity of capital or of a project as that market rate of interest at which it would just pay to undertake it. It means that we have to find the rate of interest for which the present value of the stream of earnings R_1, R_2, ..., R_n is equal to the initial investment. That is:

$$C_0 = V = \sum_{t=1}^{t=n} R_t/(1 + i)^t$$

or

$$C_0 - \sum_{t=1}^{t=n} R_t/(1 + i)^t = 0 \qquad ...(57)$$

The rate of interest i in this equation is the 'internal rate of return' of the project or 'net productivity' or 'marginal efficiency of investment' or 'marginal productivity of investment'. All these are different names for the same thing.

The equation (57) is quite complex as far as computation of the internal rate of interest is concerned. It has multiple roots. The solution of such an equation can only be done on the basis of trial and error. We use different rates of interest and compute the present value of the future stream of income and finally select the rate of interest for which the difference between V and C_0 is zero. In fact, this difference, *i.e.*, $V - C_0$, is called net present value of the investment. A capital investment is viable so long as its net present value is positive. The internal rate of return, when compared with the actual borrowing rate, provides an alternative criterion for investment appraisal. It reflects the demand side of the investment.

The expression (57) can be simplified further by assuming fixed return of R every year for a very very long time, say ∞. That is $R_1 = R_2 = \cdots = R_n = R$, such as the return from a bond or similar kind of investment security. When $R_1 = R_2 = \cdots = R_n = R$, and $i > 0$, $n \to \infty$, then (57) reduces to,

$$V = R/i \qquad ...(58)$$

That is, the present value of capital is equal to the expected fixed return per annum divided by the market-rate of interest. This formula is applicable only when the stream of future return is uniform and the life-span is very very long. These points should be kept in mind.

The formula (57) or (58) has considerable theoretical importance in capital theory. It simply says that a capital asset will be purchased only if the discounted present value of the income accruing from it is greater or atleast equal to the price of the asset. Perfect competition in the capital market will ensure that the price of the asset must be equal to the present value of its income stream at the equilibrium. This means that the price of the capital assets and, thus, total investment will be a function of the interest rate for a given income stream, and the first derivative of the function will be negative. A project or capital assets will be undertaken first whose internal rate of return (*i.e.*, the net productivity) is high. If the net productivity declines, other projects will become viable and thus they will be undertaken. This gives an inverse relationship between the net productivity and volume of investment. This is what we call as the demand function for capital, which, in conjunction with the supply of capital in the competitive market, determines the rate of interest.

There are several theories dealing with the determination of the rate of interest. A few of them are being summarised as under.

(i) The Classical Theory

According to the classical economists, the rate of interest is determined by the supply of savings and demand for savings to invest. Savings come out of current income by curtailing consumption. The relationship between interest rate and savings has been postulated as an upward sloping curve showing positive interest elasticity for savings. The demand side for savings is reflected by the marginal revenue productivity of money invested in capital assets. An entrepreneur continues to make investment in capital assets as long as the expected net return or the marginal revenue product of capital is greater than the cost of borrowing money, *i.e.*, the rate of interest. He will be in equilibrium where the demand curve for capital intersects the supply curve for savings, as shown below.

The market demand curve for capital is shown by *DD′* in Figure 11.14 Panel *B*, while the market supply is represented by curve *SS′*. These two curves intersect each other at point *E*, corresponding to which i^* is the market-rate of interest and K^* is the equilibrium market investment on capital. The equilibrium position regarding capital employment for an individual firm is given in Panel (*A*) of the figure. Since perfect competition prevails in the capital market, the market rate of interest i^* will be exogenously given for the firm. It only adjusts the employment of its capital to this rate of interest. The optimum position is, therefore, given by the point *e* on *dd′*, *i.e.*, the *MRP* curve where the interest line i^* intersects it. k^* is the optimum level of capital use for the firm for which $MRP_K = i^*$.

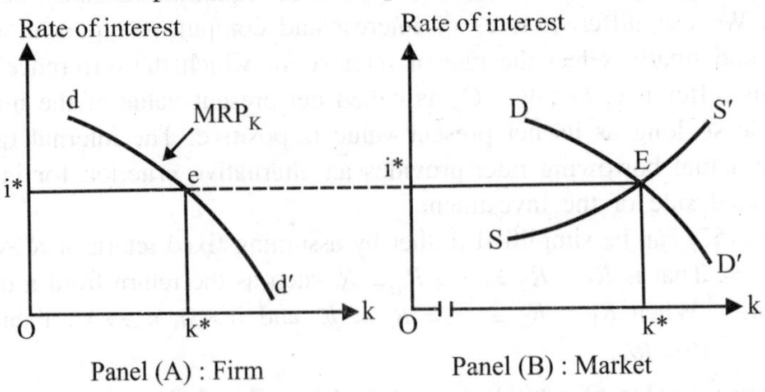

Fig. 11.14 Determination of Rate of Interest

Apart from the normal assumption of perfect competition in the capital market, the other assumptions for the classical theory of interest are: (*a*) full employment of resources including capital input, and (*b*) independence of savings schedule from the investment schedule. The macroeconomists, however, do not agree with these assumptions. According to them, a firm can increase the use of capital services when it is not utilised fully and, therefore, it need not make fresh investment for that. This implies that the increased capital utilisation may not be at the expense of consumption. In fact, as we find in macroeconomics, both investment and consumption might be positively linked together. The demand for capital investment is a derived demand. A fall in consumption may reduce the demand for investment goods and, therefore, the income and savings also decline by this. Savings and investment are not independent of each other. In the macroeconomic equilibrium, they are equal but not through changes in interest rates but through changes in national income. At least, the Keynesian economics teaches us these kinds of links between investment, savings and national income. The classical theory of interest rate is, therefore, indeterminate according to Keynes.

(ii) The Loanable Fund Theory

It is basically a neo-classical theory of interest developed independently by Wicksell, Robertson and Davenport.[7] According to this theory, the rate of interest is determined by the interaction of the demand and supply of loanable funds.

The supply side of loanable funds consists of savings from disposable income, dishoarding of funds, money created by banks, and disinvestment. Savings come from individuals, households and business units. We may take ex-ante or planned savings into account or ex-post, *i.e.*, actual savings from current period available for the next period. The relationship between private savings and the rate of interest is positively sloping one. Business savings in the form of retained earnings also show positive relationship with the rate of interest. So, the total savings are expected to be interest elastic showing positive relationship with rate of interest.

Hoarding of money by people is a result of liquidity preference. This involves cost. If rate of interest is low, people may hoard more and more money. On the other hand, if rate of interest goes up, dishoarding takes place. This means more money available for loans. Commercial banks create money and this is a very big source of loanable funds. The disinvestment component of supply of funds means raising of depreciation reserves and or withdrawal of working capital and marketable securities from the investment package. Such phenomenon takes place when rate of interest increases. All four components of loanable funds supply will have separate supply schedules, the horizontal sum of which will give us the market supply schedule for loanable funds.

The demand for loanable funds consists of investment demand based on net expected return on it, consumption demand for purchasing consumer durables, demand for hoarding of liquid money and demand of government sector for funds. All these components of demand for funds relate inversely with rate of interest. The horizontal summation of the demand curves for each of these components of demand for funds gives the total market demand for loans.

Once we have the market demand curve and the market supply curve for loanable funds, the equilibrium market rate of interest can then be found out through their interaction in the same way as we find for determination of the price of a commodity through supply and demand equality.

---

7. (*a*) K. Wicksell, "Interest and Prices," English translation by R. F. Kahn, Reprint of Economic Classic; Augustus, M. Kelley, *Bookseller*, N.Y., 1965.
   (*b*) D. H. Robertson, *Lectures on Economic Theory*, London; Staple, 1958.
   (*c*) H. J. Davenport, '*The Economics of Enterprises* (1813), Reprint of *Economic Classic*, N.Y., A. M. Kelly, 1968.

The loanable funds theory is an improvement over the classical theory of interest. It also takes into account the liquidity preference for funds which is the basic ingredient of the Keynesian theory of interest.

(iii) The Liquidity Preference Theory

Keynes, in his General Theory[8], has treated interest as a purely monetary phenomenon and provided a theory for its determination which is known as the liquidity preference theory. By liquidity preference we mean the demand for money to hold in cash. According to Keynes, the demand for holding cash arises because of (*a*) the transaction motives meaning requirements of funds for current as well as future purchases of goods and services, and inputs by house holds and business units, and others; (*b*) precautionary motive of holding cash for meeting unforeseen contingencies; and (*c*) speculative motive where cash is kept in liquid form for speculative purposes for the sake of earnings. People hold money when rate of interest is low but when it is high they release their cash and give it on loan or invest it on market securities for getting income from that in the form of interest. The first two motives do not influence the rate of interest (according to Keynes, of course), however the speculative demand for money together with the supply of money determine the rate of interest.

Let us say that M_1 is the transaction and precautionary demand for money. It will be a function of income (Y), *i.e.*,

$$M_1 = L_1(Y) \qquad ...(59)$$

The speculative demand for money is M_2, and this is a function of the rate of interest (i), so we have

$$M_2 = L_2(i) \qquad ...(60)$$

Total Demand for Money is therefore,

$$M = M_1 + M_2 = L_1(Y) + L_2(i) \qquad ...(61)$$

The supply of money is given exogenously. It consists of coins, currency notes and bank deposits subject to withdrawal by cheques. The monetary authorities determine the supply of money. The interest rate is determined through interaction of the liquidity preference curve and the supply line for money, as shown in Figure 11.15. *LP* is the liquidity preference schedule and *MS* is the money supply schedule. They intersect at E_1 point which give i^* as the equilibrium rate of interest. For a given liquidity preference schedule, if the money supply increases the interest rate falls. There may be a minimum level of interest which does not vary with increasing money supply such as i_1 in the figure

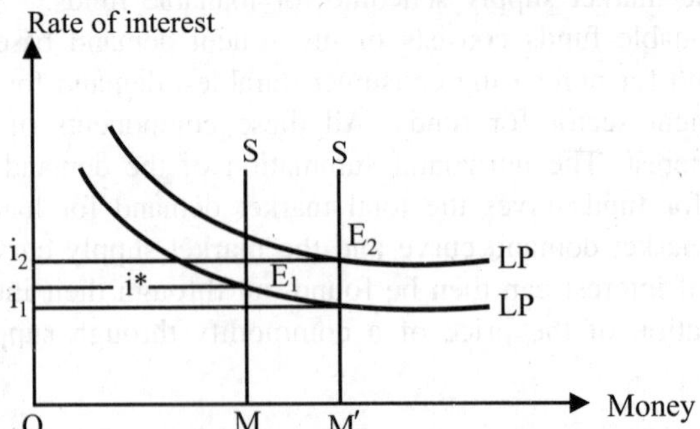

Fig. 11.15 The Liquidity Preference Analysis of Interest Rate Determination

8. J. M. Keynes, *The General Theory of Employment, Interest and Money,* Harcourt–Brace, N.Y., 1935.

This is Keyne's 'liquidity trap' situation. The liquidity preference schedule is perfectly elastic beyond this stage. If the liquidity preference schedule rises, money supply being constant the equilibrium rate of interest rises. When both the curves shift to the right, the rate of interest goes up or down depending on the relative shifts of curves. Other possibilities of a change in the rate of interest when the liquidity preference curve and the money supply curve shift in opposite directions can be examined like this.

Although the liquidity preference theory suffers from some limitations,[9] yet it is regarded as an improvement over the neo-classical theory of interest.

(iv) Hicksian Theory of Interest

Hicks[10] and Hansen[11] independently synthesized the classical, the neo-classical and the Keynesian theories and put them in a unified framework. This is popularly known as *IS-LM* approach. In this approach, the investment demand for funds or money is considered to be a function of the rate of interest alone but the supply of savings or loanable funds was considered depending on the rate of interest as well as income.

Similarly, the liquidity preference schedule is taken as a function of the rate of interest and income level and the quantity of money was taken as fixed, determined exogenously by the monetary authorities. At the equilibrium, savings are equal to investment and liquidity is equal to money supply. On solution, such model provides equilibrium level of interest rate and aggregate income. We summarize the *IS-LM* model as:

$$I = I(i) \quad \text{Investment Demand Function}$$

$$S = S(i, y) \quad \text{Saving Function}$$

$$L = L(i, y) \quad \text{Liquidity Preference Function}$$

$$M = M^* \quad \text{Fixed Money Supply}$$

$$\left.\begin{aligned} I &= S \\ L &= M^* \end{aligned}\right\} \quad \text{Equilibrium Conditions} \qquad \text{...(59)}$$

How this model works? Let us explain it graphically. In Fig. 11.16, the investment demand for funds is given by II' curve. S_1 is the saving or supply schedule for funds at a given level of income Y_1. If income increases, savings go up; so the savings schedule shifts to the right to S_2 position causing a decline in the equilibrium rate of interest. If income goes up further, savings curve shifts further to the right causing further decline in the rate of interest. If we plot a curve between the rate of interest and income levels we get a downward curve which is defined as '*IS*' curve. This is shown on the right hand side of Fig. 11.16.

9. See A. Hansen: *A Guide to Keynes*, N.Y. McGraw-Hill 1953, pp. 140-141.
10. Hicks J. R., Mr. "Keynes and the Classics: A Suggested Interpretation"; *Econometrica*, Vol. 5, 1937, pp. 147–157.
11. A. Hansen, *Ibid.*

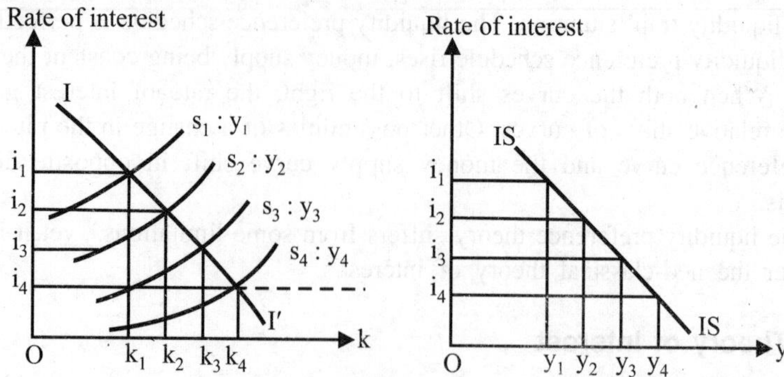

Fig. 11.16 Derivation of the 'IS' Curve

When income changes the liquidity preference schedule also changes with that. In Fig. 11.17, we have shown L_1 as the liquidity preference schedule for Y_1 income. When income increases to Y_2 level, the liquidity preference schedule goes up to L_2 position. For a given money supply schedule M^*, this implies an increase in the rate of interest. Further increases in income push the rate of interest up and up through interaction of the liquidity and money supply schedules. If we plot the relationship between the rates of interest and income levels we get a positively sloping curve as shown in the right side of Fig. 11.17. This relationship is called *'LM'* curve.

The two curves, *'IS'* and *'LM'*, on their intersection, provide the final equilibrium rate of interest as shown in Fig. 11.18. At this equilibrium situation, investment (*I*) and savings (*S*) will be equal, and the demand for money (*L*) is also equal to the money supply (*M*). If *IS* curve shifts upward due to a rise in investment demand and a fall in savings, other things being equal, the equilibrium interest rate rises; on the other hand, if the *LM* schedule shifts to the right, due to increase in money supply or decrease in the liquidity demand for money, other things being equal, the interest rate declines. When both the curves shift to the right the rate of interest may rise or fall depending on the relative shifts of the two curves.

Although there are some drawbacks of the Hicks-Hansen *IS-LM* approach for determination of the rate of interest, particularly the concept of static equilibrium, yet it is fairly acceptable to most of the economists as a modern theory of interest rate determination.

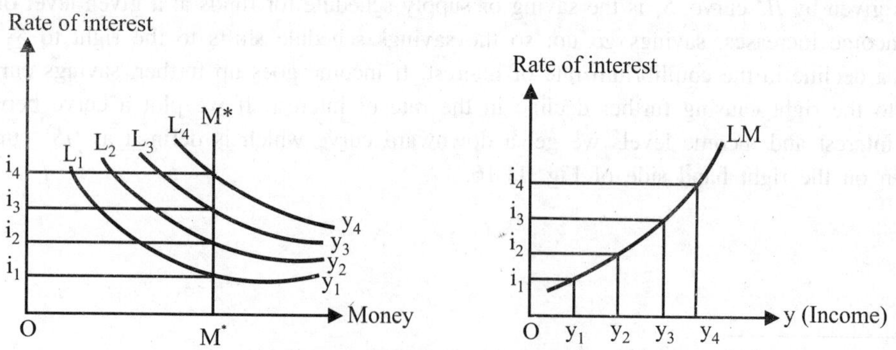

Fig. 11.17 Derivation of the 'LM' Curve

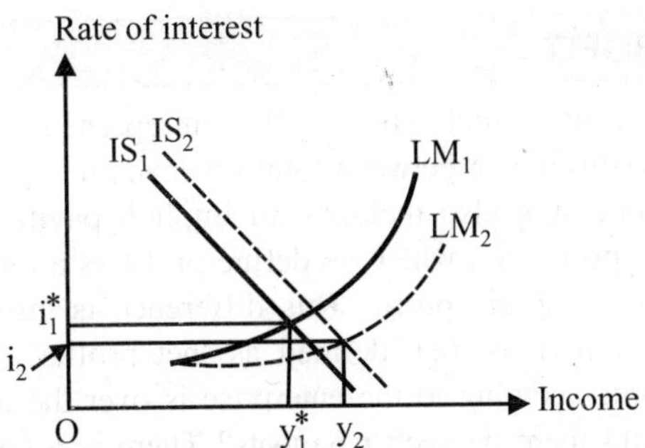

Fig. 11.18 Determination of the Equilibrium Rate of Interest: IS-LM Analysis

Apart from the theories discussed above, Bohm Bawerk and Irving Fishers have also made significant contributions in this area. The theory developed by Bohm Bawerk is known as the Agio or Austrian or Psychological theory of interest. The gist of this theory is that interest arises because men prefer present goods to future goods and, therefore, there is an 'agio' or premium attached to present consumption of goods when it is compared to the future consumption. The present satisfaction of wants is given greater importance than the future satisfaction. Thus, future satisfaction of wants undergo some discount when viewed from the present point of view. Interest is this discount which must be paid to induce people to lend their money or postpone their present consumption for some future date.

This theory has been modified further by Irving Fisher. His theory is a 'time preference theory of interest'.[12] The Fisherian theory, though different in analytical terminology and method, is similar in substance as the Bohm Bawerk's theory.

The theories discussed above are relevant for competitive capital markets free from risks and uncertainties. In practice, there are several qualifications to all such theories which make the determination of market rate of interest quite complicated. For example, presence of financial institutions, such as banks or savings and loan corporations, destroys the possibility of perfect competition in the capital markets since they are not generally small and passive entities in their business. The power of such financial institutions makes the competitive models quite inappropriate for determination of the rate of interest. On the investors' side also we do find large borrowers and, therefore, imperfections in the capital markets. One might conceive a situation that, in reality, market condition similar to a bilateral monopoly exists in the capital market and, therefore, the interest rate is not determined through interplay of the market forces but rather through a bargaining process. Thus, market imperfections and institutional forces make the process of interest rate determination very difficult. Apart from the dynamic aspects of the economy like changing technology and hence rising net products of capital overtime, the riskiness of capital investments, future uncertainties and expectations, etc., are the factors that affect the rate of interest. However, there is no accepted theory for the determination of the rate of interest which incorporates all such factors. In practice, the institutional factors play a major role in determination of the rates of interest for various capital assets. Microeconomic theories are of little use in this respect. In the short-run, we do find the rates of interest more or less fixed but in the long-run they do vary.

12. Irvin Fisher: *The Rate of Interest,* N.Y., Macmillan Co., 1907.

11.8 THEORIES OF PROFIT

Profit is the residual income which goes to the entrepreneur (an individual or a collective agency). Profit is defined as a difference between total revenue and total cost of production including selling costs. The cost of production also includes all implicit payments to the entrepreneur which constitute together the normal profit. So, when we define profit as a difference between total revenue and total cost we mean it as economic profit. This difference is gross of corporate income taxes. If such taxes are taken out of it, it is then defined as 'net profits'.

We reiterate that net profits accruing to the enterprise is óver the normal earnings or opportunity cost of the entrepreneur. Should there be such payments? There is a controversy regarding this issue. However, we will not go into its debate, rather we will simply examine the functions of the entrepreneur in the conduct of a business and then comment on the justification of paying profits to him.

A business firm is a productive entity in society engaged in supplying some product or service to people. For this, the firm employs the factors of production including raw materials in the production process. There will be several persons in the firm doing specified jobs. Who employs these persons and who coordinates their activities? We can say that there is a person or a group of persons called the 'management' which is authorised to do this job. The management may simply be the owner or owners of the firm, is the residual claimants to the firm's profits or losses after meeting the contractual obligations. In large corporations, such as the joint stock companies, managers themselves are specialized kinds of employed resources. They make contractual agreements with other resource suppliers and implement and monitor performance of such contracts. Managers, in this situation, will be acting as hired agents of the owner or owners of the firm. This means, above all contractual personnel there is a person or a group of persons having the final authority of making contracts for resource-supplies and coordinating activities of the firm. This person (or group) is the owner of the firm. Thus, there is an important decision-making aspect attached to firm's ownership. This is conventionally known as 'entrepreneurship'. The owner(s) of the firm is an entrepreneur. Apart from being a final authority for contractual decision-making, he is liable for all risks of his firm; in other words, he bears the risks. In a joint-stock company, no doubt the liability of a owner, who is one of the several shareholders, will be limited to the proportion of his or her equity participation, yet he or she is one of the owners of the firm bearing the risk. The function of decision-making and actual risk taking in such a company where there is a separation between ownership and management, are vested to elected representatives, *i.e.*, the board of directors of the firm, but from the side of *risks bearing* the shareholders, *i.e.*, owners have the responsibility and not the management.

The risks that an entrepreneur face are of two categories. One category is insurable because it is subject to the laws of probability. Such risks can be predicted with some probability of their occurrence and, hence the entrepreneur can protect himself against them through insurance. The premium that he pays for this is included in the cost of production.

The other category of risks is non-insurable. Their occurrences are unpredictable and quite uncertain. It is such uncertainties of a business that its entrepreneur faces. A few examples of such uncertainties, as one may cite, are changes in the demand for products of the firm due to changes in consumer tastes, random events like wars, strikes, unusual weather conditions do cause temporary fluctuations in the demand for products. The effects of such unforeseen events fall on the entrepreneur.

An entrepreneur introduces new products, new methods of processing and ventures in new areas of business. All this comes under innovation activities. Gains from such activities are also quite uncertain and their ultimate effect is borne by the entrepreneur.

Considering the various aspects of a business, we may summarize functions of an entrepreneur: (*i*) he or she bears the risks and uncertainties of the business; (*ii*) he or she is an innovator venturing in the new areas of business opportunities, and (*iii*) he or she is the coordinator of the entire business activities of the firm. For performing such functions the entrepreneur gets his reward in the form of profit. He or she is not a contractual claimant of income. His or her income in the form of profit or even in the form of implicit cost or opportunity cost might be negative also. In this respect entrepreneur is quite different factor of production as compared to the other factors of production. There are several view points or what we might call as theories of profit based upon the above entrepreneurial functions. A brief discussion of such theories would be useful here in order to justify profits in business activities and to get a further clarification about the various entrepreneurial functions.

(i) Walker's Rent Theory of Profit

Although most of the classical economists said something or the other about profit and its source, but a simple and consistent view-point regarding profit was put forward by Francis Walker in his article, 'The Sources of Business Profit' (*Quarterly Journal of Economics*, April, 1887). He treated rent and profit on an equal footing and so his theory is known as the rent theory of profit. According to Walker, profit is the rent of ability. Just as there is a no-rent land in the Recardian theory of rent, in the same way there is no profit firm or entrepreneur whose income just covers the cost of production, and just as rent of a piece of land is a surplus output over the output of a no-rent land, in the same way profit of a firm is a surplus above the no-profit firm. It is the surplus revenue accruing to the superior entrepreneur over the marginal one. The interest earned on the capital supplied by the entrepreneur himself is excluded obviously from the profit. The function of entrepreneur is to manage its business and provide a superintendence to it. Someone might be quite efficient in doing such jobs while others might be inefficient. So, profit is the rent for superior ability to manage the firm.

If we accept Walker's idea of treating profit as rent to entrepreneurship, the question is now: Why it is seen to be negative in a large number of firms in spite of good management? There are no such examples of rent being negative. Rent is more or less a known or expected surplus but profit is unknown and subject to several business uncertainties. Further, in a joint stock company owned by several shareholders and where there is separation between management and ownership one may not accept Walker's interpretation of profit as rent for superior entrepreneurship. The manner in which decisions regarding retained earnings and dividend payments are taken by the management in such a company is in no way related to the shareholders' ability. Further, if we interpret profit as rent, it may not be a factor determining the price of the product at least from social point of view, but invariably we do find profit margins in prices of goods and services, particularly when they are fixed through mark-up pricing procedure. So, on the whole, we can say that there might be an element of 'quasi-rent' in profit, but treating it wholly as 'rent' for superior entrepreneurial ability is far from business realities.

(ii) Marshallian Theory of Profit

Marhall's interpretation of profit is in-line with the classical line of thinking.[13] Marshall considered it as the supply price of business power in command of capital. There are three components of the business power conceived by him: (*a*) the supply of capital; (*b*) the supply of ability and energy for

13. Alfred Marshall, *Principles of Economics*, 8th Edition, London, Macmillan Co., 1956, Book 6, Chapters 7, 8; pp. 495–522.

managing the business; and (*c*) the supply of organizational capacity by which business ability and capital are put together for effective production. 'Organisation' is considered as a separate factor of production by Marshall just like land, labour and capital and he attributed to this factor "profits of capital and business power."

According to Marshall, for every business activity there is a normal rate of profit which is determined mainly by tradition and which is a part of cost of production. In the short-run, there are frictional profits which provide inducement for production. In the long-run, all abnormal profits are eliminated by forces of demand and supply operating in the market. Neither Marshall has attributed profits to business risks and uncertainties, nor he has taken the dynamic changes in the industry, like innovation, etc., affecting profits. His approach is static in nature. According to his theory, total product of the industry is exhausted when every factor is paid at the rate of its supply price.

(iii) Clark's Dynamic Theory of Profit

J. B. Clark attributed the occurrence of profit to dynamic changes in the economy.[14] In the static economy, there would be no new products, no new markets, no new inventions, no change in industrial structure, and no changes in similar other factors. The business environment remains quite static and predictable. However, in reality, we see all such factors changing over time; so an entrepreneur faces a dynamic business environment where nothing is certain. Clark's theory of profit is based on such dynamic conditions of economy about which the knowledge of businessmen is imperfect. Giving the gist of his theory, Clark argued that so long an entrepreneur starts operations with imperfect knowledge about the state of the market and the anticipated marginal products of hired factors deviate from their actual marginal products, the surplus, *i.e.*, profit would be persisting in the industry. Clark has not taken business risks into account as explicit factors determining profits, but future uncertainties of business environment were considered by him as sources of business profits.

(iv) Schumpeter's Innovation Theory of Profit

Schumpeter attributed the emergence of business profits to the changes in the technological melio of the firm which we call as innovation.[15] An entrepreneur introduces several types of innovations in his business. Some innovations like introduction of new machinery, new and cheaper techniques of processing, new and better sources of raw materials, changes in the organisational structure of the firm, etc., reduce the cost of production and thus increase the profit margin on products. Other types of innovations, such as changes in the product structure of the firm, introduction of new products, improvement in the quality of existing products, better ways of advertisement and sales promotion, discovery of new markets, etc., increase the demand for the product of the firm as a result of which the revenue of the firm increases and therefore the profit, constituting the difference between revenue and cost, increases. The entrepreneur, who introduces all kinds of innovations in his business, is, therefore, the claimant of the increased surplus over the cost of business activities. Profit is, therefore, a reward for innovation. Initially, the entrepreneur gains from innovation but later on society also gets its benefits.

---

14. J. B. Clark, *The Distribution of Wealth*, London, Macmillan, Co., 1899.
15. J. A. Schumpeter; *The Theory of Economic Development, Cambridge*, Harvard University Press, 1951, Ch. 4.

(v) F.H. Knight's Theory of Profits

Frank Knight is the leader of those economists who treated profit as a reward for business risks and uncertainties.[16] According to him, profit, a non-contractual residual accrue to the entrepreneur for his non-transferable function of bearing uninsurable future uncertainties of the business. We have already differentiated between risks and uncertainties earlier. In the situation of risk, the expected outcome of a certain course of action is known with some probability. It is therefore insurable. However, if there is uncertainty, the expected outcome is not known at all. There might be multiple outcomes of a particular course of action which are quite unpredictable. The entrepreneur would not be able to protect himself from uncertainties since they can't be insured. Knight attributed occurrence of business profits to uncertainties and not to risks. A businessman faces uncertainties, because, he would not be sure about the return from the innovations he introduces and also because of changing external factors like changes in fashion, tastes and preferences of consumers, government policies, changes in prices as a result of inflationary and recessionary conditions in the economy, changes in production technology, etc. The entrepreneur ultimately bears all such uncertainties. Therefore, he is entitled for the residual income generated by the firm.

(vi) Monopoly Theory of Profits

This is another view point regarding occurrence of business profit. Monopolistic and monopsonistic conditions prevailing in the market give rise to abnormal business profits. Firms under monopoly or monopolistic competition will be having high market power. They will be 'price-makers' rather than 'price-takers'. They will be able to protect their interests by charging high prices for their products and thus keep their profits at higher levels. They will be able to restrict the entry of new firms in the market through several barriers to entry and thus maintain their monopoly power. All this eventually give rise to profits. It is, therefore, monopoly power of the firm that is the basic source of business profits.

There are several other less known theories of profit but they do not provide us new dimensions of entrepreneurial functions. They are mere extensions of the existing major approaches developed to explain the phenomenon of business profit. We will, therefore, not go into their details.

The above discussion on profit and its sources reveals that, (*i*) it is rather difficult to define profit unambiguously, and (*ii*) there is no consensus among the economists regarding its sources and justification. After making all contractual payments to the hired factors of production and after taking into account the implicit payments to the entrepreneur(s) for his self-owned business inputs including payment for his services, whatever is left that is profit which goes to, owners of the enterprise. That is all what we can say in brief about profit.

11.9 MARGINAL PRODUCTIVITY THEORY OF DISTRIBUTION

The marginal productivity theory of distribution was an attempt on the part of economists to evolve a general theory of distribution. Although we have used marginal product or marginal revenue product as the basis to find the demand curve for a factor which in cooperation with the supply curve for the factor determines its price. Theories discussed so far for determining the factor prices are more or less demand and supply oriented. The marginal productivity theory in which we are

16. Frank H. Knight, *Risks, Uncertainty and Profit*, Houghton, Miffin CO., 1921.

concerned here is one sided approach for pricing of factors of production. It is not considering the supply side at all. This theory simply says that *if factors of production are remunerated according to their marginal products, the total product is just exhausted.* This is true in the long-run under conditions of perfect competition and perfect mobility of factors of production, all units of factors of production being equally efficient. The theory is applicable only when there are constant returns to scale prevailing in production of the product. A very clear exposition of the theory has been provided by Clark and Wicksteed in the form of 'Product Exhaustion Theorem.' It says: *In the long-run, competitive equilibrium, rewarding each input according to its marginal physical product precisely exhausts the total physical product.*[17]

This result can be explained with the help of Euler's theorem according to which we have the identity;

$$f_1x_1 + f_2x_2 = Kf(x_1, x_2) \quad \text{...(62)}$$

where $q = f(x_1, x_2)$ is the production function,

$f_1 = \partial q/\partial x_1$ = Marginal Product of x_1

$f_2 = \partial q/\partial x_2$ = Marginal Product of x_2

K = the degree of homogeneity of the production function. We can show that K = Sum of the output elasticities of two inputs, *i.e.*, dividing both sides of (62) by q we get:

$$dq/dx_1 \cdot \frac{x_1}{q} + \partial q/\partial x_2 \cdot \frac{x_2}{q} = K$$

or

$$\varepsilon_1 + \varepsilon_2 = K \quad \text{...(63)}$$

where ε_1 and ε_2 are the output elasticities of X_1 and X_2. If $K = 1$, *i.e.*, there are constant returns to scale, then the statement of the marginal productivity theory is:

$$f_1 \cdot x_1 + f_2 \cdot x_2 = q \quad \text{...(64)}$$

f_1 = 'Price' of X_1 = MP of X_1, so f_1x_1 share of x_1 in output f_2 = 'Price' of x_2 = MP of x_2, so f_2x_2 = share of x_2 in output. This result holds true even if we consider it in terms of value of marginal products for the inputs, *i.e.*, multiplying both sides by product price P we get

$$Pf_1 \cdot x_1 + Pf_2 \cdot x_2 = Pq \quad \text{...(65)}$$

$$\left.\begin{aligned} Pf_1 &= VMP \ of \ X_1 = r_1 \\ Pf_2 &= VMP \ of \ X_2 = r_2 \end{aligned}\right\} \text{for profit maximum situation Therefore, we have straightforward}$$

relationship,

$$r_1x_1 + r_2x_2 = Pq \quad \text{...(66)}$$

r_1 = Price of X_1, r_2 = Price of X_2

The equation (66) expresses the equality between total cost and revenue. There is o profit in it as it relates to long-run competitive equilibrium $P = AC = MC$. In physical term, we have $MP = AP$ as the condition at which the marginal productivity theory holds good. If there are increasing returns to scale, paying factors of production on the basis of marginal product of the last unit implies a loss to the firm while in the case of decreasing returns to scale there would be a gain. Only at the situation of constant returns to scale the total output will be equal to total factor payments on the basis of their marginal products, the surplus constituting economic profit being zero.

---

17. See C.E. Ferguson : *Microeconomic Theory,* R.D. Irwin Inc., Homewood, 1966, pp. 321–323, for proofs of this theorem.

The marginal productivity theory, as summarized above, is very restrictive in application, *i.e.*, only under long-run competitive equilibrium with constant returns to scale. It is also not taking into consideration the supply side of factor markets. The predictive power of this theory is very weak. In fact, from practical point of view it has no meaning, particularly when we have non-neutral technological changes affecting the relative shares of factors of production in total output. Modern version of this theory is what we have discussed earlier in which both demand and supply sides of the factor markets were taken into account, the demand side, no doubt, depending on the marginal products or marginal revenue products of factors of production.

11.10 CONCLUDING REMARKS

A number of issues related to the factor pricing decisions under various conditions were discussed in this chapter. This much was considered adequate to have a basic understanding of the complexities involved in the distribution theory. We have examined only micro aspect of this theory but, in the course of discussion we found that a good grasp of modern distribution theory requires both micro and macro aspects for examination. This is, however, left to readers for advance readings on the theory.

SUGGESTED READINGS

Bronfenbrenner, M.J., *Income Distribution Theory*, London, Macmillan & Co., 1971.

Carter, A.M., *Theory of Wages and Employment*, Homewood Ill., R.D. Irwin, 1959.

Hicks, J.R., *Theory of Wages*, London, Macmillan & Co., 1932.

Liebhafsky, H.H., *The Nature of Price Theory*, Dasey Press, 1968.

Sher, W. and R. Pindola, *Microeconomic Theory*, Edward Arnold, 1981.

REVIEW QUESTIONS

1. Define the problem of functional distribution of income and show how this problem can be solved through a price mechanism under competitive situations.
2. How do you derive an input demand function if the production technology, as specified by a production function, input prices, and product price are given? Why do we call the demand for an input as the 'derived demand'? Support your answers with some examples of derived demand.
3. What is the difference between *VMP* and *MRP?* How these two concepts are related with the demand function for a factor, say, labour? Explain in detail.
4. How do you get the supply curve for a factor of production, such as labour? What are the essential differences between the supply of a commodity and that of a productive factor in a perfectly competitive market? Discuss.
5. Let us assume that labour is the only variable input used in production of a commodity Q.The production function for this is given as $q = A + aL - bL^2$, where q is the quantity of output of Q, L is the amount of labour and other things are parameters. Show that the demand function for labour derived from this production function is,
   $L = a/2b - w/2bP$, where w = wage rate, P = Product Price. Also show that the demand for labour is an increasing function of product price, other things being equal.
6. The supply curve for labour may be negatively sloped in the range of high wage rates. Why it is so? Explain in terms of substitution and income effects.

7. Give an outline of how market demand for a factor is derived when the product market in whose production the factor is used is imperfect and there are multiple factors used in production.
8. By using the microeconomic framework examine how wage rate is determined when (*a*) labour market is competitive, (*b*) there is monopsony in the labour market and (*c*) there is bilateral monopoly in the labour market.
9. "Rent as price for the use of land is determined by the demand for and supply of land." Explain how. Is this the only approach to determine rent or there are alternative ways also? Examine in brief.
10. Define the term 'interest' and give a brief description of various theories developed to determine interest rate.
11. "The theory of profit is, at present, the most controversial and unsatisfactory branch of economic theory." Examine critically.
12. A set of three fundamental forces, viz. (*a*) physical marginal productivity of a factor *A*, (*b*) the values placed by consumers upon goods in whose production the factor contributes, and (*c*) the structure of the product market together determine the demand of the factor. Explain how.

CHAPTER 12

The General Equilibrium Analysis

So far we have examined the economic behaviour of individual units in economic system. Each economic agent of the system maximises something and thus attains equilibrium position. A consumer, for example, maximises utility subject to the budget constraint; a producer maximises profit subject to constraints imposed by resource availability and the production function; workers may determine their labour supply schedule by maximising satisfaction derived from leisure time subject to given wage-rates and so on. The demand, the supply and the equilibrium conditions of individual commodity and factor markets have been discussed in fairly detailed way. The assumption of 'other things being equal' has been used wherever it was required to isolate the market under study from the rest of the economy and interactions that might exist between markets if kept at the minimal level. This approach of study of the individual markets or individual units of the economy is called 'partial equilibrium analysis', because its essence is just to focus on the equilibrium position of a part of the economy and not the entire one.

In reality, an economic system is an integrated mechanism in which various elements or parts are interlinked together. Consumers, producers, commodities and factor markets, traders, creditors, and economic administration of the government, etc., have significant interdependence with each other in the system. If there is a change anywhere in the system it will have impacts on the other components of the system in varying degrees. An increase in money wage-rate, for example, in one industry might affect the price of products of that industry and then prices of all other industries, where the products are used as inputs. Further, the consumer's equilibrium position might change because of changes in the prices of consumption goods, thus affecting the demand for the products. If demand is affected, it will have effects on demand for factors of production. Factor prices change and thus impact waves of a change in wage-rate in one industry spread across the economy. To study all such impacts together economists have coined the concept of general equilibrium analysis. *This examines the interrelationships that exist among all the decision-making units and markets and studies their behaviour simultaneously with the objective of working out the equilibrium position of the* entire economic system.

The span of general equilibrium is too wide and it may be quite difficult, if not impossible, to have general equilibrium analysis, particularly when the economy is open *i.e.*, having international linkages through trade. In a limited way, one may confine the general equilibrium analysis to multi-market equilibrium in which interactions of the basic microeconomic units; the households and firms, the determination of prices and quantities of goods and services including factors of production, are analysed simultaneously. An idea of general equilibrium analysis is given by the circular flows in the economy which we have presented graphically in Chapter 2 of this book. Analytically, the general equilibrium analysis is done through solution of a set of simultaneous equations which include all the variables, prices, quantities, etc. It is argued that general equilibrium does exist when supply equals demand in all the markets for final goods, intermediate goods, services, and factors of production of the economy. This includes money markets also.

In this chapter, we will examine some approaches to develop general equilibrium model for an economy. The purpose is not to go into details of such approaches but to understand the basic economic philosophy behind using a set of equations. But before doing this, let us go through some uses of the general equilibrium analysis which justify its study.

12.1 USEFULNESS OF GENERAL EQUILIBRIUM ANALYSIS

A number of economic problems faced by individual decision-makers, such as consumers, producers, factor suppliers, can, no doubt, be solved through partial equilibrium analysis, but not all economic problems can be investigated by it particularly, when markets are mutually interdependent and the mutual interactions or influences between micro decision-making units are quite significant. Economists must ascertain the nature of influences in order to include their effects in the analysis of prices and output decisions for various markets. To some extent, by taking substitutability and complementarity among goods and productive services in partial equilibrium analysis, economists do make attempts to incorporate effects of mutual interrelatedness in the economy but that is not adequate. They have to go a bit far more by considering the general equilibrium analysis in this respect.

The multi-market analysis is quite useful from the point of view of regulating the economy. Economic decisions by individuals, particularly by firms for their own gains, might affect other firms or decision units adversely. If we do not know the ramification of such decisions or what we call as their external effects, we will not be able to control them. The general equilibrium analysis in which we do study the interrelatedness among markets and decision-making units provides us the basis for selecting issues where greater degree of control in the economy is to be exercised in the interest of the society as a whole.

The multi-market analysis helps in identifying problems of empirical research on general as well as partial equilibrium analysis. It helps to find out variables which significantly affect the economic system and suggest ways and means to control them in the policy context. Further, it also provides us an idea whether the assumption of 'other things being equal' is valid or not in the partial equilibrium analysis.

What brings an economy in equilibrium may be an important question not only from the point of view of empirical analysis but from the point of view of the economic theory also. This question can be answered only when we study the general equilibrium analysis and see the behaviour of variables in it. We can then find conditions for the stable equilibrium of the economic system as a whole.

In summary, what we can say about the usefulness of the general equilibrium analysis is that to answer certain economic problems like structural analysis of the economy, economic development and growth, sectoral interdependency in the economy, movement of general price indices, determination of macroeconomic variables, exchanges between productive sectors vis-a-vis consumers at large, the general equilibrium analysis is quite relevant. It helps in testing the validity of the partial equilibrium analysis of the markets, and, in fact, both general equilibrium analysis and partial equilibrium analysis are complementary to each other.

12.2 SOME GENERAL EQUILIBRIUM MODELS

An elaborate verbal description of the general equilibrium models is quite difficult; so most of the authors described it through a set of simultaneous equations. This approach is being followed in this section also. The basic theory of general equilibrium analysis in the form of a mathematical model has been provided by Leon Walras[1] which was latter on modified by several economists, including the neo-classicals.[2] W.W. Leontief gave it an operational usable form which is familiar with the name of 'Input-Output Analysis'[3] Let us review these models beginning with the classical approach of Walras.

(i) The Walras General Equilibrium Model

To develop the model which was eventually used for determination of outputs and prices of thc system, Walras made a number of simplifying assumptions. These are as follows:

(*a*) Each individual has a certain initial endowment of each productive factor, such as land, labour and capital. The individual can buy and sell any of the factors or commodities produced using factors at the prevailing market price.

(*b*) The individual as a consumer derives satisfaction or utility from the consumption or use of factors or commodities that he or she retains or purchases. The individual as a producer maximises profit from the production of goods or services.

(*c*) Technology is constant and is given by the production function for each commodity.

With the validity of these assumptions, Walras postulated that the first order utility maximising conditions or the first order profit maximising conditions for a consumer or firm, when the corresponding second order maximisation conditions are satisfied, provide the excess demand functions on solution for the consumer or the firm. Such excess demands, either for commodities or for factors of production might be positive, zero or negative. The sum of the excess demands of all consumers and producers for a commodity or factor of production is the excess market demand for that. The excess market demand for a commodity or factor of production will be a function of all of prices in the system. For the economy as a whole, the number of excess market demand functions will be equal to the number of the variable, *i.e.* the prices. The model specifying the excess demand functions is, thus, consistent and it, can be solved. Using symbols and equations we shall now present a formal sketch of the Walrasian general equilibrium model in its classical form.

Let us assume that there are in all n commodities in the economy, including the productive services. The market demand for a given commodity can be expressed as a function of prices of all commodities in the market, the income level and the number of consumers. The utility maximisation approach provides us the first order marginal conditions which on solution provide the demand functions for each commodity by each consumer. Aggregating all such demand curves we get the

1. Leon Walras: "Elements d'Economic Politique Pure Lausanne F Rouge 1874" (Translated by W. Jaffe, *The Elements of Pure Economics,* Homewood I 11. R.D. Irwin 1954).
2. See M.D. Intriligator, *Mathematical Optimisation and Economic Theory,* 1971, pp. 238-241 for references.
3. W.W. Leontief, *The Structure of American Economy 1919-1939,* N. York. Oxford University Press, 1951.

market demand for the commodity. (Ref. Chapter 4) Suppose we keep the income level and the number of consumer fixed, the market demand for anyone of the commodities can be written as:

$$D_i = D_i\ [P_1,\ P_2,\ ...,\ P_n],\ i = 1,\ ...,\ n. \qquad ...(1)$$

Under perfect competition the supply of each commodity, in general, will also be a function of prices of all commodities. That is, or a given number of firms, the supply function for the *i*th commodity can be written as:

$$S_i = S_i\ [P_1,\ P_2,\ ...,\ P_n],\ i = 1,\ ...,\ n. \qquad ...(2)$$

We can now define the *excess demand function* for the *i*th commodity as the difference between the market demand and market supply. Let the excess demand for *i*th commodity be denoted as E_i then we have:

$$E_i\ (P_1,\ P_2,\ ...,\ P_n) = D_i\ (P_1,\ P_2,\ ...,\ P_n) - S_i\ (P_1,\ P_2,\ ...,\ P_n),\ i = 1,\ ..,\ n. \qquad ...(3)$$

The excess demand is a function of all prices, because both demand and supply are functions of all prices.

The link between demand, supply and excess demand for a commodity can be demonstrated using a simple two dimensional graph showing quantity of the commodity on *X*-axis and its price on *Y*-axis, other things being equal as normally done for plotting a demand and/or supply curves. In Fig. 12.1, *D* and *S* are the straight line demand and supply functions for a commodity *i*.

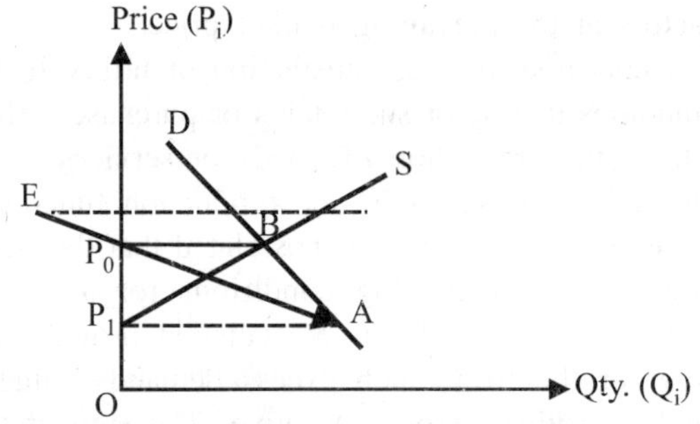

Fig. 12.1 Demand, Supply, and Excess Demand Curves

The demand and supply lines intersect at point *B*. The market for the commodity at this situation is in equilibrium which means zero excess demand for the commodity. The excess demand is, therefore, zero at the equilibrium price P_0. If the price exceeds P_0, we find negative excess demand. Further, the supply curve starts from P_1 price on *Y*-axis. At this price, there is maximum excess demand for the commodity shown by P_1A line. This provides us the origin of the excess demand line which is point *A* on the demand curve. By joining points *A* and P_0 and extending it to *E* we get the line or curve showing the excess demand for the commodity. We have derived it from the demand and supply curves (*i.e.*, lines here) for the commodity. If the demand and supply curves are straight lines, the excess demand curve would also be a straight line. This can be proved quite easily.

In derivation of the excess demand functions, there is no distinction between goods and factors of production. Same methodology is applicable to both of them. We know, consumers are owners of factors of production and they are also users of the final products. Traditionally, the demand for final products is derived from the behaviour of consumers whereas the supply of a factor of production like labour is derived from the income distribution theory. In terms of excess demand, we may treat supply as negative excess demand and thus eliminate the distinction between demand

and supply. In the case of labour, the amount of leisure time for sleep, rest and entertainment is considered as positive demand by the consumer and the rest as negative excess demand or supply. Similarly, for a producer, his own output, if used as input by him, it is positive demand, the rest of his output which is supply in conventional terms is excess demand for him which is, of course, negative. As we have said earlier, the aggregate excess demand for each commodity is the sum of the individual positive and negative excess demand functions. Same thing applies to a factor of production also. Consequently, the distinction between factor and product market disappears. In Walras model, there are n excess demand functions as specified by equation (3). Some of them are for productive services and some for produced commodities.

As we have seen in the conventional supply and demand framework, the equilibrium condition for the market is that one when supply is equal to demand, or, in other words, the excess demand is zero. We extend this concept of equilibrium to multi-market situation by simply stating that when all markets are in equilibrium, we have

$$E_i\ (P_1,\ P_2,\ ...,\ P_n) = 0,\ i = 1,\ ...,\ n \qquad ...(4)$$

In this framework, we have a system of n equations for n commodities. However, according to Walras, not all the n equations are independent of each other. For an economy, as a whole, the total monetary value of purchases is always equal to the total monetary value of sales. This means the value of excess demand for commodities is zero, *i.e.*,

$$\sum_{i=1}^{n} P_i E_i\ (P_1,\ P_2,\ ...,\ P_n) = 0 \qquad ...(5)$$

This identity is commonly known as *the Walras law.* According to this, if $n - 1$ of the n markets are in equilibrium, the remaining one will necessarily be in equilibrium. This means the maximum. number of independent equations in the system of equations expressed by (4) is $n - 1$.

When we try to solve the system of equations (4) for $n - 1$ unknowns we will be in difficulty as we do not know which of the equations for unknown prices is redundant or depending on others. This difficulty can be solved by reducing the number of unknown prices by one. That commodity is chosen as *numeraire* whose price is taken to be equal to unity. Anyone of the n commodities can be taken as numeraire. Let us consider money as the commodity whose unit is Re 1 and its price is Re 1 and so it is chosen as the numeraire. However, we will not be strict in our choice of money as numeraire. Let us be quite liberal in this regard and treat commodity 1 as the numeraire. By dividing all prices by P_1 we can express the excess demand equations systems (4) in new form as:

$$E_i\ (1,\ P_2/P_1,\ P_3/P_1\ ,...,\ P_n/P_1) = 0,\ i = 1,\ ...,\ n. \qquad ...(6)$$

We now have $n - 1$ unknown, *i.e.*, the relative prices P_2/P_1, P_3/P_1 ,..., P_n/P_1 and $n - 1$ independent equations. The model is, therefore, consistent and a unique set of values for $n - 1$ price ratios is obtained on solution.

In the above version of the Walras model, the number of firms is taken as given. In the long-run, under perfect competition, the number of firms in an industry is variable. To find the optimum number of firm in an industry we have to impose one more restriction apart from the zero excess demand to find the general equilibrium situation. This restriction is that of zero profit for the industry. That is, each firm in the industry gets long-run equilibrium which means $MR = AC = P$ implying zero profit. The condition for zero profit results in m equations, one for each industry. So, the general equilibrium model will now have n prices and m number of firms. There will be $n + m$ unknowns (n prices and m firms, $N_j = 1, 2, ..., m$ one for each industry) with $n + m$ equations. However, following the Walras law there will be just $n + m - 1$ independent equations and by converting the absolute prices into relative prices once we choose a commodity as numeraire, we can reduce the number of unknowns to $n + m - 1$ and thus solve the model. The equilibrium solution of the model satisfies the following conditions.

(*a*) Every consumer's satisfaction (*i.e.*, utility) is maximised. (The first and second order uitility maximisation conditions mentioned in the chapter on consumer behaviour are fully satisfied by this for all consumers and all goods).

(*b*) Every producer's profit is maximised. All conditions of profit maximisation, as mentioned in the chapter on the theory of production are satisfied).

(*c*) Every market is cleared. This, we have seen above.

It is true that at the equilibrium prices, given by the model, some of the excess demands will be positive and others will be negative. But the sum of the excess demand of all consumers and producers for each factor or produced commodity will be zero. Thus, the Walras model is quantitatively meaningful in a general equilibrium setting of an economy. There are two crucial assumptions for the validity of the solution: one is that prices are explicitly determined and second, all prices are non-negative. There might be complexities with the solution of the model when *number* of variables to be determined is quite large. The model being consistent might not give unique solution for some variables. All such situations are analysed by examining the stability conditions of the model.[4]

(ii) The Input-Output Model

The input-output model, popularly known as Leontief's model after the name of its inventor W.W. Leontief, has already been introduced in chapter 5 which deals with the theory of production. (see Section 5.9(IV)). This model is, in fact, a general equilibrium model which determine simultaneously the output levels of different industries and the quantities of primary factors of production, given the final demand for the output of industries and the technological coefficients of production. The model is also used to determine prices of different commodities in absolute to relative terms given some exogenous price(s) for factors of production or commodities.

The output of an industry, which is assumed to be homogeneous, is used partly by other industries as input to produce their respective outputs and partly by consumers in the form of final demand or end use. The balance equation for the distribution of the output of the industry, in this way, can be expressed as:

$$Q_i = Q_{i1} + Q_{i2} + Q_{i3} + \cdots + Q_{in} + Y_i;\ i = 1, ..., n. \qquad ...(7)$$

where Q_i = total output, Q_{ij} ($j = 1, ..., n$) is the flow of output of ith commodity of jth industry; and Y_i is the final demand representing non-production uses of the commodity, such as consumption, capital formation and export, etc. Assuming that $Q_{ij} = a_{ij}\, Q_j$, which is the standard technological relationship between inputs and output in the input-output model, we can rewrite equation (7) as:

$$Q_i = a_{i1}Q_1 + a_{i2}Q_2 + a_{i3}Q_3 + ... + a_{in}Q_n + Y_i i = 1, ..., n \qquad ...(8)$$

4. We have not gone through the full derivation of Walras model, rather used its trunkated form to discuss the main theme of the general equilibrium. Also, we are not going through the stability conditions associated with this model. For a formal derivation of the model and a discussion on the stability conditions, see Henderson, J.M. and R.E. Quandt, *Microeconomic Theory,* McGraw-Hill, 1971.

where a_{ij} is the requirement of ith commodity to produce one unit output of jth commodity (because of homogeneity of output. 'commodity' and 'industry' have the same connotation). Expanding (8) and rearranging the terms, we get:

$$\begin{aligned} (1 - a_{11})Q_1 - a_{12}Q_2 - - a_{1n}Q_n &= Y_1 \\ - a_{21}Q_1 + (1 - a_{22})Q_2 - - a_{2n}Q_n &= Y_2 \\ - a_{n1}Q_1 - a_{n2}Q_2 - + (1 - a_{nn})Q_n &= Y_n \end{aligned} \qquad ...(9)$$

There are $2n$ variables in it, n output levels and n final demands, but the number of equations is only n. To solve this model, we have to take n out of $2n$ variables as known. Normally, n final demands are taken to be known and, therefore, we can find the n output levels as:

$$\begin{aligned} Q_1 &= \alpha_{11}Y_1 + \alpha_{12}Y_2 + \cdots + \alpha_{1n}\, Y_n \\ Q_2 &= \alpha_{21}Y_1 + \alpha_{22}Y_2 + \cdots + \alpha_{2n}\, Y_n \\ Q_n &= \alpha_{n1}Y_1 + \alpha_{n2}Y_2 + \cdots + \alpha_{nn}\, Y_n \end{aligned} \qquad ...(10)$$

In matrix form we write (9) as:

$$(1 - A)\; Q = Y \qquad ...(11)$$

where I is identity matrix

$A = (a_{ij})_{n \times n}$ is the technology-coefficients matrix.

Q is a column vector of output levels; Y is a column vector of final demand. The solution of (11) is given by

$$Q = (I - A)^{-1}\; Y \qquad ...(12)$$

Once we find the output levels of different industries, we can find the requirement of primary factors of production for that. If l_1, l_2, ..., l_n be the requirement of labour per unit of out Q_1, Q_2 ,..., Q_n respectively, the total labour required across the economy would then be $L = l_1Q_1 + l_2Q_2 + ... + l_nQ_n$ and similarly, total requirement of capital can be found as $K = k_1Q_1 + k_2Q_2 + ... + k_nQ_n$ where k_1, k_2, ..., k_n are capital coefficients per unit output of Q_1, Q_2, ..., Q_n respectively. One may take, of course, the primary inputs and consumption within the inter-industry sector and, thus, determine the level of output as well as of primary input simultaneously through augmented A matrix. This is what we call as 'closed' input-output model. A closed input-output model is specified as:

$$(I - A^*)\; Q^* = 0 \qquad ...(13)$$

where $$A^* = \begin{bmatrix} a_{11} & a_{12} & c_1 \\ a_{21} & a_{22} & c_2 \\ a_{n1} & a_{n2} & c_n \\ l_1 & l_2 & l_c \end{bmatrix} \quad Q^* = \begin{bmatrix} Q_1 \\ Q_2 \\ Q_n \\ L \end{bmatrix}$$

c_1, c_2 ..., c_n are marginal propensities to consume the output of different sectoral output; l_1, l_2 ,..., $l_n l_c$ are labour coefficients per unit of output. The closed input-output model resembles the Walras model. It can't be solved except for 0 values for all variables. To get its solution, we take one variable exogenously given and thus find the rest of them. Alternatively, some components of final demand like capital formation or export might be exogenously given and so the model in semi-closed form will be soluble.

The determination of prices of different commodities simultaneously in an economy is an important feature of the general equilibrium analysis. The input-output model can be used for this purpose. For this, we take the technology matrix A and the primary input-coefficients vector

$l = \{l_1, l_2, ..., l_n)$ into consideration. Let us assume that the price of the primary input is given and it is the same for all industries. (This is just a simplifying assumption, we can extend the analysis by relaxing this). Further, let us also assume that profit-rate (as a proportion of price) is fixed and is same for all industries.

For pricing, we take the balance between price of the commodity and average cost plus profit-margin. Let the output of, say, industry 1 be one unit. The revenue or sale of the industry would then be $P_1 \cdot 1 = P_1$. The average cost of production of one unit output in this industry is the value of input coefficients, *i.e.*, $P_1a_{11} + P_2a_{21} + \cdots + P_na_{n1} + \omega l_1$ (take column 1 of A matrix, multiply each entry in this column by respective prices to get the value of input coefficients). We can now have the equation showing the equality between revenue and cost plus profit-margin when output of commodity 1 is one unit. That is:

$$P_1 = P_1a_{11} + P_2a_{21} + P_3a_{31} + \cdots + P_na_{n1} + \omega l_1 + \gamma P_1$$

Similarly, for industry 2 we have:

$$P_2 = P_1a_{12} + P_2a_{22} + P_3a_{32} + \cdots + P_na_{n2} + \omega l_2 + \gamma P_2$$

For jth col. of A matrix the corresponding price equation would be

$$P_j = P_1a_{1j} + P_2a_{2j} + P_3a_{3j} + \cdots + P_na_{nj} + \omega l_j + \gamma P_j = 1, ..., n. \quad ...(14)$$

The simplified form of (14) on expansion would give us the price system as,

$$\begin{aligned} &P_1(1 - a_{11} - \gamma) - P_2a_{21} \cdots - P_na_{n1} = \omega l_1 \\ &- P_1a_{12} + P_2 (1 - a_{22} - \gamma) \cdots - P_na_{n2} = \omega l_2 \\ &- P_1a_{13} - P_2a_{23} + \cdots - P_na_{n3} = \omega l_3 \\ &- P_1a_{1n} - P_2a_{2n} - \cdots + P_n (1 - a_{nn} - \gamma) = \omega l_n \end{aligned} \quad ...(15)$$

Given a_{ij}, γ, ω, l_1, ..., l_n, we can solve this system of equations for P_1 P_2, ..., P_n simultaneously.

Using matrix theory, we can simplify the presentation of the model and solve it. The emphasis here is, however, on the point that if there are some exogenously given prices, such as wage-rate for labour or profit-rate, prices for other commodities can then be uniquely determined by using input-output analysis. If the model is closed in prices, its solution will be obtained if at least one price is fixed exogenously as done in the Walras model.

In order to explain the method of input-output analysis, let us take a simple example: There are two industries designated as Industry 1 and Industry 2 in a hypothetical economy. The flows of outputs and inputs among these two industries vis-a-vis consumers are given as follows:

Table 12.1: Input-Output Flows in Value Terms (₹ 000)

	Intermediate Uses		*Final Uses*		*Total Output*
From/To	Industry 1	Industry 2	Consumers	Others	
Industry 1	2.0	5.0	2.0	1.0	10.0
Industry 2	5.5	3.0	3.5	2.0	14.0
Primary Inputs					
Labour	1.5	3.5	–	–	5.0
Others	1.0	2.5	–	–	3.5
Total Inputs	10.0	14.0	5.5	3.0	32.5

The interindustry flows, shown here, are in value terms rather than in physical terms. Out of 10 units of output of Industry 1, 2 units go to Industry 1 itself to produce its own output, 5 units go to Industry 2 to produce its output, 2 units to consumption and remaining 1 unit to other final uses, such as export, investment, etc. Similarly, the distribution of 14 units of output of Industry 2 is given in row 2. The use of primary inputs by Industry 1 and Industry 2 are shown in row 3 and 4. For each industry, the total output is equal to total use of inputs (sum of row 1 = sum of col. 1) and similar identity is also valid for Industry 2. Total final demand for the product of both the industries is 8.5 units which is equal to total value added, *i.e.* sum of payments to primary inputs (8.5). This is a necessary condition of balancing the input-output flows.

Now, let us derive the input coefficients. For this, entries of each column are to be divided by the column total. That is

$$a_{ij} = Q_{ij}/Q_j, \ i = 1, ..., n.$$

By applying this formula to both the industries, the technical coefficients related to produced inputs and primary inputs have been computed for them as follows. The final demand column is left out of such calculations as these are determined exogenously.

Table 12.2: Technological Coefficients Matrix

	Industry 1	*Industry* 2
Industry 1	0.20	0.36
Industry 2	0.55	0.21
Labour	0.15	0.25
Other	0.10	0.18
Total	1.00	1.00

Since we are using value flows, the technical coefficients are interpreted as value of corresponding input per Rupee worth of output. The sum of such coefficients cannot exceed unity for each industry. Also, the use of the commodity in its own production must not exceed unity in the form of the coefficient, *i.e.*, $a_{ii} < 1$. Also, the sum of produced input coefficients, *i.e.*, $\sum_{i=1}^{n} a_{ij} < 1, \ (j = 1, ..., n)$. This is true as we see above for each of the two industries.

Now, by using the input coefficients, the balance equations for the two industries can be written as:

$$(1 - 0.20)Q_1 - 0.36Q_2 = 3 \qquad ...(16)$$
$$- 0.55Q_1 + (1 - 0.21)Q_2 = 5.5$$

The solution of these two equations for Q_1 and Q_2 is the same as the total output of each of the two commodities. That is,

$$Q_1 = 10 \text{ units}, \ Q_2 = 14 \text{ units}.$$

The right hand side of the equation-set (16) represents the exogenously given final demand. Suppose this changes, the solution of the model also changes. Let the new level of final demand of output be Y_1^* and Y_2^* for the two industries respectively. The model now would be

$$(1 - 0.20)Q_1 - 0.36Q_2 = Y_1^* \qquad \text{...(17)}$$
$$- 0.55Q + (1 - 0.21)Q_2 = Y_2^*$$

This, we can write in the matrix form as

$$\begin{bmatrix} 0.80 & -0.36 \\ -0.55 & 0.79 \end{bmatrix} \begin{bmatrix} Q_1 \\ Q_2 \end{bmatrix} = \begin{bmatrix} Y_1^* \\ Y_2^* \end{bmatrix}$$

The solution of this is:

$$\begin{bmatrix} Q_1 \\ Q_2 \end{bmatrix} = \begin{bmatrix} 0.80 & -0.36 \\ -0.55 & 0.79 \end{bmatrix}^{-1} \begin{bmatrix} Y_1^* \\ Y_2^* \end{bmatrix}$$

or

$$\begin{bmatrix} Q_1 \\ Q_2 \end{bmatrix} = \begin{bmatrix} 1.250 & 0.570 \\ 0.870 & 1.265 \end{bmatrix} \begin{bmatrix} Y_1^* \\ Y_2^* \end{bmatrix}$$

This provides us the following solution for Q_1 and Q_2

$$Q_1 = 1.250\,Y_1^* + 0.570\,Y_2^* \qquad \text{...(18)}$$
$$Q_2 = 0.870\,Y_1^* + 1.265\,Y_2^*$$

We can find Q_1 and Q_2 using these equations for given Y_1^* and Y_2^*. The inverse of the matrix $(I - A)$ *i.e.*, $(I - A)^{-1}$ provides us the direct and indirect requirements of different commodities when final demand (*i.e.*, *Y*, *s*) changes by unit. The economy comes to equilibrium position regarding the levels of output of different commodities after adjusting fully with changes in the final demand.

To compute labour requirement we use the relationship

$$L = 0.15Q_1 + 0.25Q_2$$

Substituting values of Q_1 and Q_2 from (18) we have total labour required in the economy as

$$L = 0.15(1.250\,Y_1^* + 0.570\,Y_2^*) + 0.25(0.870\,Y_1^* + 1.265\,Y_2^*)$$

or

$$L = (0.15 \times 1.25 + 0.25 \times 0.87)\,Y_1^* + (0.15 \times 0.57 + 0.25 \times 1.265)\,Y_2^*$$

The brecketed figures on simplification provides the labour intensity for the two sectors, defined as the requirement of labour to sustain one unit final demand for output of the sectors. The requirement of the other factor can be computed in the similar way.

We now find 'prices' for the two commodities. The price equations for them can be written as:

$$P_1 = 0.20P_1 + 0.55\,P_2 + \omega(0.15) + \gamma(0.10) \qquad \text{...(19)}$$
$$P_2 = 0.36P_1 + 0.21P_2 + \omega(0.25) + \gamma(0.18)$$

or

$$(1.0 - 0.20)P_1 - 0.55P_2 = \omega(0.15) + \gamma(0.10)$$
$$- 0.36P_1 + (1 - 0.21)\,P_2 = \omega(0.25) + \gamma(0.18)$$

or

$$(0.80)P_1 - 0.55P_2 = \omega(0.15) + \gamma(0.10)$$
$$- 0.36P_1 + 0.79P_2 = \omega(0.25) + \gamma(0.18)$$

$$\begin{bmatrix} 0.80 & -0.55 \\ -0.36 & 0.79 \end{bmatrix} \begin{bmatrix} P_1 \\ P_2 \end{bmatrix} = \begin{bmatrix} V_1 \\ V_2 \end{bmatrix} \text{ where } \begin{array}{l} V_1 = \omega(0.15) + \gamma(0.10) \\ V_2 = \omega(0.25) + \gamma(0.18) \end{array}$$

This can be simplified by transposing matrices as:

$$(P_1, P_2)\begin{bmatrix} 0.8 & -0.36 \\ -0.55 & 0.79 \end{bmatrix} = (V_1, V_2)$$

or $$(P_1, P_2) = (V_1, V_2)\begin{bmatrix} 0.8 & -0.36 \\ -0.55 & 0.79 \end{bmatrix}^{-1}$$

or $$(P_1, P_2) = (V_1, V_2)\begin{bmatrix} 1.250 & 0.570 \\ 0.870 & 1.265 \end{bmatrix}$$

The elements of the inverse matrix have already been computed earlier. The solution for prices is therefore as:

$$P_1 = 1.250V_1 + 0.870V_2 \qquad ...(20)$$
$$P_2 = 0.570V_1 + 1.265V_2$$

So, if ω and γ are known we can find V_1 and V_2 which are value-added per unit of output in the two sectors taken here. Once V_1 and V_2 are known, prices can then be calulated by using (20).

This is a simple expository example used for demonstrating actual calculations of output levels and prices using the input-output framework. In practice, there will be several sectors in the input-output model and so several output levels and prices are to be determined simultaneously. It will be extremely difficult to solve such models manually. The only way to solve the system of equations would, therefore, be to use computers which require a skill in computer programming as well as a thorough understanding of the input-output technique.[5]

12.3 CONCLUDING REMARKS

The general equilibrium analysis is a complex concept and there exists no satisfactory explanation for this in the existing economic theory. Authors have tried to describe this through graphs focussing on two or almost three dimensional figures like contact curves, production possibility curves, and so on. But this is too far from the general equilibrium of an economy where there will be multi-dimensional aspects: several commodities, several prices, several interactions among the economic units. A graphical description of all that is impossible and there is no point of taking two or three relations to demonstrate graphically in the context of general equilibrium analysis. The general equilibrium analysis can only be undertaken in a comprehensive mathematical model involving several equations and variables. Two such models, which are quite popular from theoretical as well as operational sides of the general equilibrium analysis, are the Walrasian model, and the Leontief's input-output model. These two models have been summarised in this chapter which provided us a fairly good idea of the general equilibrium analysis. With this background one can go to the study of more complex models of economy, normally in macroeconomic framework.

5. For further full knowledge of the input-output method, (1) W.H. Miernyk, *The Elements of Input-Output Analysis*, N.Y., Random House, 1965; (2) H.B. Chenary and P.G. Clark, *Interindustry Economics,* N.Y., John Wiley and Sons.

SUGGESTED READINGS

Arrow, K.J. and F.H. Haln, *General Equilibrium Analysis;* Holden-Day, 1971.
Henderson, J.M. and R.E. Quandt, *Microeconomic Theory;* McGraw-Hill, 1971.
Kuenne, R.E., *The Theory of General Economic Equilibrium;* Prentice-Hall, 1971.

REVIEW QUESTIONS

1. Describe in simple language the meaning of general equilibrium. How general equilibrium is different from partial equilibrium and what is its practical significance?
2. Describe Walrasian general equilibrium model and explain its significance from the point of view of understanding the working of an economic system.
3. Discuss Leontief's input-output model and show why this model be considered as a general equilibrium model.
4. Derive the general equilibrium condition for a two-consumer, two-commodity pure exchange, and competitive economy with no production. The utility functions for consumers, and their initial endowments for both the commodities are given.

CHAPTER 13

Theory of Welfare Economics

While introducing the major branches of economic theory in Chapter 1, we have made a distinction between positive economics and normative economics (see, Sec. 1.5). We have also gone through the basic economic problems of every society in Chapter 2, one of the problems concerned with the efficiency of the economic system as whole (Ref. Sec. 2.2(*c*)). It was also mentioned at both the places that the branch of economics that deals with normative economics and the efficiency of the economic system as a whole is called welfare economics. This is a special branch of economics which deals with the problem of evaluating the relative desirability of economic alternatives with respect to society as a whole from an ethical point of view. Thus, it involves ethical or value judgements. This makes welfare economics as a normative branch of the discipline quite different from the positive economics in which value judgements do not play any role in decision-making concerning individuals and society as a whole. So far our analysis, presented in the various chapters of this book, was devoted to the interrelationships between economic activities concerning consumer, producer, commodity markets, factor markets and so on. This enabled us to examine the human behaviour related to a given economic phenomenon. On the basis of such studies, we can make future predictions and suggest certain policy norms to achieve some predetermined economic goals. All this can be done, of course, in the framework of positive economics. We have not said anything regarding desirability of a given economic policy. For example, we can predict that an increase in the demand for a commodity will result in both a higher market price and a higher quantity produced under given cost conditions by following laws or principles of positive economics, but we cannot say anything, whether such an increase in price and quantity of the commodity are desirable from the view point of society as a whole. A study of normative economics or what we say alternatively, welfare economics, provides an answer of to ethical questions related to the desirability of economic policies. In this branch of the subject, we study the level of satisfaction achieved by all consumers and not just one of them, and efficient allocation of resources in production from the point of view of all producers and not just one of them. Similarly, we study the interrelationships between sectors of the economy in the general equilibrium framework rather than following the partial equilibrium analysis.

In this chapter, we will go through some general issues related to welfare economics. There is no single general theory of welfare economics developed so far. Different economists have seen it from different angles and developed their own 'theories' for this. Being a normative discipline, the diversity in the approaches used in the analysis of welfare economics was quite natural. We will go through such approaches and try to synthesise them. As we know, welfare is a very broad concept. It has both economic and non-economic aspects. We may also examine welfare from the point of view of individuals as well as society as a whole. For simplicity, we will deal with the economic aspect of social welfare which is normally designated as economic welfare. Since individuals are part of society, it is quite necessary to bring them into picture while studying the social welfare. This approach is being followed by us in this analysis also.

13.1 THE OBJECTIVES OF WELFARE ECONOMICS

Every society tries to achieve certain well chosen 'ends' or 'aspirations' for itself. These aspirations might be, for example, material welfare, equity in distribution of wealth, protection of persons and property from external and internal enemies, reduction in social tensions, ethical order and religious freedom, political power, and personal aims like freedom of expression, choice, etc. The achievement weights assign to such aims may vary from society to society. The society, on the whole, will make the choice of goals and its actions will be directed towards their achievement. All this is what we call social policy which implies setting of goals for achievement and specifying measures to be adopted for this. Obviously, the social policy of a society will be directed for achievement of maximum social welfare for itself.

Economic welfare is a part of social welfare. In the context of economic welfare, we have two important goals: one is the increase in material welfare of masses, and second is the equality or equitable distribution of wealth and income among members of a society. The material welfare in the society goes up when goods and services are available in greater quantities and varieties for consumption and other uses. As goods and services are needed to satisfy human wants, they are to be produced. For production of goods and services we need various kinds of resources and, as we read in economics, the resources are normally scarce. Given the scarcity of resources, they are to be used efficiently in production of goods and services. From the point of view of material welfare mere production of goods and services is not all that is needed, it has to be supplemented by efficient consumption of goods and services by all persons in the society. Both these aspects of welfare are covered by a comprehensive term called 'economic efficiency'. An economic system will be efficient if it is technically efficient and if it succeeds in rationing out its scarce resources and the scarce products of resources in the most desirable way. By 'technical efficiency' we mean production of a given level of output of a commodity by using the optimum, *i.e.*, the least cost combination of inputs. The phrase, 'most desirable way', in this definition has normative connotation. In the case of a society as a whole, we may take it as maximisation of economic welfare of masses. From this link we find that a major objective of welfare economics is attainment of optimum economic efficiency. In this situation, as we will find soon, different segments of the society, particularly consumers and producers, will be benefited concurrently. In fact, what welfare economics really does for this is to evaluate the social desirability of alternate economic systems and then make the choice of the best keeping in mind its aspirations.

Attainment of economic efficiency for the sake of increasing material welfare is certainly important from social point of view, but equally important one is equitable distribution of wealth and income. Most of the democratic societies pursue the objective of equality in their policies. Equality as a social objective implies equal rights, privileges, ability and rank, etc., to every member of the society. It may be easy to conceive of equality from political and social angles but defining economic equality is extremely difficult. In an extreme utopian sense it implies equal distribution of wealth and income among all members of the society but it seldom happens even in a perfect democracy. In other words, men belonging to the same community and to the same country, when placed in identical circumstances, derive equal satisfaction from the same real income. We can elaborate this proposition further by saying that suppose individuals in the society have cardinal and interpersonally comparable utility functions, characterised by diminishing marginal utility, and if all such utility functions are essentially identical, total social aggregate of utilities of individuals would be maximum when income is distributed equally among individuals. This is a strong condition for economic equality. Such condition is difficult to be met in practice. Individual's preferences differ, their utilities, therefore, cannot be compared with each other. Their ability or skill to earn income differs. It is therefore difficult to argue for equal distribution of income in the society. But for equitable distribution of income depending on needs, abilities, etc., the society may have some ethical choice. Certain inequalities in income distribution might be justified on ethical grounds. John Rawl, for example, in his 'difference principle' asserts that inequality in a society is justified only to the extent that it benefits the least advantaged.[1] Similarly, Ian Bowen also defines the norm for acceptable inequalities in an economy.[2] Ethics of income equality need not be uniform or identical across the economic systems. What a society feels 'good' need not be so at all in the views of other societies. This kind of difference in the ethical choice regarding income distribution and in other aspects also makes the welfare economics as a normative discipline which has been emphasised right in the beginning of this chapter.

So, the two major objectives of welfare economics are attainment of maximum economic efficiency in the economy and having some desirable equality in income distribution in society. There is, however, a big tradeoff between these two objectives.[3] One can have equality at the cost of efficiency and vice versa. In this kind of conflicting objectives, the analysis of welfare economics becomes quite complicating, yet different authors have tackled this problem in different ways and therefore they were able to specify norms for balancing them. We will soon get an idea of this while summarising the major theories of welfare economics.

There are other aims or aspirations of social policy which have been mentioned at the beginning of this section. Some of them affect choice of individuals' and thus are related to economic welfare, but, by and large, they are non-economic in nature. So, we are not going into details of their incorporation in the analysis of welfare economics.

13.2 THEORIES OF WELFARE ECONOMICS

Basically, we have four types of welfare theories: (*a*) the classical doctrine of invisible hands; (*b*) the Piguvian theory, (*c*) the Pareto's social optimum theory; and (*d*) social welfare function approach. All these theories, together with some other criteria for welfare maximisation, are summarised as under.

1. John Rawls: *A Theory of Justice,* Cambridge University Press, Cambridge, Mass, 1971.
2. Ian Bowen, *Acceptable Inequalities,* George Allen and Unwin, London, 1970.
3. Arthur, M. Okun, *Equality and Efficiency: The Big Trade off,* New Delhi, Oxford and IBH Pub. Co., 1975. Also see (*a*) Amartya Sen, *On Economic Inequalities,* Delhi: Oxford University Press 1973, and (*b*) A.B. Atkinson, *The Economics of Inequality;* Oxford Clarendon Press, 1975.

(i) The Doctrine of Invisible Hands

Adam Smith, the founder of the classical economics, proclaimed the doctrine of the 'invisible hands'.[4] According to this, every individual, in pursuing only his own self interests, was led, as if by an invisible hand, to achieve the best interests of all. In other words, optimising behaviour on the part of individuals and firms under pure competition leads to an efficient social outcome. This doctrine or theorem is justified even by modern welfare economists like Pareto. Its validity, of course, depends upon the market conditions, *i.e.*, if there is perfect competition prevailing in the economy, the above result will hold, otherwise not. The competitive market ensures optimum conditions for exchange, for factor substitutions and for product substitution in the economy. The conditions which are provided by the general equilibrium analysis for the optimum social welfare are: (*a*) the marginal rate of substitution between any pair of consumer goods must be the same for all individuals who consume goods; (*b*) the marginal rate of technical substitution between any pair of inputs must be the same for all producers who use the inputs; (*c*) the marginal rate of product transformation in production must be equal to the marginal rate of substitution in consumption for every pair of commodities and for every individual who consumes them.

The rationale for each optimal equilibrium conditions for an individual (consumer or producer) has already been discussed in the earlier chapters (see Ch. 4 and Ch. 5). All these conditions constitute the basic foundation for modern welfare economics. The credit for this, of course, goes to the classical doctrine of the invisible hands.

As mentioned above, the doctrine of the invisible hands holds true only under perfect competition. In practice, conditions for perfect competition are rarely met. So, the doctrine of invisible hands turns out to be inoperative. Some specific market conditions under which the doctrine fails to hold true are as follows.

(a) Monopoly Markets

As we know, monopoly is opposite extreme of perfect competition, obviously a doctrine or theorem based on perfect competition will never hold true under monopoly. Monopoly can and does exist, to some degree on both sides of product and factor markets. Other types of markets, such as duopoly, oligopoly, monopolistic competition, monopsony, bilateral monopoly are all based on market imperfections and violation of conditions of perfect competition. The doctrine of the invisible hands fails to operate under such market imperfections.

As we know, a monopoly firm is a price-maker. It sets price and output by equating marginal revenue to marginal cost for profit maximisation. Its counterpart, a firm under perfect competition on the other hand is a price-taker which sets its output level by equating price to marginal cost. The monopoly output will be less than the competitive output and the price charged by the monopoly firm would be higher than the competitive price. For social welfare more output, available at less price, under perfect competition, is a better situation than the monopoly price-quantity combination. Further, under monopoly, for factor market equilibrium we equate marginal revenue product to factor price rather than value of marginal physical product to the factor price, as under perfect competition, factors of production get less reward under monopoly product

---

4. Adam Smith, *An Inquiry into the Nature and Causes of the Wealth of Nations* (1776) Modern Library N.Y. (1937 Edition), Book IV, Ch. 2.

markets when they are used. Monopoly is, thus, a market situation which exploits the consumers by depriving their surpluses and by giving them less income. The doctrine of invisible hands cannot provide maximum social welfare by adding the satisfaction of individuals in this situation since the individual consumers are not getting the maximum satisfaction that they deserve. Even public monopolies fail to fulfil the maximum conditions for social welfare since they are not controlled by the automatic market mechanism.

(b) Disequilibrium Conditions in Markets

We know that prices under perfect competition are determined through demand and supply interactions. This is an automatic market-mechanism which operates or regulates itself. In practice, however, we do find disequilibrium in markets. Prices are not allowed to be determined freely through demand and supply interactions but subject to regulations. The regulated prices may not 'clear' the market and therefore excess demand or supply might be the result which implies disequilibrium situation. With existence of excess demand or supply consumers or suppliers would remain unsatisfied and this causes sub-optimal social welfare.

(c) External Effects

External effects or 'externalities' are generated when the voluntary action of an economic agent—consumer or producer or trader or anybody else — affects the action or actions of other economic agents and there is no legally recognised right of compensation or redress for such effects. The external effects, thus, generated might be beneficial or harmful to others. Some effects might be direct and some indirect. Consider disposal of industrial effluent into a river. It degrades the quality of water by polluting it. Other firms or families using the water in the downstream of the river will be adversely affected by this. They do not find the water fit to use or to drink. Thus, the firm discharging the effluent into the river in its upstream will be causing harmful externalities directly for the firms or consumers in the downstream of the river. Similarly, one may cite smoke coming out of a factory causing air pollution and hence direct harmful externality. As said above, externalities might be beneficial also. A compost fertiliser plant using garbage as its principal raw material helps to keep the environment clean. We may find several other such examples for positive and negative externalities. In the presences of externalities the doctrine of invisible hand does not hold true. The increase in satisfaction of one consumer, when he is externality generating agent, might reduce the satisfaction of other consumers if the externality is harmful. So, there might not be any increase in social welfare in this case. But, if the external effect is beneficial, then, of course, the social welfare may go up. Whatever be situation, externalities represent the sources of social gain or loss that do not get translated into the market signals that constitute the Invisible hand. Some policy measures are taken to regulate externalities in the context of social gains. A normal process for this is to impose unit subsidies to increase outputs of firms that generate positive externalities, *i.e.*, external economies, and to impose unit taxes to decrease outputs of firms that generate harmful externalities, *i.e.*, external diseconomies. An alternative mechanism is to nationalise activities that generate harmful externalities. By doing so externalities can be controlled or regulated by a central authority and social welfare or gain is not allowed to be affected adversely by this. These are not the only ways to regulate externalities. There might be other ways which depend on the specific conditions prevailing in the economy.

(ii) Pigou's Theory of Welfare Economics

A.C. Pigou has been one of the leading welfare economists. His first book, *Wealth and Welfare* (1912) was an attempt to compile the various developments in welfare analysis since Adam Smith. However, later on, in 1920, he published his own treatise on welfare economics, known as '*The Economics of Welfare*.[5] His welfare theory was based on the neo-classical cardinal utility analysis evolved by Alfred Marshall. Because of this, the theory of welfare economics developed, by Pigou, is known alternatively as the neo-classical cardinal utility approach of welfare economics or simply as the neo-classical theory of economic welfare.

Pigou's concept of welfare is very closely linked with the satisfaction that consumers derive from consumption of various goods and services. The aggregate of the satisfaction of all individuals comprising a society constitutes social welfare. It is a broad term having several dimensions: social, political, economic, religious and so on. Pigou has not considered these aspects in his theory. He concentrated only on the economic aspect of social welfare and named it as 'economic welfare'. He defined economic welfare as that part of social (general) welfare that could be brought directly or indirectly into relation with the measuring rod of money. Pigou, however, agrees that a precise boundary between economic and non-economic welfare does not exist, but the test of accessibility to a money measure serves well enough to set up a rough distinction. Economic welfare, as loosely defined by this test, is the subject matter of economic science. Since economic welfare is a major part of total welfare, Pigou, therefore, believed that qualitative conclusions about their effects upon economic welfare would hold good also of the effects upon total welfare. In general, economic welfare will not serve for a barometer or index of total welfare.

Economic welfare, as Pigou looks it, is a function of goods and services and their relative prices. At the national level, it can be said that for most part economic causes act upon economic welfare, not directly but through the national dividend. If there is a change in national dividend or national income that represent a change in economic welfare also. A strong positive correlation has been postulated by Pigou between economic welfare and national dividend, the former being an effect and the latter one as a cause.

The whole Pigouvian welfare economics is based on certain assumptions, such as: (*i*) cardinal measurability of utility, (*ii*) inter-personal comparisons of utility, (*iii*) universal applicability of diminishing marginal utility of money, (*iv*) independence of utility functions, (*v*) similarity between individuals from the point of view of derivation of utility from money; (*vi*) prevalence of perfect competition, and, (*vii*) full employment in the economy. Given these assumptions, the Pigou's theory of economic welfare can be summarised in the form of the following two important propositions derived by him.

(*i*) "Provided that the dividend accruing to the poor is not diminished, increases in the aggregate national dividend of the community, unless they result from coercing people to work more than they wish to do, carry with them increases in economic welfare."[6]

(*ii*) "Changes in the distribution of the national dividend in favour of the poor may be brought about in several ways, the most important of which is by transfer of purchasing power to them from the rich persons. Except in very special circumstances, such a transfer must increase economic welfare. This, however, is not quite the same thing as saying that a diminution in the inequality of

---

5. A.C. Pigou: *The Economics of Welfare,* Macmillan (1920), 4th Edition, Reprint 1952.
6. A.C. Pigou, *Ibid.*, pp. 82-86.

distribution must increase economic welfare."[7] The transfer of income from rich to poor should not affect adversely the productive activities including capital maintenance and development of capital equipment.

Pigou has made 'social marginal product' as the basis for his social optimum or 'ideal output'.[8] According to him, social optimum would stand realised or the output of the economy would be ideal if the marginal social products in all industries are equal to each other. This implies maximum national dividend when values of the marginal social products in all industries are equal. In essence, for maximisation of economic welfare, Pigou's emphasis was on maximum increase in national dividend and its equitable distribution between the richer and the poorer sections of the community.

Pigouvian welfare theory has been criticised by several economists like Robbins, Hicks and others. They challenged its assumptions, particularly the 'man's equal capacity for satisfaction' which, according to Robbins, is wrong, unrealistic and unscientific. It cannot be considered as a firm and durable basis for interpersonal comparisons of utility. Pigou's emphasis on equitable distribution of national income was also criticised and so was the concept of the national dividend as a measure of social welfare itself. Nevertheless, the Pigouvian welfare theory still persists particularly in the fields of taxation, minimum wage policy and other social legislations.

(iii) The Paretian Welfare Economics

It is considered as the modern or new welfare economics originally developed by Vilfredo Pareto[9] and later on refined by several other economists.[10] The basic theme of this theory was to develop propositions which are 'scientific', free from ethical judgements, but which can nevertheless serve as a basis of conclusions with respect to policy alternatives by delimiting the area within which the final ethical judgement has to be made. By taking into account various consumers, producers, markets, and economy as a whole the theory attempted to specify the optimum efficiency conditions for them which, in turn, provided useful guidelines for economic policies. The entire theory is based on a set of assumptions like ordinal measurement of utilities, non-admissibility of inter personal comparisons of utilities and independent utility functions for individuals, perfect divisibility of commodities and factors of production, mobility of factors of production and given state of technology and substitutability of factors in production. The theory, on the whole, is quite comprehensive. Let us discuss it in a fairly detailed way in order to understand its basic structure.

(a) Basic Concepts and Theorems of Paretian Welfare Theory

As we have mentioned earlier, welfare economics is concerned with the evaluation of the desirability of various economic alternatives from the point of view of society as a whole. Every

---

7. A.C. Pigou, *Ibid.*, pp. 87-92.
8. Social marginal product is defined by Pigou as follows:
   "The marginal social net product is the total net product of physical things or objective services due to the marginal increment of resources in any given use or place, no matter to whom any part of this product may accrue" (Pigou, *Ibid.*, p. 134).
9. Pareto, V., *Cours d'Economie Politique*, Lausanne 1897; and *Manuel d' Economie Politique*; 2nd Ed. Paris, 1920.
10. Leading economists, who contributed in Paretian welfare economics are Hicks (1939), A. Bergson (1938), A.P. Lerner (1944), Myint (1948), T. Scitovsky (1941), I.M.D. Little (1950), Reder (1947), Samuelson (1956), and Nicholas Kaldor (1939). See for full details of these and other references: Fergusion C.E., *Microeconomic Theory*, R.D. Irwin, 1966, pp. 394-397.

economic alternative provides us a picture of the economic status of consumers and producers. In the context of welfare economics, this means the amount of each commodity and/or service each consumer gets as well as the amount of resources that each provides, and the amount of each input used by a firm as well as the output produced by it. So, the desirability of economic alternatives in this situation is nothing but to take into account the allocation of resources in connection with the level of satisfaction of all consumers in the society. An allocation is described by specific consumption levels for each consumer and specific input and output levels for each producer. Pareto has provided a definition of the economic efficiency of allocations which serves as a basis for the contemporary welfare economics. Before describing the definition and related aspects, however, we have to keep two things in mind. One is the consumer sovereignty which implies that the ultimate measure of the desirability of alternative allocations of resources depends on consumer's preferences and the level of satisfaction derived by consumers. The second thing is that there exists no satisfactory cardinal measure of the level of satisfaction. This implies that ordinal utility is the only way to develop a meaningful welfare theory. Further, since a good measure of the level of satisfaction (utility) for society as a whole cannot be constructed. Therefore, the social welfare function for the society cannot be specified. In the absence of a social welfare function, we cannot go ahead with maximisation of social welfare in an objective way. For this, Pareto, however, suggested the unanimity principle which is commonly known as Pareto Optimality Condition. This is a very important concept in welfare economics which requires a formal definition and more detailed explanation. But, before this, a related concept of Pareto superiority is to be defined, since, without this, it will be difficult to understand the basis for the unanimity principle. *A state A of the economy is said to be Pareto superior to another state B if, at least, one person is better off in A than in B but none is worse off.*

To explain the concept of Pareto-superiority let us consider an Edgeworth box diagram for a two person-two goods economy. Let the quantities of goods available be Q_1 and Q_2 which are shown by dimensions of the rectangle shown in Fig. 13.1. Any point in the box shows the distribution of these goods among the two persons for consumption. If one get more of anyone good the other gets less of that since the total availability of the good is fixed. The indifference curves for the two persons designated as '1' and '2' are shown with O and O′ as origins. For first person, the curves are shown as U_{11}, U_{12}, U_{13}, U_{14} ... as he moves on higher and higher level of satisfaction. For second person, curves are shown in inverted direction as U_{21}, U_{22}, U_{23} ..., showing higher and higher level of satisfaction through consumption of goods.

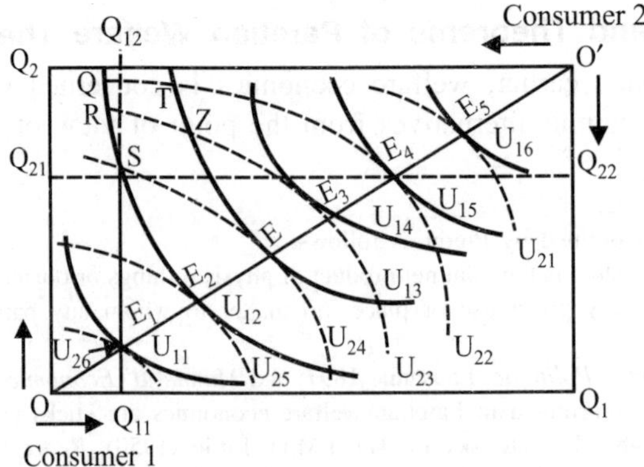

Fig. 13.1 The Edgeworth Box Diagram for a 'Two Persons-Two Goods' Economy

Let us consider a point *S* inside the box at which the indifference curves U_{12} and U_{24} for two persons meet. First person's consumption of the two goods is shown by (Q_{11}, Q_{21}) while rest of either of the two Q_{12} and Q_{22} is consumed by the second person. This kind of distribution is shown by every point on the boundary of the box or inside it as we mentioned earlier.

To explain the concept of Pareto-superiority let us consider points *Q, R, S*, inside the box. All these points are on the indifference curve U_{12} for first person and from each one of them we find one indifference curve of second person passing through. First person's level of satisfaction remains unchanged when he moves from *Q* to *S*, since he is on the same indifference curve. But the level of satisfaction (utility) of second person changes when he moves from *Q* to *S* since he is shifting to different indifference curve. For him, point *R* is better than *Q*, and *S* is better than *R* since he is on higher and higher indifference curves. It means, from his point of view, point *S* is Pareto-superior to point *R*, and point *R* is Pareto-superior to point *Q*, since the other person's utility is constant when he moves along these points.

Now, consider point *T*. This is Pareto-superior to point *Q* from the point of view of first person since he is moving on higher indifference curve and second person remaining on the same indifference curve. If we take a point *Z* then it is Pareto-superior to point *Q* from the point of view of both the persons since both of them are moving to their respective higher indifference curves. In identifying the Pareto-superior points, we have to keep in mind its definition, that is, if one person moves to higher level of satisfaction the other person's satisfaction must not be decreased by this. The Pareto-superiority expresses a transitive relationship. If there is no such transitive relationship between the points, we will have 'Pareto-noncomparability'. We consider two different states of the economy, say *A* and *B*. If neither *A* is Pareto-superior to *B* nor *B* is Pareto-superior to *A*, we have Pareto-noncomparability for the state of the economy.

In the context of welfare economics, the most important concept is that of Pareto Optimality. For a given set of all possible states, say *A*, *B*, C, *E*,... of the economy, if there does not exist a single state that is Pareto-superior to *E*, the state *E* is said to be Pareto optimal for the given set of states.

Consider Fig. 13.1 again. We have seen in the diagram that points *R* and *T* are Pareto superior to point *Q*, and point *Z* is Pareto superior to both, points R and *T*. It implies that points *R* and *T* cannot be Pareto optimal. Even point *Z* is not Pareto optimal since there exist a point *E* which is Pareto superior to point *Z*. However, there is no other point in the box-diagram which is Pareto superior to *E*. Therefore, point *E* is Pareto optimal. This is the point of tangency between two of the indifference curves U_{13} and U_{24} for the two persons respectively. When such a tangency point is obtained for the two indifference curves of two individuals it is not possible to find another point on such indifference curves which is Pareto-superior to it. Therefore, we can say that all points of tangency between different pairs of indifference curves for the two persons are Pareto optimal. The line *O.E.O′* represents the locus of all Pareto optimal points. This is known as the contract curve in the terminology of Edgeworth's box-diagram. It need not be a straight line.

Thus, as the above description reveals, the Pareto optimality represents the set of states of an economy so that it is impossible to make a single person better off without making some other person worse off. This is the essence of the unanimity principle. According to this principle, a change of any kind, cannot be considered better if it makes one person worse off but several others better off. It implies a kind of veto power to every member of a society. In Pareto, optimality there is lack of inter-personal comparison of utility and this makes room for the non-comparability of alternatives.

The Pareto approach of defining the optimality does not take into consideration distributional aspects of income in a society. Suppose there is decrease in income of one person and, at the same time, there is also an increase in the income of other person(s) because of income redistribution. This means the person whose income decreased would be consuming less and hence his level of satisfaction decreases, though the satisfaction of others might go up. In Pareto, optimality there is no room for decrease in utility even for one person. So, the income redistribution, making at least one person worse off, is incompatible with the concept of Pareto optimality. This is one of its serious limitations.

Now, let us go back to Fig. 13.1. We find that along the contract-curve, pairs of indifference curves for the two persons are tangent to each other such as shown by points E_1, E_2, E, E_3, etc. By tangency we mean that slopes of two curves are identical at the points. In the terminology of the indifference curve analysis the slope of an indifference curve is the marginal rate of commodity substitution. It implies that along the contract-curve the marginal rate of commodity substitution between the two goods for one consumer is identical to the marginal rate of commodity substitution between goods for the second consumer. That is, $(\text{MRCS}_{Q_1:Q_2})_1 = (\text{MRCS}_{Q_1:Q_2})_2$. So, in a system of pure exchange, Pareto optimality implies the equality of the MRCS for all consumers between any pair of commodities. This is reflected by the contract-curve.

We know that every point on the contract-curve is Pareto-optimal, but which point will be actually chosen to represent the social optimum? To find this, let us bring prices of commodities and incomes of consumers into the picture. Under perfect competition, all buyers face the same market price for each commodity. Hence, all consumers face the same price ratio for any pair of commodities. In the chapter on Consumer Behaviour, we have seen that the satisfaction or utility of a consumer will be maximised when, for any given income, if the marginal rate of commodity substitution (MRCS) between a pair of commodities is equal to their price ratio. This condition holds true for all consumers under perfect competition. Since MRCS for any pair of commodities is equal for all consumers, which implies that the consumer equilibrium condition under perfect competition is Pareto optimal and at this position, in the framework of the contract curve, the budget line will be tangent to the indifference curves of both the consumer at the same point where the indifference curves are themselves tangents to each other, *i.e.*, $(\text{MRCS}_{Q_1:Q_2})_1 = (\text{MRCS}_{Q_1:Q_2})_2 = P_1/P_2$. To explain this point let us consider Fig. 13.2.

AB is a common budget line for consumers (equality of income is presumed here). U_1 and U_2 are the indifference curves for the two consumers. The budget line touches them at different points E_1 and E_2 on U_1 and U_2 respectively. Point *S* represents the status quo, *i.e.*, the initial position for both the consumers. Since the budget line touches the indifferences curves for Consumer 1 and Consumer 2 at different points, this reflects a disequilibrium situation in the economy. Tangency points on the indifference curves with the budget line implies maximum utility position for either of the consumers. To reach these points consumers are making exchanges of commodities between themselves. The initial endowment of commodities with consumer 1 and consumer 2 as given by point *S* are Q_{11}^O and Q_{21}^O for consumer 1 and Q_{12}^O and Q_{22}^O for consumer 2 total availability of commodities being fixed and equal to $Q_{11}^O + Q_{12}^O$ and $Q_{21}^O + Q_{22}^O$ of commodity 1 and commodity 2 respectively.

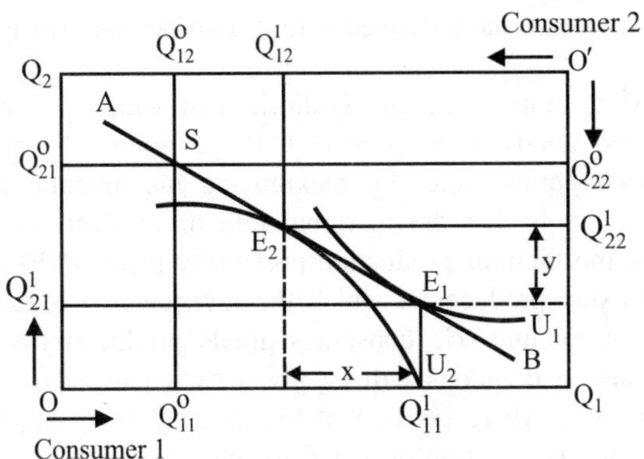

Fig. 13.2 Pareto Optimality Under Perfect Competition

At E_1 position the first consumer retains the combination Q^1_{11} and Q^1_{21} of two commodities. To reach this maximum position he gives up ($Q^O_{21} - Q^1_{21}$) amount of commodity 2 for ($Q^1_{11} - Q^O_{11}$) amount of commodity 1. Similarly, at the equilibrium position E_2 the second consumer prefers (Q^1_{12} and Q^O_{22}) combination of commodities. He gives up ($Q^O_{12} - Q^1_{12}$) amount of commodity 1 for ($Q^1_{22} - Q^O_{22}$) amount of commodity 2. Remember, both the consumers have moved away from the status quo position, *S*, to get the maximum satisfaction. Now, comparing the demand patterns for two goods at their equilibrium positions we find excess demand for commodity 1 by two consumers. It is the difference between ($Q^1_{11} + Q^1_{12}$) and ($Q^O_{11} + Q^O_{12}$) which is equivalent to *x* as shown in the figure. Similarly, we find excess supply for commodity 2 which is ($Q^O_{21} + Q^O_{22}$) – ($Q^1_{21} + Q^1_{22}$) = *y*. (The quantities of Q_1 and Q_2 are fixed that is why we have the phenomena of excess demand for Q_1 and excess supply for Q_2). Obviously, markets for the two commodities are not in equilibrium. Because of excess demand for Q_1, its price goes up and due to excess supply for Q_2 its price declines. This implies a clock-wise rotation of the budget line. With such rotation of the budget line, the equilibrium points E_1 and E_2 will come closer and closer and eventually a situation comes when the budget line is tangent to the indifference curves of both the consumers at a point on the contract-curve which means achievement of the Pareto optimality. This result holds true for any number of commodities and any number of individual on generalisation. Thus, under perfect competition we do find Pareto optimality for a pure exchange economy.

So far, we have examined the Pareto optimality from consumption side treating supply of output for the goods fixed. We now extend this concept to production sector of an economy. Production is said to be Pareto optimal if it is not possible to increase output of at least one good without simultaneously decreasing outputs of other goods. For this, optimal allocation of resources to production of goods is required. As we have found in the chapter on the theory of production, maximum output for a given cost of a firm can be achieved only if the ratio of input prices is equal to the marginal rate of technical substitution. Further, as we know, under perfect competition in input markets all producers face the same input prices. Therefore, the marginal rate of technical substitution for any pair of inputs must be equal to the input's price ratio for all producers in the economy. This will result in Pareto optimality in production at the equilibrium, *i.e.*, production takes place on the contract-curve for producers. For two producers-two input type of economy the contract curve can be derived in the same way as we have derived it for a two person–two goods comsumption analysis as described above.

Let us now examine a simple case of equilibrium in which a consumer and a producer are involved and there are two goods to be produced. If we ignore the consumer, the producer will decide to produce the two goods either by maximising his revenue or profit from goods. The equilibrium condition for this is that the marginal rate of product transformation between goods equals their price ratio. In the familiar production possibility front (PPF) analysis, this is nothing but the tangency condition for the producer at which the revenue line is tangent to the PPF. Now, let us bring the consumer into picture. He consumes goods produced for him by the producer. His preference for the combination of goods will be given by a particular position on the indifference curve. This position is the one where his budget line is tangent to the indifference curve, showing the marginal rate of commodity substitution equal to the price ratio of goods. This condition gives the proper product-mix that has to be made available for maximising consumer satisfaction or call it the welfare in the society. Any other output-mix will be sub-optimal from the point of view of consumers though that can be produced with technical efficiency but not with the economic efficiency. The Pareto optimality condition for this is that the indifference curve has to be a tangent to the production function. At this situation, the marginal rate of commodity substitution will be equal to the marginal rate of product transformation (MRCS = MRPT). Further, if we assume perfect competition, the budget line of the consumer or the revenue line of the producer must also be tangent to the indifference curve as well as the PPF at the point. This implies MRCS = MRPT = Price Ratio for the commodities. This equilibrium position is shown by point *E* in the following figure (Fig. 13.3). If the MRCS ≠ MRPT, there will not be equilibrium in the economy.

Let us now take up the Pareto optimality conditions for economy as a whole, having several consumers and many producers using multiple inputs in production several goods and services required by people. Some of the Pareto optimality conditions relevant in this connection are as follows:

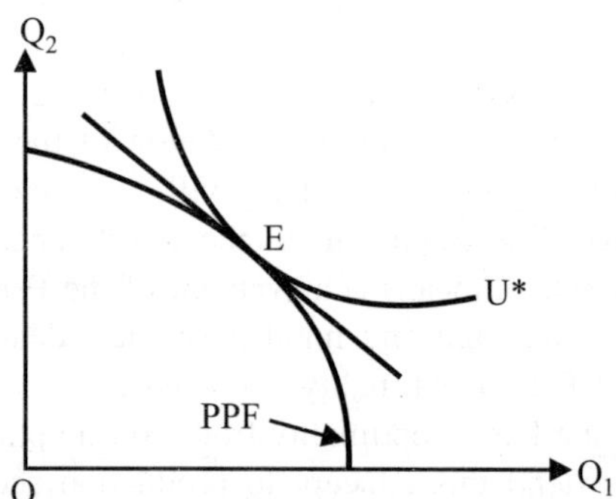

Fig. 13.3 Pareto Optimality for 'Two Goods, One Consumer, One Producer' Economy

(*i*) The MRCSs for all consumers and the MRPTs for all producers must be equal for every pair of produced goods.

(*ii*) The MRCSs for all consumers and MRTSs for all producers must be equal to every pair of primary goods.

(*iii*) MRCSs of consumers between factors and commodities must be equal to the corresponding producers' rates of transformation of factors into commodities, *i.e.*, their marginal products.

All these conditions must be satisfied to get the optimum state of the economy where it is not possible to increase the utility of one or more consumers without diminishing the utility of others by discontinuing the production of one or more goods.

The rationale for all these conditions will be clear through the mathematical derivation of results concerning them. This is given in the following sections.

(b) Mathematical Derivation of Pareto Optimality Conditions

We have described the Pareto optimality conditions for consumption, *i.e.*, the exchange of goods among consumers, for production of goods, and for economy as a whole. A mathematical exposition of such conditions is quite helpful to understand them in a much more meaningful way. Let us start this with the allocation of goods and services which maximises satisfaction of consumers (utility). The mathematical approach for this is quite simple: What we do is to maximise each consumer's utility given the utility levels for all other consumers. This ensures Pareto optimality for consumption activities.

Let us assume that there are n consumers and m commodities in the economy. All goods are already produced. Each consumer has some initial stock or endowment of commodities. However, his current consumption might be different from his initial possession of stocks.

Q_{ij}^{O} is the initial endowment of commodity j for consumer i and Q_{ij} is the current consumption for him of the commodity. Since we have taken all commodities as given, *i.e.*, the initial stock of commodities is, in fact, their total availability for current consumption. That is,

$$\sum_{j=1}^{m} Q_{ij}^{O} = \sum_{j=1}^{m} Q_{ij}. \qquad ...(1)$$

Assuming no externalities in consumption, the utility function for consumer i can be specified in terms of quantities of different goods consumed by him. That is:

$$U_i = U_i(Q_{i1}, Q_{i2}, ..., Q_{im}), \; i = 1, ..., n. \qquad ...(2)$$

For derivation of the Pareto optimality condition we have a constrained utility maximisation problem for each and every consumer. For consumer 1, this problem can be specified as:

$$\text{Max } U_1 = U_1(Q_{11}, Q_{12}, ..., Q_{1m})$$

$$\text{Subject to (1) } U_i^{O} = U_i(Q_{i1}, Q_{i2}, ..., Q_{im}); \; i = 2, ..., n$$

and
$$\text{(2) } \sum_{i=1}^{n} Q_{ij}^{O} - \sum_{i=1}^{n} Q_{ij} = 0, \; j = 1, ..., m. \qquad ...(3)$$

The first constraint says that the utility levels of other consumers are fixed, and the second constraint specifies that the total supply of commodities must be consumed fully. Writing the lagrange function for this problem, we have

$$L = U_1(Q_{11}, Q_{12}, ..., Q_{1m}) + \sum_{i=2}^{n} \lambda_i \left[U_i(Q_{i1}, Q_{i2}, ..., Q_{im}) - U_i^{O}\right]$$

$$+ \sum_{j}^{m} \mu_j \left[\sum_{i}^{n} Q_{ij}^{O} - \sum_{i=1}^{n} Q_{ij}\right] \qquad ...(3a)$$

where λ_i, $i = 2, 3, ..., n$; and μ_j, $j = 1, 2, ..., m$; are Lagrange multipliers. On taking partial derivatives of (3) with respect to Q_{11}, Q_{12} we have the first order maximisation conditions for consumer 1 as,

$$\partial L/\partial Q_{1j} = \partial U_1/\partial Q_{1j} - \mu_j = 0, \; j = 1, 2, ..., m \qquad ...(4)$$

and $\partial L/\partial Q_{ij} = \lambda_i \, \partial U_i/\partial Q_{ij} - \mu_j = 0, \; i = 2, 3, ..., n; \; j = 1, ..., m.$

We assume that the second order conditions are satisfied. By selecting any pair of two commodities, say j and k we have:

$$\frac{\partial U_1/\partial Q_{1j}}{\partial U_1/\partial Q_{1k}} = \frac{\mu_j}{\mu_k}; \; j, k = 1, 2, ..., m. \qquad ...(5)$$

We can get similar equilibrium conditions for every consumer. So, the general term for this is:

$$\frac{\partial U_i/\partial Q_{ij}}{\partial U_i/\partial Q_{ik}} = \frac{\mu_j}{\mu_k} \quad \begin{matrix} j, k = 1, 2, ..., m, \\ i = 1, ..., n. \end{matrix} \qquad ...(6)$$

Expanding (6) we have

$$\frac{\partial U_1/\partial Q_{ij}}{\partial U_1/\partial Q_{ik}} = \frac{\partial U_2/\partial Q_{2j}}{\partial U_2/\partial Q_{2k}} = \cdots = \frac{\partial U_n/\partial Q_{nj}}{\partial U_n/\partial Q_{nk}} = \frac{\mu_j}{\mu_k} \quad j, k = 1, 2, ..., m \qquad ...(7)$$

The equation (7) gives the Pareto optimality conditions for pure exchange. According to this, the MRCSs between any pair of commodities must be equal for all consumers. This condition is reflected by the contract-curve shown in Fig. 13.1.

If there are externalities, the satisfaction (utility) of consumer i is not only a function of quantities of commodities consumed by him, but also of quantities of commodities consumed by others. In this situation, the Pareto optimality conditions are quite difficult to be derived. In fact, they might not be existing at all.

Now, let us examine the Pareto optimality conditions for production. We have seen that under assumption of non-satiation of consumer wants and absence of externalities, an increase in output of one consumer good, given all other outputs constant, will result in a higher level of satisfaction for at least one consumer without reducing the level to satisfaction of others. Let us assume for simplicity that only consumer goods are produced. For Pareto optimality in production, we need that the level of each output must be maximum for given levels of outputs of all commodities. Let the number of producers be m each one producing different commodity using G inputs. Further, we take Q_j as quantity of commodity j produced by jth producer; X_g^O, as fixed quantity of input g, $g = 1,.., G$; and x_{jg} as the quantity of input g used by producer j. The inputs are fully used in production when we have,

$$X_g^O = \sum_j^m x_{jg}, \; g = 1,..., G. \qquad ...(8)$$

The production function for jth commodity is,

$$Q_j = f_j \, [x_{j1}, x_{j2}, ..., x_{jg}]; \; j = 1, ..., m. \qquad ...(9)$$

To derive the Pareto optimality condition for production, we have the maximisation problem for commodity 1 as,

$$\text{Max } Q_1 = f_1[x_{i1}, x_{i2}, ..., x_{ig}]$$

$$\text{Subject to } Q_j^O = f_1[x_{j1}, x_{j2}, ..., x_{jg}], \; j = 2, ..., m. \qquad ...(10)$$

and $$X_g^O - \sum_{j=1}^{m} x_{jg} = 0, \; g = 1, ..., G.$$

The Lagrange function for this problem can be written as,

$$L = f_1[x_{11}, x_{12}, ..., x_{1G}] + \sum_{j=2}^{m} \alpha_j \, [f_j \, (x_{j1}, x_{jg}) - Q_j^o]$$

$$+ \sum_{g=1}^{G} \beta_g \, [X_g^O - \sum_{j=1}^{m} x_{jg}] \quad ...(11)$$

where α_j, $j = 2, 3, ..., m$, and β_g, $g = 1, ..., G$, are Lagrange multipliers, the total number of which is $G + m - 1$. Differentiating (11) with respect to x_{jg} for all $j = 1, 2, ..., m$ and $g = 1, ..., G$, we have the first order partial derivatives as,

$$\partial L/\partial x_{1g} = \partial f_1/x_{1g} - \beta_g = 0, \; g = 1, 2, ..., G.$$

$$\partial L/\partial x_{jg} = \alpha_j \; \partial f_j/\partial x_{jg} - \beta_g = 0, \; j = 2, 3, ..., m_j$$

$$g = 1, ..., G \quad ...(12)$$

From these set of equations we have the conditions.

$$\frac{\partial f_1 / \partial x_{1g}}{\partial f_1 / \partial x_{1P}} = \frac{\beta_g}{\beta_P}; \; g, P = 1, ..., G \quad ...(13)$$

and

$$\frac{\partial f_j / \partial x_{jg}}{\partial f_j / \partial x_{jP}} = \frac{\beta_g}{\beta_P}; \; j = 2, 3, ..., m \; \; g, P = 1, ..., G \quad ...(13a)$$

The Pareto optimality condition for any pair of inputs for producers is therefore,

$$\frac{\partial f_1 / \partial x_{1g}}{\partial f_1 / \partial x_{1P}} = \frac{\partial f_2 / \partial x_{2g}}{\partial f_2 / \partial x_{2P}} = ... = \frac{\partial f_m / \partial x_{mg}}{\partial f_m / \partial x_{mP}} = \frac{\beta_g}{\beta_P} \quad ...(14)$$

According to this equation, the marginal rate of technical substitution for any pair of inputs must be the same for all producers at the optimum state.

To find the Pareto optimality conditions in general, we have to combine consumption and production together. For this, let us assume that there are n consumers, m commodities, P producers, and G primary inputs and variables in the model are:

Y_{ij} : Quantity of commodity j consumed by consumer i.

X_{ig}^O : The initial endowment of primary factor g for consumer i

X_{ig}^* : The quantity of factor g supplied to producers by consumer i

Q_{Pj} : The quantity of commodity j produced by producer P.

X_{Pg} : The quantity of factor g used by producer P.

$X_{ig}^O - X_{ig}^*$: The quantity of factor g consumed by consumer i.

For consumer i, we can now write the utility function as,

$$U_i = U_i \; [Y_{i1}, Y_{i2}, ..., Y_{im}, X_{i1}^O - X_{i1}^*, X_{i2}^O - X_{i2}^*, ..., X_{iG}^O - X_{iG}^*], \quad ...(15)$$

$$i = 1, 2, ..., n.$$

The production function for producer P can be written as,

$$F_P[Q_{P1}, Q_{P2}, ..., Q_{Pm}, X_{P1}, X_{P2}, ..., X_{PG}] = 0, \; P = 1, ..., P \quad ...(16)$$

Each of the producers is no longer a single product firm.

For economy as a whole, the total quantity of each primary input supplied by all consumers must be equal to the total quantity of that input used by all producers. This means:

$$\sum_{i=1}^{n} X_{ig}^{*} = \sum_{P=1}^{P} X_{Pg} , \; g = 1, 2, ..., G. \qquad ...(17)$$

Further, total consumption of each commodity in the economy must be equal to total production of the commodity by all producers.

$$\sum_{i=1}^{n} Y_{ij} = \sum_{P=1}^{P} Q_{Pj}; \; j = 1, ..., m. \qquad ...(18)$$

The maximisation problem is now to maximise total utility level of each consumer subject to given levels of utility of all consumers and constraints (17) and (18). Let us take the utility function of consumer 1 for maximisation as an example. The Lagrange function for this would be

$$\begin{aligned} L = & \; U_1 \; (Y_{11}, \; Y_{12}, \; ..., \; Y_{1m}, X_{11}^{O} - X_{11}^{*}, ..., X_{1G}^{O} - X_{1G}^{*}) \\ & + \sum_{i=2}^{n} \lambda_i \; [U_i \; (Y_{i1}, Y_{i2}, ..., Y_{im}, \; ..., X_{iG}^{O} - X_{iG}^{*}) - U_i^{*}] \\ & + \sum_{P=1}^{P} \mu_P \; F_P \; (Q_{P1}, ..., Q_{Pm}, X_{P1}, ..., X_{PG}) \\ & + \sum_{g=1}^{G} \alpha_g \; (\sum_{i=1}^{n} X_{ig}^{*} - \sum_{P=1}^{P} X_{Pg}) \\ & + \sum_{j=1}^{m} \beta_j \; (\sum_{P=1}^{P} Q_{Pj} - \sum_{i=1}^{n} Y_{ij}) \end{aligned} \qquad ...(19)$$

The total number of Lagrange multipliers in the function is $n + P + G + M - 1$. The first order maximisation conditions for this function are,

$$\begin{aligned} \partial L/\partial Y_{1j} &= \partial U_1/\partial Y_{1j} - \beta_j = 0 \\ \partial L/\partial Y_{ij} &= \lambda_i \; \partial U_i/\partial Y_{ij} - \beta_j = 0 \\ \partial L/\partial X_{1g}^{O} &= - \; \partial U_1/\partial (X_{1g}^{O} - X_{1g}^{*}) + \alpha_g = 0 \\ \partial L/\partial X_{ig}^{O} &= - \; \partial U_i/\partial (X_{ig}^{O} - X_{ig}^{*}) + \alpha_g = 0 \\ \partial L/\partial Q_{Pi} &= \mu_P \; \partial F_p/\partial Q_{Pj} + \beta_j = 0 \\ \partial L/\partial X_{Pg} &= \mu_P \; \partial F_p/\partial X_{Pg} - \alpha_g = 0 \end{aligned} \qquad ...(20)$$

where $i = 2, 3, ..., n; \; j = 1, 2, ..., m; \; Q = 1, 2, ..., P;$ and $g = 1, 2, ..., G.$

From the first equation of (20) we get,

$$\frac{\partial U_1 / \partial Y_{1j}}{\partial U_1 / \partial Y_{1k}} = \frac{\beta_j}{\beta_k} ; \; J, \; K = 1, 2, ..., m. \qquad ...(21)$$

From the second equation (20), we get

$$\frac{\partial U_i / \partial Y_{ij}}{\partial U_i / \partial Y_{ik}} = \frac{\beta_j}{\beta_k}, \; i = 2, 3, ..., n; \; j, \; k = 1, 2, ..., m. \qquad ...(22)$$

Combining (21) and (22), we have

$$\frac{\partial U_1 / \partial Y_{1j}}{\partial U_1 / \partial Y_{1k}} = \frac{\partial U_2 / \partial Y_{2j}}{\partial U_2 / \partial Y_{2k}} = ... = \frac{\partial U_n / \partial Y_{nj}}{\partial U_n / \partial Y_{nk}} , \text{ where } j, \; k = 1, 2, ..., m. \qquad ...(23)$$

That is, the MRCS between any pair of commodities (*J*, *K*) must be identical for all consumers. From the last equation of (20) we can derive the condition

$$\frac{\partial F_1 / \partial X_{1g}}{\partial F_1 / \partial X_{1h}} = \frac{\partial F_2 / \partial X_{2g}}{\partial F_2 / \partial X_{2h}} = \dots = \frac{\partial F_P / \partial X_{Pg}}{\partial F_P / \partial X_{Ph}}, \text{ where } g,\ h = 1,\ 2,\ \dots,\ G. \qquad \dots(24)$$

This says that the MRTS between any pair of primary inputs must be identical for all producers. From the fifth equation of (20) we can find the expression:

$$\frac{\partial F_P / \partial Q_{Pj}}{\partial F_P / \partial Q_{Pk}} = \frac{\beta_j}{\beta_k}, \qquad J,\ k = 1,\ 2,\ \dots,\ m;\ P = 1,\ 2,\ \dots,\ P \qquad \dots(25)$$

This is marginal rate of product transformation (MRPT) between the pair of commodities (*j* & *k*). On generalising it, we have

$$\frac{\partial F_1 / \partial Q_{1j}}{\partial F_1 / \partial Q_{1k}} = \frac{\partial F_2 / \partial Q_{2j}}{\partial F_2 / \partial Q_{2k}} = \dots = \frac{\partial F_P / \partial Q_{Pj}}{\partial F_P / \partial Q_{Pk}} \qquad j,\ k = 1,\ 2,\ \dots,\ m. \qquad \dots(26)$$

This says that the MRPT between any pair of commodities must be identical for all producers. From (21), (22), and (25) we have the relationship,

$$\frac{\partial U_i / \partial Y_{ij}}{\partial U_i / \partial Y_{ik}} = \frac{\partial F_P / \partial Q_{Pj}}{\partial F_P / \partial Q_{Pk}} \qquad \dots(27)$$

where $i = 1,\ 2,\ \dots,\ n$; $j,\ k = 1,\ 2,\ \dots,\ m,\ P = 1,\ 2,\ \dots,\ P$.

This equation reveals the marginal rate of commodity substitution (MRCS) between any pair of commodities for all consumers must be equal to the marginal rate of product transformation (MRTP) for all producers for the same pair of commodities. This is the condition for Pareto optimality for consumption and production.

Lastly, we get the relationship from (20) as

$$\frac{\partial U_i / \partial Y_{ij}}{\partial U_i / (X^O_{ig} - X^*_{ig})} = \frac{\beta_j}{\alpha_g} = \frac{\partial F_P / \partial Q_{Pj}}{\partial F_P / \partial Q_{Pg}} \qquad \dots(28)$$

where $i = 1,\ \dots,\ n$; $P = 1,\ \dots,\ P$, and $j = 1,\ \dots,\ m$, and $g = 1,\ 2,\ \dots,\ n$;

This relationship connects the substitution between a commodity and a resource for a consumer on the one hand and the transformation from inputs to commodities for a producer on the other. Its interpretation is that the MRCS between a commodity and a factor for every consumer must be equal to the marginal product of the corresponding factor for the corresponding commodity.

We have discussed the Pareto optimality conditions without any reference to commodity and factor prices. For this let us bring markets into the picture. The simplest form of commodity and factor markets is that of perfect competition. Under perfect competition, both commodity and factor prices are exogenous, *i.e.*, all concerned individuals, consumers and producers, face the same set of prices. In this situation, as we have mentioned earlier also, the Pareto optimality conditions are consistent with perfect competition. For example, a consumer's satisfaction is maximised for a given income if his MRCS between any pair of commodities is equal to the ratio of prices of commodities concerned, and the Pareto optimality implies that the MRCS between that pair of commodities must be identical for all individuals. So, we have the equality of the MRCSs with the price ratio of commodities. That is:

$$\frac{\partial U_1/\partial Q_{1j}}{\partial U_1/\partial Q_{1k}} = \frac{\partial U_2/\partial Q_{2j}}{\partial U_2/\partial Q_{2k}} = ... = \frac{\partial U_n/\partial Q_{nj}}{\partial U_n/\partial Q_{nk}} = \frac{\beta_j}{\beta_k} = \frac{P_j}{P_k},\ j,\ k = 1, 2, ..., m. \qquad ...(29)$$

The assumption for this is that the concerned second order conditions are satisfied. All commodities entering the consumption plans of consumers must have positive amounts or atleast zero when there are corner solutions and the MRCSs for the pair of commodities must be decreasing at the equilibrium.

In the expression (29), whatever role is performed by the price ratio P_j/P_k is also performed by the ratio β_j/β_k of the Lagrange multipliers. These multiplies, therefore, can be interpreted as relative prices of commodities. If we interpret them as absolute prices, the set of prices might not be unique since if we take $P_j = \beta_j$ and if $\beta_j^* = a\,\beta_j$, $a > 0$, thus $P_j^* = \beta_j^*$. So, whether to accept P_j or P_j^* it cannot be decided uniquely.

In the case of production, we know that marginal rate of technical substitution (MRTS) between two factors of production equals the factor price ratio for a firm under perfect competition. Since Pareto optimality for optimum factor employment implies equal MRTS between the pair of factors for all firms, it implies that MRTSs will be equal to the factor price ratio which is the same for all firms under perfect competition in the factor market. That is, we have the general condition,

$$\frac{\partial F_1/\partial X_{1g}}{\partial F_1/\partial X_{1h}} = \frac{\partial F_2/\partial X_{2g}}{\partial F_2/\partial X_{2h}} = ... = \frac{\partial F_P/\partial X_{Pg}}{\partial F_P/\partial X_{Ph}} = \frac{\alpha_g}{\alpha_h} = \frac{\gamma_g}{\gamma_h} \qquad ...(30)$$

where g, h = 1, 2, ..., G. In this expression, the ratio $\frac{\alpha_g}{\alpha_h}$ of the Lagrange multipliers is playing the same role as the ratio of the factor prices γ_g/γ_h. These multipliers are also interpreted as the relative prices of factors of production. The second order condition for this reflects diminishing MRTSs for firms and the factor utilisation cannot be negative.

Coming the marginal rate of product transformation between products of firms (MRPT), we have the Pareto optimality condition under perfect competition as:

$$\frac{\partial F_1/\partial Q_{1j}}{\partial F_1/\partial Q_{1k}} = \frac{\partial F_2/\partial Q_{2j}}{\partial F_2/\partial Q_{2k}} = ... = \frac{\partial F_P/\partial Q_{Pj}}{\partial F_P/\partial Q_{Pk}} = \frac{\beta_j}{\beta_k} = \frac{P_j}{P_k} = \frac{MC_j}{MC_k} \qquad ...(31)$$

where j, k = 1, 2, ..., m. This equation simply expresses the relationship of uniform MRPT for a given combination of products for producers which is equal to the ratio of prices of commodities and also equal to the ratio of their marginal cost of production. At the equilibrium under perfect competition, product prices are equal to their respective marginal costs. So, the equality between MRPTs, price-ratio, and ratio of the marginal costs of different pairs of commodities is a direct consequence of this.

The other equilibrium conditions of perfect competitive markets can also be analysed in the analogous way as we have done above. The conclusion we draw from the above mentioned results or theorems is that perfect competition in commodity and factor markets automatically leads to Pareto-optimality conditions for the economy as a whole which implies efficient allocation of economic resources for consumption and production simultaneously. For imperfect markets the Pareto-optimality conditions do not hold good. We know that various imperfect markets, such as monopoly, duopoly, oligopoly, monopolistic competition, monopsony and bilateral monopoly cause misallocation of resources. Prices are not equal to marginal costs for goods in these types of markets and the factor prices are not determined on the basis of their contribution to production or revenue (*VMP*). In all these types of markets, the commodity and/or factor prices will no longer be parameter for the decision-making by the consumers and/or firms. Prices are determined rather through the discretionary powers of the concerned party. A monopoly firm, for example, sets its price on the basis of $MR = MC$ criterion but it has every power to change the price thus fixed as we find under monopoly price discrimination. Under market imperfections, consumers' choices no longer depend on prices but on the marginal expenses of acquiring additional quantities of commodities. Firms' decisions regarding optimal choices of factors of production no longer depend on factor prices but on the cost of acquiring additional units of the factors in imperfect factor markets. We have seen that a profit maximising monopoly firm takes decision regarding factors employment on the basis of equality of marginal revenue product and factor price, rather than having the efficiency condition: value of marginal product equal to the factor price. Since $MRP < VMP$, the monopoly firm employs lesser quantity of the factor than a competitive firm. This is certainly not good from welfare point of view.

On the whole, we can say that market imperfections and welfare attainment are incompatible and the Pareto optimality conditions are violated under such situations.[11] It is true that if all markets are monopolistic, conditions for Pareto optimality might be satisfied but this is a hypothetical proposition. Some markets might be monopolistic and some competitive. Under such mixture of markets, the Pareto optimality conditions are sure to be violated.

All Pareto optimality conditions are valid under the assumption of the absence of externalities, that is, there are no external economies and diseconomies on both, production and consumption sides. The perfect competition ensures this. As defined earlier, external economy on the consumption side exists if satisfaction or utility is derived not only by the consumer who pays for goods but also someone else who does not pay for it. Similarly, external diseconomies on the consumption side arise if one's consumption give him or her satisfaction but causes someone else to suffer dissatisfaction. On the production side, we may define the external economies and diseconomies in the analogous way. We have given some examples for externalities while discussing the doctrine of invisible hands. In the presence of external economies on both the production and consumption sides we derive extra benefits and therefore social welfare goes up. But, if there are external diseconomies, there will be lesser economic welfare in the society because of reduced benefits to those who suffer from such external diseconomies. The Pareto optimality conditions specifying the efficient consumption and production in the society do not consider such external effects. In the presence of externalities, the optimality conditions might be violated seriously.

(c) Concluding Remarks About Paretian Welfare Theory

A summary of the Paretian welfare theory, by focussing on its essential character, has been presented above. Given certain basic assumptions, such as ordinal measurement of satisfaction, independent utility functions for individuals, divisibility of factors of production, mobility among the factors of production, constant technology, etc., Pareto and his followers were interested in developing 'scientific' propositions free from ethical judgements, for the choice of optimal economic system from social point of view. Basically, he developed conditions for optimum or, say, best allocation of resources for consumption, for production and for economy as a whole. The efficiency conditions developed by him are, no doubt, quite important and, in fact, very much essential from the point of view of maximising economic welfare which is a major part of the total welfare of

11. See Henderson and Quandt: *Ibid*, pp. 264-272, for a mathematical analysis of Pareto optimality conditions under imperfect markets.

a society. Conditions developed by him are compatible with the efficiency of perfect competition. If there are imperfect markets in the economy and there are external economies and diseconomies, the Paretian theory fails then. Nevertheless, the development of a concept of efficiency free from the concept of equity was a significant step in the welfare analysis which provided a character of positive economic analysis to it and the credit for this goes to Pareto. That is, we can't say that Paretian welfare theory is a normative one; it is very much positive from the point of view of economic analysis. Contemporary welfare economists might not agree with the Paretian theory since it has neglected the equity aspect completely but that is a different issue. His objective was to develop 'scientific propositions' for optimum economic welfare and to that extent he was quite successful in this objective.

(iv) Other Criteria for Judging Social Welfare

Apart from the criteria discussed so far, there are a few more for judging the social welfare. These miscellaneous criteria, as suggested by different economists, are as follows:

(a) Kaldor's Compensation Criterion[12]

This was an attempt to modify the Paretian unanimity principle. It was felt that the unanimity principle, though theoretically quite sound, had little practical value without modification. A group of economists, led by Kaldor, worked in this direction resulting in the compensation principle having its basic foundation on the Pareto criterion. The compensation principles of different economists are value-free and involve no ethical judgements. There are some basic assumptions for such principles such as unchanged preferences of individuals, ordinal measurement of utility, absence of external effects, non-interpersonal comparison of utilities, an individual being best judge of his or her welfare, and segregation of production form distribution. The last assumption is crucial as it helps in analysing the effects of changes in the level of production on social welfare without going through its distributional aspect.

Given such assumptions, Kaldor, who was, in fact, the first to advocate a compensation criterion, suggested the following one.

The state A of the economy is considered socially preferable to state B, if those who gain from A could compensate the losers, (*i.e., bribe them to accept A*) *and still be better off in A than in B.*

Let us say that the society can increase its net real income (after compensating losers) by moving from state *B* to state *A,* then this increase in real income, according to Kaldor implies, an increase in social welfare.

(b) Hick's Compensation Test

Hick's test is very much similar to the Kaldor's compensating criterion. He argued that a permitted reorganisation must be taken which would allow payment of compensation and which would yet show a net advantage. According to him *"If A is made so much better off by the change that he could compensate B for his loss and still have something left over, the reorganisation is an unequivocal improvement."*[13]

---

12. Kaldor, N., "Welfare Propositions in Economics and Interpersonal Comparisons of Utility", *Economic Journal,* 41 (1939), pp. 549-552.
13. (*a*) Hicks, J.R., "Foundation of Welfare Economics", *The Economic Journal,* Vol. 49, 1939, pp. 696-712.
    (*b*) Hicks, J.R., "The Rehabilitation of Consumer Surplus", *The Review of Economic Studies,* Vol. 8, Feb. 1941, pp. 108-116.

For example, any reorganisation of production will increase social welfare if it is possible for the state to give full compensation in the form of subsidies to losers to the extent of their losses out of funds raised by taxing gainers and still be left with a surplus. If funds raised through taxing the gainers are not sufficient to compensate the losers fully, the reorganisation of production will diminish social welfare. In essence, both Hick's and Kaldor's tests are the same as Paretian efficiency criterion, since, according, to these tests, no body is worse off as the provision of compensation maintains the losers status quo in welfare while there is an increase in the welfare of gainers through introduction of the reorganisation of production, say adaptation of a new economic policy.

(c) Scitovsky's Double Criterion

Tibor Scitovsky found a logical contradiction in the tests suggested by Kaldor and Hicks to judge social welfare. According to him, it is possible that state *A* of the economy is better than state *B* in terms of Kaldor or Hick criterion, but once a society moves to state *A* the same test may support the return of the society from state *A* to state *B* on the ground of welfare, Scitovsky, in fact, showed this possibility through an example for a two goods-two person economy. This kind of contradiction involved in Kaldor-Hick's criterion is referred to a 'Scitovsky Paradox.' Scitovsky tried to remove the contradiction from the Kaldor-Hick's criterion by suggesting his own test of welfare which is known as 'Scitovsky Double Criterion'.[14] According to this criterion:

> A state A of the economy is considered socially preferable to state B if those who gain from A could compensate (*i.e.,* bribe) the losers into accepting the change from B to A, but simultaneously the losers could not bribe the gainers into not making the change. In other words, there is no plausibility of reversibility to the old state once a change is accepted by the society.

There are several limitations of Kaldor-Hicks-Scitovsky compensation approaches of judging the social welfare. All of them are essentially concerned with potential welfare rather than actual since they do not require that compensation be actually paid. These approaches implicitly involved interpersonal comparison of utility, that most welfare economists would like to avoid, in terms of gains and losses objectively in monetary terms. Such cardinal measurement approach of welfare, as we know, was bitterly criticised by economists even by Pareto. Further, ignoring real effects of economic policies on welfare should be viewed as a serious defect of the compensation principles.

Tests are one sided in the sense that they have focussed on production as a source of increased welfare ignoring distribution aspect completely. Optimum production along with optimum distribution of economic resources are essential requirements for increase in social welfare. Tests are supposed to be free from value-judgements but, in fact, they are not so. For example, as a compromise between Kaldor and Scitovsky principles, the emphasis is given on over-compensation of losers with a net increase in social welfare. This is very much a value judgement rather than an objective principle for judging social welfare.

In spite of limitations, the compensation principle, as followed by Kaldor, Hicks and Scitovsky, is very much useful in cost-benefit analysis. This branch of economic analysis can be applied at micro as well as at macro levels. It is the basic tool to judge economic alternatives objectively in monetary terms by comparing their benefits and costs over the life-spans of projects. In case someone is adversely affected by the system, there is provision of balancing that through subsidies

14. Scitovsky, T., "A Note on Welfare Propositions in Economics", *Review of Economic Studies,* Vol. 9 (1941), pp. 77-78.

in cost-benefit analysis. This is nothing but giving practical shape to the compensating principle and, thus, forming an important part of evaluation of systems from social point of view.

(v) Social Welfare Function Approach

A number of economists, led by Bergson[15], suggested social welfare function approach to analyse and study problems of welfare economics. A social welfare function was defined by them as an ordinal index of society's welfare which was considered as a function of the utility levels of all individuals. The form of the social welfare function depends on the value judgements of its promulgators concerning effects of the utility level of the *i*th individual on the social welfare. The promulgator, might be economists themselves who are studying the problem of welfare, or legislatures or some other government authority or by some other unspecified person or group. By incorporating the value judgements in the function in some form or the other the Bergson's welfare theory becomes quite normative in nature. The entire social welfare function can be represented by an 'indifference' map ranking different combinations of the utilities which might accrue to the various members of society, as shown in the following figure.

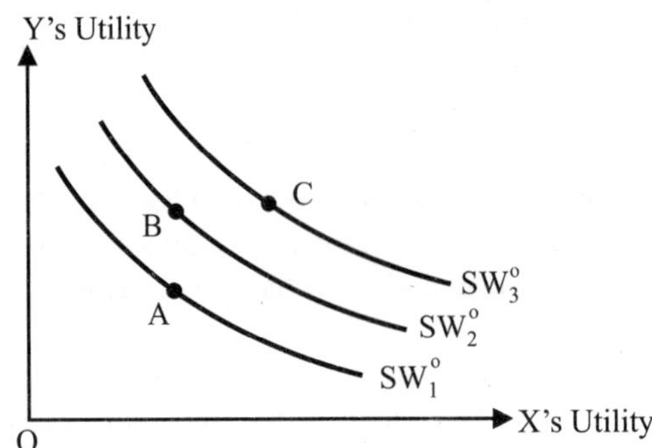

Fig. 13.4 Contours (Indifference Curves) of Social Welfare Levels

Three indifference curves for social welfare are shown in this figure. The welfare level increases with ascending order of the curves *i.e.,* $SW_3^o > SW_2^o > SW_1^o$. If we make comparison between three alternative combination of utilities for social welfare such as shown by points *A, E,* and *C,* we find that the alternative *C* is preferred over the alternative *B* which, in turn, is preferred over the alternative *A* as they are successively on higher indifference curves.

As defined above, we can express a social welfare function in terms of symbols as:

$$W = W(U_1, U_2, ..., U_n) \qquad ...(32)$$

where *W* stands for social welfare and U_i, $(i = 1, ..., n)$ is the level of utility index for *i*th individual, *n* is total number of persons in society.

For simplicity let us assume that society consists only two individuals whose utility functions are given as:

$$U_1 = U_1(q_{11}, q_{12}, x_1^O - x_1)$$

$$U_2 = U_2(q_{21}, q_{22}, x_2^O - x_2) \qquad ...(33)$$

15. Bergson, A., "A Reformulation of Certain Aspects of Welfare Economics", *Quarterly Journal of Economics*, Vol. 52, (1938), pp. 310-330.

where q_{ij} is the amount of jth commodity consumed by the ith individual (only two commodities are being taken into consideration here). x_i^O is the total availability of time at the disposal of the individual i out of which let x_i be the time devoted on work, so the rest $x_i^O - x_i$, is the leisure time. The utility derived by each individual is taken as a function of quantities of each commodity consumed and his leisure time.

Let the society's production function for goods be expressed in implicit form as:

$$F(q_{11} + q_{12}, q_{21} + q_{22}, x_1 + x_2) = 0 \qquad ...(34)$$

With two individuals, the social welfare function (32) reduces to

$$W = W(U_1, U_2) \qquad ...(35)$$

And substituting (33) in it, we have

$$W = W[U_1(q_{11}, q_{12}, x_1^o - x_1), U_2(q_{21}, q_{22}, x_2^o - x_2)] \qquad ...(36)$$

The objective of society is to maximise (36) subject to the production function (34). The Lagrange function for this would be

$$W^* = W[U_1(q_{11}, q_{12}, x_1^o - x_1), U_2(q_{21}, q_{22}, x_2^o - x_2)] + \lambda F(q_{11} + q_{21}, q_{12} + q_{22}, x_1 + x_2) \qquad ...(37)$$

By taking the partial derivatives and setting each one of them equal to zero, the first order maximum condition derived from this function are:

$$\frac{\partial W^*}{\partial q_{11}} = \frac{\partial W}{\partial U_1}\frac{\partial U_1}{\partial q_{11}} + \lambda \frac{\partial F}{\partial q_{11}} = 0 \qquad ...(i)$$

$$\frac{\partial W^*}{\partial q_{12}} = \frac{\partial W}{\partial U_1}\frac{\partial U_1}{\partial q_{12}} + \lambda \frac{\partial F}{\partial q_{12}} = 0 \qquad ...(ii)$$

$$\frac{\partial W^*}{\partial x_1} = -\frac{\partial W}{\partial U_1}\frac{\partial U_1}{\partial (x_1^O - x_1)} + \lambda \frac{\partial F}{\partial (x_1^O - x_1)} = 0 \qquad ...(iii)$$

$$\frac{\partial W^*}{\partial q_{21}} = \frac{\partial W}{\partial U_2}\frac{\partial U_2}{\partial q_{21}} + \lambda \frac{\partial F}{\partial q_{21}} = 0 \qquad ...(iv) ...(38)$$

$$\frac{\partial W^*}{\partial q_{22}} = \frac{\partial W}{\partial U_2}\frac{\partial U_2}{\partial U_{22}} + \lambda \frac{\partial F}{\partial q_{22}} = 0 \qquad ...(v)$$

$$\frac{\partial W^*}{\partial x_2} = -\frac{\partial W}{\partial U_2}\frac{\partial U_2}{\partial (x_2^O - x_2)} + \lambda \frac{\partial F}{\partial (x_2^O - x_2)} = 0 \qquad ...(vi)$$

$$\frac{\partial W^*}{\partial \lambda} = F(q_{11} + q_{12}, q_{21} + q_{22}, x_1 + x_2) = 0 \qquad ...(vii)$$

There are 7 variables q_{11}, q_{12}, q_{21}, q_{22}, x_1, x_2 and λ, which can be found out by these seven equations. The validity of all these seven equations is based on the assumption that the second order conditions related to them are satisfied. Once we find the value for the unknowns we get the welfare optimum for the society. The Pareto optimality conditions can be deduced directly from these seven equations. For example, from (*i*), (*ii*), (*iv*) and (*v*) equations yield

$$\frac{\partial U_1 / \partial q_{11}}{\partial U_1 / \partial q_{12}} = \frac{\partial U_2 / \partial q_{21}}{\partial U_2 / \partial q_{22}} = \frac{F_1}{F_2} \quad \text{...(39)}$$

and
$$\frac{\partial U_1 / \partial q_{11}}{\partial U_1 / \partial (x_1^O - x_1)} = \frac{\partial U_2 / \partial q_{21}}{\partial U_2 / \partial (x_2^O - x_1^O)} = \frac{F_1}{F_3} \quad \text{...(40)}$$

where
$$\left.\begin{array}{l} F_1 = \partial F / \partial q_{11} = \partial F / \partial q_{21} \\ F_2 = \partial F / \partial q_{12} = \partial F / \partial q_{22} \end{array}\right\} \text{These are derivatives of } F \text{ with the same product.}$$

$$F_3 = \partial F / \partial (x_1^O - x_1) = \partial F / \partial (x_2^O - x_2)$$

Also, we can find the equality,

$$\frac{\partial W}{\partial U_1} \cdot \frac{\partial U_1}{\partial q_{1j}} = \frac{\partial W}{\partial U_2} \cdot \frac{\partial U_2}{\partial q_{2j}}, \; j = 1, 2 \quad \text{...(41)}$$

This implies that the marginal social significance of consumption for each commodity must be equal for all individuals in the society. This is ensured by the point of tangency (*E*) between a social welfare indifference curve and the utility transformation curve, as shown in Fig. 13.5. The utility transformation curve shows the various combinations of utility received by individual 1 and 2 (*i.e.*, U_1 and U_2) when the economy is in general equilibrium of exchange. At the equilibrium point, the MRCS are the same for both the individuals and equal to the corresponding MRPT. Further, as reflected by (40), the rate at which individuals substitute leisure ($x_1 - x_2$) for commodities equals the marginal product of labour.

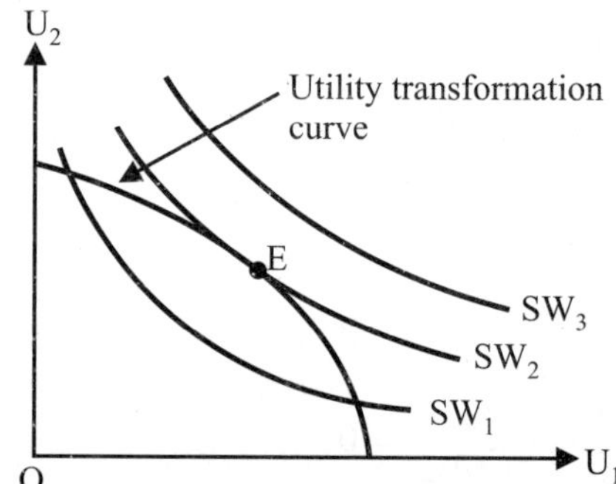

Fig. 13.5 Optimality of Social Welfare

The Bergsonian welfare theory rests on the crucial assumption of existence of a social welfare function. Such a function, as we have seen above, links the total welfare in society with the levels of satisfaction (*i.e.*, utility) of individuals. Since the level of satisfaction for an individual depends on the quantities of commodities he consumes, we can, therefore, express the welfare function in terms of aggregates of commodities consumed by all individuals in the society. This type of function will be a social analog of individual's utility function. We may call this type of function as social preference function. A social preference function helps in taking group decisions, *i.e.*, the decision, regarding optimal consumption of goods by the society keeping in mind desires or aspirations of various persons who make up the society. A social preference function is derived from the individuals' preferences. There are different ways of deriving social preferences (*i.e.*, group decisions) from the individual preferences (*i.e.*, decisions). For example, social preferences might be determined by a dictator or ruler, or they might be determined democratically by a majority votes of individual members of society or by a centralised body of representatives. All ways of translating individual preferences into social preferences may not be equally desirable or acceptable. From the point of view of desirability or acceptability of social preferences, Arrow[16] has suggested four basic conditions:

(*i*) Social preferences must be consistent (transitive) in the sense that if alternative *A* is decided to be preferred over alternative *B* and alternative *B* is preferred over alternative *C*, then *C* will never be preferred over *A*. This gives rise to the requirement of complete ordering of social preferences.

(*ii*) The social preferences or group decisions must not be dictated by anyone outside the community or any individual in the community.

(*iii*) Social choices must not change in opposite direction from the choices of members of that society.

(*iv*) A social preference, as between two alternatives, must not change so long as no individual in society changes the order in which he ranks these alternatives in accordance with his preferences. In other words, the preferred state in a set of alternatives must be independent of existence of other alternatives.

All these conditions reflect value judgements. Although they are quite reasonable, yet meeting them fully in social decision-making is not very simple. Arrow himself, through his possibility theorem, has shown that it is impossible to choose among all possible sets of alternatives without violating at least one of the four conditions. In other words, what Arrow has proved through his theorem is that social choice must be in a sense inconsistent and undemocratic. In view of this result, we may conclude that the best welfare position is unattainable in the framework of social preferences or social welfare function approach.

13.3 THE THEORY OF SECOND BEST

In the context of welfare, it is highly desirable to attain Pareto optimality conditions for the economy. However, due to several imperfections in the economy, one may find Pareto non-optimal allocation of resources and hence non-fulfilment of the Pareto's efficiency conditions. In this situation, there will be scope for making someone better off without making anyone worse off. It is generally believed that if some of the market or institutional imperfections causing misallocation of resources are eliminated, the economy moves towards better position from the point of view or attainment of economic welfare. For example, if there are market imperfections, such as perfect competition in some industries, monopoly, oligopoly and monopolistic competition prevailing in some others, then public policies that eliminate monopoly and oligopoly, but leaves monopolistic competition alone, make an improvement in economic welfare of society as a whole. According to the theory of second best developed by Lancaster and Lipsey this is however not true.[17] This theory simply states that if one or more of the first order conditions for Pareto optimality cannot be satisfied because of institutional and/or market constraints, in general it is neither necessary nor desirable to satisfy the remaining conditions. Thus, the theory of second best invalidates the piecemeal approach of attaining Pareto optimality conditions for maximum social welfare. By piecemeal, we mean treating markets in isolation and thus elimination of market imperfections or welfare impediments one by one but not all of them at a time as, for example, elimination of

16. Arrow K.J., *Social Choice and Individual Values*, New York, John Wiley and Sons, 1951.
17. Lancaster, K. and Lipsey, R.G., *"The General Theory of Second Best," Review of Economic Studies*, 24, (1956-57), pp. 11-32.

monopoly and oligopoly from certain markets but leaving monopolistic competition in certain other markets would not improve social welfare.

In the presence of market imperfections or institutional constraints, a social policy remains in the state of Pareto non-optimality, and by following the piecemeal policy of any kind, the situation of social policy does not change much. It still remains in the state of Pareto non-optimality. Of the two situations of the social policy, which are both Pareto non-optimal, if one is not Pareto superior to the other one, are not comparable for their relative desirability. This is because there is no yardstick for this in Paretian welfare theory. Such non-comparability among non-Pareto optimal situations rules out a second best alternative social policy.

If the two situations of social policy, *i.e.*, the one before the piecemeal action and the other after this are non-Pareto optimal but one of them is Pareto superior than the other, then the Pareto superior alternative or situation is better and hence preferable from social point of view. The theory of second best is not negating this kind of choice. In fact, we may argue that this is the true spirit of the theory of second best, *i.e.*, if Pareto optimality cannot be achieved due to the prevailing circumstances, then attempts should be made to eliminate the most undesirable situations by the criterion of Pareto superiority. In practice, we do find societies attempting on piecemeal basis to improve social welfare. The Pareto superiority criterion is in conformity with this and, therefore, the theory of second best if interpreted in this way, has its practical relevance.

13.4 PUBLIC GOODS

In the context of social welfare, we should examine the relevance of public goods since they are used or consumed collectively by members of society. A commodity is called a 'public good' if its consumption by anyone does not reduce the amount available for others in the community, given the existence of some total stock. In other words, providing the good to anyone makes it possible to provide the good to everyone without additional cost. Thus, supply of public goods provides a highly beneficial externality from welfare point of view. A public good is different from a private good in the sense that if one person consumes more of a stock of a private good less will be left for consumption by others. A private good is consumed or used exclusively but a public good is used concurrently by several people. Several examples can be given for public goods. The traditional one is that of a light house. If one ship receives the benefit of the light or warning signal, that in no way deprives the other ships to get and benefits from the light house. Television programmes, public roads, municipal parks, are a few more examples of public goods.

There might be some costs to users of a public good such as entry fee for a park, stationing a lookout to watch the light house and the cost of buying a television set for TV programmes. Such good for which there is users' cost are not 'pure' public goods. Many goods lie' in such intermediate range, *i.e.*, they are neither pure public goods nor pure private goods. We may call them as 'mixed goods.' A pure public good for which a user pays nothing is hardly to find. Public goods cannot be purchased and sold in the market in the same way as ordinary goods. Public goods are normally produced by public agencies on the basis of collective decisions and financed by taxation.

The theory of public goods has several dimensions dealing with important questions like finding the number of public goods that should be produced, optimal mix of public and private goods, optimal allocation of resources on these two types of goods, and so on. The conventional price and quantity determination is a part of this theory and, in the context of general equilibrium analysis, the determination of optimality conditions for production of public goods is a very important aspect of the theory.[18] It is not our purpose to review the entire theory of public goods but to deal with those aspects that are concerned with welfare analysis, *i.e.*, basically with the optimality conditions for allocation of society's resources to the provision of public goods.

There are different approaches to deal with the problem of optimal allocation of resources to public and private goods, such as Pigovian approach, Musgrave approach, Bowen/Samuelson approach, Buchanan approach, Lindahl's approach and Tiebout approach.[19] Pigou's approach is quite simple. It is a utilitarian approach. The basic core of his model is that individuals get benefit (utility) from the consumption of public goods. People pay taxes to finance supply of public goods. This implies a disutility of tax payment to individuals. This disutility may be defined as the opportunity cost of forgone private goods consumption by them. For each individual the optimal supply of public goods occurs at the point at which the marginal utility of public goods is equal to the marginal disutility of tax payments. By applying the general equi-marginal utility principle one can find the optimal allocation of his budget on public and private goods.

There are some problems with this approach; one is that it is based on the concept of cardinal utility which creates its own operational problems. Second, there is no mechanism in Pigovian approach by which individual optima could be aggregated to get social optima for allocation of society's funds on public and private goods. One way for this is to treat the entire society as 'an individual' and then the analysis could proceed by balancing the marginal social utility of goods to the marginal disutility of tax payments. For this, we must know the social preference function and we have seen earlier that this might not exist. So, there is a problem of finding the social optima for optimal allocation of funds on public and private goods following the Pigovian approach.

Economists like Musgrave, Bowen, Samuelson and Buchanan, as cited earlier, suggested partial and/or general equilibrium analysis to determine optimal allocation of resources on public goods vis-a-vis their pricing. The partial equilibrium analysis, as usual, relates to the market equilibrium for a public good for price and output determination. This analysis proceeds in the familiar supply and demand curves intersection framework as for a private good. However, there is a fundamental difference between the two. In the case of a private good, the demand curves for individual consumers are aggregated horizontally to find the market demand. The interaction of market demand and market supply curves gives the market price for the good. Such a market price will be the same for all consumers under perfect competition. At this price, individuals buy different quantities of the good as given by their respective demand curves, *i.e.*, all of them consume different amount of the good but pay the same price. For a public good, however, the situation is different. All consumers consume the same amount of the good but pay different prices for that. How? Let us examine this through a diagram (Fig. 13.6). The diagram shows the supply and demand curves for a public good. The demand for the good is taken as an inverse function

---

18. Some important works on Public Goods theory are:
    (*a*) A.C. Pigou: *A Study of Public Finance*, London, Macmillan, 1928.
    (*b*) R.A. Musgrave: "A Voluntary Exchange Theory of Public Economy," *Q.J.E.,* Vol. 53, 1938, 213-37; and *The Theory of Public Finance*, N.Y., McGraw-Hill, 1958.
    (*c*) H.R. Bowen: "The Interpretation of Voting in the Allocation of Resources," *Q.J.E.,* Vol. 58, 1943, pp. 27-48.
    (*d*) Paul A. Samuelson: *The Pure Theory of Public Expenditure*, *R.E.St.* 36, 1954, 387-9.
    (*e*) J.M. Buchanan: "*The Demand and Supply of Public Goods*," Chicago, Rand MacNally 1968.
    (*f*) Erik Lindahl: *Die Gerechtigkeit der Besteurung: Und*, 1919.
19. See Brown C.V. and R.M. Jackson, *Public Sector Economics,* Oxford, Martin Robertson, 1978, Ch. 3, for a review of these approaches.

of the price of the good, other things being equal, and supply is taken as a positive function of the price, other things being equal. The supply represents the sum of marginal costs of producers of the good under perfect competition.

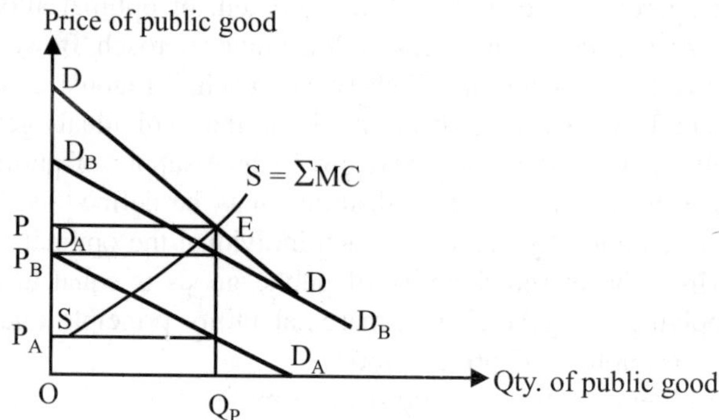

Fig. 13.6 Market Equilibrium for a Public Good

D_A and D_B are the demand curves for two individuals *A* and *B* for the public good. In the terminology of Samuelson, these are called 'pseudo-demand curves', as such demand curves are drawn by assuming that each person accurately reveals his willingness to pay for the output of the public good and there is no free rider for this. Given that, once the public good is made available it is used equally by everyone; so the total willingness to pay for the public good is found by adding the individual demand curves vertically. This is shown by *DD* curve which indicates $P = P_A + P_B$. *SS* is the supply curve for the good. The equilibrium position for the market of the public good is given by point *E* where *DD* and *SS* curves intersect. This gives *OP* as the equilibrium price for the good and OQ_p as its optimum quantity. The equilibrium price *OP* is the sum of prices that individuals are willing to pay, *i.e.*, $OP = OP_A + OP_B$. At the equilibrium position of the market, the total revenue received is equal to total cost of supplying the goods. Further, what we find at the equilibrium position is that the total willingness to pay for the output of the public good is equal to the price at which a producer is willing to supply that level of output. In this analysis, the price that an individual consumer is willing to pay for the output of the public good is directly proportional to the consumption benefit received by him.

To see why the intersection point *E* shows the equilibrium position of the market for the good, let us consider an output level of the good less than OQ_P *i.e.*, to its left. For such a level of output, the combined willingness to pay exceeds the supply price, *i.e.*, total revenue > total cost. It would be in the interest of everybody to increase output of the good. Similarly, to the right of OQ_P we find the combined willingness to pay less than the supply price resulting in a reduction in output. The only point where we have stable level for output, *i.e.*, no incentive to change it, is *E* where the demand curve *DD* and supply curve for the good intersect. On the basis of the above discussion vis-a-vis its analogy with the equilibrium condition for a private good, we have the following conclusions;

(*a*) In the case of a private good each individual faces the same market price for some level of output and the market price is equal to the marginal cost.

(*b*) For a public good each individual is willing to pay a different price for some level of output. The sum of the individual prices equals marginal cost ($P_A + P_B = MC$). The individual prices are called individualised or personalised prices for the public good.

What is the price of the public good and how the demand curve is actually derived for it is now the question that we should try to answer. The basic connotation of the demand curve for a public good is the same as that for a private good. It reveals the willingness of the individual to pay for quantities of the public good. It is downward sloping showing diminishing marginal utility for the good. It can be derived from a set of indifference curves in exactly the same way as the demand curve for a private good.[20] The essential requirements for derivation of the demand curve for the public good are that income, consumer preferences, prices of both public and private goods are given. A major controversy has arisen with respect to income variable, whether it should be money income or real income that is held constant. Musgrave and Hicks preferred money income while Bowen and Samuelson preferred real income. Samuelson's interpretation of the demand curve for the public good is in terms of 'marginal rate of substitution curve,' and this curve has been derived by him by considering the real income which is kept constant while determining the marginal price for the public good that will keep utility constant. Buchanan in his analysis of public goods used the 'marginal valuation curve' in place of the demand curves. This curve has been derived by him by plotting the slopes of successive indifference curves, as they intersect the budget line for a given price ratio.

Thus, the interpretation of demand curve is different when we compare the approach of Musgrave, Samuelson and Buchanan who are the leading economists working on the economics of public goods. The final result is, however, common, *i.e.*, the efficient supply of a public good requires that the cost of providing the public good be distributed so that the sum of the individual marginal prices equals marginal cost. In other words, the sum of individual prices or the sum of marginal rates of substitutions or the sum of marginal valuation of the good by different individuals equals marginal cost of production of the public good.

So far we have discussed the equilibrium condition for a public good. This is a partial equilibrium analysis, as we have mentioned earlier. From the point of view of economy as a whole, we have to consider several public goods and several other private goods produced by many firms for all people. This means that the resource allocation problem is to be analysed in the general equilibrium framework. As usual, we have to derive the Pareto optimality conditions for provision of public as well as private goods. This is quite a difficult task but it was simplified and analysed by Samuelson with the help of a number of assumptions.

Following Samuelson, let there be two consumers whose taste and preferences are given; there are two goods—one public and one private for consumption and the production possibility set for them is known. Further, let us assume that there is only one primary input. The utility function for each consumer can be specified as:

$$U_i = U_i\ (q_{i1},\ q_2,\ x_i^o - x_i);\ i = 1,\ 2 \qquad \text{...(42)}$$

where q_{i1} is the amount of the private good consumed by the ith consumer, q_2 is the amount of the public good consumed by the consumer. It is the same for both the consumer, $x_i^o - x_i$ is the stock of leisure time for the consumer i since x_i is the amount of his time supplied for work.

The production function for goods in implicit form is given as:

$$F(q_1,\ q_2,\ x) = 0 \qquad \text{...(43)}$$

where $q_1 = q_{11} + q_{21}$ and $x = x_1 + x_2$ *i.e.*, total output of the private good and labour supply respectively. Total supply of the public good is q_2.

20. See Chapter 4 for further details on this aspect.

21. P.A. Samuelson, *op. cit.*

To derive the Pareto optimality conditions for the economy from the public good, Samuelson followed the approach of maximising the utility function for consumer i subject to the constant level of utilities for other consumers and satisfying the production function (43). The optimal conditions for this can be mentioned as:[22]

$$(1)\quad \frac{\partial U_1/\partial q_2}{\partial U_1/\partial q_{11}} + \frac{\partial U_2/\partial q_2}{\partial U_2/\partial q_{21}} = \frac{\partial F/\partial q_2}{\partial F/\partial q_1} \qquad ...(44)$$

This says that the sum of the marginal rate of commodity substitution between the public and private goods for consumers must be equal to the rate of product transformation (RPT) of the private good (Q_1) for the public good (Q_2).

$$(2)\quad \frac{\partial U_1/\partial q_2}{\partial U_1/\partial(x_1^O - x_1)} + \frac{\partial U_2/\partial q_2}{\partial U_2/\partial(x_2^O - x_2)} = -\frac{\partial F/\partial q_2}{\partial F/\partial x} \qquad ...(45)$$

The sum of the marginal rate of commodity substitution of the primary input (X) for Q_2 must be equal, the reciprocal of the marginal product of the factor in production of Q_2.

$$(3)\quad \frac{\partial U_1/\partial(x_1^O - x_1)}{\partial U_1/\partial q_{11}} = \frac{\partial U_2/\partial(x_2^O - x)}{\partial U_2/\partial q_{21}} = -\frac{\partial F/\partial x}{\partial F/\partial q_1} \qquad ...(46)$$

The marginal rate of commodity substitution of X for Q_1 must be equal to the marginal product of X in production of Q_1.

All these conditions can be generalised for more primary factors, more than two consumers with multiple private and public goods. The basic condition for general Pareto optimality in this case is that for optimal supply of public goods the sum of marginal rates of substitution must be equal to the marginal rate of product transformation. That is,

$$\sum_{i=1}^{n} MRCS_{j,k}^{i} = MRPT_{j,k}, \quad i = 1, ..., n, \; j, k = 1, ..., m. \qquad ...(47)$$

Consider the first equilibrium condition (44). We know

$$MRCS^1_{Q_2:Q_1} = P_{12}/P_{11}; \; MRCS^2_{Q_2:Q_1} = P_{22}/P_{21}$$

where P_{12} and P_{22} are prices that consumer 1 and 2 pay for the public good and similarly P_{11} and P_{21} are the prices of the private good paid by them. This is the standard equilibrium of a consumer in the indifference curve analysis. Also, from the PPF analysis we know that the rate of product transformation equals the ratio of marginal costs of goods involved. So, we can write $\frac{\partial F/\partial q_2}{\partial F/\partial q_1} =$ MC_2/MC_1 where MC_2 is the marginal cost of production for the public good and MC_1 is the marginal cost of production for the private good. With these relations, we can rewrite (44) as:

$$\frac{P_{12}}{P_{11}} + \frac{P_{22}}{P_{21}} = \frac{MC_2}{MC_1} \qquad ...(48)$$

In the case of the private good, under perfect competition, the price will be uniform for all consumers, which, in turn, will be equal to the marginal cost of production of the good.

So $\quad P_{11} = P_{21} = P_1 = MC_1 \qquad ...(49)$

22. See Henderson and Quandt, *op. cit.*, pp. 270-272.

Therefore,

$$\frac{P_{12} + P_{22}}{P_1} = \frac{MC_2}{P_1} \qquad ...(50)$$

If we take $P_1 = 1$ *i.e.*, the private good as *numeraire* so, we have

$$P_{12} + P_{22} = MC_2 \qquad ...(51)$$

P_{12} and P_{22} are the efficiency prices of the public good for the two consumers respectively. Their sum is equal to the marginal cost of production of the public good. If there are several individuals using the public good, then we extend the equation (51) as:

$$P_{12} + P_{22} + \cdots + P_{n2} = MC_2 \qquad ...(52)$$

If prices are equivalent to the marginal benefits that individuals receive, the sum of the marginal benefits for all must be equal to the marginal cost of supplying the public good. Similar equations can be written for other public goods also. The marginal benefits that are accruing to individuals are from a marginal increase in the quantity of public good and so is the marginal cost, the private good is taken as a *numeraire* for this.

As we have explained earlier, public goods are normally produced by government or some public agencies on the basis of collective decisions and normally financed through taxation. A private manufacturer may not find production of public goods remunerative since he cannot discriminate among users for charging different prices and cannot exclude those who do not pay for goods but consume them. Seeing the welfare value of goods, governments supply them at a fairly low prices.

Without going into further details we may now summarise the above discussion on the public goods. The theory of public goods is quite complex and vast. We have gone only through some fragments of it. The basic issue for our discussion was that the theory of production concerning production and supply of public goods is different from the supply of private goods. The general Pareto optimality conditions, which define the optimum allocation of resources on production and distribution, are different in the case of public goods. Perfect competition and competitive pricing lead to under production and under consumption of public goods. Since public goods provide very powerful externality effects in the economy, and since private entrepreneurs hesitate to supply them, the responsibility of production and distribution of public goods rests on governments.

13.5 CONCLUDING REMARKS

This chapter has been devoted on the analysis of welfare economics. This branch of economics is concerned with society as a whole and so the theorems or results of partial equilibrium analysis, which constitute the subject matter of microeconomics, are not applicable to social choices between economic alternatives. Much of the present day welfare economics is normative in nature in which ethics or value judgement plays leading role in social choices.

Various types of approaches developed so far to study economic welfare of society have been discussed in this chapter. The emphasis was given on understanding the Pareto efficiency conditions for maximum welfare using the general equilibrium framework of economic analysis. The topics like externalities, theory of second best, and public goods, which are quite relevant to welfare of masses, have been discussed briefly.

SUGGESTED READINGS

Baumol, W.J., *Welfare Economics and the Theory of State* (2nd Ed.) London, G. Bell, 1965.

Baumol, W.J., *Economic Theory and Operations Analysis,* Prentice-Hall of India (E.E.E. Ed.), 1978, 2002.

Graaff, J.de V., *Theoretical Welfare Economics,* Cambridge University Press, 1957.

Ferguson, C.E., *Microeconomic Theory:* R.D. Irwin, 1971.

Henderson, J.M. and R.E. Quandt, *Microeconomic Theory: A Mathematical Approach,* McGraw-Hill 1971, 1980.

Just, R.E., *Applied Welfare Economics,* Prentice-Hall, 1982.

Pigou, A.C., *The Economics of Welfare,* Macmillan 4th Ed., 1932, Reprint 1952.

Samuelson, P.A., *Foundation of Economic Analysis,* Harvard University Press, 1947.

Sher, W., and R. Pindola, *Microeconomic Theory,* Edward Arnold, 1981.

REVIEW QUESTIONS

1. From the point of view of economic welfare of society as a whole, what are the various ways to evaluate different economic alternatives? Examine critically.
2. What is Edgeworth's box diagram? How this is considered as an analytical tool to study welfare economics? Explain in detail.
3. What is Pareto optimality and why it is so important in welfare economics? What are the difficulties associated with Paretian approach for its being applied in practice?
4. It is argued that perfect competition is a highly desirable condition for an economy according to Pareto optimality criterion for social welfare. Explain why it is so.
5. Why are externalities so important in welfare economics? Explain how production of private goods and public goods generate externalities and affect economic welfare of people at large.
6. What are the various compensating criteria and how such criteria might be compared with the Paretian optimality conditions for social welfare?
7. How do you define social welfare function' and show how it is useful for welfare analysis? What are the basic conditions for existence of a social preference function? Write in brief.
8. "Basic questions concerning right and wrong goals to be pursued cannot be settled by science as such. They belong to the realm of ethics and value judgements. The citizenry must ultimately decide such issues. What the expert can do is to point out the feasible alternatives and the true cost may be involved in different decisions"? Discuss.
9. What is the efficiency condition for optimal supply of a public good? Why such a good is generally supplied by the state and not by a private firm? Give some appropriate examples in support of your answer.
10. What is the purpose behind development of the theorem of the second best choice? How the theory of second best choice is applicable in production decision by a private firm and by a public firm? Discuss.

CHAPTER 14

Epilogue to Microeconomic Analysis

14.1 A REVIEW OF THE THEORY

The theory of microeconomic analysis presented in the preceding chapters of this book has given us a number of propositions or principles or laws for understanding human behaviour in relations to economic decision-making. We have seen how competitive markets regulate themselves through interaction of supply and demand in the short and long-runs and, thus, determine the prices, and how markets under imperfect competition are brought to the equilibrium positions. A consumer with limited income and fixed or variable prices of goods and services makes optimal decision regarding his choice. What are the laws for such optimality, how a consumer derives them, and how we can test them through facts, are the questions whose answers we find from the theory of consumer behaviour. Further, we have seen how optimisation behaviour of the producer brings equality between marginal physical products and factor prices, how the technical and economic theory of production provides the basis for the derivation of various types of cost curves and how the demand curves for various factors of production, such as land, labour, and capital, are derived and how factor prices are determined in different market situations. We have also seen the circular flows between various segments of an economy, such as consumption sector, production sector, commodity markets, factor markets, etc., showing the operation of the interdependent pricing system which brings the economy in equilibrium. This has been further demonstrated through a set of general equilibrium models in one of the chapters of the book. The analysis, in theoretical perspectives, has been extended to find the efficiency conditions for achieving optimal economic welfare for society as whole.

The entire analysis presented in this book is a synthesis of classical, neo-classical and modern approaches. It is a reading of the eocnomic theory which is, of course, abstract, based on a number of assumptions such as *ceteris paribus,* utility and profit-maximising goals for the consumer and the firm respectively and so on. Theorems or laws provided by the theory are quite useful to understand the reality as we have demonstrated on several pages of this book. Microeconomics, being the first course of economic theory, is a basic foundation for several other advanced or specialised courses of the discipline. All this is true but the theory in its present form, *i.e.*, basically neo-classical, is being seriously challenged by its rivals. Two new alternative approaches for the study of microeconomics emerged on the surface in recent times, one of them is called behavioural approach and the second managerial approach. Let us examine these approaches in brief before comparing them to the neo-classical or modern abstract approach.

14.2 'REALISM-IN-PROCESS' OR BEHAVIOURAL APPROACH

The theory of the firm is a major segment of the contemporary microeconomics. In this theory, as we have seen, a firm is defined as the smallest technical unit engaged in production and selling of some output for the sake of profit or some other gain such as revenue or income generation or consumer surplus in the case of a public firm. The economic analysis of such a firm runs in terms of maximisation of a function (*e.g.*, profit function or revenue function and so on) subject to a set of constraints. We have already discussed this type of approach in the earlier chapters of this book. The behavioural theorists are, however, not satisfied with this type of analysis of the firm. They have developed an alternative approach for this which is called the 'realism-in process' or 'behavioural approach'. To develop this approach the very concept of the firm from a holistic one, having a single person as owner-cum-manager has been changed to a coalition of individuals or groups and subgroups, such as directors, managers, shareholders, supervisors, workers, customers, suppliers, creditors and so on. In other words, a firm is defined as an organisational unit rather than a technical unit. All individuals or groups of individuals constituting the firm will have their goals and not the firm as it has no separate identity of its own. In this situation, we will have multiplicity of goals. There might be conflicts in goals of individuals. How to resolve them? A person sitting at the top of the administration, as a boss, may not be able to enforce conformity in the behaviour of subordinates to a higher level goal. The alternative way is to look at the problem in a behavioural framework, *i.e.*, through mutual consultation and bargaining between the parties concerned under the given set of rules, personal aspirations and goals. This is called 'realism-in-process' or simply 'behavioural approach' which provides us an organisational theory of the firm.

The organisational theory of the firm from which behaviourism stems has not yet been standardised. Apart from economic side it has several other dimensions, *e.g.*, sociological, psychological, administrative, managerial, and so on, each one having its own theory. However, there is no unification between such dimensions or theories and, therefore, the entire organisational theory of the firm of which they are parts looks quite loose. So far the best known organisational theory of the firm based on behaviourism has been developed by Cyert and March.[1] By taking the firm as a coalition of individuals and/or groups of individuals, Cyert and March analysed the process of goal formation, coalition formation and decision-making in the firm through bargaining, inducements and side payments, etc. Each member of the coalition will have a goal for himself which will be eventually tied with the common goals of the firm. Goals of the firm are quantifiable which can be translated into specific courses of actions. Cyert and March have listed five goals in an arbitrary order which represent the quantifiable objectives of the firm and which must be satisfied for bringing harmony in the organisation. The goals are: (*i*) Production goal which is related to the production of desired level of output and maintaining it. It represents the demand of those coalition members who are connected with production. The achievement of production goal is necessary for stable employment, ease of production scheduling, maintenance of accepted cost performance norms and growth of the firm; (*ii*) Inventory goal which reflects the interest of those coalition members connected with sales of products. For smooth marketing and to protect production from market fluctuations there should be a desired level of inventory of goods with the firm, (*iii*) Sales goal which implies achievement of target level of sales of output. It is an important goal of a firm since its stability and even survival depend on it. This. goal takes care of the interest of marketing personnel since their comparative performance is judged by this (*iv*) Market-share goal; this might be taken as an alternative to sales-maximisation goal.

1. Cyert, R.M. and J.G. March, *A Behavioural Theory of the Firm:* Englewood Cliff, N.J., Prentice-Hall, 1963.

Market-share goal reflects an interest in the firm's standing in its various markets relative to its rivals. (*v*) Profit goal; profit is necessary for the firm's continued existence in the business. This goal takes care of owner's interest. Further, profit is a source of finance for next round of operations and expansion of the firm and, also it is important for judging the overall efficiency of the firm.

All these goals may not give identical decision-rules regarding pricing, production, and finances, etc. In fact, there might be serious conflict in some of them. Consider, for example, sales and profit goals. One may argue lower prices for products to achieve the sales goal but this might affect the profit of the firm adversely. If there are such conflicts in goals of the firm, it is necessary to resolve them. Cyert and March suggested some mechanisms for this, such as quasi-resolution of conflicts, uncertainty avoidance, problematic search and organisational learning.[2]

For every goal there will be an aspiration level which signifies a desire on the part of the management to improve upon, repeat, or fall short of the previous year's performance during the coming year. Given the variability of the business environment one would expect the aspiration levels to fluctuate widely over-time but Cyert and March, however, argued for relatively little variation of the aspiration levels over time, since in the bureaucratic set up of contemporary corporations it is difficult to change them easily. The aspiration levels are fixed with lengthy discussions and backed with a set of written rules for their operations. Adjustments at the aspiration levels are made through search behaviour of the firm which is concerned with the discovery of the causes of failure and unexpected success.

The firm might face circumstances when its aspiration levels change slowly but the firm's environment fluctuates a good deal. This might result in either good or bad performance with respect to achievement of targets or aspiration levels. Suppose there is unexpectedly better performance and so the firm gets excess revenue or profit. How does the firm absorb the excess revenue or profit? Also, how does the firm make up the shortfall when its performance falls short of targets? Cyert and March introduced the concept of 'organisational slag' to take care of such situations. According to them, members of the coalition constituting the firm are often paid in excess of their opportunity costs, *i.e.*, wages, salaries and profits are generally higher than what is required to keep workers, employees and shareholders happy. Creditors might unnecessarily be paid quickly and in excess, and prices might be kept lower than what the market bears. All this is because of difficulties to assess the financial magnitudes correctly and the firm's indifference to keep the costs to their lowest possible levels. Thus, what Cyert and March say that there would be several unutilised sources of profits to the firm, such as surplus payments to coalition members, underutilisation of resources, including factors of production and sub-optimal pricing, production and marketing strategies. All this together constitute the 'organisational slag' of the firm.

If the performance of the firm is better in the sense that its target levels are achieved fully, and the firm earns excess revenue or profit, it allows the slag to develop so as to absorb the difference between aspiration and actual performance. The firm does this by allowing wages and salaries to rise, pays bonus to its staff, and undertakes unprofitable investment. In the situation of bad performance, *i.e.*, a short-fall in realisation of aspiration levels, the firm tries to eliminate the difference between aspiration level and performance by eliminating previously accumulated slag. That is, managerial perks are removed, wage claims are rejected, prices are increased and there would be drive to improve productivity by better utilisation of resources. Thus, in both the situations of surplus gains and deficit, the firm had some internal mechanism to adjust the aspiration levels.

2. See Cyert and March, *op cit.*, pp. 116–125.

One should not expect that the firm would be able to achieve its aspiration levels with respect to its goals fully. The inherent conflicts between some of the goals might restrict the firm to achieve all its targets fully.

A brief account of the behavioural theory of the firm, as suggested by Cyert and March, has been presented above. This much is sufficient to understand the difference between this approach and the conventional theory of the firm. Essentially, the two approaches are not substitutes but complementary to each other. The conventional theory of the firm has been designed to explain the way in which the price system works as a mechanism for resource allocation among factors of production and goods to be produced. The goal of profit maximisation, as pursued in the conventional theory of the firm, is quite relevant for this purpose. This theory, however, abstracts from the actual decision-making process, *i.e.*, how a firm takes internal decisions which is the major task of the behavioural theory of the firm. Profit maximisation is not necessary and sufficient for internal decision-making structure of the firm. It has to take into account the other goals as listed above.

In both the approaches, we do derive conclusions from the behavioural models. However, the models of the behavioural theory are likely to have more variables as compared to the number of variables in the models of the conventional theory of the firm. In view of this, the behavioural theory will be more complex requiring a system model for the analysis of the firm but the models of the traditional theory of the firm will be partial, simpler and abstract in nature.

We may conclude this section by saying that the behavioural theory of the firm provides several insights into the internal working of the firm, but, in any sense, it is not a substitute for the conventional theory of the firm. They supplement each other.

14.3 MANAGERIAL THEORIES OF THE FIRM

(i) Veblen's Approach

Theories of the firm emerging from the study of managerial behaviour in contemporary corporations or companies are designated as 'managerial theories'. These theories, as some economists claim, are becoming strong rivals to the conventional microeconomic theory of the firm. Although the leading managerial theories of the firm are of a very recent origin yet their foundation was laid by Thorstein Veblen in 1904 when he published his theory of Business Enterprise.[3] According to Veblen, the nature of society is determined by the machine-process which enables and necessitates extensive use of capital and large-scale methods of production. This type of technology, which stems from the machine process, also ensures the separation of owners from managers and engineers. Owners and/or entrepreneurs are concerned with generation of profits by their respective enterprises while managers and engineers aspire for attaining productive efficiency. An increase in business profits is not a guarantee that consumer welfare also goes up, in fact, Veblen mentioned the trade-off between them. Further, Veblen highlighted the role of financial capital, especially borrowing, for increase in the rate of return on business investment. On the whole, Veblen provided some useful insights for the managerial theories of the firm but not a systematic theory.

3. Thorstein Veblen, *The Theory of Business Enterprise,* N.Y., New American Library, Mentor Book, 1958, Print, Chapter 3.

(ii) Schumpeterian Approach

Closely to Veblen's theory, Joseph A. Schumpeter, in his writings, has developed a broad outline for an economic theory of corporate capitalism.[4] The starting point of this theory is the distinction between a risk-taker who provides financial capital in the form of debt and/or equity and the entrepreneur who runs the business and makes decisions regarding new products, new techniques of production, new methods of selling and new ways of organising the firm. The same person may perform these functions as we find under proprietorship particularly in small enterprises. In large firms, these functions are performed by different groups of people: creditors and shareholders as financers and managers as entrepreneurs. The crucial aspect of Schumpeterian theory is innovating function of managers. They introduce new innovations and, thus, attempt to increase revenue and reduce costs. This implies an increase in profits in the short-run. Increase in profit for the enterprise in the short-run induces rival firms to copy innovations. This reduces the comparative advantages of the firm, its prices decline and profits disappear. In this situation, the enterprise has to go through second round of innovations and maintain its profits. The process of innovation continues and, thus, the firm survives in business and maintains its profits in the long-run.

Innovation is a risky activity. It requires money as well as risk bearing ability which is provided by large firms operating under imperfect competition. This type of market structure is a necessary condition for the Schumpeterian theory. The money for financing innovations partly comes from profits earned by the enterprise but credit plays a very important role in it. The role of consumer's sovereignty is altered in the Schumpeterian system. Unlike the traditional theory of the firm producing for consumers with given preferences, the Schumpeterian firm attempts to alter the preferenees of consumers towards its product. The consumer plays the role of accepting or rejecting the product but the initiative to introduce new products lies with the firm and not the consumer.

(iii) Berle and Means Approach

An important contribution in the economic analysis of large corporations has been made by Berle and Means in 1932.[5] One of the conclusions of this study is that in large corporations there is separation between ownership and management. Managers exercise control over corporations while owners take the status of rentier. As far as operation of the corporation is concerned, its owners, *i.e.*, shareholders are quite passive. They do not exercise any control over the decision-making. It is done by a few elected representatives constituting the board of directors but largely by managers of the corporation. When the decision-making function of the corporation is vested with managers, their behaviour would be naturally different from the traditionally owner-cum-managerial firm which is covered in microeconomics. A large corporation under managerial control gains considerable market power so that it can administer its own prices, and when it is so the role of prices in resource allocation of the firm diminishes considerably. It is done by the firm by considering other factors also and not merely on the basis of prices alone.

---

4. Joseph, A. Schumpeter, (*a*) *The Theory of Economic Development* (1911), (*b*) *Business Cycle* (1919), and (*c*) *Capitalism, Socialism and Democracy* (1923).
5. Adolph Berle and Gardener Means, *The Modern Corporation and Private Property* (Revised Ed.), Harcourt Brace and World (1968).

(iv) Penrosian Theory

Edith Penrose also made significant contribution to the managerial theory of the firm.[6] Her work is primarily concerned with the growth aspect of the firm. She considers 'firm' as an administrative structure and a bundle of factor services. The goal of the firm is to increase the total long-term profit. To achieve this objective, the firm continues to make investment as long as it gets positive return from that. The firm takes advantages of its productive opportunities for expansion which it thinks profitable. The set of activities which the firm is aware of and able to undertake at a profit defines its 'productive opportunity'. The firm continues to grow further if allowed by its productive opportunity but there will be restraints to this. Normally, a firm faces three types of restraints, namely financial restraints, market restraints and managerial restraints. Penrose treated the first two types of restraints as insignificant and relied heavily on the managerial restraints limiting the growth of the firm.

Penrose emphasised both external and internal inducements for expansion of the firm. The external inducements mentioned by her include changes in demand, technology and other changes in market such as concentration, barriers to entry, etc. The competitive power of firms is affected by this. The firm grows if external forces are in its favour, otherwise not. The internal inducements are unused production resources and other potentials. There will be internal obstacles to growth in the form of scarcity of specific managerial services. The balance between the external and internal inducements and obstacles decides the direction of growth of the firm. In the opinion of Penrose, internal factors play an important role in it.

How the firm grows? Penrose mentioned product diversification as a way for this. The scope for diversification depends on the productive opportunity of the firm which is an internal dimension of the firm. Merger, being an external inducement, has been supported by Penrose as an alternative way for growth of the firm.

Penrosian theory is quite complex but there is no formal model for this. Managerial restraints on growth of the firm, which Penrose emphasised, are, no doubt, important but treating other restraints as insignificant, particularly financial one, may be considered as a serious drawback of her theory. She gave importance to non-economic factors which are often difficult to quantify, but, on the whole, her ideas regarding the growth of the firm are logically consistent. Subsequent theories of the firm accepted them without any challenge. Because of partial approach followed by Penrose to analyse growth of the firm, her theory is branded as an organisational theory of growth of the firm rather than an economic theory of the firm as argued by Marris.

(v) Baumol's Sales Maximisation Model

William J. Baumol has developed a sales or revenue maximisation model for large oligopolistic firm.[7] Instead of pursuing profit-maximisation goal, such firms, as Baumol assumed, pursue sales maximisation goal because sales revenue can be measured objectively without any ambiguity. Moreover, several business decisions, such as credit supply, managerial perks and commission, demand forecasting, production scheduling, etc., are all based on sales turnover. So, it is convenient for firms to evaluate their performances through sales maximisation rather than profit maximisation. However, it does not mean that profit is not important. It is essential for firms, what Baumol

---

6. Edith Penrose, *The Theory of the Growth of the Firm*, Oxford, Basil Blackwell, 1959.
7. Baumol, W.J., *Business Behaviour, Value and Growth* (Revised Ed.): N.Y., Harcourt, Brace and World 1967, Chapters 6–10.

proposed is the objective of sales maximisation subject to a profit constraint, which is the appropriate level of profit that the firm decides for itself. To elaborate Baumol's model, let us consider the following diagram. *TR* and *TC* are the total revenue and total cost curves for a firm in the two dimension graph showing quantity of output on *x*-axis and *TR* and *TC* on *y*-axis.

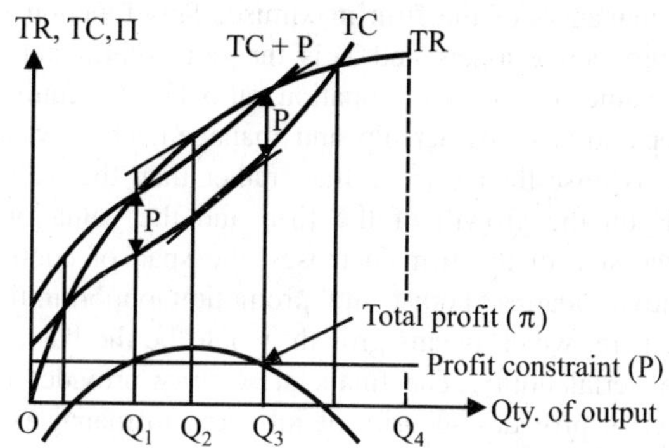

Fig. 14.1 Sales Maximisation Subject to a Profit Constraint

The firm has fixed a profit level for itself, shown by the profit constraint line (*P*). If the firm is a profit maximiser it will produce Q_2 level of output because at this level total profit (π) is maximum corresponding to $MR = MC$ situation. On the other hand, if the firm is unconstrained revenue maximiser, it will produce Q_4 level of output since *TR* curve has maximum top for this. However, profit will be negative for Q_4; so, it is not economical to the firm. The firm is interested in getting a fixed profit (*P*). The level of output for this would be Q_1 and Q_3. The firm would not produce Q_1 since this corresponds to the lower break-even point (remember $TC + P = R$ at this level) which is a disequilibrium situation, only Q_3 will be appropriate level of output for the firm to get maximum sales with profit constraint (*P*). It is possible that the firm reaches the maximum revenue before the profit constraint is satisfied. But Baumol ruled out this possibility by considering variable advertisement expenditure and a positive marginal revenue from that. So, if this is the case, the firm increases its advertisement outlay, the positive marginal revenue from this implies upward shift of the *TR* curve. This process continues till profit constraint is satisfied under increasing total revenue.

An important aspect of Baumol's model is to determine the profit constraint. Baumol has done this by extending his analysis to find that combination of current sales and growth of sales that maximises the present value of future sales.[8] Without going into formal details of the model, what we find from it is that static revenue maximisation leads to larger output for the firm than the profit-maximisation level of output. Price may or may not be lower depending on the shape of the firm's cost curve and on how much the demand curve shifts as a result of advertisement beyond the profit-maximising level.

Baumol's model is very much like a microeconomic model of the firm. There is very little managerial aspect involved in it. He has not considered, say, for example, the utility trade-off to managers between profits and sales. On the whole, we say that his model is a bit more than the model of the traditional microeconomics concerning sales-maximisation.

8. Baumol, W.J., *op cit.,* pp. 96–100.

(vi) Marris' Model

This is perhaps the most important contribution in the field. Robert Marris in his book, *The Economic Theory of Managerial Capitalism* presented a comprehensive model to analyse managerial behaviour of the enterprise.[9] The starting point of Marris' model is the specification of a managerial utility function which the managers of the firm maximise. This function is $U = U(A°, V)$ where $A°$ is the rate of growth of productive assets and V is the ratio of market value of net equity assets of the firm to their book value, *i.e.*, it is a valuation ratio for the equity of the firm.

As usual, there is separation of ownership and management in Marris model. Managers who control the firm seek to maximise their own welfare rather than the welfare of owners. Managerial welfare or utility depends on the growth of the firm and the valuation ratio providing financial security to the firm. As the size of the firm increases, the span of control of managers in running the firm increases, executive salaries, perks, and promotion opportunities increase. Therefore, an increase in the size of the firm, which means growth, would be the basic objective of the firm from the point of view of managerial utility. The financial security provides a kind of constraint to the growth of the firm. Further, it provides security of job, etc., to managers of the firm. Managers try to achieve that particular market value of the equity of the firm that prevent the threat of a take-over in the market, keep shareholders happy, and maintains a continued supply of funds to the firm.

The model proposed by Marris contains six equations as described below.

$$D° = D\ (m,\ d) \qquad ...(1)$$

which says that the rate of growth of demand for productive capacity, measured by the book value of total productive assets ($D°$) depends on the profit-margin (m) and the diversification rate (d). The relationship between the rate of growth of demand and profit-margin (*i.e.*, the ratio of net operating income including interest payments to total sales) is negative, while the relationship between $D°$ and the rate of diversification (*i.e.*, the ratio of attempted new products to existing products) is positive.

$$p = P\ (m,\ d) \qquad ...(2)$$

This equation specifies that the profit-rate (P) (*i.e.*, the ratio of net operating income to the book value of total assets) is a function of the profit-margin (m) and the rate of diversification.

$$A° = aP \qquad ...(3)$$

which means that the growth rate of supply of productive assets ($A°$) is a multiple of profit-rate. The multiplicant 'a' depends on the debt/equity ratio and the ratio of retained earnings to total income. If these ratios are constants, then 'a' is a constant. Further,

$$a \leq a^* \qquad ...(4)$$

This indicates the financial constraint. The maximum value of 'a' (*i.e.*, a^*) depends on managers' perception of financial security. Finally, we have,

$$A° = D° \qquad ...(5)$$

This is the equilibrium condition for the Marris' model showing us that the rate of growth of supply of assets must be equal to the rate of growth of demand for productive capacity.

Suppose the firm selects its optimum financial policy as indicated by a^*, then we have,

$$A° = a^*\ P = a^*\ P\ (m,\ d) = D\ (m,\ d) \qquad ...(6)$$

This is the reduced form of the above model (equation 1 to 5) showing us the growth rate of supply and demand for capacity depending on the profit-margin (m) and the diversification rate (d). At the equilibrium, *i.e.*, when $A°^* = D°^*$, the model gives optimum rate of diversification (d^*) and the implied profit-margin (m^*).

---

9. Robert Marris, *The Economic Theory of Managerial Capitalism,* N.Y., Free Press of Glencoe, 1964.

By extending the model further, Marris has developed the expression for the valuation ratio (*v*) and showed the determination of optimum retention ratio (a^*) and the optimum combination of growth and security.[10] Without going into details of all this, what Marris has finally shown that the managerial firm will not maximise value per share as assumed traditionally in the study of finance and economics, but it will increase growth at the expense of valuation until it attains its maximum level of managerial utility.

(vii) Williamson's Model

Like Marris, Williamson has provided an interesting model to understand the managerial behaviour of the firm.[11] Williamson, like others, assumes separation of ownership from management in modern corporations and concludes that managers can pursue their own self-interest once they get the goal of profit at some satisfactory level. It means that they maximise their own utility subject to a profit constraint. According to him, a manager's utility or self-interest depends upon, (*a*) his salary and other forms of compensations; (*b*) the number and quality of persons who report to him; (*c*) non-financial perquisites from business; and (*d*) the amount of discretionary spending and power he commands. Williamson's model is quite important in the sense that it provides guidelines for managers to act when either demand for the product changes or there is taxation. In other words, the adjustment in policies can be prescribed under Williamson's model, whenever there is some external factor affecting the firm. Under normal situations, a firm having a Williamson utility maximising manager will spend more on staff expenditure and will maintain more organisational slag than a profit maximising firm. Most of the government firms or public sector undertakings might come under this category.

(viii) Galbriath's Model

It will be appropriate for us to mention the model of Galbraith which has considerable implications, for industrial societies.[12] In his model, Galbraith postulated that the techniques, of modern production are dependent on specialised skills, high capital intensity, large scale of production and long-term planning. When a businessman commits investment on a project with such characteristics, he has to estimate in advance the cost of output, its price and other operational details keeping in mind the gestation period of the project. If it is not done, there might be a risk of losses from the project. All this is a part of the planning process. Once the project is commissioned, the firm has to ensure for price stability which is done through differentiated products with administered prices. Further, to ensure demand for its products the firm goes for intensive advertisement. The firm supports government policies to maintain full employment and other military and public expenditure programmes since all these might be relevant to increase the demand prospects for the output of the firm. To ensure a stable source of skilled manpower the firm supports government programmes for higher education, it helps in financing research and development programme, seeks long-term contracts with input suppliers. It supports government policies to stabilise the general level of prices and wages. The firm increasingly depends on internal sources of funds.

---

10. See J.B. Herendeen, *The Economics of the Corporate Economy,* N.Y., Dunellen Pub. Co., 1975, pp. 80–84 for further details.
11. Oliver E. Williamson, *The Economics of Discretionary Behaviour: Managerial Objectives in a Theory of the Firm*; Englewood, Cliff. Prentice-Hall, 1964.
12. John K. Galbraith, *The New Industrial State*, Boston, Houghton Mifflin Co., 1967.

On the basis of all such observations, Galbraith says that long-term corporate planning and control replaces the market as a guide to economic decision-making in modern large corporations. This gives autonomy to techno-structure of the firm. The techno-structure is the group of skilled technical and managerial personnel, *i.e.*, all professionals who make group decisions and control the firm in real sense. They are the most important people now in business units having the same prestige as capitalists or landlords who used to have it in the past. Since planning replaces market in a Galbraithian firm, therefore, profit-maximisation is not a relevant goal for this. The appropriate goal would be long-term rate of growth of sales. Constraints for this would be payment of satisfactory level of dividends to shareholders, and maintaining sufficient accumulation of internal funds for financing expansion of the firm. Further, maintenance of a level of efficient technology is a must for the firm which helps to maintain its competitive position in the business. In summary, we say that under Galbraithian system of industrial society we have a planned economy where most of the planning is done by large corporations in cooperation with governments; administered prices replace market determined prices and wages; and there is accommodation of goals of consumers, workers and government to the need of the industrial system. There is no consumer sovereignty, of course, it is replaced by the sovereign cooperation.

It is true that the large corporations, in cooperation with government, have succeeded in eliminating short-term fluctuations in demand and supply which might be the sources of insolvencies and unemployment, but this does not eliminate the market. It becomes more predictable. In this situation, prices are cost determined in the same way as the long-run equilibrium of the traditional theory of the firm. Demand and/or the ability to create it determines whether a good will be produced and what profit-margin can be expected from it. In other way, the traditional concepts of demand, supply, capacity utilisation, equilibrium and so on, still found in operation in the Galbraithian firm. The new thing is that it is subjected to planning and not left to have its own course of adjustments as we find under free market mechanism. All this is true for large corporations but what happens to small units Galbraith is silent about them.

The major managerial theories of the firm have been summarised above. The common feature of all these theories is that there is separation of ownership and management in corporations as result of which the behaviour pattern of such corporations is different from the traditionally conceived owner-cum-managerial firm. Profit-maximisation goal is, by and large, irrelevant for them, instead it is replaced by other objectives, such as sales maximisation, growth-rate maximisation, maximisation of managerial utility and like that. Naturally, the decision-rules derived from such goals would be different from the rules or laws derived from the objective of profit-maximisation. However, one thing is common in all managerial theories of the firm. All of them, in some form or other, agree that profit is necessary for the enterprise. This appears in most of the models in the form of a constraint.

Some new theories of the firm related to management or organisational behaviour have appeared on the surface in recent times which deserve some attention as they are serious challenges to the traditional neo-classical theory. In the remaining part of this section, it would be useful to have a brief summary of such approaches.

(ix) Transaction Cost Theory

In the context of understanding, the decision-making process in organizations, particularly at the firm level, this theory is a landmark development which has been proposed by Coase[13] and refined

13. R. Coase, "The Nature of the Firm", *Economica*, 4 (1937), 385–405.

further by Williamson.[14] The theory is based on the fact that the most appropriate levels of analysis for most economic behaviour are individuals and transactions among them.

A transaction refers to an exchange of goods and services between the concerned parties. It may be performed in three ways: (1) trading in spot markets, (2) long-term contracts, and (3) internalizing transactions within the firm. There will be transaction costs of specific types associated with these ways. Transaction costs are related to problems of coordination and motivation. We may list such costs as follows

(a) Coordination Costs

These are sometimes called as Coasian Costs since Coase was the first economist to examine them in detail.[13] The elements of such costs are categorised as search costs, bargaining costs, and contracting costs.

For transaction, both the buyers and sellers have to search for the relevant information related to prices, quality and transportation. In the market such an information is external while within the organization it is held by different departments from where it is to be collected and communicated to the decision-maker. Inadequate information and delays in gathering the relevant information may be quite costly depending on the nature and type of the transaction.

Bargaining costs are more relevant when markets are involved where negotiations for major transactions can be protracted and are to be carried on carefully. Even within organizations, like a firm, salaries and wage negotiations can also be costly in terms of time and efforts of party involved.

Contracting costs are associated with drawing up contracts, such as managerial time and legal expenses involved.

(b) Motivation Costs

These costs are often referred to as agency costs. There are two main categories of such costs: (1) Hidden information costs and (2) Hidden action costs. Hidden information implies information asymmetries when one or more parties of a transaction may have more information relevant to the transaction than others. For example, in the second hand market for a number of products, such as cars and other consumer durables, sellers have a big advantage over buyers. This has many consequences for the market as buyers have to devote resources to obtain more information, such as making payment to an engineer for inspecting the car.

Hidden actions are concerned with the monitoring of contracts between parties concerned when they are finalized. The behaviour of parties is to be observed and monitored carefully to ensure that terms of the contract are being upheld. Monitoring and supervision in this context are quite costly. Further, there is a problem associated with them because the often difficult to observe directly behaviour of parties. Indirect ways of observing this kind of behaviour may be too costly for the transaction dealings. This problem is known as 'moral hazard' The problem becomes more serious if legal actions are to be initiated to enforce terms of contracts.

Transactions have many attributes which affect the above costs and, therefore, affect the way in which they are conducted, particularly asset specificity, frequency, complexity and relations with

14. O. E. Williamson, "Transaction Cost Economics: The Governance of Contractual Relations", *Journal of Law and Economics,* 22 (1979), 223–261.

other transactions.[15] On the whole, transaction cost theory is a vital analytical tool useful to understand the price fixation through bargaining process in organizations.

(x) Property Right Theory

This is a new area of study in organizational economics which emerged through the writings of Grossman and Hart in 1986.[16] The focus in their work is on the issue of ownership, the nature of ownership and its relationship with incentives to invest and the bargaining power in the organization.

As we know, the institution of private property under capitalism provides strong incentives to create, maintain and improve the property assets. Owners may have absolute control over the use of properties, without any kind of regulation by the law or they may have residual control over properties when law comes in the way to have their unrestricted use. For example, consider the ownership of a music system by a person. In principle, he is free to use it, but this depends on the legal control. He cannot play it loudly during the night or even during the day time, since it would create noise pollution. He cannot use it in public places. We may cite similar examples for other private assets like car driving, houses, shops, etc., where there would be several restrictions on uses. We may, therefore, question the ownership of such assets. In fact, what we can say is that the owners will be having only residual or limited rights to use assets.

There is another important feature of ownership of an asset that it is entitled to receive a return from it. In the case of consumer durables, like a house, a car or any domestic appliance, the owner gets a rental income from that. However, there would be some expenses related to the maintenance and repair of the asset. There might be some liabilities to pay for such assets or even taxes as per the contracts or government regulation. So, what we can say that the return from the owned assests will be residual in nature. This is also applicable to properties in business organizations.

Property rights in the context of a business are the sources of bargaining power. Assets that give bargaining power should be in the hands of those people whose efforts are more significant to increase the value of the business. Such people, because of their bargaining power to get more return from investing their time and efforts in bargaining. Therefore, it is quite natural that they get incentives in the form of returns from that. Decisions about the ownership of assets in business are important to owners because the control over ownership of assets confirms the bargaining power to the owner when unforeseen or uncovered contingencies force the party concerned to negotiate about its relationship. Take, for example, the right issue related to a public limited company. There are essentially four parties in such a company who can lay claims to certain rights of ownership and control.

(*a*) Shareholders: They have ownership rights, powers to change company charter, election of directors, managers, etc., but they are not parties in day-to-day and strategic decision-making except a few having top executive positions. They don't have the residual rights as such; rights are given to them by-laws. They get dividend which is the residual income for them.

(*b*) Directors: They are policy makers, having residual control but no residual incomes.

(*c*) Managers: These are salaried executives who have full control over the working of the company. They get perks and other benefits along with salaries as incentives for their own utility.

(*d*) Other Employees: These are non-managerial staff members but no residual claims.

15. See Barthwal, R. R. *Industrial Economics*, 3rd Ed. (2010), New Delhi, New Age International, Chapter 21 for details on these attributes.

16. Grossman, S. and O. Hart, "The Costs and Benefits of Ownership: A Theory of Vertical and Lateral Integration," *Journal of Political Economy*, 94 (1986), 691–719.

As we know, in the traditional theory of the firm, the boss is the person having residual control and residual return. The entrepreneur in the neo-classical theory is seen as the owner-cum-manager getting the residual income. The sole proprietorship and partnership companies do come in this category in the joint stock companies. The situation is different where ownership rights can be sold or transferred under the provision of the law.

(xi) The Agency Theory

This theory deals with situations where one party, say an agent, is assigned the work or duties or wishes of another party called 'principal. This is a normal situation almost in all kinds of business transactions. Such transactions enable the firm to contract bilaterally with suppliers, distributors, workers, managers and even with customers. Contracting is the mechanism through which the agency theory becomes operative. A firm, in the opinion of Alchain and Demsetz, is a nexus of contracts meaning that the firm can be viewed as 'hub-in-a hub and spoke system.'[17] When there is a link between the two parties, principal and agent, through a contract, there might be conflict of interest between the two, principal interested in taking care of his own self-interest and the agent his own. This kind of conflict of interests between the two parties leads to a problem of misalignment of incentives. The agency theory deals with the correction of such misalignment in the most efficient ways.[18]

As we know, contracting is the mechanism to make the agency system operational. In the context of a transaction, for example, a contract between the concerned parties has to be in explicit terms. It will be complete in all respect. By complete contract we mean specification of rights and obligations of both the parties over the whole terms of the contract. This would eliminate the agency problems like bounded rationality, asymmetric information, adverse selection and moral hazards, and parties would be held liable in the law for any breach of the contract. A complete contract has to satisfy the following conditions as suggested by wilkinson.[19]

1. All possible eventualities must be foreseen.
2. Such eventualities must be accurately and unambiguously specified.
3. In future, it must be possible to determine which eventuality actually occurred.
4. Course of action for each eventuality must be determined.
5. The party concerned must be willing to abide by terms of the contract, with no desire for renegotiation.
6. The parties must be able to observe freely the behaviour of each other to ensure that terms of contract are followed.
7. Parties must be willing and able to enforce the contract if terms are not met.

In practice, it is very difficult to satisfy all these conditions. So, the contract in majority of the cases are bound to be incomplete. The main reason for this is the bounded rationality. By bounded. rationality we mean that people cannot solve problems perfectly, costlessly and instantaneously. There is an ultimate upper limit for such characteristics.

Incomplete contracts may lead to the problem of hidden information and hidden actions. Hidden information means information asymmetry. One party in the transaction activity is having more

17. A.A. Alchain and M. Demsetz, "Production, Information Costs and Economic Organization," American Economic Review, 62 (1972), 773–795.
18. T.V.S. Ramamohan Rao, *Contract Economics,* New Delhi; New Age International, 2004, may be referred for full details.
19. Nick Wilkinson, *Managerial Economics,* N.Y., Cambridge University Press 2005, Ch. 2.

information regarding the past that is relevant to the transaction but it is not revealed to another party at the time of contracting. For example, in a transaction relating to old car market, the seller may have more information about the condition of the car that is not given to the buyer. If the information is fully and correctly given to the buyer, his willingness to buy the car might be affected adversely by this.

There is another serious problem related to contracting. This is known as the situation of adverse selection when products or customers with worst quality characteristics are able to have or make the transaction, others are driven away from the market. Akerlof has provided an interesting analysis for this kind of problem.[20]

Problems of the agency mechanism cannot be solved precisely. Some techniques have been mentioned for this, such as monitoring of contracts to avoid inefficiencies, screening of post contract behaviour, using signaling procedures, gathering of more private information about the party concerned risk pooling, internalizing transactions and improvement in incentive structure. We will not go into details of all these as they are relevant for organizational economics rather than microeconomics.[21]

14.4 TRADITIONAL THEORY VS. NEW THEORIES OF THE FIRM: AN EVALUATION

We now have a fairly good idea about the traditional theory of the firm and the new theories which have been developed in the recent past. All theories, whether old or new, have been developed to explain the behaviour of the firm. The focus in each one of them is, of course, different. The traditional theory of the firm, that is the neo-classical theory, is concerned with optimum allocation of resources across industries, products and factors of production under different types of markets. The price mechanism does this job and the theory responds to the external conditions and abstracts from the internal factors. In the case of behavioural and managerial theories, more emphasis is given on internal factors, *i.e.*, on forces within the firm while taking decisions. They are, by and large, organisational theories of the firm. Of course, they also try to allocate their scarce resources in the best possible way. The basic elements of economics, such as demand, supply, cost, price, market and various other concepts, are essential even for the new theories since without taking them into consideration it is difficult to take economic decisions. It is true that the conventional theory assumes profit maximisation as goal of the firm but the new theories are not discarding profits altogether. They all agree that profit is essential for the firm but due to certain organisational factors, such as separation of ownership and management, divergences between the motives of owners and managers, discretionary powers to managers, etc., the other goals, like sales or growth or managerial utility maximisation, become equally important. We have seen how different models of managerial behaviour are based on pursuance of different objectives.

On examination of contents of the conventional theory of the firm, and the new ones, we do not find any clash between them. In fact, they supplement each other. The microeconomic theory is a general theory. It provides fundamentals of economics. Its applications, as we have mentioned earlier, cover several special fields, including business administration, accounting, finance and marketing. Therefore, what we can say that the various behavioural theories as well as managerial theories are nothing but mere extensions, to some extent, of the microeconomic theory of the firm.

---

20. G.A. Akerlof, "The Market for 'Lemons', Qualitative Uncertainty and Market Mechanism," *Quarterly Journal of Economics,* 84 (1970), pp. 488–500.
21. J. Hendry: "The Principals other Problems: Honest Incompetence and the Specification of Objectives;" *Academy of Management Review,* Vol. 27 (2002), pp. 98–113 and Wilkinson N., *op cit.,* Ch. 2.

14.5 CONCLUDING REMARKS

This chapter is on epilogue to the microeconomic theory covered in this book. Actually, we have provided a summary of some new theories of the firm in order to see whether there exists any alternative to the conventional classical-neoclassical theory of the firm. After seeing the content of several theories, we do find that, at present, there is no such alternative. All theories, to some extent, are supplements to each other. This provides us an opportunity to conclude that the microeconomic theory is a highly relevant basic branch of economics having several applications. This theory, in general, teaches us the rationality of economic decision-making concerning house-holds, business firms, markets, factors of production and so on. It also gives us norms for economic efficiency from the point of view of social welfare.

SUGGESTED READINGS

Chandler, A.D., *Scale and Scope*, *The Dynamics of Capitalism*, M.A. Harvard University Press.

Curwen, P. J., *The Theory of the Firm:* The Macmillan Press Ltd., 1978.

Herendeen, J. B., *The Economics of the Corporate Economy,* Dunellen Pub. Co., N.Y., 1975.

Koutsoyiannis, A., *Modern Microeconomics,* The Macmillan Press Ltd., 1978.

Machlup, F., "Theories of the Firm: Marginalist, Behavioural, Managerial", *American Economic Review,* 1967.

Mohoney J.T., *Economic Foundation of Strategy,* Sage Publications, N.Y., & New Delhi, 2005.

Shackle, G. L. S., *Expectation, Enterprise and Profits, The Theory of the Firm;* Allen and Unwin, 1970.

REVIEW QUESTIONS

1. "The theory of economics does not furnish a body of settled conclusions immediately applicable to policy. It is a method rather than a doctrine, a technique of thinking which helps its possesser to draw correct conclusions" — (J.M. Keynes).
   On the basis of your understanding of microeconomics examine the validity of this statement.
2. Is current theory of microeconomics adequate to explain the real life economic situations? Give a critical appraisal of this.
3. What are the major directions in which the received theory of the firm is going under changes? Explain in detail.
4. Do you think that the 'realism-in-process' and managerial approaches have seriously challenged the neo-classical theory of the firm or not? Give your assessment in this regard.
5. "The universality of the microeconomic theory of the firm may be adversely affected if the internal factors concerning the behaviour of firms are taken into account." Discuss.

Subject Index

Author Index